THE EGYPTIAN SUDAN

ITS HISTORY AND MONUMENTS

By E. A. Wallis Budge

ISBN: 978-1-63923-619-0

Printed: January 2023

Published and Distributed By:
Lushena Books
607 Country Club Drive, Unit E
Bensenville, IL 60106
www.lushenabks.com

ISBN: 978-1-63923-619-0

THE EGYPTIAN SÛDÂN

ITS HISTORY AND MONUMENTS

BY

E. A. WALLIS BUDGE, M.A., LITT.D., D.LITT., LIT.D.

FORMERLY SCHOLAR OF CHRIST'S COLLEGE, CAMBRIDGE,
KEEPER OF THE EGYPTIAN AND ASSYRIAN ANTIQUITIES IN THE
BRITISH MUSEUM

WITH NUMEROUS ILLUSTRATIONS

IN TWO VOLUMES

VOL. I.

I DEDICATE THIS BOOK

AS A MARK OF ADMIRATION AND ESTEEM

TO

THE DISTINGUISHED ENGINEER

SIR WILLIAM EDMUND GARSTIN, G.C.M.G.

ETC., ETC., ETC.

WHO HAS MEASURED AND CURBED

THE RIVER OF EGYPT

AND SET BOUNDS TO THE FLOOD THEREOF

AND TURNED THE WILDERNESS INTO A POOL OF WATER

AND THE PARCHED PLACES INTO WATER-SPRINGS

AND MADE THE DESERT TO BLOSSOM AS THE ROSE

PREFACE

In the summer of 1897, by arrangement with the Sirdar, Sir H. Kitchener, the Trustees of the British Museum sent me on an Archaeological Mission to the Sûdân. By the end of the year I had examined the Pyramid-fields at Nûrî, Kurrû, *Z*ûma, and Taṇḳâsî, had opened one of the Pyramids at Gebel Barkal, and had dug through portions of the ruined temples on this site. In the winter of 1898-99 I was again sent to the Sûdân, and was permitted to examine the four groups of Pyramids which stand near the site of the ancient city of Meroë, with a view of excavating the most important of them when an opportunity offered. In the winter of 1900-01 it was proposed to carry on excavations on the Island of Meroë, but as, owing to the lack of population, no labour was forthcoming, the project had to be abandoned. In the spring of 1902, Sir Reginald Wingate, who had succeeded Lord Kitchener as Sirdar, made arrangements for excavating the group of the largest pyramids at Meroë, and I was sent to the Sûdân to conduct the archaeological portion of the work. As a result of the excavations made at this time it was found that the chambers in which the dead were placed were *beneath* the pyramids, as in Egypt, and not *in* the pyramids as some had supposed; that the bodies of the native kings and queens were not mummified; and that the chambers of the dead were not filled with funerary furniture, as is usually the case in Egypt. Beneath several of the smaller pyramids large jars half filled with sand and ashes of human bones were found in small vaulted chambers, a fact which proved that the bodies of several members of the ruling class at Meroë were burned. Thus the expectation that the pyramids of Meroë would yield a rich harvest of sepulchral antiquities was not fulfilled.

In the spring of 1905 I was sent to the Sûdân to assist Sir Reginald Wingate in collecting antiquities for the newly established

Museum at Kharṭûm, or Khurṭûm, and with Mr. J. W. Crowfoot, Inspector of Education, I examined all the principal ancient sites from Sesi, or Sesebi, to Semna; the antiquities at several of these had suffered considerably since I first visited them. We collected a number of objects of importance, and were fortunate enough to discover at Semna a hitherto unknown temple of Tirhâḳâh, which was dedicated to Usertsen III., the great Egyptian conqueror of the Sûdân, about B.C. 2333. Our work at the Island of Gazîrat al-Malik also yielded good results, and we removed from the top of the hill on which the old Egyptian fortress stood a fine stele of Usertsen III. At Meroë we succeeded in clearing out the shrine of one of the pyramids, and in taking down the north and south walls; the former is now at Kharṭûm, and the latter in the British Museum.

During the years in which I was thus occupied in the Sûdân I collected materials for a history of the country, and the present work is the result. In the First Part will be found a brief narrative of the results of four Missions, and a description of the temples, pyramids, &c., which, by the friendly help and co-operation of Lord Kitchener, Sir Reginald Wingate, and their Staffs, I was able to visit, examine, and partly excavate. I have prefaced this narrative by a summary of the splendid archaeological work done in the Sûdân by modern travellers, especially by Cailliaud, Hoskins, and Lepsius, and to this a notice of the travels of Poncet, Norden, Gau, Browne, Burckhardt, Legh, Hanbury, Waddington, Russegger, and others, has been added.

The Second Part of this book deals with the history of the Sûdân. The narrative begins with the great raid made in the country by Seneferu, a king of Egypt, who reigned about B.C. 3766, and ends with a summary of the principal events which took place there A.D. 1904. We must not assume that the raid of Seneferu was the first which the Egyptians made in the Sûdân, for the Egyptian monuments of the Pre-dynastic and Archaïc Periods yield sufficient evidence to justify us in believing that it was only one of a very long series, which began some thousands of years before that king came to the throne. Details of such raids are at present wanting, but it is quite certain that every ruler of Egypt, in all periods, has considered the Sûdân simply as the country which produces slaves and gold. In spite of this, however, the history of Egypt shows that the peoples of the Sûdân influenced in no small degree the ancient Egyptian religion and civilization, and, no doubt, it is this fact which caused historians like Diodorus to assert that the civilization of Egypt had its origin in "Ethiopia," by which, of course, he meant the country of the black sun-burnt peoples, i.e., the Southern Sûdân. The Eastern and Northern conquerors of Egypt in the Dynastic Period imposed the veneer of their civilization upon the Egyptians with considerable success, but in fundamentals of belief and custom, the Egyptians, even in the Ptolemaïc Period, had more in common with the black-skinned, but non-negro, tribes of the Southern Sûdân than is usually admitted.

For the history of the Sûdân from about B.C. 4000 to the period of the rise of the Nubian kingdom under Piānkhi about B.C. 750, our authorities are the Egyptian monuments, and much light is thrown upon the state of the country, and the conquests made by its kings from about 700 to 600 B.C. by the Stelae of Tanuath-Ȧmen, Aspelta, and Nastasen. On the history of the next 1150 years, native monuments are silent, but it is clear that during this interval the great kingdom of the Sûdân was split into two parts, the Northern having its capital at Napata, or Merawi, near Gebel Barkal, and the Southern having its capital at Meroë, some forty miles south of the mouth of the Atbara. The Greek and Roman writers, especially Herodotus, Diodorus, Strabo, and Pliny, supply descriptions of the peoples of the Sûdân, excellent on the whole, even if in places somewhat fanciful, but of the history of the country they tell us nothing.

In the early centuries of our era Christianity penetrated the Sûdân *viâ* Egypt, and it had permeated the minds of the Nubians so thoroughly that, in the second quarter of the sixth century, a native king called Silko succeeded in establishing a Christian kingdom in the Northern Sûdân, and made Dongola his capital. This kingdom flourished for some seven hundred years, and proved an effective barrier to the advance of Islâm. Facts for the history of the Sûdân, from the time of its conquest by the Arabs about A.D. 650 to the end of the fifteenth century, are scanty, but Muḥammadan writers supply us with a number of statements which enable us to piece together a fairly connected narrative. It is clear that the Northern Sûdân was subject to the Khalifas and their representatives in Egypt, and that its rulers were compelled by them to pay the "Baḳṭ," or annual tribute of slaves. It is equally clear, however, that the native Christian Church made a persistent and gallant stand against Islâm, and that Christianity flourished in the country from the First Cataract to Sôba on the Blue Nile. The testimony of Muḥammadan writers proves that there were hundreds of churches in the country between these limits, and we know from other sources that many of them were fine buildings, the walls of which were decorated with painted figures of saints, &c. The form of belief which the Sûdân Christians professed was that of Alexandria, i.e., Jacobite, and the Liturgy was recited in Greek, and we may assume that the chief members of the clergy came from the Mother Church in Alexandria. In the thirteenth century, however, troubles came on the native church, and, in proportion as the power and influence of Islâm grew and spread, Christianity declined. Little by little mosques appeared in the towns and villages, and as the Patriarchs of Alexandria were unable to assist the Sûdân Church in stemming the flood of Muḥammadanism which was sweeping over the land, the clergy lost their hold upon the people, many of whom, both voluntarily and under compulsion, rejected Christianity and became followers of the Prophet. The southern portion of the Christian kingdom of the Sûdân, that of 'Alwa, came to an end towards the close of the fifteenth century, and by the time Selim conquered Egypt in 1517, the altars of Christ had been profaned or overthrown, and the churches were forsaken buildings. When the Arabs entered the Western Sûdân from Tunis, and the Eastern Sûdân from Maṣawa, and the Northern Sûdân *viâ* Egypt, Islâm finally prevailed over Christianity, and, from about the year 1520 to the present time, the population of the whole Sûdân has consisted practically of Muḥammadans and Pagans.

With the facts at present available it is impossible to write a connected history of the country between 1520 and 1820, but we know that during this period Sulṭâns ruled in Dâr Fûr, "Meks," or "Chiefs," in Shendî, Albanians in Nubia, and lines of hereditary tribal Shêkhs in other parts of the Sûdân. These waged war with each other in true Sûdânî fashion whensoever opportunity offered, the object of each being to capture as many slaves and women and as much gold as possible, and to destroy the enemy and his country. The methods employed were always the same, and seem to be inherent in the race. The accounts of the "wars" carried on by the petty kings of the Sûdân during the last three or four centuries strikingly resemble certain portions of the annals of the Nubian king Nastasen, who defeated Cambyses, and conquered the Sûdân about B.C. 525.

An excellent, though brief summary of the history of the Sûdân from 1504 to 1871, is contained in a little Arabic manuscript which belonged to General Gordon and was presented by him in 1881 to the British Museum, where it is numbered "Oriental 2345." It consists of 108 octavo pages, and was written, and perhaps also composed, by Muḥammad Abû Bakr Makki Aḥmad in 1879. Many of the facts recorded in it are to be found in Naum Shoucair's Arabic History of the Sûdân, but as a whole the little work is valuable, and is worth editing and translating. On the first and last pages are impressions of the seal of "Gordon Bâshâ," and the volume seems to indicate that his interest in the history of the Sûdân was great. For those who study the history of Abyssinia note should be made of "The Futûḥ al-Ḥabashah," or "The Conquest of Abyssinia," by Imâm Aḥmad ibn Ibrâhîm, a copy of which was also presented to the British Museum (No. 2409) by General Gordon.

From 1820 to the rise of Muḥammad Aḥmad, the Mahdi, the history of the Sûdân is comparatively well known, but it has been thought necessary to summarize the chief events in this work. The authorities for the period are the works of Cailliaud, Hoskins, Russegger, Selim, Barth, Speke, Sir Samuel Baker, Petherick, Schweinfurth, Junker, and other travellers, and the facts which they state reveal only too clearly the awful condition to which the country had been brought by the policy of Muḥammad 'Alî and his successors. Under their fostering care the clever Arab merchants in the Sûdân had brought the slave trade to a pitch of perfection which it is now difficult to realize, and the rulers in Cairo, aided by their representatives at Kharṭûm, seconded their exertions with such success that in 1880 the Sûdân was literally a "useless possession," the greater part of the country having gone out of cultivation, and most of the able-bodied men in it being brigands. I have tried to show in the chapter on the gold trade of the Sûdân in ancient times that the main object which the Egyptians had in occupying the country was the gold which it contained; the capture of slaves and cattle was of secondary importance. To attain this end they maintained a strong line of forts from the Third Cataract to Aswân, and the temples which they built at the termini of important caravan routes were not so much intended for the promulgation of the Egyptian religion, as to benefit trade. This is proved by the fact that when the mines in one portion of the country ceased to be profitable, the temples along the routes leading to them were allowed to fall into decay. The Pharaohs wanted gold, and gold was obtained at all costs. Still there is no evidence that under their rule the Sûdân ever fell into the state of misery which it had reached in 1879, when General Gordon resigned his appointment as Governor-General of the Sûdân. That a trade in slaves between the Sûdân and Egypt has existed from time immemorial there is every reason to believe, but, until the introduction of fire-arms into Africa on a large scale, it was never accompanied by such wholesale murder and destruction of innocent life and property as is described in the works of Baker and Petherick. The era of cruelty began with the rise to power of the Arab merchants, who made the Government officials partners in the flourishing business of exporting slaves, and who made an annual payment to the authorities in Cairo.

The next period of the history of the Sûdân begins with the appearance of the Mahdi in 1881, and ends with the capture of Omdurmân on September 2nd, 1898. Between those years the harvest sown by the Egyptian administrators in the Sûdân was reaped, and the civilized world stood aghast at the result, and at the atrocities which the Mahdi Muḥammad Aḥmad and his Khalîfa, 'Abd-Allah, perpetrated with such striking success, in the name of religion and liberty. For the facts I have relied on Sir Reginald Wingate's work, *Mahdiism*, which is the most complete account of the subject extant, and I have also derived much information of a supplementary character from Sir Rudolf von Slatin's *Fire and Sword in the Sudan*, and Father Ohrwalder's *Ten Years' Captivity in the Mahdi's Camp*. For the history of the reconquest of the Sûdân, Mr. Charles Royle's *Egyptian Campaigns*, the *Sudan Campaign* by "An Officer," and the Government Reports are invaluable.

In compiling the section of this book which deals with the work of the English in the Sûdân, I have drawn frequently from the annual *Reports* of Lord Cromer, from Sir William Garstin's *Report on the Basin of the Upper Nile*, from Captain Lyons' *Physiography of the River Nile and its Basin*, and from the *Sûdân Gazette*. I have also made great use of the second edition of Count Gleichen's *The Anglo-Egyptian Sudan*, which appeared at the end of 1905, and the *History of the Sudan* (in Arabic) by Naum Shoucair Bey, B.A., the Chef-du-Bureau in the Agent-General's Office of the Sûdân Government in Cairo. Count Gleichen's work is tightly packed with facts of all kinds about the Sûdân, and contains in a very condensed form a full account of the recent history of the country, and valuable Appendices. Many of his facts are drawn from official Reports, many are the result of personal experience and travel in the Sûdân, and some are derived from the published narratives of the early travellers; and all are classified and marshalled with the precision and accuracy which are demanded by military requirement. Shoucair Bey's History contains a great deal of information about the Sûdân Campaigns which will be familiar to most readers, but he has also collected in it a number of facts about the Sûdân peoples and their country which are extremely valuable, and which will be new to many. Portions of his work ought to be translated into English or French, and it is to be hoped that this may be done. The Index to the work is, unfortunately, wholly inadequate. The making of indexes is, as every one knows who has done it, a wearisome task, but if Shoucair Bey will add to future editions of his work an index which shall contain *all* proper names, he will find that his book will be used by hundreds, instead of by the few who are now obliged to read through many pages of matter before they can find what they want.

For the presence of the chapters on the work of the British in the Sûdân in a book of this kind little apology is necessary. It is the fashion to take for granted that the British have done, and are still doing, great things in the Sûdân, because of our tradition that it is the duty of every Briton, whether he be trader, traveller, sailor, soldier, or administrator, to do great things in foreign lands. Notwithstanding the letters to the press from able correspondents such as Mr. Knight and Mr. Fred Villiers, to say nothing of Government publications, few have taken the trouble really to think out and to understand the magnitude of the difficulties which have had to be overcome and the work which has been done by a mere handful of British officers in the Sûdân. Those who now visit that country, and pass over its howling deserts in a *train de luxe*, can form no idea of the state of misery to which the country had been brought within a space of fifty years by the misrule of its former masters, who sat comfortably in Cairo, and despatched one Governor-General after another to Kharṭûm to give effect to a policy the chief object of which was to "squeeze" the native and to support the slave trade. During the five months which I spent in the Province of Dongola in 1897 I saw the most abject misery everywhere. Four-fifths of the population had been destroyed, the greater part of the land had gone out of cultivation, the palm trees had been so greatly neglected that the date crops barely supported the remnant of the population which struggled for a living, most of the water-wheels had been burnt or were broken, and the Dervishes had eaten the cattle which had worked them. There was no trade and no money, the young men had been slain in the wars of the Mahdî and Khalîfa, and the young women had been carried off to fill the ḥarîms of the Baḳḳâra.

The condition of the country between Abû Ḥamed and Kharṭûm was even more terrible, as I saw for myself when I visited the Island of Meroë three months after Lord Kitchener had captured Omdurmân. Every here and there a few wretched people, chiefly old men and women, had gathered together and were trying to form a village, and how or on what they lived were things to marvel at. Thorns and briars and brambles had taken possession of nearly all the land which had been formerly fertile fields, and the few natives who had straggled back from their flight before Mahmûd sowed the seed for their scanty crops on the mud flats in the river and on the moist mud of the banks. In the courtyards of the ruined houses of the old villages were to be seen the stones on which the women were grinding their dhurra when Mahmûd's soldiers appeared, and the scattered grain which lay under the grinders testified to the suddenness of their flight. Ruin and desolation were everywhere, men and cattle were rarely seen, and even the dogs had been wiped out.

Such was the state of the country when Lord Kitchener gave it back to Egypt. On returning a year later I was able to travel all the way to Kharṭûm by railway, and on all hands there were small signs of improvement ; a feeble trade had begun to manifest itself, the astute Greeks were beginning to open shops in the ruined towns, the hand of the Sirdar had been laid with no uncertain weight on the kidnapper of slaves, and the rebuilding of Kharṭûm had begun. Lord Cromer and Sir William Garstin had been to the Sûdân, the former had created an Administration, and the latter had begun to evolve his great scheme for the control of the waters of the Nile, which must be of indescribable benefit to Egypt. One by one the former possessions of Egypt in the Eastern and Southern Sûdân were occupied, and the civil administrator followed quickly in the steps of the soldier.

Journeying to Kharṭûm again two years later, the great progress which had been made everywhere amazed me, and when, after a further interval of three years, I visited that city once more, I found the place so changed for the better as to be hardly recognizable. A handsome river front had been made, the Gordon College opened, a large mosque was in course of construction, building was going on in all directions, wide roads and streets were laid out, the mounds of rubbish and old bricks, and the large. shallow, mosquito-bearing pools had disappeared, a tramway was working, and steamers were plying between Kharṭûm and Omdurmân. And signs of material progress were not confined to the capital, for in all the towns and villages which I passed through new buildings were springing up, well-attended markets were held, and in every bazaar trade was brisk. The railways were improved, a service of steamers had been established on the White Nile, and on the Upper Nile, which had been freed from the "Sudd," telegraph lines were being extended, the Post-Office was rapidly becoming a flourishing department, and the imports and exports showed that the trade of the country was developing rapidly. Though the population was still scanty, there were everywhere signs that it was increasing steadily if slowly, and that the material condition of the people was much improved. And this great work had all been done in seven years! The men who had done it were few in number, they fared hard, they worked day and night, they lived in any shelter that came handy, and every one of them toiled with a devotion which is beyond praise. They were hampered by want of funds, and it was of the utmost importance that every piastre should be made to go as far as possible; had the money been their private property they could not have taken greater care in spending it. The splendid results achieved by the British in the Sûdân are due to the firm and consistent policy which Lord Cromer has followed with unwavering tenacity, and to his determination to make all the dwellers in that country free men.

What the exact effect of the opening of the railway from Atbara Junction on the Nile to Port Sûdân on the Red Sea will have upon the inhabitants of the country cannot at present be said, but since it has given Kharṭûm a seaport, and it will permit the produce of the Southern Sûdân and of the Dongola Province to find its way easily into all the markets of the world, it cannot fail to create a trade which must eventually be large and profitable to every class of native. Moreover, the opening of the Red Sea Railway really means the opening of the Sûdân, a country which has from time immemorial been practically cut off from the rest of the world. For the first time in history the fierce, warlike peoples of the Nile Valley, and of the neighbouring deserts, have had an easy outlet provided for the produce of their land and their own personal energies. They may now beat their swords into ploughshares and their spears into scythes, and be certain that, so far as the Government is concerned, each man will enjoy the fruit of his labours. For thousands of years the Sûdâni folk have had nothing much to do except plunder caravans, and raid each other's lands and make war; they have now the opportunity of learning that trading is more profitable than fighting, and many of them have not been slow to grasp it. The opening of the Sûdân to the world is one of Lord Cromer's greatest successes.

It is easy for sentimental philo-Egyptians to criticize and to find fault with details in the administration of the Sûdân by a Government which is only a few years old, and equally easy to complain that its motive power is too self-centred and autocratic, but every one who has lived in the country even for a few months at a time, and seen this machinery built up, knows that none but an autocrat, who was at the same time patient, wise, and strong, could do what Lord Cromer has done there. The results already achieved prove that the Sûdân is now ruled and administered with due regard to the welfare of the country; for the first time in history its peoples have been regarded as worthy of consideration. Those of us who have seen the manner in which Lord Cromer's policy has been carried out by Lord Kitchener, Sir Reginald Wingate, and their picked soldiers and civilians, and know how discipline is maintained, and the taxes collected, and the law administered, and education fostered, and trade encouraged, and the people protected against themselves, also know, especially when they are acquainted with the main facts of the history of the Sûdân, that none of its conquerors have ruled it with such patience, justice, and humanity, and with such true regard for beliefs and customs of its peoples, and that none have served it with such whole-hearted devotion and integrity as the British. The truth is that the Sûdâni folk cannot govern themselves, and that they will not be able to do so for many generations to come; in the meantime they must be ruled firmly but kindly if their country is to be developed. The great merit of British administration there is due to the fact that the Government not only rules but develops the country; for those who make its laws and give effect to them do not regard it as a gold mine, and a breeding ground of slaves, as conquerors in the past have done, but as a possession which under just and humane guidance may be made to support its inhabitants in comfort, and to play an important part in the civilization of Eastern Africa.

The work of the Administration both in Egypt and in the Sûdân, which are in reality only one country, is already very hard, and it is made harder by the writings of irresponsible critics who have no sound system of Government to substitute for the present *régime*, if it were overthrown. All that their futile suggestions do is to hamper the officials, thereby delaying progress; to increase the spirit of disaffection in the mob of ignorant peasants, who expect to gain some benefit by any change of affairs; to raise absurd hopes in the minds of the young men, who know only by tradition slavery, the hide-whip, and the *corvée;* and to fan the ever-smouldering flame of religious fanaticism in the minds of the middle-aged men throughout the country. In the last-named class are many who held appointments under the old government of bribery, corruption, and "squeezing," and these regret the good old times and sigh for their return. Such scheme with all their might for the overthrow of Lord Cromer, and seize eagerly upon any expression of opinion by Englishmen which can be made to support their own views. Those who encourage the ignorant and fanatical among the Egyptians and Sûdânî folk incur a very grave responsibility, for although, fortunately, there is small chance of their undoing or imperilling Lord Cromer's work, their words stir up strife and damage the cause of law, order, and honesty in the country. The unfitness of the Egyptian General Assembly to rule is well illustrated by the fact that this party believes that the Chambers of Commerce in Europe fix the prices of the necessaries of life!

Religious fanaticism will always exist in the Sûdân, and it must needs, from time to time, find expression in the appearance of false Mahdis, who will have to be suppressed. Those who remember the palmy days of the slave trade, and still hanker after its abominable profits, will naturally stir up trouble, and induce the idle and discontented to rise against the restraints of law and order. Such risings, however, must be provided against, and the Governor-General must have under his command, at various centres in the Sûdân, in addition to a strong garrison at Kharṭûm, troops sufficient to meet every emergency, so that if necessary he may be able to strike hard and quickly in any portion of the vast country he rules. It is impossible at present to administer the Sûdân without an adequate military force stationed in the country, and he would be indeed bold who would assert that the British soldiers at present at Kharṭûm are sufficiently numerous to meet all demands which may be made upon them. Meanwhile those who have the interests of the Sûdân truly at heart must hope that its present rulers may long be spared to continue the work which they have begun, and to put into execution the projects for its benefit which they have in their minds.

The portion of this book which describes the temples and pyramids of the Sûdân is illustrated by a series of outline drawings made from the excellent plates published by Lepsius in his *Denkmäler*, and by a number of photographic reproductions of plates from the works of Cailliaud, Russegger, and others. The former do not, unfortunately, indicate the effect produced in the sculptures by the curious system of flat relief adopted by the Meroïtic artists, but they are invaluable as pictures of the bas-reliefs in the condition in which they were about sixty years ago, i.e., when they were comparatively perfect. My thanks are due to the Comptroller of His Majesty's Stationery Office for permission to reproduce several of the illustrations in Sir William Garstin's *Report on the Basin of the Upper Nile*, and to Captain Lyons, R.E., I am indebted for a plan of the fort which he excavated at Wâdî Ḥalfa Many of the other illustrations have been made from photographs and plans kindly lent me for reproduction by Miss Hilda Burrows, Sir Reginald Wingate, Sirdar and Governor-General of the Sûdân, Sir Percy Girouard, R.E., Captain E. C. Midwinter, R.E., Director of Sûdân Railways, Lieut. P. E. Lord, R.E., Mr. J. W. Crowfoot, Inspector of Education, the Hon. N. C. Rothschild, Mr. R. Türstig, Mr. G. Mason, Lieut. E. C. A. Newcombe, and Mr. C. C. F. Mackenzie.

To the Editor of the *Times* I owe permission to reproduce passages from the speeches of Lord Cromer, and from the able letters on the Sûdân Campaigns written by its correspondent, Mr. E. F. Knight.

It is now my pleasant duty to offer to the Trustees of the British Museum my grateful thanks for the frequent opportunities which they have given me of studying the antiquities of the Sûdân, and to their Director, Sir Edward Maunde Thompson, K.C.B., for much friendly advice and helpful suggestions in carrying out their directions. The wishes of the Trustees were warmly supported by Lord Cromer, who assisted me in every possible way, and who with his strong hand brushed aside all obstacles. From Lord Kitchener and his successor, Sir Reginald Wingate, I have at all times received ready and effective help; indeed without their assistance it would have been impossible for a European to live in the Sûdân, much less to travel or to work there. Though harassed by work and worry of all kinds by day and by night, they, nevertheless, found time to make the necessary arrangements for carrying out the excavations, and continued to take a keen interest n their progress. Their officers everywhere showed me much personal kindness, and their unselfish hospitality will ever be to me a pleasant memory.

A word of praise is due to Messrs. Gilbert & Rivington and their staff for the care taken in printing this book.

E. A. WALLIS BUDGE.

BRITISH MUSEUM,
February 26th, 1907.

TABLE OF CONTENTS

VOL. I.

PART I.

MISSIONS TO THE SUDAN.

CHAPTER I.

PAGE

TRAVELLERS AND ARCHAEOLOGISTS IN NUBIA AND THE EGYPTIAN SÛDÂN 1

CHAPTER II.

FIRST MISSION TO THE SÛDÂN (1897). CAIRO TO GEBEL BARKAL (NAPATA) 64

CHAPTER III.

THE ANTIQUITIES IN THE NEIGHBOURHOOD OF MERAWI . 114

CHAPTER IV.

THE OPENING OF A PYRAMID AT GEBEL BARKAL . . 169

CHAPTER V.

MERAWI AND SANAM ABÛ DÔM IN 1897 177

APPENDIX TO CHAPTER V.—A DONGOLAH TALE . . . 235

CHAPTER VI.

SECOND MISSION TO THE SÛDÂN (1898). WÂDÎ ḤALFA TO THE ATBARA AND BAGRÂWÎYA 240

CHAPTER VII.

FERLINI'S EXCAVATIONS AT THE PYRAMIDS OF BAGRÂWÎYA 285

TABLE OF CONTENTS

PAGE

APPENDIX TO CHAPTER VII.—EXTRACT FROM FERLINI'S DESCRIPTION OF HIS EXCAVATIONS AT THE PYRAMIDS OF BAGRÂWÎYA 307

CHAPTER VIII.

THIRD MISSION, 1903. VISITS TO KHARṬÛM, SÔBA, WAD BÂ NAGAA, BÎR, MAṢAWWARÂT AṢ-ṢUERA, ETC. . . 321

CHAPTER IX.

THIRD MISSION, 1903. EXCAVATIONS AT THE PYRAMIDS OF MEROË 337

CHAPTER X.

DESCRIPTION OF THE PYRAMIDS OF MEROË. NORTHERN GROUP—FORTY-THREE PYRAMIDS 357

CHAPTER XI.

DESCRIPTION OF THE PYRAMIDS OF MEROË. THE SOUTHERN GROUP, AND THE GROUPS ON THE PLAIN 416

CHAPTER XII.

FOURTH MISSION TO THE SÛDÂN (1905) 436

PART II.

A HISTORY OF THE EGYPTIAN SUDAN, ANCIENT AND MODERN.

CHAPTER I.

THE SÛDÂN UNDER THE IVTH, VTH, AND VITH DYNASTIES 505

CHAPTER II.

THE SÛDÂN UNDER THE XITH, XIITH, AND XIIITH DYNASTIES 529

CHAPTER III.

THE SÛDÂN UNDER THE XVIIITH, XIXTH, AND XXTH DYNASTIES 561

LIST OF PLATES

VOLUME I.

	PAGE
Village in the country of Bartat	47
Ruins of Meroïtic Temples at Maṣawwarât Aṣ-Ṣufra in 1832	48
Pyramids of Meroë in 1832	55
The Pyramids at Nûri in 1832	59
Temple of Åmen-ḥetep III. at Ṣulb in 1832	60
Tawfîḳîya from the west bank	83
Sûdânî stamped leather work	216
The "Triangle" at No. 6 Station in the Abû-Ḥamed Desert	245
Grave of Lieut. Gore on the Atbara	252
Smaller Egypto-Roman Temple at Nagaa, west end	330
Smaller Egypto-Roman Temple at Nagaa, entrance	332
Scene at a well in the Eastern Desert	334, 336
Scene from the north wall of the Pyramid of Årkenkherel	372
West wall of the chapel of the Pyramid of Murtek	387
The Queen who built Pyramid No. 11, and her Consort	401
Ruins of the Temple of Seti I. near Dulgo	440
Ḳubba Idris	458
Cataract at Semna and Kumma	479
Temple of Tirhâḳâh at Semna	483
Stele of Usertsen III.	491
Doorway leading to the chapel of Pyramid No. 11	502
Stele set up in the Temple of Thothmeș II. at Wâdî Ḥalfa by Seti I.	570
Temple of Thothmes II. and Thothmes III. at Wâdi Ḥalfa	576
Sepulchral Stele in the Temple at Wâdî Ḥalfa	576
Statue of Ka-mes, a scribe of Behen	578
Plan of Cataract of Semna and Kumma, showing sites of Temples	588

ILLUSTRATIONS IN THE TEXT

VOLUME I.

	PAGE
The Temples of Semna and Kumma in 1820	39
The Town of Sennaar, on the Blue Nile, in 1842	43
Sennaar in 1821, taken from the side of the Mosque	44
Map of the Egyptian Sûdân	45
Gebel Barkal	50
Aswân in 1904	66
Aswân, showing new quay and houses on river front	67
Mountain and river near Korosko	73
Korosko (southern end)	74
New Mosque at Korosko	75
Temples of Rameses II. and Hathor at Abû Simbel	80
"Stern-wheeler" towing railway materials near Wâdî Ḥalfa	82
West bank of Nile near Old Dongola	107
Palm trees near Merawi	110
An Island in the Nile	111
An Island near Merawi	112
The town of Merawi in 1842	115
Plan of Pyramids of Nûrî, by Lepsius	116
Pyramids at Nûrî	117
Plan of Pyramids of Nûrî, by Col. the Hon. M. G. Talbot, R.E.	119
Plan of Pyramids of Tanḳâsî	123
Plan of Pyramids of Kurrû	126
Plan of Pyramids of Zûma	127
Temples at Gebel Barkal	130
Plan of Temple (A) at Gebel Barkal	131
Ruins of Temple of Tirhâḳâh at Gebel Barkal (The Typhonium)	132
Pillars, with Hathor capitals, in the Temple of Tirhâḳâh	133
Plan of Temple of Tirhâḳâh	135
Plan of Temple (E) at Gebel Barkal	139
Plan of Temple of Senka-Âmen-Seken (H)	140
King Senka-Âmen-Seken slaughtering ten rebel chiefs in the presence of Âmen-Rā	141
Plan of Temple (J) at Gebel Barkal	144
Plan of Temple of Piânkhi at Gebel Barkal	145
Plan of Temple of Piânkhi (continued)	147

ILLUSTRATIONS IN THE TEXT

PAGE

Head from the statue of a king of Napata 150
Typical Pyramid at Gebel Barkal 151
Pyramids of Gebel Barkal in 1832 153
Col. the Hon. M. G. Talbot, R.E. 154
Plan of Pyramids of Gebel Barkal (by Col. the Hon. M. G. Talbot) . 155
View of a Pyramid at Gebel Barkal, showing the arrangement of stones at corner 156
Plan of Pyramids of Gebel Barkal 157
Plan of Pyramid N at Gebel Barkal 159
Vaulted arch of the chapel of Pyramid N 159
The Solar Disk in the Boat of the Sun-God (Pyramid N) . . . 160
Scene from south wall of chapel of Pyramid O 161
Pyramid P as seen by Cailliaud 162
Drawing from north wall of chapel of Pyramid P 163
Scene from north wall of chapel of Pyramid Q 165
Pyramids at Gebel Barkal, showing chapels in 1820 167
Section of Pyramid P, with shaft and sepulchral chamber . . . 170
Headquarters of General Sir L. Rundle at Ṣanam Abû Dôm (Merawi) in 1897 178
Intelligence Department at Merawi in 1897 179
Garden of Intelligence Department at Merawi in 1897 180
Signor Calderari 181
Mess of Intelligence Department at Merawi in 1897 183
Ghânim, Sir Reginald Wingate's servant 186
Captain of General Rundle's steam launch 187
Camping ground of the War Correspondents at Merawi . . . 189
The Nile at Kassingar 191
Sûdânî harp 195
Muḥammad Wâd Ibrahîm, Shêkh of Barkal in 1897 202
Native bedstead 205
Wooden pillows used in the Southern Sûdân 205
Native house in Barkal village 208
Native sandal 209
Evening prayer under the palms at Barkal 211
Sûdânî girl's dress 213
Amulet inscribed with the words "Follower of the Mahdî" . . . 215
Leather amulet case, and suspending cord 217
Kassingar Hill 232
Palm-leaf hut of Lieut. Fitz-Clarence at Kassingar 233
Sûdân Express at No. 4 Station in the Abû-Ḥamed Desert . . . 243
The Abû-Ḥamed Desert 244
Watering tank at No. 6 Station in Abû-Ḥamed Desert 245
Locomotive drivers and officials of No. 6 Station on Sûdân Military Railway in 1897 246

ILLUSTRATIONS IN THE TEXT

	PAGE
No. 6 Station in the Abû-Ḥamed Desert	247
Station on Abû-Ḥamed and Khartûm Railway	248
Transport train on siding at Atbara Fort in 1897	249
Entrance to British Cemetery at Atbara	252
Grave of War Correspondent at Atbara in 1899	253
British Cemetery on the Atbara in 1898	254
Captain of the *Bordein* in 1898	257
East bank of Nile above Atbara Junction	259
Clearing at wooding station on west bank	260
Dhurra and jungle meeting at Bagrâwîya	261
Wooding station above Atbara in 1898	262
Load of wood for the *Bordein*	263
Dhurra	265
Clearing of Shêkh Muḥammad Ibrahîm al-Amîn	266
Boy on light platform scaring birds from dhurra	267
Boys at Bagrâwîya employed to scare birds from dhurra crop	268
Shêkh of Bagrâwîya and wife	269
Wife of Shêkh of Bagrâwîya	270
Woman of Shêkh of Bagrâwîya's household	271
Pyramids of Meroë (eastern sides)	272
Pyramids of Meroë (western sides)	273
The most northerly Pyramids of the Northern Group	275
Atbara Fort, with Capt. Swabey, the Commandant	283
View of the Pyramid (Cailliaud, F) demolished by Ferlini	289
Pyramid at Meroë demolished by Ferlini	292
Head of Dionysos	293
Bronze vessel, with handle and Dionysos masks	294
Gold-hinged armlet	298
Gold armlet with figures of goddesses	299
Gold armlet	300
Gold object made for Parei	301
Gold plaque: head of Hathor, with uraei	301
Necklaces	302, 303, 304
Gold-hinged armlets	305
Group of rings	306
Desert well near Maṣawwarât Aṣ-Ṣufra	330
Excavation Camp at Pyramids of Meroë in 1903	333
Pyramid at Meroë, with top removed between 1899 and 1903	338
Egyptian officer, overseer of works	341
Party of excavators	344
Plan of Pyramids of Meroë—Group A	345
Pyramids Nos. 14 and 15 at Meroë	347
Passage through Pyramid No. 14	350
Ruined chapel of Pyramid at Meroë	351

ILLUSTRATIONS IN THE TEXT

PAGE

Pyramids of Meroë—Groups A and B 359
Pyramid of Queen Kenthâhebit. Setting up the Standard of Osiris . 361
Scene from south wall of Pyramid of Kenthâhebit 363
Judgment Scene from south wall of Pyramid of Ȧrkenkherel . . . 371
Portrait of Amon Ship(?)alak 374
Portrait of Queen Ȧmen-Shipalta 375
The Queen of Meroë who built Pyramid No. 6, spearing captives (right and left sides of chapel pylon) 377, 379
Vignettes of Chapters of "The Book of the Dead" in chapel of Pyramid of Murtek 384, 385
Horus and Anubis, on the pylon of Pyramid No. 11 389
Section of Pyramid No. 11 391
Plan of chapel of Pyramid No. 11 392
Plan of Pyramid No. 11 and chapel. 393
Sûdânî bulls and poultry (Pyramid No. 11) 394, 395
The Queen who built Pyramid No. 11 396
The Queen making offerings 397
Offerings of the Great Queen and judgment Scene 399
Builder of Pyramid No. 12 401
Portrait of King Neb-Maăt-Rā (builder of Pyramid No. 17) . . . 403
King Neb-Maăt-Rā 405
King Tirikanletau slaughtering captives 409
Builder of Pyramid No. 32 414
Plan of Pyramids of Meroë—Group B 417
Queen Kenrethreqnen 418
Scene from chapel of Pyramid of Ȧmen-Meri-Ȧsru 419
Ȧmen-Ȧrk-Neb 422
Ȧmen-Meri-Ȧsru 423
Sepulchral stele, with Meroïtic inscription 429
Plan of Pyramids of Meroë—Fourth Group 431
Altar with Meroïtic inscription 433
West wall of Pyramid No. 15—Fourth Group 434
Ruins of the Temple of Ṣulb 445, 447
Temple built in honour of Queen Thi at Saddênga 453
Sepulchral tablet of Iêsou, Bishop of Sâî 465
Statue of King Khu-Taui-Rā and altars from the Temple of Tirhâḳâh at Semna 484, 486
Plan of Temple of Tirhâḳâh 488
Plan of Temple of Gazîrat al-Malik 491
Granite statue of Prince Tcha-Ȧb found at Gazîrat al-Malik . . . 492
The Queen who built Pyramid No. 11, making offerings . . . 499
West wall of chapel of Pyramid No. 11, showing where triad of figures stood 501
Stele of Usertsen I. found at Philae 535

ILLUSTRATIONS IN THE TEXT

	PAGE
Trace of fortress wall at Wâdi Ḥalfa and section of ditch	537
Decree against the Blacks promulgated by Usertsen III.	542
Frontier stele of Usertsen III.	545
Inscription at Semna recording level of Nile	550
Colossal statue of a king on Island of Arḳô	556
Statue of Sebek-ḥetep III. on Island of Arḳô	557
Temple of Thothmes III. on Island of Elephantine	575
Portion of painted stele of Thothmes III. in Temple at Wâdi Ḥalfa	576
Temple of Thothmes II. and III. at Wâdî Ḥalfa	577, 578, 579
Temple of Thothmes II. and III. from the south-east corner	577
Paintings in the same	579
Temple of Thothmes III. at Semna	580
Usertsen III. in his divine bark: the God Ṭeṭun embracing Thothmes III.	581
Temple of Thothmes III. at Semna, from the south-east corner	583
Door-jamb with names and titles of Thothmes III.	584
Thothmes III. dedicating offerings to Usertsen III.	585
Plan of Temple of Thothmes III. at Semna	587
Plan of Temple at Kumma	588
Thothmes III. offering a pectoral to the God Ṭeṭun	589
Uatchit, Lady of Semna	591
Usertsen III. presenting "Life" to Thothmes III.	592
Thothmes III. dancing before Hathor	593
Thothmes III. offering to a god	594
Rock-hewn Temple of Dôsha	595
Usertsen III. and Thothmes III. at Gebel Dôsha	596
Åmen-ḥetep II. with horns of the sacred ram	597
Plan of Temple of Åmen-ḥetep II. at Wâdî Ḥalfa	601
Amen-ḥetep II. offering vases to his god	602
Thothmes IV. slaying his enemies in presence of the gods	603
Plan of Temple of Åmen-ḥetep III. at Ṣulb	608
Cartouches of captive nations in Temple of Ṣulb	609, 610
Names and titles of Åmen-ḥetep III.	610
Entablature with prenomen of Åmen-ḥetep III. and name of Queen Thi	611
Åmen-ḥetep III. worshipping himself as Lord of Kenset	613
Åmen-ḥetep adoring Amen	614
Ram of Åmen placed by Åmen-ḥetep III. in Temple of Khā-em-Maāt	616, 617
Red granite lions of Åmen-ḥetep III., usurped by the Nubian King Åmen-Åsru	618, 619
Inscription on pillar in Temple at Wâdî Ḥalfa	629
Seti II. Mer-en-Ptaḥ making offerings to Horus	639
Prince Åupuath	650

PART I.

MISSIONS TO THE SUDAN

PART I.

MISSIONS TO THE SUDAN.

CHAPTER I.

TRAVELLERS AND ARCHÆOLOGISTS IN NUBIA AND THE EGYPTIAN SÛDÂN.

OUR knowledge of the Sûdân in comparatively modern times we owe to a series of enterprising travellers who have succeeded in penetrating large portions of it, both on the east and west banks of the Nile. Of such travellers many journeyed through the country on business or on pleasure bent, and contented themselves with noting much of what they saw and heard without stopping to make archæological investigations or excavations. Speaking generally, we may say that the archæological investigations of the Sûdân did not begin until the first quarter of the nineteenth century, but it will be well to mention briefly the principal travellers who visited or passed through Nubia and the Sûdân in the eighteenth century and earlier.

First and foremost comes MONSIEUR PONCET, a doctor of medicine, who made a "Voyage to Ethiopia," in 1698, and stayed there for two years.[1] His fellow-travellers were Ḥaggi Alî, an official of the Emperor of Ethiopia, and Father Charles Francis Xaverius de Brevedent, Missioner of the Jesuits. After living in tents for three months near Manfalût in Upper Egypt, the party moved on to a village near Asyût, where they stayed for four days. They left Asyût, which is described as a town "encompass'd with delicious Gardens and fair Palm-trees, which

[1] *A Voyage to Ethiopia made in the year* 1698, 1699, *and* 1700, *describing particularly that famous Empire, likewise the Kingdoms of Dongola, Sennar, part of Egypt*, &c. London, 1709.

"bear the best Dates of all Egypt," and in a short time entered a "frightful Desart," which is extremely dangerous, "because the "Sands being moving are rais'd by the least Wind which darkens "the Air, and falling afterwards in Clouds, Passengers are often "buried in them, or at least lose the *Route*, which they ought "to keep." Their caravan used to start three or four hours before daylight, and march till noon, when they stopped for half an hour. After this short rest the journey was resumed and continued till three or four hours after sunset. A march of five days brought the party to Helâwa, which appears to have been situated in a part of a large Oasis, and was the last town under Turkish rule in that direction. It contained a great number of Gardens, "watered with brooks, and a world of palm-trees," and large crops of senna. The heat by day was excessive, but the nights were cold enough. Two days' march took the party from Helâwa to Shabb, i.e., alum, a place which derives its name from the alum deposits which are found there, and in three days more they reached the Oasis of Selîma. By this time M. Poncet and his companions found the journey very "tedious and dis-"agreeable," for in these "vast wildernesses" there is "neither to "be found bird, nor wild beast, nor herbs, no nor so much as a "little fly," and "nothing is to be seen but mountains of sand "and the carcasses, and bones of camels," which "imprint a "certain horrour in the mind." Repeating, no doubt, the native view, M. Poncet declares that the kingdom of the Sûdân lies westward of that of Sennaar, and adds that the merchants of Upper Egypt trade thither for gold and slaves. In his day, even as in the time of Ḥer-khuf, whose travels are described elsewhere in this work, the kings of the two regions were almost continually at war, and this information helps us to understand the difficult position in which the ancient Egyptian official found himself when he discovered that the king of Amam was fighting against the king of Themeḥ. If Amam represents the modern kingdom of Sennaar, it is probable that Themeḥ represents that portion of the land of the Blacks from which Ḥer-khuf obtained his three hundred asses' loads of skins, &c.

M. Poncet's next stopping-place[1] was Mashu, or Moshi, near

[1] In modern maps "Bullu Narti."

the northern end of Bonarti Island, and not far from Arḳô Island. He describes these Islands as being full of palm-trees, senna, and colo-quintida, i.e., the bitter apple. The governor of the district, which was then in the Province of Fûng and under the jurisdiction of the king of Sennaar, lived at Arḳô, a town on the east bank of the Nile a few miles to the south of Moshi. After a stay of eight days, M. Poncet pushed on to the town of Dongola, that is, Old Dongola, and so passed out of the region of the Barâbara, which extends from Moshi, or perhaps Hannek, so far north as Aswân. This portion of the Nile Valley was then, as it is now, very pleasant, for the narrow strip of land on each side of the river is very fertile, and in times of peace it is well watered by means of water-wheels turned by oxen. The glimpse which our traveller gives us of the manners and customs of the inhabitants is interesting. He tells us that silver was useless in the way of trade, and that all business was carried on by barter. The bread was made of *dhurra*, from which the natives also made a "thick beer very ill-tasted." The people were healthy and stronger than Europeans and more robust. Their houses were low and made of mud, and covered with the reeds of *dhurra*. Their horses were well shaped, but were greatly fatigued by the saddles put upon them, which were very high both before and behind. Men of position went bare-headed and had their hair braided, and wore a single garment, which consisted of a sort of mis-shapen vest without sleeves; they wore nothing on their legs and nothing on their feet, except "a single sole made fast with latchets." The common people wore pieces of linen in which they wrapped themselves, and the children were almost naked. Some men carried lances, the iron ends of which were hooked, and some had swords that hung from their left arms. The morality of the Dongola folk left, according to M. Poncet, much to be desired, for he says, "Oathes and blasphemies are very common amongst those stupid "people, who likewise are so debauch'd that they have neither "modesty, nor civility, nor religion. For altho' Mahometanism "is what at present they make profession of, yet they know no "more than the bare formulary of their profession of faith, which "they repeat on all occasions."

Father Brevedent, the companion of M. Poncet, was greatly

grieved at this state of things; for, according to him, it was not long since the population was Christian, and the people only lost the faith because there was no one who had zeal enough to consecrate himself to the instruction of this abandoned race. In proof of this assertion, M. Poncet mentions that on their way they passed a great number of hermitages and churches half ruined. A contributory cause of the ignorance and misery of the district was, no doubt, the plague which ravaged Egypt and Nubia in 1696, in which year it is said that ten thousand people died daily. The town of Dongola stands on the top of a dry and sandy hill on the east bank of the river, and M. Poncet describes the houses as ill-built, and speaks of the half-deserted streets filled with sand brought down from the mountains by floods. The castle is in the middle of the town. From Dongola M. Poncet passed on to Korti, and his caravan crossed the Bayûda Desert, and struck the Nile again at Gerri, a place which seems to have been near the Sixth Cataract (Shablûka). The manner in which the Nile was crossed here struck the traveller as being "somewhat singular." The men and goods were placed in the same boat, but the beasts had to swim across, their heads being tied to the boat. The poor creatures suffered greatly by this clumsy method, and many were drowned, for, although the Nile is not wide at that place, the current is strong and the water deep. From this point M. Poncet travelled to Ḥalfâya, and thence into Ethiopia in a north-easterly direction, and the remainder of his narrative deals with that country. The information which he supplies about Nubia and the Sûdân is meagre, but it must be remembered that his destination was Ethiopia. Could he have devoted to the Valley of the Nile the same time and attention which he gave to that country he would certainly have produced a very instructive book.

The next traveller to the Sûdân of whom mention must be made was M. LE NOIR DU ROULE, who was appointed to succeed Poncet, and to conduct a mission to the King of Abyssinia on behalf of Louis XIV., the famous patron of the arts and sciences and learning generally. It seems that towards the close of the seventeenth century a serious dispute broke out between the Italian missionaries of the reformed order of St. Francis, who were settled in Cairo, and the Fathers of Jerusalem or of the Holy Land, the former claiming to be independent of the latter. Ultimately the Pope was appealed to, and, as a result, the reformed Franciscans were dismissed from their office, and they returned to Rome, where for many years they endeavoured to regain their old position and authority by any and every means in their power. For some time they were unsuccessful, because the Fathers of Jerusalem, or Capuchins as Bruce calls them, were both rich and powerful, and the Franciscans could make no headway against them. After a time the Franciscans worked out a scheme whereby they obtained the management of the Ethiopian mission. They declared that when the Jesuits were expelled from Abyssinia a great number of Catholics had fled into Sennaar and Nubia, and that though these had maintained their new faith up to the present, there was great danger of their becoming Muḥammadans unless spiritual assistance were sent to them soon.

When Pope Innocent XII. heard of this, he established a considerable fund to support a Mission to the wandering Catholics in Nubia, and monasteries were founded in three or four towns in Egypt, in which missionaries passing to and from Nubia might rest and refresh themselves. About this time the Jesuits succeeded in gaining the support of Louis XIV., and Father Fleurian, a friend of the king's confessor, was employed to direct the French Consul in Cairo, M. de Maillet, to send, in co-operation with the Jesuits, privately into Abyssinia a fit person who might inspire the king of that country with the desire to send an embassy into France, and upon the management of this political affair they founded their hopes of getting themselves replaced in the mission formerly established by them, and of superseding their rivals, the Franciscans, in directing all the measures to be taken for that country's conversion. Louis XIV. readily undertook the protection of the mission, and the Jesuit Verseau was sent to Rome with introductions to the Pope. The Pope received Verseau, and at once consented that he and five other Jesuits should go to Abyssinia without delay. Now in spite of this favourable reception of the legate of Louis XIV., the Pope had no idea of falling in with the royal wish, for without the knowledge of the Jesuits, or in any way consulting them, he appointed the superior of the Franciscans to be his legate to the king of Abyssinia, and provided him with gifts for the king and his nobles. Verseau, instead of going to Cairo, went to Syria, *viâ* Constantinople, where he remained and fulfilled the duties of head of a monastery of his own order. Thus it fell out that the Ethiopian mission at Cairo remained in charge of one Paschal, an Italian Franciscan friar, and of a French Jesuit whose name was Brevedent.

At this time there was in Cairo an envoy of the king of Abyssinia called Ḥaggi Alî, who, having known this Paschal and obtained medicines from him, now applied to him and begged him to return to Abyssinia and cure the king and his son, both of whom were of a scorbutic habit. Paschal agreed to do this on the understanding that he might take with him a friar of his own order called Anthony, and to this Ḥaggi Alî made no objection, being rather glad than otherwise to take back two physicians instead of one.

As soon as the French Consul heard of the arrangement made by Paschal with Ḥaggi Alî, he sent for the latter, and having told him that neither Paschal nor the friar Anthony was a physician, soon persuaded him to cancel his agreement with them, and take in their stead Charles Poncet, whom he lauded as a great chemist and apothecary, and one who was a supreme expert in the knowledge of the art of medicine. The French Consul also arranged that M. Brevedent, a Jesuit, should attend the physician as a servant. M. Poncet having been furnished with a medicine-chest at the expense of the "factory," set out forthwith, accompanied by Brevedent, who took the name of Joseph; and Ḥaggi Alî and they arrived at Sennaar in due course, as we have seen. There is no need to discuss here the difficulties and inaccuracies which Bruce alleges to have discovered in Poncet's narrative of his travels, for all that concerns us is the undoubted fact that Poncet did travel to Sennaar, and he certainly cured the king of his ailments, and thus performed the work which Ḥaggi Alî had intended him to do. The part of the Mission which the French Consul, M. de Maillet, wished him to carry out remained unperformed, and no wonder; for to believe that it was possible for a private person like Poncet, without a knowledge of the language, and without money and the means of making gifts, and without the power of giving or affording any sort of protection, to prevail upon the king of Abyssinia to send a party of from twenty to thirty people to France, on the word of a mere travelling physician, was the very height of ignorance and folly. The Abyssinians at that time hated the French, and they had already shown with considerable force what their opinion of their religion was, and it is quite certain that if any Abyssinians had been foolish enough to leave their own country, and to receive instruction in the religion which their countrymen abhorred, they would have been put to death on their return. The Abyssinian embassy, then, demanded from France, and recommended by M. de Maillet, was a presumptuous, vain, impracticable scheme, which must have ended in disappointment, and which never could have closed more innocently than it did.[1]

Now, although the Mission of Poncet had failed from the point of view of the Jesuits, those who were interested in forcing the Abyssinians to send a mission, which was to consist of twenty-eight persons, of whom twelve were to be the sons of nobles, determined not to let the matter drop. They therefore decided to despatch a second envoy to Abyssinia, but no adventurer or vagrant physician was to be employed in this second embassy. "A minister versed in languages, negociations, and treaties, "accompanied with proper dragomans and officers, was to be sent "to Abyssinia to cement a perpetual friendship and commerce "between two nations that had not a national article to exchange "with each other, nor way to communicate it by sea or land."[2] The man chosen by the minister who had to decide the matter was M. de Maillet, the French Consul, who, knowing all the causes which led to failure, was held by him to be the right person to bring the proposed mission to a successful issue. This selection, however, was by no means to M. de Maillet's liking, and the idea of a long and toilsome journey through waterless deserts and under a burning sun did not commend itself to him in any way, for he rarely went out of his house, and was never known to go outside the city, and for a man of such habits of life

[1] Bruce, *Travels*, vol. iii., p. 497 (Edinburgh edition, 1813).
[2] *Ibid.*, vol. iii., p. 515.

to undertake a desert journey of nearly 2,000 miles was absurd. M. de Maillet, therefore, promptly excused himself from the honour, but was careful to draw up a set of rules for the guidance of the man who was to go in his stead through a country which he himself had never seen. These rules were strictly observed by the new envoy, with what result we shall presently see.

The choice of a successor for M. de Maillet fell upon the Vice-Consul of Damietta, a young man of the name of LE NOIR DU ROULE; he had some knowledge of the Arabic language, but he knew neither the ancient language of Abyssinia (Ethiopic) nor the modern (Amharic), and he appears to have been ignorant of the manners and customs of Orientals generally. According to Bruce, he had a violent predilection for the dress, carriage, and manners of France, and a hearty contempt for those of all other nations, and as he had not sufficient address to disguise his views, his mission was fraught with danger from the beginning. He had no friends among the French colony in Cairo, but as he was the nominee of M. de Maillet and of the Jesuits, and as they were supported by the authority of Louis XIV., he troubled himself little about this matter. When the Franciscans, into whose hands the Ethiopian mission had been entrusted by the Pope, heard of the new embassy, they were extremely angry, and they determined to use every means in their power to turn du Roule's mission into a fiasco. They succeeded in making the Coptic community throughout Egypt take their view of the matter, and, before he started, his mission was doomed to failure.

On July 9th, 1704, du Roule set out from Cairo, but his followers were fewer than he had anticipated, for many of them on getting an inkling of the true inwardness of affairs promptly withdrew from the mission. At every place which he reached on the Nile between Cairo and Asyût he found that the minds of the people had been poisoned against him, and that obstruction was everywhere, in every shape and form. When he at length arrived at Asyût he saw that the chief of his caravan, one Belak, a Moor, was only prevented by fear from declaring himself an open enemy, and that every man's hand was against him and his party. Subsequently it was discovered from the confession of Alî Shalabi, the governor of Asyût, that the

Christian merchants and the friars were in a conspiracy to defeat and break up the mission, and, if necessary, to kill du Roule himself. Meanwhile the Copts had been concocting very serious mischief. They obtained access to all the principal natives in the caravan, and persuaded them that the Europeans who were travelling with them were not merchants, but sorcerers, who were going to Abyssinia on purpose to cut off the Nile at its source, or to turn it out of its course so that it might no longer send its waters into Egypt, which, in cousequence, would become a desert. In order to prove that du Roule was a sorcerer, the frequenters of the cafés and bazaars, at the instigation of the Copts, declared that whilst the party was sailing up the Nile, M. du Roule shot an arrow into the air, and that this had the effect of making appear four thousand armed men, who clashed against each other in a most alarming manner. On his way up the river from Cairo du Roule left his boat and went to visit some ancient ruins on the river bank, and those who told the story of the visit in Asyût declared that whilst there he made a sign to a high column to follow him, and that the column did so, and actually came on board the boat, and turned forthwith into a man of huge size, who held a conversation with du Roule. The result of all these absurd lies was that crowds of people assembled outside the house wherein he was lodging, and their attentions to the inmates were such that the governor of the town was sometimes obliged to send the Turkish police to drive the people away. Meanwhile the members of the mission were to all intents and purposes prisoners, and M. Lippi, in a letter written from Asyût on September 5th, 1704, pathetically complains to his correspondent that he cannot pursue his botanical studies because he is afraid to leave the house to go on excursions to collect plants. Such were the troubles which came upon du Roule in Asyût, and but for the protection of the Governor he would have found it impossible to proceed on his way.

M. du Roule left Asyût with his caravan on September 12th, and a journey of twelve days brought him to the Oasis of Khârga, where he was detained six days by the governor, who obliged him to pay 120 dollars, and at the same time to sign a paper declaring that he had been allowed free passage through the Oasis without paying anything! On October 3rd he reached Selima, and thirteen days later he came to Moshi, on the Nile, where a long halt was made by the merchants, who had much business to transact. Here du Roule learned that several Franciscan friars had passed him at Asyût, and that they had gone into Sennaar, but that they had disappeared when they heard that his caravan was advancing through the desert. About this time a report was spread abroad in Cairo that du Roule had been murdered in Dongola. Towards the end of May du Roule arrived in Sennaar, and was well received by the king, who was a young man, and fond of strangers. Du Roule received particular attention from the master of the royal household, one Aḥmad Sid-al-Kôm, who told him that he had received information from Cairo that he had twenty chests of silver with him, but at the same time expressed surprise at finding du Roule's baggage so little, both in bulk and value. Aḥmad also told him that he had been warned from Cairo not to let him pass, and that he had been given to understand that the object of his mission was to persuade Îyâsûs, the king of Abyssinia, to attack Maṣawa and Sawâkin, and to take these towns from the Turks.

Soon after du Roule's arrival in Sennaar the court decreed that a festival should be held to celebrate a recent victory of the Abyssinians over the Arabs, and he determined to do all that lay in his power to add to the magnificence of the occasion. With this object in view he shaved off his beard and resumed European garb, but the only effect of this was to shock everybody. He appears to have made some display of the mirrors, which the French Consul in Cairo had insisted on his taking with him, and because they multiplied the objects round about them, and distorted them, they caused the common people to regard du Roule and his companions as sorcerers. On all festival occasions the king's wives were allowed to leave their apartments, and to go and look on at the general rejoicings and to see what was to be seen. Without any delay they went to visit du Roule, who failed to entertain them with spirits and sweets, and to give them scent, which all Sûdânî folks love, and they left him in high dudgeon. They were, moreover, terrified at his mirrors, and, being disgusted with the scant courtesy which he had shown them, they joined in the cry that he was a magician, and tried to persuade the king to make an end of him. The king strongly objected to do this, but he made up for his self-restraint by demanding a gift of 3,000 dollars from du Roule; this demand was, of course, refused, and the king was thereby greatly offended.

Du Roule now fully realized that he was in no inconsiderable danger, and he asked leave to depart from Sennaar; twice the king gave him leave to do so, and twice was the leave withdrawn. On November 10th for the third time he received leave to depart, and as all his possessions were ready packed, he at once set out to leave the city. He walked from his lodging to the large square in front of the king's house, accompanied by two native Christians and his French servant Gentil; his dragomans MM. Lippi and Macé were on horseback, and a Nubian servant led his horse. As soon as du Roule came into the middle of the square, which was the common place of execution for criminals, four blacks attacked him, and murdered him with their sabres. All his companions were murdered at the same time, with the exception of M. Macé, who shot two of his assailants dead; he continued to defend himself with his sword, but a horseman coming up behind him drove a spear through his back, and threw him upon the ground dead. Du Roule died like a man, and, believing that his person was sacred because he was an ambassador, he in no way defended himself against those who attacked him, but left his revenge to the guardians of the law. Directly after the murder of du Roule, the friars, who had left Sennaar immediately before his arrival, returned, and they sought to lay the blame first upon the king of Abyssinia, then upon the king of Sennaar, and then upon both. Subsequently, however, it was proved that the former king was innocent, and that the latter was an unwilling agent, who had on two occasions made du Roule return to his house in order to delay the fulfilment of his pledge to have him murdered, the giving of which he much repented.

That Îyâsûs,[1] king of Abyssinia, had nothing to do with the

[1] 'Îyâsûs 'Adyâm Sagad I. was crowned in 1682, was deposed in March, 1706, and murdered in October of the same year.

murder is clear from the following facts:—Before du Roule started for Sennaar, the French Consul in Cairo, M. de Maillet, sent an Armenian called Elias to Abyssinia, with orders to proceed to Gondar by way of the Red Sea and Maṣawa, so that he might reach the king before du Roule, and so prepare Îyâsûs for his coming. When Îyâsûs had received this letter, he readily gave permission for du Roule to enter his country, and he sent one of his own men to Sennaar with orders to escort him to Gondar, and to pay the expenses of his journey. It is a pity that de Maillet had not warned the king of Sennaar that he had in his country numbers of friars who were disseminating lies broadcast, and poisoning the minds of the lowest of his people, who were naturally barbarous, brutal, and jealous. There is little doubt that the murder of du Roule was due to a plot which was hatched by the Franciscan friars, who would rather see the Abyssinians remain, from their point of view, heathen, than that their conversion should be brought about by the Jesuits.

With the above facts before us, which have been taken from the detailed narrative of Bruce, who obtained his information in Abyssinia and Egypt, it is hard to conceive how Cailliaud could write as he did of the circumstances which led up to the murder of du Roule. In the Preface to his *Voyage à Méroé* he claims for France the honour of having been the first to direct the attention of the learned to Egypt, and to have opened the mine whereout men have been able ever since to draw treasure by the handful. He then goes on to say that more than one hundred and twenty years ago Louis XIV. conceived the project of sending out learned men to make discoveries, and that they went so far as Sennaar.[1] We have seen that the missions on which Poncet and du Roule were sent were not scientific missions in any sense of the word, and that their real object was the conversion of Abyssinia. Nor is Cailliaud more correct in the cause which he assigns for du Roule's murder. He declared that it was cupidity, coupled with a stupid credulity, which led the king of Sennaar to commit such an atrocious act of treachery, and

[1] "Il est glorieux pour la France d'avoir, la première, dirigé leurs pas vers "cette terre classique, et d'avoir ouvert la mine où l'on a puisé depuis à pleines "mains."

would lead us to suppose that a contributory cause was the imprudent display of luxury which du Roule himself made, for he says that du Roule had with him sixty camels laden with merchandise and valuable goods, which was more than enough to excite the greed of the barbarians.[1]

The first traveller in comparatively modern times to deal with any portion of the Valley of the Nile was Captain LEWIS NORDEN, F.R.S., who was born October 22nd, 1708, and died September 22nd, 1742. He was despatched to Egypt in 1737 by H.M. Christian VI. of Denmark, and travelled on the Nile from November 17th, 1737, to February 21st, 1738, and embodied the results of his journey in two folio volumes, which are illustrated with plates.[2] Having arrived at Aswân, and inspected the antiquities from Elephantine to Philae, he decided to continue his journey to the Second Cataract, and announced his intention of doing so to the local authorities, who characteristically urged him to change his mind. The Aghâ of the district told him that to attempt to reach the Second Cataract was only to cause his sure destruction, for cases had happened in which men of his own religion had entered Nubia, and had never returned. After paying for his own permit to travel, and for that of the captain of the boat who allowed him to sail up the river, Captain Norden set out on his journey just one month before Dr. Pococke arrived in Aswân. The state of the country at that time was such that travelling brought with it many risks, and it is clear that only the boldest travellers ever got beyond the First Cataract. When Captain Norden landed on the Island of Philae, in order to sketch the front of the temple of Isis, some hundreds of the Barâbara collected on the bank, and threatened to burn the boat if he did not leave the place and embark. Near Kalâbsha the natives cried out to the captain of the boat, and insisted that he should stop so that they might see the Franks

[1] "La cupidité, non moins qu'une crédulité stupide, fut sans doute le "motif qui porta le prince à une trahison aussi atroce. M. du Roule "étalait un luxe imprudent ; il avait soixante chameaux chargés de bagages et "d'objets précieux : c'était plus qu'il en fallait pour exciter la convoitise de ces "barbares." Tom. ii., p. 306.

[2] *Travels in Egypt and Nubia, translated and enlarged, with observations from ancient and modern writers*, by Dr. Peter Templeman, London, 1757.

who were on board, and have some of the riches which they carried about with them. When the captain refused to stop they promptly fired at his boat from each side of the river. A few days later, at no great distance from Korosko, Captain Norden was reading over a list of names of places which they had passed on the preceding day, and making corrections in the spelling by the help of the captain of the boat and his Jewish valet, when suddenly a native, to whom a passage had been given on the boat, rushed on him, snatched the paper out of his hand and tore it in pieces; he then retired quietly to his place as if nothing had happened. The bystanders burst into a laugh, and when an explanation of the incident was demanded by Captain Norden, the passenger told him that he did not wish him to know the name of the place whence he came. The man was convinced that Captain Norden would one day return with many of his fellow-countrymen, and having made himself master of the country would force him into his service; such was the reason he gave for snatching at the paper and tearing it up.

Having continued his journey, and examined the ruins in the Wâdî Sabû'a, Captain Norden arrived at "Koroscoff," or Korosko. The governor of the little town was found seated in the middle of a field, exposed to all the heat of the sun, and employed in deciding a dispute between two men about a camel. He had the look of a wolf, and was dressed like a beggar. An old napkin, which had once been white, made his turban, and a red dress, still older, scarcely covered his body, portions of which appeared through the holes. His behaviour was insolent, and continued to be so until the valet promised him a present, when he suddenly became amiable, and told Captain Norden that there was nothing to prevent him from going to Derr. Thereupon Captain Norden set sail, but before he had gone any great distance, the master of the boat declared that nothing would induce him to proceed to the Second Cataract, or indeed to carry him any farther than Derr, that is to say, about seventy-five miles north of the foot of the Second Cataract. Continuing his journey a little above Amâda, Captain Norden found in use a curious method adopted by the natives for crossing the Nile. Two men were sitting on a bundle of reeds, which was towed by a cow swimming in front of it: one man held on to the tail of the cow, and the other, who sat behind, guided the beast by a cord fastened to her horns, and steered the bundle of reeds by means of a small oar. When a number of camels had to be taken across the river a man swam before them, holding the bridle of the first camel in his mouth; the second camel was fastened to the tail of the first, and the third to the tail of the second. The rear was brought up by a man who took care that the second and third camels should follow in line.

When Derr was reached the authorities proposed that the traveller should stay in the town until the new governor arrived, when, as it was intended to make war upon the people of the Second Cataract immediately after his arrival, Captain Norden would be able to continue his journey by land in perfect safety, for Captain Norden would be accompanied by five hundred men. This proposal was naturally rejected, whereupon the governor not only declared that Captain Norden should not go on, but also that, as the boat in which he had sailed so far up the Nile was the governor's, Captain Norden must turn out of it, as the governor needed it for his own use. As there was no other boat in which he could either go up or down the river, Captain Norden was obliged to come to terms with the governor, and to pay him handsomely for the use of the boat in sailing back to Aswân. Meanwhile a second local authority did not view with favour the idea of losing the opportunity of making more money out of Captain Norden, and he succeeded in persuading the owner of the boat to cry off his bargain, on the ground that the payment to be made for it was insufficient. When he was remonstrated with, the owner of the boat, i.e., the governor, became insolent, and on being reminded that the traveller was under the protection of the "Grand Signior," replied, "I laugh at the horns of the "Grand Signior, I am here Grand Signior myself, and will teach "you to respect me as you ought. I know already what sort of "people you are. I have consulted my cup, and have found by "it that you are those of whom one of our prophets has said, "'There would come Franks in disguise, who, by little presents, "and by a soothing and insinuating behaviour would pass every- "where; examine the state of the country; go to make a report "of it, and afterwards returning with a great number of Franks, "conquer and exterminate us all.' But I will take care of that; "you must quit the barque without delay."

To leave the boat was impossible, and Captain Norden determined to continue to occupy it at all costs, and when the authorities saw that his mind was made up to fight if necessary, they changed their tactics, and by promising to let him leave Derr succeeded in obtaining many valuable presents from him. Promise after promise was broken, and at length the governor declared he would murder the whole party. At this juncture the Effendi, or clerk to the governor, came and revealed the plot which had been hatched against Captain Norden before he arrived at Derr. He said, "You have to do with devils and not men. I have the "unhappiness to be obliged to live with them. I maintain myself "in my post because I can write, which they cannot do them-"selves; but I abhor the manner in which they treat strangers, "whence no barque comes here." He then went on to tell Captain Norden that his death was debated upon before his arrival, that it was intended to take him into the desert under the pretence of leading him to the Second Cataract, that the story of the proposed war was a lie from beginning to end, that the governor was the greatest villain on earth, that he had killed nine men with his own hands, some of them being the most powerful men in the country, that he was raving drunk every night, and that he was addicted to the incest of Lot—in short, that he was the vilest wretch he knew. Further negotiations were undertaken between the governor and Captain Norden, and little by little the former obtained nearly everything of any value on the boat. He was never tired of asking for something more, and when he saw nothing more to ask for, he begged on behalf of the bullies whom he had brought with him. In fact he was the ancestor of the Berberi camel-man to whom a modern traveller foolishly gave three days' pay more than was his due; the Berberi then asked for a compass to use in finding the direction in which to pray, and when this was given, he asked for *bakshîsh* for his camel, and then for something for himself!

Finally, seeing that there was nothing more to be had, the governor left the boat, and Captain Norden thought he had seen the last of him, but subsequently word came that he intended to visit the boat once again to bid the travellers farewell; he was prevented from doing this by hints that personal violence might be done to him if he came, but to the last he was equal to the occasion, for he sent word to Captain Norden that his wife had just been delivered, and asked for a present for the child! This he was given, and then the boat was loosed from her moorings, and the journey down stream began; in six days the port of Morrada, immediately above the First Cataract, was reached, and Captain Norden remarks quaintly that as they passed the various places on the river the people were everywhere surprised to find that the travellers were still alive, and that they had escaped out of the hands of the governor of Derr. From the above facts it is clear that in the first half of the eighteenth century the country between the First and Second Cataracts was in a very troubled state, that the Sulṭân in Constantinople had no real hold over the country, and that travellers who insisted on penetrating the upper parts of the Nile Valley did so at great risk. At this period it was extremely difficult to obtain provisions anywhere above Aswân, for the people possessed very few sheep, goats or chickens; the narrow strips of cultivable land on the river bank did not produce grain sufficient for the needs of the people, and the natives never ground more *dhurra* than they needed for their immediate use. This description of the country is not a pleasing one, but had it been written in 1885 instead of 1737 it would have been equally true.

Most prominent and most important of all the travellers in the Sûdân during the eighteenth century is JAMES BRUCE, who was born at Kinnaird, in the county of Stirling, Scotland, on December 14th, 1730. He was the younger son of David Bruce by his wife Marion, daughter of James Graham, Dean of the Faculty of Advocates, and Judge of the High Court of Admiralty in Scotland. He entered Harrow School on January 21st, 1742, and left it on May 8th, 1746. At Harrow he acquired a competent knowledge of the classics, and after his departure from the school he studied French, arithmetic and geometry, under Mr. Gordon, until April, 1747. In the same year he began to study law in the University of Edinburgh, but he made little progress. On February 3rd,

1754, he married Adriana Allan, the daughter of a merchant of Scottish extraction, who had settled in London, but she unfortunately died of consumption before the close of the year. In 1761 he withdrew from the wine business, in which he had obtained a share on his marriage with Miss Allan, and offered his services to the Government of the day; they were, however, refused. He then began a course of travel which took him through all the countries of Europe, Syria, and a considerable portion of Northern Africa, and he arrived in Alexandria at the end of June, 1768.

He left Cairo in December of that year, and sailed up the Nile to the First Cataract. In February, 1769, he left Ḳena on the Nile for Ḳuṣêr (Cosseir), and from that place he visited the emerald mines of Gebel Zumrûd, which are described by Pliny and other ancient writers. He next crossed the Red Sea to Tor and proceeded to Jidda (Jeddah), where he obtained such assistance as would enable him to travel in Abyssinia. He left Jidda in May, 1769, and arrived at Maṣawa on September 19th. Here he suffered greatly from the obstruction of the governor, who accused him of holding converse with a comet, which was then visible, for the purpose of bringing disease upon the country, and he was all but murdered on the spot. On November 15th he left Arkîks, and on December 6th he arrived at Axum, the capital of the Graeco-Abyssinian kingdom, which took the place of the kingdom on the Island of Meroë. Here he examined the obelisks [1] and other antiquities which proclaim the importance of the old capital of Tigré.

Soon after he left Axum he saw the incident which has given rise to so much discussion, viz a party of soldiers eating pieces of flesh which they were cutting from a living cow. This custom of the Abyssinians was well known to many ancient writers, some of whom state that it was introduced into Abyssinia from the interior of Africa. One writer (Lobo, *Rel. d'Abyssinie*, p. 22) says that a piece of raw beef quite warm is the greatest treat which

[1] See Niebuhr, *Kleine Schriften*, i, p. 400; V. de St. Martin, *Journal Asiatique*, vi. 2, p. 328 ff.; Dillmann, *Abhandlungen*, 1877, p. 195; Glaser, *Skizze*, ii., p. 474 ff.; D. H. Müller, *Denkschriften*, Vienna, tom. xliii., 1893, iii., p. 3 ff.

the Abyssinians can have, and that when they give a feast they kill an ox and immediately serve up a quarter of it on the table with much pepper and salt. The gall of the ox serves both for oil and vinegar! Sir William Jones declared that the country people and soldiery made no scruple of drinking the blood and eating the raw flesh of an ox, which they cut without caring whether it was alive or dead. On February 15th Bruce reached Gondar and encamped by the Anḳarab River. Here he stayed some time, and made many friends by his medical skill and knowledge. The excesses which he saw committed at the Abyssinian court troubled him greatly, and he was forced to be present at one marriage feast which lasted for some weeks. Cattle were distributed among the populace and the army, drink was given in proportion, and he considered the dissipation which followed both unimaginable and indescribable. The married women ate raw beef, drank spirits and a drink made of honey and water fermented, and smoked like men. After a time Bruce asked for and obtained permission to go and live in the village of Emfras, which is situated about twenty miles from Gondar on the eastern side of the Lake of Demba. About this time the king of Abyssinia[1] made him a gentleman of his bedchamber, a commander of the household cavalry, and a governor of a province! In return for the services which Bruce was able to render, the king gave him the village of Gish and the ground round about it, which contained the source of the river Abâî, better known in Sûdân territory as the "Blue Nile."

During the summer of that year (1770) Bruce never lost an opportunity of making his way towards the source of the Blue Nile, for he felt with the poet:—

> "Sed cum tanta meo vivat sub pectore virtus,
> Tantus amor veri, nihil est quod noscere malim
> Quam fluvii causas per saecula tanta latentes
> Ignotumque caput: spes sit mihi certa videndi
> Niliacos fontes."
>
> (Lucan x. 188 sqq.)

He believed the Blue Nile to be the source of the whole Nile, for he attached little importance to the White Nile and never

[1] The king was Takla Hâymânôt II. 'Admâs Sagad II.; he was deposed in April, 1777, and died in the following September.

imagined that it was the true Nile, and at length, early in November, he arrived at Sakkala, where he observed that the Abâi had dwindled to a small brook. He ran down to a grassy spot, where he found two or three springs of different sizes, some of which were enclosed within mounds of turf. These mounds had been made by the Agows, who had of old worshipped the river, and who, even in Bruce's time, paid adoration to it. Bruce's joy was very great, for he believed that he had really discovered the source of the Nile, and that he had seen with his own eyes that which had been unknown to the ancients and had never been seen by any European before. He then drank the healths of his sovereign and his absent friends in water from the springs before him, a proceeding which filled his companion, Strates, with wonderment. Bruce took up his abode in the house of Kefla Abâi, a descendant of the heathen priests who had in days of old worshipped the river, and he celebrated his discovery by making a feast for all the people, which lasted for five days.

From Gish Bruce returned by the Gondar road, but instead of going into the capital he turned aside and came to Koskam. It was fortunate that he did so, for, whilst he was there the usurper of the throne sallied out from the palace with his friends one night, and went to Bruce's house in Gondar with the intention of murdering him. In December, 1770, the king was enabled to take vengeance upon his foes, and for several weeks innumerable men were beheaded in the city. Besides this, men were hanged by hundreds in the public square, and their bodies were left there to be eaten by the dogs and hyenas. The result of all this was to make Bruce repent that he had ever entered Abyssinia, and he gave himself up to thinking out a plan whereby he might make his escape from that country to Egypt by way of Sennaar. He approached the king on the subject, but after many words and high disputes he only agreed to allow Bruce to go to Egypt if he would promise to stay in Abyssinia till the end of the war, and to return from Egypt very soon accompanied by his relations and friends, who were to be armed with English weapons. On May 19th, 1771, the battle of Serbraxos was fought, and victory was claimed both by the king and by his enemies. Bruce was present and seems to have taken part in it, for when the king returned to his camp he gave Bruce a massive gold chain and arrayed him in gorgeous apparel, according to the ancient custom of the country. On December 26th Bruce left Koskam and arrived at the frontier city of Tchenkîn on January 2nd, 1772. He then proceeded to Horkakamut, and then to Teawa, which he reached on March 22nd. On September 26th he arrived at Herbagi (Arbagi), and four days later he crossed the Nile by the ferry, and in the evening came to the village of Halfâya, about nine miles to the north of the junction of the Blue and White Niles. On October 4th he arrived at Shendi, which, he declared, was ruled by a woman, the sister of Wad Agib. From Shendî he proceeded by a desert route on the east bank of the Nile to Aswân, which he only reached after terrible hardships and great suffering. He left Aswân on December 11th and arrived at Cairo on January 10th, 1773.

The history of his travels, which he subsequently compiled and published, throws very considerable light on the manners and customs of the Abyssinians, and affords much information concerning the kingdom of Sennaar, but it tells nothing about the country and the antiquities which lie between the First Cataract and Kharṭûm. The most valuable portions of the narrative of his travels to the student of the Egyptian Sûdân are those which deal with Nubia and Sennaar, but it must always be remembered that, though written by an able, accomplished, and intelligent traveller, they are not the work of a scientific investigator in the modern sense of the phrase. His nautical surveys have long since been superseded, and his astronomical calculations also, and his theorizing and views as to the historical development of civilization are valueless as a whole, because he regarded Ethiopia as the birthplace of ancient civilization, and the home of the arts and sciences, especially of architecture, astronomy, and writing, and he thought that all the trade and commerce of India and of the Gulf of Arabia were originally established by the Ethiopians. On the other hand, every credit is due to him for his personal bravery, and for the tact and thoroughness with which he carried out the great object of his life, viz., the discovery of the source of the Blue Nile, and although his labours only resulted in tracing to its rise the greatest tributary of that wonderful river, the Nile, we should be thankful for the great amount of information which he gathered concerning the peoples who lived between the 11th and 24th degrees of north latitude, and who were at that time unknown to Europeans.

Our knowledge of the events which took place in Nubia and the Sûdân in the latter half of the eighteenth century is extremely small, for records written by travellers in those countries during this period do not exist. It is very doubtful if any learned European visited Nubia whilst the country was in the unsettled state described by Norden, and we know for a fact that DR. POCOCKE, who travelled in Egypt in 1737 and 1738, did not attempt to proceed further south than Aswân.[1] The eminent traveller NIEBUHR (born March 17th, 1733, died 1763), who visited Egypt in 1761,[2] contented himself with describing Cairo and its inhabitants with care, and says nothing about Upper Egypt or Nubia.[3] The only Europeans who passed through the country appear to have been priests and others who were on their way to or from Ethiopia, and such travellers, whenever it was at all possible, preferred to traverse the blazing deserts to the west of the Nile for weeks at a time, and to endure the miseries of scarcity of water, rather than trust themselves to the Barâbara tribes, and become the victims of their extortion and greed.

Towards the end of the eighteenth century a serious dispute broke out between the Mamlûks who had rule in Upper Egypt, and the governor of Ibrîm, or Primis, in Nubia, and in 1791 war broke out. The caravan traffic between the two countries was entirely stopped, and no one was allowed to pass from Egypt into Nubia under any pretext whatsoever. Such was the state of

[1] See the *World Displayed, or a curious collection of Voyages and Travels*, vol. xii., London, 1774; and *Voyages de Richard Pococke*, vol. i.-vi., Neuchatel, 1772.

[2] See *Nouvelle Bibliothèque des Voyages*, tom. xi., p. 187. Paris (no date).

[3] That such was also the case with writers in the seventeenth century is clear from Wansleben's interesting little work, entitled "*The present State of Egypt,* "*or, a new Relation of a late voyage into that Kingdom, performed in the years* "1672 *and* 1673. Printed by R. E. for John Starkey at the Miter in Fleet Street, "near Temple Bar, London, 1678." Wansleben visited many monasteries and churches in Upper Egypt, but he never went south of Thebes. Much of the information which he gives about Upper Egypt he derives from the narrative of Father Portais.

affairs when Mr. W. G. BROWNE arrived at Aswân in 1792. This gentleman visited Egypt with the view of travelling to Abyssinia in order to investigate a number of problems which had arisen in connection with Bruce's assertion that the Blue Nile was the true Nile, and of passing from Sennaar to the kingdom of Dâr Fûr on the west. He had heard that the slave-raiders of Fûr sometimes extended their journeys for forty or fifty days to the south of their chief city, and was anxious to travel with them to the region of the Equator, which no white man had ever visited. At the same time he hoped to take the opportunity of tracing the course of the Baḥr al-Abyad, or "White Nile," which he believed rightly to be the true Nile, to its source, and of thus settling once and for all the vexed question. To do this work, however, Mr. Browne found to be impossible, for on his arrival at Aswân he saw that the whole country was in a state of war, and the authorities would not allow him to proceed further south.

The following year Mr. Browne decided to visit the Sûdân by means of the desert route to the west of the Nile, and as it was impossible for him to enter the kingdom of Sennaar, owing to the civil war which had broken out on the deposition and murder of the last king, he was forced to take the road which led from Egypt to Dàr Fûr, and hoped to obtain permission to travel to Sennaar later. During the winter of 1793 the Sûdân caravan was being made up in Cairo, and on April 21st he left Bûlâḳ, the port of Cairo, and sailed to Asyût to join it. There he purchased five camels for £13 each, and on May 25th the caravan left Asyût, and set out on the road, which was practically that taken by Poncet about a century before. The caravan passed through the towns of Khârga, Bûlâk, Beris, and Mughess, the last inhabited spot in the Oasis of Khârga on the south, and reached Shabb after a journey of five days. The next halting place was the Oasis of Selima. The country between Shabb and Selima he describes as being rocky in places, and of a sombre colour. At Selima Mr. Browne noticed the small building, made of loose stones, to which Cailliaud subsequently referred, and he mentions an old tradition current among the desert camel-men to the effect that in days of old it had been inhabited by a princess, who, like the Amazons, drew the bow and wielded the battle-axe with her own hand, that she was attended by a large number of followers, who spread terror all over Nubia, and that her name was Selima. The next halting places were Lagia, Bir al-Malḥ, i.e., the Salt Well, Madwa, and Swêni, where all caravans stopped and awaited the permission of the king of Dâr Fûr to enter his territory. The remainder of Mr. Browne's narrative, though of very great interest, does not concern us here, for it deals with the events of the period of nearly three years which he was forced to pass in Dâr Fûr. During this time Mr. Browne collected a number of important facts about the government, population, and commerce of Dâr Fûr, and about the manners and customs of its inhabitants at the close of the eighteenth century. All praise is certainly due to this intrepid traveller, for his work is one of the most careful contributions to the ethnography of Dâr Fûr and Kordofân which have ever been made. The narrative of Mr. Browne came as a revelation to European geographers, for until it appeared neither the exact position nor the extent of the country was known.[1] Though in some few small details his work has been proved to be incorrect, the main facts of the mass of information which he collected have been substantiated by the investigations of such travellers and experts as Seetzen, Linant, Rüppell, Russegger, Kotschy, and Pallme.

It may be noted in passing that the most interesting work on Dâr Fûr produced in the nineteenth century is the narrative of the travels of Muḥammad ibn 'Omar of Tunis, published in Arabic at Paris in 1850. A French translation by Dr. Perron was edited by Jomard and published in Paris in 1845, and an abridgment of the French rendering by Bayle St. John was issued in London in 1854. Muḥammad of Tunis was born in 1789, and was taken to the Sûdân in 1803, and he stayed at Dâr Fûr eight years; in 1820 he

[1] "On doit à ce hardi voyageur d'avoir, le premier, assigné la situation géographique de la principale ville du Dârfour, en même temps qu'il en faisait connaître des particularités neuves, curieuses, surtout sur le climat, les moeurs et les usages. Malheureusement, cet intelligent voyageur fut malade et prisonnier dans le pays pendant la plus grande partie de la durée de son séjour. S'il eût pu mettre à profit, pendant ses trois années de résidence au Dârfour, le talent d'observation dont il était doué il aurait laissé moins à faire à ses successeurs, et il aurait évité quelques méprises où l'a fait tomber sa fâcheuse position." See Jomard, *Observations*, Paris, 1845, p. 6.

obtained permission to travel from the authorities, and he went to the kingdom of Wadaï for a year. When he had been in the Sûdân ten years he returned to Tunis, and later, in 1832, he visited Cairo, where he was given an important post in the Ministry of Public Instruction, and where he first met Dr. Perron, who translated the account of his travels in Dâr Eûr into French. His narrative forms a complete autobiography, and at all points where his assertions can be tested they have been found correct. He writes, of course, from memory, and from an Oriental point of view, and accurate geographical details are not to be expected from him. His style is easy, and his descriptions of Sûdân manners and customs reveal the fact that he possessed the faculty of shrewd and penetrating observation, together with the power of seizing in his mind and expressing in words the salient features of all that he saw and heard.

One of the most interesting features of his narrative is the light which he unconsciously casts upon the abominable traffic in men which went on merrily during his visit to Dâr Fûr. He depicts in broad outlines the conditions under which the black tribes lived in the great forests that formed a belt right across Africa, and shows that the slave trade flourished in them because there was no other business to occupy men's minds. His own co-religionists, the Muḥammadans, who had settled to the north of these forests, drew their supplies of living merchandise from them, and, possessing considerable skill and business capacity, formed slave caravans which they drove mercilessly across deserts for two whole months before they reached northern Egypt. The king of Dâr Eûr would never allow the Nile to be used as a route, for he feared that such a concession to the merchants would bring in its train an invasion of Egyptians led by Turks; he only admitted into his kingdom such merchants as had travelled by the desert route, *viâ* the Oasis of Selîma, for thus the risk of invasion and conquest of his country was reduced to a minimum. Men who had passed sixty or seventy days in marching over the sandy deserts, which lay between Asyût and his frontier towns, would be ill-fitted to undertake the fierce fighting which would follow any attempt to take the country, or in fact to overcome any armed opposition.

THE EGYPTIAN SUDAN

In the early part of the nineteenth century travellers in Nubia and the Sûdân became more numerous, and a general opening up of those countries began. Among the first to force a way into Nubia was Mr. THOMAS LEGH, M.P.,[1] of Lyme, Cheshire, who in the winter of 1812-13 journeyed up the Nile and succeeded in reaching Ibrim, the Primis of classical writers. In the interval which had elapsed since Mr. Browne was turned back at Aswân, the Barâbara, or Nubian tribes, had managed to assert their independence of the Turks, and as the power of the Mamlûks had been crushed, there was no reason why travellers should not have been allowed to proceed, except the all-sufficient one that the Barâbara hated all foreigners and determined to prevent any of them from entering the country. When VIVANT DENON, a member of the French expedition to Egypt ordered by Napoleon the Great, attempted even to visit the Island of Philae, the inhabitants utterly refused to allow him to land, and they gave him to understand that if he attempted to do so every day for two months they would not allow it. The day following that on which they had announced this decision, Denon returned with 200 men, and when the natives saw them they assumed an attitude of defence and defied the French *savant* with loud cries, which the women repeated. The inhabitants of the neighbouring island immediately armed themselves and flocked to the east side of the rock with sabres, muskets, matchlocks, bucklers, and long pikes. Denou assured them that he had no intention of doing them harm, whereupon they declared that they would never let him land, that they were not Mamlûks to fly before him, that they wished to fight, that they had defeated both the Mamlûks and their neighbours, and that they would resist him. Denon then ordered his sappers to pull down the huts on the mainland, whereupon, posting themselves in the clefts and caves of their rocks, the inhabitants began a brisk and well-directed fire. Soon after this a field-piece was brought up, and as soon as the people of the larger island saw that communication between them and Philae was broken, they drove their cattle across a narrow arm of the Nile and disappeared into the desert. As it was impossible for Denon to complete a

[1] See Thomas Legh, *Narrative of a Journey in Egypt and the Country beyond the Cataracts*, London, 4to, 1816.

raft sufficiently large to convey forty men across the river in less than two days, the natives became insolent, and told the French general that he might come alone to Philae if he would pay 100 piastres. When, however, they saw the larger island of Bigga covered with soldiers, terror seized them, and men, women, and children all threw themselves into the river to escape by swimming; and mothers were seen drowning their children whom they could not carry away with them, and mutilating the girls to save them from the violence of the victors. "Quand," says Denon, "j'entrai le lendemain dans l'ile, je trouvai une "petite fille de 7 à 8 ans, à laquelle une couture faite avec autant "de brutalité que de cruauté avoit ôté tous les moyens de satisfaire "au plus pressant besoin, et lui causoit des convulsions horribles; "ce ne fut qu'avec une contre-opération et un bain que je sauvai la "vie à cette malheureuse petite créature qui étoit tout à fait jolie."[1] The stern measures adopted by the French in dealing with the natives of Philae had a most salutary effect upon them, for they lost possession of their island, and all the stores which they had plundered from the Mamlûks fell into the hands of their conquerors, and they were in a far worse plight than their neighbours, whom they had despised as cowards.

When Mr. Legh arrived at Aswân, the Shêkh of the town encouraged him to proceed southwards, and promised that his son should accompany him, and undertook to procure a smaller boat for him in which to make the journey, for the boat in which he had travelled from Philae was too large to pass the rapids between Aswân and Philae. The reason for the Shêkh's civility was not far to seek, for he was allowed to dispose of a large quantity of salt with which Mr. Legh had loaded his boat, both for use as merchandise and ballast. The Shêkh kept his word, and in due course Mr. Legh proceeded to Sayâla, where he stopped to visit the local governor, and to present the letter to him which he had brought from Aswân. The governor received him kindly and gave him milk, flour, and butter, in return for which he received a present of coffee and tobacco, commodities which were, and still are, highly prized in Nubia. A little to the south of Dendûr he stopped again, and he reports that the natives were peaceably

[1] Denon, *Voyages*, tom. ii., p. 89.

disposed, and that they brought him dates, milk, &c.; another stoppage was made to examine the Egyptian temple of Dakka, and at length Derr was reached without mishap. Here Mr. Legh waited upon Ḥasan, the governor, who when he appeared was half drunk; he had been giving a feast to the people in honour of his marriage, and was in an excited state. In reply to his questions, "What do you want? Why have you come to Derr?" Mr. Legh replied that he had come to pay his respects to him, to see the antiquities, and to ask his permission to journey on to Ibrim. Ḥasan flatly refused to allow him to go to Ibrim, saying first that there was nothing to see, and next that he had no horses for him; in short, he clearly had no intention of letting the party proceed any further south. As he had some three thousand negro slaves, armed with spears, shields, daggers, and swords, under his command, Ḥasan certainly had the means of making his will felt.

Having appointed a lodging place for Mr. Legh and his party, and sent them a supper of goats' flesh swimming in butter, and a kind of paste made from *dhurra*, the governor set an armed negro to watch them, and they passed the night as well as they could. On the following morning Mr. Legh presented Ḥasan with a fine Damascus sword, and in return the governor gave him a negro boy, ten years old, who was afterwards brought to England and lived in the house of Mr. Smelt. Ḥasan being in an amiable mood, Mr. Legh again asked for permission to go to Ibrim, and it was given without any hesitation; he set out next day with horses and camels lent by the governor, and reached Ibrîm in about seven and a half hours. The district in which Ibrim stands was called "Maāmam" by the ancient Egyptians, and it was the seat of a governor under the XVIIIth Dynasty, about B.C. 1600. The city which stood there in Roman times was called Primis or Premnis, after it had been conquered by Petronius when he marched southward to reduce Napata. Subsequently it was fortified and held by the Blemmyes, a warlike and brave people who were sufficiently powerful to shake Roman authority in Nubia in the reign of Diocletian. The Blemmyes appear to have been of a savage and ferocious aspect, for the Romans regarded them more as beasts than as men, and classed them with baboons and satyrs. In the middle ages the Turkish lords of Egypt claimed the right of exercising jurisdiction over Ibrim, and they certainly sent there civil and military officers who attempted to rule over the natives; the right was, however, of a very shadowy kind, and the Turkish rule was ineffective except, when supported by force, in squeezing gifts from the wretched and half-starved population.

The examination of Ibrim and its remains did not occupy Mr. Legh for many hours, and finding that the Second Cataract was still a journey of three days to the south, and that there was no food to be had in the neighbourhood, and thinking it hopeless to attempt to penetrate into a country where money began to be of little use, he determined to return to Derr, and to make his way down the Nile. He had, moreover, with him no merchandise which he could barter with the natives, and there was the risk, it he proceeded further south, that he might fall in with some of the Mamlûks and their followers, and lose all his clothes, money, and provisions. Everywhere on his journey back to Aswân the natives treated him with civility, and the Egyptians between the First Cataract and Cairo rendered him every assistance, and brought dates, milk, eggs, &c., whenever they were called upon to do so. It is clear that a considerable change had come over the country since Norden's days, but to have travelled nearly 900 miles up the Nile in 1813 was a feat which any traveller might regard with complacency in the first quarter of the 19th century.

Whilst Mr. Legh was engaged in ascending the Nile, the famous Orientalist and traveller JOHN LEWIS BURCKHARDT was in Cairo planning a journey into the Nubian desert, and arranging to follow the course of the Nile to the Third Cataract. Burckhardt was born at Lausanne in 1784. At the age of sixteen he entered the University of Leipzig, where he studied for four years; from Leipzig he went to Göttingen, which he left in 1805, and then went to Basle. He came to London in 1806, and made an offer of his services to the African Association through Sir Joseph Banks and the Rev. Dr. Hamilton. His offer was accepted by the Association in May, 1808, and in January, 1809, he received instructions from its officials as to the mission on which they had decided to send him. As soon as he had offered his services to the Association he employed himself with great diligence in the study of the Arabic language, and of those branches of science which would be of use to him in his future work. He attended lectures on chemistry, astronomy, mineralogy, medicine and surgery, and in the intervals of his studies he exercised himself by long journeys on foot, bareheaded, in the heat of the sun, sleeping upon the ground, and living upon vegetables and water.[1] In March, 1809, he sailed from England and proceeded to Aleppo, and he remained in Syria for two and a half years; he was known as "Ibrahim ibn 'Abd-Allah," a name which he had adopted first at Malta, and to which the title "Ḥaggi"[2] afterwards became prefixed. His stay in Syria added greatly to his knowledge of the Arabic language, and here he obtained the deep insight into Oriental manners and customs and character for which he was afterwards so famous. He left Aleppo in February, 1812, and arrived in Cairo on September 4th, and in the November following he wrote to the Committee of the Association informing them that he intended to set out for Nubia in December. He says, "That country, further up than Derr, has never been "visited by any travellers; yet I am informed by many of the "natives, that the borders of the river are full of ancient temples "and other antiquities; resembling those of Luxor, and the "Isle of Philae. The present tranquil state of Egypt renders "such a voyage of much less danger than it might have been "during the whole of the last century; for the Pasha is "completely master of the country, and is in friendly inter-"course with the princes of Nubia. Were it not for the "Mamlouks who have settled at Dóngola, and taken possession "of the country, I might hope to reach that point. But I shall "not expose myself to their treachery, and shall be contented "with approaching to within a journey of five or six days from "Dóngola, and with making perhaps some lateral excursions "into the Nubian Desert."[3]

Burckhardt left Cairo on January 11th, 1813, and arrived at

[1] *Travels in Nubia by the late John Lewis Burckhardt*, London, 1822, p. v.

[2] "Ḥagg," or "Ḥaggi," is a title bestowed upon those who have visited Mekka.

[3] *Travels in Nubia*, p. liii.

Aswân on February 22nd; the governor of that town provided him with a guide as far as Derr, which he reached in four days, and which is about one hundred and forty miles to the south of Philae. Some fifteen miles to the north of Korosko he met Mr. Legh and his companion, the Rev. Charles Smelt, who, as we have already seen, had visited Ibrîm. Three days more brought him to the Second Cataract above Wâdî Ḥalfa, and, travelling through the rocky desert called Baṭn al-Ḥagar, i.e., "Stone Belly," he passed Sukkôt, and the large Island of Sâî, and reached Tinara, a place situated between four hundred and thirty and four hundred and fifty miles south of Aswân. The whole journey from Aswân to Tinara and back occupied only thirty-five days. On his return to Egypt, Burckhardt lived at Esna, and continued to wear his usual disguise of a poor Muḥammadan trader. Whilst here he determined to join one of the Sennaar caravans which started from Darâw, a town about twenty miles north of Aswân, and to travel across the Nubian desert to the east of the Nile, and to visit the Astaboras River, (i.e., the modern Atbara). After much waiting, and many disappointments, Burckhardt succeeded in leaving Darâw on March 2nd, 1814, and he crossed the Nubian desert by much the same route as that by which Bruce returned from Abyssinia about fifty years before. He halted at Berber on the Nile, and at Ad-Dâmar, two days further to the south, and at Shendi, the principal market for the slave-traders who journeyed between Egypt and Sennaar, and between Egypt and Dâr Fûr and Kordôfân. From Shendi he followed the course of the Atbara river for about one hundred and twenty miles, and reached Ḳoz-Ragab, whence he departed to Tâka, or Kasala; he had intended to cross the mountains and to proceed to Maṣawa on the Abyssinian sea-coast. But this he found to be impossible, and he therefore left Tâka for Sawâkin, which he reached in thirteen days.

From Sawâkin he went to Jidda, where he arrived on August 14th, and from Jidda to Tayf, where he spent the month of Ramaḍân, and met the Pâshâ of Egypt, Muḥammad Alî, who had known him in Cairo. From Tayf he went to Mekka, where he spent the months of September, October, and November, and on the 25th of the last-named month he performed the *Ḥagg*, or pilgrimage, to Mount Arafât, in the company of about eighty thousand pilgrims. From this time forward he prefixed to his name the title of "Ḥaggi," i.e., one who had made the pilgrimage to the sites held to be holy by the Muḥammadans, and it served him in good stead. From Mekka he marched through the deserts to Medina, where he was attacked by a fever, which prostrated him until April, 1815. As soon as he was able to bear the motion of a camel he marched to Yembo, on the sea-coast; a native ship took him to Râs Muḥammad, in the Peninsula of Sinai, and from this place he proceeded to Suez, viâ Tor, and reached Cairo on June 19th. During this last expedition into the Hijâz his health entirely broke down, and he himself attributed it to the climate, and to the water, which is everywhere brackish and of a bad taste. In April, 1816, Burckhardt was sufficiently well to travel through the Peninsula of Sinai, and to visit all the principal sites; he returned in June to Cairo, where he lived until his death on October 15th, 1817. He was buried according to Muḥammadan ritual, and at his funeral the greatest respect and grief were exhibited by natives of all classes.

From his reports to the African Association on the various countries through which he passed, it is evident that Burckhardt was a man of great intelligence, learning, and tact, and that he possessed to the fullest extent all the qualifications which are necessary for a traveller who wishes to live among the suspicious and crafty dwellers in the desert, and to obtain information from them. These reports were written under the greatest difficulties, for little privacy is enjoyed by the man who chooses to travel in the East as a native, and he was obliged to jot down his facts on loose scraps of paper, as he sat or squatted under the friendly shadow of his camel, whilst scorching winds laden with minute particles of sand rendered writing almost impossible. Many of his observations were put into writing whilst he was suffering from the lassitude left by fever, and from ophthalmia. In spite of such inconveniences the narratives of his journeys in Egypt, Nubia, the Sûdân, Sinai, Syria, &c., are wonderfully accurate, and, when first published, must have come as a revelation to those who were interested, pecuniarily or otherwise, in these regions. They bear upon them indelible marks of being the work of a man whose knowledge of oriental matters was wider and deeper than that of many of the most intelligent natives. It is a commonplace among the friends of many Europeans who have travelled in the East to assert that their knowledge of the Arabic language and of Muḥammadan manners and customs was so profound that both Egyptians and Arabs failed to discover that they were not natives, but all such claims must be admitted with caution. In the case of Burckhardt, however, a story, which is supported by trustworthy authority, certainly proves that he possessed a very remarkable knowledge of the Arabic language, and of the Ḳur'ân and its literature. When we remember that he resided at Mekka during the whole time of the pilgrimage, and passed through the various ceremonies of the occasion without the smallest suspicion arising among the natives as to his real character, this fact will not seem so surprising.

The story relates that at the time when Burckhardt was at Mekka, Muḥammed Alî was at Tayf, a town to the east of that city, and that when that distinguished traveller appealed to him for help in getting some of his banker's drafts honoured, the Pâshâ received him with great courtesy, and rendered him every assistance in his power, for he had heard of and known him in Cairo, and was well acquainted with the fact that, in spite of his knowledge of Arabic, and his ability to disguise himself as an Oriental, he was nevertheless a European. Muḥammad Alî knew of Burckhardt's connexion with the African Association, and, wishing to find out to what extent he was able to pose successfully as a Muḥammadan, he sent to him two of the most learned teachers of Muhammadan law that he could find in Arabia, and ordered them to test his knowledge of the Ḳur'ân and of the theory and practice of its laws, both from the historical and traditional points of view. These teachers went to Burckhardt, and having conversed with him, and discussed with him many of the doctrines about which Muḥammadans themselves split so many hairs, they were convinced by his remarks, which were supported by quotations from the Ḳur'ân itself, and from numerous commentaries upon it, that he was not only a true Muslim, but an exceedingly learned one, and they returned to their master and reported accordingly. This story ought not to be taken to indicate that the two teachers of the law did not recognize Burckhardt as a foreigner, for there is little doubt that they did; but they assumed, probably, that he came from India, and were surprised in consequence to find his knowledge of the theological literature of the Arabs so extensive.

A few years after Burckhardt travelled in the Sûdân, the countries over which he passed on the west bank of the Nile were visited by GEORGE WADDINGTON, Fellow of Trinity College, Cambridge, and by the Rev. BARNARD HANBURY, and it is to the labours of these travellers that we owe the first attempt made to describe the remains of the ancient Egyptian occupation of Nubia and part of the Sûdân. Burckhardt had collected in his notes on these countries several facts concerning the ancient Egyptian temples and forts which he visited and examined, but Messrs. Hanbury and Waddington published views and plans of the pyramids, etc., which they found within the boundaries of the old kingdom of Dongola, and with their work the archæological examination of the Sûdân may be said to have begun.

Their work and travels may be thus summarized:—They arrived at Wâdi Ḥalfa on Nov. 10th, 1820, and at Ferket (the scene of the defeat of the Dervishes by General Kitchener on June 7th, 1896) five days later; on the 17th, near the island of Sâî, they were visited by Ḥasan, the governor of Derr, who was wearing the sword which Mr. Legh had given him some years before; he had been shorn of all his importance by Muḥammad Alî, and was so much reduced that he subsequently sent to beg a little tobacco, which, their supply being low, the travellers refused without any fear of what the result of his anger would be. On the following day they were opposite the Island of Sâî, on the north end of which are the ruins of large buildings, but there was neither ford nor ferry there, and passing southwards they arrived at Koye, a village of Dâr Mahass, from which place the temple of Soleb (Ṣûlb) became visible. Up to this point they followed in the steps of Burckhardt, whose book had been their constant guide, and they take leave of him with well-merited expressions of admiration for his work and character. Mr. Waddington says, "His acquired qualifications were, I believe, never "equalled by those of any other traveller; his natural ones appear to "me to be even more extraordinary. Courage to seek danger, and "calmness to confront it are not uncommon qualities; but it is difficult to court poverty, and to endure insult. Hardships, exertions, and privations of all kinds are easy to a man in the "enjoyment of health and vigour; but, during repeated attacks of a "dangerous disease, which he might have considered as so many "warnings to escape from his fate, that he should never have "allowed his thoughts to wander homewards—that when sickening "among the sands and winds of the desert, he should never have "sighed for the freshness of his native mountains—this does, "indeed, prove an ardour in the good cause in which he was "engaged, and a resolution, if necessary, to perish in it, that made "his character very uncommon, and fate most lamentable; and "perhaps none are so capable of estimating his character, as surely "none can more lament his fate, than those who can bear "testimony to the truth of his information; who have trod the "country that he has so well described, and gleaned the fields "where he reaped so ample a harvest."[1]

On Nov. 18th they were opposite the temple of Soleb, but were unable to visit the ruins because they found no means of crossing the river; on the 20th they passed Delligo, or Dulgo, and reached Koke. On the 22nd they crossed the frontier of the kingdom of Dâr Mahass, and entered that of Dongola; the frontier was then marked by a large hill called Arambo, which stands about four miles from the river, and by five palm trees which were by the river side. On the 24th they visited the Island of Arḳô, and examined the two gray granite statues which lie there, the measurements given by Mr. Waddington being 22 ft. 6 in., and 23 ft. 5 in., respectively. On the 25th they reached Maragga, or New Dongola, and on the following day they embarked in a boat to sail up to Gebel Barkal; on the 28th they arrived at Old Dongola, and were greatly disappointed at the barrenness of its site. On Dec. 7th they arrived at Korti, near which had been recently fought the battle between Muḥammad Ali's troops, led by Isma'il Pâshâ, and the Shaiḳiyas. Isma'il's loss was one officer and sixteen men wounded, whilst the Shaiḳîyas

[1] Waddington and Hanbury, *Journal of a Visit to some Parts of Ethiopia, with maps and other engravings*, London, 1822.

left six hundred men dead on the field. On Dec. 13th Merawi was reached, and here Messrs. Hanbury and Waddington made a somewhat prolonged stay for the purpose of examining the antiquities at and in the neighbourhood of Gebel Barkal. Their investigations of the pyramids and temples occupied them about ten days, and they left the site of the city of Napata on Dec. 24th. On their way down the river they made a small excavation on the Island of Arḳô, but "it was only by the strongest application of "terror that seven men were at length prevailed upon to work for "six or seven hours." Their labours were not quite useless, for they found the head of a seated statue of black granite, and the foundations of a thick wall.

Mr. Waddington records the existence of a curious belief at that time among the Shaiḳîya people as to the use to which Egyptian monuments might be put. The arms of the black granite statue were broken off by the men at the request of their wives, who hoped, either by the violence of the act or by the possession of fragments from the breakage, to obtain the power of producing large families, or at least to avoid the stigma of barrenness. He goes on to say that similar acts, by which, even if effectual, the increase of the human race would be too dearly purchased, have been, and are still, frequently performed by the Arabs of Egypt, and lamented by the travellers who describe them. The women of many of the tribes in the Egyptian Sûdân believe implicitly that, if they touch or rub colossal or large statues of men and animals with their bodies, they will produce large families of strong children. Until quite recently it was no uncommon thing on Fridays and holidays to see Sûdâni women from Cairo hovering near the large wooden staircase which formed the main entrance of the palace at Giza, wherein the National Collection of Egyptian Antiquities was housed for some years. At the foot of this staircase were two large stone statues of the clever African ape which the Egyptians held sacred to Thoth, and Sûdânî women used to come to them, mutter prayers for offspring before them, and then rub their hands and bodies against them, and try to sit upon them. The custom is the more curious from the fact that the Sûdânî folk declare all such statues of men and animals to be the work of unbelievers and idolaters; but at the same time they admit that they possess powers which may be of use to the true believers.

Near Moshi Messrs. Hanbury and Waddington met Messrs. CAILLIAUD and LETORZEC with their interpreter and servant, and Mr. Waddington remarks concerning the meeting, "We merely "exchanged a few words of civility in passing, and proceeded on "our respective destinations with as much indifference as if we "had met in the park or on the boulevard." M. Cailliaud also mentions the meeting, but was disappointed because he failed to obtain from Mr. Waddington any information about the antiquities of Gebel Barkal; he was struck by Mr. Hanbury's "courteous manners," and would have liked to see more of him, for he thought that he might have been able to obtain from him the information which his companion had denied him. With reference to Mr. Waddington's published account of his travels, he thought it interesting, but believed that it would have had more value if the illustrations, which he declares only give a false idea of the antiquities which they profess to represent, had been omitted.[1]

On their return journey Messrs. Hanbury and Waddington took care to visit the temple of Soleb, or Ṣûlb, as the natives call it, and to make a plan of it;[2] from the description which they gave of it it is quite clear that the remains of the temple were

[1] "Là je rencontrai MM. Waddington et Hanbury, voyageurs anglais qui "arrivaient de la province de Chaykyé, terme de leur voyage. Ils retournaient "au Caire. Les voyageurs aiment toujours à se faire accueil à d'aussi "grandes distances de leur pays : je me flattais que cette rencontre inattendue "allait me procurer l'avantage d'apprendre en quoi consistaient les antiquités "que les Arabes me disaient exister dans la province de Chaykyé : je devais "moi-même y arriver sous peu de jours. M. Waddington, à qui j'adressai "cette question, qui n'avait rien d'indiscret, ne jugea pas néanmoins à propos "d'y répondre ; il me laissa dans une ignorance complète. Aussi ma surprise fut "extrême, quand je fus arrivé à Barkal, à l'aspect de ses grands monumens. "Je ne pus voir qu'un moment M. Hanbury : ses manières affables me firent "regretter de n'avoir pu jouir longtemps de son entretien ; j'aurais peut-être tiré "de lui les éclaircissemens que m'avait refusés son compagnon de voyage. "L'ouvrage intéressant de ces voyageurs est aujourd'hui publié : il aurait plus "de méri e, s'ils n'y avaient pas inséré des dessins qui ne peuvent donner que "des idées fausses sur la nature de ces antiquités." "Voyages à Méroé," tom. i., p. 395.

[2] See the plate facing p. 286 of their work.

more numerous, and in a better state of preservation, than in the latter half of the nineteenth century. A few miles north of Ṣûlb they visited the tomb which is hewn out high up in the rock at Dosha, but they failed to recognize the cartouche of Usertsen III., which is cut on the wall nearest the river. On January 25th they were opposite to the Island of Sâî, which is about eight miles long and three miles wide, but were, as on a former occasion, unable to visit the ruins on it because they could not obtain a boat to take them across the river. On February 1st, 1821, they returned to Wâdi Ḥalfa, having occupied about eighty-four days, including intervals for rest, in travelling to Merawi and back. They were the first to publish any detailed account of the antiquities of Gebel Barkal, and the study of the monumental archæology of the Sûdân may be said to have begun with the publication of their travels.

It has already been said above that on their return journey Messrs. Hanbury and Waddington met the French travellers Cailliaud and Letorzec, who were actively employed in examining the antiquities of the Sûdân, and in visiting the places on each side of the Nile where history or report declared that ruins of ancient temples, &c., existed, and here a brief account of the travels of these distinguished Frenchmen naturally follows. M. CAILLIAUD,[1] the author of the famous work "Voyage à Méroé," began his career as archæologist and traveller by spending a period of three and a half years (1815-1818) in examining the antiquities of Egypt, and he even succeeded in visiting some of the Oases in the Western Desert.[2] He had for guidance in his work the results obtained by the great expedition inaugurated by Napoleon I., but, as is well known, the Island of Philae at the south end of the First Cataract marked the limit of its labours to the south, and we are quite justified in asserting that none of the *savants* among the members of that expedition had the remotest idea of the number and importance of the antiquities which existed between Aswân and Kharṭûm. That remains of ancient cities and monuments must be there was no doubt assumed by every one who had read the works of Herodotus,

[1] He was born june 9th, 1787, and died May 1st, 1869.

[2] See his "Voyage à l'Oasis de Thèbes."

Strabo, Diodorus, and later classical writers, but the antiquities of Egypt alone formed a field sufficiently large for their exertions, and as the physical difficulties which barred the way against a scientific mission into Nubia were of no light character, Napoleon's *savants* decided, and no doubt rightly, that an archæological examination of the country south of Philae might be left to the scholars who would succeed them. As soon as an

THE TEMPLES OF SEMNA AND KUMMA AS THEY APPEARED IN 1820.

A.—The temple of Kumma (west bank).
B.—The temple of Thothmes III. (east bank).
C.—The temple of Tirhâḳâh (east bank).

efficient system of police was established between the First and Second Cataracts, travellers were able to enter Nubia, and to proceed so far as Wâdi Ḥalfa, and at the beginning of 1816 M. Cailliaud was among the number of those who were in the happy position of having actually seen Abû Simbel and the other ancient Egyptian remains which are to be found in that district.

On November 25th, 1820, M. Cailliaud, accompanied by

Letorzec and six men, including the guide, set out on his journey through Nubia; he arrived at Abû Simbel on December 4th, and visited a second time[1] the temple, which he was now able to enter. On the occasion of his first visit the whole temple was filled to its mouth with sand, and the natives of the neighbouring village agreed to clear it out for the sum of three hundred piastres. When Cailliaud and Drovetti returned there from Wâdi Ḥalfa they found that the natives had not touched the work, for the simple reason that they were afraid to undertake it. A local shêkh had assured them that the opening of the temple would be followed by a series of dire calamities which would fall upon their village, and that the foreigners would carry off the treasure which it contained; that the natives believed these forebodings is proved by the fact that they sent back the money which had been given them in advance as payment for their work. Six months later Belzoni went to Abû Simbel, but although he succeeded in overcoming the prejudices of the natives sufficiently to make them start the work, he had, for various reasons, to leave it unfinished; six months later, however, he returned and cleared out the temple from one end to the other at the expense of Mr. Henry Salt. On December 21st Cailliaud arrived at Semna; he stayed there to examine the antiquities, and afterwards succeeded in crossing over to the west bank, where stand the fine remains of the temple of Kumma. Early in January he reached the Island of Sâî, and having crossed over to it on a raft made of pieces of palm trunks and reeds, he visited the ruins of the Coptic church which still exist on the northern end of the Island. A mile or so to the east he found the ruins of a modern fort, which was built by Turks or Arabs upon the remains of an ancient Egyptian fortress or temple. Passing up the river, he examined the tomb hewn out of the rock of Dosha, which forms such a striking feature of the landscape, and then came to Soleb, or Ṣûlb. In this portion of Nubia he found great difficulty in feeding himself and his camels, for meat was not to be had, and *dhurra* and straw were very scarce. The fact is that then, as now, the people of Sukkôt produced just enough for their own wants, and no more.

[1] His first visit took place on March 5th, 1816, and he was accompanied by M. Drovetti.

Dates, of course, grow in great abundance, but their production entails very little labour upon the natives, and as a large export trade in them has always existed, the traveller can obtain as many as he pleases.

At Soleb or Ṣûlb, M. Cailliaud stayed three days, which he spent in making plans of the famous Egyptian temple, and in drawing up a description of it. He notes that his sleep was broken by the cries of a hippopotamus, and those of the natives who drove him away from their crops. On January 19th, 1821, MM. Cailliaud and Letorzec visited the Island of Arḳô, which is famous for the two colossal statues that date from the period of the early Nubian kingdom; and on the 31st they arrived at Dongola. For reasons which need not be given here, Cailliaud left the exploration of the pyramids of Gebel Barkal for his return journey, and passed on to examine those of Nûri; a difficult and fatiguing journey brought him to Berber, and soon after he arrived at the site of the ancient capital of the Island of Meroë, where he found the ruins of large temples, and several groups of pyramids. The name given to pyramids in the Sûdân is *ṭarâbîl*, the supposed singular form being *ṭarbûl*.[1] Cailliaud's joy was great when he first saw the pyramids in the distance, and when he came near them he ran up to the top of a hill, so that he might obtain a complete view of them at a glance. His next care was to ascend the largest of them, and on it, "As a humble tribute of homage to the illus- "trious geographer whose intelligence had guided his steps," he cut on one of the stones the name of d'Anville. This done, he decided to take up his abode in the neighbouring village of As-sûr, and whilst there he spent his days in measuring the pyramids, and in drawing plans, and in describing the shrines. M. Letorzec meanwhile devoted himself to practising medicine on the natives with extremely good effect. From Kabushîa Cailliaud journeyed on to Shendi, from Shendi to Ḥalfâya, and a few hours later he passed a "place called Omdurmân," on the west bank of the Nile, where the Egyptian army had encamped near a wood filled with acacia trees. Continuing his route, he came to the junction of the White and Blue Niles, and it is interesting to note

[1] طربول, plural طرابيل. See Captain Amery, *English-Arabic Vocabulary*, Cairo, 1905, p. 282.

that he made up his mind that the springs which Bruce had discovered near the village of Gish in Abyssinia were the source of the Blue Nile only. At this time it is difficult to understand how Bruce can ever have laid claim to have discovered the source of the Nile, and how he can have been satisfied to ignore the information possessed by the natives, with which he must have been acquainted, to the effect that the White Nile was both longer and more constant in its flow than the Blue Nile. We should expect a man who enjoyed a reputation for thoroughness at least to have tested the truth of ancient and modern belief and tradition, which, after all, in such cases is usually based upon facts, before he committed himself to such definite assertions as to bis discovery.

The crossing of the river to the point of land between the White and Blue Niles called Râs al-Kharṭûm, or simply Al-Kharṭûm, was not accomplished without difficulty, and Cailliaud draws a vivid picture of the way in which the Egyptian Army sent up by Muḥammad Alî to occupy the Sûdan, managed it. For three whole days the surface of the river for a considerable distance up and down stream was covered with camels, horses, Turks, and Arabs, all in an indescribable state of noise and confusion, and all struggling to reach the opposite bank. Some of the soldiers swam across, others supported themselves on blown-up skins and pieces of wood, others clung to their horses' tails, or climbed on the backs of camels. In this way five thousand five hundred men crossed the river; thirty men and one hundred and fifty camels and horses were drowned, and the only thing to be wondered at is that the loss was not greater. When Cailliaud reached Soba, a few miles up the Blue Nile on the east bank, he disembarked and succeeded in obtaining a horse and a guide, who led him to the ruins of the old town, but he was considerably disappointed with what he saw there. He found nothing but heaps of earth and pieces of stone, and not a single fragment of any size. He made the tour of the old town, the extent of which is still plainly discernible, and among the rubbish in the centre he found a sphinx, made of black quartzite sandstone, hewn in the Egyptian style. Cailliaud's examination of the ruins of Soba cannot have been very thorough, for when I visited them in 1903, under the able guidance of the Mudir of Kharṭûm, Colonel E. A. Stanton, the remains of the side buildings of several of the city gates were considerable, and the ruins of the old Coptic church were far from insignificant. The latter indicate that in the early centuries of the Christian era a heathen temple was turned into a church, a fact which is proved by the crosses that have been found carved on portions of some of the drums of the pillars, and from the small bronze crosses which have been found among the ruins. The church was probably attached to some religious house or monastery which stood close by, and it may have been used for purposes of worship until the early part of the thirteenth century of our own era, but probably not later. That the ruins are not more

VIEW OF THE TOWN OF SENNAAR ON THE BLUE NILE, SHOWING THE FORT AND MOSQUE, IN 1842.

[From Russegger, *Reisen*, Plate 13.

considerable is due to the custom which the inhabitants have of carrying away large stones from old buildings to turn into mill-stones, and to form the foundations of graves, water-wheels, &c.

From Soba Cailliaud set out for Sennaar, a kingdom which he had the greatest desire to see. On his way thither he visited the mountain of Mûîl, where local tradition asserted ancient ruins and statues were to be found; these, however, turned out to be nothing more than rocks and boulders of granite which had been worn into fantastic shapes by the action of wind and water, and the imagination of the natives had turned them into pyramids and statues. He was told that on another mountain, called Sakâdî, there was the colossal figure of a man wearing a long cap or helmet on his head, but a view of it obtained at some distance from the mountain itself convinced him that the so-called figure was nothing but a *lusus naturae*, and a mere figment of the native imagination, like the rest. An opportunity of visiting the mountain occurring later, Cailliaud embraced it, and there he obtained many specimens of new and rare plants, but saw no reason for altering his opinion. Continuing his travels to the south and east of Sennaar, he visited many remarkable towns and villages, and collected much information about the manners and

A VIEW OF SENNAAR IN 1821, TAKEN FROM THE SIDE OF THE MOSQUE.
[From Cailliaud, *Voyage*, Plate VII.

customs of the inhabitants of Karabîn, Kilgû, Yara, Fâzôglî, Kamâmîl, &c., and he penetrated into the region of Abkûlgui, which has from time immemorial been famous for the production of gold. Here the natives were in the habit of turning over with great care the sand in the beds of the mountain torrents after the rains had ceased, and of collecting the gold dust which they found in them in the hollow shafts of the feathers of vultures, which then took the place of money and were given by their owners to the Arabs of Singue in exchange for sheep, cattle, and clothes. The Arabs carried the gold dust to Fadâssi, on the borders of Abyssinia, where it was melted and cast into small rings. Cailliaud about this time visited the tribe called "Barta,"

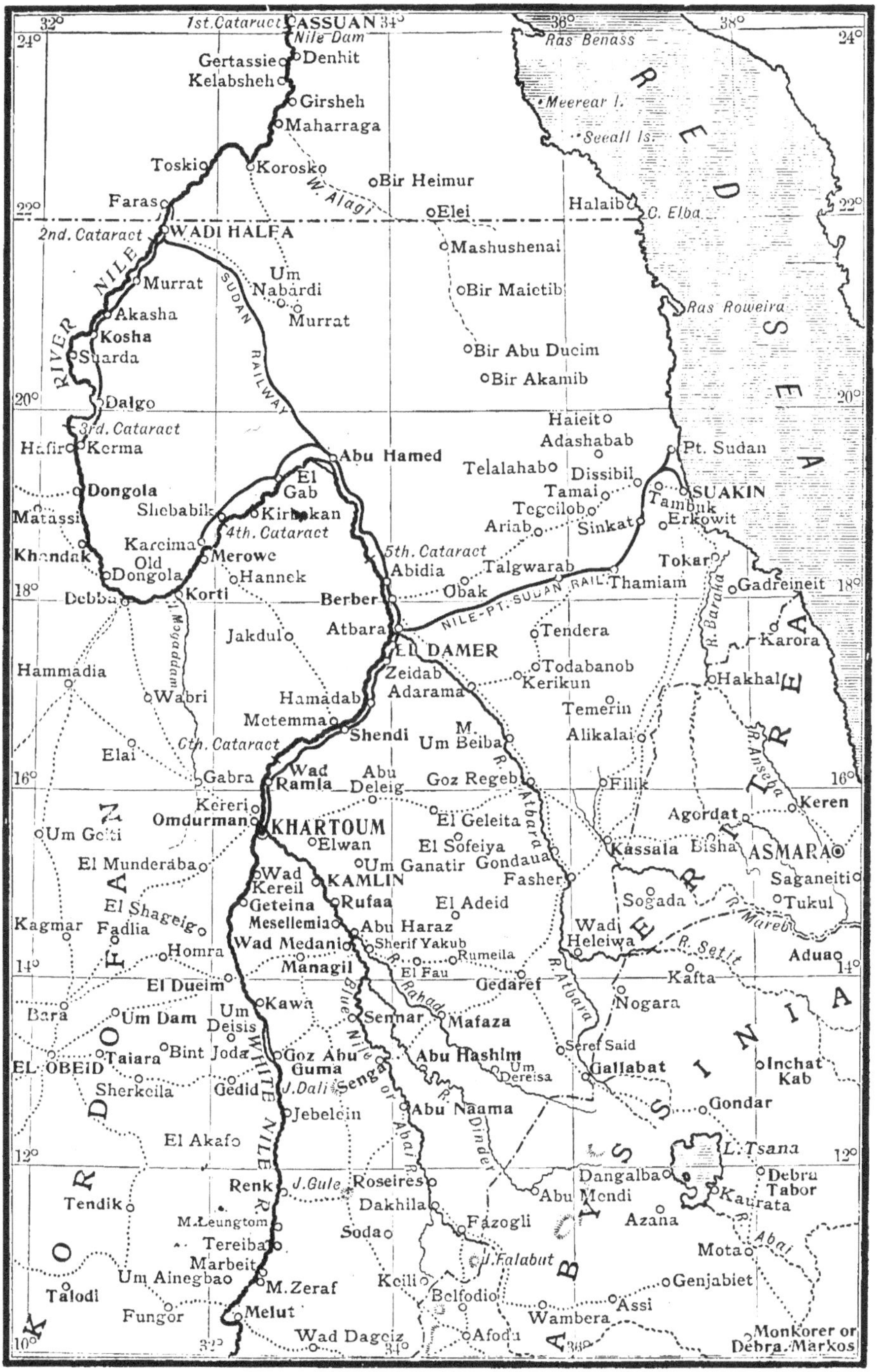
1st. Cataract
ASSUAN
Nile Dam
Denhit
Gertassie
Kelabsheh
Girsheh
Maharraga
Toski
Korosko
W. Alagi
Bir Heimur
Faras
Elei
Ras Benass
Meerear I.
Seeall Is.
Halaib
C. Elba
RED SEA
2nd. Cataract
WADI HALFA
Mashushenai
RIVER NILE
Murrat
Um Nabardi
Murrat
Bir Maictib
SUDAN RAILWAY
Akasha
Kosha
Suarda
Dalgo
Bir Abu Ducim
Bir Akamib
Ras Roweira
3rd. Cataract
Hafir
Kerma
Abu Hamed
Haieit
Adashabab
Pt. Sudan
Telalahab
Dissibil
Dongola
El Gab
Tamai
SUAKIN
Matassi
Shebabik
Kirbekan
Tegeilob
Tambuk
Erkowit
4th. Cataract
Ariab
Sinkat
Khandak
Kareima
Merowe
5th. Cataract
Tokar
Old Dongola
Hannek
Abidia
Talgwarab
Thamiam
Debba
Korti
Berber
Obak
NILE-PT. SUDAN RAIL
R. Baraka
Gadreineit
Jakdul
Atbara
Tendera
Karora
EL DAMER
Wadi Mogaddam
Hammadia
Zeidab
Adarama
Todabanob
Kerikun
Hakhal
Wabri
Hamadab
Temerin
Metemma
Shendi
M. Um Beiba
Alikalai
ERITREA
R. Anseba
Elai
6th. Cataract
Gabra
Wad Ramla
Abu Deleig
Goz Regeb
R. Atbara
Filik
Keren
Kereri
Omdurman
KHARTOUM
El Geleita
Agordat
Um Geiti
Elwan
El Sofeiya
Kassala
Bisha
ASMARA
El Munderaba
Um Ganatir
Gondaua
Wad Kereil
KAMLIN
Fasher
Saganeiti
Geteina
Rufaa
El Adeid
Sogada
Tukul
R. Mareb
El Shageig
Kagmar
Fadlia
Mesellemia
Abu Haraz
Wadi Heleiwa
Wad Medani
Sherif Yakub
Rumeila
R. Setit
Aduao
Homra
Managil
El Fau
Gedaref
Kafta
El Dueim
R. Rahad
R. Atbara
Kawa
Nogara
Bara
Um Dam
Um Deisis
Sennar
Mafaza
Blue Nile
Seref Said
Taiara
Bint Joda
Goz Abu Guma
Abu Hashim
EL OBEID
Um Dereisa
Gallabat
Inchat Kab
Sherkeila
Gedid
J. Dali
Senga
WHITE NILE R.
Blue or Abai R.
Abu Naama
Gondar
KORDOFAN
El Akafo
R. Dinder
L. Tsana
Renk
J. Gule
Roseires
Dangalba
Debra Tabor
Tendik
Dakhila
Abu Mendi
Kaurata
M. Leungtom
Fazogli
Azana
R. Abai
Tereiba
Soda
Marbeit
J. Falabut
Mota
Um Ainegbao
M. Zeraf
Keili
Genjabiet
Talodi
Belfodio
Assi
Fungor
Melut
Wambera
ABYSSINIA
Wad Dageiz
Afodu
Monkorer or Debra Markos
24°
22°
20°
18°
16°
14°
12°
10°
32°
34°
36°
38°

A VILLAGE IN THE COUNTRY OF BARTAT.

[From Cailliaud, *Voyage*, Plate 11.

and appears to have been the first to discover this interesting people. From Abkûlgui Cailliaud marched to Singue and then returned to Fâzôglî; from Fâzôglî he returned to Sennaar, and from Sennaar to Ḥalfâya on the Nile, a few miles to the north of Kharṭûm. After a short stay at Ḥalfâya he set out for Shendî, and visited the interesting ruins of Wad Bâ Nagaa on the way.

From Sennaar to Shendi he followed Bruce's route, and it is impossible not to agree with him in wondering why that traveller makes no mention of the important ruins of Nagaa and the pyramids which lie about thirty miles to the north of Shendî. The only explanation possible is that Bruce was exhausted by his travels and sojourn in Abyssinia, and that he was in such a hurry to escape from the strife and wars of that country, and to return home, that he had neither the inclination nor time to visit and examine such extensive remains; indeed that he should press on to Egypt as fast as possible is not to be wondered at when we remember his experiences. Cailliaud stayed at Nagaa, which he says was also known by the name of "Kanîsa ul-Faḳir Maṣawwarât," and made a plan of the ruins and of the temple, and to him belongs the credit of being the first European to depict their character. A day's march brought him to Shendi, where he met M. Linant, who had recently returned from Sennaar, and from visiting the ruins to the south of Shendî. Before leaving Shendi Cailliaud set out to examine the ruins of Nagaa, in Gebel-Ardân, and those of Al-Maṣawwarât. The remains which he found at the former place proved beyond all doubt that a large city stood there in ancient times, and that it was one of no small importance, and every one who takes the trouble to examine them cannot fail to appreciate the question which Cailliaud put to himself: "What has become "of the people who dared to found a city and to build splendid "edifices, on this parched land, in the middle of the desert, where "at the present day the traveller is unable to find the smallest "spring whereat he may quench his thirst, and in such a spot that "even the wild animals avoid it as a dwelling place?" (p. 125, tom. iii.).

The examination of Nagaa which Cailliaud made enabled him to identify the sites of several temples and other buildings, and the plan which he published (plate xi.) represents the first attempt made by any European to give to the learned world an idea of the importance and extent of these ruins. His description and drawings of the small, well-preserved temple, the walls of which are ornamented with bas-reliefs after the manner of the large temples of Thebes, attracted well-merited attention, for no scholar or historian had the least idea that such interesting buildings were to be found in the Eastern Desert so far from the Nile. Cailliaud rightly deduced from the bas-reliefs on this temple that the rulers of the kingdom which existed in that part of the country were women, and that they enjoyed prerogatives which women did not possess in his day, either in Egypt or Nubia. Their ornaments and dress differed in many particulars from those of Egyptian queens, and their physique proclaimed them to be not Egyptians; their heads were small, their bodies heavy, and their hips and thighs massive. It seems clear that the natural steatopygy of the women of this region of Africa was developed by artificial means. The natives told Cailliaud that other remains, similar to those of Nagaa, were to be found at a distance of two days' journey from Nagaa, and that a journey of another day and a half would take him to a place called Kély, where a large surface of ground was covered with the remains of another ancient city. It was quite clear that the city which stood on the site now called Nagaa was on the main road which led from the Nile into Abyssinia and to ports on the Red Sea, and that it was one of a series of cities at which caravans to and from Egypt and North Africa halted and were taxed.

Cailliaud found it impossible to follow up the hints which the natives gave him, for his supply of water was running short and he had yet to visit Maṣawwarât; he therefore left Nagaa as soon as possible, and set out for that place, which he reached in about five and a half hours. When he entered the great valley of Maṣawwarât, at the northern end of which are the ruins, he was struck with astonishment in approaching the vast ruins which appeared before his gaze. "I did not," he says, "know in which direction I should "at first turn my steps, for every part of the site attracted my "attention equally. I set myself to wander from court to court, "and from temple to temple, and from one chamber to the other, "ascending and descending, and passing along the corridors and

VIEW OF THE RUINS OF THE MEROITIC TEMPLES AT MASAWWARAT AS-SUFRA AS THEY APPEARED IN 1832.

[From Hoskins, *Travels*, Plate 15.

"galleries which joined the various buildings. In this hurried "ramble I counted eight temples or sanctuaries, forty-one dwelling "rooms, twenty-four courts, three galleries, and fourteen ramps; "all these were enclosed within walls, and they occupied a piece of "ground which was 828 metres in circumference." He was not struck by the proportions of any of the buildings, for they were not in any way remarkable, but he was, like many a later traveller, much puzzled to discover among the confusion which reigned supreme, what was the purpose for which the group of buildings had been designed. Having ascended the highest wall of the central building, and studied the general arrangements of the ruins which he saw about him, he came to the conclusion that the temples, galleries, rooms, &c., formed parts of a place devoted to teaching, in fact, a college. The reasons for his conclusion are best set forth in his own words,[1] but those who are acquainted with teaching institutions in the East will hardly accept it. From Maṣawwarât, Cailliaud visited the Wâdî al-Banât, where he examined a small temple built and ornamented in the same style as the shrines of the pyramids of As-Sûr, and then proceeded to the north, arriving in due course at Berber.

[1] "Cette solitude silencieuse, me dis-je, a donc été animée par les jeux "bruyans d'une jeunesse folâtre? Ce monument sur les débris duquel je me "trouve a donc retenti de la voix des professeurs? Oui, ces figures informes "d'oiseaux et de quadrupèdes, tracées sur les murs, sont bien l'ouvrage d'une "main enfantine; ces noms gravés en caractères éthiopiens sont bien ceux de "quelques élèves: et qui ne reconnaîtrait, à cet indice certain, l'intérieur d'une "classe? Ces autres noms grecs, sans doute ils sont ceux d'étrangers amis des "sciences que la célébrité du lieu y attirait. Ces trois longues galeries qui "partent de cette salle, ne conduisaient elles pas à divers lieux consacrés à des "cours particuliers? Ces logemens qui avoisinent ces salles d'étude, n'étaient-"ils pas destinés aux professeurs? Ces grandes cours nues, desséchées par "les rayons d'un soleil brûlant, peut-être alors étaient des jardins et des bosquets "où les jeunes étudians allaient goûter les délices de la récréation; où les "maitres, assis à l'ombre d'un arbre touffu, méditaient et préparaient leurs "leçons? Cet enclos qui renfermait un grand nombre de cellules, et hors de "l'enceinte, était-il le quartier des gens de service? ou bien ces cellules "avaient-elles pour objet d'offrir aux voyageurs un abri hospitalier? Hélas! "ces lieux autrefois si fréquentés, ces lieux où régnaient le mouvement et la "vie n'existent plus que pour être un nouveau témoignage de l'instabilité des "choses humaines; les hyènes, les chakals et autres animaux sauvages, en "parcourent les vastes décombres, sans y trouver rien qui puisse repaître leur "faim" (tom. iii., p. 142).

So far as can be seen from his narrative Cailliaud made no attempt to discover if there were any ruins in the hilly deserts on the east, and he seems to have been anxious to reach Gebel Barkal, at the foot of the Fourth Cataract. His account of his journey to this place is not particularly interesting, but it is worthy of note that he identified the remains on and near the Island of Kabenât as Christian, and that he found on them traces of paintings of figures of Saint George and other Coptic saints. There were no inscriptions to assist him in assigning a date to

GEBEL BARKAL, 302 FEET HIGH, OPPOSITE TO THE ANCIENT NUBIAN CAPITAL OF NAPATA.

them, but from what I saw of them myself it seemed to me that they belonged to the twelfth or thirteenth century. A journey of a few hours brought Cailliaud to Gebel Barkal, where he stayed for some time, and made drawings and plans of the pyramids, &c. He measured Mount Barkal, and found it to be 1,340 metres in circumference, and, on its southern side, sixty-four metres high; but it may be mentioned in passing that its altitude was taken in 1897 by Major the Hon. M. G. Talbot, R.E., who found that its height was 302 ft. We need not here follow Cailliaud through his descriptions of the pyramids, for they tell us nothing of the history of these buildings, and do not help us to assign a date to them; it must, however, be noted that with the help of Champollion's observations he identified the ruins of the temple of Tirhâkâh, which lie between the mountain and the river.

Leaving Gebel Barkal in May, Cailliaud determined to avoid the Nile route, and to cross the desert by the route which would bring him to the Island of Arḳô; he thought that there was nothing worth examining on either of the river banks between Gebel Barkal and Dongola, but in this he was mistaken, for there were several pyramid-fields to be met with on the way, and at that time large numbers of the pyramids must have been standing, and in a tolerably perfect condition. The desert between Gebel Barkal, or Merawi, and Arḳô in May is one of the hottest that can be imagined, and the sufferings of Cailliaud and his companions must have been considerable. At one o'clock in the morning the temperature was about 47° centigrade, and before noon it rose to nearly 53°; the heat, and the glare, and the want of wind almost made them think they were passing through a fiery furnace heated with red-hot sand, and soon after they had started they were met by a prolonged sand-storm, which once experienced can never be forgotten. This storm was, of course, caused by the terrible wind commonly called the "Khamsin,"[1] because it blows, off and on, for a period of fifty days; as a matter of fact, however, a storm only lasts for two or three days at a time, while the Khamsîn period contains sometimes more and sometimes less than fifty days. By taking the desert route Cailliaud shortened his journey by six days, and he took the opportunity of visiting Al-Kirmân, Askan, and Tombos. Near the last-named place he found the large granite quarry which supplied the stone for the colossal statues now lying on the Island of Arḳô, and among the rocks he saw an unfinished statue of a king about 12 ft. long.

So soon as the natives discovered that Cailliaud was interested in antiquities, they hastened to assure him that ruins of considerable size and extent existed in the Oasis of Selima, and, as they described them as being similar to those in the Oasis of Khârga,

[1] More correctly "Khamâsin," which is really the vulgar plural of "Khamsin," i.e., "Fifty." The correct name of the period is "Khamsûn."

he determined to go and see them. He crossed over to the Island of Dakartî, and thence to Hannek, and, proceeding by way of Kôka and Sesha, arrived at Ṣûlb (Soleh) and Gebel Dôsha, which marks the frontier of the province of Sukkôt. It was not, however, until he reached the Island of Sâî that he was able to obtain a guide to the Oasis of Selima. Here he found that the province contained many natives who knew Selîma well, for they were in the habit of travelling there in the winter and of bringing back with them rock salt. Leaving the greater part of his baggage at Bir Daffer, and taking with him his companion, M. Letorzec, and two Arabs, he set out for Selima. As he journeyed on he questioned his guides closely about the antiquities which were said to be at Selima, and began to feel some doubt as to their existence, especially as the two travellers, Browne and Hornemann, had made no mention of any such things. The extremes of heat and cold were very trying, for at 5 a.m. the thermometer registered 16° centigrade, and at 2 p.m. it marked 48°! On the road Cailliaud passed a number of petrified tree trunks, some being 15 ft. long, and after thirty hours of hard riding he arrived at the Oasis. The restful green of the palms was very comforting to the weary-eyed traveller, but look where he would he could see no trace of ruins which resembled those of the temple at Khârga. The palm trees stood in two groups, one of which was about 750 metres in circumference, and the other 1,000 metres; between the two groups was a marsh filled with reeds. The palm trees were in number three or four hundred, and there were with them several *dûm* palms and tamarisks.

The only ruin in the Oasis was that of a small stone hut, on the walls of which were some Greek or Coptic letters, and native tradition asserted that it had once been the dwelling of a princess called Selima, who by means of a band of warriors succeeded in terrifying Nubia. Selima was, as we have already seen, a halting-place for the caravans which travelled between Egypt and Dâr Fûr, and so long as the slave trade flourished might be termed an important place. To all intents and purposes it was under the rule of the king of Dâr Fûr, who in Cailliaud's time was called Muḥammad al-Fâdl, and who marched at the head of an army containing from 20,000 to 25,000 warriors, including infantry and cavalry. His bodyguard was formed of slaves armed with rifles. The slaves were captured in Dâr Fertît, several days to the south of Dâr Fûr, and brought to Kôbi, the capital, where the caravans were started; such products of the country as could be sold with advantage in Egypt were committed to the *gellâbs*, or merchants, who paid the king for permission to trade in them, and then took the wares from Kôbî to Swêni, a journey of five days. Each caravan was placed in the charge of a *habîr*, or chief, whose power whilst on the journey was absolute. The poor slaves were driven forward in fetters from halting-place to halting-place, being treated with far less consideration than the camels, and when a caravan arrived at Asyût, after forty days' journey, it was no uncommon thing to find that at least four hundred of them had perished on the way.

Having assured himself that there were no ancient ruins at Selima, Cailliaud left the Oasis after two days' rest, and returned to Bir Daffer, whence he paid a second visit to the temple of Ṣûlb. Then, marching northwards, he came to Semna, where he stayed four days, and made plans of the temple of Thothmes III., and copied the inscriptions on the walls. From Semna he travelled by a desert route to Dêr Sûllah, where he measured the ruins of a massive brick fortress, and then, taking the direct road to the famous rock of Abûṣîr, he arrived shortly afterwards at Wâdî Ḥalfa. On his way through Nubia he visited the temple of Abû Simbel, which was blocked with sand, but he says, "Me couchant à plat ventre, je pus passer sous le fronton du temple et me faire glisser sur le sable dans l'intérieur." A little further down the river he met a boat sailing up, and having on board an Englishman called Gorthon, who was travelling to Dongola, with the view of tracing the White Nile to its source. This brave man, however, behaved in a very imprudent manner, for he stinted himself of proper food, wore insufficient clothing, and threw himself into the river for a swim whensoever the whim took him. The result was the natural one: soon after he entered the region of the Third Cataract he fell ill, and he died before he could reach Sennaar.

M. Cailliaud's journey from Aswân to Cairo it is unnecessary to describe in detail, and it will be sufficient to say that he examined the temples at Luxor, Karnak, Abydos, and other important sites on the west bank of the Nile. He published a careful account of his travels in 1826, under the title, " Voyage à Méroé, au Fleuve Blanc, "au-delà de Fâzoql dans le midi du Royaume de Sennâr, à Syouah "et dans cinq autres Oasis, fait dans les années 1819, 1820, 1821 "et 1822." This work was accompanied by a valuable series of drawings, plans, and sketches, which appeared in folio form, and to it I am indebted for many of the illustrations printed in this book. Cailliaud's narrative is, unquestionably, one of the most important contributions to the archæology of the Sûdân which has ever appeared, and his plans and drawings, though they leave much to be desired from the modern point of view, are of the greatest value, for they serve to give us an idea of the condition in which were the monuments of that country at the beginning of the nineteenth century, and they supply copies of reliefs and inscriptions which no longer exist. That one man with such limited resources should have accomplished so much is in itself a matter for wonder, and when we remember the trying climate of the Sûdân, and the difficult physical conditions under which he worked, the wonder is greatly increased. The publication of his "Voyage" came as a revelation to the learned world of Europe, and many were moved by his example to visit Nubia and the Egyptian Sûdân, which was then called " Ethiopia," and was regarded as the land whence sprang the arts and learning of Egypt, and ultimately those of Greece and Rome.

In 1819 F. C. Gau, a French architect, visited Egypt and Nubia, and made a series of plans and drawings of the buildings and monuments in these countries. These were intended to form a supplement to the great work published by Napoleon's *savants*, and appeared under the title, *Antiquités de la Nubie, ou Monuments inédits des bords du Nil, situés entre la première et la seconde Cataracte*, Stuttgart and Paris, 1822.

In 1829 Lord Prudhoe made a journey from Cairo to Sennaar. He arrived, on March 10th, at Kharṭûm, which he describes as consisting of a collection of mud-houses and straw huts, resembling wheat-stacks or bee-hives. The governor lived in a "tolerable house" of mud. He visited some Shilluks and notes that they swore by the Sun. During his journey he kept a

VIEW OF THE PYRAMIDS OF MEROE IN 1832 FROM THE NORTH-EAST.

[From Hoskins, *Travels*, Plate 8.

"Journal," from which a series of very interesting extracts were published by Sir John Barrow, Bart., in the *Journal of the Royal Geographical Society*, vol. v. 1835, p. 38 ff.

Among those who set out to emulate Cailliaud was the Englishman G. A. HOSKINS, who made a journey to the "higher parts of Ethiopia," in 1833, and published, in 1835, an account of the same, entitled "Travels in Ethiopia above the Second Cataract of "the Nile: exhibiting the state of that country and its various "inhabitants under the dominion of Mohammed Ali; and illus-"trating the Antiquities, Arts, and History of the Ancient "Kingdom of Meroe." This account was illustrated by maps, plans, and drawings of the temples, pyramids, &c., of Meroë, Gebel Barkal, Ṣûlb, &c., made by the author and by an artist who accompanied him. Hoskins' travels may be thus summarized. He proceeded from Cairo to Korosko, which he left on February 16th, and arrived at Abu Ḥamed on February 23rd; his camels marched for eighty-six hours, and he estimated the length of the journey at 250 miles. He reached Berber on February 28th, and sailed to the mouth of the Atbara, the Astaboras of Strabo, and the Mugrum of modern writers; on March 3rd he sailed from Unmatur, which is opposite the junction of the Atbara with the Nile, and reached Bagromeh on the 8th. He notes that on the way he passed several crocodiles and hippopotami, but they caused him no inconvenience. Bagromeh must have been the nearest village to the pyramids of the Island of Meroë, and close to the villages of As-Sûr and Dankelah, but no village of this name is to be found in the neighbourhood at the present time.

Hoskins set out without delay for the main group of the pyramids of the Island of Meroë, which he describes as a "magnificent necropolis," and when he found himself in the midst of them, he was gratified beyond his most sanguine expectations. He says, "The pyramids of Geezah are magnifi-"cent, wonderful from their stupendous magnitude; but for "picturesque effect and elegance of architectural design I "infinitely prefer those of Meroe. I expected to find few such "remains here, and certainly nothing so imposing, so interesting "as these sepulchres, doubtless of the kings and queens of "Ethiopia. I stood for some time lost in admiration. From "every point of view I saw magnificent groups, pyramid rising "behind pyramid, while the dilapidated state of many did not "render them less interesting, though less beautiful as works of "art" (p. 68). Hoskins noted the existence of only *three* groups of pyramids, containing the remains of eighty monuments, and he appears not to have noticed the large group, in a terribly ruined state, it is true, which lies a little to the north of the village of Kabûshía. His plans are very useful, and he rightly concluded that the orientation of the pyramids was the result of a "religious observance"; that their builders had no astronomical object in view in making the pyramid shrines face the rising sun he considered certain from the variation in their directions, and from there being no attempt at mathematical precision. And he was certain that "the scientific object conceived by some "to have been contemplated in the location of the pyramids "of Memphis," could not be attributed to them. He concluded that the pyramids of Meroë were tombs, and that they were probably constructed over wells in which bodies were deposited, and he thought it highly improbable that any of them contained galleries or corridors. It must be noted that Hoskins stated that attempts had been made, either from motives of curiosity or avarice, to open many of the pyramids, a fact which I shall comment on later in the description of the site.

Having made plans of three groups of pyramids, and measurements of the sides at their bases of large numbers of pyramids, Hoskins moved on to Shendî, and two days later he reached the ruins called by the Arabs "Maṣawwarât-aṣ-Ṣufra" He describes their appearance as very imposing from their immense extent, and says that they were the "most curious and inexplicable" which he had yet seen in Ethiopia. "They consist of chambers, courts, "corridors, and temples, in an enclosure or parallelogram, 760 by "660 feet; but in more accurate numbers the entire circumference "is 2854 feet." The style and variety of the remains at this place puzzled Hoskins, and he found it difficult to say for what purpose the buildings were intended. Cailliaud, as we have already seen, made up his mind that they formed a college, and Prof. Heeren believed that they represented the famous Ammonium, or the original seat of the oracle of Jupiter Ammon, "at whose command "those religious colonies issued forth, which carried civilization, "arts, and religion from Ethiopia to the Delta." Cailliaud's view Hoskins found to be wholly untenable, and that of Heeren he thought most improbable, but, curiously enough, he was ready to explain the paucity of remains of sacred edifices in Ethiopia by assuming that, at the time when "the religion of the Gospel was "widely spread in this part of Africa, some Christian king of "Ethiopia, zealous, and desirous of obliging his subjects to embrace "the true religion, and aware that, if his faith prevailed at all, it "must prevail, to use the language of Paley, by the overthrow of "every statue, altar and temple of the world," utterly destroyed not only the Ammonium, but also many of the other temples. He was prepared also to regard the ruins of Maṣawwarât as the remains of a *château de chasse* of the king, or palace in which he passed the rainy season, which might then, as now, be unhealthy near the Nile. The evidences of pomp and ceremonial in the buildings were, however, too few to permit him to maintain this view seriously, and he therefore thought it more reasonable to hold that they formed a hospital to which invalids, particularly those suffering from malaria, were sent during the rainy season. Hoskins' views as to the date of the ruins are tolerably correct, for in them he saw the "last architectural efforts of a people whose greatness was passed "away, their taste corrupted, and all the lights of knowledge and "civilization just extinguished. The elegant pyramids of Meroë "differ as widely in taste and execution from the immensely "extensive but ill-planned ruins of Wâdi al-Awâiteb, as the best "sculpture at Thebes, during the age of Rameses II., differs from "the corrupted style under the Ptolemies and Caesars."

From Maṣawwarât Hoskins returned to the Nile, a journey which he accomplished in six hours, and on the following morning he marched to Abu Nâga[1] (Maṣawwarât al-Kirbikan), where he found the remains of two pillars, each ornamented with sculptured reliefs of the God Bes, who appears to have been introduced into Egypt from some part of the Sûdân in very early times. At this place the Arabs of course told Hoskins of the existence of some fine ruins called "Maṣawwarât an-Nagaa," which lay at about eight hours'

[1] More correctly BAN NAGAA, or BÂ NAGAA; the site lies near the river, and the small temples stood here.

distance in the desert, and he was most anxious to visit them. His guide, however, declared that the site was infested with lions, that it was folly to attempt to go there without an adequate guard and escort, and finally declined to undertake the responsibility of his safety if he went. Whilst he was revolving the matter in his mind, and forming plans whereby he might camp in one of the buildings at Nagaa, and so defend himself against the lions, his artist raised so many objections that he told him, in disgust, that he might go or not as he thought proper. The artist took him at his word, and promptly refused to go, and as Hoskins was unable to make satisfactory arrangements for him if he should himself go alone, which he had fully intended to do, he was obliged to give up the expedition. Hoskins puts the best face possible on the matter, and mentions his lack of funds, and the difficulty of replenishing them in that country, and refers to the excessive heat and to his health, which had for some days not been very good, and tries to show that he estimated the giving up of his expedition to Nagaa as a matter of "little importance;" but it is easy to read between the lines and see that his chagrin and disappointment were great. As a matter of fact, the temples of Nagaa are the most interesting of all the monuments in the Sûdân! and every one who does see them and knows that Hoskins did not, will greatly regret that this bold and enterprising traveller was, through the timidity of his artist, obliged to leave the Island of Meroë without seeing the best preserved and most characteristic of all its antiquities. Having given up the idea of going to Nagaa, he abandoned his intention of going to Sennaar and all hope of tracing the White Nile to its source. He therefore made up his mind that Sennaar was very much like Shendi, and was not worth a journey of twenty-two days, that the source of the White Nile could only at that period be successfully discovered by an armed force, that certain death would certainly await the individual who undertook such an expedition, and—he returned to Shendi!

From Shendi Hoskins crossed the river to Matamma, whence, having obtained camels, he set out to cross the Bayûda Desert to Merawi, a distance of about two hundred miles. At Abûlay he found wells of water, at which he refilled his water-skins, and he then pressed on to Gakdûl Wells, and arrived at the Nile, a little

VIEW OF THE PYRAMIDS AT NURI AS THEY APPEARED IN 1832.

[From Hoskins, *Travels*, Plate 31.

above Merawi, without mishap. Near Merawi is the striking mountain called Gebel Barkal, at the foot of which the Nubian king Piânkhi, and his immediate successors, including Tirhâḳâh, built temples; on the hills close by are a number of pyramids which form their tombs. Hoskins devoted much time and trouble to the making of plans of these monuments, which are of considerable importance. The drawings made by himself and his artist are useful in checking the results obtained by Cailliaud. Recent travellers to Gebel Barkal have been surprised at the chaotic state of the ruins, but in connection with this it may be noted that Hoskins thought (p. 153) that the pyramids there had been the object of some "learned curiosity" or avarice. He believed that some persons, having been deceived by the false doors at the west ends of the shrine-chambers, had endeavoured by means of blasting to discover inner chambers, which they expected to contain objects of value, and that others having come to the conclusion that the dead, with their treasure, were hidden beneath the pyramids, set to work and systematically destroyed several of them.

From Gebel Barkal Hoskins proceeded to the pyramid-field of Nûri, which lies on the opposite bank of the Nile, about ten miles farther south. On sailing down the river, he stopped at Old Dongola, and made a brief inspection of the ruins of its famous Christian church, but neither he nor his artist made any plans or drawings of it. We may note in passing, however, that he was prepared to believe that Old Dongola, and not Gebel Barkal, as has been usually supposed, was the site of the ancient city of Napata. Pliny states that the distance from Napata to the Island of Meroë is 360,000 paces, i.e., about 340 miles, but according to Hoskins the distance from Gebel Barkal to the Island of Meroë is only 240 miles, and he felt obliged to look for the site of Napata at some place about 100 miles to the north of Gebel Barkal, and he therefore fixed upon Old Dongola as the probable site. Now the distance from Gebel Barkal to Abû Ḥamed is about 130 miles by river, and the distance from Abû Ḥamed to Hamadab, the village which is nearest to the ruins of the city of Meroë, is about 220 miles according to recent measurements, and thus we see that Pliny's statement is substantially correct.

THE EGYPTIAN SUDAN

Continuing his journey northwards, Hoskins visited the antiquities on the Island of Arḳô and the quarries of Tombos, and he stopped at Ṣûlb, and made a plan of the temple there. The views of the ruins which he made are of some importance, for they serve to give a general idea of the state of preservation of the remains of the temple in the first half of the last century. Hoskins believed that the ruins which lay round about the temple marked the site of the city of Phthouris which is mentioned in Ptolemy's "Itinerary." A short ride brought Hoskins to Gebel Dosha, which is the boundary mark between Dâr Mahass and Dâr Sukkôt, and with the aid of Champollion's list of kings he correctly identified the cartouches of Usertsen III., the first true Egyptian conqueror of Nubia, and of Thothmes III. Judging by his own narrative, Hoskins cannot have visited all the remains which exist between Gebel Dosha and Amâra, for he only mentions the ruins of what he calls the "Temple of Sukkot," with its solitary pillar,[1] and the remains of a Christian church on the Island of Sâî. It is curious that he did not examine the ruins of the huge modern fortress which stand on the eastern side of the north end of the island, for their existence must have been well known to the local authorities. He thought so little of the ruins of the Christian church, the pillars of which certainly came from an Egyptian temple, that he set no value on the drawing of them which "Mr. B." had made, and he mislaid it! We may note, too, that he did not examine the Christian remains on the small islands south of Sâî. At Amâra he visited the ruins of the little temple and made a plan of it, and thought that it marked the site of Berethis, which is mentioned in Ptolemy's "Itinerary."

After leaving the village of Ḳaṣr Towaga, Hoskins entered the Baṭn, or Wâdi al-Ḥagar, which, he says, "is desolate and fright-"ful, beyond any I have ever seen. After a short space its "appearance became still more terrible, resembling a sea agitated "and driven into the most awful shapes by wild winds" (p. 264). In due course he arrived at Semna, the temple of which he describes in some detail. He saw there a portion of a headless statue of Osiris, of a late period; Mr. Crowfoot and myself found

[1] It was still standing when Mr. J. W. Crowfoot and I visited the site in February, 1905.

A VIEW OF THE TEMPLE OF AMEN-HETEP III. AT SULB IN 1832.

[From Hoskins, *Travels*, Plate 42.

this object lying inside the temple at the north end, and we took it to Kharṭûm, where it stands in the Government Museum. From Semna Hoskins crossed the river to visit the ruins of Kumma, which consist of the lower parts of the walls of a temple of the XVIIIth Dynasty, whereon the cartouches of Thothmes I., Thothmes II., and Thothmes III. and Ȧmenhetep III. appear frequently. With his arrival at Wâdi Ḥalfa the travels of Hoskins in Ethiopia may be said to terminate, and his archæological researches to cease. The account of his journey is more useful from the anthropological than the antiquarian point of view, but his plans and views will always possess a certain value, for they represent the work of a careful and intelligent traveller.

In 1836 J. Russegger set out from Europe to visit Egypt and Nubia, and he travelled in those countries from November 11th of that year to July 27th, 1838. He went to Korosko, crossed the Abû Ḥamed Desert to Berber, and then went on to Kharṭûm; from this place he visited Kordôfân, and passed some time among the Nûbas. He next went up the Blue Nile to Sennaar, Fâzôglî, Ruṣêreṣ, &c., and penetrated the Negro land as far as the Galla country, to the south-west of Abyssinia. On his return he crossed the Bayûda Desert from Matamma to Gebel Barkal, and he visited Gebel Barkal and Dongola on his way to Ḥalfa. He published an account of his travels under the title *Reisen in Europa, Asien, und Afrika*, Stuttgart, 1843, and he illustrated them with a number of plates which were published in six parts at Stuttgart, 1842-1849. His book is valuable, and is a mine of information, but it is heavy to read. His Egyptian travels are described in the second volume of his work.

The next traveller of importance who examined the antiquities of the Sûdân scientifically was the eminent Egyptologist RICHARD LEPSIUS, who in 1842 was appointed director of the scientific expedition to investigate the "remains of ancient Egyptian and "Ethiopian Civilization, still in preservation in the Nile Valley and "the adjacent countries," which was sent out by H.M. Frederick William IV. of Prussia. Lepsius was accompanied by G. Erbkam, a land-surveyor from Berlin, E. and M. Weidenbach, draughtsman and painter respectively from Naumburg, J. Frey, a draughtsman from Basle, O. Georgi, a painter from Leipzig, H. Abeken, a Counsellor of Legation, Franke the *formatore*, J. Bonomi, an artist, and J. Wild, an architect. The members of the expedition met at Alexandria on September 18th, 1842; Lepsius' examination of the antiquities of the Sûdân began on January 8th, 1844. He crossed the desert between Korosko and Abû Ḥamed, and proceeded to the village of Bagrâwîya, close to which lie the pyramids of the Island of Meroë; from the Pyramids he went to Shendi, and having examined the remains of Nagaa and Maṣawwarât, he passed on to Kharṭûm. From Kharṭûm Lepsius sailed up the Blue Nile and visited Soba and Sennaar, and whilst he was thus occupied the other members of the expedition returned to Bagrâwîya, where they were joined by Lepsius and Abeken on April 5th. When all the drawings, plans, &c., had been made, the party left the pyramids, and marched by the desert of Gilif to Gebel Barkal in six days. From Gebel Barkal they descended the Nile, stopping at Dongola, Arḳô, Tombos, Sesebi, Soleb (Ṣûlb), Saddênga, the Island of Sâi, Amâra, Semna, and, of course, all the ancient sites which lay on each side of the Nile between Wâdî Ḥalfa and Aswân. The sketches, drawings, plans, copies of inscriptions, &c., which were made by the members of the expedition, were published under the editorship of Lepsius in that magnificent work the "DENKMÄLER," in many large-folio volumes. The material collected by Lepsius is of the greatest importance, and it must form the base of all future work on the archæology of the Sûdân; its value increases as time goes on, for many of the monuments with which it deals have either disappeared entirely, or are in imminent danger of being destroyed. In the course of his travels in the Sûdân Lepsius caused a number of stelae, &c., which he considered to be of special importance, to be dug out from the ruins of buildings and sent to the Royal Museum of Berlin; similarly, under the rule of Mariette over the Bûlâk Museum, a limited number of monuments were brought from certain sites in Nubia, and placed among the National Collection of Egyptian Antiquities in Cairo. Neither Lepsius nor Mariette carried out excavations on the sites of any of the ancient cities of the Sûdân, and nothing was done towards solving the problem of the construction of the pyramids of the

Sûdân, which still exist there in large numbers, until the summer of 1897, when the Trustees of the British Museum, with the help and approval of the Sirdar, Lord Kitchener, sent me out to begin work at Gebel Barkal. The following chapters describe the results of four Missions to the Sûdân.

CHAPTER II.

FIRST MISSION TO THE SÛDÂN (1897).

CAIRO TO GEBEL BARKAL (NAPATA).

LEAVING London early in August, 1897, I made my way as fast as possible to Cairo, where I received instructions about my journey to Merawi, where were at that time the Headquarters of the Egyptian Frontier Field Force. I was ordered by the British authorities to proceed to Aswân, and to report myself to the Commandant, Captain O. Pedley, to whom I had introductions. I proceeded by rail to Nagh Ḥamâdi, which was then the terminus, and embarked on the stern-wheeler which carried mails and passengers to the south. Looking at the country and the good-humoured crowds which filled the stations, it was hard to imagine that Egypt was then engaged in a life-and-death struggle with Sûdânî hordes for the possession of the country containing the sources of the mighty river on which her very existence depended, and a few hundred yards away from the river and railway the natives pastured their cattle and watered their crops with as much unconcern as if the Sûdân and its Khalîfa did not exist. The war mattered nothing to them. They had obtained, thanks to the British irrigation officers in Cairo, all the water they needed for their crops, their cattle had multiplied, and were not raided by the local governors, as in the "good old days" of Turkish rule, their taxes were light, bread and onions were cheap, and even if their sons were taken and made to serve in the army, it was God's Will, and "God is Good," they said.

It was, however, impossible to be near the railway and the river without noticing that matters of urgency were in progress throughout the country, and the railway sidings, which were filled with laden trucks, more nearly resembled the goods yards of some great English railway terminus than temporary resting-places of trains full of stores and war material in the land of the Pharaohs. The trucks were of many shapes and sizes, and the locomotives of various powers and of all kinds of build, but it was clear from the way in which they were worked from station to station that their movements were directed by one all-compelling master-mind, which spared neither man nor machine until its commands had been performed. The river was full of craft, some drifting down empty, and others sailing up heavily laden with wooden sleepers and rails for the Sûdân Military Railway, and machinery of all kinds ; and their crews worked by day and by night. The scene at Nagh Ḥamâdî was an extraordinary one. At the place where the line stopped short many scores of boats were being loaded and unloaded, and the river-bank was lined with workmen and idlers who never seemed to sleep at all. By day the air rang with the clang of the hammers and the shouts of the men who were working on the iron bridge which was to carry the railway over to the east bank of the river, the sing-song of the natives who were unloading trucks and loading boats, the whistlings of locomotives, and the crashes of trucks being shunted, the hooting of steamers, the braying of donkeys, and the hundred-and-one noises which are the accompaniments of Egyptians engaged in manual labour. At night the work on the bridge ceased, and the river-bank was lit up by the glare of electric lamps and by innumerable fires, round which squatted groups of men cooking their food, eating, smoking, and talking and laughing to their heart's content. Every now and then the shriek of a locomotive announced the arrival of another train, and hundreds of human forms sprang up, as if by magic, and transferred the contents of the trucks to the places most convenient for stowing them in the boats.

The journey up the river from Nagḥ Ḥamâdi to Aswân was uneventful, but the views which the passengers on the steamers obtained of the country on each bank of the Nile were of the greatest interest, for from the upper deck it was possible to see, near the foot of the mountains, villages, the existence of which is unsuspected by the ordinary traveller in Egypt. The Nile flood of 1897 was a fairly good one, and its waters covered the fields completely, and turned into islands many villages which stood even so much as a mile or so from the river; on the edges of these were groups of inhabitants anxiously observing the effect of the inundation on their mud houses, and near them stood fine cows, which watched the scene with their large, solemn eyes. The river itself appeared to great advantage, and was a wonderful sight, and, as one looked at the speed and volume and irresist-

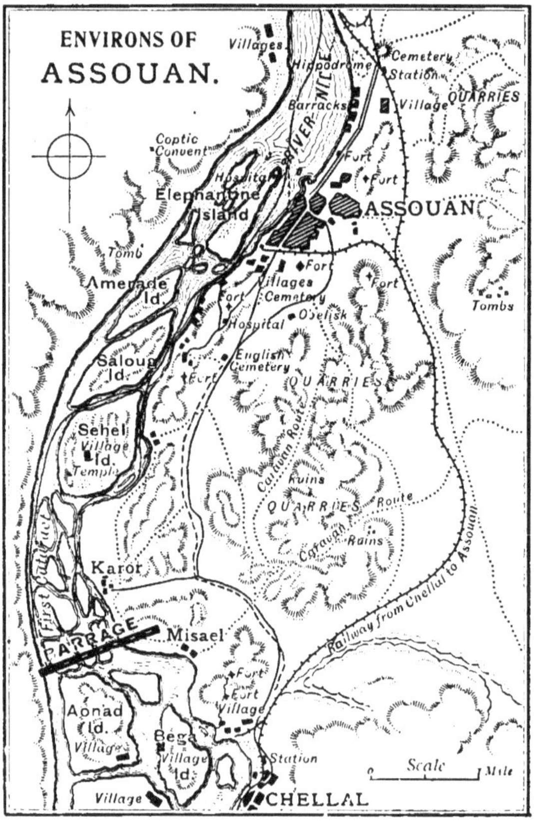

ASWÂN IN 1904.

ible force of the flood of muddy water which spreads life and fertility over the land, it was impossible not to acknowledge the suitability of the seemingly extravagant and exaggerated praises which the ancient Egyptians addressed to Ḥâpi, the god of the Nile. We know now that the composers of such hymns had no exact knowledge of the source of the Nile, and that its origin was to them, as to later nations for centuries, a "mystery"; but they well understood that the stream which brought them life, and formed the great highway of their country, was the starting point of their religion, civilization, commerce, and conquests. To them the Nile on earth was merely a continuation of the everlasting Nile of heaven, and their theologians set the throne of Osiris, the king of the gods of the Other World, at the spot near Philae, where it left heaven and began its course on earth. As the flood stretched away on the vast plains to the north of Thebes it produced a curiously dwarfing effect upon buildings of every kind. The temples and obelisks of Karnak and Luxor lost much of their majesty, and the famous Colossi of Ȧmen-

ASWÂN, SHOWING THE NEW QUAY AND THE HOUSES ON THE RIVER FRONT.

ḥetep III., which have stood in the waters of successive inundations for nearly thirty-five centuries, only served to emphasize the vastness of the flood about them.

We arrived at Aswân late in the evening, and having found a guide who possessed a lantern, I set out to report myself to Captain O. Pedley. There was no moon, and it was no easy task to find a way up the steep bank, on which lay sleepers, rails, ropes, chains, and bags, and boxes of foodstuffs in apparently inextricable confusion. Having reached the road near the railway station, I learned that Captain Pedley's house was in the old Rest Camp compound, wherein I had lived in 1886, when excavating the tombs on the other side of the river with General (now Lord) Grenfell. It was about eight years since I had been in Aswân, and the developments which had taken place in the town came as a revelation to me. The first quay, which was built by Colonel Leach, R.E., in 1887, had been removed, and a fine, broad road had been built along the river front, extending nearly as far as North End, and along it were numerous shops kept by Greeks and other Europeans. The rocky barrier, and the houses which marked the limit of the town in 1886, and the old offices of Messrs. Thomas Cook and Son had been taken away, trees had been planted, and everywhere signs of prosperity were apparent. Aswân had, in short, become a fashionable health resort, and the squalor and misery which filled the town in 1885 and 1886 no longer existed.

We found Captain Pedley in his garden, trying to eat a late dinner and to answer the batches of telegrams from the Sirdar, General (now Lord) Kitchener, and from the Egyptian War Office in Cairo. He was the only British officer in Aswân, and in order to keep pace with the work of all kinds which poured in upon him he had to be on duty all the day, and often a part of the night, for boats had to be unloaded as soon as they arrived, no matter when they made their appearance. His duty was to receive and to pass on without any delay the supplies necessary for some twenty thousand men, to say nothing of the materials required for the Sûdân Railway, and this great work went on day and night without any serious hitch or fuss. In the intervals between the reading of telegrams, Captain Pedley told me that the Sirdar had instructed him to "take me over" on my arrival, and to "pass me on" by the first boat leaving for the south, and he went on to inform me that he would "despatch" me on the following day.

The improvements in the town, which could only be guessed at by night, became plain in the light next morning, and their effect was heightened by the peculiar natural beauty of the surroundings. Aswân had grown greatly towards the south, and new streets had been built on the east side which testified to the prosperity of the householders. The new municipal buildings were, considering the size of the town at that time, large and spacious, and the legal tribunals were well-housed. In former days courts of justice were held under the magnificent tree, which, I rejoice to say, still stands, near the site of the old post-office, and summary chastisement was often administered to transgressors both cheaply and effectively. Many of the natives would even now prefer the rough-and-ready justice of the Ḳâḍi to the machinery of the modern law-court in Egypt. Access to the river was gained from the road on the high quay by means of long flights of stone steps, and low platforms which stretched out from the bank into the water, and it was a sign of the times that not only the professional water-carriers, but even the women made use of these. In 1887 Colonel Plunkett, R.E., built a wooden platform from the bank at the foot of the Rest Camp into the river for the use of the women who came down to fill their large jars in the morning and evening, but none of them would use it, and declared openly that they preferred to wade through the mud to the river, as their grandmothers had done. Their descendants are not so conservative, and scruple not to make use of the contrivances which the "infidels" have devised for their convenience. Aswân was cleaner, larger, and better lighted in 1897 than it was eight years previously, and at the present time it is better suited for the habitation of Europeans than almost any other town in Upper Egypt; but it has undoubtedly lost for ever the picturesque and half-barbaric look which it possessed twenty years ago, and which was its chief characteristic and charm.

The north and south ends of the First Cataract, that is to say, Aswân and Shellâl, are joined by a short railway, built by Isma'îl Pâshâ, who at an enormous cost cut the road-bed through the rocks which separate the south end of the town from the desert on the east. Soon after I had made my way to the shed which has for many years been dignified by the name of "railway station," a long train, made up of a score or so of long trucks filled with stores and railway material, backed into the siding, and soldiers, workmen, and natives of all kinds promptly climbed up the sides and found seats wherever they could. The din and confusion were horrible, and everybody fought with appalling vigour for his place on the top of the already filled trucks, shouting as he did so after the manner of the Egyptian, and everybody yelled orders to everybody else. At length with much straining and groaning the wheezy engine moved out of the siding with its load, and as we passed an adjoining building a glimpse was caught of the Commandant employed in giving instructions to his subordinates on all points connected with the working of the machinery which had to feed an army some six hundred miles away, and to provide the materials for keeping three thousand men at work in the desert between Wâdî Ḥalfa and Abû Ḥamed. In the office of the Commandant there was no confusion, and the sight of the solitary British officer quietly shouldering his responsibilities, and carrying out the orders of a Sirdar, who would not only be obeyed, but obeyed quickly, was one not easily forgotten.

Once through the cutting, the tents of the Bishârin Arabs to the left of the line became visible, and, as of old, we saw some of the men trying to sell wretched camels which they swore by God were as "strong as railway engines, and swifter than birds." A little further on we came to the place where the line from North End joins the Shellâl Railway. Nineteen years ago the points at the junction were worked by a man who was mortally afraid of the pack of fierce jackals which made their way from the desert through the railway cutting into the town each night. As soon as he heard their cries he took refuge in a sort of sentry-box which stood near, and refused to come out whether trains were waiting to pass over the points or not. The whole line was in 1887 infested with jackals, which were attracted thither by the carcases of the stray camels that were either killed outright or were badly wounded by passing trains. When a camel finds himself in front of a train he appears to become fascinated by it, and loses his head completely; sometimes he tries to run away from it, but in the end he stands still on the line and looks at it, and is then overtaken and run down. The sentry-box had now disappeared, and in its place stood a station with platforms, and at one end of it a signal-box with semaphores and all necessary machinery. On one platform was a weighing machine, which, I was told, had been brought there for the special purpose of weighing passengers' luggage; it was another sign of the times, but also a contrivance of the Frangi, or European, which the natives would have been quite willing to do without.

The desert on one side of the line was covered with a thin layer of mud, which was cracking and warping in all directions, and the courteous railway superintendent, who happened to be a passenger on the train, told me that it had been caused by the recent floods of rain, which, he asserted, were more frequent than formerly. In the previous winter large quantities of rain had fallen, and it was declared that during the extremely cold nights which followed, thin layers of ice had been seen among the rocks. It is a mistake to suppose that rain never fell in Upper Egypt, but it is certain that the rainfall has much increased in recent years. According to some, this is the result of the cutting of the Suez Canal; and according to others, the efforts of the Irrigation Department are responsible for the change. It may be as well to mention here the rain-storm which broke over Aswân in January, 1887, when as yet the Irrigation Department had hardly begun its laboûrs. The rain began to fall gently before noon one Tuesday, but about three o'clock in the afternoon the gentle rain turned into a fierce downpour, which was accompanied by frequent and vivid flashes of lightning and long peals of thunder. The Rest Camp wherein I lived was soon inches deep in liquid mud, and the lightning played among the palms, and seemed to glide over the surface of the water. The mud roofs of the houses in the town sucked in the water like sponges, and in a very short time dissolved and dropped into the rooms below them in the form of little streams of liquid mud. On the rising ground outside the town the water washed down the sand and pebbles which covered the graves of the Muḥammadan population, and many corpses were left exposed; the next morning, when the rain ceased, a gruesome sight met the eye of the spectator, for the jackals had been busy during the night.

On arriving at Shellâl, almost before the train stopped, it was boarded by crowds of labourers, who began to unload the trucks, and to throw bags of rice and grain, planks, sleepers, &c., upon the ground, where busy hands grasped them and carried them to the barges lying in the river. The Nile itself presented a wonderful sight, for the inundation had filled all the valleys near the Islands of Philae and Bigga, and the stream poured through the defiles to the north of these islands at the rate of from six to eight knots an hour. The mountains on both banks appeared to have lost much of their height, and the great temple of Isis looked insignificant. The pylons stood out clear and sharp against a background of shiny, blackened granite rocks, and, with the deep blue of the sky, and the muddy flood which rushed by each side of Philae, presented a picture not easily forgotten.

Very soon after my arrival I was "taken over" by a Turkish officer in the Egyptian Army, who caused my kit, after it had been weighed, to be taken to the stern-wheeler *Semneh;* the regulations allowed me to take on board three hundred-weight of luggage, and considering how difficult questions of transport were in those days, I wondered at the Sirdar's generosity. The captain of the *Semneh* was in a hurry to be off, and the engineer chafed at the delay which made it necessary to blow off so much steam from his boiler. One by one four barges, loaded with stores and soldiers, were lashed to the sides of the stern-wheeler, two each side, and soldiers on their way to the front filled the body of the steamer from the boiler, which is near the bows, to the engines, that are set aft. Never did I see craft so crowded, and it seemed impossible for a steamer so heavily laden to make headway against such a current. So soon as the mails were on board, a scrutiny of the passengers took place, and tickets were demanded by the officer who had brought me on board. I never expected to be asked for a ticket, and no one had thought of supplying me with one, and but for the fact that I had with me a private note from Captain Pedley, whose signature was known to the examining officer, I believe I should have been made to disembark. Subsequently he explained to me that he knew I was an *abu antika*, or "father of antiquities," i e., one whose business or profession was connected with antiquities, and that it had been his duty on one or two occasions to turn off the steamers those who under the pretence of being archæologists had tried to force their way into the Sûdân without the Sirdar's permission. When he was satisfied that all the passengers were what they professed to be, he gave the word, and we pushed out into the stream, which we began to ascend at the rate of from two to two and a half miles per hour.

As the day wore on the heat became great, for the sun's rays were fierce, and whenever we passed one of the black rocks in mid-stream heat came out of it as from a hot fire-grate; the breeze from the north afforded no relief, for we were travelling about as fast as it was. The longer the engines worked the hotter the steamer became, and the Egyptian soldiers betook

MOUNTAIN AND RIVER NEAR KOROSKO.

themselves to the barges which were lashed alongside, and fraternized with the ordinary native passengers; they thrust their rifles between the bags of grain, and made little tents by stretching their blankets on these supports, and having taken off most of their garments, they sat down to pass the day in smoking, chatting, or sleeping. On the other hand, some of the Sûdânî folk clustered round the boiler, and some of the crew actually sat under it and ate their meals. Kalâbsha, the Talmis of classical writers, was passed early next morning; we had taken eighteen hours to cover thirty-five miles! The current ran very strong in the "Gate of Kalâbsha," and boats floating down stream passed swiftly and were soon out of sight. Dendûr, Garf Hussên, Dakka (Pselcis), Ḳubbân, Wâdi Sabûa, and other sites of ancient Egyptian towns, were passed in due course, but the monotony of the journey was only broken by the steamer stopping for a few minutes here and there to let some passenger alight, or to enable the soldiers to buy a few eggs or vegetables. An idea was prevalent among the natives on board that we should receive

KOROSKO (SOUTHERN END).

some startling war news at Korosko, and every one was, therefore, most anxious to arrive there. At length we turned the bend of the river a little to the north of that town, and then steamed up the reach to the landing-place, where rumours of the most fantastic kind abounded, but few facts. The telegraph clerk, by virtue of his office, was supposed to be a mine of information as to the intentions of the authorities and the progress of the war in the south, but the Sirdar's telegraphic arrangements were such that leakage among his clerks was impossible.

KOROSKO

The most prominent feature of Korosko is the steep rocky hill which stands at the back of the plain whereon the town is built, and is famous among the Muḥammadans as the resting-place of the body of a saint called Awâs al-Guarânî, who is said to have lived *min zamân*, i.e., a long time ago. Nobody knew anything about him, but every one agreed that he was a very holy man and an ascetic, and many people visit his tomb in the course of the year. Some go there to pray, and for the purpose of acquiring religious merit, and formerly boatmen and camel-men

THE NEW MOSQUE AT KOROSKO.

from the caravans that passed through the town were in the habit of filling little bags with dust from his tomb, which they tied on their camels and boats, and relied upon for protection against the *afarît*, i.e., "spirits," or jinn, and the evil eye. In 1885 the British established a "look-out" station on the top of the hill, and cut a pathway to it, and the older inhabitants of Korosko at that time were convinced that by so doing they were honouring the local saint and putting themselves under his protection! For many centuries Korosko was a place of some note in Nubia, for it was the terminus of the route by which caravans arrived from

Morocco and other places in north-west Africa, and here the Sûdânî and Mugrabi merchants effected the exchange and sale of their wares. Formerly this town was the starting point of travellers who wished to enter the Sûdân, for the road to Abû Ḥamed on the Nile from Korosko viâ the desert is less than one half of that by river. Sir Samuel Baker performed the journey in seven days, but to do this he bad to ride fifteen hours a day, and General Gordon did it in about the same time more than once. A considerable amount of trading by the natives is still done at Korosko, and in recent years a new mosque has been built there, the Government wisely supplying some of the funds required for the purpose. The stripes of brilliant colour with which the walls are painted render it a picturesque and prominent object. Like all other places in the Sûdân and Egypt on which the hand of the British has rested, the town is cleaner than formerly, the people are better off, and in the new shops which enterprising natives have opened most of the small necessaries of native life can be bought cheaply. The admirable postal and telegraphic arrangements have brought it into close touch with Egypt, and life and property are as secure there as anywhere. In 1887 it was not an uncommon thing to see a crocodile or two on the river banks, and in that year Masadâglia Bey showed me in tanks in his garden several small ones which he had found lying on the mud, where they had crept from the river, and one of considerable size, for which he had made a little lake. The crocodiles have been driven away from the Nile in northern Nubia by the noise of the paddles of stern-wheelers, which for years ran up and down by day and by night. The "important" war news which the engineer and crew expected at Korosko was not received, and in due course we resumed our journey.

Two or three hours' steaming brought us to Tushki, or Toski, which will be ever memorable as the scene of the defeat of the Dervish Amîr, Wad an-Nagûmi, by General Grenfell, on August 3rd, 1889. Wad an-Nagûmî, or the "star-child," was called by the Dervishes the "Amîr of Amirs," or "Prince of princes," and was a brave soldier. In his early days he led the hard, miserable life of the founders of Mahdiism, but subsequently he married many wives and lived so luxuriously that Sherîf

Maḥmûd, the Mahdî's uncle, persuaded the Mahdî to order Wad an-Nagûmi to reduce his *harîm* by twenty wives, who were afterwards sold as slaves. After the Mahdi's death the Khalifa sent him to invade Egypt, a venture which had been planned by the Dervish leaders since 1886, and in the early summer of 1888 he set out from Dongola to carry out his mission, at the head of six or seven thousand men, and a very large following of women and children. All went well with him until he reached Argin, a village a few miles to the north of Wâdî Ḥalfa, whence his men marched in from the desert in order to drink at the Nile. Here he came upon the Egyptian forces under Colonel Wodehouse, who was making a reconnaissance, and who promptly tried to drive the thirsty Dervishes back into the desert without their drink. Now the Sûdânî men love fighting for fighting's sake, and their love for Nile water at all times is very great; backed by two such strong incentives, Wad an-Nagûmî's men fought with fury, and to such good purpose that half a battalion of Egyptian soldiers found themselves driven gradually towards the river, until the rear rank was actually standing in the water. But the result of this fight was a victory for Colonel Wodehouse, and Wad an-Nagûmî lost one thousand of his men.

In spite of his defeat, however, Wad an-Nagûmî marched on to Toski, and, knowing that the Dervish army was nearly starving, and that men were deserting from it in considerable numbers, General Grenfell wrote to him and advised him to surrender. The Dervish leader's answer was what was to be expected: If General Grenfell would become a Muḥammadan and a true follower of the Khalîfa, he would bestow upon him every kind of happiness; but if not, he would come and destroy the General and his army. General Grenfell attacked Wad an-Nagûmî's position at dawn, and before noon twelve hundred Dervishes were slain, four thousand were taken prisoners, and the rest were in full retreat, leaving behind them their whole camp, and Wad an-Nagûmî himself was among the slain. This decisive action rendered the invasion of Egypt by the forces of the Khalifa impossible, and such a crushing defeat of the Dervishes was a severe blow to his power; its importance in assuring victories for the Egyptians subsequently cannot be over-estimated. The relief felt by all classes between Aswân and Kharṭûm at the news of the death of Wad an-Nagûmi was a proof of the universal fear and detestation in which that cruel but able fanatic was held, and there is little wonder that Christian and Muḥammadan alike regarded General Grenfell as the instrument of God's justice.

The steamer stopped late at night near Toski to enable the boiler fire to be drawn and the furnace bars scraped, and every one took the opportunity of going ashore. Here we heard the sounds of tom-toms and reed pipes, and singing, and inquiries showed that the people of the district were celebrating the marriage of a local magnate. Several fires had been lit, and by the side of each was a group of men engaged in eating the mutton and rice which the bridegroom had provided. The boiled rice was heaped up on trays, and on the top of each tray were laid pieces of boiled mutton. So soon as the guests were seated, each with his right hand and arm bared ready to reach forth into the tray, a woman came carrying a metal bowl filled with hot mutton fat, or oil, which she poured over the savoury heap. As the fat ran down the sides of the heap of rice each man reached out his hand, saying as he did so, "Bismillâhi," i.e., in the Name of God, and began to scoop some of the contents of the tray into his mouth. If the happiness of the newly-wedded couple was in proportion to the amount of mutton and rice which their guests consumed, they must have been very happy indeed! When the trays were empty and all had drunk water, a youth came and sat by one of the fires and began to sing some tune, which sounded more like a dirge than a wedding song, but he was greeted with the customary applause from time to time. The pity was that he sang through his teeth, and with partly closed lips, and that he finished each cadence with a jerk, for his voice was tuneful, and his skill was undeniable. After a brief allusion to the generosity of the bridegroom, which he said "filled the earth," and was "like unto the goodness of God," he proceeded to describe the physical beauties of the bridegroom and bride, and the happiness which each would find in the other, with the plainness of speech which characterizes Oriental songs of the kind. Every here and there he made topical allusions which, owing to my ignorance of the people in question, I failed to understand, but which were greatly appreciated by the audience and were received with loud guffaws of admiration.

Meanwhile the master of the wedding ceremonies was organizing a dance, and when the tom-tom began to sound the guests and others formed themselves into a circle, into the middle of which stepped a number of Sûdânî men, who began to amble about and bend their bodies and beat their hands together to the sound of the tom-tom. As a dance the performance of the first group of men was a failure, but the scene was remarkably picturesque. There was no light of any kind except that given by the fire, which was reflected from the great curving palm branches overhead, and the shining faces and bodies of the cheerful dancers and their audience, and the shadows cast by the performers added to the somewhat weird nature of the scene. When the dancers were tired their places were taken by another group of a very different character. Each man had a club or weapon of some kind in his hand, and they leaped and jumped about, brandishing these, shouting at the same time the words of a Berberi war song; their eyes flashed, their looks became fierce, and they engaged in hand-to-hand encounters which came perilously near actual fighting. When this performance was ended, a number of women entered the arena and began to dance in the manner with which all who know the Sûdân are familiar. The words which they sang were obscene, and their gestures suited the words; after a time they threw off all their garments except their fringed girdles, and when a number of Egyptian soldiers from our steamer rushed in to join their dance, it was evident from the applause of the bystanders that the most popular part of the entertainment had begun. The black women danced with absolute *abandon*, and the soldiers rushed about in a sort of delirium, to the great delight of the onlookers, who shouted "Allah, Allah," and cheered them on to fresh exertions. Just, however, as the dance was developing into the final stages of such entertainments the whistle sounded with such vigour that we knew the captain was in a hurry to be gone. A rush was made to the river, and in a few minutes every one had scrambled on board and we were off. The noise of the tom-tom reached us as we went up the river, and it was clear that the people of Toski meant to dance until daylight. The most interesting feature of the entertainment at Toski was the songs, and it seems a pity that some one with means and leisure cannot be found to go and live among the Berberi people for a few months, and take down the songs in writing and make copies of the tunes, so far as our modern system of musical notation will permit. It would, no doubt, be difficult to express the thirds of tones wherein Berberi tunes abound, but one would think that some way might be found of overcoming the difficulty. Both words and tunes are probably very old; they may even date from pre-Islamic, or earlier days. Lepsius published four songs in his "Nubische Grammatik," p. 287 ff., but every one will lament the loss of the copies of seventeen others which he wrote down and sent to a friend.

THE TEMPLES OF RAMESES II. AND THE GODDESS HATHOR AT ABÛ SIMBEL IN THE EARLY MORNING.

A few hours' steaming brought us abreast of Abû Simbel, which we reached almost as the sun rose, and we obtained a beautiful view of the four colossal statues of Rameses II. The expression of indescribable dignity and wisdom on the faces of these wonderful monuments changed every few minutes as the light grew stronger and brighter, and it seemed easy to imagine that the souls of the great king who were believed to inhabit them were holding converse with the sun-god, Rā-Harmachis, to whom the temple was dedicated. At this point the river is very wide during the inundation, but the deepest water runs swiftly at the foot of the hill in which Rameses II. dug out his temple; this hill is nearly one hundred feet high, but it is hard to realize this fact from the river. Rameses set up these statues to remind the Nubians and the "Nine Nations" of the Barbarians who were armed with bows that he had conquered and crushed them, and that his souls were watching their actions, and for thirty-two centuries they have formed a striking monument of his far-reaching power and greatness. On the walls inside the temple this king caused the history of his defeat of the confederation of the kings of North Syria to be inscribed, and reliefs illustrating his prowess to be sculptured; but, seeing that very few of the Nubians could read his bombastic language, these have served chiefly to commemorate his inordinate vanity. In the train of the conquests of Rameses II. in the Sûdân there only followed desolation and misery, but the victories of the British were succeeded by true liberty for the native and material prosperity for his country; the ruin wrought by the former is, nevertheless, commemorated by a unique temple of a stupendous character, which stands in a prominent spot on the great highway of the country, the river, plain for all men to see; but no public monument of any kind has been set up to record the great benefits which the latter have conferred on the country, and the great loss of life and expenditure of money which they have borne in carrying out the work of civilization.

Between Korosko and Abû Simbel there are on both banks of the river the ruins of many ancient buildings, Egyptian temples and forts, Roman forts, Coptic churches, &c., and it is interesting to note that often the Greeks, Romans, Arabs, and even the British have, sometimes unwittingly, chosen for their forts sites which had been employed for the same purpose by the ancient Egyptians. There is a large field here for exploration, but the cost of systematic exploration will be considerable, and not very remunerative in respect of material results. To the natives on the steamer, however, no ancient building evoked the same interest as the modern village of Argin (which we reached early in the morning of the fourth day after leaving Shellâl), where, as said above, Colonel Wodehouse defeated Wad an-Nagûmi. Argin stands on or near the site of a flourishing little town which existed in the early centuries of the Coptic period, and the painted vases,[1] which Mr. Somers Clarke obtained here when making researches in Nubia, indicate that it must have been of some importance, perhaps even at the time of the conquest of Egypt by the Arabs in 641 (?).

A little to the south of Argîn is the Island of Dabrôs, and when abreast of this we obtained an excellent view of Tawfîḳîya, and its pretty little mosque, which is a prominent object on the east bank. Tawfîḳîya is quite modern, and lies about two miles to

A "STERN-WHEELER" TOWING RAILWAY MATERIALS NEAR WÂDÎ HALFA.

the north of the old Sirdarîya, or General's quarters, at Wâdî Ḥalfa. It is built upon a part of the site of the old village of Dabrôs, which was looted and burned by the Dervishes during a raid which they made on the district in 1888. Tradition says that a relative of the prophet preached Islâm here, and that he died and was buried close by: be this as it may, the village was held to be a holy place, and Muhammadans made pilgrimages to it, and declared that special blessings were to be obtained there.

[1] See in the Fourth Egyptian Room of the British Museum, Nos. 20,712 and 30,709.

VIEW OF TAWFIKIYA TAKEN FROM THE WEST BANK, SHOWING THE MOSQUE, AND THE NEW HOTEL WHICH HAS NOW BEEN CONVERTED INTO GOVERNMENT OFFICES.

Tawfîḳîya has grown rapidly in recent years, and it now contains numbers of well-to-do merchants, who continue to thrive on the trade which the Anglo-Egyptian Expedition to the Sûdân has attracted to the place. It is now the terminus of the railway, and passengers to Khartûm start from it instead of from the old landing-place as formerly.

At Tawfîḳîya the steamer stopped to unload certain stores, and when the four barges had been "cast off" we moved up the river. It was ten years since I had visited Wâdî Ḥalfa, and the change which had come over the place was very great. In 1884 it was a small and miserable Sûdânî village, with a very limited number of inhabitants, who lived chiefly by work on the river in connexion with the exports from the south and imports from the north. Its chief importance was due to the fact that it was connected with Sarras, thirty-three miles to the south, by a line of railway; the gauge of the line was, and still is, 3 ft 6 in., and its road-bed had been made, exclusive, of course, of bridges, for fifty-five miles. New life was brought into the place by the arrival of half a battalion of British troops in September, 1884, and when, in the following month, the "whalers" appeared which were to convey Lord Wolseley's Expedition into the Sûdân to relieve General Gordon, with their crews, Wâdi Ḥalfa, or simply Ḥalfa as it is now called, presented a scene the like of which was unknown to the "oldest inhabitant."

After the return of the Expedition early in 1885 the authorities decided to consider Ḥalfa as the frontier of Egypt on the south, and by April 15th all the troops and stores were withdrawn from the stations further up the Nile, and a garrison of Egyptian soldiers was established there. In November Major-General the Hon. R H. de Montmorency (the late Lord Frankfort) took command of the troops at Ḥalfa, for a body of Dervishes, from 7,000 to 10,000 strong, 1,500 of whom were armed with rifles, were on their way north with the view of capturing Argîn, and thus to cut the line of Egyptian communications. In this they were unsuccessful, but in December they made good their hold on Sarras, and again threatened Ḥalfa. Colonel (now Sir) Herbert Chermside, and Major (now Sir) Leslie Rundle attacked them, and after a severe hand-to-hand fight defeated them; Nûr al-Kanzi, their leader, and nearly the whole of their force of about two hundred men were killed. This was the first fight in which the Egyptian soldiers attacked the Dervishes without the support of British troops. In June, 1886, the Dervishes came back to Sarras and plundered the unfortunate inhabitants who had returned, but they did not threaten Ḥalfa again until the following October, when they again occupied Sarras, and a body of the enemy, about 1,000 strong, marched on Ḥalfa. This force was met by Colonel Wodehouse about seven miles south of Ḥalfa, and was duly repulsed with loss, and the leaders of the Mahdi's movement decided to postpone the invasion of Egypt until a more fitting opportunity. Sarras, however, remained in the hands of the Dervishes, and although it was impossible for them to maintain a large number of troops there, owing to the difficulty of feeding them, it formed an ideal place as a centre from which to organize raiding expeditions on the villages which stood on the east bank between Ḥalfa and Aswân. The British did their utmost to prevent such raids, which terrified the natives of the whole country round about, and established fortified posts along the Nile, and patrolled the river by gunboats.

The Dervishes, however, light of movement, and knowing every foot of the ground, as well as the nature and habits of the Nubians, frequently eluded the gunboats, and keeping well out of the reach of the fortified posts on the river bank, attacked village after village, and plundered the people, murdering such as resisted them, with comparative impunity. It will be remembered that the last detachment of British troops was withdrawn from Aswân in June, 1888, and this act put fresh heart into the Dervishes. In August following they made a determined attack on the fort of Khôr Mûsa, about four and a half miles south of Ḥalfa, and captured it. A small detachment from a body of about five hundred Dervishes succeeded in creeping up to the fort about 11 p.m. on the night of the 29th, using the river bank as cover. The sentry at one corner of the fort, hearing a noise, challenged and was promptly shot; the corporal of the guard, hearing the report of a rifle, opened the western gate, went out, and was also shot. The Dervishes rushed into the fort through the open gate, and for two hours a fierce fight raged inside, the Egyptians getting the worst of it. On the first alarm the native Bimbashi, or Major, had telephoned to Ḥalfa for help, and three hours later Lieut. Machell arrived with troops, and the gunboat "Metemmeh" began to shell the portion of the fort held by the Dervishes. The Dervishes, greatly surprised at the turn events had taken, fought bravely, but all were soon killed or wounded, and when the Egyptians regained possession of the fort they found the dead bodies of eighty-five Baḳḳâra and Jaalin Arabs. A considerable number of the enemy had also been killed in trying to escape. The Egyptian loss was nineteen killed and thirty-four wounded. This defeat made the Dervishes ponder for a while, and for two years Ḥalfa remained undisturbed. The Egyptian troops were unable to take the offensive, but in 1890 Sâba Bey made a reconnaissance towards Abû Ḥamed, and captured and held for a few hours one of the Dervish outposts. It is satisfactory to be able to say that in the fight which took place as Sâba Bey retreated Sulêmân Wad Ḳamr, who murdered Colonel Stewart on September 18th, 1884, was killed.[1]

By the end of 1892 the Dervishes had gained sufficient strength and boldness to advance towards Ḥalfa once more, and in January, 1893, they attempted to cut the railway between that town and Sarras, but failed. Six months later they descended on the town of Beriṣ, to the south of the Oasis of Khârga, hoping to be able to make a way into Egypt on the western bank of the Nile, but success did not attend their efforts, and nothing more was heard of an invasion of Egypt. In 1895 the Ḥalfa district was raided by the Dervishes once more, and they became so bold that on one occasion they descended on the officers playing polo outside Ḥalfa, causing them to leave their game and run for the Ḥalfa gate. On another occasion, when General Knowles was reviewing the Ḥalfa garrison, the parade was broken up quickly to allow some of the troops to go in pursuit of raiding Dervishes. Only a few months before the Dongola Expedition, the raiders had galloped through Tawfîḳîya, slashing at the unarmed and inoffensive inhabitants, several of whom were drowned in attempting to save themselves by the river.[2]

In March, 1896, as a result of the defeat of the Italians by the Abyssinians at Aduwa on February 29th, the British and Egyptian

[1] Royle, "Egyptian Campaigns," p. 472.

[2] "Sudan Campaign," p. 5. By An Officer. London, 1899.

Governments decided to send an expedition to Dongola. It was clear that if, as was possible, Kasala fell into the hands of the Dervishes (for the Italians were unable to protect their garrison in that town), the whole Nile Valley would be at the mercy of the Mahdiists. On March 12th, Colonel (now Sir) Archibald Hunter was ordered to advance from Ḥalfa and to occupy Akâsha,[1] and British troops began to move up the Nile the same day. In a very short time the little frontier town of Ḥalfa became a vast depôt for stores and the munitions of war, and the base from which all supplies had to be sent to the front. It was well-nigh impossible to believe that the Ḥalfa to which I came in 1897 was the same place which I had seen ten years before. In 1887 there was neither quay nor landing stage, and disembarking from a boat of any considerable size was a matter of difficulty. Strewn along the bank, lying in the mud, were a number of fine machines for workshops, and pieces of large machines which had been brought to Ḥalfa by Isma'îl's orders, but as no means existed for lifting them from their barges to the top of the bank they had been dropped into the mud, and, of course, left there. There they lay for years until the inevitable Englishman or Scotsman arrived, and dragged them into the Ḥalfa workshops, where I have seen some of them working at the present day. On the bank itself I saw a few locomotives tied up in bazaar cotton, but as the working parts of many of them had been removed, and they belonged to an obsolete class, it was some time before they could be used. Between 1887 and 1897 a strong river wall had been built along the bank for a considerable distance, and lines of rail to connect it with the main track had been laid. Storehouses and workshops had come into being, and work went on in them by day and by night. In 1890 the Nile gauge now in use was built by Captain H. G. Lyons.

After leaving the steamer I made my way to report myself at Headquarters, where I was received by my old friend Colonel (now Sir) J. Grenfell Maxwell, the Commandant. With characteristic kindness he gave me quarters in his house until such time as a train started for the south. There was no time for talk, for every minute of his day, and sometimes a great part of his night

[1] More correctly 'Ukâsha.

also, had to be devoted to his work. Theoretically, every one knows what a serious matter the transport of goods and materials is in time of war, but when to this is added the task of providing the sleepers and rails necessary for laying from one to three miles of railway each day, and food and water for 3,000 workmen in the desert along one single line, and for 10,000 soldiers at the end of another single line, about two hundred miles long, very few who have not actually seen transport operations in progress are able to realize how great the burden becomes.

After the heat of Kalâbsha and Korosko the comparatively cool temperature of Ḥalfa was very pleasant, and the afternoon of the day was profitably spent in obtaining tinned food and stores necessary for a six months' sojourn in the Sûdân. In this matter I found the help of Captain Blunt invaluable, and many of the creature comforts which I enjoyed later in the year at Gebel Barkal I owed to his forethought. I was quite accustomed to preparing for journeys in Mesopotamia, where villages are to be found on the road comparatively often, and where food, more or less bad, can be generally obtained, but the arid wastes of the Sûdân were new to me, and, but for the friendly and practical advice of Colonel Maxwell and his colleague, Captain Blunt, I should have fared badly. Speaking generally, the country between Ḥalfa and Kerma, i.e., for at least two hundred miles, produced nothing which was available for purchase by the traveller, and everything he was likely to require he had to carry with him. The Dervishes had cut down palm trees by the hundred, they had eaten up nearly all the sheep, goats, and cattle which they found north of Kerma, and when the Egyptian army arrived the inhabitants of scores of villages were on the verge of starvation.

On the day following my arrival at Ḥalfa, Colonel Maxwell arranged that I was to leave for Kerma by a train which started about noon. As a rule a train consisted of a locomotive, one or more water tanks, and as many loaded trucks of all classes and sizes as the engine could haul, but on this occasion the railway authorities attached to the train for my use an old and battered four-wheeled coach which was commonly known as "Yellow Maria." It was a coach with a history. It was made for Isma'îl Pâshâ, and had been employed for some years on his railway between Ḥalfa and Sarras; the body had never been painted or varnished since it left the maker's hands, and the fact that the sides held together and clung to the frame spoke volumes for the excellence of the work which had been put into it in the first instance. Large numbers of tourists had travelled in it, and every British officer in the Sûdân at that time knew it well. At one end of it was a small compartment in which a large water-pot was kept, and along each side of the remaining portion was a low bench, which served as a seat by day and a bed by night. Most of the glass in the windows was broken, and the frames were so loose that when the coach was in motion they rattled incessantly. This coach had been in many an accident, and everywhere bore on its body marks of its experience. It was, nevertheless, a means of conveyance for which to be most thankful, as every one who has travelled on camel or donkey through that awful region of rocks,[1] sun, and sand, the Baṭn al-Ḥagar, will admit, for it afforded protection from the scorching heat of the day, and from the bitter cold which comes in the Sûdân between midnight and dawn. When one remembers how glad every one who was accustomed to caravan travelling, from the Sirdar downwards, was to avail himself of "Yellow Maria," the complaints of those who travel from Ḥalfa to Kharṭûm in luxurious trains at a uniform speed of twenty-five miles an hour, with food, cool drinks, lavatory accommodation, electric light, electric fans, always at hand, seem unreasonable.

Shortly after noon a bag of official documents for the Sirdar, General Sir H. Kitchener, was committed to my care, and the picturesque guard of the train, whose dress consisted of one shoe, one boot, and parts of a pair of trousers, and the body of a shirt, having taken both them and me under his charge, the train started. For a few miles we ran at a speed of about fifteen miles an hour, and the gradient was very slight, but as soon as the line ran into the hills, our pace slackened, and it became evident that the train-load was a heavy one. One by one, however, the curves and gradients were overcome, and at times, when it was possible to catch a glimpse of the river, the view was charming. From the elevation of the

[1] See the "Report on the Blackened Rocks of the Nile Cataract, 1905," published by the Egyptian Government.

line the traveller could look down at the little villages which the natives had built wheresoever the Nile had deposited sufficient mud to enable them to grow *dhurra*, and though the houses were mere hovels, the fact was not conspicuously apparent from a distance. In places the waters of the Nile were a mile wide, and the river appeared to be much larger than it is really, for it was the season of its flood, and hundreds of rocks and small islands and sand-banks were submerged. On some of the larger islands there were vegetation, trees, shrubs, &c., and their vivid green was in striking contrast with the polished blackened granite rocks below, and the blue sky above, and the bright yellow sand which streaked the sides of the rugged banks that led down to the water-side. In places a very few palms were seen, but these striking characteristics of Nile scenery were, and still are, wanting in this portion of the Nile Valley, for the Dervishes cut down every palm they could in order to starve the Barâbara into joining their ranks. This act was a peculiarly cruel one, for the dwellers in the Cataracts can grow very little *dhurra*, for the simple reason that there is no mud to grow it on.

A run of three hours brought us to Sarras, where we stopped for some time. The engine needed water and a certain amount of oiling and cleaning, and the soldiers on the train who were on their way to the front took the opportunity to light fires and cook their dinners, which they intended to eat at sunset. The scene was an interesting one, and even the civilian could see what a surprising change had come over the Egyptian soldier since the British occupied Cairo on September 15th, 1882. Years of hard work and drill under Grenfell, Kitchener, Rundle, MacDonald, Hunter, Maxwell, Lewis, and other indefatigable officers, had produced a fighting machine which had learned not only to do as it was told, but to do it at the proper time; and good rations, suitable uniforms, and regular pay, without vexatious deductions and pilferings on the part of his superior officers, had produced a man who had confidence in his officers, and was now ready to respect himself. The Egyptian soldier in 1897 knew that his brothers in arms had fought side by side with British troops against the Dervishes at Ginnis and had conquered, and that without the help of British troops they had destroyed the army of Wad an-Nagûmî at Argin and Toski. Between 1887 and 1897 they had met the Dervishes in many a frontiér skirmish, and they had found that the troops of the Mahdi and Khalifa were not invincible.

At Sarras itself there was absolutely nothing to see, and until one realized that it offered a very convenient site for an outpost, it was difficult to understand why the Dervishes had fought for its possession so tenaciously. The banks of the Nile are high and comparatively steep, and the fort on the hill commanded an excellent view of a fine broad reach of the Nile, which here bends away to the west, and of the track which runs south to Akâsha viâ Ambigôl Wells. On the flat ground, not far from the railway, a considerable number of graves were to be seen. Up to this point the railway runs by the river, but soon after leaving Sarras it enters one of the most stony regions it is possible to imagine, and does not touch the Nile again until it reaches Akâsha. The railway embankment from Sarras to Akâsha was first made by the engineers of Isma'il Pâshâ, but rails were not laid on it; the route chosen was, according to experts, the worst possible, and it seems as if the object of those who surveyed it was to make as long and difficult a road as they could. During Lord Wolseley's Expedition in 1884 rails were laid on it for about fifty-seven miles, but these had been torn up by the Dervishes between 1884 and 1896, and much damage done to the embankment. When the advance to Dongola was ordered there was no time to make a survey for a new road; the old embankment was therefore repaired, and all the rails which the Dervishes had not carried off were re-laid as fast as possible.

What travelling on this portion was like we had an opportunity of learning so soon as we left Sarras, and the experience was an exciting one. The curves in many places were very sharp, and it was not difficult to understand why two engines had fallen from the line to the bottom of a fifteen-foot bank, and why engines and trucks left the line daily. The wreck of a train frequently interfered with the water supply, but the British officers who worked the line were equal to all emergencies, and the men under them responded with amazing alacrity.

The short and less steep gradients were ascended without

difficulty, but frequently the power of our engine was tried to the utmost. More than once we were unable to ascend a gradient at the first attempt, and the drivers were compelled to let the train run back and stand on the level until a fresh supply of steam had been generated. When once the top of the hill had been reached, and we began to run down the other side, the pace became alarming, and one's whole mind was occupied in wondering how long the train would keep on the metals. None of the trucks were provided with breaks, and the break-blocks on the engine were so much worn that they were almost ineffective; the last vehicle on the train, "Yellow Maria," rattled and rocked very badly, and in going down any incline rarely travelled on all four wheels at once. However, the special Providence which presides over all things Egyptian prevailed, and so far as our train was concerned no accident happened. The stations of Mughrât Wells, Ambigôl Road, and Ambigôl Wells were passed safely, the last-mentioned being particularly interesting. The well at Ambigôl, from which the water supply for engines is obtained, is from sixteen to twenty feet deep, and more than twelve feet in diameter. Its water is of a purgative character, and not very wholesome; during the campaign, however, it was invaluable, and lightened the labours of the transport service. At a little distance from the Wells, in the desert, is the tomb of that gallant officer "Roddy" Owen, who died of cholera during the very hot summer of 1896; on the head-stone is inscribed, "Under the Shadow of the Sword is Paradise." It may be noted in passing that the name "Ambigôl" is of interest. It can hardly be Arabic, but it may well represent the Coptic words *Amba Pedjoul*, i.e., Father Pedjoul.[1] It is well known that during the Coptic period of the history of Egypt a number of recluses and anchorites took up their abode in the islands of the Cataracts and in places on the mainland, and it is quite possible that one of these bearing some name like Pedjoul may have lived near the Wells, and that he may have worked cures by means of their waters, which possess certain medicinal properties. In any case, the first part of the name Ambigôl suggests a Coptic derivation.

[1] On the other hand, *ambi* or *ambu* means in the language of the Barâbara the "dûm palm."

After climbing the steep gradient from Ambigôl Wells, we ran down a long incline amid most weird and striking scenery, if this word can be applied to the wild and shapeless masses of rocks which were piled up in fantastic heaps on both sides of the line. The khôrs and ravines were brilliantly lit by a moon nearly at the full, which hung clear of the sky like a mass of shining silver, and shone with such splendour that the stars were almost invisible. The yellow wind-blown sand, which lay in ridges on the slopes of the hills and in patches at their rocky feet, had a slightly ruddy tint, and the shadows cast by the rocks were strikingly inky in their blackness. As the speed of the train slackened from time to time, the shrill cries of the "children of yells,"[1] as the Arabs call the jackals, could be heard, and they added a strange weirdness to what was an enchanting fairy scene. The locomotive, leaving behind it a trail of black smoke, did not seem out of place in the primeval chaos which surrounded us; on the contrary, it might well have appeared to the denizens of that rocky wilderness to be one of the rushing fiery monsters with which the ancient inhabitants of the country peopled the desert.

Quite close to the caravan road from Halfa to Akâsha, and about five miles to the north of the latter place, is the sulphur well of Ukmah or Okmah, which is famous among the Cataract folk for its cures of scrofulous diseases, and we had on the train two natives who had come from Cairo to bathe in its waters. Above the well are the remains of a building which is called after the name of "our lord Solomon" (*sayyidna Sulêmân*), but the construction is quite modern. Under it several little hot springs rise, and he who seeks a cure there causes his friends to dig a hole in the warm mud near them large enough to hold him, and then they place him in it and cover him over with mud. The place is, of course, under the protection of the Prophet, and no cure can be effected without his blessing. There is no doubt that those who suffer from rheumatism obtain benefit from such bathing in the warm sulphur mud, but the supply of water is limited at the best of times, and during the Inundation the place is entirely swamped by the flood, and the healing waters are lost in it. There are other hot springs in the neighbourhood, but none has the reputa-

[1] *Banât âwa.*

tion of the spring of Okmah. Burckhardt mentions[1] that he slept near the tomb of Shêkh Okâsha, which is close to these springs, but he makes no mention of them. This shêkh was, he says, much revered by the Nubians, and he saw offerings of earthen vessels, mats, and pieces of linen spread within the enclosure of his tomb, and all around it. The inhabitants of Dâr Sukkôt make frequent pilgrimages to this tomb.

A little before midnight Akâsha was passed, and we saw the remains of the heaps of stores and material which had been piled up here by the Sirdar when preparing to make his famous onslaught on the Dervishes, who were collected at Farka, or Ferket, about fifteen miles further south. The first fight of the Dongola Expedition took place near Akâsha on May 1st, 1896. Major Burn Murdoch, with about two hundred and forty of the Egyptian cavalry, encountered unexpectedly a Dervish force consisting of three hundred mounted Baḳḳâra, and one thousand men on foot. The Egyptian cavalry was ordered to retire, but the order was barely carried out before the Dervish horsemen were upon them, with the result that several of the Egyptians were speared in the back before their companions could turn and defend them. A halt was called, and when the Egyptians wheeled round they charged the Dervish horsemen with such vigour that, after a fierce hand-to-hand fight, the enemy turned and fled. Meanwhile the Dervish men on foot were advancing to help their comrades, but when the Egyptians dismounted, and began to fire volleys into them, they turned round and retreated to Ferket. This fight lasted from noon till 3 p.m. The Egyptian loss was two killed and ten wounded, and the enemy's eighteen killed and eighty wounded.

A further run of fifteen miles brought us to the miserable village of Ferket, which, however, looked picturesque enough in the moonlight. This place is memorable as the scene of the battle fought there on June 7th, 1896, but the importance which it possesses in the eyes of the natives is due to the fact that it is situated at the end of the open stretch of river which lies between the foot of the Third Cataract, and the head of the Second. After the fight at Akâsha mentioned above, the Sirdar decided that it

[1] "Travels in Nubia," p. 50.

was time to attack the large Dervish force of three thousand men gathered together at Ferket. On June 4th he began to move up his troops to Akâsha, and by the afternoon of the 6th nearly ten thousand Egyptian soldiers were concentrated at that place. This force was divided into two parts, which were known as the River Column and the Desert Column, the former being placed under the command of Colonel Hunter, and the latter under that of Major Burn Murdoch. The Sirdar decided that the River Column was to advance along the Nile bank to Ferket, and the Desert Column was to make a detour in the desert and march to the same place, his intention being that both Columns should arrive at the same time, and so hem in the Dervishes. The time of the starting of both columns was fixed, it is said, by Major Broadwood, who knew both routes well, and they arrived simultaneously at Ferket hills at dawn. The marching had been carried out so silently that the Dervishes knew nothing of the projected attack until they saw the Egyptian troops all round them. The Dervishes, seeing that all chance of escape was gone, prepared for action, and began the engagement at 5 a.m. on June 7th, by opening fire from an outpost on Ferket Mountain, which lay on the north side of the village, close to the river, by the side of which the Egyptian troops had to pass. As the River Column advanced from the north the Desert Column shelled the enemy from the south, and though the Dervishes fought with the utmost bravery, their losses were severe.

When all organized resistance was at an end, a certain amount of hut-to-hut fighting had to be gone through, and when all the huts were cleared a general rout of the Dervishes took place. In fact, the enemy were cleverly trapped, for those who ran away from one column fell into the hands of the other, and those who managed to avoid the columns, and who fled either to the river or the desert, were pursued by the cavalry and cut down. Within two hours the fight was over; the Dervish loss was about one thousand killed, and five hundred wounded, and of the Egyptians twenty were killed and eighty wounded. Among the killed were about forty Amirs, or "commanders," many of whom were identified by Sir Rudolf von Slatin Pâshâ; of these was the infamous Osmân Azrak,[1] whose

[1] According to some authorities Osmân Azrak, "Osman the Blue," was not

fate gave satisfaction to many. Osmân Azrak was a man of considerable intelligence, and he had enjoyed the protection of the British at Ḥalfa so long as it suited his purpose; but when he thought that the power of the Dervishes was in the ascendant, he went over to them, and organized raids with conspicuous success. Like Osmân Diḳna (i.e., Osmân of the beard)[1] he always arranged the preliminaries of a fight, but so soon as the fight began he promptly disappeared by the means of escape which he had taken care to provide.

The destruction of the Dervish frontier army enabled the Sirdar to establish his advance post at Suwarda, about thirty miles south of Kôsha, and permitted the continuation of the railway; all the country round about was cleared of Dervishes, who fled to Dongola, and there is no doubt that the Khalifa realized that a crushing blow had fallen on his troops.

From Ferket to Kôsha the railway runs between low hills, and gradually descends to the plain in which that village lies. The neighbourhood of Kôsha is famous as the scene of some hard fighting which took place there in 1885. In November of that year the Dervishes had assembled in large numbers at Kôsha, and their leaders believed that, since the British had retreated after the fall of Kharṭûm and the murder of General Gordon, it would be comparatively easy to invade Egypt. On December 12th three thousand Dervishes attacked the fort of Mograkeh, a village near Kôsha, and though they succeeded in getting within one hundred yards of it, they were repulsed by the three hundred Egyptians who were inside it. On the 15th the Dervishes opened fire on Kôsha from a battery erected on the sand-hills on the western bank, but it was soon silenced, and the men with it were driven away. On the 29th General (now Sir) Frederick Stephenson, who commanded the British Army of Occupation, and General Grenfell, the Sirdar of the Egyptian Army, marched

killed at Ferket, and he is said by these to have taken a small box of treasure and to have swum across the river with it on his head so soon as he heard the firing begin.

[1] *Dikna* is said to mean "ugly" in the Hadanduwa language. This nickname is further said to have been given to him on account of the light colour of the complexion of his father, a Turk or Levantine; his mother was a Hadanduwa woman.

to Kôsha from Ferket, and on the following day they defeated the Dervishes both at Kôsha and at Ginnis. The British battery shelled the village, the houses were rushed by the Cameron Highlanders and the Ninth Sûdânî Battalion, and the fire of the gunboat *Lotus* did great execution on those who attempted flight. After two hours' fight the Egyptians moved on and attacked Ginnis, which fell into their hands after another two hours' fight. The Dervish loss was three hundred wounded, and five hundred killed, among the latter being the Amir Abd al-Magîd and eighteen minor chiefs. The Khalîfa was greatly disturbed at the result of this fight, for all his calculations were upset; what his feelings were eleven years later, when his frontier army of three thousand men was wiped out, it is difficult to say.

The village of Kôsha has nothing of interest in it, but a considerable amount of trade was done there formerly. It was, and still is, the centre of the date trade of Sukkôt, but it is uncertain how long it will remain so. After the railway was brought there on August 4th, 1896, the merchants were in the habit of sending their dates by it in sacks weighing about three hundredweight, but now that the rails from Kôsha south have been taken up, and freight trains no longer run at regular intervals, the dates must be sent in to Ḥalfa by camel, and the cost of camel transport is practically prohibitive. The Sirdar, Sir F. R. Wingate, has, however, built a rest-house at Kôsha and established the head-quarters of an inspector there, and he will undoubtedly find some means of maintaining and increasing the trade of the district. In former days caravans for the Oasis of Selima started from a village on the west bank of the Nile, a little to the south of Kôsha, and rock salt from that place was sold in the bazaar of Kôsha.

After a delay of some two hours at Kôsha our train resumed its journey, and set out at dawn to cross the desert between Kôsha and Delligo, or Dulgo, a distance of about forty-four miles. The route was surveyed by British officers, and as this portion of the line was laid with new rails, travelling over it was easier and quicker than over the section to Kôsha. When for various reasons it was decided in 1904 to abolish the Ḥalfa-Kerma line, these same rails were sufficiently good to take up, and to carry away viâ

Ḥalfa and Atbara for use on the Atbara and Sawâkin Railway. Between Kôsha and Dulgo the railway is carried over the beds of summer torrents by good bridges, which must have cost the builders much anxious thought and care. The embankments are well made, with generous side-slopes, and it is regrettable that so much good work must be abandoned. Rather more than half-way to Dulgo we passed a tent on the right of the line, and soon after saw a young Royal Engineer officer, Lieut. Micklem, I think, engaged in taking levels and inspecting portions of the line. The appearance of this solitary officer in the heart of the desert was a convincing proof of the constant vigilance with which the Sirdar caused his line of communication to be watched.

At Dulgo another long halt was made, for the train had to be re-made, the engine fire had to be thoroughly cleaned, and a certain amount of overhauling of parts had to be gone through. Whilst these important works were going on, the soldiers left the trucks and lighted fires and made coffee, for the morning was relatively cold, and every one was glad to gather his cloak about him. The most prominent feature of Dulgo is a large mountain on the east side of the plain whereon the village is built; in the early hours of the day it obstructs the sun's rays, and casts a long shadow, which the natives who seek warmth avoid. At mid-day the plain becomes a veritable sun-trap, and the flat stony side of the mountain sends out heat like a furnace. Under the rays of the setting sun the appearance of the mountain is a thing of beauty, for the tints and colours of the various layers of stone in it vary from moment to moment, changing in the after-glow from bright orange to a warm deep red. On the west bank of the river, about two miles from Dulgo, stand clearly against the sky the few remaining pillars of the temple built by Seti I., in the fourteenth century before Christ. The village of Dulgo played no part in the rebellion of the Mahdi and Khalifa, but in November, 1885, the plain close by served as the place of concentration of the eight thousand Dervishes who were sent to cut the Ḥalfa railway at Khanak, and invade Egypt.

Between Dulgo and Kerma the line passed through a very wild tract of country, and it is easy to understand what an almost insuperable barrier it must have proved to the invading host of the Pharaohs when they made a raid into the Sûdân. We passed Kaddin and Farêg, the site of the Sirdar's advanced out-post in 1896, and then crossed the desert to Kabôdî, thus cutting off a great bend of the river. A run of three hours brought us to Kerma, the terminus of the Ḥalfa line, and we arrived about noon in a sand-storm. A strong wind was blowing, and the air was so full of sand that the sun was almost invisible; but for the heat and the sandy air the day had all the appearance of a "gray day" in England. There was neither station nor shed for the train to pull up at, and we stopped about fifty yards from the point where the rails came to an end. After a short time the Sûdânî soldiers loomed in the sandy air, and, telling me that they had been sent to fetch me by Captain Oldfield, proceeded to take my luggage and self into this officer's tent. Captain Oldfield rose from his table, and welcomed me cordially. His first words were, "What have you done with the bag of papers for the Sirdar?" then, "Will you have a bath and breakfast?" The precious bag being duly forthcoming, he pounced upon it and put it in a safe place, and then quickly dropped into his ordinary character of a courteous, but much harassed, British gentleman in the Egyptian Army. What Captain Pedley was at Aswân Captain Oldfield was at Kerma, and as transport officer his duties were multifarious, and his work was never done. Whatever time a steamer arrived from Merawi, whether by day or night, it had to be loaded at once, and despatched forthwith; telegrams by the dozen came to tell him what to load in the steamers, and what not to load, and he was responsible for all the food and stores which were consigned to him until he had passed them on to the south. And all this with the thermometer at 118° in the tent! At Kerma I had the pleasure of meeting Count Calderari, who had been deputed by the Italian Government to report to them on the military operations which were taking place in the Sûdân, and subsequently we lived in neighbouring huts at Merawi for many weeks.

When I arrived at Kerma a number of barges were being loaded, and Captain Oldfield hoped to have been able to lash them to a stern-wheeler, and set them on their way south the same day, and myself with them; but this was found to be impossible, and as the loading could not be finished before the evening, it was decided not to start until dawn the following day. This arrangement set the afternoon free, and we were able to go and look at the Dervish fort, which lies to the north of the village. Its position was well chosen, and it consisted of a very thick wall, with loop-holes and embrasures for guns, and an inner fort; its area of fire was extensive, and in the hands of a determined foe would have caused an attacking force a good deal of trouble. The idea of visiting the famous granite quarries on the Island of Tombos was mooted, but boats were scarce, and the Nile being in high flood the possibility of returning by a given time was very doubtful. Tombos lies a little to the north of Kerma, just opposite Hannek, where the series of rapids called the Third Cataract begins. The only antiquities to be heard of consisted of a few pillars, situated about three miles from Kerma, and an examination of these showed them to have belonged to a small Egyptian temple, built probably under the XIXth Dynasty. Close by, the lower part of a seated stone figure of an ancient Egyptian official was found; it passed into the hands of Mr. Page, the engineer in charge of all the machinery at that time in Kerma, who presented it to the Trustees of the British Museum. It is tolerably certain that a town of some importance stood at or near Kerma, under the XVIIIth Dynasty, though probably on the west bank of the Nile, and as the natives declared that "written stones" used to be found there, it might be well for the Sûdân Government to make trial examinations there.

The loading of the barges being completed by sunset, Captain Oldfield took me and my kit, including the bag of papers, to the stern-wheeler, *Abu Klea*,[1] and I was "handed over" to the officer in command of the steamer. The whole of the lower deck was crammed with boxes and stores, and all the space at the sides and front of the boiler was filled with logs of wood for the fire. In the barges which were lashed alongside were hundreds of Egyptian soldiers, and I recognized many of my fellow-passengers in the train. The upper deck also was crowded, and it was with the greatest difficulty that space could be found for a roll of blankets. At the end of it, seated on any odd box that

[1] The correct form of the name is "Abû Ṭaliḥ."

came handy, were five Englishmen; they were clothed somewhat scantily, and were very hot, and were horribly bored at the delay which they had to suffer. They were five war correspondents from England, namely, Mr. Payne Knight, the brilliant author of "Where Three Empires Meet," and correspondent of the *Times*: Mr. Fred Villiers, the veteran correspondent of the *Standard;* Mr. Scudamore, who represented the *Daily News;* the late Mr. Maud, whose excellent pictures of Sûdân towns and scenes of native life have charmed thousands of readers of the *Graphic;* and Mr. Gwynne, Reuter's "Special Correspondent" in the Sûdân. They all were exceedingly kind to me, but were sorely puzzled to know what my business was in the Sûdân, and why it was I had been allowed by the Sirdar to travel from Cairo to Kerma in ten and a half days, while the same journey had taken them several weeks to perform. They were all very earnest, and very anxious to get to the front and wire home news as to the events which were happening in the neighbourhood of Abû Ḥamed and Berber, and they chafed sorely at the delays imposed on them by the Sirdar. They were provided with tents and a good supply of tinned food, which they carried in long, narrow boxes very suitable for camel transport, and it was good to find that the managers of the newspapers which they represented supplied their wants in no niggardly manner. Their supplies permitted them to give me several meals, and as in those days in the Sûdân ordinary food was scarce, and could not be bought, such kindness was most acceptable. The heat on the steamer was stifling, and we wandered about in the night vainly trying to find a place where the heat thrown out by the boiler and smoke-stack could not be felt; there was no room for unrolled beds, so each man slept as best he could on his blanket or rug, in any place which seemed cooler than the rest of the deck.

Soon after the "false dawn," and about that time of the night when a wave of cool air passes over the desert, the crew began to haul in chains and ropes, and after a great deal of pushing with poles, the *Abu Klea* got under way, and steamed out into mid-stream. The coolness of the dawn was very refreshing, and under the influence of early tea the Sirdar's restrictions seemed less galling to the correspondents. The scene on the steamer and barges was interesting and characteristic. Little groups of soldiers perched on the sides of the barges, or squatted round handfuls of fire watching the *ibrîks* (metal pots) boil, and as they smoked with great deliberation their small cigarettes they discussed the future of the war, and told stories, as amazing as amusing. At the ends of the barges down-stream others washed themselves, and then climbing up on to any tolerably clean place slipped off their shoes and said their prayers. An Egyptian bugler began to practise, and the crew employed themselves in stacking the boxes in a more ship-shape fashion, to the words, "Ya Muḥammad an-Nebi," i.e., "O Muhammad the Prophet!" Above all the noises rose the steady beat of the great paddle-wheel aft on the water, and the noisy clang of the door of the boiler fire when, at short intervals, fresh logs were pushed into the furnace. Everybody seemed to make as much noise as he could, and everybody seemed as happy as if there were no such thing as war in the world. Our progress was very slow, for the steamer herself was heavily laden, and she had besides to tow four barges, two on each side; in addition to this the Nile current ran swiftly and strongly, and in some places we cannot have covered more than two and a half miles of ground in the hour.

Two or three hours' steaming brought us opposite Al-Hafir, a village on the west bank, famous in the annals of the Dongola campaign as the scene of the artillery duel between the Egyptians and the Dervishes on September 19th, 1896. A few days before this date the Sirdar learned that the forces of the Khalifa were strongly entrenched at Kerma, but on the evening of the 18th, Captain Mahon[1] reported that he had been close up to the fort at Kerma and had found it empty. Next morning the Anglo-Egyptian troops marched through Kerma and on to a spot opposite Hafir, where Wad al-Bishâra had taken up a very strong position. "The Dervishes were occupying some excellently "placed low trenches connecting six earth gun emplacements. "Several Dervishes could also be seen firing from the tops of the "palm trees, from which they were soon dislodged by the "maxims, and if they were not killed by the bullets, they certainly

[1] Now Col. Mahon, C.B., D.S.O. He led the Mafeking Relief Column in 1900.

"must have been by their fall to the ground. Behind in the "desert could be seen about three thousand Dervish horse and "foot, waiting out of range of the gunboats to fall on any "force that attempted to cross the river."[1] This position was protected by deep morasses at each end. Soon after the Egyptian artillery had opened fire, Commander Colville, R.N., arrived in his flagship, the *Tamaai*, accompanied by the *Abu Klea*—the gunboat on which we were—and the *Metammeh*, and so soon as they were abreast of the Dervish forts they poured in their fire, and then dropped down stream until they were out of the enemy's range.

During the three hours' engagement which followed the Egyptian gunboats were struck several times by the Dervish shells, one of which entered the magazine of the *Abu Klea*, but fortunately did not explode. Seeing that the Dervish fire was not silenced, the Sirdar sent three batteries of artillery and the Maxim battery to take up a position on the Island of Artaghâsi, which lay about three quarters of a mile from the Dervish position, and within two hours the Dervish fire was silenced. Whilst this was going on the gunboats were ordered to proceed to Dongola, and the carrying out of this order made it necessary for them to run the gauntlet of the five Dervish guns, which were worked by ex-Egyptian gunners. As they did so, the Dervishes made such good practice that scarcely a square inch of the gunboats escaped being hit by the rifle bullets of the enemy. Whilst the gunboats were making their way south to Dongola the Dervishes fired shots at intervals, chiefly from the place on the west bank where were moored a gun-boat, built by General Gordon at Kharṭûm and called *At-Tahra*, and twenty five large sailing vessels laden with grain, which they were trying to discharge. The Dervish loss that day is unknown; the Egyptian loss was twenty-one killed and wounded.

Wad al-Bishâra, the Dervish general, finding out late at night that the gunboats had arrived at Dongola, and being deceived by false information, decided in his mind that the Sirdar intended the Egyptian troops to march on until they were opposite Dongola, and then to make them cross the river. His answer to this

[1] "Sudan Campaign," p. 60. By An Officer.

supposed move was to withdraw his forces from Hafir at about 3 a.m. on September 20th, and he marched with all haste to Dongola in order to be ready to resist the passage of the river by the Egyptians. Within a few hours of their leaving, the Sirdar knew what had happened, and ordered his troops to begin to cross at once to Hafîr; this was done, and the whole day was occupied in bringing soldiers, guns and ammunition, transport animals, &c., to the west bank. As the river was high and the steamer stood in tolerably close to the west bank, we were able to see some of the loop-holes in parts of the walls which the Dervishes had held so bravely. It is generally admitted that Wad al-Bishâra chose his position with great judgment, and, but for the wound in his head, inflicted by a piece of shell on the "day of Hafir," his resistance would have been prolonged.

As the day wore on the heat became great, and natives and Europeans alike found the time hang heavily on their hands, and no matter with what subject a conversation started, it always ended with the war. The correspondents had sufficient information to know that stirring events were taking place "up the river," and they were intensely eager to find out exactly what was doing. For some reason or other they expected news of current events at Dongola, and they awaited our arrival there with impatience. In the afternoon we began to pass the Island of Arḳô, which so far back as the XIIth or XIIIth Dynasty must have been the site of a large town, with temples, &c., built according to ancient Egyptian designs. As reference has already been made to the granite statues on this Island, and their measurements by Mr. Hoskins and others, nothing need be said about them here. The Island is a long one, and the village of Arḳô is on its western side.

In due course we arrived at Dongola, i.e., New Dongola, known among the natives as Al-Ordi, i.e., "the Camp," to distinguish it from Old Dongola, or more properly "Tunkul," and there the steamer stopped for the night. The newspaper correspondents rushed ashore to find out what news there was to be had; but though rumours were abundant, the amount of fact elicited by their questions was exceedingly small. The natives gave graphic accounts of the capture of Abû Ḥamed by General

Hunter on August 7th, and declared that the Dervish corpses which they had seen floating down the river were so numerous that the crocodiles had returned to the Dongola reaches. It will be remembered that General Hunter left Merawi on July 29th with about 2,500 men for Abû Ḥamed. When he arrived at Abû Ḥamed he found the village held by about fifteen hundred Dervishes, three hundred of whom had rifles, and one hundred and fifty were mounted. The position was a very strong one, but it was captured after a fierce fight, and over twelve hundred Dervishes were slain ; the Egyptian loss was eighty-seven killed and wounded, and Major Sidney and Lieutenant Fitz-Clarence were killed. The Sirdar then ordered his gunboats and sailing boats with men and stores to hurry up through the Fourth Cataract to Abû Ḥamed, so that he might press on and attack Berber, but before this order could be carried out news reached him that the Dervishes had evacuated Berber, and withdrawn to the south. A large party of "friendlies" were sent on to occupy the town, and their leader, Aḥmad Bey Khalifa, arrived there on September 6th; a week later General Hunter arrived with the greater portion of his force. Now all the details of these important operations were kept a profound secret by that strong silent man the Sirdar, and even some of the British officers at Merawi were surprised when General Hunter and his battalions suddenly left Kassingar, about fifteen miles south of Merawi, to carry out the Sirdar's plans. The evacuation of Berber by the Dervishes and its reoccupation by the "friendlies" actually took place while we were steaming up the river to Merawi, and though it was generally known that "something was up," no one had the slightest idea what that something was. Questions and surmises were alike fruitless, and all the European passengers went ashore to look at the town.

Dongola, or Tunkul, was at one time a very important town, and the capital of a large and thriving province. When Hoskins visited it in 1833 the province contained five thousand water-wheels, each of which watered from four to five acres, and the population was estimated to be about fifty thousand. The town was fortified with walls and towers, on which were mounted a few pieces of cannon sent there by

Isma'il Pâshâ; its garrison consisted of from three to eight hundred men. In the bazaar were sold silk, linen, cotton stuffs, tarbushes, shoes, glassware, earthenware, medicines for the eyes, pipes of all sorts and sizes, thread, needles, rock salt, amulets, coffee, sugar, tamarinds, weapons of every kind, ginger and spices of all kinds, seeds possessing certain medicinal properties, oils and pomades of various kinds, scent, &c. Dongola also possessed a flourishing slave market; this is not to be wondered at when we remember how closely it was connected with Dâr Fûr and Kordofân, and that main caravan routes ran to both these places and to Sennaar and Eastern Abyssinia. Hoskins tells us (p. 184) that he saw "one extremely beautiful Abyssinian girl" on sale for one hundred and fifty dollars, and that for one who was not beautiful eighty dollars were asked. Business was transacted by barter, but he saw some rudely shaped pieces of iron which he was told were Dâr Fûr money. In the first quarter of the nineteenth century Dongola was famed, according to Burckhardt,[1] for a breed of horses, of Arabian origin, of great strength and beauty, and with all four legs white as far as the knees. A prime stallion was worth from five to ten slaves. Burckhardt also mentions that there were no elephants in Dongola in his day, but says that the hippopotamus (called *barnîk*, or *faras al-baḥr*, i.e., river-horse) was very common in the river. In 1813 there were three in the Nile between the second and Third Cataracts, and in 1812 one was seen so far north as Darâw, "one day's march north of that place" (i e., Aswân). The reputation of the men of Dongola is not high among certain Sûdânî folk, for they have a proverb to the effect that a "man of Dongola is a devil in the skin of a man."

For some time after the beginning of the Mahdi's rebellion, the people of the Dongola province refused to join him, but eventually they were forced to do so, and though they afforded him great assistance, they were very glad when General Kitchener freed them from his rule. After the bombardment of Hafir, which has been mentioned above, the gunboats steamed up the river, and began to fire on the fortifications of Dongola, and on the huge Dervish camp which was at the back of the town. A

[1] "Travels in Nubia," p. 66.

fourth gunboat, the *Zafr*, which had been repaired in some marvellous manner, joined them, and materially assisted Commander Colville. The Dervishes did not return the fire, and Dongola fort was silent; about 9.30 a.m. on September 23rd, 1896, the blacks who garrisoned the fort hoisted the white flag, and Commander Colville ceased firing, and landed with one hundred Sûdânî soldiers and hoisted the Egyptian flag. As the Sirdar's land force came near Dongola the Dervishes retreated, for they appear to have realized that resistance was useless. Time after time they halted, and seemed to be going to attack, but they always changed their minds. When the Egyptians arrived in Dongola they saw the Egyptian flag flying over the Government buildings, and then learned that the blacks had surrendered. Meanwhile the Dervishes fled, pursued by the Camel Corps and Horse Artillery, and they were in such a hurry to escape that mothers dropped their babes, and the Dervish general forgot to take with him some seven hundred Sûdânî riflemen! These surrendered in a body, and four hundred of the finest of them were enlisted in the Egyptian army, and sent to Ḥalfa to be trained, while the remainder were sent to work on the desert railway from Ḥalfa to Abû Ḥamed. The inhabitants grasped the hands of the soldiers and kissed them, and manifested the greatest joy at being freed from the Khalîfa's rule. The once flourishing town of Dongola was found to be a ruin, for under the Dervishes its trade had died, and its inhabitants had either been killed or had gone away. The loss of life consequent on the recapture of Dongola was very little. When we were there a year afterwards it was said that some of the old inhabitants were returning, and that signs of a new growth of trade were already visible.

During the next three days the steamer stopped at intervals to take in wood, and to enable the soldiers to buy small supplies of provisions; such stoppages were eagerly awaited by every one, especially by the correspondents, who were thirsting for news of passing events, and even the goat on board rushed ashore to stretch its legs, and to nibble the blades of grass on the bank. On the afternoon of the fourth day from Kerma, we passed Old Dongola, which is built on a rocky height close to the river, and stands on the east bank, and must always have been a place of great strategic importance. It was an important stronghold in the seventh century before Christ; it became the capital of the kings of the country, who appear to have embraced Christianity in the fifth century, and it continued to hold a position of great importance until the Muḥammadans overran the land in the thirteenth and fourteenth centuries. The river opposite Dongola forms in flood time a fine sight, and is broader than at any place I have seen in Egypt. It rushes along with great strength and swiftness, and the current is so powerful that loaded steamers

THE WEST BANK OF THE NILE NEAR OLD DONGOLA.

going south travel with difficulty two miles an hour. Details of the antiquities at Dongola are given elsewhere in this book. In the evening we passed Hammar Island, and soon after arrived at Abû Ḳûs, or Abû Ḳussi, on the west bank.

A few hours later brought us to Al-Debba, where we received news which was for the correspondents and myself somewhat startling. A telegram from the Sirdar at Merawi had been sent to Colonel E. F. David, Commander of Debba, to the effect that the five correspondents and myself were to disembark at Debba, and to await further permission to proceed to Merawi. It was eleven o'clock at night when we arrived, and nearly every one on the steamer was asleep. We could hardly believe our ears, but Sergeant-Major Kelham, who brought the order to the boat, was quite definite as to the instructions which he had received, and he had been told not only to see us out of the steamer, but that we were to leave it without any delay. Fatigue parties were standing by the side of piles of stores and telegraph wire which had to be loaded on the steamer, and when these and a certain number of troops had been embarked she was to start at once. Then began a scene of hurry and scurry which it was hard to describe. The black "boys," or servants, were running in all directions to collect the property of their masters, and every approach to the gangway was blocked by a mass of soldiers and civilians, the former trying to struggle out of the boat with their kits, and the latter trying to get into it. Most of the men were shouting after the manner of the Egyptians, and no one would give way to his neighbour. Then the fatigue parties began to push their stores on to the steamer, wherever they could find room, and when some of these slipped off into the river, the din and confusion became appalling. Everybody seemed to be cursing everybody else, and men threatened to do violence to each other as they heaped insults of a truly Oriental character upon the memories of their mothers, and alluded joyfully to the torments which their fathers were suffering in hell. Meanwhile nothing was being done, for every one's energies were devoted to shouting. In the nick of time, however, Captain N. T. Borton appeared, and those who know that energetic officer will readily understand how under his vigorous commands, which were punctuated by the light whip which he carried in one hand, the tumult ceased, and the gangway was cleared, and work was done.

The removal of my small effects required a very few minutes, and I was glad to transfer the bag of papers for the Sirdar to other hands. The correspondents were, however, not so fortunate, for they were encumbered with tents, and with many "Press Mess" boxes of considerable length and weight. They themselves were in despair, for it had somehow leaked out that events of importance were happening at Merawi, and that our being turned out on the river bank, in the middle of the night, was due to the Sirdar's intention of keeping the knowledge of his plans to himself and his officers. One of the correspondents telegraphed up to him, asking if he might buy camels and proceed to Merawi at once, and the necessary permission was given forthwith, but an embargo was at once laid on all camels, as they might be required for the army, and no Arab dared to sell any. Hence the permission to buy camels was useless! Soon after I left the steamer Sergeant-Major Kelham was so kind as to offer me the use of a spare *anḳarîb*, or native rope bedstead, which he had by chance in his hut, and in a very short time the troubles of the day were forgotten. The correspondents were not so fortunate, and they slept near their baggage on the river bank.

The following day there was nothing to do but to explore Debba, and wander about and look at the fortifications which had been built there by the Turks, and at the old gun which they had left there. Colonel David was most courteous and hospitable, and Mr. Kelham and another brother non-commissioned officer, called Blake, showed me much kindness. Mr. Maud, of the *Graphic*, ensconced himself under a gauze mosquito tent, and made some capital sketches of natives, and his companions wrote up their diaries. When the evening came we had not the slightest idea when we should be able to continue our journey, and in due course we went to bed; about 1 a.m., however, we were awakened by the hoot of a steamer from the north, and a few minutes later we were ordered to pack up and get aboard at once, as orders had been received to send us on. Then came a repetition of the scene of the previous night. The steamer from the north, called the *Khaibar*, was towing four barges loaded with grain, and on board were considerable numbers of civilian natives, and a company of soldiers, who were to be landed somewhere on the way up. She had to take on board several hundred *kantars*[1] of wood, all the stores which the *Abu Klea* had left behind, a number of soldiers, and ourselves and our baggage; this work took several hours to perform, and we all regretted the absence of Captain Borton.

The village of Debba has nothing in it to make a visit worth

[1] The *kantar* = 99·05 pounds, or 44·93 kilogrammes.

while, and it was only important because it was formerly the starting point of the direct caravan road to Omdurmân. We left Debba at dawn, and appeared to be steaming straight into the sunrise, for the river makes a sharp bend at Debba, and we travelled in an easterly direction as far as Korti, a place famous as the Headquarters of Lord Wolseley in 1884, during the Gordon Relief Expedition. Early in 1885, the "Desert Column," under Major-General Sir Herbert Stewart, marched from Korti to the Gakdûl Wells (ninety-five miles), then on to the Wells of Abû

PALM TREES NEAR MERAWI.

Klea (forty-three miles), near which it fought the famous battle, then on to Metamma (twenty-three miles), where its gallant leader was severely wounded, and then under the greatest difficulties it marched back to Korti, all in less than sixty days. It was one of the most glorious marches ever performed by British soldiers, and every one must be of the opinion of the highest military authority in Europe, Count von Moltke, who said of the men who took part in it, "They were not soldiers but heroes."

From Korti to Merawi the course of the river is north-east, and a few miles from Korti one of the most beautiful stretches of country on the Nile is entered. Both banks are lined with fine palm trees of various kinds, and in the summer time the air is filled with the slightly aromatic scent of the flowering shrubs and trees. In most places the cultivable mud on both banks extends some distance from the river, but as we steamed on to Merawi we saw that most of it was lying waste. For some years past the palms had been neither tended nor fertilized, and under the rule of the Dervishes the water-wheels had in many places been ruined, and the channels which supplied them had become choked with

AN ISLAND IN THE NILE.

mud and rubbish. The huts everywhere were in ruins, and very few cattle were to be seen. The little islands which we passed from time to time were veritable paradises, and they stood up like large gems of living green from the yellowish-brown waters of the river. The trees on such islands were filled with large numbers of little birds of the most brilliant plumage, and it was satisfactory to think that the tourist sportsman had not yet made his way into that portion of the Sûdân. Here and there we saw on the banks contrivances of reeds which the natives had placed there for catching fish, and some of them reminded me of the fish-traps which the people of Mesopotamia set along the banks of the River Tigris.

Soon after leaving Korti, the heat became very trying, for there was a dampness in it which is a characteristic of the time of the year when the Nile begins to fall. A thermometer in the shade marked 123°, the double covering over the deck had to be removed because we began to feel the effect of the north wind, which drove the smoke and sparks from the chimney aft over the steamer, instead of forward as was the case when we were

AN ISLAND NEAR MERAWI.

steaming on the other side of the great bend of the river. This had the effect of increasing our general discomfort, and all the Europeans on the steamer were truly thankful when the engineer announced that Merawi, our destination, was in sight. Almost immediately afterwards we saw the ruddy mass of what seemed, when compared with the flat country about us, to be a huge mountain looming above the tops of the palms, and we knew from pictures of it which we had seen that it must be Gebel Barkal. In two hours more the steamer anchored, and as we saw tents stretching away up the river for a mile or two, we knew that we had arrived at the Headquarters of the Frontier Field Force. We were met by Colonel (now Sir) F. R. Wingate, H. E. Slatin Pâshâ, my old friend Major Drage, now Colonel W. H. Drage Pâshâ, and other officers, who gave us a hearty welcome.

At length the correspondents learned what had been happening since they left Ḥalfa and its neighbourhood. That Abû Ḥamed had been taken on August 7th they knew before they started, but they did not know that Berber had been evacuated by the Dervishes as a result of this, nor that it had been reoccupied promptly by "friendlies" on behalf of the Sirdar, and that General Hunter was at that moment on his way to support them. They learned too that the stop which we had been forced to make at Debba was due to the fact that the Sirdar was about to despatch a company of the Camel Corps to Berber by the desert route, and that he wished it to start before we arrived. The correspondents were eager for permission to ride across the desert, either to Berber or to Matamma, which the Sirdar was about to attack from the river, but it was refused, and they departed sadly enough to the place assigned them at the down-stream end of the camp. Owing to the great kindness of Colonel Wingate, I was allowed to mess with the officers of the Intelligence Department, and on the following day General (now Sir) Leslie Rundle had a tent pitched for me near the officers' *tukuls*, i.e., rectangular structures with the framework formed of branches of trees, and the roofs and sides of palm-leaf mats. Having arrived at a spot quite near to the site of the ancient town of Napata, where the Trustees of the British Museum ordered archæological investigations to be carried out, it only remained to get to work as soon as possible.

CHAPTER III.

THE ANTIQUITIES IN THE NEIGHBOURHOOD OF MERAWI.

THE portion of the Nile Valley in which Merawi is situated was occupied by the victorious troops of the Sirdar immediately after the capture of Dongola, on September 23rd, 1897. The Nile is easily navigable for steamers the whole way from Dongola to Kasingar, a village on the east bank at the foot of the Fourth Cataract, but the Sirdar decided that the Headquarters of the Frontier Field Force of the Egyptian Army should be established on the west bank of the river, opposite to the village of Merawi, about nine miles down stream of Kasingar. The camp lay, in fact, quite close to the village of Ṣanam Abû Dôm, which stands at one end of the comparatively long valley that runs parallel with a range of mountains extending from Al-Makhêrif (Berber) on the Nile, not far from the mouth of the Atbara River, to the Nile, nearly opposite Gebel Barkal. This valley is called "Wâdî Abû Dôm," i.e., the "valley of the *dôm* palms," because numbers of this tree are, or were, found in certain portions of it. The village of Ṣanam Abû Dôm has always been of some importance, for it formed the halting-place of the caravans which travelled from the Nile across the Desert of Gilîf to the Nile again. The first portion of its name, which means "image," or "idol," suggests that it stood near the site of some ancient buildings containing figures of gods, and it is probable that the whole name has reference to a temple built by some Nubian king at the north-west end of the Wâdi Abû Dôm a few centuries before Christ. That a temple with two or three courts and many columns actually stood on the site where the camp lay is proved by the fact that the bases of several sandstone columns, similar in shape and size to those which are to be seen to this day at Nûrî and Gebel Barkal, were found in 1897, when the soldiers were digging out trenches in which the foundations of block-houses were to be laid. The route from Merawi to Berber *viâ* the Desert of Gilîf cuts off the great bend which the Nile makes between these places, and is much frequented; it was actually traversed by the Camel Corps in 1897, when they marched to strengthen Berber after its evacuation by the Dervishes, and it is used as a trade road to this day. Lepsius was of opinion "that once, though perhaps not in historic "times, there must have been a connection by water which cut off "the largest portion of the great eastern bend of the Nile, now

VIEW OF THE TOWN OF MERAWI, SHOWING THE FORT AND MOSQUE IN 1842.
[From Russegger, *Reisen*, Plate 22.

"formed by the rocky elevated plateau at Abû Hammed, driving "back the stream above a degree and a half towards the south, "contrary to its common direction."[1] Whether this was so or not, geologists must decide.

At a distance of from eight to ten miles up stream, according to the road taken, on the same side, i.e., the west of the river, is the great pyramid field of Nûri, or Nurrî; the journey may easily be made on a camel in a little over two hours, but in a sailing boat rather longer time is required. The pyramids of Nûri stand on a

[1] "Letters from Egypt, Ethiopia, and Sinai," p. 218.

slightly raised plateau about a mile and a half from the river bank, and they present a very picturesque appearance, especially in the early morning or evening, when they cast shadows of considerable length. Speaking generally, they are all oriented to the south-east, and it is clear that their builders intended the light of the

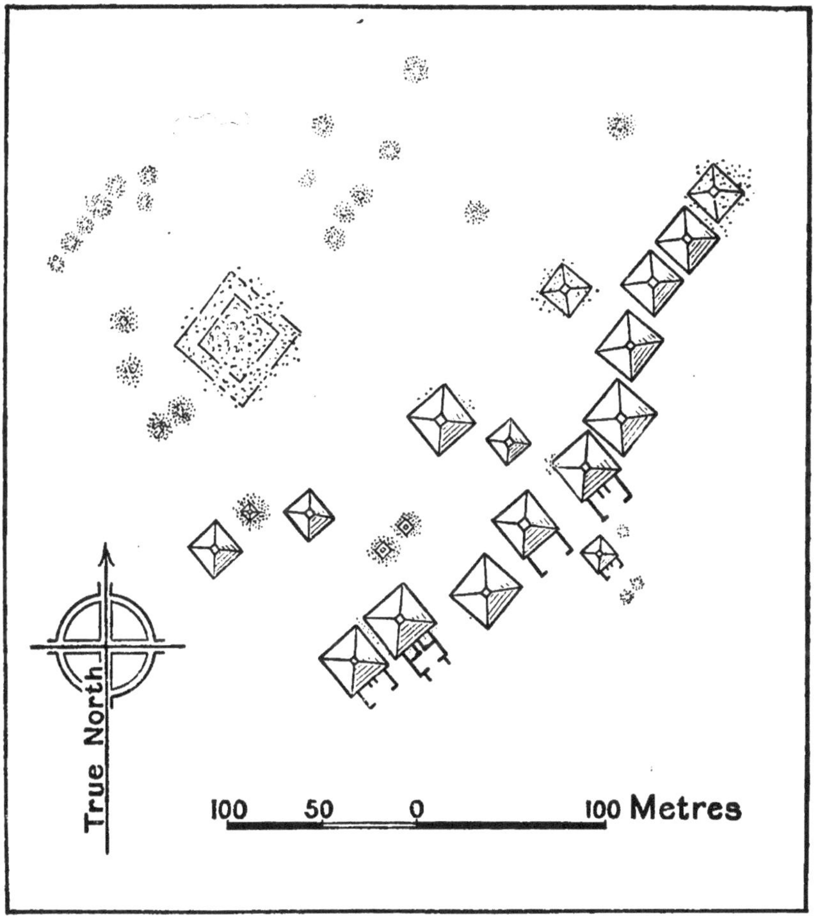

PLAN OF THE PYRAMIDS OF NÛRI, ACCORDING TO LEPSIUS, *Denkmäler*, I. 130.

same celestial body to penetrate all the chapels which stood before the pyramids on a certain day in the year. The orientation of every pyramid which I examined here is slightly different from each of the others, but their state of ruin is such that, without careful excavation, it is impossible to give any angle in terms mathematically correct. These pyramids vary greatly in size, some being only about eight feet square at the base, whilst one measures at least one hundred and sixteen feet at the base. They all appear to have been truncated, and the height of the largest is, so far as could be made out, about ninety feet; the fallen stones and drift-sand which lie at their bases make the taking of accurate measurements impossible. As to the number of the pyramids at Nûri authorities differ; Hoskins counted the remains of thirty-five, Lepsius twenty-five, and I saw remains of only seventeen or eighteen. This variation is probably to be explained by the fact that

PYRAMIDS AT NÛRI.

for the last eighty years the pyramids have served as quarries for the natives, who have used the stones of which they are formed to build the foundations of their water-wheels, graves, &c. Hundreds of graves lined and covered over with pyramid stones may be seen in every part of the Sûdân which is near a pyramid field, and their existence explains the disappearance of scores of pyramids. Nearly all the Sûdân pyramids are formed of masses of loose stones of a comparatively small size, with well-built stone casings; when once the casing is removed from a pyramid the wind alone will complete its ruin.

The largest of all the pyramids at Nûri is the most interesting; each side of its base measures about one hundred and sixteen feet in length, and the decay of one portion of it shows how it was built. We see from the general appearance of the remains that this pyramid once had three stages, in fact that it was a sort of step-pyramid. One side, the west, bulged, owing either to some subsidence, or to a piece of bad work, or perhaps to the decay of a layer of stones, and a smaller pyramid beneath it stands revealed. Thus it seems clear that the original pyramid structure was quite small, and that it was subsequently increased and heightened simultaneously on all sides. It will be remembered that Dr. Lepsius believed that the Step Pyramid of Mêdûm was built in this manner, and that he applied his theory to the Pyramids of Giza. His view was that each king began the building of his pyramid as soon as he ascended the throne; he only designed a small one so as to ensure himself a complete tomb, even were he destined to be but a few years upon the throne. But with the advancing years of his reign, he increased it by successive layers until he died, then the external covering was completed, and the monument of death finally remained proportionate to the duration of the life of the king.[1] The theory of Lepsius is somewhat similar to that enunciated by Hoskins[2] in 1835; he saw the pyramids of Nûri in 1833, about twelve years before Lepsius visited them, and speaking of the largest of the group he says, "It consisted of three stages. "Part of one having fallen discovers another pyramid underneath. "They seem to have added this second pyramid around the inner "one, in order to increase its size, or, perhaps, to make the body "underneath doubly difficult to get at. The Egyptian method of "building pyramids with stages was, I think, by first erecting a "pyramid with a very acute angle, and then building around it "the first stage from the summit, and so on, in like manner, as "many as were required." Thus the credit of being the first to publish an intelligent theory as to the manner in which the pyramids were built is due to Hoskins, and since the pyramids of Egypt were the models copied by Nubian builders the results obtained from the examination of the pyramids at Nûri may well be

1 "Letters," p. 65.

2 "Travels in Ethiopia," p. 165.

used in explaining the system followed by the architects of ancient Egyptian pyramids.

In one respect the pyramids of Nûri differ from the other pyramids in the Sûdân. Instead of being formed of heaps of loose, uncut stones and sand, with one or two outside casings of well-hewn stones, an examination of several of them shows that they

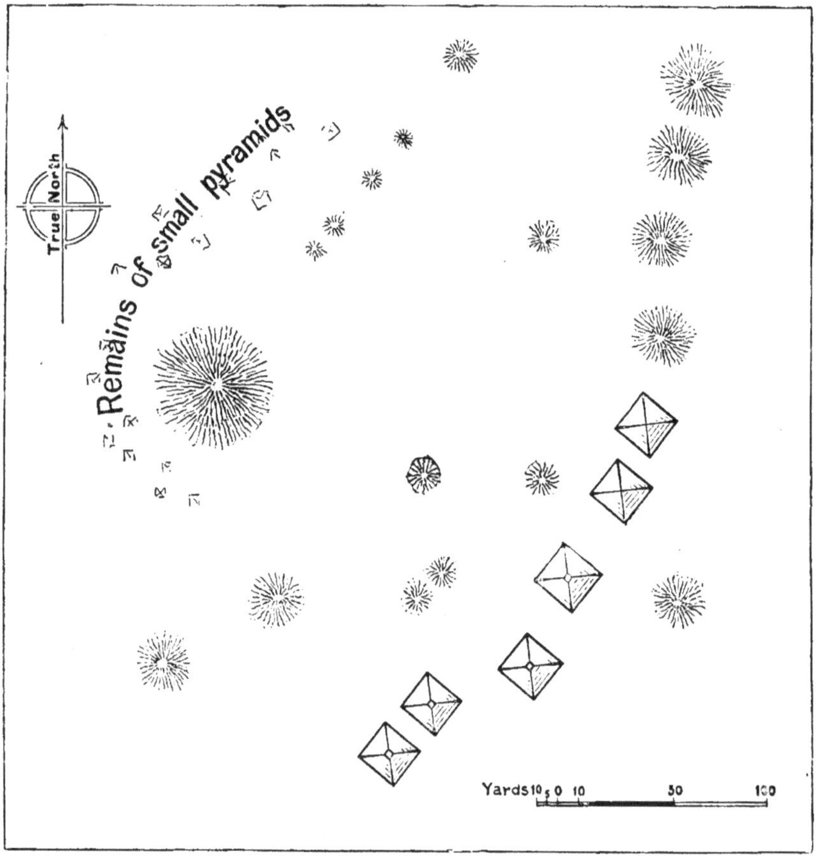

PLAN OF THE PYRAMIDS OF NÛRI.
By Colonel the Hon. M. G. Talbot, R.E.

are built of hewn stones throughout. This fact proves that their builders copied the great pyramids of Egypt, and as the stones in the layers are well hewn and well laid, there is every reason to suppose that had the Nubian quarries yielded stones as hard and close-grained as those of Egypt, the pyramids of Nûri would have remained to this day in a good state of preservation. It is uncertain if all the pyramids of Nûri had smooth, sloping sides like those of Egypt, but on one or two of them are found angle stones which seem to have been placed there to form a flat side. Another peculiarity of these pyramids is that but few appear to have been provided with chapels in which services in commemoration of the dead were recited and offerings made. The pyramids at Gebel Barkal, just across the river, had chapels, which, judging from the views published by Cailliaud and Hoskins, were of considerable size, and it is difficult to believe that the builders of such large monuments as the pyramids of Nûri would have omitted to provide suitable accommodation for the priests who ministered to the souls of dead kings and queens buried beneath them. Major M. G. Talbot, R.E., and I spent some time in examining the south-east sides of the best preserved of the pyramids, but only in one case did we find traces which might have been left by the bonding in of the stones ot the side walls of a chapel. Four times subsequently I spent whole afternoons in exploring this pyramid field, and the result was always the same.

At the present time it is impossible to assign a date to the pyramids of Nûri, for none of their stones have inscriptions upon them, and there is nothing exactly like them in Egypt with which to compare them. Systematic excavations might result in the discovery of inscriptions containing the names of the kings who built them, but unless such inscriptions are on objects buried with the dead beneath the pyramids, the hope of finding such is not very good. Every one with any knowledge of the subject who has seen them has believed them to be older than the pyramids of Gebel Barkal and of the Island of Meroë, and it seems impossible to come to any other conclusion. Their position, i.e., their being on the west bank of the Nile, according to true ancient Egyptian custom, their size, their solidity of construction, and the general air of good workmanship about them, all tend to suggest that they are the oldest pyramids in the Sûdân, and that they were built before the rise of the kingdom of Piānkhi in the eighth century before Christ.

Under the Vth and VIth Dynasties the Egyptians at Memphis knew a great deal about the Sûdânî folk, and it is a very significant fact, in respect of the intercourse which went on between the people of Ta-kenset (Nubia) and the Egyptians, that the name of the great god of Ta-kenset, i.e., TETUN, appears in the funeral texts compiled for Pepi I.[1] This king claimed, and certainly possessed, a certain amount of authority over Nubia, and he expected its chief god to render him service in the other world. It is assuming nothing to say that the fame of the pyramids of Egypt would penetrate far into Nubia under the Vth and VIth Dynasties, and that the Nubians would have a general idea of their size and height. After the complete conquest of Ta-kenset by Usertsen III., of the XIIth Dynasty, still more would be known of Egyptian funeral customs by the native officials from the Egyptian officers who were sent there to rule the country in the interest of Egypt. It is not here suggested that all the pyramids of Nûri date from the VIth, or even from the XIIth Dynasty, but the Egyptians built few pyramids under the XIIth Dynasty, and very many under the Vth and VIth Dynasties, and it is the pyramids of the earlier period which are copied at Nûri. The size of the largest pyramids at Nûri suggests that their builders were independent kings, who had the command of labour in abundance. We know that Egypt possessed little power in Nubia after the downfall of the XXth Dynasty, and that the palmy days of her sovereignty over that country were under the XIIth, XVIIIth, and XIXth Dynasties. While Egypt's rule was most effective in Nubia, it seems to me unlikely that any native ruler would have been able to build even the smallest of the larger of the pyramids of Nûri. If this were so we have the choice of three periods in which to think they were built, i.e., between the VIth and XIIth, the XIIth and XVIIIth, and the XXth and XXIVth Dynasties. The difficulty cannot, of course, be settled until the pyramids have been opened, and inscriptions found inside them, but at present there is no evidence which proves that they are not contemporaneous with the oldest introduction, on a large scale, of Egyptian influence into Nubia.

Quite close to the pyramids of Nûri are the remains of a temple of considerable size, but much sand would have to be cleared

[1] The words are, "Behold Ṭeṭun the Great, at the head of Ta-kenset 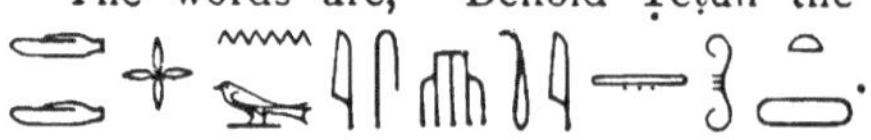. Pepi I., line 200.

away before its complete plan could be made out. It seems tolerably certain that it was built for funerary purposes by some king or queen of Nubia, who either established or restored services for the dead at Nûri, for the bases of its columns are of the same size and style as those in the temple of Tirhâkâh across the river, and probably belong to the period of his reign. Cailliaud imagined that Nûri represented the necropolis of Gebel Barkal, but this is unlikely, and it is far more probable that the remains of the city, over which ruled the kings who built the pyramids of Nûri, lie under the Sirdar's camp at Sanam Abû Dôm. Near the pyramids Hoskins traced the remains of the banks of a canal which ran some distance inland from the Nile; these, as he rightly says, indicate that the cultivated land extended much further into the interior, and it is probable that the bodies of the dead were brought by water from the city to Nûri for burial.

Down stream, at a distance of about seven miles from Ṣanam Abû Dôm, and on the same side of the river, lies the pyramid field of Tanḳâsî. At this place the cultivable land runs back from the river for nearly a mile, and just beyond the edge of this, on the skirt of the desert, the remains of a number of pyramids are to be seen. The pyramids are represented by mounds of sand, earth, and small stones, and in every instance the stone casing has disappeared. With one exception, all the pyramids here were small, and were, no doubt, poorly built, and it seems as if they marked the tombs of the ordinary native folk who belonged to the city which must have stood near Ṣanam Abû Dôm. I could neither hear of nor find the remains of any pyramids or temples on the west bank down stream of Tanḳâsî, or up stream of Nûri, and it seems that these places form the limits of the great Nubian settlement which was made in pre-Christian times at the western end of the Wâdî Abû Dôm.

Two hours' ride from the site of the Sirdar's camp in 1897 are some low stone hills in which are still to be seen a number of chambers, short passages, and irregularly shaped excavations; some of these may be gold miners' workings, but a few are certainly the remains of tombs. One chamber was noteworthy, for its walls had been covered with a thin layer of plaster, and it resembled the principal room of an Egyptian tomb; it is possible

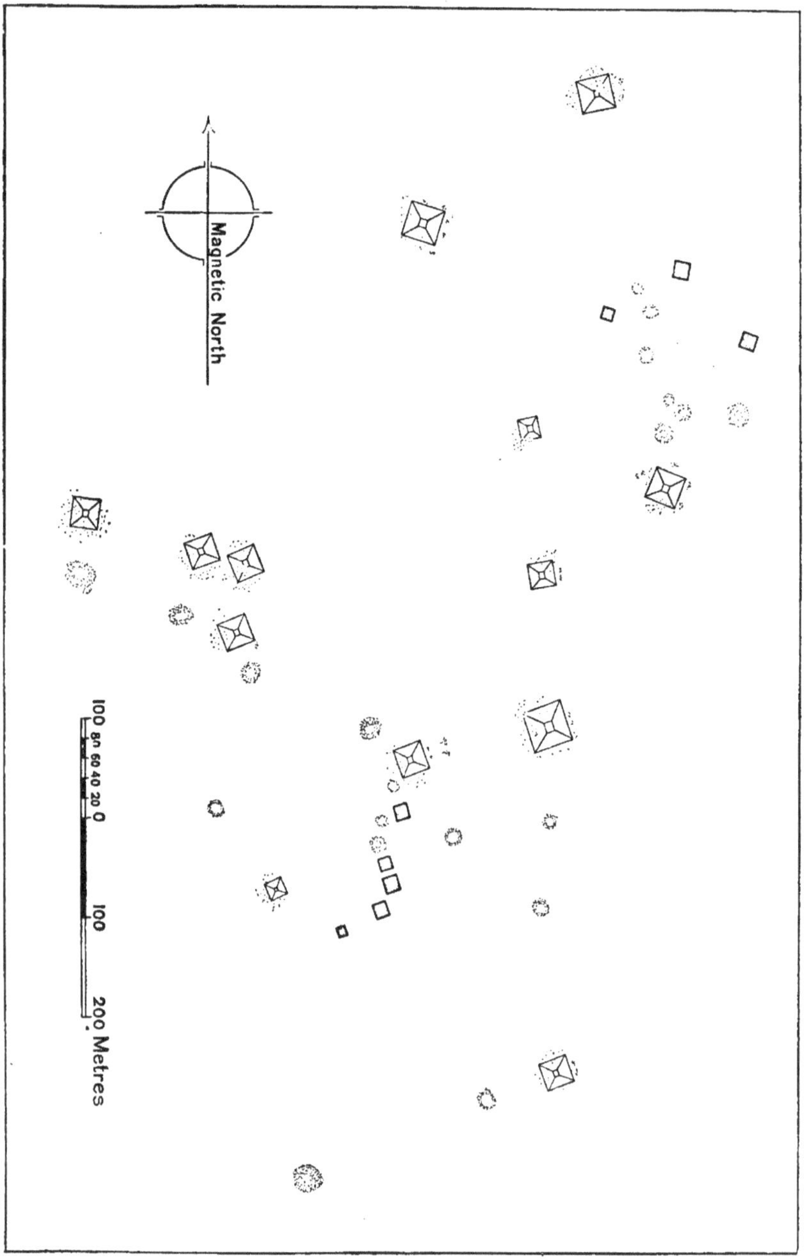

PLAN OF THE PYRAMIDS OF TANKÂSÎ.

[From Lepsius, *Denkmäler*, Abth I. Bl. 124.

that an inscription may have been painted on this plaster, but there were no traces of it remaining. A few of the excavations which I assumed to have been made for tombs contained two rooms, one large and one small, either opening directly one into the other, or joined by a very short passage. If these were tombs the dead must have been buried in a hole in the rock, beyond the second chamber. In another excavation, close to the end wall, were the remains of what appeared to be the base of a statue; not a trace, however, of any inscription was to be seen. On the whole, it is tolerably certain that some of these excavations were actually tombs, which were made for the Egyptian officials who were stationed in the neighbourhood between the XIth and the XXth Dynasties. It is impossible to think that such an energetic king as Seti I., B.C. 1370, would have allowed the fertile and wealthy provinces of Dongola and Merawi to have remained independent.

The only other ruins in the neighbourhood were those of a Christian monastery and church, which have already been described by Lepsius;[1] these lie off the track some distance, and are near Gebel al-Ghazâl, or "Gazelle Mountain," so called because of the number of gazelles which passed there on their way to drink at the river. Herr Erbkam made a plan of the church, which Lepsius published, and if it was correct the ruins must have been in a much better state of preservation than they are at the present time. As this church will be referred to elsewhere in this book, we may pass on at once to the consideration of the antiquities on the eastern bank.

Almost opposite the pyramid field of Tanḳâsî, on the east bank, is the pyramid field of Kurru. It was visited by Lepsius, who saw there the remains of twenty-one small pyramids and two large ones; the largest of the latter was thirty-five feet high, and was called by the "strange name of Qantur," probably a corruption of some ancient Nubian name. It was quite easy to trace in 1897 the sites of a very considerable number of pyramids, but scarcely a stone could be seen. On the river side of this necropolis once stood the largest pyramid of the group, which must have been well built and was probably of stone throughout.

[1] "Letters," p. 219.

Nothing of the pyramid now remains, but the space of ground which it occupied is well-defined, and its foundations went down to the bed-rock; the rock was, in fact, scarped to receive them. It is interesting to note that here, as at Nûri and Tanḳâsî, there stood one pyramid larger than any other on the field, and it seems as if, in each case, the builder of the largest pyramid was the first to occupy the site, and that the other smaller pyramids mark the graves of his kinsfolk and chief officials. The clearance which has been made of the great pyramid at Kurru is most

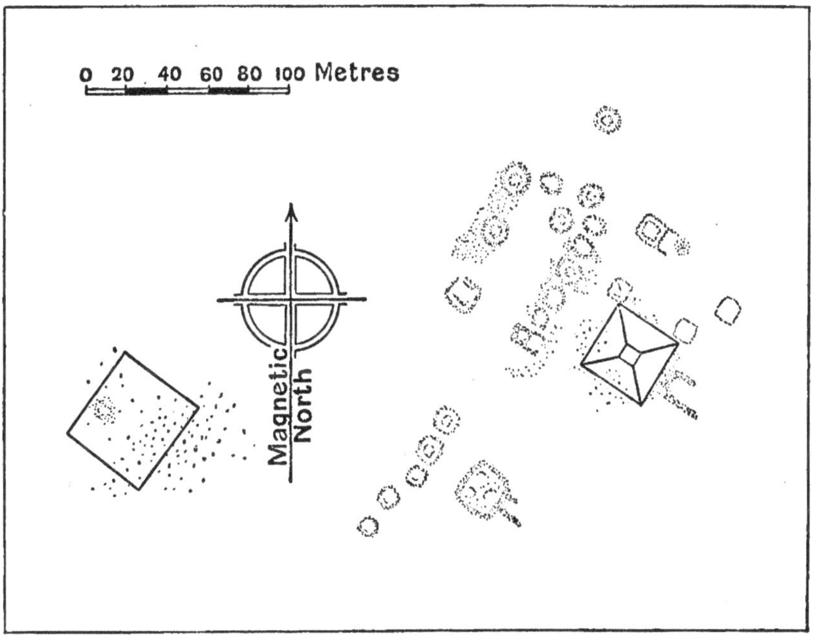

FLAN OF THE PYRAMIDS OF KURRU.

[From Lepsius, *Denkmäler*, Abth I. Bl. 122.

complete, and suggests that it was effected not by mere filchers of stones for building purposes, but as the result of a determination, either political or religious, to make the whole pyramid disappear. It is important to note that the rock on which its foundations rested is scarped, for it proves that the earliest pyramid builders in the Sûdân copied the works of Egyptian pyramid architects and masons in every particular.

A few miles to the south-west of the pyramid field of Kurru are the remains of nearly two-score pyramids, which must have

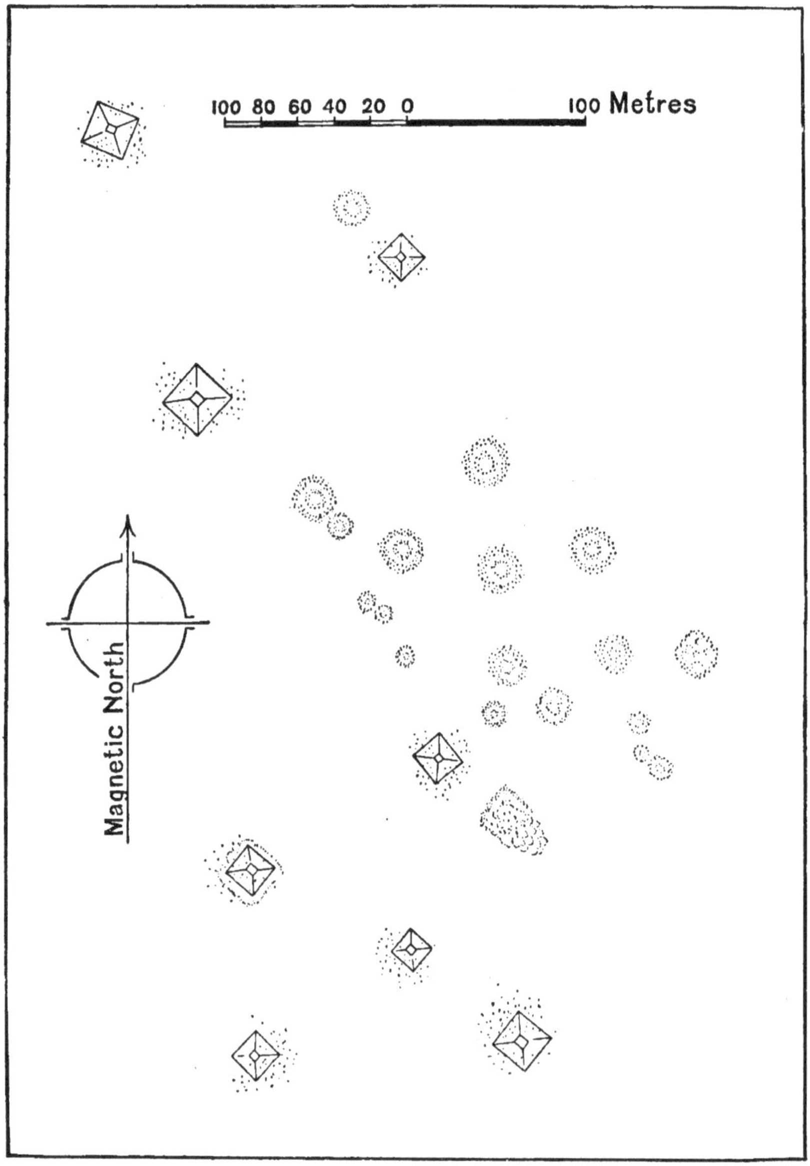

PLAN OF THE PYRAMIDS OF ZÛMA.

[From Lepsius, *Denkmäler*, Abth I. Bl. 122.

formed the necropolis of another royal Nubian family. They are called the "Pyramids of Zûma," and stand near the village of that name, between the mountains and the river. Behind them, near the mountains, is the ruin of an old fort, called "Ḳal'at An-Nagîl," i.e., the "Castle of Nagîl": the natives said that it was built by an ancient king of the country, but in reality nothing is known of its builder. Lepsius states [1] that the front walls were "only destroyed and thrown down about fifty or sixty years ago," i.e., about 1780, when the inhabitants of Zûma settled there, and he records a tradition to the effect that when the fort was built the surrounding land, now dry, was still within reach of the Nile, and it is said to have been fertile. During the last hundred years a large quantity of land on both sides of the river has gone out of cultivation, chiefly through the supineness of the natives. They build water-wheels, and dig shallow canals to carry the water to their fields, but they take no trouble to remove the sand which drifts over their ground, and chokes the canals, and buries the plots wherein the *dhurra* is grown, and in a few years the land becomes unworkable. No man takes the trouble to grow more grain than he wants, and no man will take any trouble about his property unless he considers it absolutely necessary. In ancient times this district must have supported a large population, and whole tracts of country which are now covered with sand must at one time have been cultivated, and one of the chief causes of the decay in the cities which once stood near the foot of the Fourth Cataract was, undoubtedly, the failure of the land to supply sufficient grain for their inhabitants. The freaks of the Nile and the drift-sand of the desert were probably responsible in the first instance for this failure, and the laziness and apathy of the people completed what the river began.

Between Kurru and Merawi there are no remains of ancient Nubian buildings or pyramids, but not far from the latter village, close to the mountains, small, rectangular slabs of stone, inscribed in Coptic with funeral texts, have been found, and these seem to indicate that a Christian community was settled there perhaps before the Muḥammadan conquest of Egypt. From Shibba, a village just beyond Merawi, the striking mass of sandstone known

[1] "Letters," p. 230.

as Gebel Barkal, i.e., Mount Barkal, is seen to great advantage. In ancient Egyptian inscriptions it is called "Ṭu-āb," i.e., "Pure, or Holy, Mountain." It stands about one mile from the river, and rises abruptly from the plain. Hoskins believed it to be three hundred and fifty feet high,[1] and Cailliaud thought it had "sixty-four metres of elevation,"[2] but its height was carefully measured in 1897 by Major M. G. Talbot, R.E., who pronounced it to be just three hundred and two feet. The end near the river has been used as a quarry, and from it came all the stone

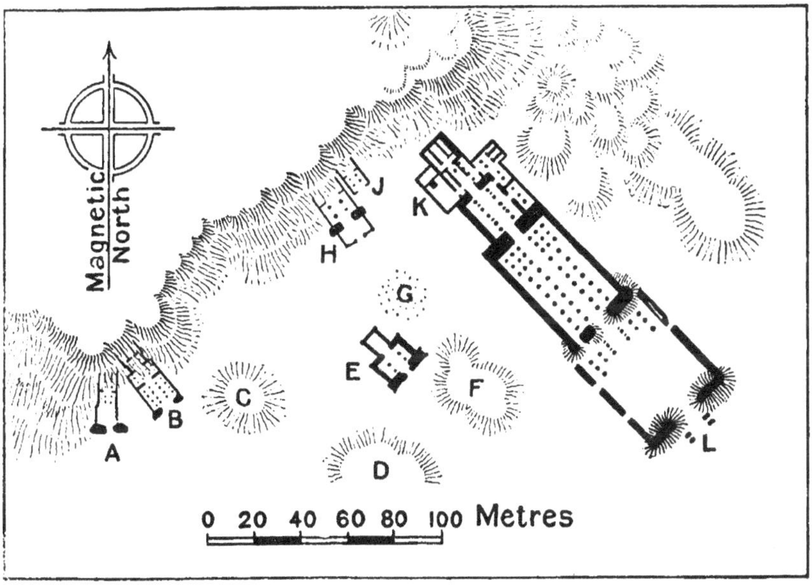

THE TEMPLES AT GEBEL BARKAL.

[Drawn from Lepsius, *Denkmäler*, Abth. I. Bl. 125.

used in building the temples and pyramids close by. The whole form of the mountain is very picturesque, and highly imposing, especially when seen from a distance. At the south-west corner a large perpendicular mass of sandstone has become separated by a deep fissure from the body of the mountain, and when looked at from a distance of a mile or two up stream it has all the appearance of a colossal statue. The Arabs declare that it is a statue of one of the kings who reigned in the "time of

[1] "Travels," p. 134.

[2] "Voyage à Méroé," tom. iii., p. 200.

ignorance," i.e., before the time of Muḥammad the Prophet, and in its profile some Englishmen have seen representations of the features of certain prominent British statesmen. As Cailliaud says, however, the form of this rock is due to a freak of nature, and is purely accidental.[1] A town of some size stood on the east

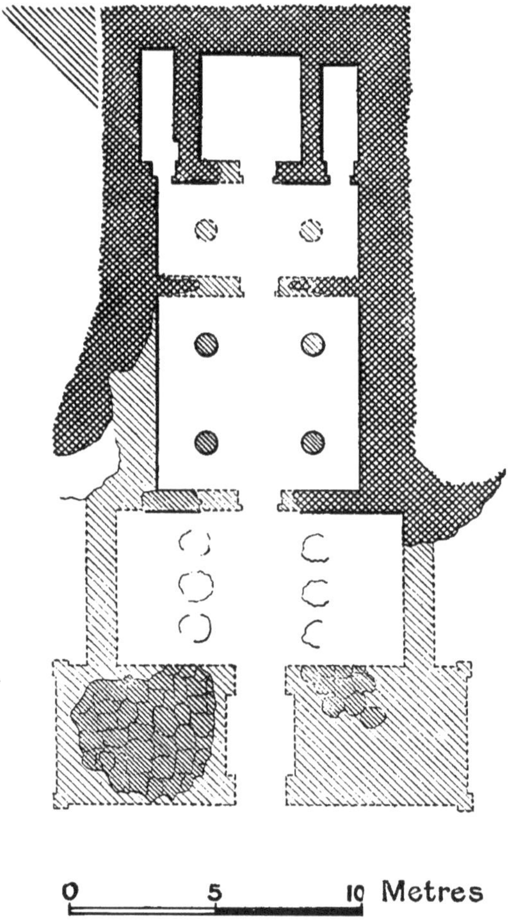

PLAN OF TEMPLE (A) AT GEBEL BARKAL.

[From Lepsius, *Denkmäler*, Abth. I. Bl. 127.

side of the mountain, but the shape and material of the fragments of bricks found there, and the fragments of pottery, do not suggest that it was pre-Christian. On the west side are two groups of pyramids, one group being on the slope, and the

[1] A view of it will be found in Cailliaud's volume of plates (i. 58).

other on the crest of the rocky ridge which rises at right angles to the mountain. On the south side are the ruins of several temples, and close in by the mountain itself are the ruins of two others, which appear to have been destroyed by the fall of huge masses of stone from the mountain. Beginning at the south-west angle of Gebel Barkal, we may now briefly describe the principal ruins there :—

I. The first ruins seen are those of a small temple (A) which was cut into the mountain to a depth of about 50 feet ; here and there

RUINS OF THE TEMPLE OF TIRHÂKÂH AT GEBEL BARKAL (THE TYPHONIUM).
[From Hoskins, *Travels*, Plate 20.

traces of sculptures are visible on the walls of the chambers which were formerly in the mountain, but it is impossible to tell from them to what period the building belonged. According to Cailliaud, this temple consisted of a small hall containing four columns, a smaller chamber with two columns, and a sanctuary. It seemed to me, as the result of turning over large numbers of the stones which now lie in front of it, that this building was approached through a hall of six columns, of the bases of which many fragments still remain. Of the pylon or gateway a few remains exist.

II. A few yards from the ruins of the little rock-hewn temple described above are the remains of the large temple (B) built by the Nubian king called Tabarqa, better known under the Biblical form of his name, "Tirhâḳâh," who was reigning B.C. 693. This temple was called the "Typhonium," because Cailliaud and Hoskins wrongly identified the figures of the god Bes which are sculptured on some of its pillars as those of Typhon, a god of

TWO PILLARS, WITH HATHOR CAPITALS, FROM THE TEMPLE OF TIRHÂKÂH AT GEBEL BARKAL (THE TYPHONIUM).
They were standing in 1897.

evil; Bes and Typhon were, however, gods with totally distinct attributes, and there is no evidence to show that Tirhâkâh ever wished to pay honour to one of the Egyptian gods of evil. The door of the temple of Tirhâḳâh faces 143° from the true north,[1]

[1] I owe this fact to Colonel M. G. Talbot, R.E. Cailliaud says, "Son axe fait avec le nord magnétique un angle de 23 degrés vers l'est."

and the total length of the building is about 115 feet. The measurements here given are substantially those of Hoskins, who differs frequently from Cailliaud, and it must be understood that they are only approximately correct. Accurate measurements could only be obtained by clearing the whole site. The breadth of the temple was about 50 feet, and Hoskins supposed the pylon to be about 11 feet deep, and 62½ feet wide. In front of the pylon there appears to have been some building, perhaps a portico, the roof of which was supported by four pillars. Beyond the pylon is a court containing sixteen columns, arranged in double rows, a double row being on each side of the pathway; beyond this court is a second, with eight columns, also arranged in double rows. According to Hoskins, these two courts formed "a portico, 59 feet long, and 50 feet 2 inches wide;" Cailliaud and Lepsius, however, found traces of the wall which divided the two courts, and they are still visible. The columns which stood immediately on each side of the path were rectangular, and were ornamented with full-length reliefs of the god Bes, wearing lofty plumes; these columns were about 17 feet high, the height of the figure of Bes on each was 12 feet 4 inches, and the diameter of the column was 4 feet 3 inches.

The rows of columns which stood between the Bes columns were somewhat higher (17 feet 6 inches), but their diameters were only 3 feet 6 inches, and they stood on round instead of square bases. Each column had a Hathor-headed capital, and it is interesting to note that the faces of the goddess looked towards the walls of the temple, which, according to Hoskins, were only about 5 feet 6 inches high. Had the Hathor faces been placed on the north and south sides of the capitals, it is clear they would have been hidden by the Bes columns which stood in front of them.

After passing through the second court, the path leads into a small chamber hewn in the living rock; on each side of the path stood a rectangular column ornamented with a figure of Bes, and inscribed with the names and titles of Tirhâḳâh. On the portions of the cornice which still remain runs an inscription which records the king's devotion to the ram-headed god Amen and his consort Mut, the lady of Ta kenset, or Nubia, and several of Tirhâḳâh's titles. On the walls are the remains of a

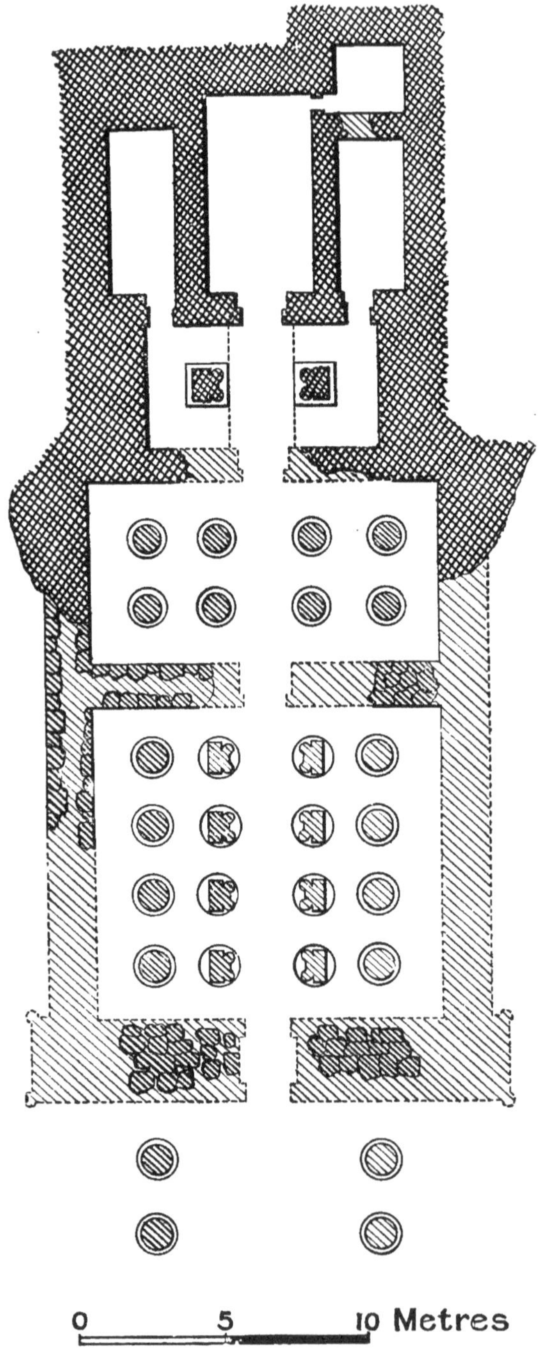

PLAN OF THE TEMPLE OF TIRHÂKÂH AT GEBEL BARKAL (B).

[From Lepsius, *Denkmäler*, Abth. I. Bl. 127.

series of reliefs in which the king is seen adoring and making offerings to the gods of the "Holy Mountain," i.e., Gebel Barkal, and in one of them we see Tirhâkâh's queen, who was called Ȧmenṭākhet , making an offering of a sistrum, that is to say, rattling this instrument in honour of the goddess Mut. The hieroglyphic texts leave no doubt as to the builder of the greater portion of this temple, but in one or two passages the words[1] "making great the temple, renewing with stone," &c., appear to indicate that after all Tirhâkâh was only the restorer and enlarger of the temple. It is evident from the remains of colours which still adhere to the walls in places that this portion of the temple at least was painted, and though to modern taste the ornamentation would appear crude, there can be no doubt that it would appear pleasing to native artists. In looking at the colours in the temples and tombs of Egypt, the spectator forgets, in his admiration of the faded greens and reds and blues, that when those same colours were first laid on, from two to four thousand years ago, the effect must have been very startling.

The path now leads into the sanctuary, which is about 23 feet in length and 13 feet in breadth; the walls are ornamented with a series of reliefs in which Tirhâḳâh is seen making offerings to a number of Theban gods and goddesses, and to certain deities who belong to the company of Thoth of Hermopolis. This sanctuary probably contained a figure of Ȧmen, or Ȧmen-Rā, the god to whom, in conjunction with Mut, the temple was dedicated On the left is a chamber of similar length, but of less width by 5 feet than the sanctuary; on the walls the king is seen making offerings to the gods. On the right of the sanctuary are two chambers, one behind the other; the first is 17 feet long and 7 feet 7 inches wide, and the second 5 feet long and 7 feet wide. In the larger chamber the reliefs represent the king making offerings to the gods of the dead, but the smaller chamber is without ornamentation, and seems not to have been finished. The scenes and texts on the walls of the chambers tell us nothing of the history of Tirhâḳâh's reign, but from first to last the whole bûilding proclaims that it

1 

is a copy of a funerary temple in Egypt; in fact, it was probably built in connection with the king's pyramid, and commemorative services for the dead were no doubt performed in it. The reliefs and decorations of the walls were copied from temple-chambers in Egypt, but it is curious that Tirhâḳâh did not imitate the great kings of Egypt, and cause the records of his conquest of Egypt to be inscribed on the outer walls of his temple. Another striking peculiarity about the temple is the pillars with Bes reliefs upon them; we find these at Nagaa and other places in the Sûdân, and we are almost driven to believe that Bes must have been a native Sûdân god. The name Bes is thought to be Egyptian, and it was probably bestowed upon the god because he wore the skin of the *bes* animal,[1] which has been identified with the *Felis Cynailurus*. The fact that the figures of the god are represented with a head-dress of feathers indicates a savage or semi-savage origin for him, and his characteristics are rather those of an African than Asiatic deity. The figure of Bes suggests that his home was a place where the dwarf and pygmy were held in esteem, and the association of the name of the God with Punt and the "Land of the Spirits" points to the existence of an ancient belief that his cult was the product of the peoples of the eastern part of Central Africa.

III. The plain on the east side of the temple of Tirhâkâh is covered with fragments of stones which must have formed portions of buildings, and at a distance of about 100 yards from it we reach a low pile of ruins which marks the site of a small and unimportant temple (E). It consisted of a small hall, with four pillars, and a sanctuary; the length of the building was about 85 feet, and the breadth about 65 feet. The uninscribed block of polished green stone which was intended to serve as an altar was *in situ* a few years ago. The builder of this little temple is unknown.

IV. Immediately to the east of the temple mentioned in the preceding paragraph is another heap of ruins, which marks the site of another temple. We turned over large numbers of the stones, and dug a few trenches here, but we were just as

1 .

unsuccessful in finding any traces of the plan of the building as Cailliaud, Hoskins, and Lepsius were. The last-named archæologist was, during the course of the investigations which he carried out on this site, fortunate enough to discover two stone altars bearing the cartouches of two kings who probably reigned between B.C. 525 and 260. The cartouches are those of Sekheper-en-Rā, who as the son of the sun was called Senka-

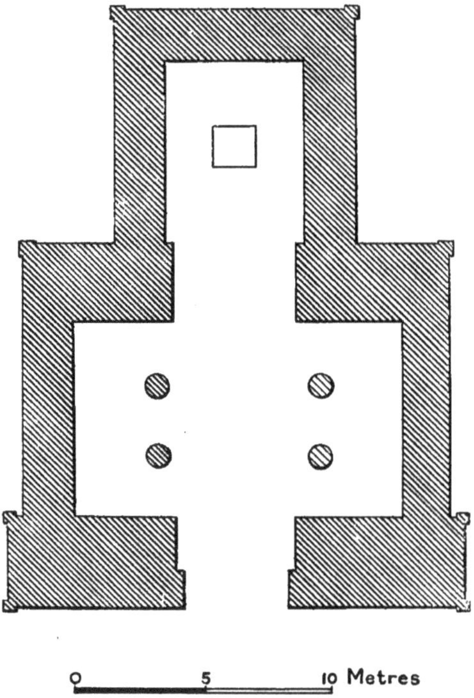

PLAN OF TEMPLE (E) AT GEBEL BARKAL.

[From Lepsius, *Denkmäler*, Abth. I. Bl. 127.]

Åmen-seken,[1] and of Khu-ka-Rā, who as the son of the sun was called Atlenersa;[2] nothing is known of these kings, and the order in which they reigned is uncertain.

V. Close to the end of the mountain, about forty yards to the north of the ruin described in the last paragraph, is a mass

1 

2 

of stones which originally formed part of the pylon of a small temple (H). Before the pylon was a small court enclosed by low, thin walls, but there were no pillars in it, and it was probably without a roof. The inner court of the temple contained four

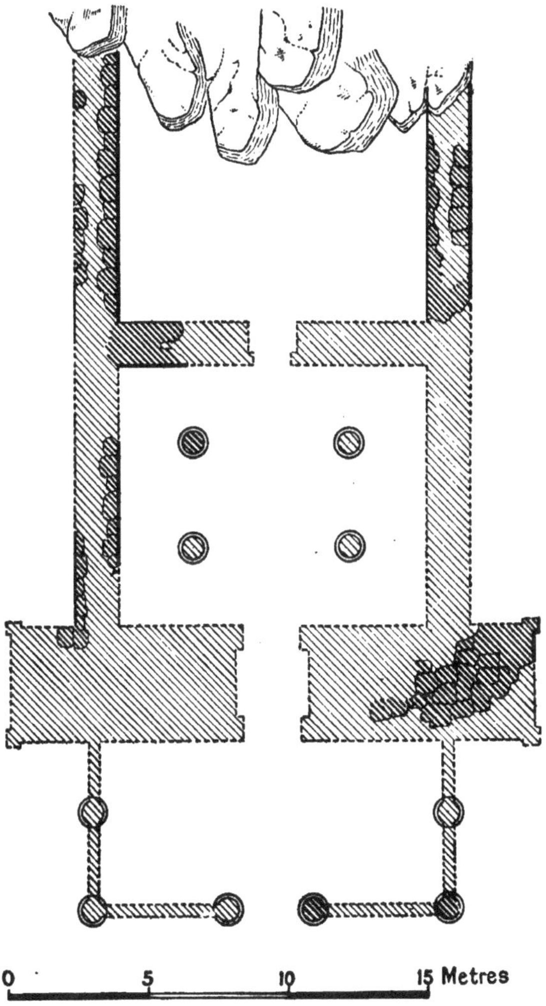

PLAN OF THE TEMPLE OF SENKA-ÀMEN-SEKEN (H).

[From Lepsius, *Denkmaler*, Abth I. Bl. 127.

columns, and beyond it, terminating in the rock itself, was the sanctuary. The walls of the court were ornamented with reliefs, which are now ruined. On the south side of the remains of the pylon are traces of sculptured scenes, in which the king is

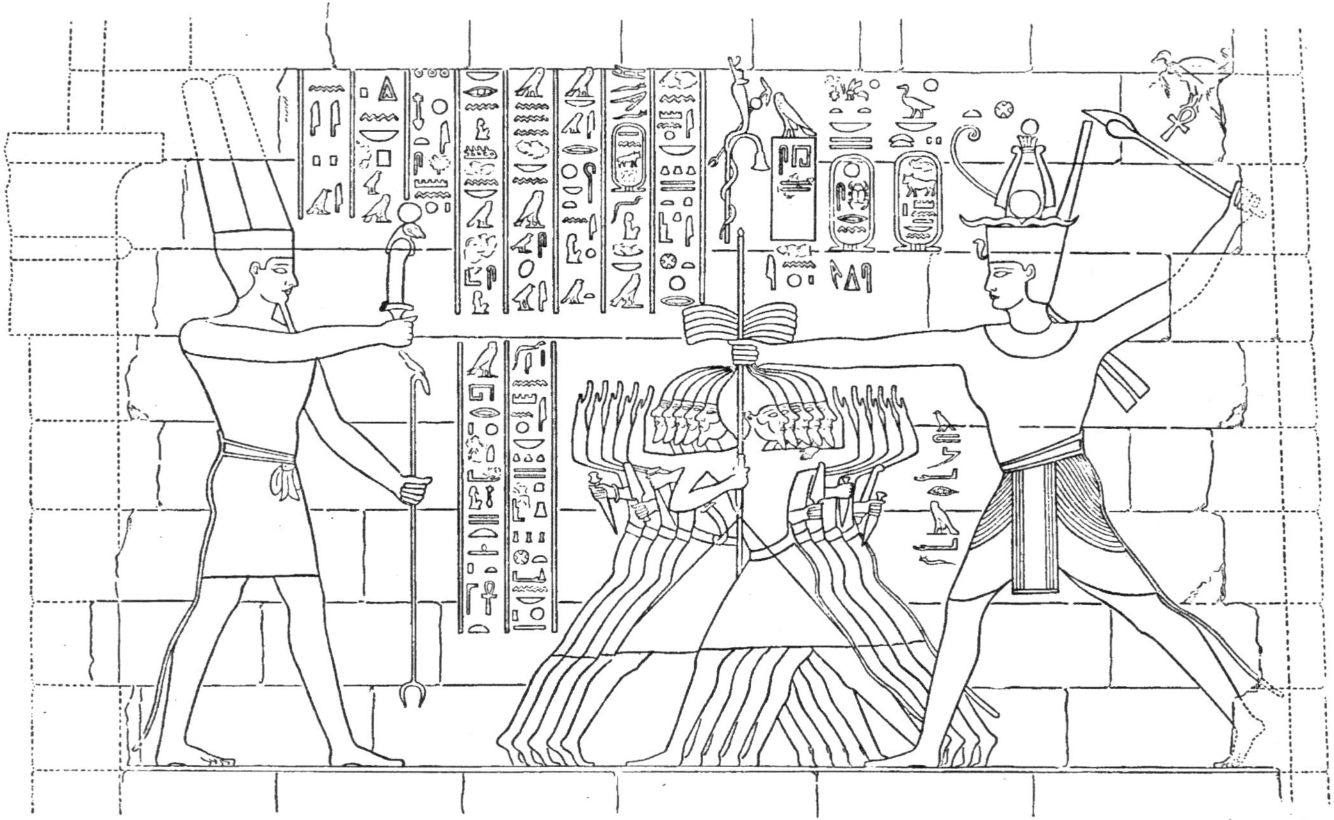

THE NUBIAN KING SENKA-ȦMEN-SEKEN SLAUGHTERING REPRESENTATIVES OF TEN REBEL NATIONS IN THE PRESENCE OF ȦMEN-RĀ, THE LORD OF THE THRONES OF THE WORLD.

[From Cailliaud, *Voyage*, Plate LXI.

represented slaughtering members of the prominent tribes of the country which he had conquered, in the presence of the god Åmen of the Holy Mountain. This scene was, of course, copied from Egyptian temples, and probably is rather the outcome of the desire of the king's courtiers to please him than an illustration of an historical fact. On the north side of the pylon were also elaborate sculptures and many columns of hieroglyphics, which clearly refer to the offerings made by the king to the god. As the text here mentions only the name of Senka-Åmen-seken, and as figures of this king occupied the most prominent place on the walls, we are justified in assuming that he was the builder of this temple. Its small size seems to indicate that he was not a great or wealthy king, and the characteristics of the reliefs, judging by what still remain, suggest that he reigned towards the end ot the period of which the probable limits have been given above. Why an altar bearing his cartouches should be found among the ruins of the temple of another king cannot be said, it may have been carried there from the place in which it originally stood, or it may have been made by a later king, and set up in his own temple to commemorate his predecessor's reign. An examination of the ruins at Gebel Barkal shows that no attempt was ever made to repair the temples, and that most of them perished prematurely owing to poor work and the exceeding softness of the sandstone employed in their construction. Two or three appear to have been pulled down wilfully, probably because their stones were required for new buildings. In the case of the temple now under consideration, it is clear that the sanctuary was wrecked through a fall of stones from the end of the mountain, and it is difficult to understand how any architect could have been bold enough to build a temple so close to its foot. The shrine of the temple was undoubtedly hollowed out of the rock, and pieces of stone above it would be loosened in the process; as time went on cracks would develop, and at length the day came when a rush of stones ruined one end of the temple.

VI. Close to the remains of the temple of Senka-Åmen-seken are those of another small temple (J), which consists of a small court with four pillars, and a sanctuary; it also was built close in under the mountain, and was destoyed by a fall of stones. There is nothing here to show by whom this temple was built, and no reliefs, from which the date of its construction might be guessed at, have been found among the ruins.

VII. The largest and finest of all the temples at Gebel Barkal is that of which the remains lie at the foot of the north-west corner of the mountain, covering a considerable space, and presenting the appearance of a shapeless mass of stones over 500 feet long. Looked at from any point of view it is almost impossible to believe that the countless fragments of pillars, cornices, walls, pylons, &c., which are scattered here in hopeless confusion could ever have formed a temple, which for size and grandeur was only second to that of Ṣûlb (Soleh). This temple was built by the Nubian king Pānkhi 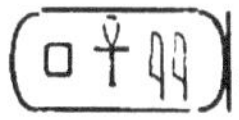, or Piānkhi, who reigned about B.C. 750, and is famous as the conqueror of Egypt. He carried his victorious arms so far north as Memphis, which he captured. There is little doubt that he built his temple at Gebel Barkal according to an Egyptian plan and design, and the work appears to have been executed by Egyptian workmen, who must have been imported into Nubia for the purpose. The entrance door of Piānkhi's temple faces 127° from the true north, the difference in the orientation of the temple of Piānkhi and that of Tirhâḳâh thus being sixteen degrees. Piānkhi's temple was about 500 feet long, and the width of its largest court was about 135 feet. This court was entered through a pylon, the exact size of which cannot be accurately given. The towers have not only been pulled down, but the stones of which they were built have been removed. On each side of the gateway were two figures of rams or lions (*a-d*).

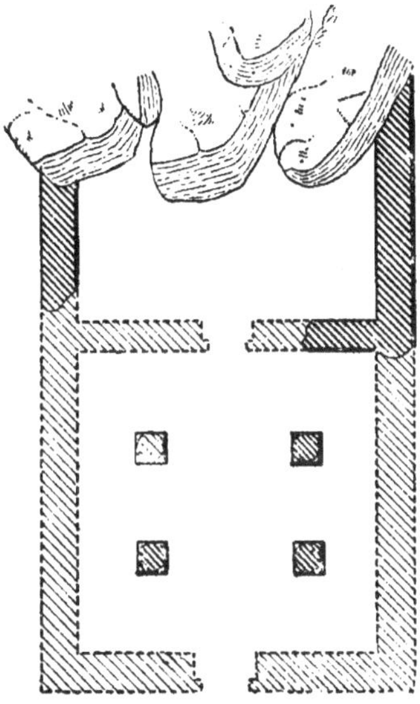

PLAN OF TEMPLE (J) AT GEBEL BARKAL.
From Lepsius, *Denkmäler*, Abth. I. Bl. 127.

Round the four sides of the first court (A) ran a colonnade, which, on the north side, was supported by a double row of columns; this court was 150 feet long, approximately. The pillars were nearly six feet in diameter, and they rested on bases about one and a half feet larger.

The second court (B) was 125 feet long and 102 feet wide, and was also entered by a pylon, about twenty-eight feet deep. At the east

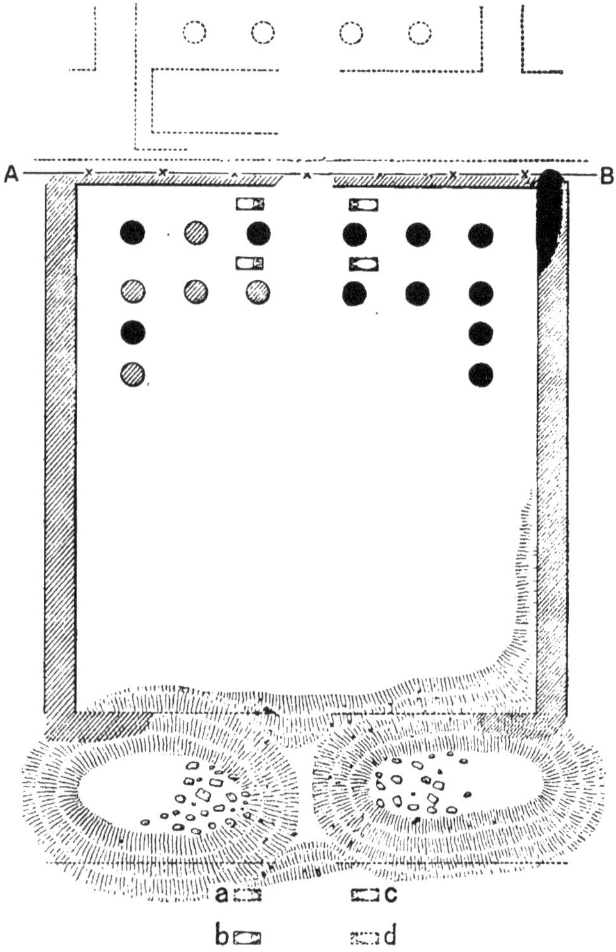

PLAN OF THE TEMPLE OF PIÂNKHI AT GEBEL BARKAL—THE GREAT PYLON AND MAIN HALL.

[From Lepsius, *Denkmäler*, Abth. I. Bl. 128.

side were three rows, each containing six pillars, three on each side of the door, and a double row of columns stood on each side of the pathway which was about seventeen feet wide, from pylon to pylon. On each side of the entrance to the pylon in this court were two seated figures of rams or lions (*a*, *b*). The walls of this court were ornamented with sculptured reliefs illustrating scenes in Piānkhi's battles, arranged, no doubt, according to the plan followed in the great Egyptian temples. On one side of the pylon wall are the remains of a scene familiar to all from the pylons of Egypt, i.e., the king doing battle with his foes.

The third court (C) was much smaller, only measuring fifty-one feet in length and fifty-six feet in width, and contained ten columns, five on each side of the pathway ; it was provided with a pylon. In the wall on the right-hand side of this court were two doorways, each of which led into a small chapel (D, E). Passing into the pronaos (F), we see that this chamber was practically divided into three parts by two walls which ran nearly the whole length of it. A doorway in the wall led into a long narrow chamber, with four columns (G), and beyond this was a small chapel (H) containing two columns and a shrine. Retracing our steps, and passing the inner and outer walls on the left, we enter another chapel (I), which contained four pillars. At the end of it stood a fine granite altar inscribed with the names and titles of Tirhâḳâh, the builder of the temple at the other angle of the mountain which has already been described. This indicates that Tirhâḳâh added a chapel to Piānkhi's temple, and it is very probable that he built it with stones taken from other parts of the edifice. Behind this chapel is a long room (J), which was entered by a door on the left.

The plan of the sanctuary (K) can be easily traced. The figure of the god Ȧmen was placed at the far end, at no great distance from the massive stone altar, which still bears the cartouches of its maker, Piānkhi. On the right was a small chapel (L), which could be entered from the end of the sanctuary proper, and in this probably were kept the dress and ornaments of the god and his priests. Considering the state of ruin in which Piānkhi's temple now is, it is impossible to speak definitely, but it seems tolerably certain that every chamber in that building was employed by the priests for purposes in connection with the cult of the god, and that the king and the priests had their habitation elsewhere, probably on the other side of the river.

Whilst at Gebel Barkal in 1897 I kept a party of men occupied for some weeks in clearing portions of the courts of Piānkhi's

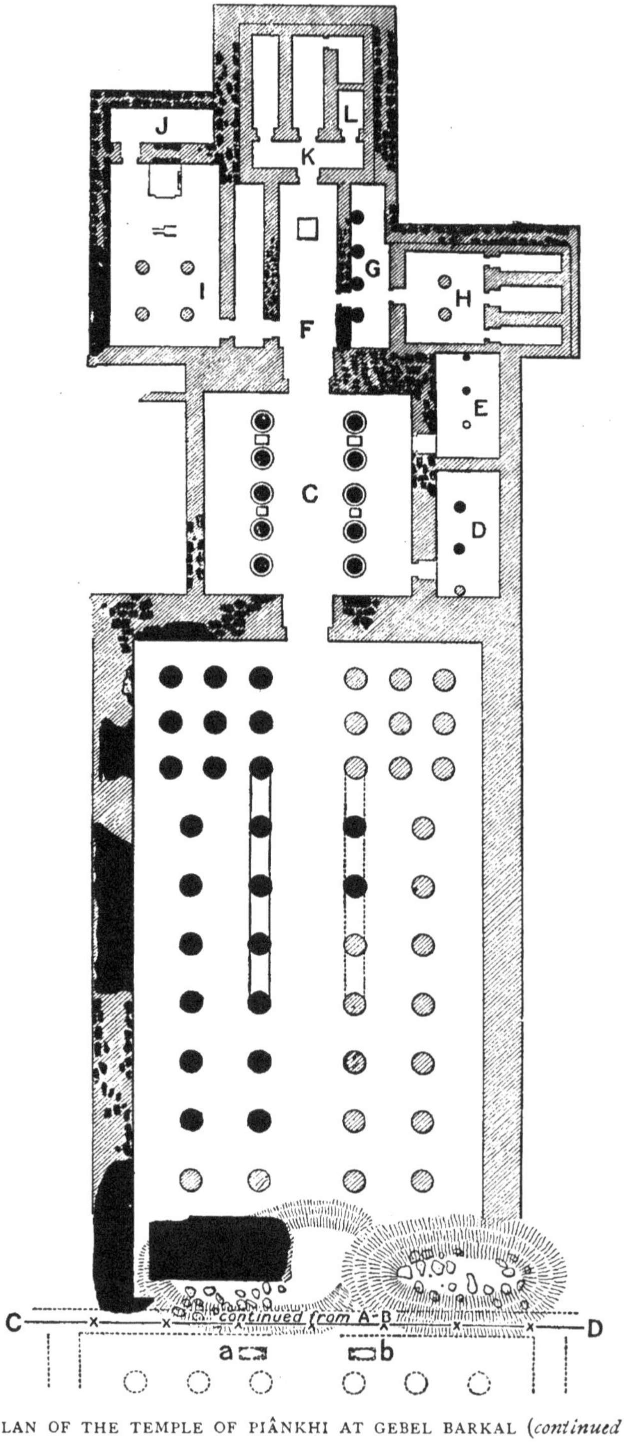

PLAN OF THE TEMPLE OF PIÂNKHI AT GEBEL BARKAL (*continued*).

temple. This was done for a double purpose, i.e., to compare the variations between the ground plans published by Hoskins and Lepsius, so far as possible with the actual site, and to find out if any more inscribed stelae were to be found lying face downwards among the ruins. It will be remembered that about the year 1860 the eminent French archæologist Mariette asked Sa'id Pâshâ, Khedive of Egypt, to give him permission to make excavations in the Sûdân, and the reason he gave for doing so was that antiquity dealers from Egypt went into the Sûdân from time to time and brought away with them sufficient loot to pay their expenses, and to make it worth their while to return for more. Natives at places like Gebel Barkal and Ṣûlb welcomed such visitors, for they gave them gold for, to them, useless stones. The first to teach the people of Meroë that antiquities were valuable things was "Al-Nimsâwî" (i.e., the German) Lepsius, who carried off some boat-loads from the Sûdân, and, be it said to his credit, paid the natives well for their trouble. One day he bought a headless statue of King Amather, or Amtel, which had been found in the village of Merawi,[1] and from that time onwards the villagers lost no opportunity of exploring the ruins, and of carrying off anything that was at all portable to their houses. Any monument which was too large to remove they re-buried in the sand.

In 1862 an official of the Egyptian Government was obliged to pass some days in the neighbourhood of Gebel Barkal, and whilst he was wandering about among the ruins some of the natives showed him, it is said, in one of the courts of the temple of Piānkhi, a group of five inscribed stelae. He understood enough of Egyptian antiquities to know that cartouches contained royal names, and as he felt that he had made an important discovery, which was indeed true, he copied the hieroglyphic text on the largest of the stelae and sent it to Mariette. His

[1] The king's names read , and he styles himself "Beloved of Åmen-Rā Ḥeru-khuti" . A picture of the statue is given by Lepsius in *Denkmäler*, Abth. V. Bl. 15, and it is described on p. 312 in the official *Verzeichniss*, published at Berlin in 1894.

copy was full of mistakes, but it was sufficiently good to permit the general nature of its contents to be made out. Mariette at once caused steps to be taken for the removal of the stelae, and the Mudîr of Dongola was ordered to place them on a raft and send them to Cairo; their transport was effected with difficulty, and they did not arrive at Bûlâk until the end of 1864.[1] When we consider that Hoskins carried out extensive excavations at Gebel Barkal, and that the whole site was surveyed with the

HEAD FROM THE STATUE OF A KING OF NAPATA AT GEBEL BARKAL.
[From a photograph by the Hon Charles Rothschild.

greatest care by Lepsius and his colleagues, it is astonishing that five such large monuments were overlooked. With this fact in mind we searched the ruins of Piānkhi's temple with the greatest care, and though many scores of tons of sand and stone were removed in the process, the labour spent was in vain.

VIII. A little to the north of Piānkhi's temple a portion of the plain is littered with fragments of pottery, stone, and bricks, but there is nothing left which serves to show what class of buildings

[1] Descriptions and translations of the inscriptions on these stelae are given in the second volume of this work.

stood here. Hoskins says (page 148) that he found at this place "fragments of the same description of bread stamps which are "found at Thebes, but these are without hieroglyphic inscrip-"tions." By "bread stamps" he appears to mean terra-cotta models of sacrificial cakes, or loaves of bread, of a conical shape ,

TYPICAL PYRAMID AT GEBEL BARKAI.

of which so many examples exist in all museums; if his assumption be correct, the ruins where they were found must mark the site of some funerary building.

IX. At one or two places to the south of Piānkhi's temple are the remains of pillars, which probably belonged to small temples, but if this be so, every trace of a building has disappeared.

From what has been said above it will be seen that all the

temples which existed at Gebel Barkal were built between the southern end of the mountain and the river. All of them were oriented to some point between the south and the east, but it is at present only possible to give the orientation of two of these with accuracy. We may now pass on to describe the pyramids of Gebel Barkal, that is to say, the tombs of the kings who built the temples enumerated above, and of other royal personages.

The PYRAMIDS OF GEBEL BARKAL, like nearly all the others in the Sûdân, are truncated, and each stands upon a platform formed of two or three layers of stone, which project everywhere on each side, except the south-east, where the chapel is built. The sides of all Sûdân ordinary pyramids form a series of steps, from twenty to seventy in number, each of which stands from four to eight inches behind the one below it; these stones were never filled up with stones so as to form smooth, inclined surfaces, as was the case usually in Egypt. The angle stones are generally carefully cut and smoothed, and give grace and symmetry to the appearance of the pyramid. High up the pyramid, on the side facing the south-east, is sometimes found a rectangular opening, which, I cannot help thinking, was intended to be used by the soul of the person buried beneath the pyramid as a door by which it might enter the building and descend to the place where its body lay. At the present day such openings serve as shelters wherein birds build their nests, and it is no uncommon thing to see a hawk standing in one as if keeping guard over the building. The Egyptians believed that the souls of the dead entered hawks, and that they visited the tombs under this form, and, if that belief was not common to all primitive peoples in the Nile Valley, it was probably introduced into Nubia from Egypt. The flat top of each pyramid is covered with a layer of well-cut, close-fitting stones, which in some cases appear to have been laid in a bed of lime and sand. There is no evidence to justify the view of Hoskins that the flat top was designed to hold a statue, and it is far more likely that the pyramids were finished off in this way because the builders were unable to make and raise a stone pyramidion to the required height, than that their builders intended to place ornaments on the flat top.

The greater number of pyramids in the Sûdân consist of: 1. A foundation of two or more layers, according to the thickness of the stones in each layer and the size of the pyramid. 2. A casing of stones, single or double, according to the size and height of the pyramid. 3. A core formed of pieces of sandstone, basalt, &c., the interstices of which are filled with sand, mud, or any earthy substance available. 4. A chapel or shrine which is always built on the side of the pyramid which faces nearest to the south-east. The building of the Sûdân pyramids must have presented little difficulty, for it is clear that the stone casings

VIEW OF THE PYRAMIDS OF GEBEL BARKAL IN 1832.
[From Hoskins, *Travels*, Plate 26.

were filled with the core as soon as they were laid, and an inclined plane made of sand, which could be heightened and lengthened without very much trouble, was all that the workmen needed to give them access to the pyramid. The only pyramids in the Sûdân built of stone throughout are those of Nûri.

The pyramids of Gebel Barkal fall naturally into three groups. The first group stood immediately on the western side of the mountain, and contained four pyramids. The two northern pyramids of this group (A, B) had lost their casing and chapels even in Lepsius' time, and neither Cailliaud nor Hoskins thought them worthy of mention. The two southern pyramids (C, D) were about 30 ft. and 23 ft. square respectively; when Lepsius made his plan of the site the lower courses of D and of its chapel were still *in situ.* The second group contained at least nine pyramids, though Caìlliaud only mentions six, Hoskins seven, and Lepsius eight. The pyramid E at the base measured 30 ft. by 26 ft.; F

COLONEL THE HON. M. G. TALBOT, R.E., AT SURVEY WORK ON THE PYRAMIDS OF GEBEL BARKAL.

was about 27 ft. square; G and H were each about 36 ft. square; I was about 88 ft. square, and J and K were about 25 and 23 ft. square respectively. When Hoskins was at Gebel Barkal the pyramid J was in an extremely good state of preservation, for he says, "It is scarcely at all injured;" in 1897 all traces of stonework had disappeared, and its remains resembled a natural mound of earth and stones. The third group contained at least eight pyramids, which are marked in the plan opposite by the letters L-S; of pyramid R the casing has wholly disappeared, and it must have been in an utterly ruined state in Cailliaud's time, for there is no trace of its existence in his map.

The following is a list of the bearings of these pyramids taken by Major Talbot, R.E., in 1897, from a prismatic compass, the variation of which has been determined by comparison with an astronomical azimuth; but owing to the irregularity of the masonry they cannot be relied upon to nearer than 2°.

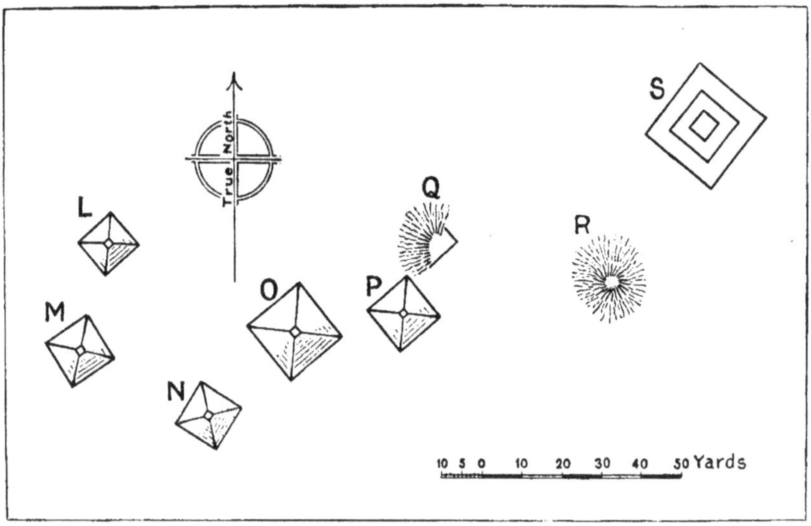

PLAN OF THE PYRAMIDS OF GEBEL BARKAL.

[By Colonel the Hon. M. G. Talbot, R.E.

Pyramid	L.	Door faces	139°	from true	north.
,,	M.	,,	147°	,,	,,
,,	N.	,,	122°	,,	,,
,,	O.	,,	140°	,,	,,
,,	P.	,,	140°	,,	,,
,,	Q.	,,	140°	,,	,,
,,	S.	,,	129°	,,	,,

The FIRST pyramid of the group, L, is about 36 ft. square at the base, and is well built; several layers of stone from the top have disappeared, and the south-east corner is very much damaged. The ornamentation of the angle stones of the lower layers is different from that on the angle stones of the upper layers. This pyramid appears not to have been provided with a chapel, for in Cailliaud's time there was no evidence that any had ever existed.

The SECOND pyramid of the group, M, is about 41 ft. square at the base, and its height is between 47 and 48 ft.; its angle of inclination is roughly 19°. The pyramid was perfect in Cailliaud's time, and he rightly called attention to the raised border on each face formed by the angle stones and the topmost layer of the

A PYRAMID AT GEBEL BARKAL, SHOWING THE ARRANGEMENT OF THE STONES AT ONE CORNER.

pyramid. In the platform itself is a square hole, which Cailliaud noted, and which he thought had been intended to serve as a socket for some ornament.[1] On the S.E. side was a small chapel, and in front of this stood a pylon, about 20 ft. wide at the base; the chapel, or sanctuary, had an arched roof, and over the entrance of the pylon was the solar disk, with uraei "[illegible]." Above the shrine, at the end of the chapel, was sculptured in relief the

[1] Un trou carré, sur cette plate-forme, a dû servir d'emboîture à un ornement quelconque qui couronnait le monument. "Voyage," iii., p. 201.

III.

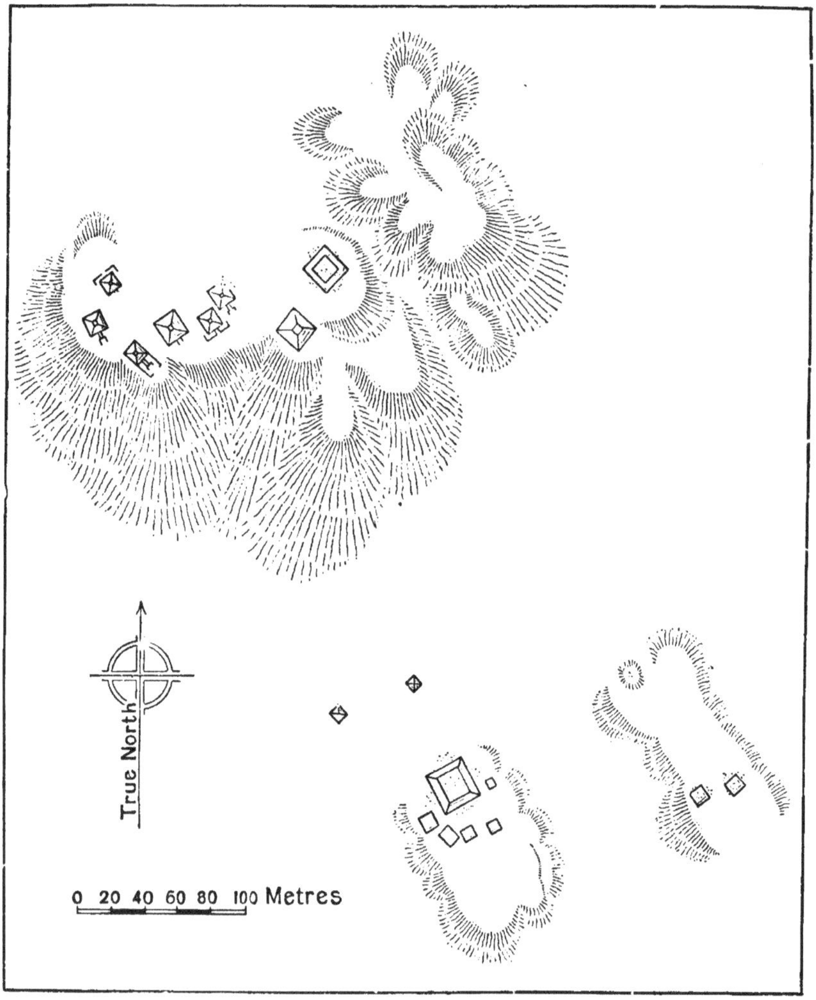

I.

II.

PLAN OF THE PYRAMIDS OF GEBEL BARKAL.

[From Lepsius, *Denkmäler*, Abth. I. Bl. 125.

boat of the sun-god. The greater part of both chapel and pylon was standing when Hoskins was at Gebel Barkal, but in 1897 every trace of them had disappeared, and in addition the great holes which had been made in the lower layers of the pyramid showed that attempts had recently been made to find the passage into it. Destruction of this kind was the work of natives, not of the Sûdân, but of Egypt; for several men from the neighbourhood of Thebes succeeded in entering the Sûdân after its re-conquest by Lord Kitchener, and they did much injury to the pyramids, both at Gebel Barkal, and on the Island of Meroë.

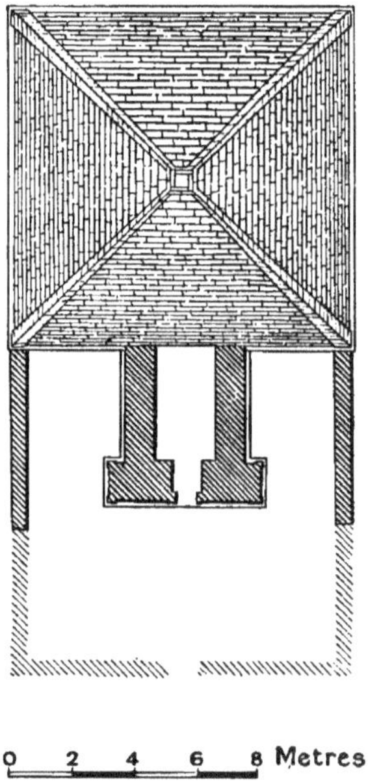

PLAN OF PYRAMID N AT GEBEL BARKAL.
[From Cailliaud, *Voyage*, Plate LVI.

The THIRD pyramid of the group, N, is about 35 ft. square at the base, and its height is between 48 and 49 ft.; it is the most complete of all this group, and still possesses a pleasing and stately appearance. The faces of the stones of the twelve topmost layers have been rubbed smooth on all four sides of the pyramid, and form a curious contrast to those of the other layers. The chapel possessed an arched roof, and the little court before it was surrounded by a wall; the walls of the chapel were ornamented with very rough reliefs, which appeared to Cailliaud to have been left in an unfinished state.

VAULTED ARCH OF THE CHAPEL OF PYRAMID N AT GEBEL BARKAL.

The FOURTH pyramid of the group, O, is about 53 ft. square at the base, and its height is between 58 and 59 ft. Its form is exactly the same as that of pyramid N, but it is now in an almost ruined state. When Cailliaud saw the pyramid its chapel, which had a vaulted roof, was still standing, but its pylon was a mere heap of stones. The reliefs represented a king and a queen seated on thrones, with priests making offerings of incense to them. The king wore the double crown of the South and North , and the queen had on her head the disk, horns, and plumes of Isis. Each personage holds in one hand the flail, , and crook, , and a palm branch (?), and a curious sceptre something like , in the other.

The FIFTH pyramid of the group, P, is about 44 ft. square at the base, and nearly 52 ft. high. It was almost perfect in 1897, and is one of the best built pyramids in the group. The platform at the top was complete, and the socket in it was well-cut and in a good state of preservation. The faces of all the stones in the twelve topmost layers had been carefully chiselled and rubbed smooth, and the angle stones were modified accordingly. When Cailliaud was at Gebel Barkal the chapel was still standing, and

THE SOLAR DISK IN THE BOAT OF THE SUN-GOD (PYRAMID N).
[From Lepsius, *Denkmäler*, Abth. V. Bl. 24.

its roof was well-preserved, but a portion of the pylon had been thrown down. The reliefs on the wall represented the performance of ceremonies connected with the making of offerings to the dead, and from Cailliaud's drawings (see "Voyage," planches, liii., liv.) we may note the following:—The deceased personage is seated under a canopy, holding a bow and other weapons in one hand, and a palm branch in the other. A priest stands in front of the canopy and burns incense, and behind him are rows of beings, including Anubis, Mut (?), Thoth, Ta-urt, Isis, Nephthys, and Osiris, preparing offerings. Men are bringing gazelle on their shoulders, a woman leads a cow and a calf for sacrifice, and processions of men and women bear palm branches. In one part of the relief we see the god Osiris seated, with offerings of fruits, flowers, vessels of incense, wine in jars, &c., arranged in rows before him. The flat raised portions which are seen in many parts of the reproduction were in the original relief intended for inscriptions, but either because the sculptor did not know hieroglyphics, or did not know how to cut them, he left them blank. The Egyptian origin of the details of the decoration

SCENE FROM THE SOUTH WALL OF THE CHAPEL OF PYRAMID O.

A priest is offering incense to a Queen of Napata, who wears the crown of Isis and holds the emblems of Osiris.

[From Lepsius, *Denkmäler*, Abth. V. Bl. 22.

is beyond question; the canopies are like those seen in Egyptian tombs; the capital of its pillar is Hathor-headed; the ornament of the pillar is lotus-shaped; and the influence of the Nubian element is only seen in the dresses of the priests and others, and in the jewellery of the deceased. When Cailliaud described the pyramid its chapel was standing with its roof intact, and only a part of the pylon was ruined; the reliefs on the walls were in a sufficiently good state to enable him to make copies, and the shrine, with its cornice of uraei, surmounted by the boat of the sun, could still be easily distinguished. Writing about twelve years later, Hoskins states that the "portico" was still standing, but "very few figures were distinguishable." He goes on to say

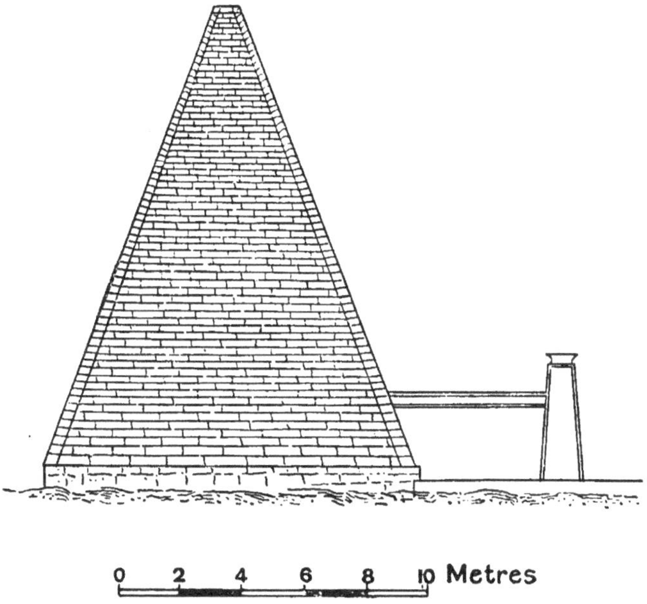

PYRAMID P AT GEBEL BARKAL AS SEEN BY CAILLIAUD.

that the style is "decidedly Ethiopian," and mentions the existence of an inscription in "Ethiopic" characters. Between Hoskins' visit to Gebel Barkal and that of Lepsius about twelve years later, some damage, though not a great deal, appears to have been done to the chapel,[1] but by 1897 the whole of the chapel and pylon had completely disappeared, and there was not one stone near the pyramid which would lead one to suppose that buildings of the kind had ever existed. From the drawings made by Cailliaud I was convinced that this pyramid was one of the

[1] Compare Lepsius, *Denkmäler*, V., plates 20 and 21.

best examples of Nubian tombs available for examination at Gebel Barkal, and it was here that excavations were carried on by me during the autumn and winter of 1897-8. An account of these excavations will be found on p. 169.

The Sixth Pyramid of the group, Q, is about 38 ft. square at the base, but the upper portion is so much ruined that no useful guess can be made as to its height. Cailliaud states that the pylon was destroyed, but that the walls and roof of the chapel were standing, and that the walls had been covered with plaster, having figures

DRAWING FROM THE NORTH WALL OF THE CHAPEL OF PYRAMID P.

In the upper register are the Scales of Judgment, and gods and goddesses bringing offerings for the dead, and in the lower men bringing flowers, &c.

[From Lepsius, *Denkmäler*, Abth. V. Bl. 20.

of the deceased painted upon it in bright crude colours. Hoskins speaks of "some remains of painting, rather indifferently executed," but Lepsius succeeded in producing very interesting copies of the painted figures,[1] and, judging by the specimens of this kind of decoration which exist in other places in the Sûdân, they are tolerably correct, and give a very good idea of the gaudy appearance which an ancient chapel at Gebel Barkal presented. This

[1] See *Denkmäler*, V., pl. 19.

pyramid was built for a royal personage, as the cartouche shows; the only signs, unfortunately, which Lepsius was able to read are 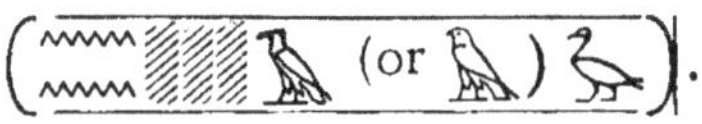. The two Meroïtic inscriptions which were traced on the walls were also copied by him. At the west end of nearly every pyramid chapel, either cut in outline on the wall, or sculptured in very high relief on a separate slab of sandstone, were the figures of three deities, usually Osiris (in the centre), Isis (on the left), and the deceased in the form of some god or goddess. Such a group Cailliaud says he found at the end of the chapel, but detached from its place, where it had formed part of a "false door" to the pyramid.

The Seventh Pyramid of the group, R, was, according to Hoskins, about 33 ft. square at the base, and he describes it as a "mass of ruins;" Cailliaud does not even mention it, but its position is worthy of note.

The Eighth Pyramid of the group, S, is in reality a step-pyramid, and is the largest of all the pyramids at Gebel Barkal; it measures about 66 ft. at the base, but the platform upon which it rests covers a large area. The angle stones are entirely without ornament, and even in Cailliaud's time no traces of the chapel, if it ever had one, were visible; he says that about one-third of it was in a ruined state, and that the bottom "step" had suffered considerably.

From what has been said in the descriptions of the eight pyramids given above it is possible to arrive at some general conclusions about the decoration of the chapels at Gebel Barkal. At the west end of the chapel was a "false door," the cornice of which was ornamented with winged disks with uraei, and large uraei in relief. Above the "false door" was the boat of Ȧmen-Rā in relief, and the deceased was represented as one of the occupants. Within the "false door," either cut in outline or sculptured in high relief, were figures of Osiris, the Egyptian god of the dead, and Isis, and a third deity, who was usually the deceased, who was assumed to be a god. On the north and south walls were figures, sometimes painted, of the king or queen who was buried under the pyramid, and in these the ornaments of the neck, arms, wrists, &c., were represented with most elaborate detail. The

SCENE FROM THE NORTH WALL OF THE CHAPEL OF THE PYRAMID Q OF A QUEEN OR PRINCESS OF NAPATA.

[From Lepsius, *Denkmäler*, Abth. V. Bl. 19.

dress in which the deceased is represented is Nubian, and the physical characteristics indicate that the reigning family was of local and not Egyptian origin. The reliefs which accompanied the large figures of the dead represented priests burning incense, and rows of members of the royal household and slaves bringing offerings to the tomb. The Nubians accepted the cult of Osiris, as they did that of Rā, and we find figures of the gods of the cycle of Osiris in many places on the reliefs; but whether they understood much of the Egyptian doctrines of immortality, or even of

VIEW OF THE PYRAMIDS AT GEBEL BARKAL, SHOWING THE CHAPELS AS THEY EXISTED IN 1820.

[From Cailliaud, *Voyage*, Plate LII.

the scenes which were cut on the walls of the chapels, is doubtful. The door of the chapel, which sometimes consisted of one chamber, and sometimes of two chambers, was in the form of a pylon, more or less elaborately sculptured with reliefs. In the space immediately behind the pylon of the chapel I believe a stone altar stood, for the altar seems to have been an important feature in all Nubian religious or funerary buildings. If such an altar existed, it would probably be inscribed with the name and titles of the deceased, and on the top of it the offerings made to the deceased would be laid. Outside the pylon was a small court, enclosed by a wall, wherein assembled the relatives and friends of the deceased, who assisted at the periodic funerary ceremonies. Having briefly noticed the principal characteristics of the pyramids of Gebel Barkal and their chapels, as deduced from actual remains of them, we may pass on to consider such information as we possess about the arrangements made inside the pyramids for the reception of the dead.

CHAPTER IV.

THE OPENING OF A PYRAMID AT GEBEL BARKAL.

THE official instructions which I received before I went to the Sûdân in 1897 authorized me, subject to the approval of the Sirdar, to attempt the opening of one pyramid at Gebel Barkal. When therefore we had finished an examination of Piānkhi's temple, and the excavation of some parts of it, we began work on one of the pyramids of the north-west group, viz., that called "N" by Hoskins, "No. 16" by Lepsius, "No. 6" by Cailliaud, and "P" in this work. The reasons for selecting this pyramid from the group were many. The pyramid itself was in an almost perfect state, the workmanship was very good, and the scenes from the walls of the chapel, which had been published by Cailliaud and Lepsius, showed that the architect had followed an Egyptian model closely. No expectations were entertained of finding the tomb either of Piānkhi or Tirhâḳâh in it, for those kings were probably buried near Nûri, but it was hoped that we might find that the arrangements made beneath the pyramid for the reception of the deceased resembled those of a good pyramid tomb, built after the XIth Dynasty, in Egypt. The details of the reliefs, judging by the published copies, suggest that the ornamentation represents a style of art which came into being after the Ptolemies had made their influence felt in Egypt. Still, the reliefs proved clearly that the Nubian personage for whom the pyramid was built professed, outwardly at all events, the religion of Osiris, and it was only reasonable to assume that provision would be made in the tomb for the preservation of the body of the deceased, which formed such an important object in that religion.

Before beginning work at the pyramid it was important to decide whether the person for whom the pyramid was made was buried within it or under it. Many attempts had been made to open the pyramids previous to 1897, but none had succeeded. Some people had set to work by making holes at the corners and in their sides, but in both cases they merely succeeded in laying bare the cores of the buildings, and their efforts only resulted in the destruction of the pyramids. Others, led astray, no doubt, by the "false doors" at the ends of the chapels, were convinced that the sepulchral chambers lay behind these, and broke away the pyramid casings behind them in the hope of entering them. It is only fair to say that such attempts were usually made by travellers, who, knowing nothing about the construction of the pyramids, thought it would be easy to effect an entrance into them. The natives in the neighbourhood, who during the last few generations have stripped the stone casings from the pyramids of Tanḳâsî, Kurru, and Zûma, knew better than to waste their time and trouble in digging through the cores, and contented themselves with carrying away stones when they wanted them. It seemed to me only too certain that the dead were not buried in chambers inside the pyramids, and no one who had examined the tombs of all periods in Egypt could do otherwise than believe that the dead lay in receptacles under ground. In order, however, to make quite certain about the matter, the stones were removed from one corner of pyramid P, and a clean boring several feet long was made; nothing came out of the hole except stone, sand, and lime roughly mixed together, and the hole was therefore filled up, and the stones replaced in the casing work.

When this experimental work was over, a party of from thirty to forty men was set to work to find the opening of the pit or shaft which, we assumed, existed and would lead to the place or chamber wherein the deceased was laid. We dug a trench some two feet deep round all four sides of the pyramid, and laid bare the platform on which it rested, but found no trace of any pit or opening. Still assuming that such a pit did exist, the trench was deepened on the east side, and finally about half way along it the picks struck a stone so hard that we could not break it in the ordinary way. When the surface of the stone was cleared it appeared to be a huge slab of ironstone, about ten feet long, six feet wide, and ten inches thick. The fact that it was set in a bed of lime proved that its position was not the work of nature, and its presence suggested

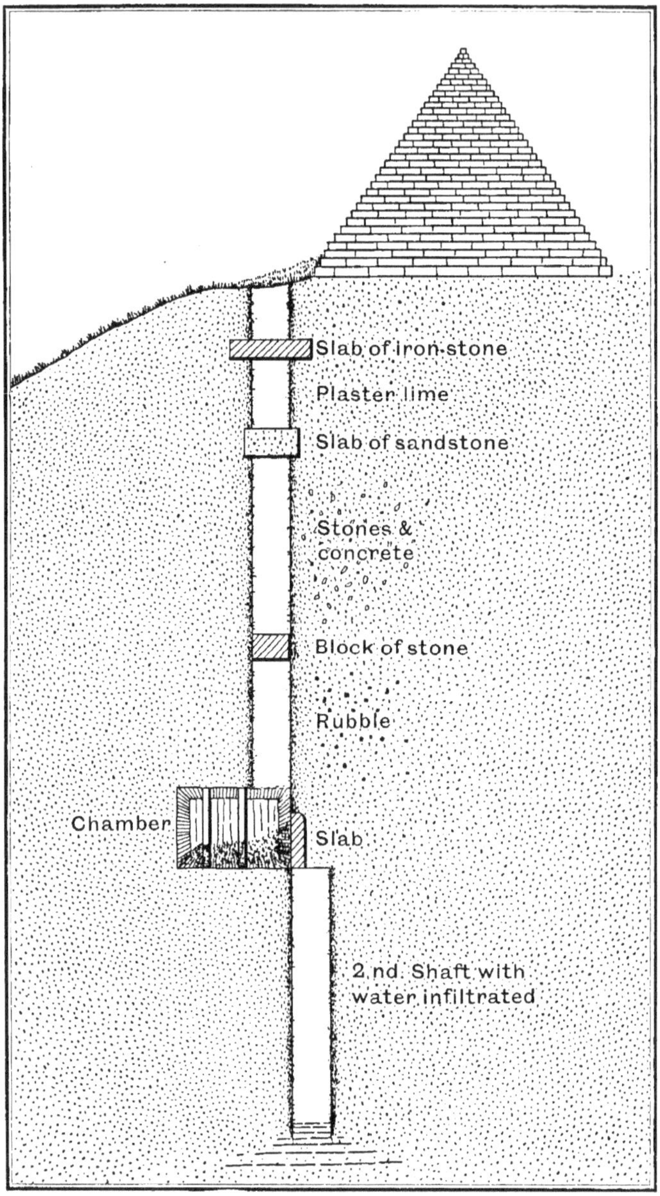

SECTION OF PYRAMID P AT GEBEL BARKAL WITH ITS SHAFT AND SEPULCHRAL CHAMBER.

that we had reached the mouth of a pit, or shaft, or "well" (*bîr*) as the natives called it. We had no tackle with which to move this stone, and it was decided to break it piecemeal; whilst doing this one of our two large iron spike crowbars broke in half, and several days were consumed in the removal of the stone. The natives declared that there was no stone of the kind to be found in the country nearer than Omdurmân; it turned out to be iron-stone, heavily charged with ore, and a piece of it is in the British Museum.[1]

Beneath the stone was a layer of solid lime plaster about one foot thick, and the removal of this caused great difficulty, for it would only come away in white dust which was unpleasant in the mouth and actually dangerous when it got into the eyes. Beneath this layer was another very thick one formed of a kind of rough concrete, and very hard, and under this was a thick block of sandstone which completely filled the opening of the shaft. Then came more concrete, and another block of stone, and after this there followed a bed of rubble some feet thick. When we had cleared all this out we saw that notches had been cut in the sides of the shaft in ancient days whereby the workmen had ascended and descended, and we found them very convenient. At the bottom of the rubble we came upon a very large flat slab of stone, which we proceeded to break with hammers and a crowbar in the same way that we had broken the others. This stone, however, gave out a hollow sound when struck, and before long cracks appeared in it, and a piece disappeared into a chamber below. We then saw that the stone was one of three that had been placed in a row to form the roof of a rectangular funeral chapel, hewn out of the living rock, about sixty feet below the level at which we had begun to dig.

The chamber is rectangular and its roof was supported by two square pillars. A narrow passage on the south-east side of it leads into another rectangular chamber, which also has square pillars; there is no inscription of any sort or kind on the faces of the pillars or the walls of the chambers. The chamber nearest the pyramid was about half full of fine yellow sand, and the narrow passage and the outer chamber were filled with it to within a few

[1] Nos. 42,150, 42,154.

inches of the roof. Lying loose on the sand of the inner chamber were a number of bleached bones of some small animal, which suggested a part of a sheep's skeleton, but they crumbled into white powder when touched, and were therefore not worth removing. By the side of the bones was a fragment of the upper part and neck of an amphora,[1] on which were inscribed the words, "Rhodian wine," **ΟΙΝΟΣ ΡΟΔΙΟΣ**, and the other portions of the jar lay round about. Thus it seems that before the filling up of the shaft began meat was eaten and wine drunk in commemoration of the dead, and that when all the wine had been drunk the jar was smashed.

When the sand had been removed from the inner chamber and from the passage and chamber beyond it, we examined the walls carefully to see if there were any concealed openings in them, but found none. Special care was taken in examining the end wall of the outer chamber, for it was possible that a doorway had once existed and had been filled up; none, however, was found. On tapping the walls with a hammer it was found that all rang solid, with the exception of the south-east wall, i.e., that which was immediately in a line with the edge of the pyramid. Closer examination showed that in it was set a slab of hard limestone about seven feet high, and six feet broad, and when this had been broken through, we found behind it a low vault, with a rounded roof, but there was nothing in it. The slab of stone which had been removed suggested that the vault had been built for some purpose, and it was decided to dig through the floor of it. When this had been done, we came upon a quantity of concrete, and shortly after it became certain that we had found the second shaft, by which the deceased had been lowered into the place set apart for him. In this shaft our excavations had to be made by candlelight, and the atmosphere was stifling. When the shaft had been cleared out to a depth of about forty feet, it began to widen out towards the pyramid and we began to come near to the short passage which we expected would lead to the mummy chamber. Here, however, the sides of the shaft became very damp, and every piece of stone which we took out was thoroughly wet; a foot or two lower down the men found themselves in standing water, and finally the work

[1] Brit. Mus. No. 30,440.

had to be abandoned. A depth had been reached which brought us down to the level of the Nile, or perhaps below it, and it seemed that its waters had forced their way by infiltration into the shaft.

This discovery was both vexatious and disappointing, for since I had no pump or pipes I was obliged to leave this portion of the year's work unfinished. For twelve weeks we all had worked hard in the intense heat, and under considerable difficulties, and it was disheartening, after the expenditure of much time and money, to have our labours suddenly brought to an end from such an unexpected cause.

From what has been said above it is clear that from first to last there is nothing in the pyramid, or in its shafts, which enables us to fix the date of its building. The reliefs in its chapel, as made known by Cailliaud, suggest, it is true, that the pyramid was built towards the end of the Ptolemaic Period; but the first shaft, and the little chambers at the bottom of it, with their squat square pillars, were not unlike those which are found in rock-hewn tombs of the XIIth Dynasty in Egypt. One thing is certain, the shafts and the chambers were made after an Egyptian model. The inscribed fragment of the wine jar mentioned above is important, for the writing upon it is sufficiently distinct and good to indicate roughly when the jar was broken in the tomb. The expert to whom it was submitted a few years ago thought it belonged to the period of the first or second century before Christ, but Sir Edward Maunde Thompson, K.C.B., Director of the British Museum, and Mr. F. G. Kenyon, Assistant Keeper in the Department of Manuscripts, British Museum, are in favour of a later date, and are inclined to assign it to the second century *after* Christ. If the wine jar were broken at the conclusion of the sacrificial meal which was eaten in connection with the ceremonies performed when the deceased was buried under the tomb, then we must believe that the pyramid was built in the second century of our era. On the other hand, we know that in Egypt the tombs of royal personages, and of people of high rank, were kept open by the priests for the express purpose of inducing relatives and friends to contribute offerings, chiefly in kind, at stated seasons of the year, and we are justified in assuming that the same custom obtained in Nubia. But in the case of the pyramid under consideration it is difficult to see how the offerings were to be brought into the chamber in which the bones and the jar fragments were found, for it is unlikely that they were let down the shaft from inside the chapel, and, so far as we could find out, there was no entrance into it from the side of the hill. The facts, however, are as given above, and it is possible that future excavations at Gebel Barkal may solve the difficulty which we now have in explaining them.

CHAPTER V.

MERAWI AND ṢANAM ABÛ DÔM IN 1897.

HAVING now mentioned the principal ancient remains which exist in the neighbourhood of Merawi on the east bank, and of Ṣanam Abû Dôm on the west bank of the Nile, it may not be out of place to describe briefly the appearance which this portion of the Nile Valley presented in the summer of 1897, when those two masterful men, the Sirdar and the Khalifa, were engaged in fighting for the possession of the Sûdân. Taking first the Sirdar's camp, we know that it stretched along the west bank for about two and a half miles, and though in the day time it seemed insignificant, by night, especially when there was no moon, the lights and fires which twinkled from one end to the other of it made it appear to be endless. The Headquarters of the Frontier Field Force of the Egyptian Army were nearly opposite to the village of Merawi. The most prominent building there was the comparatively large mud house occupied by General Leslie Rundle. It was built by a Greek merchant, and was said to possess a roof which would keep out rain, but as it was never subjected to the test, the statement was merely regarded as one invented by the owner to obtain the highest rent possible. The house contained one large room, which the owner had intended for a reception room, and one small one; in the former General Rundle transacted business, and in the latter he and some of his officers messed. Outside the larger room was a courtyard with a low wall running round it, and behind the small room was a kind of shed which served as a kitchen. In the summer this house was comparatively cool and comfortable, but in the winter it was almost the last place a man would choose for a dwelling, on account of the draughts. Turning to the left by the path along the river bank, the first hut met with was that of Colonel C. Long, R.A., the kind and fearless officer whose artillery did such excellent work at the Battle of the Atbara on April 8th, 1898, and at the Battle of Omdurmân on September 2nd of the same year.

Next came the Headquarters of the Intelligence Department. These practically consisted of two large, rectangular huts, or structures formed of a framework of branches of trees with sides and roofs made of *gerîd* and *salatîk*, i.e., the leaves and sticks of palms. To such huts the word *tukul* is often applied, but it is

HEADQUARTERS OF GENERAL SIR LESLIE RUNDLE AT ṢANAN ABÛ DÔM (MERAWI) IN 1897.

said that, correctly speaking, a *tukul* is a round structure, with a roof in the shape of a bee-hive. Between these two huts ran a narrow, covered-in passage. One hut was occupied by Slatin Pâshâ, and the other by the chief of the Intelligence Department, Colonel F. R. Wingate. These huts formed one of the most interesting features of the camp; for, at almost any hour of the day or night, he who was so fortunate as to be allowed to enter them would see these officers engaged in receiving the reports of men who had been to Omdurmân, and spied on the actions of the Dervishes, of envoys from the Gakdûl Wells, and from Matamma, and of fugitives from the wrath of the Khalîfa. Besides these, scores of men came asking for help for their starving relatives and friends, and for assistance to enable them to remain loyal to Egypt. From the stream of words which these men poured out as they squatted on a mat laid on the ground, Colonel Wingate would pick out the essential facts, whilst a shrewd question quietly asked by Slatin Pâshâ would indicate that he had discerned where the truth in the story ended and the fiction

THE INTELLIGENCE DEPARTMENT AT MERAWI IN 1897.

began. Natives from every tribe in the Sûdân came to these huts, and no matter what dialect of Arabic they spoke, either Wingate or Slatin would understand it. These officers would sit there hour after hour, patiently listening and noting, and advising or directing, through the men before them, the course of events which were taking place hundreds of miles away, in Abyssinia, Sennaar, and even in the remote places of Kordôfân. It is a pity that there were no means available for taking down the stories of the cruelties which the Dervishes were perpetrating at that time, to say nothing of the valuable information about peoples and places in the out-of-the-way corners of the Sûdân which such visitors brought in.

The next hut we came to was that of Colonel the Hon. M. G. Talbot, R E., who was employed by the Egyptian Government to make the triangulation and general survey of the Sûdân for military purposes. All travellers in the Sûdân owe a debt of gratitude to this officer for the accurate maps which he has produced year after year, and all must regret his decision to resign

THE GARDEN OF THE INTELLIGENCE DEPARTMENT AT MERAWI IN 1897.

the directorship of the Survey, which he has carried on with such conspicuous success. During my stay at Merawi he found time to make the plans of two groups of pyramids which are printed in this book, and to determine the orientation of certain pyramids and temples, and to render me much assistance in many ways. Proceeding down stream, we next pass the hut of Signor Calderari, the Italian Military Attaché on the Sirdar's staff; when this gentleman left for Berber, General Rundle very kindly placed this hut at my disposal. Beyond this hut we came to the ground where large numbers of the cavalry horses lived, and away some distance beyond these was the camping-ground of the newspaper correspondents. Still further on was the landing stage to which Mr. Loiso, the well-known army-contractor, brought his cattle and his stores, and close by were the fields in which they pastured for a short time after their arrival.

Returning now to General Rundle's house, and passing up stream, we came to the large open space, in the centre of which was the flagstaff, from which flew from dawn to sunset the

SIGNOR CALDERARI, THE ITALIAN MILITARY ATTACHÉ ON THE SIRDAR'S STAFF.

Egyptian flag. In one corner of this space was the tent of Major W. H. Drage (now Colonel Drage Pâshâ), the chief of the Army Service Corps at Merawi. This officer controlled all the supplies of every sort and kind which were required by an army of ten or twelve thousand men, and it was popularly believed that, if called upon to do so, he could at any time of the day or night tell the Sirdar the exact position cf every stern-wheeler on the river, what stores she was carrying. how long they would last, and also the number of boxes, and bags, and logs of wood which were to be found with each section of the Army at every place in the Sûdân! He spent most of the day in writing orders, and giving directions to a legion of subordinate officials, and in seeing that his commands were carried out promptly, and a good deal of the night he devoted to official "paper work." His practical, shrewd common sense and great experience enabled him to attend to half a dozen things at a time, and to grasp the details of each in a surprising manner; nothing escaped his notice, nothing disturbed him, and he was just as sagacious in discussing with the General the number of times which a soldier's boots ought to be soled, as the preparations necessary for the despatch of a company of Camel Corps to Berber or elsewhere. At Merawi in 1897, and at Aswân in 1886, 1887 and 1888, I was indebted to Major Drage for much timely assistance.

A little further up the river was Major Drage's *nuzûl*, or "place where things were set down," i.e., the place where all the stores and ammunition were set down by the men who unloaded the stern-wheelers which anchored alongside. Here were stacked in rows hundreds and thousands of bags of grain, rice, lentils, &c., and the stores which were required for feeding and arming the Frontier Field Force. At the end of the *nuzûl* was a wall of logs of wood, three or four feet long, and at each end of it stood a sentry. These logs were intended for fuel for the stern-wheelers, and were supplied by natives who went about in gangs, and either cut down or dug up by the roots such trees as they found in the desert *khôrs* and valleys on each side of the Nile. It is worthy of note that the natives were paid for every load of wood which they brought in at remunerative rates, and many native officials have expressed surprise that the British officials who were leading a victorious army into the Sûdân, for the benefit of the natives, should insist on paying the inhabitants for that which cost them nothing but their labour and the price of a few cheap tools; for they might reasonably have demanded and obtained the wood without payment. Beyond the *nuzûl* were placed at intervals on the river bank the huts, tents, and mud-houses of many of the British officers, H.S.H. Prince Francis of Teck, Captain Bunbury, Captain Borton, Colonel Townshend,

C.B., Colonel Lewis, Colonel Broadwood, Captain Mahon, Major Tudway, and others, and behind these were the mud-barracks.

Close to General Rundle's house were a number of tents in which some non-commissioned British officers, assisted by Shahîn Effendi, did the "paper work" connected with the administration of the army at Merawi, and two large tents which served Colonel Wingate and Slatin Pâshâ for offices. In a comparatively good, but new, mud-house lived the *mamûr*, a native official who held

THE MESS OF THE INTELLIGENCE DEPARTMENT AT MERAWI IN 1897.

authority under General Rundle, and who tried to carry out the functions of the governor of a town with a settled community. Immediately behind his house, looking towards the desert from the river, was the *sûk*, or "market," in which the shopkeepers were mostly Greeks. Here in small mud-houses these enterprising and most useful people lived, and it was astonishing to see how they managed to store so many varieties of useful articles in a small space. They successfully catered for everybody, from the General to the "boy" or servant, and from the *mamûr* to the camp-followers. They found out by some mysterious means when the army was about to move on, and on more than one occasion when the Sirdar's troops arrived at a place they found the Greeks there already in possession, with their wares spread out in booths, ready to do business. A legend was current in 1897 to the effect that, once when the Sirdar sent on messengers to a certain place to arrange with the tribes in the neighbourhood for a supply of camels, they found on their arrival that the services of every available camel had been bespoken by Greek traders two or three days before, notwithstanding the fact that the purposed expedition had been kept a secret! I was told at Berber later that the Greeks who were not allowed to go to Abû Ḥamed in July, 1897, made arrangements with their countrymen settled in Sawâkin to send goods across the desert by camel, and that when the Egyptian troops advanced to Berber on its evacuation by the Dervishes, they found a small Greek bazaar established there. Be this as it may, the boldness and enterprise of the Greek traders in the Sûdân are astonishing, and if their ancestors who entered Egypt under the favour of the kings of the XXVIth Dynasty possessed the same business qualities as their descendants, it is small wonder that they obtained such a firm footing in the country.

The needs of the soldiers and their officers were represented in the Greek shops by tinned biscuits, meat, fish, jams, milk, fruit, tobacco, cheap knives, razors, scissors, soap, cooking pots of all kinds, enamelled ironware, &c. Bowls, dishes, cups, saucers, &c. sold readily, and it was interesting to note how quickly the followers of the Prophet found out the superiority of such articles over the gourds and coarse earthenware vessels which they were accustomed to use in their villages. Besides merchandise of the kinds mentioned above, the Greeks dealt largely in brilliantly coloured cotton goods, which were bought chiefly by the Sûdânî women, who love bright colours and plenty of them. Strong European scents, musk, oil of geraniums, patchouli, &c., and strongly scented soaps and hair oils found a ready sale at Merawi, and the demand for one kind of highly perfumed pomade was so great that at that time it was impossible to obtain supplies from Europe fast enough. An extraordinary quantity of pins, needles, and cottons was sold when we consider how little clothing is worn by natives, and the demand for small circular mirrors was steady. The Greek shops were exceedingly useful, and their keepers maintained their stock surprisingly well. This is more than can be said for some firms of another nationality, which, notwithstanding the gift of free transport by the Sirdar for their goods, allowed their stocks to dwindle to such a degree that finally officers and men were driven to buy everything from the Greeks. The Greeks were ready to take trouble, and the others were not; within a few days of their arrival at a place they would have a soda-water machine in full work, and also an oven capable of baking long rolls of bread. Another peculiarity about the Greeks was that they did business without making use of any currency; very few people at Merawi could get any money at all, and bills were paid by cheque.

A great deal has been said and written about the evil influence which the Greek shopkeepers have upon the lower class natives, especially in the cities and towns of Egypt where many of the drinking shops, or "brasseries," or *bakkâls*, as they are termed, are kept by them. There is no doubt that they have everywhere in Egypt done harm to improvident Egyptians, whom they have helped to drink and gamble, and caused them to mortgage and sell their lands, and even the crops on them before they were grown, but there is equally no doubt that in the Sûdân their business qualities were most useful to the Government authorities, and that in establishing shops in almost every place where white men are to be found, they have done a considerable amount of good work. Certainly no other people have attempted to do in the Sûdân what they have done, and done well.

Near to the market of the Greeks was the native market, which consisted of a few rows of wretched shanties, that contrasted strongly with the shops of the Greeks, with their walls white-washed outside, and their wooden window-frames and doors. The stock-in-trade of most of these shops consisted of very bad matches, tobacco, sugar, lentils, rock salt, &c., and little gourds filled with dried native fruits, pepper pods, and seeds; some of the last named were supposed to possess medicinal properties, and others were bought and used as aphrodisiacs. One or two shops in the native "bazaar" had a small stock of Syrian turban cloths, and gaudily coloured stuffs. A little beyond this market were some rows of straw huts, wherein the wives of some of the Sûdânî soldiers lived.

GHÂNIM, SIR REGINALD WINGATE'S SERVANT.

The day began in the camp at Ṣanam Abû Dôm with a bugle-call by the bugler of each battalion about one hour before dawn, and I have often noticed that the call sounded about the time when the wind which Arab writers[1] call the "breath of dawn" began to blow On hearing the call, pious Muḥammadan soldiers rose and said the dawn prayer, and then prepared for the work of the day. With the dawn the whole camp was astir, and every one rejoiced in the prospect of the hour or so of comparative coolness which comes with the sunrise. The British officers made their appearance on the river bank, where they drank their early tea, and in a very few minutes each was off to his duties, and was not seen again till his return from the march, or parade, or gun practice, or whatever his work might be. On certain days the black battalions started at dawn, marched to Tanḳâsî, a distance of seven miles, and having performed what seemed to me to be marvellous evolutions for two hours, marched back again to the camp, which they reached by about 10.30. It was a fine sight to see those magnificent "blacks" striding along in the desert in open formation, with a "go" and vigour about their every movement which showed that the love of fighting was to them as the breath of their nostrils. They often came back singing, and seemed to treat the fourteen miles' march and their work at Tanḳâsî as a rather pleasant morning's occupation. Small wonder is it that the "black battalions" and their British

[1] The poets, especially Persian poets, love to describe this wind.

officers were always the best of friends, and the enthusiasm with which the blacks received them, and the pains they took to carry out their orders, spoke volumes for the training which they had received from Grenfell, Kitchener, Rundle, Maxwell, Lewis, Macdonald, Hunter, Townshend, and others.

During the hottest hours of the day, i.e., between 12.30 and 3.30 p.m., a certain amount of relaxation was permitted, but the click of the needles in the telegraph tent rarely ceased, and so long as they were moving work of some kind or other had to go on somewhere in the camp. From one point of view this was an exceedingly good thing, for without plenty of occupation life in the Sûdân at that time would have been almost unendurable. To a civilian the number of British officers employed at Merawi seemed too few, but the Sirdar had very little money at his disposal, and he had to consider carefully the spending of every pound. The result of all this was that every officer was working at high pressure, and the few civilians who were permitted to come to Merawi marvelled at the spirit which they put into their work and the cheeriness which they displayed. Camping at Merawi was no picnic, for everything had to be done "on the cheap," especially as the Sirdar was obliged to maintain another force at Berber, and to keep his sternwheelers going between that place and Matamma, and to provide for the laying of the Ḥalfa-Abû Ḥamed Railway, and the support of the three thousand men who were occupied in its construction. Every officer too was in a state of tension, for no one knew exactly what was going to happen. The Dervishes had evacuated Berber, it is true, but only because

THE CAPTAIN OF GENERAL RUNDLE'S STEAM LAUNCH.

the Khalifa knew that the place was of no use to him, since the Egyptian gun-boats, having command of the river, could bombard it at any time. There was a strong Dervish force concentrated at Matamma, and it was rumoured that the Khalîfa believed the Sirdar had collected an army at Merawi preparatory to marching across the desert to attack it; in fact, that he thought the tactics employed in Lord Wolseley's expedition of 1884 would be repeated. As the weeks passed on after the occupation of Merawi, rumours reached our camp from time to time that the Dervishes had decided to rush from Matamma to the Gakdûl Wells, and, having slaughtered the Gaalin Arabs who held them, to march on and engage the Sirdar's force at Ṣanam Abû Dôm. Such rumours were credited in certain quarters, but the responsible authorities, beyond taking care that the "black battalions" were ready to fight at any time of the day or night, paid little attention to them, and possessed their souls in patience.

There was, however, one uncertain element in the situation, and that was whether the Frontier Field Force would be called upon to advance either to Abû Ḥamed or Matamma, and if so, when? It need hardly be said that every man in the camp was eager to push on and to enjoy some of the fighting which was believed to be imminent, but no order to advance came, and when we saw Colonel Wingate depart for Abû Ḥamed, and leave Slatin Pâshâ behind to watch over the Intelligence Department at Merawi, it seemed tolerably clear that the battalions at Merawi were intended to remain where they were.

Meanwhile day succeeded day, and although each brought its own work in abundance, a feeling of monotony prevailed. The arrival of the mail stern-wheeler from Kerma with letters and newspapers was the great event of the week, for ordinary people at Merawi learned more of what was said to be going on up the river from the newspapers than from the officers in camp. Of course this was as it should be, but thirst for news of the war was great, and it was rarely slaked! The position of the newspaper correspondents of that time was a very trying one, for the Frontier Field Force was not fighting, in fact it was doing nothing but marching, parading, exercising, and manoeuvring, and there was exceedingly little news to be had which was worth telegraphing to

England. Each day they would go to Colonel Wingate's hut either to ask if there was anything to report, or to get their telegraphic drafts censored, but this proceeding occupied very little of their time, and had they not devoted themselves to the study of the country and the native, they would have had practically nothing to do. It was impossible for them to make excursions in the desert or on the river, for every native boat was in the hands of the authorities, and every beast belonged to them; and the

A PORTION OF THE CAMPING GROUND OF THE WAR CORRESPONDENTS AT MERAWI.

correspondents could neither go forward nor backward. Mr. Maud, the artist sent out by the *Graphic*, found plenty of work to do in sketching the members of the various tribes who came to Merawi, and camp scenes, &c., and many of the excellent drawings which he sent home after he left Merawi bear testimony to the value of the "studies" which he was able to make there comparatively at his leisure. To every one's great regret, Mr. Fred Villiers, of the *Standard*, fell sick of the fever of the country, and was ill for weeks. Merawi in October is not a good place for fever-stricken men. The site on which the war correspondents had been allowed to camp had its drawbacks, and he betook himself to a great cleft in the river bank which had formerly held a water-wheel; a cluster of palm trees stood above it giving pleasant shade, and its sides were lined with grass, altogether an attractive place so far as appearance went. To this spot Mr. Villiers moved his bed and stores, and for a few days he rejoiced in his new abode; to keep off the wind at night he hung palm-leaf matting all about him, but this in the end only caused trouble. We know now, thanks to experiments and researches made by Dr. Andrew Balfour, of Kharṭûm, that water-wheel cuttings in the river banks serve as nursing homes for the *anopheles* mosquito, and Mr. Villiers fell an easy prey to the legions of this insect which throve in his new home. In a very short time malaria seized upon him, and each day its effects became more serious. One night, from some unexplained though suspected cause, the matting about him caught fire, and he was only rescued from the flames with difficulty; for many weeks the trunks of the palms above the cutting were blackened and scorched to the height of several feet. Soon after he was well enough to travel, the Sirdar sent permission for him to return to Ḥalfa by steamer and rail, and thence by rail to Abû Ḥamed, and a day or so later the war correspondents were allowed to move higher up the river. One morning the whole party of them, with their stores and baggage, was sent by boat to Kassingar, where the following day they made up a caravan, and set out to march up the east bank of the Fourth Cataract to Berber, a distance of about 260 miles. They left Merawi about the middle of October, and as the Battle of the Atbara was not fought until April 8th of the following year, their patience must have been tried considerably.

A subject of never-failing interest of that time was the progress of the railway across the desert between Ḥalfa and Abû Ḥamed, and each evening the General received by telegraph a statement as to the advance which it had made during the day. It will be remembered that the first rail was laid on May 15th, 1897, only eleven days after the line between Ḥalfa and Kerma was completed. For a few weeks progress was very slow, and but little more than twelve miles were laid; but so soon as the railway battalion at Kerma had been transferred to the scene of its new labours, and an abundant supply of materials had been provided, work on it began in earnest. By the end of July the railway reached a point in the desert 115 miles from Ḥalfa, i.e., about half-way to Abû Ḥamed, and each day brought rail-head nearer to that place, which was actually in possession of the Dervishes. In spite of this, however, the work went on, and the rails were laid at the rate of from one to two miles a day. On August 7th General Hunter took Abû Ḥamed, and the railway battalion was free to

THE NILE AT KASSINGAR.
The boat was General Rundle's steam launch.

advance as quickly as it could; towards the end of October, on a day when every circumstance was favourable, a little over three miles of railway were laid. This was of course the "record" day, and we heard that its work elicted an expression of great satisfaction from the Sirdar. It would have been interesting to have heard the Khalifa's views on the subject, especially as he had begun to realize that the "steam-devil" which ate coal and breathed out fire and smoke, and could carry more baggage than 2,000 camels, was likely to work his downfall. On October 31st the railway reached Abû Ḥamed; thus in less than three months after the capture of that place by General Hunter, trains were running into it. It really was a marvellous piece of work, for between May 15th and October 31st two hundred and thirty miles of line had been laid, i.e., at the rate of about one and one-third miles per day, during the hottest time of the year, through a waterless desert, which about six months previously had been unmapped. Every man employed on the line did his best, of course, but the great success which attended the undertaking proved once more how correct was the Sirdar's choice of the man who directed the work, and lasting credit is due to Lieutenant (now Sir Percy) Girouard, R.E., and to the little band of young Royal Engineer officers who so thoroughly justified their Chief's expectations.

The weather at Merawi was not all that could be desired. During the early part of September the days were very hot, and in the afternoons even well-seasoned Egyptian officers found the heat sometimes nearly unbearable. Between 1 and 3.30 p.m. the heat could be seen moving the air above the sand in wavy lines, and the great glare added to the discomfort of every one. Every animal sought the slightest shade that could be found, and the small birds flocked to the shelters where the dripping water-jars were protected from the sun. Close to the river at night the heat was steamy, but with the dawn came a most agreeable coolness which lasted for an hour or two. Every few days came a heat wave, which was usually followed by a violent storm of wind laden with desert sand. A few hours before the *habûb*—for such is the Arabic name of the storm—came, the sky in the quarter whence it was coming became dark, and quite suddenly one saw as it were a dense grey wall advancing with the speed of a fast train and overthrowing everything that stood in its way. When it reached the camp it snapped the ropes and levelled many of the tents with the ground, and papers and small objects were driven before it like chaff. This, however, was not the worst effect of the *habûb*, for when it had passed on it left the air behind it heavily charged with sand and dust, and this was unpleasant to breathe and tasted very nasty. In the open desert, where the *habûb* stirs up sand only, it is disagreeable enough, but when to the sand there is added the dust of the offal of a camp like that at Merawi, where thousands of men and hundreds of animals have been living for weeks, its noxiousness to human beings may be better imagined than described. The effect which storms of this kind had on the Nile was astonishing, for in about half an hour such large waves were ashed up out of its water that to cross it in a native boat was impossible. Whilst returning with a few natives on one occasion from Gebel Barkal to the village of Merawi, we were caught in a *habûb*, and on passing a particularly exposed place near the hills some of the party were blown off their donkeys, and we had to wait until the wind had gone by. When the ferry was reached the ferryman refused to attempt to take us across the river, and there was nothing to be done except to sit on the bank until sundown, when the waves abated.

The heat waves which visited the camp from time to time were most disagreeable, and it was easy to understand how much they are dreaded by the desert tribes. No Arab will travel at such times if he can possibly help it, for he knows that any attempt to do so will probably be followed by disaster. A famous instance of this happened in August, 1897. The Sirdar ordered that 500 camels should be loaded with supplies and sent to Abû Ḥamed, and they set out from Korosko in two convoys, each containing 250 camels. Soon after they started, a heat wave of unusual strength came on, and marching through the air-less, red-hot desert was like marching in an oven. The proper rate of travelling could not be maintained, and the camels of one convoy, having broken loose, finally stampeded. The other convoy, which was under the charge of Lieutenant Mackay, managed to get to the Murat Wells on the fifth instead of on the third day, his own camel being so much exhausted that he had to walk the last sixteen miles of the way on foot and without water. When search was made for the other convoy, several camels were rescued, but it was found that eleven men and two hundred camels had perished of thirst.[1]

In the beginning of October the Nile suddenly rose to a higher level than it had done the whole of that summer, but it fell again very rapidly, and as it fell the weather became more and more unpleasant. The temperature by day was not so high, but the air was heavily charged with moisture, and as the night began to grow cooler, mists were seen over the *dhurra* fields about dawn. Men

[1] "Sudan Campaign," p. 114.

no longer slept in the open, but were glad to withdraw to their tents or *tukuls*, and the early mornings and evenings were decidedly chilly. In November the nights were very cold, curiously so, and the cold was of that peculiarly penetrating kind which is characteristic of the Sûdân. Neither the Greek nor the native bazaar could produce blankets, but one Greek merchant had, seemingly by accident, laid in a good stock of large cotton table-cloths ornamented with a striking pattern of huge flowers and leaves in blue, and these served excellently as blankets and dressing gowns. The servants, who had no clothes to speak of, felt the cold very much, and some of them were dressed up in these table-cloths, with most picturesque results; the men were delighted, for the love of the Sûdâni folk for garments decorated with large flowered patterns is very great. As the winter advanced the "blacks" felt the cold very much, and all felt it to be regrettable that the funds allotted to the Sirdar to carry on the war were not sufficient to provide these fine fellows with a few comforts in the way of extra blankets, &c. Cases of sickness increased considerably after the river began to fall, and Surgeon-Captains C. S. Spong and P. H. Whiston were kept hard at work the whole day long.

The amusements of the camp were of a limited character. The "blacks" organized dances among themselves from time to time, and these generally took place at night by the side of a fire. The men ambled about, swaying their bodies and clapping their hands as they shouted doggerel lines about love and war. The more excited grew the dancers the more interesting became the dance; for they forgot for the moment that they were soldiers in a disciplined army, and reverted to the actions and movements of body which had come down to them from a long line of savage ancestors. I noticed that when the "blacks" danced among themselves and for their own special amusement, their performances and the words which they shouted were quite different from those with which they favoured their officers. That the blacks attach great importance to this exercise is clear, and I cannot help thinking that they believe they will acquire fresh strength, or some other benefit, by dancing a certain "set" a given number of times. Sometimes after a long morning's work in the sun at the pyramids of Gebel Barkal, a number of the men would arrange themselves in groups and rows, and then advance towards each other, and retire, and raise their right hands to each other, and sing and utter cries for half an hour at a time. Dancing among many Oriental peoples was regarded as an act of devotion, and among African folk generally it was, and still is, cultivated to an unusual degree. One of the oldest Egyptian objects extant, namely, the wooden plaque of king Semti, now preserved in the British Museum,[1] represents this king dancing before the god Osiris, and we know that Usertsen I. danced before the ithyphallic god Menu, and Seti I. before the goddess Nekhebet. Again, Pepi I., a king of the VIth Dynasty, declares in one of the texts[2] cut on his pyramid that he will be "the pygmy who danceth "for the god [Osiris] and who maketh "glad the heart before the great "throne." That the Hebrews regarded dancing as an act of worship is proved by the fact that David danced before the Ark of the Lord (2 Samuel vi. 16). Whether the Sûdânî folk at the present day know exactly what their dances mean it would be hard to say, but it is probable that they do; in any case, it is to be hoped that this and many another anthropological question may be finally answered now that British officials are being stationed at all important places in the Sûdân.

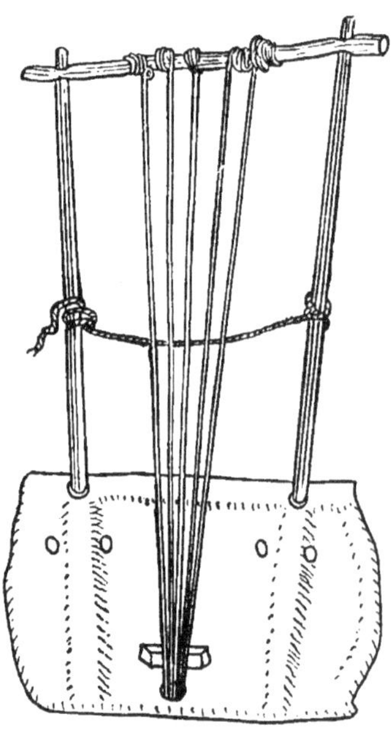

SÛDÂNÎ HARP.

The amusements of the officers at Merawi were almost as limited as those of the "blacks." The little gatherings which took place on the river bank near the huts of the Intelligence Department each evening were an important feature of the day, for thither came the officers commanding the Battalions, and the officers of the Artillery, Cavalry, and Camel Corps. The

[1] See Fourth Egyptian Room, Table-Case L, No. 32650. This object dates from about B.C. 4200.

[2] *Recueil de Travaux*, tom. vii., p. 162, line 401.

impromptu dinners given from time to time by Colonel Lewis and Colonel Townshend were greatly appreciated. Colonel Lewis had taught the band of his Battalion to play numbers of European airs and marches, and his grave "blacks" rendered many a familiar tune with considerable accuracy and skill, seeming to enjoy the result of their efforts as much as we did. Colonel Townshend was himself no mean musician, and as he possessed a fine voice and an extensive repertory of songs, most of which he accompanied on the banjo, his concerts were a great pleasure. Such entertainments were few and far between, but while they lasted the Khalifa and all his evil works passed out of the mind, and the audience forgot that they were sitting on a mudbank fourteen hundred miles up the Nile, stewing in the sun by day and shivering in the desert wind by night.

To a civilian like myself the camp was a source of perpetual interest, for one saw and realized for the first time numbers of facts which most of us only knew from books. It was quite easy to take for granted the acts of heroism which officers and men perform in battle, but not so easy to conceive the ceaseless strain which had to be borne for weeks and months by the officers who were responsible for the efficiency and well-being of the Egyptian Army, until the details were worked out under one's eyes. Every likely move of the enemy was calculated beforehand, nothing was forgotten, nothing left to chance, nothing wasted; men and animals were worked so as to get the utmost out of them, and marvellous economy was practised unflinchingly. Only picked men, with a practical knowledge of the country and its people and their languages, could have achieved such results at such small cost in money. The Egyptian Army at Merawi in 1897 puzzled greatly the natives who remembered the Gordon Relief Expedition of 1884-5. According to legends current in the villages the British bought any supplies which were forthcoming at fabulous prices, and money was spent freely. One old woman at Shibba declared that she had sold her eggs in 1884 for five large piastres (one shilling) apiece, and lamented loudly because she could do no business on those terms in 1897; she was quite convinced that the British officers she met in 1897 were not of the same race as those whom she had seen in 1885. Every native told the same story, and viewed with surprise the economy which was practised in all departments.

One of the things which astonished them greatly was the care of the Sirdar for his camels. Before the completion of the Ḥalfa-Abû Ḥamed Railway all supplies sent from Merawi to Abû Ḥamed had to be carried south on camels, and every camel had a full load. The road along the east bank of the Fourth Cataract is a peculiarly difficult one, and the greater portion of the distance—one hundred and forty miles—is over low, stone hills, and much climbing has to be done. During the journey ropes broke and caused the loads to slip, and the result was that large numbers of camels had their backs and sides rubbed into sores. Whatever happened, caravans were obliged to go on, and they did go on, but when the camels returned to Merawi many of them were in a sorry state. In this condition they were handed over to Captain G. B. Griffith, who knew everything which a man could know about camels, and who had established a sort of open-air hospital for them behind the camp. Here were seen camels suffering from every kind of camel ailment, but Captain Griffith's surgery, and pads, and lotions, coupled with rest and food, quickly set many of them on their legs, and they were soon carrying loads as before. Arab poets never tire of describing the bond of love and friendship which exists between the dweller in the desert and his camel, but the cases in which this bond affects his treatment of the camel are usually very few. Many of the natives overloaded their camels shamefully, and when it entered their heads, as it sometimes did, that they had put on the poor beast more than he could carry, they would unload him, and pull off the padded saddle which protected his sides by way of reducing his load! When they had reloaded him and hung about him loose articles which would bang against some portion of his body every step he took, and which were calculated to irritate the most patient of beasts, one of their number would jump on the top of the load, and the animal was allowed to scramble on his legs and stagger on his way. The camel will endure a great deal of ill-treatment so long as he is allowed to travel at his own pace, and to meditate at intervals, but if he be hurried he becomes distressed, and he will die on the slightest provocation. It is true that he is often perverse, vicious, and ill-tempered, but the fine animals which the Camel Corps rode showed what the beast could develop into when properly rested, fed, and watered. When travelling on a short allowance of water the animal closes every opening of his body, and as he only perspires behind the ears, no moisture escapes from him. He is easily frightened, and does very foolish things when in this state, and when his allowance of food has been insufficient or has not pleased him, his grumblings and bleatings are maddening; but like his friend the ass he rarely deserves all the abuse which is often showered upon him.

The stay at Merawi also enabled one to understand the policy which the Sirdar and his officers pursued in respect of the people they had conquered. One of the burning questions of the time was domestic slavery, and in the practical handling of this delicate subject General Rundle showed consummate tact So soon as the English arrived, slaves were quick enough to find out that dealing in slaves was prohibited, and many of them promptly ran away from their masters, sometimes actually leaving the oxen standing idle on the water-wheels, and therefore the growing crops perished for want of daily watering. Many were married, but they left their wives and children behind to live as best they could, or starve. Most of the runaways escaped to comparatively distant places, where they loafed and begged, and some few succeeded in joining passing caravans. The result of this was that a good deal of land began to go out of cultivation, and the authorities had to consider the matter seriously, for many natives complained that, whilst the Dervishes who had robbed them of most things, had left to some of them a few slaves, the British had been the cause of the flight of such slaves as remained. An aged farmer at Tanḳâsî told us that he once had forty slaves, who, with the help of some twenty bulls and cows to work the water-wheels, watered his fields and raised his crops. When the Dervishes came they carried off the young women and all his slaves except four, and left him only cattle sufficient to turn two water-wheels. When the British came to Dongola his remaining slaves ran away from him, and as the women of his house were old, there was no one left to water the crops, and then the rest of his cattle died. As he pointed to his sun-cracked fields, and told us how many acres had formerly been cultivated, he cursed God and man, and lamented the defeat of the Dervishes, which he declared had brought him to the state of misery in which he then was. This and less serious cases were carefully inquired into by General Rundle, and no pains were spared by him in attempting to secure substantial justice for the sufferers.

Many of the runaway slaves who were skulking in the neighbourhood were brought back to their work, and many, finding that the delights of freedom were not so great as they anticipated, returned of their own free will. The fact was that the slaves had mistaken notions about the meaning of the words "abolition of slavery," and they construed them into meaning abolition of work and a right to live an idle life at the expense of some one else. The negro slave is indolent and indisposed to work, and even the Sûdânî man who is not a negro will not do any more than he is positively obliged to do to maintain himself. Still, if the Sûdân is to prosper the land must be worked, and the prosperity of the country must depend ultimately upon the amount of work done in it under some system of labour. Forced labour of every kind is, of course, an abomination, and has long been abolished by the British in Egypt and in the Sûdân, but any attempt to overthrow hurriedly the system by which for thousands of years one class of men has worked for another in return for the maintenance of themselves and their families is to be deprecated. The conditions under which "domestic slaves" live and work have entirely changed under the rule of the British, and the time is probably not far off when men will be paid for their labour in money instead of in kind. In these days no Sûdânî man need suffer oppression in any form, and what I have seen in his country has convinced me that British officials, whether military or civil, are far more likely to take the side of the "domestic slave" than that of his master.

Disputes as to the ownership of land also formed another subject of difficulty with which the military officers had to deal at Merawi. During the years in which the Dervishes were masters of the country, misappropriation of estates had gone on on a very large scale, and hundreds of people had been grossly wronged. Many who had been dispossessed of their estates appealed to the British for a redress of their wrongs, and some went so far as to claim that the losses which they had suffered in every way through the Dervishes should be made good. In all cases careful examination of the claims were made, and it is satisfactory to be able to say that the people were generally satisfied with the decisions which were arrived at by the authorities. General Rundle had not only to command the Frontier Field-Force, but he had to create and work a new civil administration at Merawi, with a staff wholly inadequate for the purpose. Still, substantial justice was done, and the natives quickly realized that their new rulers were impartial and not amenable to bribes.

In order to arrive at a decision in one case the General determined to pay a visit to a certain local shêkh so as to obtain some necessary information. The shêkh lived some miles distant, and the General decided to take with him Slatin Pâshâ and other officers, and to go by river to his village. I was invited to form one of the party, and we all went down the river in the launch. A messenger had been sent on in the morning to warn the shêkh that the General was coming, and to tell him to be in attendance. When we arrived we found some fifty or sixty men drawn up on the river bank, each wearing a long garment of some dark-coloured cotton stuff, and a clean white turban neatly twisted. Many of them were grey-bearded, and each man stood in the dignified attitude which is characteristic of the native when assisting at any solemn function. The shêkh received the General with many warm words of welcome, and then Slatin Pâshâ, whose history every man knew, was accorded an ovation. When the business which occasioned the visit had been discussed, the General made his way towards the launch, accompanied by the shêkh and Slatin. Then the shêkh made a little speech to the General which was of singular interest, for it threw much light on the difference which he had noted between the old and the new *régimes*. "Formerly," he said, "when a "high Government official came to visit my father, all the women "in our *ḥarîms* fled to the fields, and every slave who could get out "of the way did so. When the official arrived he at once demanded "grain and dates for his followers, and we were obliged to kill sheep "and feed all his party. We had to make him presents of donkeys, "and of anything to which he took a fancy, and he and his men "paid unwelcome attentions to our women. Now your Excellency "comes with your honourable Pâshâs, and you ask us for nothing, "and you take nothing from us; our women no longer run to the "fields, for they are not afraid, and all our men are here, and they "are your servants." Then, after many wishes for the long life and success of the General, he said, "You shall take Omdurmân, "you shall kill the Khalifa, and you shall marry his mother!" The General's reply to the last portion of the prophecy was inaudible, but as if to emphasize the shêkh's remarks a very good-looking donkey, which had been solemnly looking on for some time, began to bray loudly, and the meeting between the General and the shêkh ended with a laugh in which every one joined.

Now, although the British authorities were fully occupied with work, they managed to find time to assist me in carrying out the examination of the antiquities in and about Merawi, which I had been sent out to make by the Trustees of the British Museum. I was well acquainted with all that Cailliaud, Hoskins, and Lepsius had done, and a preliminary visit to Gebel Barkal convinced me that the complete excavation of the site would require more time and cost more money than I had at my disposal. After consultation with Colonel Wingate, it was decided that we should explore the ruins of Piānkhi's temple (see pages 145 ff.), and clear out any portions which seemed promising, and attempt to open one of the pyramids at Gebel Barkal. It was estimated that this work might be done in three months, and as no one except the Sirdar knew how long the Frontier Field Force was going to remain at Merawi, it was clearly unwise to begin work on too ambitious a scale.

This conclusion arrived at, Slatin Pâshâ summoned the Shêkh Muḥammad Wad Ibrahim from the other side of the river, and informed him that the Sirdar had given me permission to make excavations near his village. Muḥammad replied that the Sirdar had already told him that I was coming to do this work, and that, if God willed, I should find the untold treasures which the ancient kings of the country had hidden in the pyramids. He and the men of his village would take care that nothing was stolen, and as for himself he was the faithful servant of the Sirdar, and of his Excellency Salatin Pâshâ. It will be noticed that the shêkh pronounced Slatin's name "Salatin," and in doing so he wished to pay this distinguished man a great compliment, for "salatin" is the plural of "Sultân," i.e., "king," or "governor," and by this play of words he intended to express his belief that the power of all kings was in him. Many natives of the Sûdân consistently spoke of "Salatîn Pâshâ." After

MUHAMMAD WAD IBRAHÎM, SHÊKH OF THE VILLAGE OF BARKAI, IN 1897.

Slatin's escape from Omdurmân the Khalîfa also made a play of words on his name, and called him "Shayatîn;" now "shayatîn" is the plural of "shetân," i.e., devils," and by giving him this name the Khalifa expressed his opinion that Slatin was a whole legion of devils! From compliments we proceeded to business, and found that there were only about twenty men available for the excavations, because nearly all the inhabitants were busily employed in watering the *dhurra* which had just been planted. Next came up the knotty question of wages, and after much talk these were fixed at five piastres per day. The shêkh was as keen in money matters as any Oriental I ever met, but that he should be so exacting in this case was not remarkable, considering that about a year previously his village was actually in possession of the Dervishes, who forced him to provide them with grain and dates, and tortured him till he told them where his money was buried.

The question of wages having been settled, the General gave me authority to apply to Major W. H. Drage for baskets, ropes, planks, picks, crowbars, &c., and this officer rendered me every assistance in his power. We were old friends, for he had helped me at Aswân in 1887, when I was clearing out the tombs in the hill opposite the modern town for General Sir Francis Grenfell, and again in 1888, when I made a collection of ancient Egyptian skulls at the same place for Professor A. Macalister, of Cambridge. Besides tools, Major Drage lent me some large Egyptian water-jars and buckets, so that we might attempt to filter the Nile water, and at some inconvenience to himself he arranged to provide me with a boat to take my tools and stores across the river. The crossing of the river was at that time a very difficult matter. Owing to the scarcity of boats, every sailing boat had been seized by the Sirdar, and was employed in transport work, and of rowing boats there was none. There was a ferry at the southern end of the camp, but the ferryman only worked when he liked, and the crossing occupied anything from half an hour to two hours. His method was to tow his boat a considerable distance up stream of the point which he wanted to reach on the opposite bank, and when it was loaded to allow it to drift down stream and to steer it aslant the river to its destination. This method was theoretically good, but in practice we found that about halfway across the river the current took command of the boat, and carried it along until the ferryman managed to get it under a bank, a mile or more lower down the river than the place where the passengers wanted to land. Two narrow planks served him as oars, and it was a matter of wonder how he managed to bring his boat at all to the other side. The boat was a crazy thing, and seemed to have been built up of odd bits of wood of different sizes and thicknesses nailed together at random, and how the mass of rags, of all sizes and colours, which served as a sail, held together was marvellous. No load, however, seemed able to sink the boat, and I have seen twenty-three men, eight women and children, a couple of donkeys, and several bags of fodder in it at one time. On any other river the boat would have foundered, and all its passengers would have drowned, but the special providence which watches over native concerns in that country never permitted such a thing to happen, to my knowledge. As the river fell the boat often stuck on a mudbank, and then the captain and many of his passengers would jump into the water, take off their garments and throw them into the boat, and, having pushed her off, swim contentedly to shore. On one occasion the captain had managed to refloat his boat without any help, and as he was jumping in, many of the passengers raised a cry, and we heard the click of a crocodile's teeth! For several days afterwards passengers were very chary about getting into the water to shove off the boat when it ran aground

For the first few days after my arrival at the camp I was occupied in getting together the tools necessary for the work to be done at Gebel Barkal, and in making arrangements for living in a village across the river, for it was out of the question to attempt to return to the camp each night. Some delay was caused by the illness of the man I had hired as a servant, and I could neither take him with me nor leave him without attention. I engaged him at Ḥalfa, and his testimonials were excellent, but I had reason to believe after we had started that they referred to some other man, and that my man had either hired or stolen them. He had been a servant in Cairo, and had learned to drink intoxicating liquors, and at every place where the boat stopped on the way up he went ashore, and enjoyed a carouse in some Greek's shop. When he arrived at Merawi he was suffering from fever, and as he continued to get worse Colonel Wingate made arrangements and sent him back to Ḥalfa. There was some difficulty in finding another servant, but at length this was overcome, and a *saïs*, or groom, was found who was ready to leave the delights of a camp life and go with me.

MERAWI IN 1897

We started in a boat from the camp one Saturday afternoon towards the end of September, intending to sail up the river to the water-wheel nearest the village of Gebel Barkal, but so soon as we got well out into the stream the wind dropped, and the

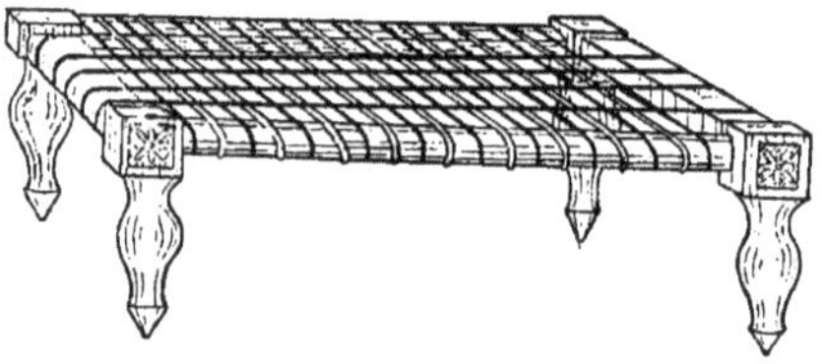

ANḲARÎB, OR NATIVE BEDSTEAD.

current carried us down the river. When at length we succeeded in reaching the bank on the other side, we found ourselves more than a mile from the point for which we had set out. The crew got out and began to tow the boat, but progress was so slow that the night fell before we were a quarter of the way to the mountain, and in the darkness two of the towers slipped into the river. After this they argued the case with the Egyptian orderly whom Colonel Wingate had sent with me, but as they talked the Berberi language I could not follow the drift of their remarks; when the orderly had turned them into Arabic it appeared that the crew wanted to return to the camp and make a fresh start on the following day. This, of course, was absurd; so the towing began again, and all went well until we came to a reach of the

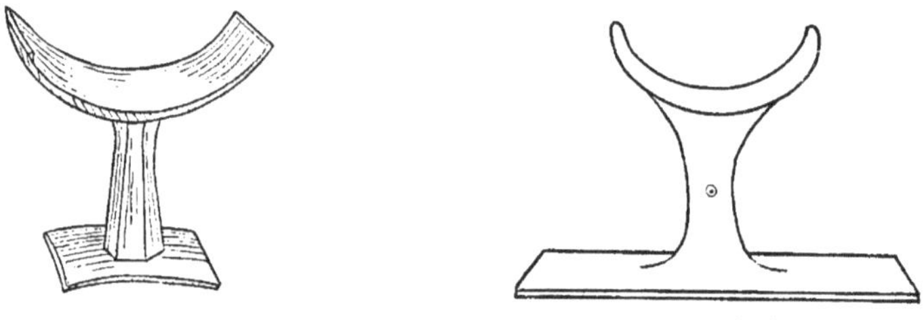

WOODEN PILLOWS USED IN THE SOUTHERN SÛDÂN.

river where water-wheels are numerous. The men climbed up the staging of several of them and passed the tow-rope over, but at one place, where the current ran very strongly, the rope caught in a forked branch of a tree which had fallen into the river near the bank, and the men, who were at that moment climbing over a water-wheel, were brought to a standstill. Suddenly the branch broke, and the weight of the boat pulling the rope taut with a jerk, the same two men who had slipped before were again thrown into the river. How they got out was a puzzle, but they were very cold and much exhausted, and we then decided to camp on the bank at the place where a palm trunk in the river had stopped the downward course of the boat. A fire was lit, and after warming themselves the men declared they were no worse, and having brought some *anḳarîbs*, or native bedsteads, to sit upon, the party had supper and went to bed. In the darkness no one noticed that the bedsteads had been placed in one of the small patches of ground into which the cultivable land is divided for convenience in watering, and when we woke at dawn we found that, through the water-wheel having been set going during the night, our beds were standing several inches deep in water, and that shoes, socks, the orderly's putties, tarbush, &c., were quietly floating about us. We quickly re-embarked, and in a short time reached the village of Barkal.

We were met by the Shêkh Muḥammad Wad Ibrahîm, his son Osmân, his brother, and a few of the "elders" of the village, each of whom was anxious to let me a house. Having stored the picks, shovels, baskets, &c., in the shêkh's house for safety, and my precious water-jar with its iron stand in his "guest-chamber," we set out to examine the mud huts which were to be let. There were at one time some good mud houses in Barkal village, but during the Dervish rebellion they had been allowed to become uninhabitable. Few had a roof of any kind, none had whole walls, and the only room in them all in which one might have lived had no window, and had to be entered by crawling on hands and knees. In most of the rooms donkeys, goats, and sheep had lodged, and had left behind them abundant traces of their occupation. A glance at the thick layers of dust and sand on the floors, and the thought of the creatures which it hid, made one's flesh creep. The natives had long since abandoned the mud houses which were offered to me, and had gone to live in *tukuls* [1] made of palm-leaf mat-work tied to stakes driven in the

[1] The word *tukul* seems to be the Amharic *tĕkĕl* ተክል፡ which means in Abyssinia both "tent" and "tent-pole;" its primary meaning appears to be a booth made of green leaves.

ground. Things being thus, I returned to the shêkh's house, and hired his guest-chamber, wherein he had already placed the baggage, and had, I believe, intended me to live all along. This chamber was built on to the end of his house, but could not be entered from it, and was to all intents and purposes a separate building; it was about fourteen feet long, eight feet wide, and eight feet high, and was roofed with palm-branches. High up in an outer wall were several openings, and along the same wall ran a *maṣṭăba*, or "bench," made of mud, on which the occupants might spread their mats and bed-carpets, and sit or sleep. When several inches of the floor had been shovelled out and a new roof put on it became habitable. The sloping sides and flat roof gave it something of the appearance of an Egyptian tomb, and Slatin Pâshâ neatly expressed the general opinion of the officers when one day he chalked on the front in large capitals the name "Mummy House." The chief drawback to this hut was the heat in the day-time, for the sun's rays poured on its front for hours each day, and then it was impossible to live inside it. There was a small court in front with a wall about two feet high running round it, and this we decided to roof over. The shêkh and his brother readily agreed to build a *râkûba* for me, and set about it without delay. The methods of the workmen were primitive and interesting. They dug the holes in the ground for the supports with their hands, they burned the ends of the palm trunks for the roof in a fire until they were of the right length, they twisted ropes of palm fibre, which was stripped from the trees as wanted, and they made a palm tree, which they declared God had placed there for my special benefit, serve as the support for one end of the *râkûba*. I pointed out that the use of the palm-tree as a support was unsatisfactory, for the simple reason that when the tree, which was a high one, rocked, it must loosen the ropes, and let the poles fall. The shêkh's brother, who was said to be very clever in such matters, assured me that the *râkûba* would "never fall;" but all the same, three nights later, during a high wind, it *did* fall, and had I not moved my bed to the other end earlier in the night, it would have fallen upon me. The builder was not at all disturbed by this, for he told me that my escape was a proof of the special favour in which

I was held by Providence, and of the luck which the villagers enjoyed in securing my presence among them. There was, of course, nothing more to be said. The next duty was to build a hut for the native servant, and when we had been provided with a mud fire-place our domestic arrangements were complete.

In front of the hut there was a little canal which carried water from the water wheel into the remote parts of the village, and with all its branches it must have been a couple of miles long. At first we drew our water for cooking and drinking from this

A NATIVE HOUSE IN BARKAL VILLAGE.

source, but subsequently we found that the members of several households whose doors it passed washed in it, and we made other arrangements for our water supply. The natives, however, and the animals drank regularly from it, and seemed none the worse.

A few words may now be said about the shêkh of Barkal village and his people. In the days before the Mahdi and Khalîfa rose to their evil eminence, the family of Shêkh Muḥammad Wad[1] Ibrahim had been a power in the land, and he asserted that for

[1] Wad = weled, i.e., "Son."

five generations the head of his house had been shêkh of Barkal. Hardly a day passed without some elderly man coming to see him and discuss the war; and inquiries showed that nearly every one of them had held some Government appointment under the old *régime*. Muḥammad was a tall, spare man, with good eyes, regular features, a short dark beard and a very dark skin; he was quick-witted, intelligent, and active. His son Osmân was a tall, broad-shouldered young man, about eighteen years of age, with large eyes set in a broad face; he had very fine teeth, and between the two large front top ones was the division called *fulga* by the natives, which is always regarded as a sign of luck in the Sûdân, and is much prized. His father always wore a dark robe, but his garments were always white, and he carried in his waist-band two steel daggers which were said to have been made at Berber from the fish-plates which the Dervishes carried off when they wrecked the Ḥalfa Railway south of Sarras. His father often went bare-footed, but he walked in red leather sandals with long pointed toes, the ends of which turned upwards and then curved backward towards the ankle, being fastened just above the instep. Sandals of the same pattern were worn by Sûdânî kings two thousand years ago, and representations of them are to be seen on the reliefs in the pyramid chapels on the Island of Meroë, and elsewhere.

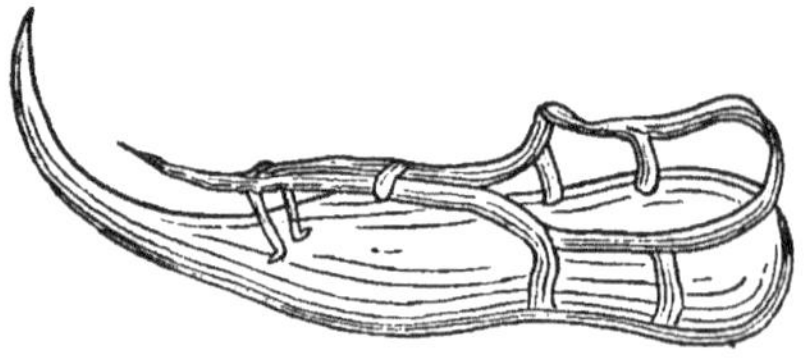
NATIVE SANDAL.

Muḥammad had always been a loyal supporter of the Egyptian Government, and his loyalty had cost him dear. It was difficult to get him to talk about the events of the last few years, and his remarks showed that he was unwilling to express his real opinion about the Khalifa; for it will be remembered that in 1897 Omdurmân and Kharṭûm were still in the hands of the Dervishes, and the Khalifa's final overthrow had not been effected. One evening, however, a friend arrived at Barkal from Berber, and he brought with him news of the Sirdar's entry into Berber, which he himself had witnessed, and as he told his story the shêkh began to be agitated. Presently he took his string of prayer beads in his fingers, and as he told every bead he cursed the Dervishes with a series of very comprehensive curses. When he had ended his cursings, after some persuasion he told me how the Khalifa's followers had treated him. It seemed that when the British left the Sûdân in 1885 the Dervish movement made great progress, and a Dervish horde, blatant and elated after the fall of Kharṭûm, came to Ṣanam Abû Dôm, and crossed the Nile and appeared in Merawi. The Dervishes hated the people of Merawi, Shibba and Barkal, because they had refused to join the Mahdi's followers, and because they belonged to the Shaiḳiya tribe, which, like the Gaalîn Arabs, denied his pretensions to be a reformer sent by God. The Dervishes seized all the young women, both married and unmarried, and dishonoured them, and then began to loot the houses. They forced the men to show them where their grain and dates were stored, and when they had smashed the mud bins which held the family stores, they compelled them to carry their property to the Dervish depôt, which was always established near the place where any plunder was to be had. Day by day cattle were killed to feed the Dervishes, parties of whom went about in the villages harassing the men and terrifying the women until they revealed the places where their money was hidden.

Now Muḥammad, the shêkh, was reputed to possess much money, and when certain of his enemies told this to the Dervishes, he was seized and ordered to give up his hidden dollars. He was laid on the ground and beaten with a whip made of hippopotamus hide,[1] or sinew, until the skin of his back was in strips, but he made no confession. A few days later he was dragged from the hut into which he had been taken and beaten on the feet until his toe-nails dropped out. The Dervishes would have killed him, only they felt sure that he had money hidden somewhere, and they knew they would lose it if he died. They therefore allowed time for his wounds to heal, and then they finally determined either to make him confess where his money was, or to kill him. When they had brought him out of his hut again they drove stakes in the ground and tied him to them securely, and then they kindled four fires near him, one at each side, one at his back, and one in

[1] The *kirbâg*, commonly called *kurbag* or *kurbash*. The Arabic form of the word is كرباج, and it exists in Amharic as *akûrbâg* አኮርባጅ :

front of him. As the fires burned they well nigh roasted him, and the effect of the heat on the new skin can well be imagined; all water was kept from him, and after some hours of agony he admitted that his money was in the ground under his house. Without extinguishing the fires the Dervishes rushed to his house, dug up the floor, pulled down the walls, and at length found eight thousand dollars tied up in small bags. Having released the unfortunate man, they carried off everything of use or value from

EVENING PRAYER UNDER THE PALMS AT THE VILLAGE OF BARKAL.

his house, and then they sent out parties of men to lay waste his fields and to destroy his water-channels and water-wheels. As proof of the truth of his words the shêkh showed me his broken and twisted nailless toes, and the weals across his back, and the scars of wounds made by the fires. When the Dervishes had "eaten up" all the villages of the Shaiḳiya Arabs in the neighbourhood they moved on and ate up villages elsewhere in the province, and when nine years later they fled before the Sirdar from Dongola, in 1896, the inhabitants consisted for the most part of old men and women, children and babies. The young men had been carried off to fight, and the girls of eight or nine years of age and upwards had become the wives of the Khalifa's followers.

The poverty of the villagers of Barkal was abject; their drink was usually water, which as often as not they scooped up with their hands from the channels in the fields, and their food consisted of thin cakes made from *dhurra*, partially baked either in the ashes or on a hot stone, and dates. The shêkh told me that fifteen different kinds of dates grew at Barkal, and the soil is especially good for date palms. It has always been a matter of wonder to me that the Dervishes did not cut them down as they did further north, in the villages along the banks of the Nile at the Second Cataract. Each kind of date had its own name, which indicated its characteristics, but that which most Europeans appreciate is the *sultânî*, or "royal" date. It is short, fleshy, and dark-coloured, and when ripe is very good. The Shaiḳiya, like the Prophet, love dates and water-melons, and they remember that he said, "Honour your paternal aunt, the "date palm, for she was created of the earth of which Adam was "formed." Coffee I saw in very few houses, but tea was more common, and though tobacco was greatly prized, only here and there would be found a man who could afford to buy it.

The greater number of the natives of Barkal lived in palm-leaf houses among the palms; in summer these abodes were pleasant enough, but at the end of the year their inhabitants suffered greatly from cold. Many houses, or *tukuls*, contained a sort of inner room, into which the family huddled at night and slept, but frequently, for the sake of the handful of fire which was kindled in the outer room, the men and boys squatted there and talked most of the night The furniture of a house consisted of one or two *anḳarîbs*, or native bedsteads, a few water-pots, cooking pots, and a gourd or two, in which liquids were carried. Any store of *dhurra* and dates was kept in coarse earthenware jars, or in holes in the ground. Most people were astir at dawn, when the matrons went down to the river and bathed, and brought back jars full of water for drinking purposes. The men looked after the crops, and, whilst I was at Gebel Barkal, spent most of the day in watching the gathering and the drying of the dates. A great many men seemed to have nothing to do, and a number of them sat the whole day in front of my hut; they came about seven in the morning, and when I returned from the excavations about eleven they were still there; I left them sitting on palm trunks when we resumed work at three, and in the evening I found them again. When the *râkûba* was first built they used to come and sit on the little wall that ran round the court; but there were drawbacks to these assemblies, for they frequently left behind them most unwelcome visitors; so we had a space cleared outside, the ground of which was swept and watered every morning, and we had some palm trunks brought for our visitors to sit on. This arrangement was much appreciated, for the men found they could sit down without soiling their garments. It was

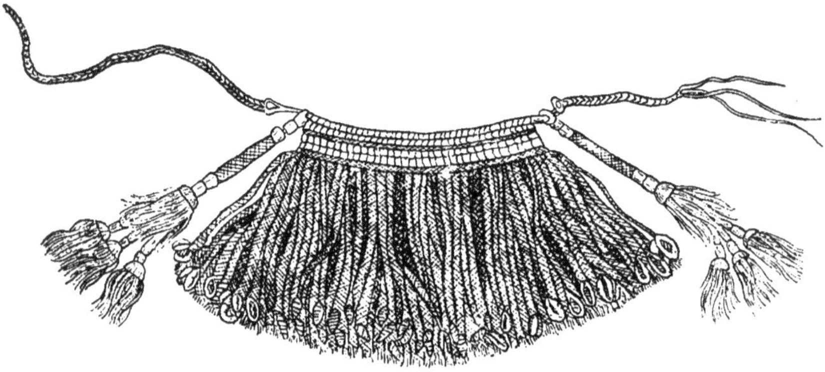

LEATHER *rahât*, OR SÛDÂNÎ GIRL'S DRESS.

interesting to note how their habits were gradually modified by clean surroundings. At first they came and sat down in their ordinary garb, which was full of dust and vermin, and with their feet caked with mud and sand. They saluted no one, and when they felt thirsty they went to my water-pot, and helped themselves without remark. Soon, however, they began to shake their garments before they sat down, and then they took to washing their feet in the water which ran past the hut, and finally they got into the habit of appearing in clean white garments! We were visited by many strange folk, among others by a curious shrivelled old man, who was said to be a *fiḳi*, i.e., religious teacher. One day he brought his sheepskin with him, and throwing it on the ground in the *râkûba* he knelt down and began to pray, among other things for the "Apostle of God, Abd-Allah the Khalifa." This however, I would not stand, and he was promptly thrown out, skin and all, to his great astonishment. On Fridays the shêkh's son brought his Ḳur'ân, and read some Suras, or chapters, for the edification of our visitors, and sometimes other natives brought their own tattered copies and read to themselves.

The dress of the villagers at Barkal was extremely simple. The men wore a pair of cotton trousers and a long blue or black cotton garment, which reached from the neck to the feet, and of course a thick turban made of some white cotton stuff. A few turned the brightly-coloured *kefiyas*, or kerchiefs, made in Syria, into turbans, and those who wore such were accounted men of substance. Certain men, who claimed descent from holy ancestors, wore green turbans, and some possessed red leather shoes, which, however, they oftener carried than wore. The dress of the women was nearly as simple as that of the men, and young children in the daytime ran about naked. Little girls had cords tied round their waists from which were suspended amulets of various kinds; these were often made of pieces of metal cut out of the sides of the rectangular boxes in which kerosene is carried. The Sûdân amulet is usually made of some substance which shines or is brightly coloured, or is in some way very conspicuous; its object is to attract to itself the glance of the "evil eye," whether it be that of an evil spirit or a human being. When a piece of bright metal is not available, a shell or a large white or yellow bead takes its place.

In each house of any importance there appears to be laid up a number of ornaments and articles of women's apparel which are only brought out on special occasions, and the character and variety of these are surprising. During his enforced stay at Ṣanam Abû Dôm, the late Mr. Maud, the artist sent to the Sûdân by the *Graphic*, came over to Barkal village for a couple of days, and sketched and made "studies." He was particularly anxious to make a drawing of a Sûdânî woman in full native dress, and after a good deal of persuasion the shêkh promised that a member of his household should array herself in the family finery, and allow herself to be sketched. After waiting for a very long time in the court of my ḥut, one of the plainest negro women we had ever seen appeared, and stood for her portrait to be drawn. Her hair, which had been specially dressed for the occasion, was done up in little rolls all round her head, and these were stiffened with bits of sheep's wool and mud, and perfumed with castor oil and some very strong European scent, probably recently purchased at the Tanḳâsî market. In her ears were enormous earrings made of silver and studded with red and green stones. She had a massive silver armlet on each arm near the shoulder, some half-dozen large, hollow bracelets on each wrist, and very heavy anklets on her ankles. Her apparel was made of

MOTHER-OF-PEARL AMULET INSCRIBED IN ARABIC WITH THE WORDS "FOLLOWER OF THE MADHÎ."

some pretty silken material, with a large flowered pattern, and she wore a necklace of huge beads, made of coral, amber, quartz, shell, &c., which descended to her waist. There were several very quaint rings on her fingers, but she had no sandals for her feet. She had been brought straight out of the dhurra field to be drawn by Mr. Maud, and the mud was in cakes on her feet and ankles in spite of all her finery. All the ornaments and the dress belonged to the shêkh's wives, and many of them must have been in his family for generations, and have come originally from Constantinople, for the intricate silver work, inlaid with green enamel, was certainly never made in the Sûdân. Mr. Maud worked at his sketch, and in about an hour had made an excellent portrait of the negress and her finery. The natives who crowded round the court were much interested as they saw the picture growing under his skilful fingers, but the woman herself was afraid that his possession of her likeness would put her in his power. When the drawing was ended Mr. Maud gave her two twenty-piastre pieces (about eight shillings), which was double what the shêkh suggested, but she took them unthankfully and walked away saying, "*Galîl, galîl*," i.e. "Little, little."

With the arrival of the Anglo-Egyptian army at Merawi in 1896 a new era of prosperity dawned for the natives there, and one of the strongest evidences of this was the improvement in the quantity and quality of the apparel worn by both men and women, and especially in the number of ornaments worn by the latter. In the wake of the army followed the enterprising Greek, and employment for the native, who was well paid both for his work and for the things which he supplied to the troops, such as dates and *dhurra*. The regular employment of the men brought a steady flow of money into the villages, and before I left Gebel Barkal there was a sufficient demand for cotton goods, ironware, crockery, &c , to make it worth the while of the merchants to re-open on one day each week the market, which had been discontinued during the Dervish rebellion. For some time past the villagers of Merawi, Shibba, and Barkal had been obliged to make their purchases at Tanḳâsî, seven miles down the river, but times were so much changed that the merchants of Tanḳâsî now came up to Barkal, and did a considerable amount of business.

A Sûdân market is an interesting sight, and there is nothing like it anywhere else known to me, except, perhaps, the bridge at Stambûl, and the camel-market at Ṣûkhna, between Tudmur and the Euphrates. The people alone afford a fine subject for study, and the variety of faces and types of countenance seem endless. At Tanḳâsî we saw Gaalîn Arabs from the Western Desert, men partly Arab and partly Negro, Dongolâwîs, men of the Shaiḳiya tribe, dwellers in the deserts to the west of the Fourth Cataract, full-blooded Negroes, a few Abyssinians, and many other kinds of men too numerous to mention. The apparel of nearly every man showed some slight

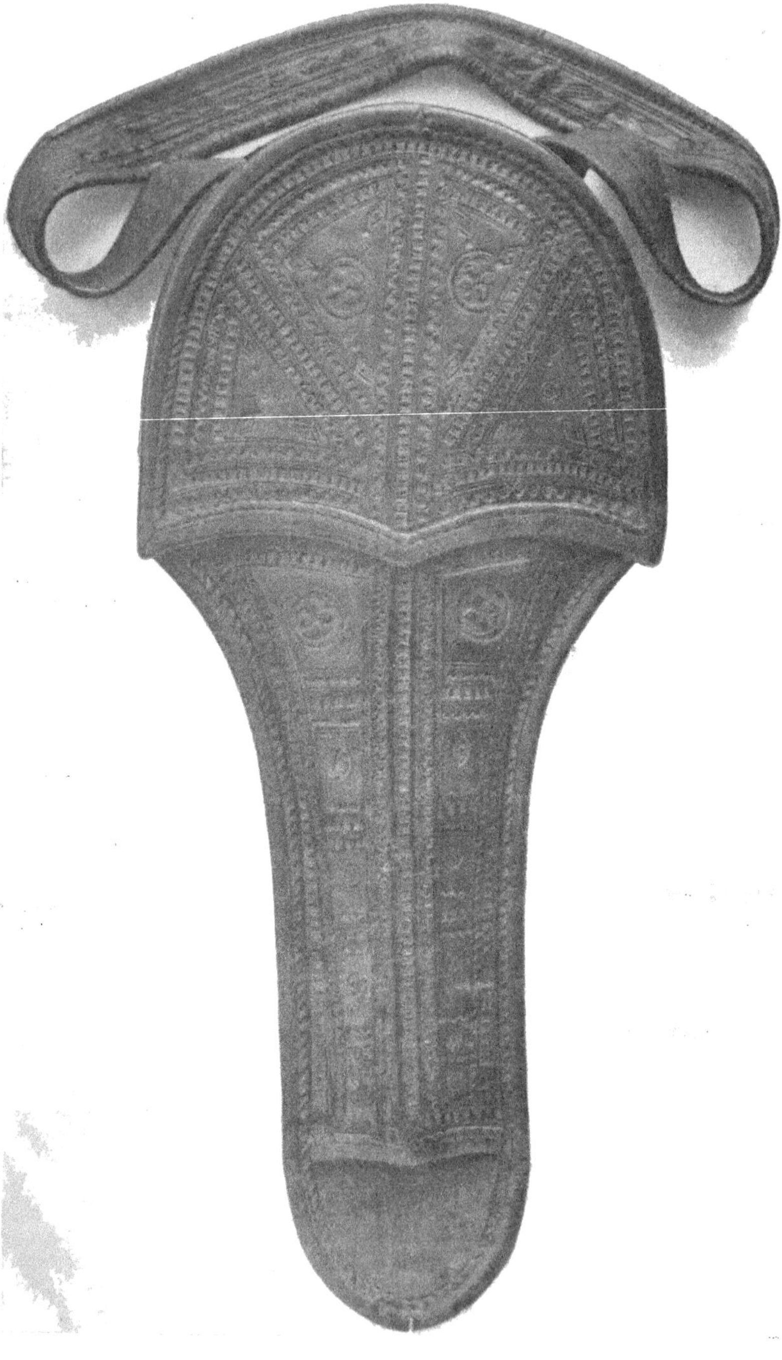

SUDANI STAMPED LEATHER WORK.

variation, and an expert like Slatin Pâshâ could tell at a glance from what part of the country each man hailed, and the tribe to which he belonged. It was interesting to note that many Arabs had the small regular features and short beards which one sees in Arabia, and even in the deserts of Southern Mesopotamia, and it is difficult not to think that the original[1] home of the ancestors of such Arabs must have been situated beyond the Red Sea, in Southern Arabia. In one portion of the *sûk*, or market, camels and donkeys were offered for sale, and close by were some cattle, near these were both men and women who sold vegetables, *mulukhîya*, *bâmia*, &c. Numbers of native women offered the products of their villages, mats, rough earthenware jars and other vessels, &c., and skins of all sorts sold readily. Sellers of leather sandals, short daggers in leather cases, with straps for attaching them to the arms, beads, stamped leather cases containing pieces of paper with verses from the Kur'ân written on them, and all articles of cutlery, did a roaring trade, and brightly coloured stuffs of all sorts and kinds were bought by the women readily. Sugar was sold in small canes weighing about three pounds each, salt both crushed and in bars, alum, and anything in the nature of condiments, were in great demand.

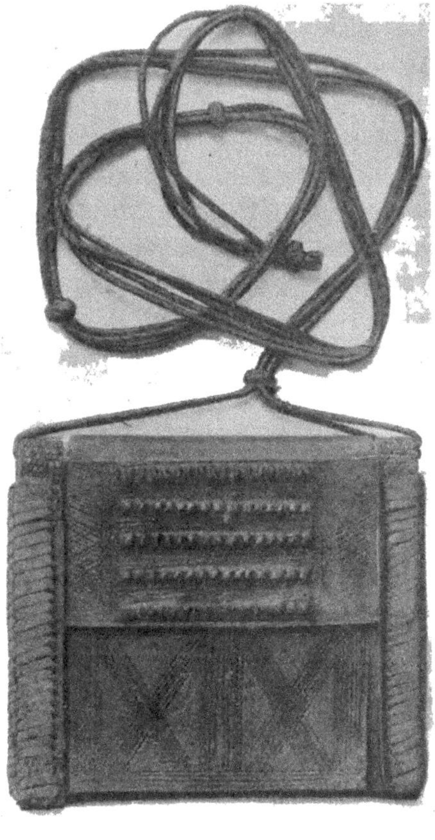

LEATHER AMULET CASE, WITH LEATHER SUSPENDING CORD.

Modern Omdurmân work.

In the centre of the market the merchants seated themselves in two rows, forming a kind of street, and before each of them was a series of small receptacles filled with the seeds and berries which are used as drugs and medicines and aphrodisiacs by the Sûdânî folk. Nearly every one had coarse native soap for sale, and some had little boxes containing three or six or a dozen small cakes of scented soap of Western manufacture. Cheap scents, small round mirrors made in Germany, boxes of pins and needles, and small articles for personal use, were in great demand. Most of the business was done by barter, especially in the case of small dealings, but a large number of Maria Theresa dollars changed hands. There was very little change available, for at that time hardly any small pieces of money were to be found in the Sûdân; so far as possible every transaction was settled in whole dollars. The want of pieces of money of the value of one, two, five, and ten piastres caused great inconvenience, especially when men's wages had to be paid, and articles of food, such as milk, eggs, vegetables, &c., bought daily. Many merchants possessed scales, but the weights were usually pebbles or pieces of stone, and it is certain that numbers of them cheated their customers. Water was hawked round by men who carried it in skins, and dispensed it to the thirsty in gourds. The busiest time in the market was between the hours of 11 a.m. and 2 p.m., when the noise and shouting were deafening, and the jostling and pushing, the heat and glare, and the dust and confusion rendered a visit to a Sûdân market, held at a place like the plain of Tanḳâsî, a thing never to be forgotten.

The market at Barkal was quite as interesting as that of Tanḳâsî, and not so fatiguing to visit, for it was held in the afternoon and only lasted two hours or so; it began about 2 p.m., and so soon as the shadows of the hills began to touch the plain the temporary booths were pulled down, and the villagers returned to their homes. Trade was brisk while it lasted, and more money changed hands for clothes than for food. One afternoon a man appeared there who called himself a "merchant" (*tuggâr*), and he dealt in beads, metal ornaments, and scents; he spoke French and Arabic, and was, apparently, a Syrian, and said he had been to school in Beyrût. After a little talk he said that he had come to the villages on that side of the river to see if he could buy up from the native women any old gold ornaments, and he wished to be introduced to Shêkh Muḥammad. His method was to persuade the women to exchange their old gold bangles, which were usually made of soft pure gold, for modern nine-carat bangles and a few strings of pretty glass beads made in Austria, making of course a handsome profit on each transaction. He hoped that he would be as successful in the Sûdân as he had been in Egypt, but the Dervishes had stripped the country so bare that he could do little more than sell his beads.

As the cold weather came on at Barkal, cases of chill and fever increased in the village, and the natives came to me daily for medicines. They knew that the soldiers across the river fell ill and were cured by the English *hakîm* (doctor), and they assumed, naturally perhaps, seeing that the British officers sometimes came over to look at the excavations, that I could obtain for them the medicines of the effects of which they had heard such fantastic stories. Natives all over the East assume that every traveller has a knowledge of medicines, and that he carries with him the things which will enable him to destroy the effects produced by the peculiar class of evil spirits which, they believe, attack the European. It is beyond them to understand that a knowledge of the effects of drugs and medicines has only been acquired by Europeans after long study and careful experiment, and they are firmly convinced that it was obtained in the first instance by magical means, and that the healing skill of the doctor is only a form of what mediaeval writers called "white magic." Men, and women also, would come and tell me gravely that early in the morning a "devil" had attacked them and hit them inside, but inquiry would show that they had been sleeping partly in and partly outside their huts, with insufficient covering, and that the cold about 3 a.m. had given them a chill. Others would come having eaten a large quantity of new dates, presumably unripe, and the pains of indigestion which followed were attributed not to the fermentation of the date juices, but to "spirits" of a malignant character.

This is not to be wondered at when we remember that many Sûdânî peoples believe that the world about them is filled with spirits, which live in the air, and water, and mountains, and have the power of taking the form of the birds, animals, reptiles, &c., that live in them. Then there are numbers of spirits which live among the trees and in thickets, and enter into men, women, and children by force, and make them to become workers of their will, which is generally evil. Lonely deserts and mountains, to say nothing of tracts of land where there are large collections of trees, are fearsome places on moonless nights to the natives, and in some cases men from the West have been affected by the weird silence and awesomeness of such. Even experienced travellers like Stanley have felt the terrifying effects of the darkness and silence of the night among trees and in deserts, and have to some degree understood the feeling of the native who declares that the very air is filled with spirits. And it must not be forgotten that some of the admiration and respect which the natives felt for British officers in the Sûdân was, and still is, due to the fearlessness with which they move and go about on the darkest night.

The villagers of Barkal were very fond of medicines, and the more unpleasant they were to the taste, and the swifter and more drastic they were in operation, the more they respected them. Native medicines were compounded of nasty ingredients, e.g., portions of the bodies of snakes, lizards, and scorpions, excrementa of men and animals, &c.; salt and oil were also often given by native medicine-men. These they swallowed without a murmur, and, strange to say, seemed to be better for them; but whether it was faith in the medicine or belief in the man which effected the cure I could never decide. Theoretically Muḥammadans believe that whatever happens to them, for good or ill, is the result of the decrees which are inscribed by God each year on the 15th day of the month Sha'bân,[1] on the "Preserved Tablet," which is kept in heaven. Speaking generally, it is held to be a wicked act to dispute such decrees, which concern the destinies of men in the most minute particulars, and more than twelve and a half centuries of Muḥammadan history testify to the implicit obedience which the Arabs have rendered to the Divine will. But in practice many believe that God can be induced by earnest prayer to erase from this Tablet an unfavourable decree, and to insert a more favour-

[1] The eighth month of the Muḥammadan year.

able one in its place. Whether the Sûdânî folk ever think this matter out it is hard to say, but their belief in medicines is unbounded.

It was impossible to send every sufferer over to the camp for treatment, for the doctors were overworked, and medicines and bottles were by no means plentiful. I found the stock of tabloids with which my friend, Mr. Henry Wellcome, of the firm of Burroughs and Wellcome, had furnished me most useful, for I was able to supply the natives with medicine for weeks. They did away with the necessity for weighing and measuring drugs, and it was a comfort to feel that the old medicine case, with its breakages and leakages, was a thing of the past. Fortunately the complaints commonest in the villages were the result of injudicious food and of chills, and as I had a good store of simple medicines and quinine many patients were relieved. Some of the older men applied for "cognac," and my reputation as a medicine-man suffered when I said I had none; one applicant went so far as to declare that I was no Englishman, as I had no boxes of *maya ḳawwî*, or "strong waters," with me. We discussed this matter one evening over the fire, and the greybeards said that Muḥammad the Prophet permitted his people to drink water in which dates had been soaked, and the juice of the grapes, but the obvious answer to that was that the Prophet himself declared that there was both sin and advantage in wine, as in games of chance, but that the sin was greater than the advantage. One of the party then observed that I must be a *fiḳi*, or religious teacher, which was strange; for it seemed that, although some were ready to deny me my nationality because I had no cognac, others considered me sufficiently good to be a religious teacher! A little learning went a long way in Barkal.

Another class of troublesome "patients" were the older men who begged for *ḥashîsh* (i.e., *cannabis Indica*, or Indian hemp), and the juices of cucumber seeds and poppies, opium, &c. When obtainable these drugs are used as intoxicants, and when mixed with honey or raisins, and swallowed, after the recital of certain prayers, they are said to form powerful aphrodisiacs, and both men and women in the East have for many centuries taken them with the view of obtaining large families. In the days when the slave trade flourished, opium and *hashîsh* were imported openly into the Sûdân, both from Egypt and Sawâkin, but when Great Britain took the management of the Nile Valley into her hands the importation of the latter drug was prohibited, and it could only be obtained by smuggling. In spite of the prohibition, however, quantities of *hashîsh* found its way into the country, and the shifts and devices invented by the natives to get it were worthy of a better cause. It is said that the sailors and labourers at the ports of Egypt used to walk ashore in sandals, the soles of which were stuffed with the leaves of Indian hemp. Little by little, however, the importation of the drug diminished, and Lord Cromer tells us ("Egypt," No. 1, 1904, p. 42) that the price of *hashîsh* in Egypt that year was higher than it had ever been before. Two grains were placed in a pipe, which was passed round among eight men until it was empty. The value of two grains was five farthings, and the eight men paid for it in all ten farthings, i.e., the retail profit on the drug was one hundred per cent. In the Sûdân, however, it was sought after chiefly as an aphrodisiac, for the desire there for offspring is very strong. Amulets and spells of every kind were employed by the natives for obtaining children, and an employé of the Egyptian Government at Manṣûra told me that Sûdânî women eat the bodies of bright green beetles after they have been fried in oil, believing that they will make them prolific. This is an interesting fact, for it shows that the ideas which the ancient Egyptians held about the beetle being the symbol of generative and creative power, and the type of fertility, have survived in the Sûdân. The head and wings of a beetle boiled in snake fat formed a potent charm against the powers of evil, according to old Egyptian belief, and the modern Egyptian boils the insect in sheep fat and eats it, with the object of curing internal disorders.

In some cases at Barkal the belief in the immutability of a Divine decree was ineradicable, as the following instances will show. One night Shêkh Muḥammad came and asked for some medicine for a specific purpose, saying that his "house," i.e., some woman member of it, was ill. He took the tabloids and went away, and next day told me that they had had the desired effect. A few days later he asked for medicine of a different kind, and as I had none, I promised to get the help of the military doctor when I went to the camp. He was disappointed at the answer, and the following morning asked me to come and see his "house," and tell her what to do. When I entered his courtyard, I found it was the shêkh's chief wife who was ill, and that she was suffering much from one of her feet. It seemed that one day when she was going to the river she struck her foot against a branch of prickly acacia which was lying on the ground, and cut her big toe. The wound had festered and spread, and she had not been able to walk for two or three weeks. She was lying on an *anḳarîb*, covered up with a mass of dirty clothes which her women had heaped on her, and only with the greatest difficulty could she be persuaded to let her foot be looked at. When at length the foot was uncovered it became clear that hers was no case for any but a professional man, and after suggesting that the foot should be bathed with warm water and wrapped up in lint, of which, thanks to Mr. Wellcome, I had a supply, I went over and told General Rundle. With characteristic kindness he spoke to one of the military doctors, who promised to dress the wound if the woman were brought over, and the next day Major Drage sent over a boat, with a staging in it to bring her to the camp. The shêkh was overjoyed, but when we went to his house to carry the woman to the boat, we found that she had refused to have anything to do with warm water or lint, and she declined absolutely to let herself be carried to the boat, for she declared that she was going to die, and said she preferred to die where she was. To every entreaty on the part of the shêkh she replied, "I have never been to the other "side of the river, and I will never go there. I am afraid of the "boat, and the English doctor will work magic on me. If I die, "it is the business of God, and if I live, it is the business of God; "but I will not leave this house. If the Englishman in the "village will give me the drink of medicine, let him do it, but I "will not go over the river." So the boat returned without her. The disease (gangrene?) spread with wonderful rapidity, and on the fourth day she died soon after daybreak.

The funeral took place the same day, and was very simple. The body was wrapped in some new whitish yellow cotton stuff, the ankles were tied together, and the hands folded over the breast. When the body had been laid on a stretcher with a light wooden cover above it, over which a coloured cloth was thrown, two men came, and, lifting up the bier, carried it away feet foremost for burial. The women of the house followed, uttering the familiar *lulu* cry, and these were joined by a number of friends and relations of the deceased, some of whom marched before and some behind the bier. The men began to sing verses from the Ḳur'ân, among them being the Shahâda, or "Testimony,"[1] and the Fatha,[2] or opening Sura (chapter). When the procession reached the hill to the west of the village the coloured cloth and wooden cover were removed from the stretcher, and the body was lifted into a shallow trench dug in the sandy soil, the sides and bottom of which were lined with rough flat stones. The body was laid with its face towards Mekka, and when it was being covered up with sand it was noticeable that cavities were left at the head and feet.

Pious Muḥammadans believe that the angels Munkar and Nakir come to the grave on the night after the burial of the body and question the soul of the deceased, which awaits them there, as to its belief in God, and His Prophet Muḥammad, and concerning its views about the religion of Al-Islâm, and the Ḳur'ân, and the Ka'aba[3] at Mekka, and the Unity of God. If the answers of the soul convince the two angels of its orthodoxy, they say, "Sleep, "O servant of God, in the protection of God," and they allow the body to rest in peace, and to breathe the air of Paradise. If, on

[1] It runs, "There is no god but God, Muḥammad is the Apostle of God, may "God bless and preserve him."

[2] It runs, "Praise be to God, the Lord of all creatures; the most merciful, the "King of the day of judgment. Thee do we worship, and of Thee do we beg "assistance. Direct us in the right way, in the way of those to whom Thou hast "been gracious; not of those against whom Thou art incensed, nor of those "who go astray." (Sale's translation.)

[3] The Ka'aba is a rectangular building at Mekka, 24 cubits long, 23 cubits wide, and 27 cubits high; it has a door on the east side. In it is the famous BLACK STONE, which is set in silver, and is placed in the south-east corner about 2⅓ cubits above the ground. This stone is said to have come from Paradise with Adam, and to have been given by Gabriel to Abraham when he built the original Ka'aba; originally its colour was white. The Muḥammadans always turn when praying towards the Ka'aba. See Sale's "Preliminary Discourse," p. 91, and Masudi, "Prairies d'Or," iv. 125-129.

the other hand, they are not satisfied with the soul's answers, they beat it with bars of iron. On this the soul utters piercing cries which can be heard from one end of heaven to the other, but none comes to its assistance. Men, however, and the beings called *Ginn* cannot hear these cries. When the beating is over Munkar and Nakir press down the earth on the body of the deceased, and they hand it over to ninety-nine monsters, each of which has seven heads, and they bite it and gnaw it until it is consumed.

When the body was covered with sand the men who were present laid several flat stones on the grave, and then began to heap pebbles on them, taking care to push many into the grave itself. Every traveller in the Sûdân has seen numbers of graves covered with long heaps of pebbles, which have always seemed to me to be the equivalent to the poor Sûdânî folk of the stone and mud buildings which stand above the graves of the rich. Of old the Nubian kings built themselves large pyramids, the less important members of their families and a few high officials lay under small pyramids, and the poorer folk under heaps of stones. The barrows which are seen in many places in the desert, some miles from the river, are formed of long low heaps of stones, and bear the same relation to the pyramids as the long low heaps of pebbles laid on modern Sûdânî graves bear to the barrows.[1] The piles of stones, whether hewn and built into pyramids, or unhewn and loosely piled over the body, were no doubt at a primitive period intended to protect the dead from prowling hyenas, wolves, and jackals, but gradually they came to be regarded as honourable memorials of the dead, and, according to their size, represented the rank and dignity of those buried beneath them.

[1] On this point compare Burckhardt (*Travels*, p. 269): "After a hearty meal, we "recommenced our reading. One of the Shikhs produced a basket full of white "pebbles, over which several prayers were read. These pebbles were destined "to be strewed over the tombs of the deceased in the manner which I had often "observed upon tombs freshly made. Upon my inquiries concerning this "custom, which I confessed to have never before seen practised in any Moham-"medan country, the Fakyr answered that it was a mere meritorious action, "that there was no absolute necessity for it, but that it was thought that the "soul of the deceased, when hereafter visiting the tomb, might be glad to find "these pebbles in order to use them as beads in addressing its prayers to the "Creator."

Now as regards the pebbles on modern graves, a native of Barkal told me that many Sûdânî folk nowadays consider them to take the place of the thousand beads of the rosary, the telling of which plays such an important part among the religious rites which are performed in the houses of well-to-do folk in Cairo and other large Muḥammadan cities. According to Lane,[1] after a funeral a number of religious men go to the house of the deceased, one of them carrying a string of 1,000 beads, each as large as a pigeon's egg. When they are seated three Suras of the Ḳur'ân are recited, and a blessing on the Prophet and his companions is said three times. The words, "There is no god but God," are then said three thousand times, and after every three repetitions the man who holds the rosary passes one bead from one hand to the other. This done, all drink coffee, and two texts are repeated one hundred times, and a third text fifty times; the last three verses of Sura xxxvii. are said, and another short extract from the Ḳur'ân is recited. Then one of the men asks his companions, "Have ye transferred [the merit of] what ye "have recited to the soul of So-and-so?" and they reply, "We "have transferred it," adding, "And peace be on the Apostle." The performance of a ceremony of this kind in the Sûdân was out of the question, for the expense incurred by it would have been prohibitive. The shêkh, having seen the grave covered over, gave gifts to the poor, who were there waiting to receive them, and then men and women went to their homes. The burial of a woman in the Sûdân is usually quickly performed, but those who believe in the words of the Prophet have no doubt that good women will have their portion in that part of heaven which he declared would be specially set apart for them. There, he said, old and elderly women would become maidens again, who would be free from all blemishes, and would be able to compete successfully for the affections of beatified men with the maidens of Paradise, who are created of pure musk, and live in large pearls, and have very large eyes, the black pupils of which stand out in striking contrast to the whites round them.[2]

[1] "Modern Egyptians," vol. ii., p. 270.

[2] The Arabic name for such a being is *ḥûriah* from which is derived "*houri*," the "white-eyed." In the Ḳur'ân (Sura lvi., verse 22) we have *ḥur 'în*.

The superstition which existed in the minds of the people of Barkal, of which mention has already been made, showed itself in many ways, and sometimes in a most inconvenient manner. The smallest incident which happened out of the usual course, in connection with the excavations that were being made, was sufficient to make them declare that the "Satans" were abroad, and were bent on doing mischief to the workmen, because they were intruding on the privacy of the spirits of the "shêkhs" who had built the pyramids. Shêkh Muhammad told me that so long as he could remember, no villager would go up the hill to the pyramids by night, and that even by day the men who were working in the fields near the pyramids would keep as far away from them as possible. The villagers had seen the figures of the kings and gods which were sculptured on the sides of the rock-hewn chambers of the temples at Barkal, and their fathers had told them that similar figures had existed on the walls of the chapels which had stood before the pyramids. These simple folk believed that each sculptured figure was the abode of some spirit, whether of a god, or a devil, or a human being, and that at night such spirits left the stones, and came out and talked with each other, and wandered about and looked at the places familiar to them. They thought, moreover, that the only way to rid themselves of the attentions of such spirits was to smash the stones in which they dwelt by day, and it is probable that this belief is partly responsible for the wholesale destruction of chapels which went on during the last century.

This belief is not confined to the Sûdân, and I met with it in a very unpleasant form near Môṣul (Nineveh) in Northern Mesopotamia. Whilst excavating there for the Trustees of the British Museum in 1888 and 1889, I went to Baibûkh, a few miles from Nineveh, to examine the site of the great palace of Sargon, king of Assyria (B.C. 721-705). One door of the palace was still standing, and on one side of it there still remained one of the colossal bulls that guarded the entrance. It was a grand object, and in a good state of preservation, and was quite as fine as either of the bulls which the late Sir Henry Rawlinson obtained for the British Museum. On my return to England I tried to get the archaeological authorities at Constantinople to arrange for its transport to Europe, and I was asked to find out if it could be sawn up by the natives, and removed piecemeal, as was the case with the Sargon colossi in the British Museum. When I returned to Môṣul the following year I again went to the site of Sargon's palace, where I found a heap of fragments of limestone in the place where the colossus had stood. Inquiries elicited the information that the last remaining colossus had been smashed in pieces by two men from a neighbouring village, and that its destruction had only recently been effected. It seemed that one night one of the two men had a dream, in which a divine messenger appeared to him and told him to go at once and smash in pieces the "idol." When he awoke he rose up, called his son, and, each taking a hammer, they set out, and in a very few hours the colossus was in fragments. When I reported the matter to the Wâli of Môṣul, he was most sympathetic so far as I personally was concerned, but he refused to punish the two men, or to make any inquiry into the matter, and he remarked that the colossi, which he called *khaiwânât*, or "animals," when burned made the very finest lime for plastering houses! At Barkal, as at Môṣul, religion and practical utility went hand in hand, and by wrecking a pyramid chapel the natives freed themselves from spirits and obtained stones for building purposes at the same time.

I asked Shêkh Muḥammad why, since his people were so much afraid of the spirits of his "dead fathers," as he called the old Nubian kings, the villagers dared to carry off the stones from the pyramids.[1] He admitted that they had formerly done so, but added that nothing had been removed in recent years, for the Dervishes told them that the pyramids were the tombs of the Mahdi's ancestors, and that there was laid up in them great treasure, which was guarded by legions of ever-watchful spirits. The latter part of this statement was believed implicitly, for most

[1] Throughout the Sûdân the common word for pyramids is *ṭarâbîl*, in the singular it is assumed to be *ṭarbûl*, but I have never heard it used by the natives. It is probably a word of Sûdânî origin, and its exact meaning seems to be unknown; it may have some connection with the root *ṭarābi* ጠረበ፡ and, if so, the pyramids are called *ṭarâbîl* because they are built of hewn stones.

natives thought that the pyramids were full of gold, and when as the weeks went on treasure was not forthcoming, they were much disappointed. They were willing enough to work during the day, but so soon as the sun began to cast shadows on the plain they were eager to get back to their villages. They began to work about seven in the morning, and went on till about 5 p.m., with a break of three hours in the middle of the day during the hot weather; in the cold weather they started an hour later, and the break in the middle of the day was reduced to two hours. Sometimes it was necessary when moving large stones to go on working till sunset, but the dread of walking two miles or so to their homes in the short Sûdânî twilight made them work in a half-hearted manner, and the money which they were paid for overtime was practically wasted. One evening the men were kept at work half an hour or so after sunset, by a promise of *bakshîsh*, but the wives of several of them came in a body and carried off their lords to the village; they strongly disapproved of their husbands being overworked, and said so in characteristic Sûdânî fashion. Several men left the diggings, some saying that they heard the Satans talking at the bottom of the shaft, and that the diggings were "Satanic work," and others saying that it was wicked to dig up the works of idolaters, which, on account of the iniquity of their makers, God had buried so deeply in the ground.

For the needs of the men who were working at the pyramids and were in number from twenty-five to forty, two donkeys were kept occupied all day in fetching water in skins from the river, about three miles distant. As the skins arrived they were hung up on pegs driven between the stone courses of a pyramid, on the shady side, and it was not long before the animals of the desert found that water was to be had nearer than the river. The wolves and the jackals came each evening when there was no moon to lick the outsides of the skins, and to get as much drink as they could, and the imaginations of some men turned these thirsty animals into devils, and made them more than ever afraid to stay on the hill after sunset. One morning we found a thick-bodied snake of a grayish blue colour, about eight feet long, lying on the damp sand under the water-skins, and the men killed it at once, because, they said, it contained a devil, and we were bound to have bad luck or ill-success. The creature was quite harmless, and had only crept to the water-skins for coolness. A few days later our water-skins were besieged by large numbers of gaunt Sûdânî bees, the largest I had ever seen; they settled on the dripping skins for hours at a time, and only disappeared in the cool of the late afternoon. The men regarded the bees with favour, for they believed them to be heralds of good luck, and they felt sure we were going to find some of the treasure laid up in the pyramid by the Mahdi's ancestors! In their approval of the bee the men followed the example of the Prophet, who called one of the Suras of the Ḳur'ân the "Bee," and said that the "variegated liquor," i.e., honey, was a "medicine for men." On one occasion the Prophet told a man to give honey to his brother, who was suffering from colic; the man did so, and reported afterwards that his brother was no better for the honey. On this the Prophet replied, "Go, and give him more honey, for God speaketh truth, and thy brother's belly telleth lies." According to the commentator Al-Bêdâwî the second dose of honey cured the sick man. In ancient Egypt honey was an ingredient in almost every prescription, and to this day it is a favourite medicine all over the Muḥammadan East.

Every one who knows the average Sûdânî man knows that he is not fond of work, and that there is nothing which he hates so much as having to do the same kind of work every day, and at the same time of the day. The men who worked on the excavations were very poor, but though they prized highly the regular wages of five piastres (one shilling) per day, with occasional overtime, very few of them could resist their unconquerable desire for two or three days' "loafing" each week. I am convinced that nothing but the Sirdar's orders to Shêkh Muḥammad enabled us to get through the amount of work we did, and but for the friendly visits of General Rundle and Slatin Pâshâ, and the good-natured pressure which they put on the men, that work would have occupied as many months as it did weeks. The shêkh was in wholesome awe of the Sirdar, who, he said, was "a king, and greater than a king," and he did his best. But it must be admitted that at times the work was hard, for the heat was great and the iron tools were often so hot that they could hardly be handled. The second shaft, i.e., the shaft under the pyramid, was dug out by the light of candles, and its atmosphere was stifling. The muscular Egyptian soldiers would have thought nothing of the toil, but the native of the Sûdân is not muscular, and he likes to be able to work or lie down and sleep, as the humour takes him.

On the whole I found the villagers of Barkal and Shibba a kindly folk, and ready to do anything for the British except work hard. They admired and respected the British officers, of whose ways they had had about a year's experience when I arrived at Merawi, for they knew that from them they would obtain consideration and justice. Many things puzzled them in connection with the soldiers, and they were indignant because money was not spent so freely by them as by the Gordon Relief Expedition in 1884-5. They could not understand why the Sirdar wanted to open the pyramids, or why I went there unless it was to dig up buried treasure. As time went on, however, they learned to trust me, and little by little they brought me many private difficulties to settle. One wanted the help of Colonel Wingate, another wanted a petition about his land given to the General through Slatin Pâshâ, another wanted the *tupgî* (i.e., gunner), Colonel Long, asked to obtain a rifle or revolver for him, another wanted to have sent back to him a wife who had run away with a soldier and was living on the other side of the river, another wanted a slave to be flogged, and so on. They regarded the occupation of digging at the pyramids as a means to an end, and that end was usually the settlement of some long-standing dispute with a neighbour about land, or a proprietorship of slaves. To interfere in matters of this kind was a thing I naturally avoided, but there were several smaller disputes about which I was consulted, and it was surprising to see how readily my decisions were accepted. The people of Barkal were mixtures of shrewdness, cunning, and childish simplicity, but when once they were convinced that their referee had no personal interest in the matter before him, they were usually amenable to common sense.

Owing to some remarks made by one of the newspaper correspondents as to the thieving propensities of the natives of Merawi, it has been thought that these men were greater thieves than other Sûdânî folk, but I did not find this to be the case. During the whole time I was at Barkal I lost nothing which my *sais* did not steal, and he was not a native of that part of the Sûdân! The Sûdânî folk are greedy for money, grasping, and quite insatiable as regards presents or *bakshîsh*, but those are qualities not confined to the Sûdân! It is impossible for any one who has lived in the country to preserve any illusions he may have once had about their habits and character, but

KASSINGAR HILL.

too much must not be expected, even under British rule, from people who have been ill-ruled and ill-used for thousands of years, in a land where slavery in one form or another has been a permanent and universal institution, and where wrong and oppression have dogged the lives of all but a few for untold generations.

But for the pyramids and remains of temples at Barkal the neighbourhood of Merawi was an uninteresting place, and the visitor was driven to explore the country for a few miles up and down the river. In 1897, in comparison with the camp at Ṣanam Abû Dôm, the village of Kassingar, about twelve miles up stream from Merawi, was a place full of life and interest, for it was the starting point of the camel transport to Abû Ḥamed. In September and October the banks of the river were piled high with stores of all kinds, and the arrival and departure of camels seemed to be incessant. These curious and perverse creatures were everywhere, and they always appeared to be eating. They would scramble along the banks until they came to a thorny shrub or tree, and then tear off its branches one by one and eat them, with their faces wearing that peculiarly idiotic expression which the camel puts on when he is contented. They delighted

THE TUKUL OR PALM-LEAF HUT OF LIEUT. FITZ-CLARENCE AT KASSINGAR.

in the coarse, dry fabric of the dôm palm, and would break off and chew with relish the stumps of withered shrubs and plants, and they thrive on substances which would, I believe, have killed any other animal. The Commandant at Kassingar was Colonel F. W. Kitchener, the Sirdar's brother, and from him and Captain F. I. Maxse I received much kindness. The latter took me through the camel lines and gave me a great deal of information about the working of the camel transport, and about the arrangements which were made for the care and treatment of sick camels. Even a civilian could see that every detail of the organization was thought out, and every eventuality provided for, and yet that the strictest economy prevailed in everything. Among other things, Captain Maxse showed me the *tukul* of Lieutenant

Fitz-Clarence, who was killed, with Major Sidney, at the taking of Abû Ḥamed; it was unoccupied and empty. A very good view of the river at the foot of the Fourth Cataract can be obtained from Kassingar Hill, and, looking towards Merawi, Mount Barkal forms a striking feature of the landscape. . .

An afternoon may profitably be spent in visiting the little village of Dûwêm, which is about three miles from Merawi. It is famous throughout the Sûdân as the dwelling-place of one Abd ar-Rakhmân, in whose honour a large *kubba* known as the "White *Ḳubba*" has been built. It is said to be the only white *ḳubba* in the Sûdân. It contains a mosque and school which is famous for teaching the Ḳur'ân. Other places well worthy of note are the small islands in the river, which in the summer time are full of birds of many colours. Many hours may be spent in watching their flight, and to see them passing from tree to tree, with their brightly coloured feathers flashing in the sunlight, is a very pretty sight. One species with bright green wings splashed with scarlet was greatly admired, and the tameness of all the birds in the neighbourhood was remarkable. They would come close to the visitor, and pick up crumbs, and perch on the edge of a tray of water and drink without any shyness. It is said that most of them come in from the Bayûda Desert in the summer and return there in the winter. As the native is not cruel to the birds, and the sporting tourist does not readily find his way to Merawi, we may hope that they will not be exterminated for some years.

Other places of antiquarian interest are the Pyramids of Nûri, which have been described elsewhere (see pp. 115-122), and the ruins of the Christian monastery in the Wâdî Ghazâl. Between the villages of Belal and Nûri is the "station" of the religious man, Ghûzêr Alî, whereto large numbers of the inhabitants resort in order to obtain a blessing. These villages are on the west bank of the Nile, as was Napata, and there is little room for doubt that if the site occupied by the Sirdar's camp in 1897 were carefully excavated, a number of important facts bearing on the extent of the ancient city of Napata would be ascertained. It is unlikely that antiquities of any great importance would be discovered, or that any great light would be thrown on Nubian history before the eighth century B.C., but the complete excavation of the site is a work which should be undertaken, for the size and number of the Pyramids of Nûri prove that the kings who built them were mighty men in their day, and that their capital was no mean city.

APPENDIX TO CHAPTER V.

A DONGOLAH TALE.

A TRAVELLER in the Sûdân who has been fortunate enough to be treated as an honoured guest in the house of a native of position will often see his host and his friends gather round a fire in the evening to listen to a *râwî*, or teller of stories, narrate a tale of love or war. Such a tale is usually based upon some incident related in the "Thousand Nights and a Night," to which are added such modifications as the story-teller pleases, and a number of allusions of a topical character, which are intended to refer to the greatness and bravery of the host, and his successes in love, the chase, and war. Sometimes the story refers to events in the history of the country, but in this case the facts are usually swamped by fiction, and the result is unsatisfactory to the European listener unless his object is merely to learn Arabic. The stories which deal with love adventures are for the most part unprintable in an English book, a fact much to be regretted, for in these the powers of native invention are at their best. It is, however, necessary in a work dealing with the Sûdân to give some idea of the class of fiction with which, in comparatively recent years, the Sûdâni folk have amused themselves, and as an example of it, we quote the story of the beautiful maiden Amnah, which Hoskins [1] heard related by a little girl of the ‘Abâbda tribe of Arabs, aged thirteen. It runs thus :—

Amnah was the most lovely of the daughters of the Nile : fair as the sand of the desert, the gazelle was not more elegant in form, or more graceful in its movements. Her bust was beautiful, and her skin soft and pliant to the touch. Her face was as the light of day ; her eyes were bright as the stars ; her teeth whiter than the polished ivory ; and a lovely and ever-constant smile illumined her countenance. Nature had done her utmost ; Fortune equalled her rival in loading her with its favours. Her

[1] See his "Travels in Ethiopia," p. 194.

necklaces were numerous, and of the finest gold; and great was the weight of gold on her wrists and ankles. Her hair was beautifully plaited, and decorated with the largest and rarest pearls, and broad plates of gold [were] above her forehead; and two large and most precious ornaments set with diamonds hung gracefully from her ears. Her *râhat*[1] possessed every variety of colour; the skin of the hippopotamus was never cut so fine; it was ornamented with the most curious shells and pieces of gold and silver attached coquettishly in the most becoming manner; and the border of the *rat* around her waist consisted of coral and pearls. From her waist to her knees, only, this graceful ornament screened her form; and there was not one of the youths of the village and of the neighbourhood, who had ever seen Amnah, who did not sigh and regret bitterly his being unworthy that her *rahât* should be broken for him. "The houris of the paradise of "the Prophet cannot," said they, "be more enchanting, endowed "with such ravishing beauty, or such extraordinary talents."

She was, at the same time, the gayest of the gay, and also acquainted with all the learning of her tribe. Her father and other travellers had related to her the history and customs of their countries, and from them she had learnt the traditions and wars of her native land. Every passage of the Koran was familiar to her; and it was whispered she had devoted herself secretly to the study of astrology, and the more hidden sciences of the Arabians. At midnight she was often seen alone, gazing at the heavens; and for this reason the homage she received for her beauty and understanding was blended with a certain feeling almost approaching to fear. Too beautiful, pure, and learned to be of this world, she was considered by the ignorant peasants more as an angel of light than a frail inhabitant of earth

At the death of her father, after she had accompanied his remains to the grave, and for some time had lamented his loss, Amnah, weary of the constraint to which her sex subjected her, and anxious to visit those scenes which she had so often heard described, left her native village. The morning after her departure, at the entrance of a small town, she observed an old man covered with vermin. "My father," said she, "let me free you from those "tormentors"; and she began killing the animals, until suddenly the man fell dead at her feat. "It is the will of God!" she exclaimed, and immediately dressed herself in his clothes, and pursued her journey. Thus disguised, and safe by the power of

[1] The *rahât* is a covering worn by unmarried girls, and is made of thin thongs of hippopotamus hide. It reaches from the waist almost to the knee, and is coquetishly ornamented with masses of silver, and a variety of shells and beads It is considered sufficiently modest in this country, where no consequence is attached to the exposure of the body and limbs: otherwise, so far as it extends, it forms an elegant and impenetrable screen. The *rahât* is torn to pieces by the bridegroom before marriage. For a drawing of the *rahât* see above, p. 213.

magic from detection, she procured a dromedary swift as the wind, and visited the different regions she had heard described; sometimes joining one caravan, and sometimes another. The immense treasures on her person were little diminished by this expense; when, one day, the people of the caravan with which she travelled perceived a cloud of sand approaching them, and shortly afterwards distinguished a troop of horsemen at full gallop. Amnah and her companions urged on their camels, but, finally, finding flight useless, they endeavoured to hide themselves in a large well, which the heat of the summer had dried up. But the horsemen had seen them enter, and, delighted to have their prey secured, they offered to the young leader of their band his choice, whether he would have for his portion the first or the last of the persons whom they should find in the well.

Their chief, called Mustapha, was only twenty-one years of age, but renowned for his skill in the use of the matchlock, the sabre, and the lance. His shield, of the hide of the hippopotamus, was almost useless; for with his sabre he parried the blows of his enemies; with a slashing cut of his Damascus blade, which his father, who had travelled far towards the north, had brought him, he separated the limbs of his foes, and even severed the iron chain. At the shake of his lance all fled before him; and never was a matchlock in more skilful hands. In form, he was the perfection of manly beauty and vigour, and his mind was richly endowed, displaying a judgment beyond his years, and greater presence of mind in danger than the oldest warrior. The Koran he knew by heart, and his chief delight was in listening to the traditions of his country. Young and generous, he could never repress his indignation at the recital of the evil deeds of the tyrants who had reigned over the land; his eyes kindled with enthusiasm, and his cheeks glowed with pleasure and emulation when they told him of the valorous exploits of his ancestors, their generosity and hospitality. Like the rest of his race, much of his time was spent in excursions against the tribes with whom they were at war.

Perceiving where the caravan had taken refuge, Mustapha, having the first choice allowed to him, said, "I will take for my "share the captive at the extremity of the well: he who has most "to lose will have fled to the farthest." His companions cast lots for their portions. Some had young women, others young active male slaves; all with some treasure. None were apparently so unfortunate as Mustapha, who found at the extremity of the well Amnah disguised as an old man, miserably clad, the picture of poverty. His companions, with the freedom of friends, rallied him on the wisdom of his choice, in the following lines, which one of them sang, and the others joined in chorus:—

> Our chief, what wisdom he has shown!
> God has blessed him with great judgment,
> O, what a prize he has gained!

So young and so active a slave ;
So splendid and costly his dress ;
So sweet the scent of his body !

Our chief, what wisdom he has shown !
God has blessed him with great judgment,
O, what a prize he has gained !

He will lead your horse to the field ;
Give you your lances in battle,
And ward off the treacherous blow.

Our chief, what wisdom he has shown !
God has blessed him with great judgment,
O, what a prize he has gained !

Mustapha bore good-naturedly the jests of his companions, and, not wishing to appear to despise the gift of Providence, although apparently useless, he led to his castle, as prisoner, the disguised Amnah. On his arrival, he asked her what she could do :—"Can you cut wood ?" said he. "No," replied Amnah, "I have "no strength ; see you not that my arm is shrivelled up with "age ?" "Can you carry it ?" said the chief. "No," she said, "my back is already double ; I should sink under the lightest "weight." "Can you guard the cows, or sheep ?" "Alas, no !" replied Amnah, "they walk too fast and far for me." "Can you "clean the horses ?" "I know not how." "Can you wash the "sand for gold dust ?" "My eyes are not good enough." "You are too dirty to make bread, can you attend the geese ?" "I think I can," said Amnah ; "at all events I will try."

Mustapha gave her for her companion a dumb youth, called Yabibi. After some days, when Yabibi was bathing in the river, Amnah took off her disguise, and showed herself, to the astonished peasant, as the perfection of beauty, covered with gold and precious stones, her hair ornamented with fine pearls and plates of gold, and her earrings studded with diamonds ; laughing, she sang to him the following lines :—

Open your eyes, Yabîbî ; See ! I am young and lovely,
Covered with gold all over ; my necklace of gold,
My earrings of gold, my bracelets of gold,
And gold round my arms, and gold round my legs,
Gold on my forehead, and gold on my *rat ;*
Pearls and silver also.
Open your eyes, Yabebe ; See ! I am young and lovely,
Covered with gold all over !

The astonished peasant left the river, and Amnah, laughing, resumed her disguise. On his return to the castle, the dumb youth made signs to his chief that Amnah was a woman, beautiful, and covered with gold. They surveyed her, and, not finding out her disguise, beat the boy for his improbable falsehood.

The day afterwards they were at the same river ; Amnah threw aside her disguise, put her ornaments together, and bathed herself, with the lad, in the shaded stream. The peasant went first out of the water, and unobservedly stole one of her rings. Amnah, having counted them, found one missing. Yabebe denied having taken it. Amnah beat him, but still he denied, and, escaping from her, fled to his master, and gave him the ring, describing, by signs, that she had similar ones on all her fingers, and was covered with gold and precious stones; that she was a woman, and that her beauty was, as the mid-day sun, too powerful to gaze at. Mustapha sent for Amnah, and, flying suddenly upon her, tore open the rags that covered her, but fell senseless at the sight of such exquisite beauty. Great was the *fête* of the marriage, countless the camels and sheep that were killed. The music was incessant for seven days and seven nights, and they danced until they could dance no more. None, for many years, saw the brilliancy of her face, being ever in her harem, or closely veiled, when, occasionally, she appeared in public. The fame of her beauty, knowledge, and goodness was spread abroad through all lands; the learned were anxious to converse with her; but none, except her husband, had seen her face.

One day her dearest son fell from a tree that he was climbing. His cries reached the ears of his anxious mother. Without a veil, without a garment, she rushed forth. The crowd, on seeing her, fell as dead. They knew not if the effect was produced by magic, or by the power of her exquisite beauty. At her touch her son was restored; and, having clothed herself with a gourbah, and thrown a veil over her head, the crowd recovered; but the tree withered from that day: the branches decayed fast; the leaves fell on the ground, and it no longer afforded shade.

CHAPTER VI.

SECOND MISSION TO THE SÛDÂN (1898).

WÂDÎ ḤALFA TO THE ATBARA AND BAGRÂWÎYA.

THE examination of the pyramid fields of Tanḳâsî, Kurru, *Z*ûma, Gebel Barkal, and Nûri, and of the remains of the Nubian temples on both sides of the river near Merawi, which I made in 1897, produced few material results, but it succeeded in showing the plan according to which certain of the pyramids were built, and proved the necessity of making further investigations among the other pyramid fields of the Sûdân. The descriptions and plans published by Cailliaud, Hoskins, and Lepsius suggested that a great deal of archaeological work still remained to be done in the Island of Meroë, and as general interest centred in the antiquities which were known to exist near Bagrâwîya, a village on the east bank of the Nile, about forty-four miles south of the Atbara, and at Nagaa and Maṣawwarât, the Sirdar most kindly offered every facility for proceeding thither, and the Trustees of the British Museum sent me to the Sûdân a second time. The instructions which I received directed me to visit in particular the Pyramids of Bagrâwîya, and to report on the possibility and advisability of making excavations on the site. With this object in view I left London early in the winter of 1898, and proceeded to Aswân, where I found Captain O. Pedley and Sergeant-Major Kelham, who had given me such valuable assistance in 1897. The journey from Shellâl to Ḥalfa was uneventful, but there was abundant opportunity of examining the change which was beginning to manifest itself everywhere as the result of the Sirdar's signal victory over the Dervish forces at Omdurmân on September 2nd. A new impetus had been given to trade in every direction, and the natives who lived to the south of Aswân felt that they could now enjoy the fruits of their labours without further fear of the Khalîfa.

On arriving at Ḥalfa I heard that my friend Colonel Maxwell had become Governor of Omdurmân, but the Commandant of Ḥalfa had received instructions to send me to the south by the first train, and without delay I made preparations for the journey. None of the officers whom I met at Ḥalfa that year had visited the site on the Island of Meroë which I wished to examine, and no one could give me any information about the state of the country there. Colonel Wingate and Slatin Pâshâ, who knew every mile of the country well, were both at Kharṭûm or Omdurmân, so no information could be obtained from them. Good fortune, however, put me in the way of Lieutenant A. G. Stevenson, R.E., one of the gallant little band of Royal Engineers who had built the Ḥalfa-Abû Hamed Railway, and Lieutenant M. G. E. Manifold, R.E., whose work in connection with the telegraphs in the Sûdân is too well known to need mention here, and from them I learned many important facts. These gentlemen told me that there were very few inhabitants on the east bank of the Nile, that no supplies of any sort or kind could be bought anywhere on the way, and that for all practical purposes the Island of Meroë was as bare of the necessaries of life as the Abû Ḥamed desert. As a result of the information I set to work to obtain stores of tinned meats, rice, &c., and in a few hours those invaluable Greeks, Messrs. Angelo Capato, collected for me a comprehensive selection of stores which a long experience in the service of British officers had taught them were likely to be needed. Through the friendly help of Lieutenant Stevenson I obtained the loan of a couple of tents, and the opportunity of purchasing second-hand a Berkefeld filter, with a supply of new strainers. In the course of the afternoon the Commandant told me that a goods train would be leaving for the Atbara in the evening, and that he had arranged for me to travel by it in one of the covered-in waggons, with sliding doors at the sides, which were then used for transport of everything from a Pâshâ to a goat. In due course myself and my baggage were deposited in this waggon, and about six o'clock the train started.

The train was made up of two huge water-tanks, each containing many thousand gallons of water, bolted on trucks, several long trucks, uncovered, and with a flap-door on each side, three waggons of the kind I was in, and a brake van; the whole was drawn by a mighty engine, which must have weighed forty or sixty tons. The contents of the train were miscellaneous. Several trucks were filled with sleepers for the continuation of the railway from the Atbara to Kharṭûm, and above these were stacked piles of small boxes full of light merchandise of all kinds. Behind the trucks of sleepers came a number of trucks of small coal, and upon this were camped numbers of soldiers, both Egyptians and blacks, native merchants, Greeks, Italians, and several Sûdâni women with their families. By the help of a few sleepers and odd boxes and their own loose garments, many of the black women had made for themselves shelters from the night wind, and soon after the train steamed out of Ḥalfa they kindled little fires in flat earthenware pans and cooked their suppers. Each woman had her *ḳulla*, i.e., native water-bottle made of porous earthenware, which had been filled before we left Ḥalfa, and many of them had brought their stone *dhurra* grinders with them. They seemed very contented, and chattered for hours, in fact far into the night, and shared their dates with each other in, apparently, sincere good fellowship.

Just before we left Ḥalfa a young Royal Engineer attached to the railway entered the train, and he came and shared the waggon with me; he had "worked" the train which had arrived that morning in Ḥalfa from No. 6 Station, and was returning there. He was a very intelligent man, and naturally knew every mile of the line; he was one of the first Englishmen to drive an engine on the Ḥalfa-Abû Hamed Railway, and told me many an interesting story of the difficulties which beset pioneer railway engineering in the Sûdân. His knowledge of the peculiarities of every engine in and out of work was wonderful, and to him they were certainly living beings, with likes, and dislikes, and caprices just like human folk. Apparently he had been ordered to "keep an eye" on the driver of our train, and, whether talking or eating, his ears were always listening to the beat of the engine, which in some way told him what the driver and the stoker were doing. For the first hour or two nothing happened to disturb him seriously, but so soon as we had left Ḥalfa some twenty miles behind us, and were well out in the desert, a strong wind began to blow, and the clouds of sand which it drove southwards before us gave him anxiety. The fine sand of the desert penetrates everywhere, and works mischief in locomotive machinery at the best of times, but when driven under an engine by a strong wind it clogs all the oiled parts, and if any of its bearings be not in as good a condition as they should be, it works its way into them, and becomes dangerous. And this is exactly what happened on the night in question; about half-way between No. 3 and No. 4 Stations we stopped,

THE SÛDÂN EXPRESS AT NO. 4 STATION IN THE ABÛ-ḤAMED DESERT.

because one of the bearings was greatly over-heated. The young Engineer was soon out of the waggon and by the engine, and he decided that we must stay where we were for two or three hours. On his return to the waggon he discoursed on the wickedness of native drivers, and related many instances of their "sinful carelessness about locomotives and people's lives," their waste of good oil, the reckless way in which they burned their furnace bars out, &c. All that he then said I have learned since was true, and that not only did native stokers and drivers waste the oil, but they sold it and gave it away to their friends at the various stations through which they passed. I heard at that time of a native driver who, when he found bearings running hot, would stop the engine and get down and unscrew the bolts, and then go on again without the least misgiving as to the result! Strange to say, nothing serious happened for a time, but the day came when his engine wrecked itself, and hurt him badly in doing so.

When at length we were able to go on again the dawn was breaking, and a more wonderful sight of its kind cannot be

THE ABÛ-HAMED DESERT.

imagined. As the light grew stronger it showed at all points of the compass a sandy waste, which seemed to be absolutely interminable. Here and there were seen in the distance some low hills, but nowhere was there any sign of life except on and near the narrow track whereon the train rolled. A very few yards away from the railway, on each side, the desert had all the appearance of never having been disturbed from the time when, according to some, it emerged from the sea. The railway itself did not seem out of place in that desert, nor did the gaunt telegraph posts, to which the sun, and the wind, and the driving sand had

THE NORTHERN END OF THE "TRIANGLE" AT NO. 6 STATION IN THE ABU HAMED DESERT.

given a worn and ancient appearance, but a wrecked truck, a wheel broken off an axle, a stray sleeper, or a kerosene can, stood out like scars on the face of the sandy plain. It was impossible not to pity the station officials who lived in huts made of railway sleepers covered with palm-leaf matting to keep out the keen night

WATERING TANK AT NO. 6 STATION IN THE ABÛ-HAMED DESERT.
The water is pumped up from a well.

wind, and were literally giving their whole time to the working of the Sirdar's railway. Their natural fatalism must have served them in good stead at this time.

We reached No. 6 Station, 127 miles from Wâdi Ḥalfa, and 1,555 feet above sea level, a few hours after sunrise, and there we were again obliged to stop for a considerable time; the damage done by the sand in the night made it necessary to "lift" the engine, and carry out some repairs. This work, however, gave one the opportunity of examining the station, which was full of interest. Its most prominent feature is the large "triangle," which takes the place of the turn-table in European termini and works. The next point of interest is the well, from which about twelve thousand gallons a day are pumped up by steam into a large tank built upon pillars; it is about seventy feet deep, and its water, though not pleasant to take, is

LOCOMOTIVE DRIVERS AND OFFICIALS OF NO. 6 STATION ON THE SÛDÂN MILITARY RAILWAY IN 1897.

drinkable. It is not so heavily charged with salts as the bitter water of Ambigôl Wells, and is far less injurious to the constitution of locomotive boilers. There were no residents at No. 6 except railway employees, and no habitations except their little houses, and nothing could be bought there, and yet this desert railway centre was of singular interest. My companion on the train introduced me to his colleagues, who kindly invited me to cook my breakfast on their stove, and subsequently took me round the place and explained the working of the well, and showed me many things of interest connected with the working of the line. They were a cheery, kindly party, and allowed me to take a "snap-shot" at them and their beloved dog, which is here reproduced. The figure on the extreme right is that of my friend the Engineer. At the present day the Egypt and Sûdân Mining Syndicate, who are engaged in developing the Umm Nabâdî Mine, have an office at No. 6, and when I passed through in February, 1905, a few miles of their 2 ft. gauge railway to their mine, which lies about forty miles to the east, had been laid.

Soon after we resumed our journey another lengthy stoppage

NO. 6 STATION IN THE ABÛ-ḤAMED DESERT.

took place, for a bolt of the engine broke, and the replacing of it occupied five hours. None of these things is to be wondered at; on the contrary, the wonder is that the railway worked as well as it did, for, owing to want of funds, the officials had to overwork their engines, as well as themselves. The same engine hauled a heavy train from Ḥalfa to Abû Ḥamed, i.e., over 230 miles of one of the sandiest deserts in the world, and if it broke down anywhere on the road it had to be patched up somehow, and wait until it reached the shops at Ḥalfa for systematic repair. Frequently the exigencies of the service made it necessary for the same engine to haul the train on to Berber, another 130 miles. At Abû Ḥamed

Mr. Adams, a civilian railway engineer, who had come out from England to assist the Royal Engineers in establishing workshops, repairing sheds, &c., came out to meet the train on a trolley, and as a further delay was impending, he took me back to his quarters and showed me much kindness. After some hours the engine appeared, and we set out for Berber a little before dawn. As a brief statement about the Sûdân Railways will be made elsewhere in this book, there is no need to describe here the

A STATION ON THE ABÛ-ḤAMED AND KHARṬÛM RAILWAY.

route of the line, and it is sufficient to say that we arrived at Berber about 11 a.m.

We passed several places near Berber, where large numbers of natives had been buried during the past year, and the sticks and short branches of trees, with bits of rag and feathers tied to them, which marked the graves of the men, reminded one more of scarecrows than of sepulchral monuments. We stayed at Berber for some hours, for several trucks had to be unloaded, and the engine again required attention. The delay gave me the opportunity of looking about the place, and of noticing the various types of natives who were gathered together there, and their, to me, unfamiliar costumes. Though only fifteen months had elapsed since Berber had passed into the hands of British officers, they had already writ their mark large in the town. The Government buildings had been repaired, roads had been marked out by rows of stones, the market had been re-established, and the natives of the town and of the deserts round about it, being sure by this time that the Khalifa's rule was

TRANSPORT TRAIN ON A SIDING AT ATBARA FORT IN 1898.

dead, had begun to trade with a feeling of confidence and security hitherto unknown. The "key of the Sûdân," as Berber has often been called, is admirably adapted by nature for native markets, though Europeans and natives alike find its winds and sandy atmosphere very trying. It was proposed many years ago by Sir Samuel Baker to make Berber the inland terminus of a line between Berber and Sawâkin on the sea coast, but the modern requirements of the Sûdân suggest that Atbara is the better place for the line to start from. It is undoubtedly a wise policy which has made it the terminus of the new line from Sawâkin, and probably no one will regret the disappearance of Berber as the chief market town of the district. As the capital of the province it has been superseded by Ad-Dâmar.

From Berber we proceeded to the camp on the Atbara, which was situated quite close to the junction of that river with the Nile. During their stay at this place the soldiers had built rows of small mud houses, which were used for administrative purposes, barracks, &c.; huge stacks of bags of rice, grain, and mounds made of tree trunks to be used as firewood rose in all directions, to say nothing of thousands of sleepers, and layers of rails for the continuation of the line to Kharṭûm. There was a post-office, and the general public was allowed to despatch telegrams both to Cairo and Kharṭûm, a striking proof of the rapidity with which the country was settling down. To the north of the camp was the market where the Greeks carried on a fair amount of business, though nearly all bûying and selling was done without the help of money. From time to time the Greeks told their English customers how much they owed them, but, whether they were paid or not, they went on supplying goods just the same. The officers paid by cheques, which pleased the Greeks, for they could be more easily taken care of than cash at that time, and the Englishman's word was as good as his money. A little beyond the Greek bazaar was the native market, where most Sûdâni products were obtainable. One fact in connection with the advance of the Anglo-Egyptian Army up the Nile is very noteworthy, I mean the strict supervision which the Sirdar exercised over the admission of strong drink into the Sûdân. The supplies which the Greeks brought into the Sûdân, whether by camel or railway, were closely examined, and if any merchant imported more spirits or spirituous drinks than the Sirdar thought necessary, effective measures were taken to prevent their finding their way down native throats. I have even heard of instances in which the bottles were broken in the cases in which they arrived, and their contents allowed to sink into the desert sand! People of Negro origin and many black-skinned tribes in the Sûdân love strong drink, especially that of European manufacture, for it affects them more quickly and more powerfully than the home-made article.

ATBARA

The train pulled up a few yards from where the rails abruptly came to an end, and an orderly took me to the office of the Commandant, Captain W. S. Swabey, who told me what facilities could be afforded to me. The Sirdar did not wish me to go further south than Wad Ḥabashi, about 55 miles from the Atbara, but I was free to go where I liked north of that village. Means of transport I was to find for myself, for every camel in the service was employed on military business. Captain Swabey thought that some means of sending me up the river might be found after he had made some inquiries, and in the meantime he kindly gave me a hut to live in near the Atbara Fort, and I was free to look about the camp for some hours.

The river Atbara[1] was a source of interest, for preparations were being made for building a temporary bridge across it for the transport of railway material; the foundations for the pillars had already been laid, and a few supports set on them. The bridge which now carries the railway is of iron, and has six spans of 200 feet each: the rock on which the piers rest is about 30 feet below the bed of the river. The average width of the Atbara is about 450 yards, and in the rainy season it is from 25 to 30 feet deep. For several months of the year it is perfectly dry, and Sir Samuel Baker says that when he saw it in June, 1861, it was "a mere sheet of glaring sand; in fact, a portion of the desert "through which it flowed." In some years the course of the river is marked by a number of shallow pools which are found at long intervals. From the beginning of March to early in June the last 150 miles of its course is dry. The storm period in Abyssinia lasts from the middle of May to September, and by the end of June the Atbara has become a deep, swift stream. About this time the storms are terrific. "Every "ravine becomes a raging torrent; trees are rooted up by the "mountain streams swollen above their banks, and the Atbara "becomes a vast river, bringing down with an overwhelming "current the total drainage of four large rivers—the Settite, "Royân, Salaam, and Angrab—in addition to its own original "volume. Its waters are dense with soil washed from most fertile

[1] The natives make all the vowels short. In Amharic the last vowel is long—Atbarâ.

"lands far from its point of junction with the Nile; masses of "bamboo and driftwood, together with lárge trees, and frequently "the dead bodies of elephants and buffaloes, are hurled along its "muddy waters in wild confusion, bringing a rich harvest to the "Arabs on its banks, who are ever on the look-out for the river's "treasures of fuel and timber."[1] The velocity of the Atbara current is so great when the river is in flood, and its waters so dense, that it forces the water of the Nile across on to the western

ENTRANCE TO THE BRITISH CEMETERY AT ATBARA.

bank. Even in December the Nile is so wide at the mouth of the Atbara that it forms a kind of bay, and the shallowness of the water in the winter renders the passage from one bank of the river to the other a long and tedious business.

About a mile from Atbara Fort, on the right bank of the Atbara, is the English cemetery, which is enclosed within a high mud wall, and is provided with wooden gates. The graves were well kept, and all the crosses were in position, and Captain Swabey took special care to see done everything which would

[1] Sir Samuel Baker, "The Albert Nyanza," London, 1870, p. 6.

THE GRAVE OF LIEUT. P. A. GORE, OF THE SEAFORTH HIGHLANDERS, ON THE ATBARA.

[From a photograph by Lieutenant S. F. Newcombe, R.E.

serve to keep in remembrance the names of the brave men who were buried there. The Battle of the Atbara was fought on April 8th, 1898, at Nakhêla, a village on the right bank of the river, about 30 miles from its mouth. The position of Maḥmûd, the Dervish leader, "was more or less of an oval resting on the river, honey-"combed with trenches, and surrounded by a *zeriba*. It resembled "Abû Ḥamed on a larger scale, in that it lay at the bottom of a "kind of crater, of which the radius was about 600 yards, so that

THE GRAVE OF A WAR-CORRESPONDENT AT ATBARA IN 1899.

"it would be impossible to open fire at a greater range, which "was evidently the reason which caused the Dervishes to take "up such a position."[1] The fight lasted less than half an hour, and in this time 2,500 Dervishes were killed, including all the Amirs with the exception of Osmân Diḳna, who, as usual, escaped before the fight began, and many hundreds were wounded. At least 2,000 more were made prisoners, and all the Dervish stores, arms, and ammunition fell into the Sirdar's

[1] "Sudan Campaign," p. 151.

hands. Some 8,000 Dervishes, the remainder of Mâḥmûd's force,[1] fled up the Atbara to Adârama, where one part of them set out for Gedâref, and the other for Abû Dulêḳ. As they went several hundreds, who had been wounded but had managed to get away, sank from exhaustion and died, and many hundreds perished from hunger and thirst. The total Anglo-Egyptian loss was 568 killed and wounded. Maḥmûd himself was found hidden in a hut, and was brought before the Sirdar, whose questions he answered in a very insolent manner. He was subsequently made

BRITISH CEMETERY ON THE ATBARA IN 1898.

to walk after the cavalry, with his hands tied behind his back, when the Sirdar made his triumphal entry into Berber.

In the course of the afternoon Captain Swabey told me that a steamer had returned unexpectedly from the south, and that they were going to send her up the river again as soon as possible to fetch wood, and he told me that if I cared to embark in her he would instruct the captain to let me land as near the Pyramids

[1] The above figures are Mr. Royle's. but according to the writer of "Sudan Campaign, 1896-1899," Mahmûd's force consisted of 17,000 men. Of these, he says, 5,000 were killed, and 1,000 made prisoners, 4,000, or 5,000 perished from wounds and hunger during their flight, and the remainder were scattered.

of Bagrâwîya as possible. This was a piece of good fortune not to be thought lightly of, and we went to look at the steamer, and to make the best arrangements we could. The steamer was the *Bordein*, or *Burdên*, and her looks were not inviting. All her deck and cabins, and all her woodwork had been removed, having been used by the Dervishes to feed her fire, and all that remained in her were the iron deck-beams, a narrow iron bridge aft the boiler, and the small iron platform at each end of her. These were all that were required for military purposes, for at that time she was only used for fetching wood, but they were not conducive to the comfort of passengers. A friendly British officer, Captain Hobbs, was, however, equal to the occasion, and he had some planks laid across the deck beams, to form a floor, and then had my tent pitched on them. The centre pole was lashed to a beam, and the ropes were tied to the twisted railing or to anything that came handy. This done, a rug and a sheepskin made a very good carpet, and when a native bed had been taken inside the tent with the rest of the baggage, the general appearance was not unsatisfactory. With the arrival of a large *zîr*, or water-jar, the equipment was complete.

The day was Friday, or "mosque day," and the captain and crew wanted to go and see their friends and say their prayers before they started, but their devotions took so much time that when they returned the sun was about to set. When it was nearly dark the black engineer reported that he had enough steam to go on with, and we pushed off into the stream. It was necessary to make a circuit in order to reach the main channel, and for about an hour we steamed along fairly well, but in the dark, for there was no moon, the captain did not allow sufficient margin for turning round into the channel, and we ran aground on the mud flat which he had managed to avoid with such success hitherto. The crew jumped into the river with ropes and small anchors, and worked very hard for a couple of hours in hauling the steamer off the bank, but when she floated it was found that there was not enough steam to work the engines; for the engineer had made up his mind to start in the morning, and, whilst the crew were hauling at the steamer, had gone to bed! Therefore, dropping out two or three small anchors to keep the steamer from drifting on to the mud, the crew lit a fire and cooked their supper, and everybody tried to go to sleep.

This, however, was difficult, for the cold was, relatively intense, and lying out in the broadest part of the river we felt the full strength of the north wind. The tent was a poor shelter, because it was impossible to keep the wind away from beneath it, and after a short time the few native merchants who were on the steamer and myself joined the crew, who were squatting by a fire close to the engines, and were thankful to be welcomed by them. The gift of a tin of tobacco and two or three briar-root pipes put us on very good terms with each other, and as the pipes passed round the shyness wore off the black faces of the smokers, and they cracked jokes with each other, and were full of fun. After a little time the engineer woke up, and he and the *rais*, or captain, joined us. About two o'clock it became bitterly cold, notwithstanding the good fire kept up with the Sirdar's wood, and then one of the party having produced a few handfuls of coffee berries, the engineer, who said "he knew this business," pounded and boiled them, the whole company giving their advice at critical moments. There were no cups available, but two tin mugs served the party very well, and when my "black boy" produced a lump of loaf sugar about two pounds in weight, great satisfaction was felt. The crew were very good-natured fellows, easily pleased, and quickly touched by a little act of kindness, and though it seemed incredible that many of them had been fanatical Dervishes less than a year previously, such was the fact. When the false dawn appeared the company became quiet, and most of them huddled themselves together and slept as best they could.

About 6 a.m. we got under way, and in a short time turned the bend in the river and lost sight of Atbara Fort. Every one welcomed the sun, and, turning his back to the wind, tried to get as much of the heat as possible. When it was sufficiently warm to leave the friendly shelter of the iron bridge over the shaft of the paddle-wheels, and to wander along the sides of the steamer, it became evident that the gallant little boat had seen a considerable amount of service, and that she had been knocked about a good deal. The funnel was pitted with bullet marks, and had had several holes made in it at one time and another; very few inches of it possessed proper shape, and there was scarcely a particle of paint upon it. The hull, too, had been much knocked about, and was patched in dozens of places where bullets had made holes. The paddle-boxes were scarred and

THE CAPTAIN OF THE "BORDEIN" IN 1898.

battered, no two floats were of the same size, length, or thickness, and the iron frames were bent into fantastic shapes; what surprised me most of all was that the *Burdên* made any headway at all. Compared with all this ruin most parts of the engines were in first-class condition, and though the cranks knocked, and the shaft turned in badly worn bearings, and the piston-rods wanted packing, and the whole framework lifted at each revolution, they drove the steamer against the current at the rate of a mile and a half per hour. On the frame was the brass label which stated that they were the work of Messrs. Penn & Co., and that the steamer was built by Messrs. Samuda Brothers; that the *Burdên* was capable of doing the work upon which she was then engaged after some twenty years' service in the Sûdân said much for the soundness and strength of the materials, and for the excellent workmanship which her builders put into her. Looking at the boiler, one felt astonished at seeing how thin its plates had become, and how many tubes leaked, but the most amazing thing of all was that it had no safety valve! The engineer kept heaping in logs of wood, but so far as I could see he had no guide at all to tell him what the pressure in the boiler was. A little watching, however, showed that when he thought the engines were working too fast, he left the furnace door, and went and turned a tap projecting from the top of the boiler, and let out as much steam as he thought necessary. This done, he returned to his furnace and heaped on more wood. In any other country that boiler would have exploded, and killed many men, and wrecked the steamer, but in such respects Egypt and the Sûdân are under the care of a special Providence. The natives have ways of their own in such matters which do not commend themselves to Europeans, but the results are singularly successful.

The *Burdên* closely resembled one of the "penny steamers" which used to ply on the Thames between London Bridge and Greenwich about the year 1865, and was one of a group of paddle-wheel steamers which were bought by the Egyptian Government, on the advice of Sir Samuel Baker and General Gordon, for service on the White Nile. Sir Samuel Baker was the first to recognize that it was impossible to deal effectively with the slave trade without the means of moving quickly up and down the river; and it was he who persuaded the Khedive Isma'il to order three steamers of 251, 108 and 38 tons respectively, and two steel lifeboats of 10 tons each. The *Burdên* obtained her name[1] from a place in Upper Egypt, where Sherif Pâshâ, who was at one time Prime Minister of Egypt, had a large estate, and her sister steamers were called *Ismaïlia, Embâba, Mansura*, and *Sasia*. She had a very honourable record, and had done

[1] I.e., the "cool of the morning and evening."

splendid work. In the year 1880 she played an important part in the deliverance of Gessi Pâshâ and his followers from a serious position. Gessi Pâshâ, the loyal friend of Gordon, having crushed the rebellion of Sulêmân, left Meshra ar-Rek in the *Sasia* on September 25th, 1880, taking in tow boats containing 400 Arabs and officials. Near Ghâba Jer Dekka the whole flotilla got hemmed in by the "Sudd," i.e. masses of vegetation which blocked the river, and could not move. Provisions ran short, and scores of men died from hunger and fever, and the

EAST BANK OF THE NILE ABOVE ATBARA, SHOWING NATIVE BOATS.

living were eating the bodies of the dead. When things were at their worst Marno, an Egyptian official, appeared on January 4th, 1881, with the *Burdên*, bringing with him food and medicines, and so saved the life of the remainder of Gessi's party. The "Sudd" was broken up and towed away piecemeal by the *Burdên*, and the *Sasia* was able to proceed to Kharṭûm.

As we steamed up the river there was abundant opportunity of examining the state of the country on each bank, and a more desolate region it would be difficult to imagine. The west bank is lower than the east, and except on the very edge of the river no traces of cultivation were to be seen. The little islands we passed in the river were covered with bright green vegetation, shrubs, and trees, and a few natives had already returned and were cultivating the ground. The men I saw wore loin-cloths only, and the women very little more; how and on what they lived it was hard to imagine. The east bank is usually from eight to

CLEARING AT A WOODING STATION ON THE WEST BANK.

twelve feet high, and its soil is extremely good, but when I saw it the ground was wholly covered with a dense mass of thorny bushes of all kinds, and a thick matted crop of ḥalfa grass, which must have been in undisturbed possession of the land for many years. The palm trees were in a decaying state, and a Turkish merchant on the steamer, who had lived in the country for many years, and had witnessed the fall of Kharṭûm, told me that the mass of withered leaves at their tops showed they had not been attended to for several years. We know from Sir Samuel Baker's testimony that the banks of the river between Berber and Kharṭûm about the year 1862 were crowded with populous villages, and that the land was everywhere cultivated, and produced heavy crops, and it was evident that the rule of the Turk, seconded by the atrocities of the Dervishes, had in thirty-five years turned a flourishing country into a howling wilderness. The frequent gaps in the bank showed where water-wheels had

THE DHURRA AND THE JUNGLE MEETING AT BAGRÂWÎYA.

once stood, but these structures had entirely disappeared, and the channels which they once filled must have been choked for years.

About twenty miles up the river we stopped on the west bank to take in wood, and whilst the work was going on I went to the group of *tukuls* which had recently been put up close to the river, on the site where a thriving village now stands. The men who brought in the wood from the desolate plains were nearly all naked, and must have been starved for months; the few sheep and goats they had were, I believe, better fed, and far better clothed than they. The Sirdar paid for every log of wood taken from them, and for all the work they did, but piastres had for once lost their power in the Sûdân, for there was nothing to buy. In the afternoon we stopped at another wooding station, this time on the east bank, and here the desolation was made more evident by the thorn jungle which had pushed its growth over the edge ot the bank, and almost down to the water. There were several fine trees there which afforded pleasant shade, and we all took the opportunity of cooking and eating a meal whilst the "wooding"

WOODING STATION ABOVE ATBARA IN 1898.

of the steamer went on. The men who loaded her slept between the heaps of wood, and had neither *tukuls* nor huts; they lived on dates, *dhurra*, and water, the last-named article alone being abundant. At the south end of the station they had made a sort of clearing which enabled them to work at digging up the tree stumps and at cutting off branches from the larger trees, but it would have been very difficult for any one to penetrate the thorn jungle for more than a few hundred yards.

We left the station as soon as possible, and steamed till about an hour after sundown, when the captain stopped for the night. The crew were very glad to reach some place where they could find a shelter to sleep in, for they did not appreciate the night which they had been obliged to spend on the river, and every one devoted himself to the preparation of his evening meal. In the course of talk with some of the natives I was told that at some little distance from the river-bank, in the desert, there were three British officers, but exactly what they were doing I could not make out. On being questioned, the engineer of the steamer said they were making a

A LOAD OF WOOD FOR THE "BORDEIN."

railway, and were making men drive "sticks" into the ground! A man was found who knew the whereabouts of their tent, and for a consideration he promised to take me there. We set out on our way through an opening in the scrub, and, after an hour's rough going in the dark, came to an open, sandy patch on which was pitched a large rectangular tent.

On coming to the front of it I saw three officers seated at a camp-table with large scale plans open before them, and it was evident that they were engaged in surveying and planning the route of the continuation of the railway from the Atbara to Kharṭûm. The three officers were Lieutenant E. C. Midwinter, R.E., D.S.O., Lieutenant G. C. M. Hall, R.E., and Lieutenant W. R. G. Wollen, R.E. They received me most kindly, and gave me accurate information about the pyramids I wished to reach, and told me how to get there. This was most fortunate for me, for no one on the steamer knew the whereabouts of the pyramids, and I was as much in the dark about their exact position as Cailliaud had been eighty years before. The natives of the Sûdân call the pyramids *tarâbîl*, and as I had always used the common Egyptian word *ahrâm* in making inquiries about them,. they may have failed to understand what I meant. Midwinter, however, knew the exact spot on the river which was nearest the pyramids, for it corresponded with mile 44 from Atbara on his plan, and he sent word to the captain of the *Burdên* that he was to stop at this place and land me and my baggage. When travelling in the Sûdân in those days I met with many surprises, but one of the greatest was coming suddenly across three young officers seated quietly in a tent in the open desert, and working out by night the route of a railway through the desert of the Island of Meroë, which less than nine months previously had been in the possession of the Dervish leader Maḥmûd. The responsibility, of course, rested with the Sirdar, but he selected his men, and invariably got the best results out of them.

Early next morning the *Burdên* continued her journey, and two or three hours later we were passed by the stern-wheeler which was carrying Lord Cromer to Kharṭûm to discuss with the Sirdar on the spot the system under which the Sûdân was to be ruled. The only member of his party visible was Mr. Harry Boyle, Lord Cromer's lynx-eyed Oriental Secretary, who seemed surprised at the condition of the *Burdên* and her passengers, as he well might be. In the course of the morning we stopped at another station for wood, and about noon we arrived at the place on the east bank where I was to land. This was not easy, for the bank was steep, and the *dhurra* came down to the water's edge; it was almost the only sign of cultivation which I had seen for miles. Just as the tent was landed an old man appeared at the top of the bank, and he turned out to be the owner of the *dhurra* which we had been trampling upon, and the shêkh of the district. He was tall and thin, and his features were of the regular Sûdâni (not Negro) type; his head was clean-shaven, and his only garment was a long strip of native cotton stuff which he wound round him. His name was Muḥammad Ibrahim al-Amin, and he saluted me by uncovering his right shoulder.

When the steamer had gone on up the river the shêkh took me

DHURRA.

by a winding path through the scrub to the clearing where his *tukul* was, and showed me a place where the tent might be pitched. In the course of conversation with him I found that he had formerly been in the Egyptian Army, and had served under General Gordon in 1877, and he produced papers containing instructions to him which had been signed by Gordon himself. Like most people in the Sûdân he had suffered greatly under the rule of the Dervishes, and was practically reduced to beggary. I never understood how he had escaped death, or how he had managed to settle himself on the land again, but there he was, and quite willing to give me help if he could. The *tukul*, wherein he lived with his wife and children, stood at the far end of the clearing, which was 200 or 300 yards long, and close by was a small hut occupied by a former slave and his wife and child. The shêkh had a baby donkey, a few goats and two or three fields of *dhurra,* which was then nearly ripe; he complained bitterly of the thefts of the grain by the birds, and he kept two boys, perched aloft on wooden platforms ten or twelve feet high

THE CLEARING OF SHÊKH MUḤAMMAD IBRAHÎM AL-AMÎN.

among the crops, to drive off the feathered thieves by shrill cries and pellets of mud which they threw at them from slings. Every few minutes he would jump up and run towards the *dhurra* and exhort the boys in most vigorous language to drive away the birds. On all sides of the clearing the thorn jungle and halfa grass grew luxuriantly, and the labour spent in making the ground ready for the *dhurra* crop must have been enormous.

So soon as the tent was pitched I began to make inquiries for the pyramids, and the shêkh took me through the scrub to a place from which they could be seen. There was no path, and the long, straggling thorny bushes made progress slow, but eventually we came out of the belt of scrub and entered a sandy plain which was bestrewn with large bits of stone of brownish-black colour and having a shiny surface.[1] In the distance ahead of us was a range of low stone hills, and in looking at these I saw in front of them a number of smaller hills, with regularly sloping sides, and, remembering the drawings of Cailliaud and Hoskins, it was easy to recognize in them the Pyramids of Meroë. They did not

A BOY ON A LIGHT PLATFORM SCARING BIRDS FROM THE DHURRA.
The Shêkh of Bagrâwîya is exhorting him to greater diligence.

appear to be more than a mile from where we were, and I wished to press on to see them closer, but so soon as we came to the well-defined series of tracks running from north to south, which the shêkh said was the Berber road, he was afraid to go any further and begged me to return. He said that in the early evening the spirits of those who had built the *ṭarâbîl*, or pyramids, left their abodes and came out and talked with each other, and that some of them, i.e., those who had been wicked on

[1] Specimens of these are in the British Museum, Nos. 42,151 and 42,152.

earth, were visited by evil spirits, which took the form of jackals and wolves and other animals. It is not the "custom of our country," he said, to go to such places except in the daytime, and it was "not nice" to intrude upon the ground of the dead kings. The natives of Barkal had said much the same kind of thing, and it was evident that their belief concerning the spirits

PORTRAITS OF TWO BOYS AT BAGRÂWÎYA EMPLOYED TO SCARE BIRDS FROM THE DHURRA CROP.

of the dead kings was general in the country, but the shêkh's idea that evil spirits dwelt in wolves and jackals was new to me. In Ethiopian lives of saints we often meet with the statement that the king of the devils rides on a fire-breathing wolf in a forest, and that he is accompanied on his journeys by fiends in the form of wolves, and it seems that the modern Sûdâni folk must have inherited a phase of this belief from earlier peoples in the country.

A glance at the sun, which was dropping fast, told me that it would be impossible to get to the pyramids and back before it set, and having made the shêkh promise to go to the pyramids the next day; we turned back. As we did so, we heard the shrill cry of jackals somewhere in the desert, and the shêkh, declaring that

THE SHÊKH OF BAGRÂWÎYA AND HIS WIFE.

the evening meeting had begun, set off at a good rate for his clearing.

It was nearly night when we arrived, and I was glad I had come with him, for I could not have found the way through the scrub by myself. The shêkh's wife and the other woman had evidently been very anxious about him, and thanked God fervently that we had returned in safety from the desert. In the evening the shêkh told me many interesting details about his life and the period of his service under Gordon, and if only one-twentieth part of the things he narrated about the cruelty and villainy of the governors who had been sent from Egypt to administer the country were true, no one need wonder at the success of the Mahdi's rebellion. He had seen Sir Samuel Baker, whom by reason of his strength

THE WIFE OF THE SHÊKH OF BAGRÂWÎYA, ARRAYED IN DAMÛR CLOTH AND WEARING HER COLLECTION OF AMULETS.

and energy he called a "steam engine" (*babûr*), and he praised Gordon, for whom he had the greatest admiration; but he said that both these men were made toys of by the local governors of **Kharṭûm**, who, whilst pretending to help them to suppress the slave trade in every way, were really in secret helping the "traders" to carry on their infamous business. So long as the governor of Kharṭûm sent money regularly to Cairo, no one there cared by what means it was obtained. By accident the Khedive Isma'il once appointed a man, who was personally both honest and God-fearing, to be Governor of Kharṭûm, but the natives did not profit; this Governor committed his territory to the care of Provi-

A WOMAN OF THE HOUSEHOLD OF THE SHÊKH OF BAGRÂWÎYA.

dence, but took every opportunity of increasing the taxes, and in one year he sent to the Khedive £100,000 in dollars. All this money must have been squeezed out of the wretched *fellaḥîn* of the Sûdân, and if this sum was actually paid by the Governor, it is easy to imagine how much besides must have been squeezed out of the people by the officials who collected it. In the course of our talk the shêkh produced the papers signed by General Gordon, already referred to, and asked me to give them to Colonel Wingate when I returned to Cairo, for he thought that he was entitled to arrears of pay, or a pension, or both. This I did, but I do not know whether his expectations were realized or not. In February, 1905, on the occasion of the visit of T.R.H. the Duke and Duchess of Connaught, and their daughters, Princesses Margaret and Patricia, this shêkh came to the Pyramids of Meroë arrayed in a bright scarlet "robe of honour," with which he had been recently invested by Sir F. R. Wingate, Governor-General of the Sûdân,

VIEW OF THE PYRAMIDS OF MEROË (EASTERN SIDES).

and it was good to see that he had not been forgotten by the authorities.

From talking of the past we went on to the present, and I asked the shêkh if he could hire a donkey to ride to the pyramids; he said that he would send that night the native who lived with him in the clearing to a family he knew of to try to borrow one, but thought it very doubtful if it would be lent. This family lived some miles away, and his messenger unwillingly prepared to go there, for he was greatly afraid of the dark, and nothing less than a present in hard cash induced him to go at all. Next morning we were stirring betimes, but no donkey appeared, and just as the sun rose the shêkh and myself set out for the pyramids on foot. The morning was comparatively cool, and we reached our destination in an hour, but the shêkh sat down on the pebbles at the foot of the hill on which the pyramids stand, for he said he was afraid to go any further. When I reached the top of the hill, and had walked over the rocky ridge to the most easterly pyramid but

VIEW OF THE PYRAMIDS OF MEROË (WESTERN SIDES).
Showing the difference in the angles of orientation.

one, the scene I saw was one of singular interest. The pyramids were grouped on the highest points of the hill in a kind of semi-circle, and the rays of the sun shone into the chapels in front of them, lighting up most of the chambers thoroughly. A little lower down the side of the hill was a second row of pyramids, and at its foot was a third row of pyramids, which were quite small. A little to the south-east, and across the valley, tops of another group of pyramids were just visible, and away to the west, on the flattest part of the plain was another group, and still further away, on the extreme edge of the plain, close to the belt of scrub on the river, were the remains of the tombs which Cailliaud called the "Pyramids of As-Sûr." The place was a veritable city of the dead, and with the exception of the necropolis of Nûri, there is no other place like it in Egypt or the Sûdân. Its surroundings were wild and picturesque. Low rows of bare hills, with circular pointed peaks worn by the winds, stretched away to the north and east, and the plain between them was full of thorn bushes and ḥalfa grass, which near the channels made by the summer rains was still green. To the south there were more low hills, and on the west, seen dimly, was a long confused mass of a greenish-black colour which, when approached, resolved itself into the palms and other trees growing on the river bank. Beyond this the western desert stretched away to an apparently infinite distance, and the few hills which were dotted upon it seemed only to emphasize the flatness of the barren wilderness surrounding them. The site of this necropolis of Meroïtic queens and kings was well chosen, for, saving the rustling of the ḥalfa grass at the foot of the hill, not a sound of any sort or kind was to be heard.

On comparing the views and the plan of the group of pyramids at this place made by Cailliaud about 1820 with the buildings before me, I saw at once that the pyramids had suffered greatly since his day, and that many of them, which had been perfect when he visited them, had since fallen into ruin. The views published by Hoskins, who examined the pyramids twelve years later, show that little change had taken place in their condition since Cailliaud was there, and thus it is tolerably clear that the greater part of the damage which had been done to the chapels and to the pyramids to which they belonged, had been effected between 1832 and 1898. Now it was quite impossible for any European to visit these pyramids between 1884 and the spring of 1898, for the simple reason that the whole of the Island of Meroë was in the possession of the Dervishes, and therefore no excavations could have been made there during that period. A month or two after the battle of the Atbara, on April 8th, 1898, a few of the British officers rode over to look at the pyramids, but they made no excavations and disturbed nothing; had they done so, the marks of their work would have been visible in January, 1899.

On the north side of Pyramid No. 14, on the sixth layer of stone from the ground, is cut the name H. E. Price, R.E., 1889, but the cutter of the name made a mistake in his date, which was probably intended to be 1898, for there was no British soldier of any kind on the Island of Meroë in 1889. There is no record that Sir Samuel Baker ever did any work at these pyramids, and it is very unlikely that he ever had any time to devote to practical investigations of the ancient history of the country by means of

THE MOST NORTHERLY PYRAMIDS OF THE NORTHERN GROUP.

spade and pick, and so we are driven to the conclusion that whatever damage was done to the pyramids since Cailliaud's time, was effected between 1832 and 1884. Now the only Europeans who made excavations on this site between these years were Ferlini and Lepsius, and it seems to me that any damage which they did to the pyramids or to their chapels was a result which was bound to follow the work of any one who attempted to examine these buildings.[1] The slightest examination of the chapels will

[1] As the investigations made by these explorers were on a much larger scale than is usually supposed, they will be dealt with in a separate chapter.

convince the visitor that their foundations are rarely well laid, and that in consequence some of their walls have "settled" so deeply at the corners that whole sides and ends have fallen out. Besides this, the stones used for the lintels of the doors and for the roofs were not well chosen in the first instance, and the damage caused by "weathering" has been considerable. Another cause of the ruined state of many of the chapels is the wind, which, blowing fiercely from the north, and being laden with sand, acts upon the stones in their corners like a sand-blast, and erodes them deeply. It is important to mention these details, otherwise misconception may arise in some minds as to the true causes which have contributed to the ruin of some of the chapels and their surrounding walls.

So soon as I began to go about among the pyramids it became evident that it was impossible to make accurate measurements of them, because the lower parts of the sides of all were buried in the loose stones which had fallen, or had been thrown down from their tops, and in masses of loose rubble. I checked the measurements given by Cailliaud and Hoskins, and though many appear to have been arrived at by guesswork, they are sufficiently correct for all practical purposes. Nearly all the pyramids are oriented a little to the south of east, but with very few exceptions the angles of orientation are all different. It is clear, in my opinion, that all were oriented to the same celestial body, and that the differences in orientation corresponded to the changes in position of that body. The pyramids throughout the Sûdân seem to me to prove beyond doubt the truth of Sir Norman Lockyer's theory of orientation as propounded in his "Dawn of Astronomy," but no group so clearly makes it manifest as that which I was then examining, partly because of the semi-circular arrangement of the pyramids, and partly because of their large number.

Passing over the narrow valley which divides the two groups of pyramids, I found that the southern group was as instructive as the northern one, and it was interesting to note how careful the builders of the pyramids had been to arrange each in such a way that its shrine should receive the light directly into it from the celestial object.

Returning to the northern group, and proceeding along the foot of the hill on the east side, it was easy to see where Ferlini had excavated one of the small pyramids, for the heaps of rubbish lay untouched at the side, and they looked as if they might have been taken out of the ground only a few months previously. I examined with interest the pyramid marked F on Cailliaud's plan, and its chapel, and the hole in the masonry from which Ferlini is said to have taken out the treasure of the great queen of Meroë, and it was clear that many people since his day must have dug in the pyramid in the hope of finding further collections of jewellery, or money. From nearly every shrine which was easily cleared out I saw that blocks of stone were missing from one or other of the side walls, generally above or near the most important figures in the scene or procession. A reference to the monumental publication of Lepsius[1] shows at once that some of the missing stones were inscribed with texts in the Meroïtic character, and the official Guide[2] to the Egyptian and Nubian Antiquities in the Berlin Museum proves that they are now in that institution. No one can blame Lepsius for removing these precious relics of an important, but dead and forgotten language, to a place of safety in Europe, and it is to be hoped that when the Governor-General of the Sûdân is in a position to have cleared out the chapels of the two great pyramids to the north of the northern group, which are still buried under many tons of fallen stones, he will take steps to have removed to Kharṭûm any Meroïtic inscriptions which may be found on the walls.

The examination of the Pyramids of Meroë which I was able to make in 1899 made it clear to me that further excavations ought to be made on the site; for nothing whatever was known about the funerary customs of the ancient people of Meroë, and there was the possibility that bilingual inscriptions in the Egyptian and Meroïtic languages might be discovered among the buried chapels. Moreover, it was important to prove, or disprove, the theory which was held by some to the effect that the queens and kings of Meroë were buried in their pyramids and not beneath them. The examination of the site also showed that the work of excavation and clearing would be a very serious one,

[1] *Denkmäler*, Abth. V.

[2] *Ausführliches Verzeichnis*, Berlin, 1899, p. 401 ff.

and that it would cost a great deal of money. No antiquarian society could be expected to spend a large sum of money on such a site, and the absence of population on the Island of Meroë would make it impossible for some years to carry out excavations there on any considerable scale, even if the necessary funds were forthcoming.

Meanwhile the shêkh, who had sat down at the foot of the hill in the morning, had been joined by the man whom he had sent the night before to borrow a donkey (which he had now brought), and finding that it was very hot there, he came up and rested in the shade of one of the pyramids. As time went on he became very impatient and nervous, and finally declared that he would stay no longer, for he was afraid of what might happen to the donkey if he remained anywhere near the pyramids. We therefore returned to the clearing, after what the shêkh regarded as a most dangerous undertaking! In the late afternoon we went along the river bank and visited one or two of the villages. The shêkh showed me the mud huts wherein many of his friends had lived formerly, and in some of them I saw on the ground the stones on which the women used to grind the *dhurra* and roll the oblong dough into thin flat cakes. Remains of both dough and *dhurra* were on several, and the shêkh told me that they had been left thus by the women who had to flee for their lives before the Dervishes, led by Maḥmûd, who about a year previously had swept the Island of Meroë from one end to the other, and slain all who would not join him. Not a living thing was to be seen, and the desolation of the place was complete. Many of the huts were in good condition, but all the mud bins in which the natives had stored their grain were destroyed, and in some rooms the ground had been dug through by seekers after buried treasure.

On returning to the clearing, we found a number of men and women, and children, who had walked several miles in order to ask for medicines. Fortunately I had plentiful supplies with me, and I was able to give them away freely. Three of the children had very sore eyes, the result of sand, dust, glare, and want of washing, and both eyes of a fourth were caked over to such a degree that he could not see at all. For some reason the women were very anxious that this boy should be attended to first, and I heated some water which had been passed through the Berkefeld filter, and began to wash the accretions from the eyelids. In a short time the eyelids were cleared, but the child, who lay on his back, howled continuously; a little cocaine mixed in a tube and poured on the eyelids gave him great relief, and very soon after this he was asleep. The simple folk were very pleased, and the gift of a few dozen tabloids of different kinds for future use evoked warm expressions of gratitude; but the chief need of our visitors was not medicine, but food, and clothing in which to wrap their bodies during the cold nights.

Life at the shêkh's clearing was pleasant enough, but it was difficult to see how I was to get back to the river Atbara, where at that time the railway ended, for no one knew when the steamers which plied between Atbara and Kharṭûm would pass the clearing, and I had no authority to signal for one to stop. To obtain camels or donkeys was impossible, for there were none in the neighbourhood, and the shêkh had neither the power nor the desire to facilitate my departure, for he wished me to stay with him indefinitely. Fortunately, however, the young Engineer officers, who had given me such valuable information as to the position of the pyramids, remembered the difficulty in which I was likely to be placed, and Lieutenant Midwinter most kindly sent the *Burdên* on from her last stopping-place to fetch me. Thus whilst we were sitting in the clearing one afternoon, having made all preparations for passing the night there, the evening meal being actually in the saucepan, the beat of paddles sounded on the still air, and soon after the steamer was sighted. When she had tied up, an orderly landed and brought me a message from Midwinter to the effect that I was to embark on the *Burdên* and to come and stay with him that night. The orderly was followed by the friendly engineer and several of the crew, and in less than half an hour the tent was struck, the saucepan with our dinner in it taken off the fire, the water-pot and all else were transferred to the steamer, and I was trying to thank the shêkh for his kindness. Money he absolutely refused to take, saying, correctly enough, that it was useless, as there was nothing to buy, but he approved highly of a Swedish razor—for at that time he had shaved off his beard and was cultivating a moustache—a supply of shaving soap, a pocket knife, and a compass, things which previous experience had shown me were greatly prized by the natives both in Mesopotamia and in Egypt. Some brightly coloured handkerchiefs, two little cases filled with needles of all sizes and kinds, and a couple of cakes of very highly-scented soap, gave great pleasure to his wife and her friends, and a small sugar-loaf, about three pounds in weight, won for me the temporary affection of the two boys who scared the birds from the *dhurra*.

The shêkh was very anxious to go to Cairo with me, so that he might press his claims on the Government in person, but I explained to him that before he could travel on the steamer he must have the Sirdar's permission. Finally we parted, and when I caught a last glimpse of him as we passed down the river, he was standing on the river bank in that dignified attitude which is so characteristic of the natives of the better class, looking after the boat; just behind him were the two ladies of the clearing, and near them were the two boys, who were evidently more ready to watch the steamer than to scare the birds. The shêkh was very kind and hospitable, and I was glad to see him again in February, 1905, when he appeared at the pyramids in his gorgeous "robe of honour." He had prospered greatly since I saw him in 1899, and had married more wives, and been blessed with offspring; but it seemed to me that the condition of his finances left something to be desired, for he wished to borrow money to pay his train fare to and from Kharṭûm, whither he was most anxious to go in order to present a petition praying for the restoration of certain lands to which he laid claim. He was too old to work, but he had left in him sufficient energy and strength, to which we may add foolishness, to embark in what most Orientals revel in and enjoy above all things—a lawsuit!

A few hours' steaming brought the *Burdên* to the place where Midwinter and his colleagues were camped, and they welcomed me most kindly. The following morning they took me to see the works which were in progress in connection with the making of the bed of the railway, and described the methods they followed in building culverts, drains, &c. The portion of the Island of Meroë through which they were then passing was full of stone hills, and the difficulties which they had to surmount before the bed of the railway could be made were considerable. The urgent need for economy developed their inventive faculties to a wonderful degree, and their ingenious makeshifts and contrivances were singularly successful. In the course of the morning the captain of the *Burdên* reported that the steamer was loaded with wood and ready to start, and, as there was no possibility that year of visiting the ancient sites in the southern portion of the Island of Meroë, I left my kind friends and returned to the Atbara. The train for Ḥalfa had left about half an hour before I arrived, and as there would not be another for two days I had plenty of time to look about the camp, and watch other people work. Almost the first person I met was a young Egyptian whom I had known as a boy in the school of the American Mission at Cairo. He spoke English very well, and had been helped by the Mission into the Government engineering works in Cairo, where he stayed for some years and learned his trade, and he was then employed in connection with locomotives at Atbara. He was one of the many young men who have been educated by the American Mission, and made good and useful members of society. The Post and Telegraph Office was an interesting place, and the number of natives who frequented it was surprising. Natives of various towns and villages in Egypt were continually telegraphing to their relations to say that they were well, and the business done in money orders was, comparatively, large.

Wandering one morning by invitation into the Commandant's office, I was the witness of an interesting ceremony, namely, the setting free of some slaves. The British authorities had, it seemed, for some time past, suspected certain natives of Berber of carrying on, though on a much reduced scale, their old traffic in slaves. These men had their agents posted at different points on the various caravan roads in the desert, and from time to time they were able to seize small companies of travellers, and stray wayfarers, and carry them off across the desert to the sea-coast near Sawâkin, where they managed to export them. When British officers began to open up the old trade routes in the Eastern Desert, and to establish patrols under Egyptian officers, the Berber merchants found such proceedings highly inconvenient, and as British officers could not be bribed, they were placed in a difficult position. The natives, moreover, had discovered quickly what manner of men their new rulers were, and they plucked up courage, and began to give the authorities information which sometimes turned out to be of value. The day I returned to Atbara Fort a Berber slave agent was arrested in the desert some miles from the river, with a number of slaves in his possession, and he was promptly brought in to Atbara and examined by Captain Swabey. The agent's statements were soon found to be false, and as the charge of kidnapping was clearly proved against him and his assistant, they were put under restraint until the punishment to be meted out to them was decided upon. Captain Swabey then had the party of slaves brought in before him, and asked them questions, and found that they had been greatly ill-used; the party consisted of an old man, three elderly women, and a boy. Having satisfied himself on all points connected with their capture, Captain Swabey then declared each one of them to be free, but they seemed dazed and hardly to understand that they had been set free. At that moment freedom did not mean much to them, for they were hungry and penniless, and far from their homes. They were, however, helped out of their difficulties, for Captain Swabey took steps to have them fed, and by his wish one of the Egyptian officers found them shelter, and made arrangements whereby they received rations. The party left the Commandant's office in a most dejected state, and I believe they would even then have welcomed a life of slavery with any one who would have taken the responsibility of providing them with food and drink and enough cotton stuff to cover them.

A day later a train was made up for the north, and in company with Captain Oldfield and Captain (now Colonel) Henry I returned to Ḥalfa in about two days. We occupied one of the new saloon coaches, wherein provision was made for sleeping and cooking, and I have often travelled with much less comfort on an English railway. We frequently attained to a speed of twenty-five miles an hour, and if the protracted delays at some stations, caused by an insufficiency of locomotives, be not taken into consideration, no one had any cause for complaint. At Ḥalfa I was met by Mr. Somers Clarke, who showed me great kindness and welcomed me on his *dhahabîya*. The following morning we visited the little XVIIIth Dynasty temple on the western bank of the river, a few miles south of the camp, and he showed me a number of his excellent plans of the temples, churches, &c., which are found on both banks of the Nile between Philae and Ḥalfa. These plans are the most accurate and comprehensive of any yet made, and they throw a great deal of new light upon the architectural knowledge and methods of the ancient Egyptians, and of their Christian descendants, the Copts. Mr. Somers

ATBARA FORT.
In the foreground is Captain Swabey, the Commandant.

Clarke's exhaustive examinations of the remains of the Coptic churches so far south as Semna are most important, and when he has worked out his results we shall be able to understand for what uses many portions of these buildings were employed, and the peculiarities of churches in monasteries and nunneries as opposed to churches in villages and towns. He has done for the churches of Nubia what Waddington did for the churches of Syria, and it is to be hoped that his monograph on the subject will soon appear.

From Aswân to Luxor I travelled by the narrow-gauge railway

which had recently been opened, and seventeen and a half hours were occupied in performing the journey of one hundred and twenty miles. The dust was suffocating, the rattle deafening, and the road-bed was so uneven and the curves so short that it was a marvel how the coaches kept on the rails at all, and all this in spite of the fact that tens of thousands of tons of railway material and stores had rolled over the line on their way to the Sûdân. I thought with regret of the Sirdar's Military Railway, and wished that the line I was on had been surveyed and laid by my friends the young officers of the Royal Engineers.

CHAPTER VII.

FERLINI'S EXCAVATIONS AT THE PYRAMIDS OF BAGRÂWÎYA.

THE first European who attempted to excavate the temples and pyramids on the Island of Meroë was Joseph Ferlini, an Italian doctor of medicine, who entered the service of the Egyptian Government as a Surgeon-Major in 1830. His first appointment took him to Sennaar, but he was afterwards sent to Kordofân, and finally, in connection with the rearrangement of the medical branch of Muḥammad Ali's army in the Sûdân, he was despatched to serve in Kharṭûm. When he had been in this town for a few months, he asked permission of the Governor of Kharṭûm, Kurshîd Pâshâ, to make excavations on the ancient sites in the country; but the Pâshâ, assuming his wish was to dig for buried treasure, advised him to be content with what he had already saved during his four years' residence in the Sûdân, and not to run the risk of losing everything. He further pointed out that if Ferlini were to find any valuable object, the blacks would certainly kill him and take possession of it. These remarks produced not the smallest effect on Ferlini, and so soon as his successor had been found, and he had left Cairo for the south, Ferlini set to work to prepare for his archæological researches. There was at that time in Kharṭûm an Albanian called Antoine Stefani, who had lived in the country for fifteen years, and carried on business as merchant. Him Ferlini made a partner in the undertaking, and promised to give him one-half of the proceeds, and putting 400 dollars (?) into his hands, he sent him to Masallamîya to buy camels, ropes, grain, water-skins, &c. He next hired 30 young men for their food and two Spanish dollars per month each, and laid in a large stock of meat, which he cut into strips, and dried in the sun according to the custom of the country. The day after his successor arrived from Cairo (August 10th, 1834), Ferlini sent off the camels by land, and he and Stefani, with their families, slaves, &c., set out for Wad Bâ Nagaa by boat. From Wad Bâ Nagaa they marched to the ruins at Nagaa, at the head of the valley, a journey of eight hours, and there they were obliged to build shelters to protect themselves from the lions which at that time abounded in the neighbourhood. Ferlini began to clear out one of the larger temples, the sides of which were decorated with reliefs and hieroglyphics, but after a few days he had to stop work, for five of his camels had died, and the others were either ill or exhausted by the long journeys to and from the Nile for water. Besides this his men were ill, and a young negro had died. Ferlini then moved nearer the river, and finding another temple, he began to clear it out, but after three days he again stopped work, and he and Stefani returned to their families, whom they had left at Wad Bâ Nagaa.

At this place Ferlini found several pillars of an ancient temple still standing, but he determined to let temples alone for the future, and to search for his reward among the tombs of those who built them. Having found the site of the cemetery, he began to dig there, and very soon after he discovered a large corridor which resembled a gallery of the catacombs at Rome. This corridor widened out into a circular space having an area of several square yards, and here he found many terra-cotta jars, the mouths of which were carefully sealed [with plaster]. The workmen naturally imagined that these contained gold, and were much disappointed when Ferlini broke one open, and they saw that they held nothing except a sort of plaster cake. At the far end of the corridor was a hollow, and at a depth of some feet a number of bodies were discovered by the light of a lamp; the body in the centre of these lay under a stone, and had on one side a sword and lance, and on the other a bow and some arrows. When the weapons were touched they fell to pieces, with the exception of a few arrows which were plated with some hard metal.

Not being satisfied with the results which he had obtained from the tombs, Ferlini began to dig at a spot on the site of the town where he saw the remains of some columns. Here he discovered a rectangular block of red granite, ornamented with figures of gods, and inscribed with hieroglyphics. What he had found was, of course, an altar belonging to the ancient temple of Wad Bâ Nagaa, probably that which is now preserved in the Royal Museum at Berlin.[1] Finding it impossible to carry off the altar on account of its weight, Ferlini tried to break off the lower portion of it, so that he might be able to remove the upper inscribed part, but all he could do was in vain, and he only succeeded in detaching a large fragment. He next tried to saw it in half, but this attempt was more hopeless still, and finally he was obliged to commit the care of the "superbe pilastre," as he calls the object, to the care of the shèkh of Wad Bâ Nagaa, telling him not to give it up to any person without his orders. When he arrived subsequently in Cairo, he presented the altar to the French Consul, M. Mimant. Ferlini being dissatisfied with the results of his excavations on this site, struck his camp and travelled northwards until he came to the group of villages which at that time appear to have been known by the general name of "Bagrâwîya," or as he writes the name, "Bégaraviah." In Cailliaud's time these villages were As-Sûr, Dankêl and Tenedhbai, and they were situated on the edge of the cultivated land, close to the desert; their sites were about forty-five miles from the Atbara river.

On their arrival at Bagrâwîya Ferlini and Stefani pitched their tents near the village, at no great distance from the river, and having set some of their men to make leather baskets out of cow-hides, and the remainder to keep watch over the camels, they went to look at the pyramids. They passed over the site of the old city of Meroë, which was then, even as it is now, buried in sand, and all the ancient things they saw were the black basalt sphinxes which are still *in situ*, and are hardly worth removal. They passed on to the east and saw the ruined pyramids which are close to the modern Berber road, and continuing in an easterly direction they came to the hills where the two most important groups of the Pyramids of Meroë are situated. Ferlini counted the groups, and declared the larger contained twenty-one pyramids, only one being nearly intact, and the smaller eight. Here he wished to begin to dig, but, as Stefani insisted on his making a beginning on the site of the ancient city near the sphinxes, he did so. The first

[1] See Lepsius, *Denkmäler*, Abth. V. Bl. 55.

structure excavated was a kind of house, which "appeared to have "been destroyed by the hand of man," and there they found a green, enamelled terra-cotta plaque, and a serpentine ichneumon, but nothing further. At this point Ferlini left Stefani, and, taking one hundred men, he set out for the pyramids on the hill, about three miles distant. He began to work on the east side of the hill, and attacked one of the small pyramids at its foot. Having removed the pyramid proper, he found some flat slabs of stone at the level of the ground, and removing these he found beneath them a flight of steps cut in the sandy soil. Further digging brought to light a second and then a third flight of steps, but as it was becoming dark Ferlini decided to postpone his examination of the tomb until the next day. The next day he sent for Stefani, who had found meanwhile nothing but a small glazed figure, and adding Stefani's workmen to his own, he began to clear the tomb out in a systematic manner. He tells us that the people who were employed on this work were 350 in number, but it is difficult to understand how so many men could be occupied in connection with what was a very small monument.

The steps having been cleared, Ferlini was able to enter a small cavern wherein he found the bones of a camel, of a horse, and of some small animals, which he thought might have been dogs, a camel saddle, a horse saddle, and some metal bells, on which were inscribed figures of birds and of gods. At the end of the cavern was a large stone, and when this was removed he saw the outline of an oval opening, cut in the rock, but carefully plastered over. This opening formed the entrance to a second chamber, in which Ferlini saw lying a mass of human bones piled one above the other. Besides these there was nothing in the chamber. The clearing out of the chamber was only accomplished with difficulty, for no man could endure for long its suffocating atmosphere which was exceedingly hot and damp.

Whilst Ferlini had been excavating one pyramid, Stefani attacked another, and in due course he found the flight of steps, and the chambers, which closely resembled those described above, and a number of bodies. One of these was covered by a stone, and as the workmen were digging by the side of it, one of them struck with his pick a round object, as large as an ostrich's egg, and a number of solid white, transparent objects, presumably made of glass, rolled out of it. When Ferlini and his friend had opened two other pyramids, and had found nothing of special interest, they began seriously to consider their position, which was certainly not an enviable one. They were engaged on a piece of work which was costly, and their personal discomfort was very considerable; the heat was great, their food was bad, and they distrusted the natives so much, that one or the other of them had to keep watch during the night lest they should be robbed and

VIEW OF THE PYRAMID (CAILLIAUD F) DEMOLISHED BY FERLINI.

murdered. Ferlini decided to continue the work for a short time longer, and to make a last attempt. The smaller pyramids he abandoned, and, after a careful examination of the large pyramids, he decided to attack the one which Cailliaud has marked F on his plan, and has described at some length in his *Voyage*, tom. ii., p. 157 ff., plates (tom. i.) xli. and xliii. It was one of the largest pyramids of the group, and was about eighty-eight feet high; the length of each side at the base was about sixty-one feet. As will be seen from the view of it reproduced here from Cailliaud's work, the pyramid was nearly complete, and its chapel and pylon were in a good state of preservation. A portion of the casing of the east face was badly cracked, due, no doubt, to some settlement of the foundations, but this defect must have existed in ancient days, for the south face was strengthened by means of a low wall which had been built against it at the base. The chapel was, and still is, remarkable for its ornamentation and reliefs, and especially for its roof, which is a rounded arch, formed of correctly hewn arch-stones. This pyramid was built for a queen, who in the reliefs is seen wearing over her shoulders a garment of unusual character, and most elaborate jewellery, and there is no doubt that she was one of the greatest of the large-bodied women, each of whom bore the name of Candace, who had gained ascendency both in the Island of Meroë and at Napata.

Having come to a decision, Ferlini, acompanied by four workmen, ascended the pyramid, and saw at the first glance that the work of demolition would not be difficult, for the uppermost part was already falling. So soon as he had removed the top stone[1] he brought up his workmen, who began to hurl the blocks of the casing to the ground, and on account of the fierce heat, 48° Réaumur (= 140° Fahrenheit) Ferlini and Stefani beat a retreat and took shelter in the shadow of a neighbouring pyramid. "Then," he says "I was called by my faithful servant. I ran "with my friend to the top of the monument and I already felt "my heart open to sweet hope. I saw my servant lying on his "belly on the flat space which had been made, and seeking to "cover with his body the hole which had just been uncovered. "The Blacks, incited by greed, wished to drive away my servant "by force, and to plunge their hands down to the bottom of the "opening; but with our weapons in our hands we made them go "down, and then calling to us other servants whom we trusted, "we had the excavation continued in our presence. The open-"ing permitted us to look across an empty space and at every "object which it contained. This empty space was formed "by large stones roughly joined together. We made the men "remove the largest of the stones which covered the upper part, "and then we were able to see that the chamber was rectangular

[1] Ferlini in his drawing makes the pyramid terminate in a single block, but we know from Cailliaud's drawing that it had a flat top, composed of many stones, like the other pyramids.

"in shape, and that its walls were formed of large stones laid one "upon the other, and that [they were parallel] with the steps [of "the pyramid]. The chamber was from six to seven feet long, "and about five feet high. The first object that met our gaze "was a large 'masso,' covered over with a white piece of linen "or cotton cloth, which however, so soon as it was touched, fell "into dust. Under this was a rectangular funerary couch, or "bier of wood, which was supported on four cylindrical legs, and "was surrounded by a framework, wherein small and large bars of "wood were arranged alternately. These bars were carved and "represented symbolical figures. Under this bier I found the "vase (Catalogue No. 108) which contained objects, wrapped up "in a piece of linen similar to that which I have just mentioned. "Close to the vase, on the floor of the chamber, there were "arranged symmetrically by means of thread, necklaces formed of "beads made of glass, paste, [coloured] stones, &c., a number of "amulets, small figures of gods, a metal eye-paint case, little "round boxes [filled with a powder, of which I give the analysis "further on],[1] a saw, a chisel, and several other objects of which "I have given a description in my Catalogue."

Ferlini says that he promptly placed in little leather bags the valuable objects which he had found, taking care not to allow the Arabs to see the gold. When he came down from the pyramid his workmen crowded round to see what he had found, but grasping his weapons, he ordered them to continue their work, and they obeyed him hurriedly, because they thought that the sight of fire-arms alone was sufficient to kill them. That night, when the Blacks were in their huts, and the servants fast asleep, Ferlini and Stefani examined carefully the objects of their find; they were greatly surprised at the beauty of the workmanship, for Ferlini considered that it was finer than any to which the Greeks had attained. Whilst he was rejoicing in his good fortune, he noticed that Stefani's countenance was sad, and, when he asked the reason, his friend replied that the Blacks could not be trusted, and that they had better fly for their lives with their treasures. This, however, Ferlini refused to do, and having dug a hole in

[1] See Ferlini's Catalogue, No. 107. The words in brackets are from the French.

the ground near his tent and laid his "find" in it, he covered it over with sand.

The next morning, with the help of five hundred men, he continued the work of pulling down the pyramid. He first pulled down the chamber wherein he had found the treasure and the "masso,"[1] and then dug up layer by layer the stones beneath it. The removal of the upper part of the pyramid from A to B occupied fifteen days, and at B, that is to say in the centre of the pyramid, he found a niche, or small chamber, formed of three blocks of stone. Having removed the stones,

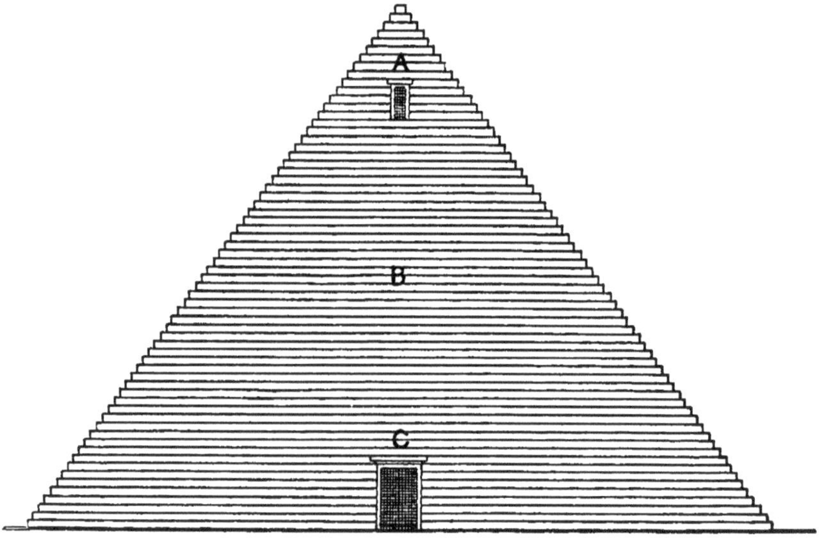

THE PYRAMID AT MEROË DEMOLISHED BY FERLINI.

A—The chamber where the jewellery was found.
B—The chamber where the two bronze vessels were found.
C—The place where Cailliaud's name was cut.

he saw a piece of linen stuff, and beneath it were two vases in bronze, "of the most beautiful forms, and so well preserved that "one would have said that they had just left the hands of the "workman." The work of twenty days more enabled Ferlini to clear away the remainder of the pyramid down to the level of the hill, where he found large slabs of black stone. The chapel, on one of the walls of which was cut the name of "Cailliaud," he left standing, but he broke off and carried away the portion of the

[1] About the disposal of the "masso" he is silent.

stone which faced the door and contained the cartouche of the royal person for whom the pyramid was built.

Ferlini next noticed, on the east side of the hill, traces of a path which seemed to lead directly under the chapel; he began to dig there, and found at the depth of about eight feet several huge blocks of stone set in lime. He seems to have thought that he was about to make some important discovery, and to have wished to keep it to himself as much as possible, for he began to dismiss

HEAD OF DIONYSOS.
From the handle of a bronze vessel of the Ferlini Collection.

a large number of his workmen; they, however, refused to be dismissed, and returned to the diggings without being summoned, bringing their lances and other weapons with them. Their truculent manner excited Ferlini's suspicions, and having had them watched, he learned after about six days from one of his faithful servants, who knew their language, and had made friends with them, that they were determined to attack Stefani and himself, and to take possession of their treasure. Ferlini first thought of fighting the Blacks, but Stefani persuaded him not to do so, and then remembering his own family, and that of his friend, and also reflecting that if there were a disturbance, and if the report of it reached the ears of the Government officials, he would certainly lose everything he had found, he determined to make his escape that very night. He despatched his camels to Berber, under the charge of his confidential servants, and he and Stefani sailed thither in a Government vessel which had been placed at

BRONZE VESSEL, WITH HANDLE, ORNAMENTED WITH DIONYSOS MASKS.

From the Ferlini Collection, and now in the Antiquarium at Munich.

his service. Abbâs Aghâ, the Governor, received him kindly, and made him his guest for eight days; at the end of that time Ferlini left Berber, and a journey of two days brought him to Abû Ḥamed. Here he laid in a supply of water, and then set out across the desert for Korosko, which he reached in about fifteen days. Thence he proceeded to Cairo by the ordinary route, and, having obtained the balance due to him of his salary, and permission to depart, he returned with his spoil to his own country.

Such is, in brief, the narrative of the excavations made at the Pyramids of Meroë by Ferlini as told by himself. It has been condensed from an account of his excavations and travels written in Italian, and published at Bologna in 1837, under the title "Cenno sugli scavi operati nella Nubia." To this work he added a Catalogue of the objects which he found,[1] and one plate on which several of them are depicted in outline. In 1838 a French translation of the narrative appeared at Rome, entitled "Relation "Historique de Fouilles opérées dans la Nubie par le Docteur "Joseph Ferlini de Bologne;"[2] appended to this was a French translation of the Catalogue, and descriptions of the deserts of Korosko, Sennaar, and Kordôfân. Here and there the French translation contains modifications of the statements made in the Italian original, and certain additions. As these pamphlets are somewhat rare, the portions which relate to Ferlini's excavations at the pyramids of Meroë are reprinted in the Appendix at the end of this chapter.

The narrative of Ferlini is certainly circumstantial, but it leaves many points unexplained, and the reader is left without guidance in his difficulties. There is no doubt that Ferlini and Stefani excavated four small pyramids at Meroë, and it is pretty certain that they pulled down the pyramid marked F in Cailliaud's plan, because the tradition which was common in the neighbourhood when Lepsius was in the Sûdân, and is still repeated, says that they did. That treasure, consisting of necklaces, bracelets, rings, and other articles of jewellery, was found during the excavations may also be true, but Ferlini's statement that the greater number of the objects which he describes in his Catalogue were found in a chamber five feet high and six or seven feet long,

[1] Catologo della Raccolta dei Monumenti Antichi la maggior parte d'oro trovati nella cuspide di una delle Piramidi della Citta di Meroe in Etiopia di stile Egizio-Etiopico.

[2] The title continues:—"suivie d'un catalogue des objets qu'il a trouvés "dans l'une des quarante-sept pyramides aux environs de l'ancienne ville de "Méroé, et d'une description des grand déserts de Coruscah et de Sinnaar."

seems to me open to doubt. Lepsius, in his *Letters from Egypt, Ethiopia*, &c. (p. 197), says that he tried to prove to Osman Bey "that the discovery of Ferlini was pure chance, that he had not "found the gold rings in the sepulchral chambers with the "mummies, where they alone might reasonably have been "searched for with any hope of success, but walled up in the "stone, in which place they had been concealed by a whim of the "owner;" but unfortunately, further than this he gives no opinion about the place in the pyramid where they were found. In the upper portion of no other pyramid in the Sûdân, up to the present, has any chamber been found, and it is impossible to believe that any one who wished to hide valuable jewellery securely would choose such an unsafe place. According to Ferlini's own showing it was only necessary to remove a few layers of stone, which four men were able to do in a very short time, before the entrance to the "chamber" was found, and the treasure secured. I cannot believe that any queen of Meroë would have her jewellery hidden away in a place which would be known to many people, and whence it could be easily abstracted by a very few men in a very short space of time.

It is, moreover, not quite clear what Ferlini saw in the chamber when it was first opened. He says there was a "grande masso," which was presumably some large object, covered over with a cloth that fell to pieces as soon as it was touched. Under the cloth there appeared a rectangular wooden bier (un cataletto, o bara di legno di forma quadrilatera), supported on four carved legs, and under it was the metal vase or bowl, which contained all the gold objects. In the French translation "masso" is rendered by "corps," which, however, does not make the meaning any clearer, unless we accept the translator's explanation that the "masso" or "corps" was a kind of table or altar (une espèce de table ou autel), either a *mensa sacra* or an *ara domestica*. Ferlini, however, says distinctly that the object which was under the cloth that crumbled into dust was a bier, or funeral bed (cataletto o bara), and that it had a wooden frame with bars, and if this were so, the object must have resembled the broad wooden *dîwân*, or couch, on which the natives sit and sleep at the present day, and was probably intended to receive a dead body.

Ferlini refers the reader to No. 153 of his Catalogue for a description of the bars of the bier, but if we compare that given by him in Italian with the French translation made by B. B. already referred to, we shall see that it is in many particulars quite different. The translator also adds that the bars were fourteen in number. This interesting piece of information he must have obtained from Ferlini, and it is important as suggesting that the additional details which are given in the French translation were derived from that source.

We have next to note that Ferlini tells us that after fifteen days' work in pulling down the pyramid, when the upper half of it had been removed, he found a niche formed by three slabs of stone, wherein were two metal vessels of most beautiful workmanship. The narrative is quite explicit, and he says that he saw the vessels himself in the niche, but as the statement stands it is to me incredible. The vessels could serve no useful purpose when buried in an inaccessible niche in the interior of the pyramid, about twenty-four feet from the ground, and neither the piety nor the superstition of its builder would be served by hiding vases in this manner. Vessels in bronze, earthenware, &c., ornaments and jewellery, arms and weapons, &c., when buried with the dead, were intended to be used by the dead in the Other World, and were always placed near the bodies in their last resting-places, or at any rate somewhere in the sepulchral chamber, or in neighbouring chambers, which were connected with it by a corridor.

Ferlini's narrative of the "find" in the pyramid closely resembles the stories which natives all over Egypt tell travellers to whom they wish to sell some article of unusual interest or importance, and they have been in the habit of telling marvellous stories for some generations, hoping thereby to make sure of selling their antiquities. It is most probable that most of the objects which Ferlini describes in his Catalogue were found somewhere in or near the pyramid, but not in any chamber or niche in the building itself. Their number and variety suggest to me that they represent the loot collected by some thief from several tomb chambers, and not the ornaments and jewellery of one queen only. Or it is quite possible that they

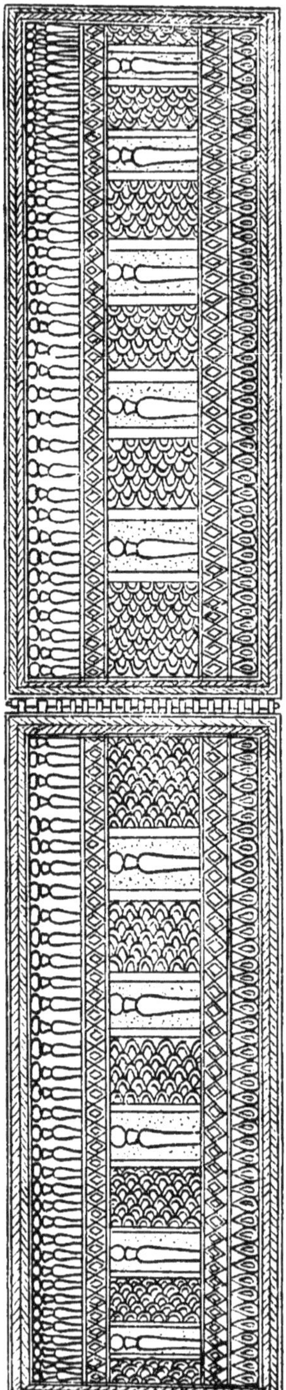

NO. I.—GOLD HINGED-ARMLET, IN THE BERLIN MUSEUM. (From the Ferlini Collection.)

were collected from the sepulchral chambers during a period of national calamity, when there was every likelihood of their being stolen, and were hidden in some safe place, just as the mummies of the kings and queens of Egypt, with their possessions, were removed from their tombs at Thebes and hidden at Dêr al-Baḥari. But in any case it is incredible, to me at least, that a chamber, even if we admit its existence in the upper half of a pyramid, which could be easily entered by merely removing a few layers of stones of moderate size, should have been chosen either by pious man or thief, as a hiding place for such treasure. Personally I believe that Ferlini bought his collection at Ḳûṣ, or some similar place where rich burials of the Graeco-Roman Period are frequently found, and that the narrative which he printed is a mixture of his own experiences, and those of natives in Egypt with whom he had come in contact.

It is now time to give a brief summary of the objects which Ferlini has enumerated in his Catalogue. These are divided by him into groups, thus:—Necklaces, Nos. 1-20; Bracelets, Nos. 21-25; Rings with hinges, Nos. 26-34; Ordinary rings, Nos. 35-88; Silver rings, Nos. 89-93; Miscellaneous objects, rings in stone, cameos, &c., Nos. 94-104; Objects in metal, Nos. 105-117; Objects in stone and pastes, Nos. 118-148; Stones, Nos. 149-151; Objects in wood, Nos. 152-155. At the end of his Catalogue he published a plate of illustrations of some of the objects in outline, and a few of these have been reproduced in the present work. Soon after Ferlini returned to his native country he began to exhibit his collection to archaeologists and others, and it received considerable attention from the learned world in Europe, which was at that time profoundly interested in the decipherment of Egyptian hieroglyphics, chiefly through the results obtained by Young, Champollion, and Rosellini. Whether Ferlini had in his possession all the objects which he obtained through his researches

NO. 2.—GOLD ARMLET WITH FIGURES OF MUT AND OTHER GODDESSES, IN THE BERLIN MUSEUM.

From the Ferlini Collection.

in the Sûdân, or whether he had only one-half of them—for it will be remembered that in his contract with Stefani the merchant he promised to give to him one-half of all his findings—cannot be said, but in any case his collection came into the market, and one part of it was purchased by the Royal Museum at Berlin and the other went to the Museum at Munich.

Dr. Birch, of the British Museum, viewed many of the objects with suspicion, and many others he regarded as imitations of ancient Egyptian jewellery made long after the kingdom of the Pharaohs had come to an end, and therefore declared them to be "forgeries." On the other hand, Lepsius (*Letters*, p. 207) had no doubt that the collection "belonged to a well-known, and as it happens, the "greatest of all the queens of Meroë, who built "almost all the temples still in tolerable preservation on the "Island," and, from this circumstance, Ferlini's jewels, Lepsius says, "become infinitely more valuable for the history of Ethiopian "art, in which they now occupy a fixed position." Further, he considered "the purchase of that remarkable discovery" as a "most important acquisition" of the Berlin Museum. In referring to the value of Ferlini's jewels, it is important to note that Lepsius says they were found hidden in the "wall work"[1] of the pyramid, a statement which suggests that he did not believe in the existence of a chamber at the top of the pyramid.

NO. 3.—GOLD ARMLET, IN THE BERLIN MUSEUM.
From the Ferlini Collection.

With the help of the splendid plate of coloured reproductions of the jewellery published by Lepsius in the *Denkmäler* (Abth. V. Bl. 42), and the list given in the official *Ausführliches Verzeichnis*,[2] the principal objects of the Berlin portion of Ferlini's collection may be thus enumerated:—

1 and 2. Pair of gold armlets with hinges. In the centre is a row of gold figures wearing disks, set in green enamel, on the top edge is a row of uraei wearing disks in gold, in a setting of blue enamel, and on the bottom edge are designs of diamonds and buds inlaid with red and blue enamel. (See illustration No. 1.)

[1] "Die Pyramide mit römisch gewölbter Vorkammer, in deren Mauerwerk "Ferlini den Schatz verborgen fand." Lepsius, *Briefe*, p. 218. Berlin, 1852.

[2] Page 314 of the 1894 edition, and p. 407 of the 1899 edition.

3 and 4. Pair of gold armlets, ornamented with figures of four goddesses with outspread wings, inlaid with red and blue enamel; a central figure of Mut is all of gold, and wears the double crown, , and the vulture headdress. Above these is a row of uraei, and below them a diamond pattern in gold. (See illustration No. 2.)

5 and 6. Pair of gold armlets, ornamented with rows of circles, buds, uraei with disks, diamonds, &c., inlaid with blue enamel. In the centre is a group of small temple doors, and aegis, &c., in red, blue and gold. (See illustration No. 3.)

7. Large gold object, part of a necklace (?), with inscription recording the name Parei. (See illustration No. 4.)

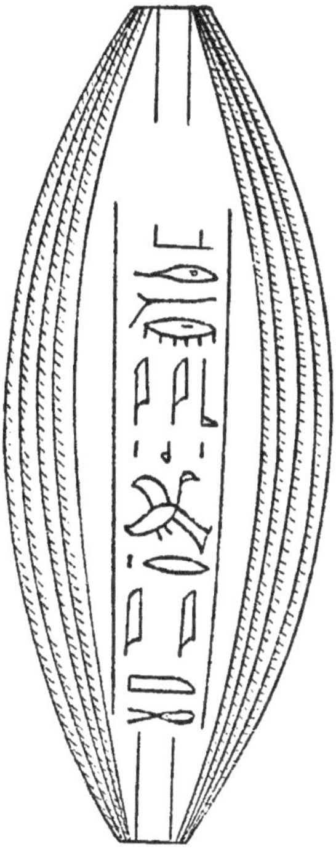

NO. 4.—GOLD OBJECT MADE FOR PAREI, IN THE BERLIN MUSEUM.

From the Ferlini Collection.

8 and 9. Pair of ornaments, with bands of gold and eyes of Horus, inlaid with black, white, and green enamel.

10 and 11. Pair of oval silver ornaments, inlaid with eyes of Horus.

12. Gold ring, with blue glass or paste bezel, inscribed with the figure of a bird.

13. Silver ring, inscribed with the figure of a bull.

14. Gold ring with rectangular green paste bezel, inscribed with the figure of an animal.

NO. 5.—GOLD PLAQUE. HEAD OF HATHOR, WITH URAEI.

15. Gold ring, inscribed with the figure of a pig.

16-19. Gold plaques; heads of Hathor, with uraei, inlaid with blue and green paste. (See illustration No. 5.)

20-23. Gold figures of Anubis, with uraei.

24 and 25. Gold figures of Sekhet and Harpocrates.

26. Necklace, formed of twelve eyes of Horus, four symbols of "life," and a lotus bud pendant, in gold, inlaid with blue and green enamel. (See illustration No. 6.)

NO. 6.—NECKLACE, IN THE BERLIN MUSEUM. (From the Ferlini Collection.)

NO. 7.—NECKLACE, IN THE BERLIN MUSEUM. (From the Ferlini Collection.)

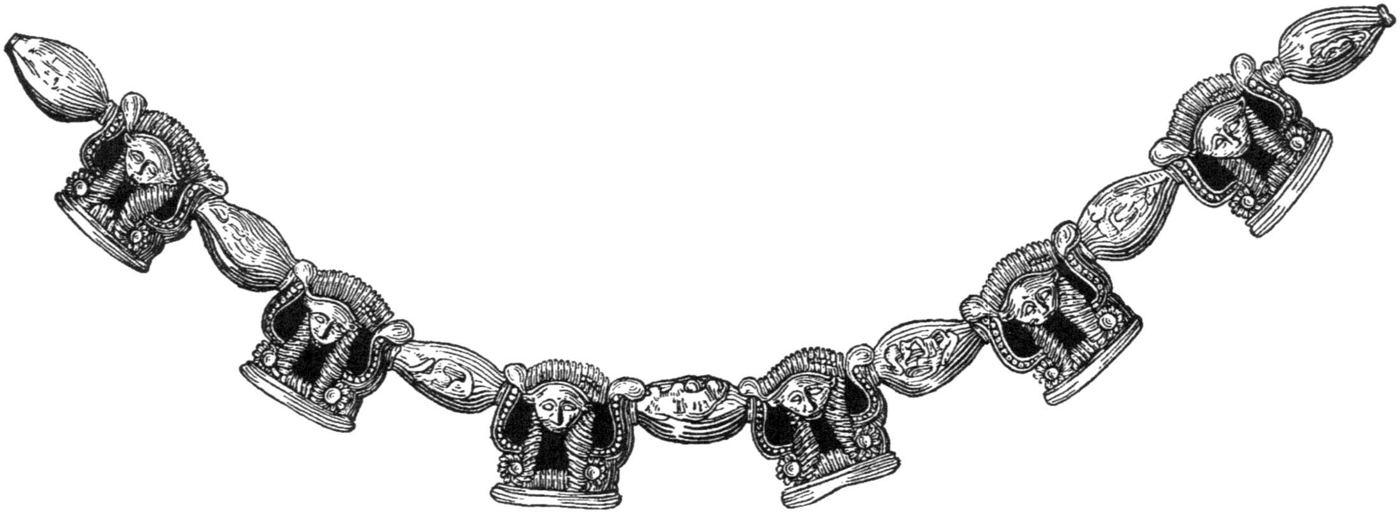

No. 8.—NECKLACE, IN THE ANTIQUARIUM AT MUNICH. (From the Ferlini Collection.)

27. Gold necklace of beads, made in the forms of shells, symbols of "life," eyes of Horus, &c., with four ☥ pendants. (See illustration No. 7.)

NO. 9.—GOLD-HINGED ARMLET, IN THE ANTIQUARIUM AT MUNICH.
From the Ferlini Collection.

28-31. Small gold bells.
32 and 33. Pair of large gold rings.
34-37. Four small gold lions.
38-41. Four gold scarabs.
42. Gold bangle, with ends terminating in heads of serpents.

NO. 10.—GOLD-HINGED ARMLET, IN THE ANTIQUARIUM AT MUNICH.
From the Ferlini Collection.

43. Massive copper ring, inscribed with the figure of a lion, &c.

44-47. Silver rings, inscribed with figures of gods, &c.

48-53. Three pairs of silver rings, with projections (earrings ?).

54-59. Ornaments in silver.

60-100. A series of gold finger-rings inscribed with figures of the gods, Åmen, Khensu, Isis suckling Horus, Isis holding

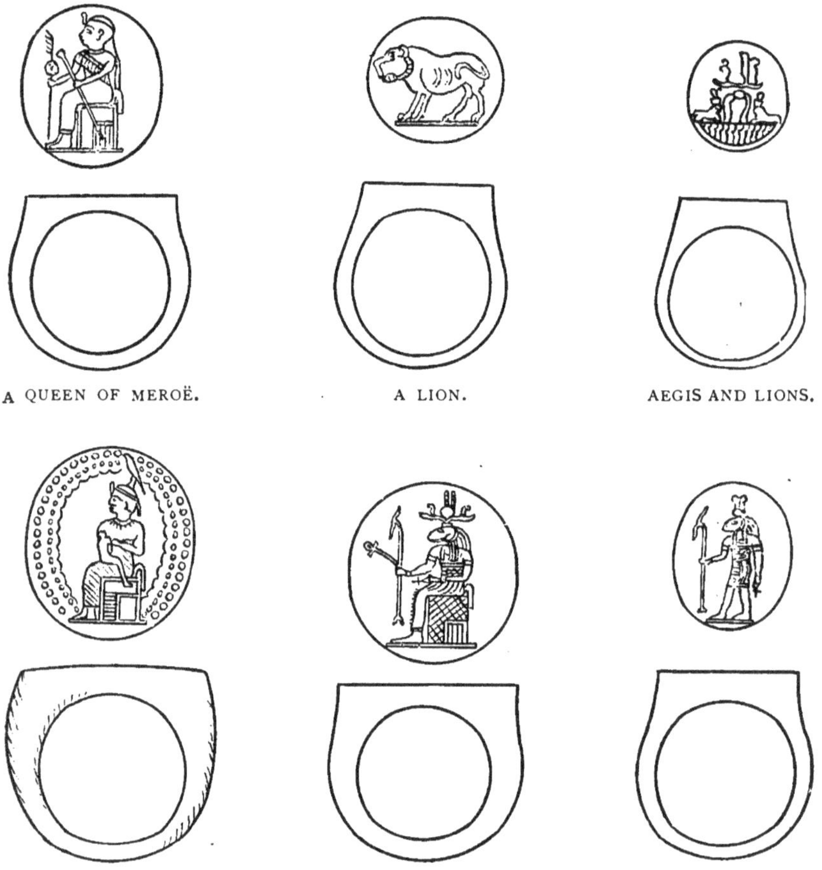

A QUEEN OF MEROË. A LION. AEGIS AND LIONS.

ISIS SUCKLING HORUS. THE RAM-HEADED ȦMEN OF NAPATA. THE RAM-HEADED ȦMEN OF NAPATA.

Group of rings, from the Ferlini Collection.

symbols of "life," Mut wearing the crowns of the South and North, and holding symbols of "life," a man-headed bird, &c. On others are figures of lions, heads of rams, and serpents, a vulture, an eagle, a bee, a dove, a symbol of "life," &c.

101. Bronze bowl, in which the above mentioned objects were found.

For a number of other objects from Bagrâwîya see the official *Verzeichniss*, Berlin, 1899, p. 411.

The portion of Ferlini's "find" which was acquired by the "Antiquarium" at Munich is thus summarized in the official Guide[1]:—

703. Necklace made of beads of gilded glass, scarabs inlaid with *utchats*, symbols of "life," hearts, and heads of Hathor. (See illustration No. 8.)

704. Richly decorated finger rings, with shield-shaped bezels engraved with heads of sacred animals, ram, cat, or figures of Osiris; the heads wear elaborate crowns, and frequently have above them the plumes of Ȧmen, the rams' horns with disks, uraei, &c. One ring is inlaid with an *utchat*, or Eye of Rā or Horus, and one is inscribed with a figure of a small temple.

705 and 706. Hinged armlets, ornamented with squares, annules, "Nile keys," scale or feather patterns, heads, &c., the intervening spaces being filled with red, blue, and green enamels. (See illustration No. 9.)

707 and 708. Hinged armlets, smaller and of better work, the ornamentation being similar.

Where the hinges come in Nos. 705-708 are figures of Mut or Isis with outstretched wings; they wear double crowns, and diadems with serpents and hawks. (See illustration No. 10.)

709 and 710. Bronze boxes, with handles, for holding costly unguents or perfumes; the handles of the small one are in the form of the "knot of Hercules," and those of the large one in the forms of bearded Dionysos masks. Dr. Christ believes these to be of Greek, probably Alexandrine work, and he thinks that the other objects of the group belong to the late Greek Period.

APPENDIX TO CHAPTER VII.

EXTRACT FROM FERLINI'S DESCRIPTION OF HIS EXCAVATIONS AT THE PYRAMIDS OF BAGRÂWÎYA.

ITALIAN ORIGINAL.

"Di là ci recammo verso *Begaravia* ove esistono le grandi Pira-
"midi, le quale più volte mi aveano messo il pensiero di cercare tra

[1] "Führer durch das K. Antiquarium in München," von W. Christ, p. 40.

" questa muta regione seggio di antica grandezza qualche avvanzo, " che potesse illustrare la storia di quella parte del mondo.

" Si posero le tende in vicinanza del piccolo Villaggio di " *Begaravia* poco distante dal Nilo ; e presa ad affitto qualche " capanna de' neri fu spartita la nostra servitû parte alla cura de' " cammelli parte a formar con pelli di bue vasi concavi per gettar " la terra scavata. In questo tempo andammo col' Albanese a " visitare le Piramidi che si fanno vedere a un ora di distanza. Si " passo dapprima all' antica città di *Meroè* tutta coperta dalla " sabbia, dove null' altro si scorge fuori che alcune sfingi di granito " nero ordinate in due fila, ma guaste, e sfigurate in parte. A " poca distanza da questa si vedono molte piramidi unite " rovinate dal corso degl' anni. Dopo breve cammino giungemmo " ad un colle la cui cima è coronata da ventuna Piramidi, tutte " guaste, e rovinate nella parte superiore ; fuori di una che ancor " conservasi intatta. A levante se ne veggono altre otto piû " piccole, ma intere, ed alle falde della collina se ne vedono molte " altre più piccole di cui non mostrasi intero che il portico, ovvero " santuario con iscrizioni Geroglifiche. Qui io divisiva di " intraprendere il lavoro, ma dissuaso dall' Albanese tentammo la " fortuna nella Città in vicinanza di quelle catene di Sfingi. " Quattro giorni dopo il nostro arrivo posta in ordine tutta la nostra " gente chiedemmo al capo del villaggio, detto Sech lavoratori a " paga ; ne' primi giorni, non isperando di ottenere il guiderdone " che loro si promettava, accorsero in poco numero, ma dappoi " tanti ne vennero che conveniva rimandarli. Dopo pochi giorni " si rinvenne un' abitazione, che aveva segni di rovine operati per " mano d'uomini, e nelle tre camere che di essa rimanevano non " si trovò che una piastra di pasta con vernice a smalto turchino " segnata al N. 146. ed un Ichneumone di serpentino segnato nel " catalogo al N. 118. Invano si cercò di scavar piû al fondo " per andare in cerca di alcuna cosa pregevole ; laonde passammo " ad altro luogo, poco distante, e qui lasciato l'Albanese, mi recai " con cent' uomini a visitare le grandi piramidi. Il mio compagno " dopo pochi giorni trovò un' altra abitazione più grande della " prima, ma con avversa fortuna, non avendo ritrovato che un " solo idoletto di terra cotta inverniciata come al N. 147. In " questo tempo io aveva già demolito gli avvanzi di una piccola " piramide posta al piede del colle, e giunto alla falda della " montagna la trovai di color nero formata di lastre, come se " fossero poste per mano d' uomo ; cercai col ferro la via piû " facile per riuscire alle fondamenta, e dopo aver levata poca terra " si offri al mio sguardo un gradino che facea capo di una scala, " e quindi appresso un seconde, ed un terzo. Sopravenuta la sera " si dovè stare dal lavoro ; ma nel giorno seguente chiamai a me lo " Stefani, e le sue genti, cogli Arabi che gli si erano aggiunti, e " che s' annoveravano a trecento cinquanta. E tanti si richie- " devano al lavoro, dovendosi levare la terra, ed altrove sulle " spalle trasportarla. Ma gli Arabi che vedevano distribuirsi un "giornaliero stipendio, cosa a loro inusata, avevano poste in "vicinanza ai lavori le loro capanne formate di lunghe paglie "intrecciate a foggia di stuoie dette da loro *Birs*. Continuai per- "tanto lo scavo della scala, e giunsi a scoprire il nono, che era "l'ultimo de' gradini. Metteva questo in una piccola spianata "ove ritrovai molte ossa di Cammello, e Cavallo, ed altre ossa di "piccoli scheletri che a me parvero di cane; poscia due arnesi, "uno dei quali aveva la forma di una sella di Cammello, e l'altro "di Cavallo; quindi pezzi di metallo rassomiglianti a campanella "(N. 113) con sopravi incisioni rappresentanti volatili e deità. "La spianata faceva capo ad una gran pietra siccome porta di un "monumento. Rimossala, si trovò uno scavo ovale formato nel "vivo masso a punta di scalpello, ripieno di terra impastata con "acqua, che feci subito smuovere, e via portare. Ma il calore "soffocante per la soverchia umidità tanto eccedeva che i lavora- "tori, quantunque usati al caldo stemperato di quei climi, non vi "potevano durare che lo spazio di cinque minuti, e si dovevano "dar cambio. Levata la terra di quel luogo, trovai in faccia all' "ingresso un altro ambiente simile nella forma a quello testè "descritto ma di minore grandezza ripieno della stessa terra, "con entrovi molti cadaveri gettati senz' ordine, e senza l' "ornamento delle armi. Lo Stefani che in questo tempo erasi "posto a demolire un altra piramide assai più grande, in otto "giorni non era giunto a demolirla che all' altezza del porticato. "Dopo alcuni giorni di lavoro trovò anch' egli la scala, e la "tomba. Tra i moltissimi cadaveri uno era coperto d'una "pietra, e scavando dalla parte della testa per rimoverla, un "lavoratore diede con la mazza in un masso rotondo della "grandezza di un uovo di Struzzo, che a quel colpo si ruppe, e "mostrò gran quantità di cristalli d' una calce fluata trasparente "di color bianco.

"Mentre l'Albanese era intento a quest' opera, io aveva già tutta "esaminata la piramide demolita, ma senza frutto; solo dal "porticato, o santuario tolsi un pezzo di macigno con due figure "segnato al N. 150. Non volendo rimanermi, avea già impreso ad "atterrarne un' altra. Recherà forse meraviglia ad alcuno, che io "con tanta paziente ostinatezza seguitassi nelle ricerche, e nell' "impresa, e cosi distruggessi tanti antichi monumenti sulla incerta "speranza di coglier frutto delle mie fatiche. Confesso anche io "che spesse volte era preso da grave tristezza, quando cessati gli "scavi, mi riconduceva alle tende coll' Albanese, e la truppa de' "scavatori che urlando, e saltellando seguivano a piedi per lungo "spazio lo Stefani, e me, e poi si mettevano diffilati a ricevere la "mercede. Oltredichè il pessimo cibo di che ci nutrivamo, le "veglie continue[1] per campare dai pericoli la vita, il caldo del "cocentissimo sole, e molte altre pene che si accompagnavano al

[1] L'Albanese ed io metà della notte per ciascheduno vegliavamo per sospetto de' servi poco fedeli, e de' Neri avari, e crudeli.

"timore di perdere il frutto di quasi cinque anni di fatiche facevano "talvolta tanta forza sul mio animo che mi mettevano al punto di "abbandonare l'impresa. Ma l'aspetto de' lavoratori, che più di me "s'affaticavano, di poco e duro cibo contenti per la speranza di "scarso guadagno mi rinfrancava l'animo, anzi lo accendeva per "modo, che risolvetti o di tornarmene deserto d'ogni avere, o "coll' acquisto di qualche raro tesoro; ed ecco la ragione perchè "appena distrutto un edifiizio si poneva mano ad un altro. "Quando lo Stefani ebbe compite le ricerche nella sua piramide, "gli ordinai di incominciare un nuovo lavoro in altro luogo, posto "tra il villaggio, e le grandi piramidi situate sul colle dalla parte "di levante, dove si veggono avvanzi di antica Città. Questa "ricerca però non ebbe alcun prospero successo; ma gl' indigeni "facevano coraggio assicurandomi di sapere per tradizione di "antichi libri esservi nascosti tesori in Oro per quaranta *Ardeb*, "che equivarebbero a quattro milla libbre delle nostre; io però "m' avvisava essere questa una favola inventata per farmi "proseguire i lavori, e procacciare ad essi vitto, e danaro. La "quale mia opinione si avverò, perchè dalle ricerche praticate "dallo Stefani non si ottenne alcun frutto, non avendo trovato "che una figura di legno rosa dal tempo nella parte destra del "volto e nel destro braccio, la quale è segnata al N. 154. Io non "fui più avventurato del compagno, essendo giunto a demolire la "quarta piramide senza aver trovato nulla di pregevole, salvo che "un gran cerchio prolungato a cono coll' apice troncato, di "Calcedonia Zaffirina (N. 148.)

"Dolente delle ricerche infruttuose fatte nelle piccole piramidi "mi decisi per ultimo di tentare miglior sorte in una delle più "grandi che restavano alla vetta del colle, e mi determinai di "lavorare su quella che era sola intatta. Era questa piramide la "descritta dal Cailliaud di Nantes nel suo viaggio al fiume bianco, "ed azzurro nel secondo volume a Pag. 157 e disegnata colla Fig. F. "Non accade che io descriva la forma e la costruzione esterna "perchè uguale all' altre ed a tutti nota. Sessantaquattro "gradinate alte ciascuna mezzo braccio formavano la piramide, "sicchè l'altezza era di braccia trentadue corrispondenti a metri "ventotto; e da ogni lato si stendeva in quarantotto braccia di "lunghezza che corrispondono a metri quarantadue come alla "Fig. I. Asceso alla vetta con soli quattro operanti per "incominciare il lavoro, conobbi, che in breve tempo si poteva "demolire la cima perchè già cadente, e levato il primo masso di "macigno si fece luogo ad altri lavoranti. Mentre si gettavano "a terra gli altri massi delle sottoposte gradinate, arso pel "soverchio calore che era segnato dal termometro di R$^{r.}$ al 48 "grado, m'era posto coll' Albanese a riposarmi all' ombra della "vicina piramide. Mentre io cosi mi ristorava fui chiamato da "un fedele servo; ond'io m'alzai col compagno, ed accorsi aprendo "l'animo a larga speranza di lieta avventura. Saliti sulla piramide "trovammo il servo disteso col ventre sul piano che aveano

"formato, e precisamente sopra un pertugio che si era scoperto. I
"neri rapaci volevano per forza cacciare il servo per porre le
"mani entro il pertugio; ma noi coll' armi alla mano li sforzammo
"a discendere. Chiamati altri servi fedeli, facemmo alla nostra
"presenza proseguire il lavoro. Il pertugio scoperto, e che
"lasciava travedere un vacuo e qualche cosa in esso contenuto,
"era formato da mal messi macigni. Fatti levare i larghi e
"grossi che coprivano il piano superiore, a noi si mostrò una cella
"di forma quadrilunga formata da macigni disposti in quattro
"muri laterali alle gradinate, alta circa cinque piedi, e lunga sei o
"sette. Per prima cosa appari a nostri occhi un grande masso
"coperto da un drappo candido tessuto di cotone, o di bisso, che al
"solo tocco andò sfasciato in pezzi, e sotto ad esso si scopri un cata-
"letto, o bara di legno di forma quadrilatera sorretta da quattro piedi
"lisci come bastoni rotondi, e le cui sponde erano formate di varii
"pezzi di legno posti alternativamente, un grande ed un piccolo,
"e rappresentanti figure simboliche come si vede al Catalogo N.
"153. Sotto questa bara trovai il vaso descritto al N. 108,
"che conteneva gli oggetti ravvolti in panni tessuti della medesima
"natura del sopradetto. Appresso al vaso, e sul piano della
"celia erano disposti per mezzo di fili con ordine, ad uso di
"Collane, paste vitree, pietre; v'erano alcuni talismani, ed
"Idoletti, un astuccio di metallo, scatolette fatto al torno, una
"sega, uno scalpello, e molti altri oggetti quali vengono descritti
"nel mio Catalogo.

"Raccolto tutto ciò che trovai, lo posi entro a sacchetti di pelle,
"e per tal modo nascosi agli Arabi l'Oro. Discesi al piede della
"piramide, costoro ci si strinsero in cerchio, ansiosi di vedere le
"cose trovate. Ma io coll' armi alla mano, e con faccia fiera
"comandai loro di salire, e proseguire il lavoro, ed essi perchè
"credono che l'arma da fuoco col solo presentarla uccida, in un
"baleno si ricondussero al travaglio. Sul far della sera, essendo
"andati i neri verso le loro capanne, portammo alle tende le cose
"trovate, e nella notte quando tutti i nostri servi, e schiavi si
"erano dati al sonno, in compagnia dell' Albanese trassi fuori de'
"sacchetti gli oggetti preziosi che verrò nel mio catalogo
"descrivendo, e li contemplai coll' animo pieno d'allegrezza.
"Trovai mirabile il lavoro degli ori, e vedendone la quantità
"conobbi che dovevano superare di gran lunga tutti quelli che
"sapea essere sparsi ne' Musei d'Europa; nè potea saziarmi di
"ammirare lo squisito lavoro de' Cammei, e delle pietre, che potea
"non pure emulare, ma superare le più pregiate opere de' Greci.
"Intanto che io esultava per allegrezza, lo Stefani erasi fatto
"oltremodo tristo, perchè temendo i Neri, e pensando alla loro
"avidità voleami persuadere a salvar noi ed il tesoro colla fuga.
"Ma io avvezzo da quasi cinque anni alle guerre contro d' essi, e
"conoscendo da loro viltà non perdetti punto il coraggio, e vago
"di nuovi ritrovati volli restare. Cercai però di rassicurare
"l' animo pauroso del compagno col divisamento di seppellire nel

"deserto il tesoro; diffatti scavata una fossa a poca distanza "della tenda e postivi entro gli ori gli ricoprimmo di terra, e di "sabbia. Allo spuntare dell' alba, essendoci recati alla piramide "trovammo i Nubiani accorsi al lavoro pressochè in numero di "cinquecento. Quantunque per l' opera della grande piramide "questo numero fosse soverchio, tuttavolta credei buon consiglio "non aspreggiarli rimandando i nuovi lavoratori; per la qual cosa "feci incominciare in altra piccola piramide un lavoro, che "continuossi per qualche tempo, ma senza alcun frutto. "Seguitando il racconto dell' atterramento della grande "piramide dirò, che levati i materiali che formavano la "celletta dove era raccolta la bara, ed il tesoro, la trovai di nuovo "costrutta di grandi macigni uniti con terra impastata a foggia "di cemento; per la quale costruzione l' atterramento lungo, e "malagevole ci riusciva. Dall' altezza segnata nella figura I colla "lettera A si giunse, dopo un lavoro di quindici giorni, "a demolire la piramide sino al punto segnato nella figura "sopradetta colla lettera B; nè si trovò in questo spazio che "paglia del deserto intrecciata a guisa di funi, e pezzi di legno "lavorati ad uso di mazza rotti, e guasti dal tempo. Nel punto "segnato colla lettera B e nel mezzo della piramide era formata una "nicchia da tre macigni; levati questi s' appresentarono "a' miei occhi alcuni tessuti forse di cotone, che dimostravano "avvolgere qualche oggetto. Mi corse all' animo nuova "allegrezza per la speranza di nuovi oggetti preziosi in oro. Se "questa mia speranza fu delusa per l' oro, fu però paga pel "ritrovato di due vasi di composizione simile al bronzo ele-"gantissimi nella forma, e nel lavoro, perfetti, come ciascuno per "se stesso vedrà, leggendo nel mio catalogo i numeri 105, e 106, ed "osservando nella tavola le figure 15 e 16. Dall' altezza segnata "colla lettera B dopo un lavoro di venti giorni, aveva demolito la "piramide fino al piano del colle, ed apparivano lastre di pietra "nera dette da Nubiani *Galla*. Il vestibolo però era ancora "intatto; sotto e da un lato di esso era inciso sopra un macigno "il nome di Cailliaud, come alla lettera C della figura I. Era "questo vestibolo tutt' inciso di geroglifici a molte linee; di fronte "all' entrata era un uomo maestosamente seduto sopra un leone, "che non so qual cosa stringeve nella destra. Per utilità della "scienza archeologica, e della storia avrei desiderato di staccare "tutti questi macigni. Ma pensando che per la mole, ed il peso di "essi non avrei potuto transportarli pe' deserti, staccai una parte "di quello posto di fronte all' entrata, da me creduto il più "interessante, perchè in esso è scolpito il cartello, ed è segnato "nel catalogo col N. 149.

"Sperava ritrovare nell' interno della piramide, come nelle più "piccole, la scala per discendere nella tomba, ma inutili riuscirono "le ricerche di due giorni per l'ostacolo degli strati di *Galla*. "Allora tentai di aprirmi una via lavorando sulle traccie di un "viale scavato sotto il vestibolo, alla distanza di circa otto piedi, "e che estendevasi verso il basso del colle. Lavorando al "termine del viale, e sotto il vestibolo, lo trovai chiuso da massi "di macigno, uniti con terra ad uso di cemento. Volendo rivol-"gere le mie ultime ricerche sopra questo luogo, nè abbis-"ognando di tanta copia di operai, decisi licenziarne buon numero. "Nulladimeno venivano i Nubiani ogni giorno egualmente, "senza essere chiesti, al lavoro, e stavano armati delle loro lancie "a riguardarci. Venuto io perciò in qualche sospetto, feci "vegliare su di essi i miei neri, ed i miei servi; quando passati "sei giorni di lavoro, i Nubiani armati, e messisi in cerchio, "s' accordavano d' assalirmi per derubarmi il tesoro; e n' ebbi "avviso da un mio schiavo fedele intendente del loro linguaggio, "che si era ad essi frapposto; io era di consiglio di batterli "coll' armi, quando fossi assalito, ma il compagno me ne distolse, "e mi prese compassione delle donne, e del figlio dell' Albanese; "pensai anche tra me che se accadesse alcun grave fatto, e fosse "riferito al Governo si sarebbe sparsa la fame de' miei ritrovati, "con pericolo di perdere il tesoro; laonde deliberai di mettermi "in salvo colla fuga di notte. Spediti tre de' più fedeli servi coi "cammelli per terra alla volta di *Berber*, luogo ove radunansi le "carovane per trapassare i grandi deserti di Crusca, m' imbarcai "alla vicina sponda del Nilo sopra una barca del Governo, che "stava sempre pronta al mio volere . . . giunsi a *Berber* . . . "dopo due giorni di cammino da *Berber* arrivammmo ad Abu "Acmet . . . m'avviai pel vasto deserto di *Crusca* . . . Nel "settimo giorno giungemmo ad un luogo dove è una sorgente di "cattivissima acqua, . . . e nel duodecimo giorno giungemmo ad "un luogo chiamato le *ponte* . . . seguitammo il cammino per "altri due giorni, e pervenimmo in Crusca . . .

APPENDIX TO CHAPTER VII.

EXTRACT FROM FERLINI'S DESCRIPTION OF HIS EXCAVATIONS AT THE PYRAMIDS OF BAGRÂWÎYA.

FRENCH TRANSLATION.

"NOUS n'allâmes pas plus loin dans nos recherches de *Vod-*"*Benaga*. Nous quittâmes la ville et nous nous dirigeâmes vers "*Bégaraviah*, oû existent les grandes pyramides. J'avais déjà "depuis long-temps le projet de chercher dans ces régions muettes, "siége de l'ancienne grandeur, quelque monument propre à "illustrer l'histoire de cette partie si intéressante du monde, qui "à cette époque n'avait encore été visitée que par M. Belzoni et "moi.

"Nous plaçâmes donc nos tentes près du petit village de
" *Bégaraviah* peu éloigné du Nil, et nous louâmes quelques
" cabanes de nègres. Nous employâmes une partie de nos gens à
" faire avec les peaux de bœuf des corbeilles propres à transporter
" la terre ; le reste de nos esclaves devait veiller à la garde des
" chameaux. Puis nous allâmes visiter les pyramides qu'on
" apercevait très distinctement à une heure de distance. Nous
" traversâmes d'abord l'ancienne ville de Méröé, presqu'entière-
" ment couverte par le sable; nous n'y vîmes que quelques sphynx
" en granit noir, dégradés et en partie détruits. Non loin de la
" ville on trouve beaucoup de pyramides unies et tombant en
" ruines ; près de là nous nous trouvâmes devant une colline dont
" le sommet était couronné de 21 pyramides ruinées surtout dans
" la partie supérieure. Une seule était encore presque intacte.
" À l'est nous en aperçûmes 8 autres plus petites et très bien
" conservées ; au pied de la colline nous en vimes plusieurs autres
" encore plus petites qui n'avaient d'intact que le portique, ou
" sanctuaire, chargé d'inscriptions hiéroglyphiques. C'est ici que
" je voulais commencer mes travaux, mais mon ami M. Stefani
" m'engagea à faire un premier essai dans la ville située à
" proximité des allées des sphynx.

"Quatre jours après notre arrivée, nous campâmes tout notre
" monde, et demandâmes au *Scheick*, ou chef du village, des
" ouvriers. Dans les premiers jours ceux-ci, croyant que nous ne
" leur paierions pas leur salaire, n'arrivaient qu'avec défiance,
" mais par la suite ils se présentèrent en si grand nombre que
" nous fûmes obligés de les renvoyer. Nous fouillâmes d'abord
" une espèce d'habitation qui semblait avoir été détruite par la
" main des hommes. Nous y trouvâmes une plaque composée
" d'une espèce de pâte enduite d'un vernis émaillé en bleu, et un
" ichneumon en serpentin. C'est en vain que nous poursuivîmes
" nos recherches dans l'espoir de trouver quelqu'objet précieux ;
" nous dûmes aller ailleurs.

"Je quittai M. Stefani, et j'allai avec cent hommes visiter les
" grandes pyramides. Peu de jours après mon ami découvrit une
" autre habitation plus grande que la précédente, mais ce fut sans
" aucune chance de bonheur puisqu'il ne trouva qu'une petite idole
" en terre cuite vernissée. Sur ces entrefaites j'avais déja démoli
" les restes d'une petite pyramide située au pied de la colline;
" parvenu au bas de la montagne, je la trouvai formée de dalles
" noires qui semblaient y avoir été placées de la main des hommes.
" Je cherchai, à l'aide du pic, à pénétrer plus avant dans les
" fondemens, et après avoir enlevé peu de terre, je vis distincte-
" ment un gradin. C'était la première marche d'un escalier
" pratiqué au centre du monument. Après ce gradin j'en
" découvris un second, puis un troisième et ainsi de suite. La
" nuit survint, il fallut suspendre l'ouvrage ; mais le jour suivant
" j'appelai M. Stefani, ses gens et les arabes qui s'étaient joints à
" lui ; nous étions en tout 350 personnes ; c'était précisément le

" nombre d'hommes qu'il nous fallait pour creuser la terre et " emporter les déblais. Et les arabes qui voyaient que nous " payions chaque jour nos ouvriers (chose à laquelle on ne les " avait pas accoutumés) s'empressèrent du (sic) placer leurs tentes " à proximité des travaux. Ces tentes sont faites avec de longs " brins de paille tressés; les arabes les appellent *birs*.[1]

" Je continuai à découvrir l'escalier, et je parvins à la neuvième " marche qui était la dernière. Il conduisait à un petit caveau où je " ne trouvai d'abord que des ossemens de chameau, de cheval, et " d'autres petits squelettes que je pris pour des chiens. Puis je " trouvai deux espèces de harnais paraissant l'un un bât de " chameau, l'autre une selle de cheval; enfin des pièces de " métal ayant la forme de clochettes, sur lesquelles étaient gravés " des oiseaux et des divinités. Au fond du cavean je vis une grosse " pierre qui était la porte d'un monument sépulcral; je la " fis enlever et je trouvai une ouverture ovale taillée dans le roc au " moyen d'un ciseau; elle était remplie de terre pétrie avec de " l'eau; je la fis remuer et emporter. Mais dans cette ouverture, " la chaleur causée par l'humidité etait tellement suffocante, que " les ouvriers, habitués à la température extrèmement élevée de ce " climat, ne pouvaient rester dans le grotte plus de cinq minutes. " Je les faisais relever. Après avoir entièrement déblayé cette " chambre sépulcrale, je trouvai vis-à-vis de la porte d'entrée un " autre caveau semblable à celui que je viens de décrire; il " contenait un grand nombre d'ossemens humains entassés les " uns sur les autres, sans armure et sans aucune autre espèce " d'ornement.

" Pendant ce tems-la, M. Stefani, qui avait commencé la démo- " lition d'une autre pyramide, ne l'avait abattue dans huit jours " que jusqu'à la hauteur du portique; il parvint toutefois, peu " de jours après, à trouver l'escalier et les caveaux. Parmi les " cadavres il y en avait un qui était couvert par une pierre.. On " creusait du côté de la tête pour enlever cette pierre, lorsqu'un " ouvrier, en donnant un coup de pioche sur un corps rond, gros " comme un oeuf d'autruche, il en fit sortir une grande quantité " d'objets en verre, ou chaux fluée, d'une composition solide, " blanche et transparente.

" Pendant que M. Stefani surveillait cet ouvrage, j'avais examiné " la pyramide démolie de laquelle je ne présageais pas un résultat " heureux, puisque je n'avais pu extraire du portique qu'un bloc " de pierre où étaient sculptées deux figures (No. 150). On sera " peut-être étonné de voir avec quelle patience et quelle persévé- " rance je poursuivais mes recherches, dans l'espoir bien douteux " de cueillir le fruit de mes travaux. J'avoue franchement que " j'étais souvent accablé de douleur lor[s]qu'après les travaux de " la journée je rentrais dans ma tente avec mon ami, et que les " ouvriers qui nous suivaient en sautant et en poussant des hurle-

[1] I.e., بِرْس

"mens affreux, nous tendaient la main pour demander le salaire "d'un ouvrage que je regardais comme perdu. En outre de cela "notre nourriture était exécrable, nos veillées continuelles[1] pour "mettre notre vie à couvert contre les embûches que nous redou- "tions à chaque instant; une chaleur insupportable, la crainte "de perdre en un instant tout espoir de réussite dans une entre- "prise couteuse que je poursuivais avec persévérance! il faut "convenir que cette perspective était bien faite pour abattre tout "autre esprit plus fort que le mien; toutefois elle agissait sur "moi avec tant de violence, que souvent j'étais sur le point de "renoncer à mes projets. Mais quand je voyais les ouvriers mal "nourris travailler avec assiduité dans l'espoir de se procurer un "faible profit, je reprenais courage et à tel point, que je résolus "de revenir sans le sou, ou bien possesseur d'un trésor. Et "voilà comment après avoir fouillé un édifice, je pénétrais dans "un autre.

"Quand M. Stefani eut terminé les travaux de sa pyramide, je "lui ordonnai de commencer un autre ouvrage ailleurs, c'est-à- "dire entre le village et les pyramides situées à l'est sur la colline "où sont les restes d'une cité antique. Cette tentative ne "produisit aucun résultat satisfaisant; mais les indigènes "m'encourageaient et m'assuraient qu'ils savaient positivement, "d'après une ancienne tradition de leur pays, qu'il y avait des "trésors cachés pour plus de quarante *ardeb* d'or; (environ "quatre mille livres) je ne voyais là qu'une fable inventée dans "le dessein de m'engager à poursuivre mes travaux, et à donner à "ces barbares des vivres et de l'argent. Je me confirmai d'autant "plus dans cette opinion que les excavations de M. Stefani ne "produisirent rien; car il ne trouva qu'une figure en bois dont le "côté droit du visage et le bras droit étaient à-demi rongés "(No. 154). Je n'eus guères plus de bonheur que mon compagnon, "car, étant parvenu à fouiller la quatrième pyramide sans rien "trouver d'important, en m'en allant, je découvris un grand "cercle en chalcédoine *saphirée*, allongé en forme conique, et "tronqué aux extrémités; je l'ai placé au No. 148.

"Affligé de l'inutilité de mes perquisitions dans les petites "pyramides, je me décidai à faire une dernière tentative sur l'une "des grandes situées à l'extrémité de la colline, et précisément "sur elle que j'avais remarquée presqu'intacte. Cette pyramide "était celle dont M. Cailliaud de Nantes avait donné la descrip- "tion dans la relation de son voyage aux *rivières blanche et bleue*, "*tom.* ii., *page* 157, *fig.* F. Il est inutile que je m'étende ici sur ce "beau monument qui est assez généralement connu; je dirai "seulement qu'il avait 64 degrés, hauts chacun d'une demi-brasse, "formant l'ensemble de la pyramide, de manière que la hauteur "totale était de 32 brasses, ou 28 mètres. De chaque côté elle

[1] "M. Stefani et moi nous étions obligés de veiller chacun la moitié de la nuit redoutant l'infidélité de nos gens et la cruauté des nègres."

" s'étendait environ 48 brasses de longueur, c'est-à-dire qu'elle " avait 168 mètres carrés.

" Monté au sommet de la pyramide, avec quatre ouvriers, pour " mettre la main à l'ouvrage, je reconnus au premier coup-d'œil " que la démolition pouvait se faire fort facilement, et que " le monument tombait déjà de vétusté; les premières pierres " enlevées, je relevais mes ouvriers. Pendant qu'on jetait par " terre les pierres des gradins, ne pouvant plus résister à l'ardeur " du soleil dont les brûlans rayons donnaient jusqu'à 48° de " Reaumur, j'allai me reposer avec M. Stefani à l'ombre d'une " pyramide voisine. Tout-à-coup je fus appelé par mon fidèle " domestique. J'accourus avec mon ami au haut du monument . . . " et je sentis déjà mon cœur s'ouvrir à la douce espérance . . . Je " vois mon domestique couché sur son ventre, sur l'emplacement " qu'il avait pratiqué, et cherchant à couvrir de son corps " l'ouverture qui venait d'être découverte. Les noirs, poussés par " la cupidité, voulaient à toute force chasser mon domestique et " plonger leur mains avides dans le fond de l'ouverture . . . " Nous fîmes bonne contenance, et les armes à la main, nous les " forçâmes de descendre ; nous appellâmes d'autres domestiques " de confiance, et nous fîmes continuer la fouille en notre " présence.

" L'ouverture nous laissait entrevoir un vide qui contenait des " objets que nous ne pouvions distinguer. Ce vide, ou cellule, " était formé de grandes pierres grossièrement assemblées. Nous " fîmes enlever les pierres les plus larges qui couvraient le plan " supérieur et nous reconnûmes une cellule ayant la forme d'un " carré long et composée de grosses pierres superposées qui " formaient les quatre murs latéraux correspondant aux gradins " de la pyramide. Cette cellule avait quatre pieds de hauteur " sur six ou sept de longueur. La première chose qui frappa nos " regards ce fut un grand corps couvert d'un tissu en coton d'une " éclatante blancheur qui, à peine touché, tomba en poussière. " C'était une espèce de table ou autel, (*mensa sacra* ou *ara domestica*) " soutenue par quatre pieds cylindriques et entourée d'une " balustrade de barreaux en bois, grands et petits alternativement " placés. Ces barreaux étaient sculptés et représentaient des " figures symboliques (No 153). C'est sous cette table que se " trouva le vase en bronze porté au No. 108, et qui contenait les " objets précieux enveloppés dans du linge semblable à celui dont " je viens de parler. Près du vase et sur le plan de la cellule, " étaient symétriquement disposés, au moyen de fils, des colliers, " des pâtes en verre, des pierres de couleur, &c. Il y avait aussi " quelques talismans, de petites idoles, un étui cylindrique en métal, " de petites boites travaillées au tour remplies d'une matière " pulvérisée dont je donne plus loin l'analyse, une scie, un ciseau, " et plusieurs autres objets dont j'ai donné la description dans mon " catalogue.

" J'enfermai tous ces objets dans de petits sacs en cuir, et je "dérobai ainsi aux arabes la vue de l'or. Je descendis de la "pyramide; tous les ouvriers se pressèrent autour de moi pour "voir ce que j'avais trouvé. Mais je montrai de la fermeté, et "ayant saisi mes armes, je leur ordonnai de continuer leurs travaux. "Quand ces nègres aperçurent les armes, ils s'enfuirent pré-"cipitamment, parce qu'ils croyent que la seule vue des armes "suffirait à leur donner la mort. Le soir, lorsque les nègres se "furent retirés dans leurs cabanes, et que nos domestiques étaient "profondément endormis, M. Stefani et moi nous examinâmes "avec plus d'attention cette grande quantité d'objets précieux "dont la vue remplit mon cœur d'une joie inexprimable. (Cette "riche collection forme la plus grande partie de mon catalogue.) "Je fus surpris de la quantité et de la beauté des ouvrages en or, "et je reconnus qu'ils devaient surpasser de beaucoup tous ceux "de ce genre qui existent dans les différens musées de l'Europe. "Quant aux pierres gravées, je jugeai qu'elles pouvaient, non seule-"ment approcher des meilleurs ouvrages des grecs, mais même les "surpasser. Pendant que je me livrais ainsi aux douces émotions "que me causait naturellement cet événement aussi heureux qu'in-"attendu, je remarquai une grande tristesse empreinte sur la "figure de mon ami. Je lui en fis l'observation et il me répondit "qu'ayant tout à redouter de la cupidité des noirs, il croyait que "nous ferions bien de nous enfuir avec nos trésors. Mais moi "qui depuis cinq ans étais habitué à faire la guerre à ces barbares, "et qui connaissais leur lâcheté, je refusai cette proposition; je "courais d'ailleurs la chance de faire de nouvelles découvertes. "Je rassurai donc mon ami et je proposai d'enfouir nos trésors "dans le désert: en effet, nous creusâmes une fosse à peu de "distance de notre tente, nous y plaçâmes nos objets précieux, et "nous les couvrîmes de terre et de sable. Le lendemain, au point "du jour nous revînmes à la pyramide; tous nos ouvriers étaient "accourus à l'ouvrage; ils n'étaient pas moins de 500. Quoique "je n'eusse pas besoin de tant de monde pour les travaux de la "grande pyramide, je jugeai prudent de ne pas indisposer ces "gens en renvoyant les nouveaux ouvriers: j'ordonnai qu'on fit "des fouilles dans les environs, mais ce fut sans résultat.

"En continuant le récit de la démolition de la grande pyramide, "je dirai que, l'ayant débarrassée des matériaux qui formaient la "petite cellule où étaient la table et le trésor, je trouvai que le "reste était construit en grosses pierres assemblées par une espèce "de ciment composé de terre pétrie. Cette construction compacte "rendait l'opération extrêmement difficile. Nous employâmes "quinze jours a démolir la pyramide depuis le point A, jusqu'à la "hauteur B. Dans cet espace nous ne trouvâmes que de la paille "du désert tressée en manière de cordes, et des morceaux de bois "qui avaient la forme de maillets; tous ces objets étaient presque "détruits. À la hauteur B, c'est-à-dire au centre de la pyramide, "était une niche ou cellule, formée de trois blocs de pierre. Nous "enlevâmes ces blocs et la première chose qui se présenta à nous,

" ce furent des tissus en coton qui semblaient couvrir d'autres " objets. . . . Mon cœur battit avec nouvelle force: je croyais " trouver d'autres objets en or. . . . Mais si ce précieux métal ne " s'offrit pas à ma vue, je n'en fus pas peu dédommagé par la " découverte de deux vases en bronze, de la forme la plus élégante " et si bien conservés qu'on eût dit qu'ils sortaient de la main de " l'ouvrier. Chacun pourra s'en convaincre en jetant les yeux sur " les N. 105 et 106 du catalogue, et sur les figures 15 et 16 de la " planche; ces vases contenaient également une matière noire " pulvérisée dont nous rapportons l'analyse. Depuis la hauteur B, " j'étais parvenu, en vingt jours, à démolir la pyramide jusqu'au " plan de la colline; je ne trouvai que de larges dalles d'une pierre " noire, appelée en Numidie *gallah.* Le vestibule (let. C) était " encore intact; au-dessous, et d'un côté était gravé sur la pierre " le nom de *Cailliaud.* Ce vestibule était couvert de hiéroglyphes " sculptés sur plusieurs lignes. En face de la porte d'entrée on " voyait une figure d'homme majestueusement assise sur un lion, et " tenant en main un objet dont il fut impossible de déterminer " les formes. Pour le bien de la science j'aurais vivement désiré " m'emparer d'une de ces pierres si interessantes, mais elles " étaient d'une telle pesanteur que le transport devenait impossible " dans cet immense désert; je me bornai à detacher un morceau " de la pierre qui était en face de la porte d'entrée et que je crus " être le plus curieux à cause du cartouche qui y était gravé " (No. 149).

" J'espérais trouver à l'intérieur de la pyramide l'escalier que " j'avais découvert dans les petites, et par lequel on descendait à " la chambre sépulcrale; mais mon attente fut trompée; je fus " arrêté par les nombreuses couches de pierre dite *gallah.* Alors " j'essayai de m'ouvrir un passage en suivant les traces d'un " sentier creusé sous le vestibule, à la distance d'environ huit " pieds, et qui se prolongeait vers le bas de la colline. Je fis donc " creuser à l'extrémité de ce sentier, sous le vestibule, mais je fus " également arrêté par des blocs de pierre assemblés avec du " ciment. Je voulus toutefois poursuivre mes recherches en cet " endroit, et comme je n'avais pas besoin de tant d'ouvriers j'en " congédiai bon nombre; mais ils ne manquaient pas de revenir " à l'ouvrage sans être requis, et nous regardaient travailler d'un " air menaçant et armés de leurs lances.

" Cette attitude fière éveilla mes soupçons. Je chargeai mes " nègres et mes domestiques de surveiller ces hommes qui " commençaient à devenir dangereux pour nous, lor[s]qu'au bout " de six jours je fus informé par un de mes esclaves fidèles qui " connaissait leur langage et qui s'était introduit parmi eux, que " ces barbares armés se disposaient à me surprendre dans le " dessein de s'emparer de mes trésors. Je voulus d'abord les " attaquer et les disperser à l'aide des miens, mais M. Stefani " m'en détourna: j'eus pitié de nos femmes et de la famille de " l'albanais. Je réflechis en outre que s'il arrivait quelqu' "événement sérieux qui parvint aux oreilles du gouvernement, "mes découvertes auraient eu du retentissement, et je courais le "risque du (sic) tout perdre. Je résolus de prendre la fuite; "j'attendis la nuit. Je dirigeai trois de mes plus fidèles "domestiques avec mes chameaux sur Berber, lieu où se "réunissent les caravanes qui traversent les grands déserts de "*Coruscah*, et je m'embarquai avec M. Stefani et nos familles sur le "Nil, à l'endroit le plus rapproché de mon campement, sur un "navire du gouvernement qui était toujours à ma disposition. "J'arrivai à *Berber*, après trois jours de navigation; . . . Je "quittai donc *Berber*. Après deux jours de marche j'arrivai à "*Abu-Achmet* . . . et je me dirigeai vers le grand désert de "*Coruscah*. . . . Le septième jour nous trouvâmes une source "de très mauvaise eau. . . . Au douzième jour j'arrivai à un "endroit appelé *les portes*. Là commence une très-longue chaine "de montagnes de granit noir; nous les traversâmes pendant "deux jours et nous parvînmes enfin à *Coruscah*, &c. . . ."

CHAPTER VIII.

THIRD MISSION, 1903.

VISITS TO KHARṬÛM, SÔBA, WAD BÂ NAGAA, NAGAA, BÎR, MAṢAWWARÂT AṢ-ṢUFRA, ETC.

ON my return to London in 1899 I reported to the Trustees of the British Museum on the condition of the pyramids of Bagrâwîya, and that it was impossible to carry on at that time excavations on the Island of Meroë, because there were no men available for digging purposes among the civilian population. The few natives who dwelt on the river bank were busily employed in cutting down the small trees and shrubs, and in digging up the thorn bushes and making small clearings on which to grow *dhurra*, and they had neither the time nor the desire to take part in excavations for antiquities. The only men on the Island capable of doing real hard work were the Egyptian soldiers of the Railway Battalion, but all these were employed in the important task of continuing the Sûdân Military Railway from the Atbara to Kharṭûm.

In the winter of 1900-1901 I was sent to Egypt on business by the Trustees, and whilst I was in Luxor Sir F. R. Wingate, K.C.B., who had succeeded Lord Kitchener as Sirdar of the Egyptian Army and Governor-General of the Sûdân, gave me the opportunity of going to meet him at Kharṭûm to talk over the possibilities of the Sûdân as a field for archaeological research. I gladly accepted his very kind offer, and ten days after the receipt of his telegram I arrived in Kharṭûm.

The British had been in possession of the town for sixteen months only, but the progress which had been made in building and in laying out roads and streets was extraordinary. The most prominent object in the town was, of course, the new palace, part of which stood on the site of the old Egyptian Government Palace wherein General Gordon was murdered. The British and Egyptian flags were flying over the roof, and a 40-pounder siege-gun stood on each side of the main gate, which was guarded by British and Sûdânî soldiers. A road had been marked out along the river front, and was in process of construction, and most of the natives in the town seemed to be engaged in making bricks and building Government Offices, houses, &c. An hotel had been started under the management of Mr. Arnaud, about a mile down the river, and there several of the officers lived. Lord Cromer was visiting Kharṭûm at the time, and was arranging and inspecting with Sir F. R. Wingate the work of every branch of the Administration.

Through the kindness of the Sirdar I was allowed to witness a very interesting ceremony at the Palace. A number of men and two or three women of the Shilluk and Dinka tribes had walked from their native land, which lies some hundreds of miles to the south of Kharṭûm, in order to present their fealty to the "great chiefs" of the "White Queen," and it was arranged that the ceremony should take place one day at noon on the verandah of the Palace, which faces south. The Delegates of the tribes were led in before Lord Cromer, who was wearing a large number of orders, the Sirdar, and a few British officers and ladies, and having taken up their position, one of them stepped forward and with appropriate gestures and in simple language told his Lordship that they had come to tender their allegiance to him as the representative of the "White Queen," to express their undying loyalty to him, and to ask his protection so that they might henceforward live in their own country in peace, and carry on their trading arrangements in security. They went on to say that they now regarded him as the head of their tribes, and as a proof of this they said they had brought with them the head-dress or crown which could only be worn by the chief of their tribes, and this they wished to be allowed to put on his head. Lord Cromer then made a suitable reply, which was at once translated to the Delegates in good and fluent Arabic by Mr. Boyle, and which gave them great satisfaction. Two men, one a Shilluk and the other a Dinka, then produced a wonderful object which resembled a black-green flower-pot more than anything else, and, advancing to Lord Cromer, placed it on his head, saying as they did so formulae which were probably many centuries old, and had been repeated from time immemorial over the heads of newly-crowned Shilluk and Dinka kings. His Lordship having made a fitting answer, the crown was removed.

Now as Lord Cromer had become a Shilluk king, he was obliged to receive from his subjects the gifts which testified to their loyalty and service. The Delegates therefore produced a few small elephants' tusks and other things, and laid them at his feet, uttering appropriate words of homage as they did so. It was now Lord Cromer's turn to make gifts to his subjects and "children," and in answer to a sign from him some Egyptian soldiers came forward with rolls of Sûdâni cloth, and some gaudily coloured Manchester stuffs, &c., and he and the Sirdar gave to every man a useful gift. Special care was taken to give each of the Shilluk and Dinka women a very liberal allowance of the bright-flowered stuffs, and they were so delighted with their new apparel that they wanted to undress and wind the strips of stuff round their bodies then and there! The tusks which the Delegates had brought as tribute and the other gifts were returned to them as *bakshîsh*, and the Shilluks and the Dinkas went down the steps in great happiness.

Before I left Kharṭûm, a few days later, Sir Reginald Wingate thoroughly discussed the question of excavations at the Pyramids of Bagrâwîya. He was most anxious to preserve all the ancient remains in the Sûdân, whether Pagan or Christian, and declared it to be his intention to investigate the sites of the ancient cities as soon as possible. However, nothing could be done that winter, for the want of population in the country formed one of the most serious of the difficulties which the Government had to contend with, and there was no money available to import labour from Egypt. Thus matters stood until the summer of 1902, when Sir Reginald Wingate came to the British Museum, and, having described to the Director, Sir Edward Maunde Thompson, K.C.B., his plans for archaeological work in the Sûdân, applied to the Trustees for the loan of my services during the coming winter. The Trustees ordered me to go to the Sûdân again, and I therefore left England at the end of December, and proceeded to Kharṭûm. On my arrival I found that the Governor-General had gone up the White Nile on a tour of inspection with Lord Cromer, and that excavations either at the Pyramids of Bagrâwîya, or elsewhere, could not begin until their return. This delay placed about ten clear days at my disposal, and through the kindness of Colonel F. J. Nason, Civil Secretary to the Governor-General, and Lieut. Percy Lord, R.E., I was able to spend them in a profitable manner. Lieut. Percy Lord proposed that we should visit Wad Bâ Nagaa, Nagaa, and the Wâdî Aṣ-Ṣufra, and with characteristic energy and kindness set to work to make arrangements for our journey. At that time it was quite impossible to travel anywhere in the Sûdân without the countenance and help of the Government, and, but for the friendly assistance of the British officers and the kindness of the British railway officials from one end to the other of the Ḥalfa-Kharṭûm line, all attempts to visit ancient sites in the Sûdân would have been in vain.

Whilst Lieut. Lord was making arrangements for a supply of camels, &c., an opportunity of visiting Sôba, the site of the capital of the Christian kingdom of 'Alwa, presented itself, and I went there with Colonel E. A. Stanton, the Mudir of Kharṭûm, who had already made a careful examination of the ruins, and made some excavations there. Sôba lies on the right bank of the Blue Nile, about thirteen miles above Kharṭûm. Whilst there, Colonel Stanton collected a small party of men, and we went to the ruins of an ancient temple which had been subsequently used as a Christian church, and began to dig among the pillars near the east end of it. After clearing away a considerable amount of sand and earth, we found a number of maṣṭabas, or rectangular benches, about 3 feet high, built of mud, and they so much resembled in form the tombs of ecclesiastical officials which I had seen in the churches of monasteries in Mesopotamia that for me it was impossible not to regard them as tombs. We dug through two of them and found bodies at a depth of about two feet below the surface of the ground, and the supposition was thus proved to be correct. There was nothing found in the graves which served to indicate the period when they were made, but they appear to belong to the Christian Period of Sûdân history. On some of the pillars the Coptic cross was cut, and it was clear that we were digging among the ruins of a building which had been used for Christian worship. We, of course, did not disturb the bodies, and we filled in the holes which we had made. We then went and examined the remains of a stone gateway, which did not appear to be so old as the temple which we had just left.

Soon after returning to Kharṭûm I found that Lieut. Lord had secured camels for our journey to Nagaa, and we left Kharṭûm by train for Wad Bâ Nagaa, where we arrived in the evening. The following morning we were joined by Mr. Nevile, of the Sûdân Civil Service, and we all set out to ride up the *khôr* to Nagaa, which lies on the right bank of the Nile, about eight hours' distance from the river. The ruins of the ancient city, the site of which is marked by the remains of some temples, are in the Wâdî al-Kirbikân, a few miles to the north of the point from which we started. We rode through a barren, stony waste for some three or four hours, and soon after passed Gebel Buwêrib; we then entered the Wâdî Awateb, and journeying through a region filled with bushes, small trees, and halfa grass, all of which grew in a soft rich soil, we came in three hours more to the side of the stony hill on which are to be found the remains of several temples. In some places we found the ground still wet with the rains of the previous summer, which had been dammed up by long barriers made of earth, stones, &c. Every here and there we saw traces of patches of cultivation, which proves that the natives on the river bank walk from sixteen to twenty miles in order to grow crops, and to lead their flocks to good grazing ground. On the way we passed a few gazelle, and as we came near Gebel An-Nagaa we saw a very large herd of *ariel*. Hoskins and Ferlini relate that the Wâdî Awateb was infested with lions when they were in the Sûdân, and it will be remembered that the former was prevented from visiting the temples at Nagaa chiefly through the great fear which his men had of the lions in that place. Ferlini went to Nagaa, and began to clear out one of the temples there, but he tells us that he was obliged to spend a day in making a sort of *zerîba* to prevent the lions from attacking them at night.

The site of Nagaa is a very interesting one, and the extent of the ruins indicates that the city which once stood here was great and flourishing. As a description of the temples and buildings there is given in another part of this book, it will be sufficient to say here that no traveller who is really interested in the antiquities of the Sûdân should fail to visit the temple of the Great Queen at Nagaa, and the pretty little building in the Egypto-Roman style which stands quite close to it. In the Gebel an-Nagaa are the quarries from which the stone for the temples was taken, and in two or three places, generally near the temples, are still to be seen the sites of the artificial reservoirs from which the ancient inhabitants drew their water supply. Hitherto travellers have been prevented from undertaking a journey to Nagaa by the difficulty of carrying a sufficient supply of water with them; for the road is not an easy one, and the water-skins of the natives frequently leak, owing to careless loading up and tying. Thanks to the forethought of Lieut. Lord and Mr. Nevile we had an abundant supply, for they took with them several of the little light iron tanks, with screw-mouths, two of which when filled with water formed a camel's load. Much of the difficulty of visiting Nagaa from this cause has now been removed, for Sir Reginald Wingate has had a well dug there, and the traveller need only take with him sufficient water for drinking purposes. Lieut. Lord knew the site of Nagaa very well, and a few hours sufficed to visit the ruins of the temples, &c., which looked extremely picturesque at sunset and sunrise.

We pitched our tent between the pretty little Romano-Egyptian temple and that of the great Queen of Nagaa, and on the following morning we left Nagaa, more fully Maṣawwarât an-Nagaa, i.e., the "sculptures of Nagaa," and set out for the ruins of Maṣawwarât aṣ-Ṣufra, which lie in a circular hollow in the mountains, about twenty miles north of Nagaa. The track runs on the west side of Gebel an-Nagaa, over ground the greater part of which is covered with scrub and patches of halfa grass. My companions sighted some gazelle and went after them with one of the camel-men, who tied his camel to a small tree. Whilst they were away the camel took the opportunity of breaking or untying the rope which held him, and bolted in a direction the exact opposite to that in which we were going. Then began a hunt after the camel, during which the animal showed such wickedness and cunning that it seemed quite possible to believe, with the natives, that "devils" sometimes make camels their dwelling-places; but finally he was captured. After a four hours' ride we turned off to the right, and passing over a series of low stony hills for two hours more, we came to the famous *Bîr*, or desert "well," which is about one hour's distance from Maṣawwarât aṣ-Ṣufra.

There is a shorter way by two hours to the Wâdi aṣ-Ṣufra, but Lieut. Lord was emphatic about the interest which attached to the well, and we therefore took the longer and more difficult way. As we drew near to the well we saw enormous numbers of sheep and goats, and some very fine cows of a rich tawny brown colour, with big patches of white on their backs and sides. They had the large soft eyes which we see in ancient Egyptian pictures of the cow of the goddess Hathor, and the creatures stood in great contentment by the sides of the shallow troughs made in the ground, from which they had been drinking. The sight of so many sheep, goats, and cows in the desert, about twenty miles from the river, was to me extremely surprising, and I was more astonished still when the natives told me that the tribes pasture their flocks in the mountain valleys and plains, where grass grows after the rains, some twenty miles still further eastwards. Generally speaking, the flocks go from one to three days' journey from the well, according to the season of the year, and they return and drink every few days. So soon as we arrived the shêkh of the well came and greeted Lieut. Lord with respect and friendliness mingled, and it was evident that he liked that very popular officer as much as every one else does in the Sûdân. The shêkh next drove away, with scant ceremony, a party of men who were seated under a good shady tree, and made us take their places, and when we had eaten our meal we set off with a guide for Maṣawwarât aṣ-Ṣufra.

After an hour's ride over very rich ground, thickly covered with grass, shrubs, and small trees, we came to a place where the track forked, and taking the path on the right we arrived in a few minutes at a mass of ruins which covered some acres of gound. The buildings stand at the head of the valley, and even in their decay are both picturesque and imposing. The general appearance of the ruins has changed perceptibly in recent years, owing chiefly to the rain-water which every summer now flows down from the hills round about, and washes out the foundations and makes the walls fall in places. The remains of the temples, especially some of the columns, were very interesting; for they illustrate a kind of architecture in which we may see blended the characteristics of Egyptian, Ptolemaïc, Roman, and ancient native Meroïtic buildings. The stones which form the walls are almost puny when compared with those in Egyptian temples, and the details of the decoration of the columns, and their slenderness, gave the ruins of the temples a somewhat effeminate appearance. When in a perfect state the temples were, no doubt, pretty, but they certainly lacked the solidity which the architects of the Ptolemaïc Period managed to give to their buildings in Egypt, without sacrificing too much of the beauty of form and design, of which they were such consummate masters. To me the ornaments on the bases and capitals of the pillars appeared too delicate for a country where nature is sometimes majestic, but always grim.

No one has as yet succeeded in arriving at a reasonable conclusion as to the use to which the buildings round about the temple were put, but the hypotheses on the subject advanced by Cailliaud, who maintained that the buildings were those of a college, and by Hoskins, who thought that they were the remains of a hospital, seemed to me untenable. Some parts of the ruins resembled those of a palace, and others reminded me of the fortresses which are found in Northern Mesopotamia, e.g., at Birejik, on the Euphrates, and on the plain of Darâ, to the west of Mardin; on the other hand, it was impossible not to think that a portion at least of the main building was at one time used as a fortified "khân," wherein the masters of caravans could rest themselves and their animals, and deposit their wares during the night in safety. All suggestions on such points, however, must remain purely tentative until the site has been carefully excavated, and the remains examined by some competent architect who has studied buildings of the kind in other parts of the East. Meanwhile it is important that the remaining pillars should be removed to a place of safety, and that channels should be cut across the courts, so that rain water may escape at once and not collect in pools, which undermine the foundations. In the winter of 1905-6 Mr. P. Scott Moncrieff, of the British Museum, under the direction of Mr. J. W. Crowfoot, repaired one of the pillars at Maṣawwarât aṣ-Ṣufra. In the hills on one side of the site are the remains of a large circular reservoir, from which in ancient days the natives, no doubt, obtained their water supply. We saw a great gap in the edge of it, but if this were repaired, it would again form a valuable natural cistern.

We returned to Bir a short time before sunset, and when we had pitched our tent, and made arrangements for the evening meal, there was plenty of time to go and examine the well. The approach to it on all sides is protected by layers of palm trunks covered over with a layer of lime, earth and sand, so as to form a floor; immediately over the mouth is a square opening through which the water is drawn up. The buckets consist of squares of goat-skin tied together at the corners, and they bring up remarkably little water at a time. The well is said to be over one hundred and fifty feet deep, and a portion of its sides is lined with stones; when, and by whom, it was built is uncertain. The cords attached to the buckets are very long, and they work in grooves which they have cut for themselves in the palm trunks that frame the opening over the mouth of the well. I understood that a representative of each great tribe in the neighbourhood had a right to a place at the well, but that all arrangements as to the time when each man might draw water, and as to the quantity, were in the hands of the shêkh of the district. When we first saw the well, in the early afternoon, every place at its mouth was occupied by fine tall, solidly built black women, and by a very few men. Some of the women were dressed in scanty strips of native cloth, and others simply wore the *rahât*, or girdle made of leather cut into strips like fringe. All were working hard, and singing and laughing loudly as they drew up the buckets, which were carried away and emptied into the shallow trough in the ground near the well. When we returned from Maṣawwarât we saw that a new lot of drawers of water had taken the place of the women at the well's mouth, and were told that they drew water for payment. The scene was most picturesque, and when we saw women with small flocks standing there patiently waiting for their turn to water their animals, the sight recalled the story of the daughters of Jethro waiting at the well, and how Moses came and drew water for them and helped them to such purpose that they returned to their father before he expected them.

After we had visited the well there was nothing left to do but eat our meal and go to bed, but it was impossible to sleep, for the men at the well sang songs nearly all night, and during the few intervals when they ceased to sing, they talked with their friends who were

THE DESERT WELL NEAR MAṢAWWARÂT AṢ-ṢUFRA.

[From a photograph by Lieutenant S F Newcombe, R.E.

sitting round fires not far from the well, at the top of their voices. On the following morning Lord and I started early (Mr. Nevile had been obliged to leave the previous afternoon on business), intending to reach Wad Bâ Nagaa by one o'clock, but though the track ought not to have been difficult to follow, we lost our way, and did not manage to strike the railway until about four o'clock ; we then found that to reach the station we had to ride some miles to the south, and therefore did not arrive at our starting place until sunset. We had been wholly in the dark as to the whereabouts of the railway, but fortunately for us a train passed on it towards Nagaa, and the smoke of the locomotive

THE SMALLER EGYPTO-ROMANO TEMPLE AT NAGAA. THE OUTSIDE OF THE WEST END.

[From a photograph by Lieutenant S. F. Newcombe, R.E.

formed a dense black cloud in the sunlight, and showed us the direction in which to ride. Lieutenant Lord's inspection coach proved to be a most welcome haven of rest, and we were in need of the tea which his servant brought quickly; for having sent our baggage camels on before we left the well, we had no other food nor drink with us on the way. Food we could not get because the said baggage camels had not arrived. Whilst we were waiting for these we heard the beat of an engine in the distance, and a few minutes later we rejoiced to see the dark bulk of a locomotive emerge from the thick vegetation, and advance until it stopped close by our coach. Presently from the "cab" of the locomotive descended a grimy giant who turned out to be Mr. Stenning, one of the civilian officials in the Shendî workshops. He was taking one of the large engines on a trial trip, and his duty, fortunately for us, brought him to Wad Bâ Nagaa; after a little delay he backed on to the siding where we were, and coupled on the inspection coach, and we left for Shendî, which we reached about half an hour after sunset.

We stayed the night in the railway mess, which thanks to its large and commodious quarters, built by the Royal Engineer officers, is the most comfortable in the Sûdân, and the following day I went to Kharṭûm to meet Sir R. Wingate. In a brief interview he explained the arrangements he had made for the excavations at the Pyramids of Bagrâwîya. He had decided to form a camp of exercise at the pyramids, and about one hundred and eighty artillerymen, under the command of two British officers, Captain W. H. Drake, R.F.A., and Captain H. F. F. Lewin, R.F.A., were to do the digging. The performance of some manoeuvres and a review to be held at Mutmîr, in which these officers and men were to take part, would prevent our beginning the work for a few days, but as soon as these were over the men would be drafted to Bagrâwîya, near which they would encamp. The camp was to be as near the pyramids as possible, so that the men might march out to them in the morning, and return in the evening. A few days later accordingly we went to Kabushîa, the station on the railway nearest the pyramids we intended to excavate, and rode from there to the place which Captain Lewin had chosen for the camp. This spot was close to the railway, on the west side of it, and was, as the crow flies, about three miles from the pyramids; it was about half a mile from the river, and was thus very convenient for watering the horses. In order to get the best results possible from our work, Captains Lewin and Drake decided to have their tents and mine pitched on the hill just below the pyramids, and to live there whilst the excavations were going on. This was an excellent arrangement, for it enabled us to begin work soon after sunrise, and to continue, with an interval for food and rest in the middle of the day, until sunset. So soon as the two batteries were encamped we rode out early one morning to the pyramids, and before the day was ended our tents were pitched on the hill, and the men who were with us had established themselves in their tents in the little valley between the two groups of pyramids to the south of us. With the loose stones on the hill-side a kitchen was built, and so soon as wood arrived the cook was able to get to work. His stoves were primitive and were made of stones, but in spite of the high winds which blew through the crevices in the walls and made it at times very difficult to keep the fire going, he managed very well. At the further end of the kitchen was a raised bench of stones, which, with a sheep-skin upon it, served him for a bed; the soldier-servants lived in a little tent pitched close by.

All the arrangements necessary for supplying us with food and water were made by Captain Lewin. Early every morning mules arrived, each carrying two of the little regulation tanks filled with water, which was at once emptied into the large water jars that stood on wooden frames on the north sides of the tents, as much in the shade as possible. The mules returned to the camp near the river for the day, and came back in the evening with another load. Milk was supplied by the native women near the river, who sent it out to us each morning. Chickens were very scarce, and eggs scarcer still, but so soon as the women in the villages began to realize that we paid for things on the spot, they looked after their chickens, and fed them sometimes, and by degrees a fair supply of eggs was produced. At first the women thought that they would be expected to provide the officers with eggs, poultry, and sheep for nothing, and every inquiry for eggs was met by the answer that the "chickens would not lay." One day

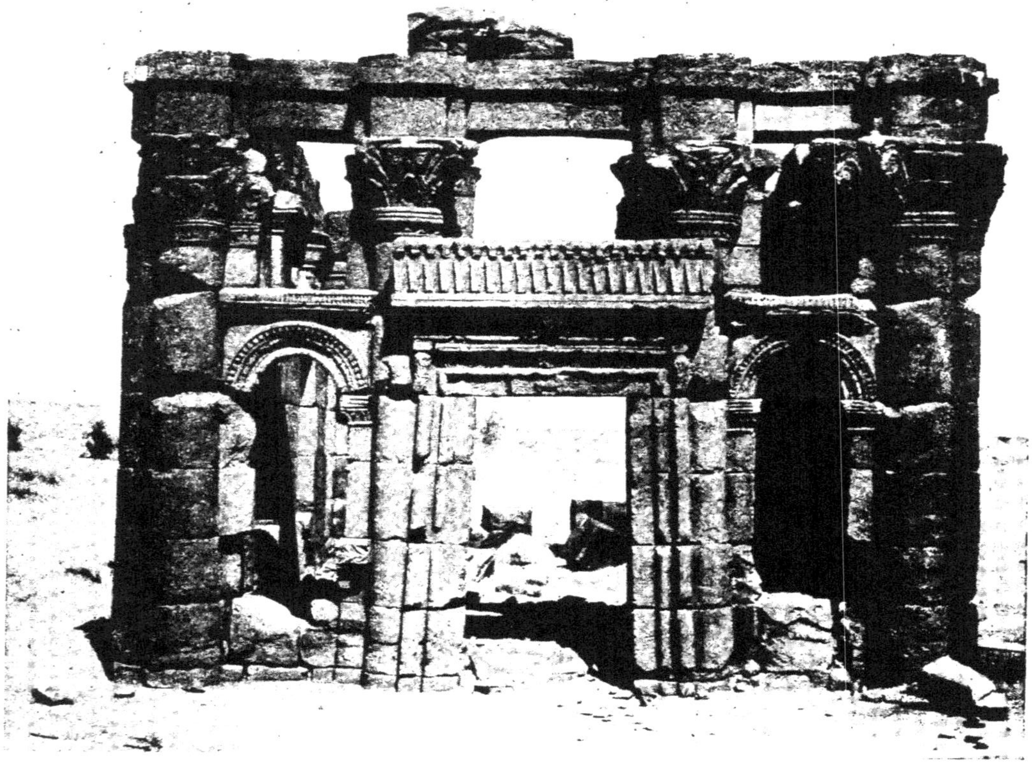

THE SMALLER EGYPTO-ROMANO TEMPLE AT NAGAA. THE ENTRANCE.

[From a photograph by C. C. F. Mackenzie, Esq.

Captain Lewin interviewed the black matrons in the village, and having told them that they would be paid for their goods, he made them a few little presents, and left them to consider the matter. A little later in the day one of the Egyptian officers also visited the matrons, and told them that the Sirdar had given orders that the hens were to lay, and that if they did not, he, i.e., the officer, would not be surprised if great trouble fell on the village. The result was satisfactory, whatever may have been the cause, for the very next day six good eggs appeared instead of two, as

THE EXCAVATION CAMP AT THE PYRAMIDS OF MEROË IN 1903.

was usually the case, and and the supply increased until the last day we were at the pyramids, several weeks later, when the number of eggs brought in the morning was forty-four. The Sûdâni eggs, like the Egyptian, are, however, very small. The experiment was interesting, as showing that the natives are quite willing to work when ready money is to be obtained. Fresh meat could generally be obtained by buying a sheep, which cost from fifteen to twenty piastres, and every few days we obtained a basket of vegetables, i.e., the egg plants, mulûkhîa, tomatoes,

&c., with occasionally a large water melon, from Mr. Morgan, an *employé* of a land company in the Sûdân whose headquarters were near Bagrâwîya. Bread we obtained from a Greek merchant at Shendi who for some weeks sent it regularly by train to Kabûshîa, whence it was brought to the pyramids by the men. One day, however, he went to Kharṭûm and got married, and for several days no bread appeared; but when he returned to his shop he made up for his neglect by sending us at one time fourteen four-pound loaves, two for each of the days he was away!

For the first fortnight or so a body of artillerymen used to march out to the pyramids at sunrise, and work there all day, and time their departure in the afternoon, so that they might reach their camp near the river at sunset. Captains Lewin and Drake decided, however, that this arrangement was not a good one, for the men having walked about three and a half miles in the morning before they began their work, and having the same distance to go after they had ended it, naturally spared themselves during the day. The new plan which these officers made was a much better one. The men came out on shifts of three days, and then went back to the river for three days, and in this way duties connected with the care of the horses and the labour of digging were distributed equally among all the men in the two batteries. It necessitated an increase in the transport work, but a great deal more digging was done than would have been possible under the first arrangement. One or other of the British officers, and sometimes both, rode into the camp near the river each day to see that all was right with the men, guns, and horses, and they were indefatigable in the discharge of both their military and antiquarian duties. That more constant supervision might be given to their men two heliostats were obtained from Kharṭûm, and thus instant communication between the camp on the river and that at the pyramids was established; at night, signals were made between the camps with lamps. By means of these instruments much time was saved, and supplies of all kinds were obtained quickly.

A word may be said about the weather which we had at the pyramids. The nights were very cold, so cold that we cordially

SCENE AT A WELL IN THE EASTERN DESERT.

[From a photograph by Lieutenant S. F. Newcombe, R.E.

welcomed the sunrise; as we were some miles from the river there was no damp in the air, and we escaped the bitter cold which is always felt in a camp pitched close to the Nile, even when there is no vegetation near. The first two or three hours of the day were generally pleasant, but from eleven in the morning to three in the afternoon the heat was tremendous. The hill on which the pyramids stand is of stone, and by noon the air near the surface was moved into waves by the heat reflected from it, as by a heated furnace. The only thing to do then was to take refuge in some pyramid chapel, but even there the absence of moving air would make the atmosphere inside it stifling. Towards sunset a breeze would often begin to blow from the north, but when, as was frequently the case, the gentle breeze turned into a strong wind, we were glad to seek the shelter of the tents. Occasionally the absence of wind would tempt Captain Lewin to arrange for us to dine in the open air, but more often than not we were driven into our tents by the wind by nine o'clock. When the weather is propitious nothing is more lovely than a Sûdân night, especially if there be a moon. The whole desert becomes flooded with brilliant white light, the rugged face of the desert disappears, the shrubs and small trees turn into shapes of mystic beauty, and the whitish blue of the sky casts a reflection of soft beauty over the remote stretches of the desert which are filled with dimly seen silver-grey mountains, and turns them into Fairyland. At certain times of the month several reaches of the river, which were many miles away, revealed themselves by moonlight, and when seen under these circumstances they looked like lakes of silver mingled with white fire. When there is no wind the "outgoings of the morning and evening" are things of great beauty, but in a strong, continuously blowing north wind, the deserts of the Sûdân are unbearable. In February, 1903, a fierce wind blew from the north for three days, and on the third day we could not see the sun; the air was filled with sand to such a degree that we felt as if we were shut in by walls of sandstone, and the fine sand got into the food and water, and filled the eyes, and ears, and nostrils, and made life most uncomfortable. For several days after the gale had blown itself out, the atmosphere was charged with fine dust stirred up from the desert, and though this made the sunsets glorious, every one was thankful when the hills resumed their wonted clear-cut outlines, and it became again a pleasure to breathe the wonderful Sûdân air. On the whole, the climate of the Sûdân in January and February is good, and the air is dry and invigorating, but care must be taken to guard against chills, which are very easily contracted in the early morning, and against the heat of the sun between noon and three o'clock. In February the alternate spells of heat and cold are trying, but they need cause no inconvenience to the traveller, especially if he takes care to keep warm at night, or can sleep in a thick-walled mud hut. Many of the native huts are very comfortable, especially those possessing an inner room which is inaccessible to the north wind. It would be unfair to judge the Sûdân climate in the early spring from the weather which we experienced on the hill of the pyramids, for there we were exposed for several weeks to the full heat of the sun by day, and to the whole force of the wind by night. There was on the hill no soil into which to drive the tent-pegs, and our tents were only kept in position by tying the ends of the ropes to large stones. Thus by night the north wind blew under the tents and made them very cold inside, and by day they were filled with hot air which came in in the same way; and when a storm was raging outside, every object inside was soon covered with a thick layer of sand, and the air was charged with dust. The Sûdân Government has, very wisely, spared neither pains nor money in providing for the housing of the officials, and in building rest-houses for the use of inspectors when journeying through their districts, but it seems a pity that sun-dried bricks are not more frequently used in the construction of the houses built for the officials at Kharṭûm. Walls made of burnt bricks absorb much heat by day, and radiate it by night to the great discomfort of those who live within them.

SCENE AT A WELL IN THE EASTERN DESERT.

[From a photograph by Lieutenant S. F. Newcombe, R.E.

CHAPTER IX.

THIRD MISSION, 1903.

EXCAVATIONS AT THE PYRAMIDS OF MEROË.

DURING the first two or three days of our stay at the pyramids we were occupied in settling ourselves, and in making arrangements for the well-being of the artillerymen who were to do the digging. This seems a simple affair when soldiers are in question, but as a matter of fact, much thought and care had to be expended, and much time was consumed, before we could begin work and hope to continue it uninterruptedly. We were some three miles from the Nile, and every drop of water and every meal for men and horses had to be brought from the camp to the hill. There were no villages or towns near in which necessaries could be bought as in Egypt, and the nearest town where stores could be obtained was Shendî, forty miles distant. Whilst Captains Lewin and Drake were occupied in establishing the camp, I spent my time in examining the pyramid chapels, and in sketching out a plan of work on the lines which Sir F. R. Wingate, the Governor-General of the Sûdân, had discussed with me in the previous year. He was anxious to make the pyramids yield up their secrets, and especially to find out definitively whether the dead were buried in chambers built in the masonry of the pyramids, or in chambers or pits beneath them. It was very important to settle this question, for so long as the natives believed that there was treasure hidden in chambers in the pyramids, so long would attempts be made to reach it by pulling down their tops, or otherwise destroying them. When I arrived at the pyramids in 1903, I found that much damage had been done to some of the most northerly of them since I first went there in the winter of 1898-99, and also that an attempt had been made to dig down through the mass of fallen stones which covered the shrine and chapel of the second of the two largest pyramids at the north end of the hill. He who made the attempt had gone to work systematically, and it was evident that it was only the difficulty of getting rid of the sand and stones which he dug out, that stopped his work. That the attempt should be made was not

PYRAMID AT MEROË, FROM WHICH THE TOP HAD BEEN REMOVED BETWEEN 1899 AND 1903.

surprising, for I knew that some of the antiquity diggers from Upper Egypt had gone into the Sûdân, and the site of the pyramids of Bagrâwîya formed an ideal place for excavations for the native digger. In the first place, there were no watchmen to be reckoned with ; and in the second, the pyramids were miles from any human habitation, and at a considerable distance from any desert road, and he could work all night without fear of being disturbed, and hide himself during the day in one of the chapels, or among the stones of a half-ruined pyramid. The only difficulty he had to contend with was the water supply, but this was not hard to overcome, for he could easily arrange with a partner to bring out water to him by night. I heard subsequently that diggings had been carried on by two or three Egyptians, assisted by Sûdâni men from a village near Bagrâwîya, but their labour yielded no antiquities, and when they returned to Egypt they loudly denounced the pyramids as useless. They brought a few scarabs from the Sûdân, which they said they had found whilst digging, but it is far more likely that they bought them from the natives.

One very sad result of Ferlini's excavations, and of his alleged discovery of treasure in a chamber in the pyramid of the "great Queen," has been the total destruction of several pyramids on each of the great pyramid fields of the Sûdân. Very few natives really believe the statements of the Europeans when they say that they excavate ancient sites for the love of science, and because of a desire to learn the ancient history of the country, and in their heart of hearts they think that the foreigners have learned from old, native books where treasure is buried, and that they have come to dig it up. The traditions about Ferlini's "find," which are still extant in the Sûdân, have confirmed them in this view, which is often held by educated Egyptian officers quartered in the country, who ought to know better. Lepsius tells us in one of his Letters (English ed., p. 197) that on April 8th, 1844, he was surprised to receive a visit from Osmân Bey, who was returning with an army of five thousand men from Taka (Kasala), where he had been employed in putting down a rebellion with a strong hand. In the course of conversation Osmân Bey told Lepsius that he wished to turn his men into treasure-diggers, and that he was about to order some of his battalions to come and pull down the pyramids in order to find the treasure which rumour said still existed in them. The people in Kharṭûm, both Europeans and natives, believed there was treasure in them, because Ferlini had found some. Lepsius says: "I constantly endeavoured to prove to "them all, that the discovery of Ferlini was pure chance, that he "had not found the gold rings in the sepulchral chambers with "the mummies, where they alone might reasonably have been "searched for with any hope of success, but walled up in the "stone, in which place they had been concealed by a whim of "the owner. I endeavoured to convince Osmân Bey of this also, "who even offered me the aid of his companies of soldiers to "conduct the work of destruction. I naturally declined this, "though perhaps I should have accepted it for the sake of laying "open to view the sepulchral chambers, which necessarily must "have their entrance in front of the Pyramids in the natural rock, "had I not feared that here also we might not arrive at any "brilliant result, and even if our own expectations were not so, "yet those of the credulous general might be bitterly disappointed. "I succeeded in diverting him from his idea, and thus for the "present, at least, the existing Pyramids have been saved. The "soldiers have departed without having made war on the "Pyramids."

Now besides the scientific interest which Sir Reginald Wingate took in the pyramids of Bagrâwîya, he wished, if possible, to make them and their chapels accessible to the visitors to the Sûdân, and this could only be done by clearing away the sand which had drifted up the sides of several of them, and by making roads, with side-paths between the most important of the pyramids. In fact, he decided to do for the chief pyramid-field in the Sûdân what Mariette and Maspero have done with such conspicuous success for so many of the great temples of Egypt. When I first went to Meroë in 1898-1899 only three of the chapels could be entered, and even these were half filled with sand; all the rest were choked with stones which had fallen from the pyramids, or had formed the roofs and walls of the chapels, and with drift-sand, and to reach any one of them was a tedious piece of work. The artillerymen started by making a good broad path, several feet wide, along the west sides of the pyramids, and then, having cleared away the masses of stones which lay round the most northerly pyramids, they turned round and made a road in front of the chapels, on the east side, from north to south. Paths were then made between the pyramids to join these roads, and thus the men were enabled to save much time in getting to their work. Paths were next made from the road in front of the chapels down to the pyramids at the foot of the hill, and in the course of this work we found portions of the pillars which had stood in the fore-court of the chapel of the largest of the pyramids on the hill. It was hopeless to attempt to replace them, and they were therefore hauled out from the stones and sand under which they had lain

AN EGYPTIAN OFFICER WHO ACTED AS OVERSEER OF WORKS.

buried for many years, and rolled to the sides of the paths, along with other inscribed blocks, where they could, at least, be easily seen. In the course of the road-making many scores of tons of stone-blocks were "shifted," but the work took a very few days to accomplish, for the Egyptian artillerymen worked with a will, and Captain Lewin's excellent arrangements prevented loss of time.

So soon as the roads and paths were made a large number of soldiers were turned on to clear out the chapels, and to remove the broken slabs from their roofs; whilst this was being done we attacked, with about twenty men, the four small ruined pyramids which stood on each side of the pylon of pyramid No. 11 in the plan (Cailliaud L, Hoskins H, Lepsius No. 10). Each pyramid was about twelve feet square at the base, and its core was made of mud, sand, and small blocks of stone, chippings from the quarry, pebbles from the desert, &c.; the casing was formed by rows of small slabs of sandstone, piled one above the other, and no mortar was used in its construction. On the east side of each were the remains of a small stone false door and of a very shallow chapel, but no traces of inscriptions were to be seen on them. We began by trying to sink a shaft at the exact spot where the chapel had stood before one of these pyramids, but, as we came almost immediately on the living rock, which showed no signs of having been touched by a mason's tool, it was quite evident that no shaft existed there. We then removed the remains of the pyramid, and on coming to the bed-rock, we found the entrance to a shaft about five feet in diameter; the shaft was an irregular square in shape, and was filled with clean desert sand. When this had been cleared out to a depth of about thirty feet, we found on the side facing the east two slabs of stone, about two feet six inches long and a foot wide, leaning backwards, with a space of about six inches between them. They seemed to be intended to represent the two towers of the pylon of a funerary chapel, and if this were so, the space between them must have been meant to serve as the door. On moving these, we saw behind them the traces of an oval-shaped opening which had been stopped with mud, and behind this was a small hollow, hewn in the rock, about three feet high, two feet wide, and eighteen inches deep. The lower part was filled with sand, and in the sand was a tall narrow earthenware jar of the Roman Period, about two feet high. We took out the jar carefully, and it appeared to be half full of mud plaster, which closely resembled that used in stopping the entrance to the hollow in the rock wherein the jar stood. The mud plaster in the jar fitted loosely, and when it was taken out we found in the bottom of the jar a quantity of very fine sand and bone ashes. Thus it was clear that the body of the man for whom the pyramid had been made was burned, and not mummified. The jar seemed to me to belong undoubtedly to the Roman Period, but it also strongly resembled in size and shape the jars which are found in the Parthian graves of about B.C. 150 and later in Mesopotamia, and which also contain the ashes of the dead mixed with lime, earth, &c. Nothing but the jar and its ashes was found in the tomb, and having searched everywhere in it, we filled up the shaft with the sand which had come out of it. We then levelled the remains of the other three small pyramids, and found the shafts, which we cleared out as before. At the bottom of each shaft we found two slabs of stone, standing as before, and a small hollow hewn in the rock, having its entrance filled with mud plaster. Two of the hollows contained a jar, the third held two jars, but three of the four jars were broken, apparently owing to the pressure exerted by the sand which filled the shafts, for this had driven the slabs through the openings, and they had crushed the jars. The broken jars were made of a reddish kind of material, not unlike that of the *zîrs*, or water jars, produced by modern potters in the Sûdân. We made no attempt to collect the scattered ashes of the dead, but the whole jars were carried to the surface and then kept in a tent until they were taken to Kharṭûm. The pyramids under which we found the ashes of burnt bodies appeared to me to belong to a very late period; it is probable that they covered the tombs of foreigners, perhaps of Roman officials, who were quartered at Meroë, and died there. In all the other tombs under the pyramids in the Sûdân, the bodies were found in an unburned and unmummified state.

So soon as the shafts of the four small ruined pyramids referred to in the preceding paragraph had been filled in, the men who had dug them out were moved to the foot of the hill, and we began to work at the small pyramids there. We found without difficulty the shafts which Ferlini and Stefani had cleared out, but, as nothing was discovered of interest in them when they had been excavated, they were again filled in, and we passed on to the largest pyramid of the row. The stone casing had been removed, but a portion of the chapel, with its pylon, was still standing. A trial excavation in front of the chapel proved that the entrance was not there, and we therefore proceeded to remove the core of the pyramid. This work was completed in two or three days, and when the surface of the ground was reached we found that the pyramid stood immediately over a trench three or four feet wide. This was filled with sand and mud, and when the clearing out began, a short flight of steps appeared. They were deeply cut in the ground, and were most useful for the men to stand on when passing the baskets of sand and mud to the surface. The floor of the chamber was literally covered with a mass of bones of horses, sheep, oxen, a camel, and a gazelle, and they filled about thirty baskets. A selection was

A PARTY OF EXCAVATORS.

made from these, which was subsequently taken to Kharṭûm for examination by experts. The remainder lay by the tomb for a time, but the jackals came by night, and either ate them or carried them off; many of the bones were hard and firm and even moist, but one would hardly expect even a jackal to find much nourishment in them.

At the west end of the chamber, close to the ground, we saw an opening, which was almost covered by two slabs of sandstone. The slabs were about thirty inches high, and fifteen inches wide, and there was a space of about six inches between them ; on the ground, immediately between the slabs, stood a small bronze pot, which was empty. This pot was sent to Kharṭûm. On removing the slabs the opening was found to be in shape an irregular square, and on passing through it a chamber about five feet high, hewn in the sandstone, was entered. On each side of the chamber were a

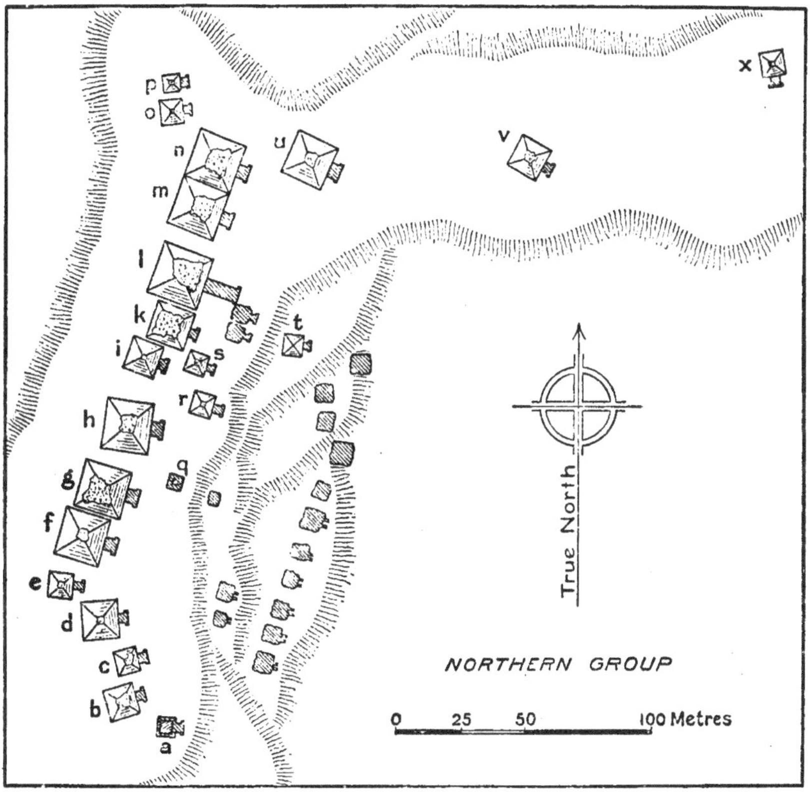

PLAN OF THE PYRAMIDS OF MEROË—GROUP A.

[From Cailliaud, *Voyage*, Plate XXXV.

number of dead bodies, each of which appeared to have been buried in a single cotton garment that had perished. In one corner of the chamber were some large earthenware jars, but they were empty. The bodies had apparently never been disturbed, and we left them as we found them. At the end of this chamber, i.e., on the west side, was another opening close to the ground, but smaller than that through which we had passed. This led into a much larger chamber, with a concave roof, which was almost filled with dead bodies piled one upon the other. By the opening were several skulls, which were thrown there in ancient times. With the exception of a few small earthenware pots nothing was found with the bodies in this chamber.

In clearing the surface round the pyramid, signs of another shaft, which was immediately beneath the chapel of the pyramid, were noticed. The remains of the chapel walls were removed, and we at once came upon the mouth of the shaft, which was filled to a depth of nearly twenty feet with a pinkish-coloured sand. In clearing this out, we found that the shaft turned westwards, in fact that it went right in under the steps already described, and led to a chamber, which was built on the same plan as those mentioned above, and contained dead bodies. In the course of all this work we found nothing which helped us to identify the personage for whom the original pyramid was built, and as the small pylon and the chapel walls were only ornamented with figures of the deceased and his gods in outline, and contained no inscriptions, these portions of the tomb gave no clue. The tomb, in the first instance, was certainly made for a man of importance, and it was probably kept open after he was buried in it, and used as a sepulchre for members of his family for a few generations. The oldest sepulchral chamber of the group is, of course, that which is reached by the shaft over which the chapel stood. At a later period, when the pyramid to which the chapel originally belonged had either fallen or been pulled down, the sandstone above the deeper tomb chamber was excavated, and other chambers made above it to receive the dead. When the newer chambers had received the bodies for which they were intended, the trench containing the steps was filled up, and a new pyramid was built above it. All the lower layers of the casing of the newer pyramid were made of burnt brick.

To the north and west of the pyramid referred to above we opened the shafts of three or four others, but the arrangement of the chambers was the same in each case, and in none of them did we find anything but reddish-yellow earthenware vases, mostly broken. We dug a few trial pits on the slope of the hill in the soft sandstone, and generally ended by breaking through the roof of some chamber containing dead bodies. It seemed that the whole of this portion of the site was honeycombed with common tombs of the kind, and several were joined by means of narrow passages; nothing whatever was found with the dead in them. From what has been said above, it is clear that the people of Meroë sometimes burned their dead, and sometimes buried them without mummification. This being the case, it followed of necessity that it was useless to expect to find under the pyramids large quanti-

14 15

PYRAMIDS NOS. 14 AND 15 AT MEROË.

14—Pyramid through which a passage was driven from side to side.

15—Remains of a pyramid selected for removal.

ties of miscellaneous funerary objects and furniture such as are found in the tombs of royal folk, nobles, and high officials in Egypt, and the experience which was subsequently acquired during the excavations at the pyramids proved that very few things were ever buried with the dead on the Island of Meroë.

By the time the excavation of the eight small pyramids was finished the soldiers had removed from the larger pyramids the masses of stone which threatened to fall so soon as work on the shrines was begun, and had collected the materials necessary for making a thorough examination of the system on which the pyramids were built. Sir Reginald Wingate approved of the suggestion that, if necessary, one or two of the smaller pyramids should be taken down layer by layer, and the base uncovered, and the ground on the east side thoroughly dug through, in order that we might arrive at a correct view about the statements of Ferlini, who asserted that in Pyramid No. 6 (Cailliaud F, Hoskins R, Lepsius No. 15) near the top he had seen a chamber six or seven feet long, and about five feet high. The first pyramid chosen with this object was No. 15 (Cailliaud P, Hoskins D, Lepsius No. 15), which is one of the most northerly on this site. Its sides at the base measured twenty feet six inches, and it belonged to the class called "step-pyramids," and it seemed to have been intended to match No. 1, the most southerly pyramid of the group on the hill. The upper portion was in a half-ruined state, and the work of clearing it away only occupied two days; the lower portion was well built, and its removal gave a good deal of trouble. Finally we reached the bed-rock, and found that the hill had been scarped in order to obtain a good foundation for the pyramid. We cut down into this to a depth of from two to three feet, but found nowhere in it an entrance to a shaft. On the east side there remained *in situ* the lower stone blocks of the chapel, but there were no inscriptions on them, and the style of the reliefs which remained suggested that this pyramid was not so old as the large ones on the hill. When these stones were removed we began to dig down into the hill, at the place where the chapel had stood, and it was found that we were cutting into stiff reddish clay, which must have been brought there. At all events it was not natural soil, and this fact was proved by our finding at a depth of three feet some fragments of a green glazed, red earthenware table of offerings, and some pieces of pottery. A foot or two lower down another and larger fragment of the table of offerings came to light; it was a corner piece of the object, and had on it signs in the Meroïtic character. Both fragments are now at Kharṭûm. When we had dug down to the depth of twelve feet, marks were distinctly traceable which showed that a trench had been made, and that it had been filled up, and it was quite clear that the trench ran from east to west, gradually sloping down from the hill-side into the hill until it went in under the pyramid to the sepulchral chamber. Thus it was perfectly certain that there had never been any chamber in the pyramid, and that the body of the deceased for whom the tomb was made was laid in a little cave, hewn in the rock, which was reached by means of a sloping trench cut in the hill-side. The trench was filled up after the deceased was deposited in his last abode, and a chapel was built, close to the east side of the pyramid, immediately over its deepest part. The demolition of this pyramid proved that the masonry work of the pyramid was not sufficiently good to have permitted the making of a chamber inside it.

We next attacked Pyramid No. 14 (Cailliaud O, Hoskins E, and Lepsius No. 7), the upper part of which was in a somewhat ruined condition; the lower half was, however, in an excellent state of preservation, and was well built. The base of this pyramid is not a true square, for the north and south sides are thirty-one feet long, and the east and west sides twenty-eight feet long. This pyramid was built for a man, for on the remains of the chapel walls were figures of an officer or prince, who in one hand grasped a bow and arrows, and in the other held the end of a rope which was tied round the necks of a number of kneeling captives, who had their arms tied behind their backs in agonizing positions. The remains of the chapel were removed, and then we decided to drive a passage from the east to the west side of the pyramid. So soon as the middle stones were removed from the lower layers of the casing on the east side, the upper layers of stone began to bend in the middle and, where the weight was greatest, to crack. It was manifestly impossible to make the passage through the pyramid without relieving the upper portion of it from the strain, and, as no proper timbers were available, we obtained permission to use the old railway sleepers which were lying by the side of the line about three miles off. When a number of these had arrived, we cut and prepared uprights, and then laying three sleepers on their edges, and nailing them together, we laid them on the uprights, which were placed one on each side of the passage, and, having driven them in with hammers, they carried the whole weight of the east side of the casing of the pyramid without difficulty. The work of making the passage then continued, and at every foot of advance made inwards, we added sides and roof made of sleepers. At the end of a few days the passage was completed, and as it was about five feet high and five feet wide, we could walk through from one side to the other without difficulty. It was quite clear now that there was no chamber of any sort or kind in the lower half of the pyramid, and we therefore attacked

THE PASSAGE THROUGH PYRAMID NO. 14.

the upper half. We were unwilling to demolish it, so we decided to dig a hole downwards from the centre at the top until we reached the passage which we had made. This was done without trouble, and the big Egyptian artilleryman who was wielding the pick finished digging the hole much quicker than he expected by suddenly slipping through the loose stones into the passage below. He arrived in a shower of large black stones, a little bit frightened, but quite unhurt. Here, then, was conclusive proof that in a pyramid which must have been quite forty feet high when complete, and was then at least twenty-eight feet square at the base, there was no chamber of any sort or kind.

The next step was to sink a shaft at the place where the chapel once stood, in order to save the trouble of excavating the whole length of the trench which we saw must run from the hill-side towards and under the pyramid. We passed through the foundations of the chapel, and then came upon several slabs of hard stone, and, when a depth of about 20 feet was reached, we

RUINED CHAPEL OF A PYRAMID AT MEROË.

found clearly marked on the side of the shaft nearest the pyramid the outline of the passage which ran in under the pyramid. The materials with which it had been filled up had contracted in the course of centuries, and had "drawn away" from the sandstone. Thus we had found the entrance to the sepulchral chamber, and at the depth which was suggested by the slope of the passage from the hill-side. Having made the bottom of our shaft large enough for two men to dig and two to load the baskets, we began to work inwards towards the pyramid; very soon, however, cracks began to appear above the men's heads, and it being impossible to foresee how far they might extend, it was decided to abandon the shaft, at least temporarily. The work which was done at the other pyramids subsequently convinced me that no addition would be made to our knowledge by digging out the remainder of the passage and the chamber under that particular pyramid, and, as we did not consider it worth the time and labour which would have to be expended on it, the shaft was left as it was.

After a careful examination of the other pyramids, we made arrangements to carry on work next at No. 2 (Cailliaud B, Hoskins V, Lepsius No. 19). This pyramid is the most southerly of the northern group of pyramids except one; its north and south sides at the base are nearly forty feet long, and its east and west sides nearly thirty-eight feet long. We found the upper half of the pyramid in ruins, and as the pylon of the chapel had completely disappeared, it was thought that the investigations which we wanted to make beneath it could not add greatly to the damage which it had already suffered. The triad of figures at the west end of the chapel was mutilated even in Cailliaud's time (*Voyage*, tom. ii., p. 155), and the decorations on the walls are so poor that Lepsius did not consider them worth recording in his *Denkmäler*. We first removed the stones which had fallen from the pyramid on to the chapel, and then cleared away the blocks from the chapel walls outside, making visible the fine reliefs of bulls with which they are decorated. The next work was to clear out the chapel, which was filled nearly to the roof with fallen stones and drift-sand. The hill immediately in front of the chapel falls away somewhat abruptly, and this was the cause of the destruction of the pylon of the chapel; the builders of the pyramid made a small platform to support the pylon, but it was not sufficiently well bonded into the bed-rock, and it slipped away, carrying the pylon with it. Some fifteen or twenty feet below the level of the floor of the chapel there was a hollow in the side of the hill, which was due evidently to the settlement of some artificial filling, and it suggested that the entrance to a passage leading towards and under the pyramid might be found here. When we had cleared away the stones from this hollow we saw a level surface, much resembling the bed of a small lake or pool which had dried up, and containing many cracks. Now as there could never have been an artificial or natural lake at this place, we concluded that the surface of reddish mud which we saw before us was the sediment of a pool of rain water which had collected here. A few hours' work enabled us to remove the dried mud, which turned out to be some feet in thickness, and then the sides of a narrow rectangular trench, some thirty feet in length, became apparent. When this had been cleared out, a low opening was seen at its west end near the ground, and beyond this we found a low passage ; this ran on towards the pyramid for about 40 or 50 feet, and led into a sort of vaulted chamber, which, so far as I could judge, was exactly under the middle of the pyramid. To about two-thirds of its height the chamber was filled with sand and mud, and nothing was found inside with the exception of some bones and a skull. It is possible that there was another chamber beyond, but to have settled that question we should have been obliged to line the trench and passage with timbers carefully strutted and stayed, and to have put in balks of timber to take the weight of the chapel under which the long passage ran. The question was really of no importance, and we therefore let the matter drop. We had again found that the sepulchral chamber was beneath the pyramid, and that it was approached just in the way to be expected considering the conformation of the hill-side. In the pyramid itself there was no sign of the existence of a chamber.

We next attacked Pyramid No. 4 (Cailliaud D, Hoskins T, Lepsius No. 17). This pyramid is well and solidly built, and is about 47 feet square. The layers of stone in the casing are twenty-two in number, and the slope of the sides is greater than that of any other pyramid on the site. The stones are large and well cut, and afford good foothold. The chapel had disappeared, and only a few foundation-stones marked the site whereon it had stood. These were removed, and we proceeded to dig out a sloping trench about 40 feet long. The shaft was found immediately under the west end of the chapel, close to the pyramid, and as this was being cleared out, a trench was dug to the north of it, because small pieces of pottery and fragments of green glazed earthenware objects were found. At a depth of about 30 feet in the shaft some bones of animals were dug up, which showed that we were on the right track. The diggers then turned inwards, towards the middle of the pyramid, and out of the passage which they made several other bits of pottery were taken. Up to this point, we had been working with some risk to everyone concerned, for, though we had made every possible use we could of the railway sleepers, and all shoring up had been most carefully done under the personal supervision of Captains Lewin and Drake, it was found that the best of our available material was not strong enough to take the weight of the side of the pyramid which now began to press upon it. This being so, we decided to cover over the shaft, and to put in more sleepers at the entrance of the passage which leads in under the pyramid, so that no part of the casing might fall. As we had found the passage to the shaft, there was no reason for doubting that the direction of the way into the sepulchral chamber had been discovered, and we therefore made no attempt to demolish any part of the pyramid itself. Three or four layers of stones from the top of the pyramid were thrown down some years before we began to work there, presumably by seekers after treasure, who expected to find a chamber there; but being satisfied that no such thing existed, they disturbed the pyramid no further. Whilst we were at work here, it was suggested by a visitor that the sepulchral chamber might be easily reached by sinking a shaft on the west side of the pyramid, because, as we had already seen in the case of the small pyramids down the hill, the sepulchral chamber sometimes extended beyond the limits of the pyramid. We therefore sank a shaft to a depth of 12 or 15 feet, but no trace of the chamber was visible, and the stone through which the men had to cut was so hard that the work was abandoned.

It is unnecessary to describe here in detail the work done at all the pyramids which we attacked, for it will be summarized in the brief account of each pyramid at Meroë which immediately follows these remarks. It is, however, important to state that in no pyramid did we find any evidence which would justify us in assuming that it either had contained, or did still contain, a sepulchral chamber, but that everywhere we saw proofs that the sepulchral chambers were under the pyramids, and that they were approached by means of passages which passed under the chapels, and continued beyond them into the chambers. Speaking generally, we had found nothing except unmummified human bodies, ashes of human bodies which had been burned, a small bronze pot, several earthenware jars, bones of animals, human skulls, and fragments of green glazed earthenware. Of the twelve pyramids which we had opened, six of them, at least, were royal, but still they contained in the way of funerary paraphernalia nothing but a few jars, and it seemed to me quite clear that we were no longer justified in expecting the Pyramids of Meroë to yield large numbers of coffins, biers, boxes, alabaster jars, &c., which they were at one time thought to contain. The passages and sepulchral chambers which our hard-working Egyptian soldiers had laid bare proved that the workmen of the old Meroïtic kingdom were not able to hew in the solid rock passages and chambers like those which the Egyptians made under the XIIth, XVIIIth, XIXth, and XXth Dynasties, and that having once cut a hollow under the pyramid wherein to lay the dead, it concerned them not whether or no it possessed regular proportions.

The hills near the Pyramids of Meroë which contain the quarries whence came the stone for building the casings of the pyramids and their chapels were most suitable for rock-hewn tombs, yet the tomb-builders of Meroë made no use of them for this purpose. The architects of the great queens of Meroë devoted their energies rather to the decoration of the chapels than to the building of the pyramids against which they stood. There is a great deal of good work in some of the pyramids of Meroë, but it lacks the solidity, durability, finish, and simplicity of the work of the best builders and architects of ancient Egypt. And in both pyramids and chapels may be observed the effeminacy and ostentation which are noticeable in the temples at Maṣawwarât an-Nagaa, and at Maṣawwarât aṣ-Ṣufra. The people of Meroë copied ancient Egyptian funerary customs in nearly everything so far as outward show is concerned, but they lacked the ability to construct tombs comparable even to the pyramids of Gebel Barkal. Perhaps the most interesting characteristic of the pyramids of Meroë is the reliefs on the walls of the chapels, and, as they are important in illustrating the survival of ancient Egyptian religious ideas and beliefs in the Island of Meroë in the early centuries of the Christian era, some description of them must here be given. In the following detailed account of the pyramids it is proposed to mention first the work which we did at each pyramid, and then to give a description of the reliefs, making full use of the drawings of them published by Lepsius in his *Denkmäler* (Abtheilung V. Band X). These are, undoubtedly, the best illustrations extant, and it is impossible to make any better, even in these days, for the chapel reliefs are now in a far less perfect state than they were when Lepsius had them drawn in 1844.

CHAPTER X.

DESCRIPTION OF THE PYRAMIDS OF MEROË.

NORTHERN GROUP—FORTY-THREE PYRAMIDS.

PYRAMID No. 1. A step-pyramid. (Cailliaud A, Hoskins W, Lepsius No. 20). This is the most southerly of the pyramids of the Northern Group. The length of each side at the base is about 21 feet; the first "step" is about 10 feet high, and the second about 8½ feet. The pyramid is well built and well preserved, and is made of blocks of sound stone; it stands on the basalt bluff at the south end of the semi-circular hill whereon stands this group of pyramids. The layers of stone are sixteen in number, nine in the lower "step," seven in the upper. The chapel is also well built, but most of its roof is wanting, as well as the pylon. In front of the chapel the hill drops abruptly, and twelve feet below the floor the place where the passage leading to the sepulchral chamber ends is distinctly visible. We cleared the front and all the sides of this pyramid, and then made a road all round it.

This pyramid was built for Queen KENTHȦḤEBIT, who was also called ȦMEN-ĀRIT, or ȦMEN-ĀR,[1] but nothing is known of her reign, and at present her name cannot be placed in chronological order. She was a worshipper of Ȧmen, or Ȧmen-Rā, the Sun-god, whose name she compounded with her own. The name "Kenthȧ-ḥebit" was believed by Lepsius to be the Meroïtic equivalent of the name, or title, "Candace," and it is boldly stated to be so by some writers, but surely if this were so we should find it in

[1] 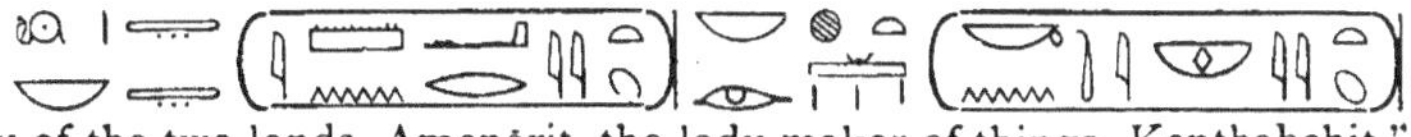, "Rā, lady of the two lands, Amenȧrit, the lady maker of things, Kenthaḥebit."

[2] *Ausführliches Verzeichnis*, Berlin, 1899, p. 404, "der Pyramide einer Königin Ȧmen-ari Kandake."

many other pyramid chapels on the Island of Meroë. So far as we know now, the chapel of Pyramid No. 1 is the only one in which it has been found. The slab on which it occurs, which formed part of the door of the chapel of this pyramid, is preserved in the Royal Museum at Berlin (No. 2259).[1]

On the west wall of the chapel is sculptured the Boat of Rā, with a ram, the symbol of the god, standing in it. Below this we see the mummied form of the deceased queen lying on a lion-bier within a funeral coffer, with a vulture near her head; at her feet stands a bearded god wearing a disk. Under the bier lies the mummied hawk-headed form of Seker, and at its head are the scales of the Judgment Hall of Osiris, wherein the heart is being weighed with the figure of Maāt as the counterbalance. At the head and foot of the coffer are figures of the goddess Isis "pouring out water at the tomb of the deceased Osiris."

On the north wall is sculptured a figure of the queen sitting on a throne ornamented with lions' heads, wearing a tight-fitting cap, with uraeus over the brow, surmounted by a headdress formed of plumes, horns, and a disk. Her ornaments consist of a necklace, armlets, and bracelets; in her right hand is some object, symbolic of authority (?), and in her left hand is a long staff. Under her throne are nine bows, emblematic of her sovereignty over nine barbarian tribes whose chief weapon was the bow. The queen sits under a canopy, and behind her stands the goddess Isis as Maāt (?), wearing the vulture head-dress, with disk and horns, and holding up the feather of Maāt in her left hand. In front of the queen we see the goddesses of the South and North, setting standards, with rams[2] upon them, on pedestals whereon lie the jackals of Ȧnpu (Anubis) and Ȧp-uat. Close to these pedestals are two smaller ones, with a lion on the top of each. In the middle is set up the standard with a box surmounted by the head-dress of Ptaḥ-Seker-Ȧsȧr on the top of it; the box was supposed to contain the head of Osiris. During a solemn ceremony, which was performed annually at Abydos in Egypt, this standard was "set up," and it was supposed to typify the resurrection of the god Osiris. All the standards and pedestals in this scene rest

[1] Published by Lepsius, *Denkmäler*, Abth. V. Bl. 47.

[2] Symbols of Ȧmen of Thebes, and Ȧmen of Napata.

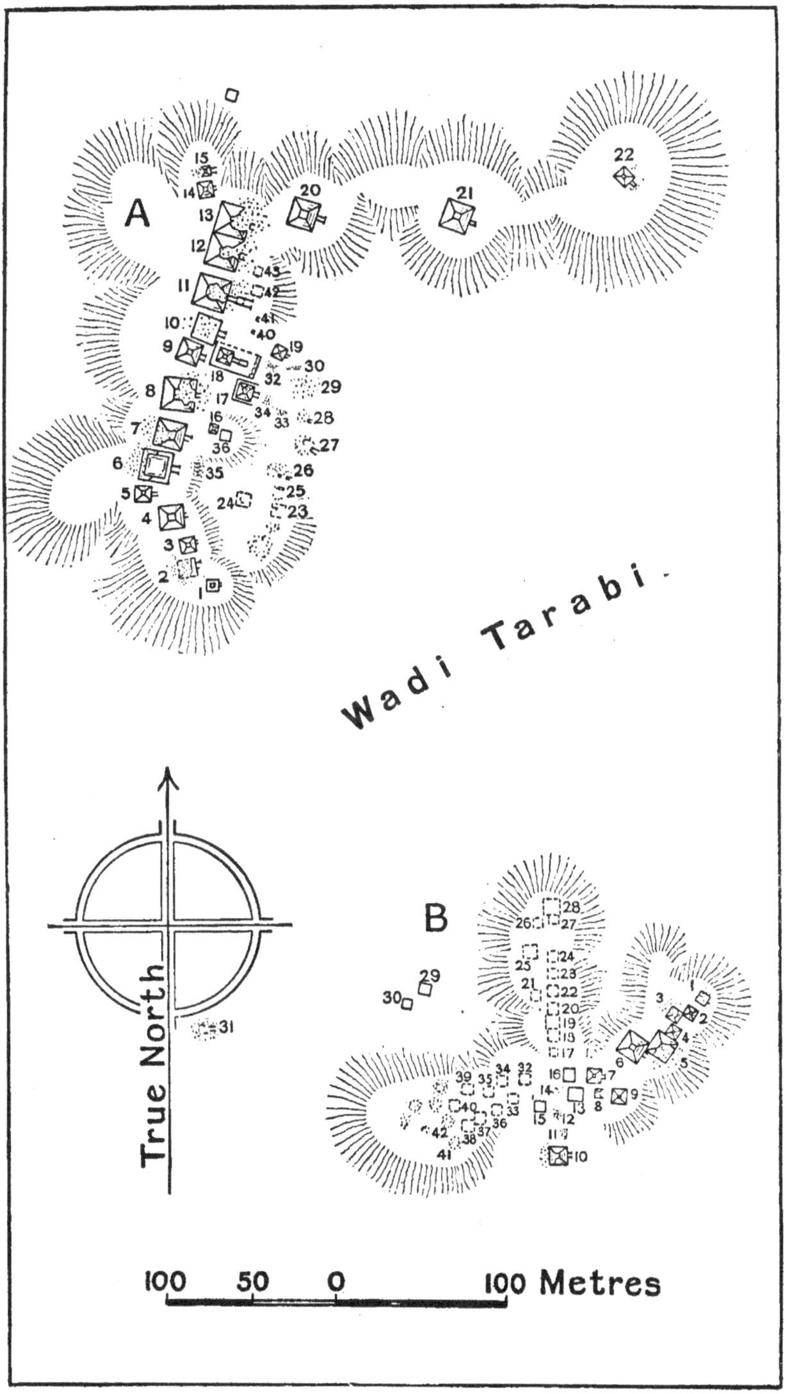

THE PYRAMIDS OF MEROË—GROUPS A AND B.

upon a coffer on the side of which are depicted the forms of the four children of Horus, who were called Mesthạ, Ḥāpi, Ṭuamutef, and Qebḥsennuf. This coffer is of the kind which was carried

PYRAMID OF QUEEN KENTHÀḤEBIT (NO. 1). SETTING UP THE STANDARD OF OSIRIS.

[From Lepsius, *Denkmäler*, Abth. V. Bl. 46.

about from place to place by means of poles, or staves, the ends of which are represented. Next to the above group stands a priest, who is making an address to the queen ; in his right hand, which is raised and stretched out, he grasps a short sceptre, and in his left he holds a bow and several arrows, and a long sceptre, or staff, with a top in the form of the head of Horus, and a rectangular base, on which is depicted a prostrate foe. His tight-fitting cap has plumes at the sides, round his neck is a collar, over his shoulders hangs a panther-skin, and he wears sandals. This priest is called the "priest of Maāt," and his name may be ÅMEN KA-ĀNKH. The inscriptions which refer to these reliefs are mutilated, but it is quite clear that they were drawn up by some one who was acquainted with ancient Egyptian religious lore, especially that section of it which referred to "Osiris, lord of Tattu," and to "Osiris Khenti-Åmenti, great lord, lord of Abydos," i.e., to Osiris of the Delta, and Osiris of Upper Egypt. The values assigned to some of the characters prove that the inscriptions were drafted at the end of the Ptolemaïc, or at the beginning of the Roman, Period.

On the south wall we see the funeral procession represented. First come four men with shaven heads, the third bearing the standard of the Hawk nome, and the fourth that of the Ibis nome; behind these come Anubis, jackal(?)-headed, and Nefer-Tem, with his characteristic head-dress of lotus flowers and plumes. Next come eight men with shaven heads, who carry on their shoulders the poles to which is attached a boat containing a coffer, wherein is the body of the dead queen lying on a bier. The bier stands within a funeral coffer, on the four corners of which stand hawks, wearing plumes. On one side is the hawk of Horus, and on the other the vulture of Mut, and below these are figures of gods and goddesses with hands raised in adoration of the queen. In this scene we have the apotheosis of the queen depicted. In the space between the two groups of bearers are standards, one of which is surmounted by a star within a frame. Round two of them are twisted objects which are, I believe, intended to represent the skins of bulls, but the mason did not know what they were meant to be. It will be remembered that in papyri of the *Book of the Dead* we often see, tied to a pole by the shrine of Osiris, the skin of a pied bull, dripping with blood from the neck, whence the head has been cut off; the god is supposed to have taken refuge in the skin, which in some way conduced to his immortality. In the lower registers on this wall we see a table of funeral offerings,

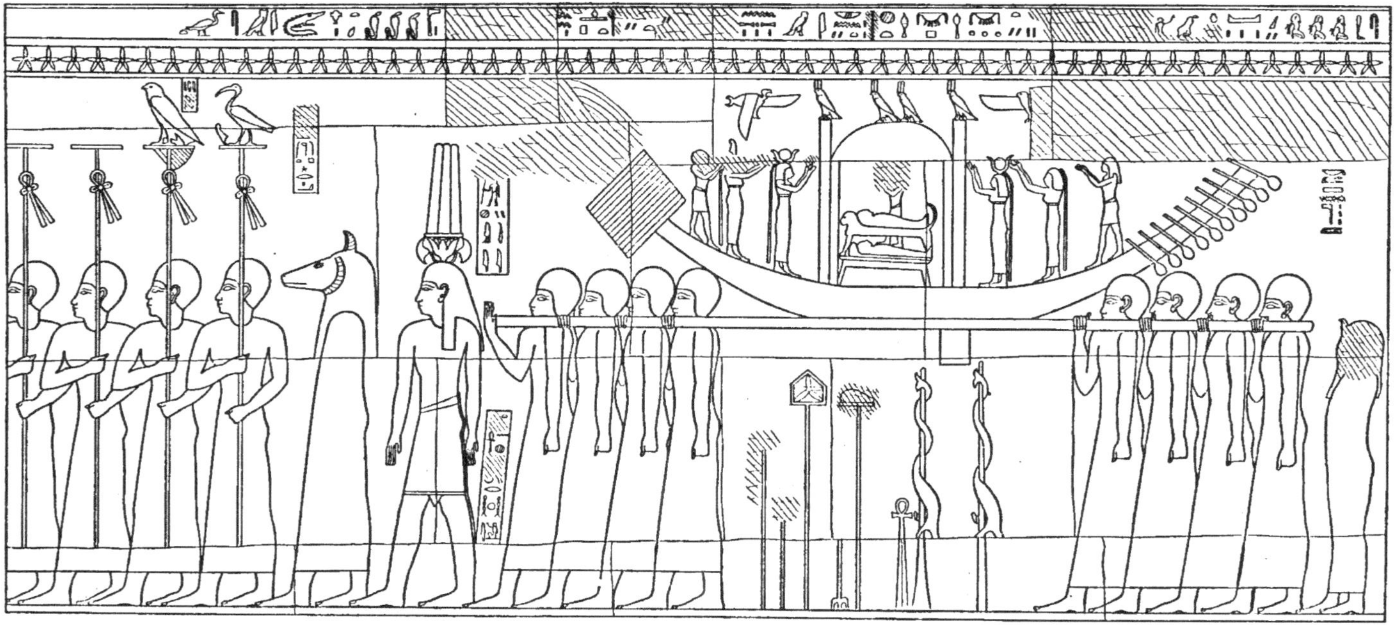

SCENE FROM THE SOUTH WALL OF THE PYRAMID OF KENTHÀḤEBIT (NO. I).

[From Lepsius, *Denkmüler*, Abth. V. Bl. 47.

laden with bread-cakes, fruit, flowers, vegetables, &c., and beneath it are jars of wine, beer, &c. To the right is a bearded, man-headed lion embracing the head of a ram, and behind him are: 1. A winged serpent, with four human legs, before a tree. 2. A many-coiled serpent, before a tree. 3. A priest, wearing an animal's tail, and an attendant. Round the upper parts of the north and south walls runs a line of well-cut hieroglyphics, but the breaks in the text make it impossible to give any connected reading of it. On the north wall the queen's names and titles were given, and on the south wall enough of the text remains to show that queen Ȧmen-Arit boasts of her overthrow of certain enemies, and says that she carried off from them gold and silver and much spoil.

PYRAMID NO. 2 (Cailliaud B, Hoskins V, Lepsius No. 19). This pyramid is in a very dilapidated state, for the north and west sides are in ruins, and its upper half has almost entirely disappeared. It stands more to the west than No. 1. Its north and south sides at the base are nearly forty feet long, and its east and west sides are nearly 38 feet long, but these measurements are only approximate. The path between this and the next pyramid is blocked by masses of fallen stones. The chapel is solidly built, and is 15 feet long, 5½ feet wide, and 6½ feet high; one jamb of the doorway is wanting. The work done in connection with the clearing of this pyramid was considerable, and, in addition to that already described (see above, p. 352), we removed a large number of stones which threatened to demolish the chapel and we made two paths about it.

At the west end of the chapel are the remains of a false door, ornamented with uraei wearing disks, the winged disk, &c.; the triad of gods originally within it was mutilated even in Cailliaud's day. In some places in the chapel bees have built their nests. On the north wall is a relief in which a prince or king is seated on a throne. He wears an elaborate crown, with a bandlet coloured green, and he holds in his hand a palm branch, which is also coloured green. Behind him is a figure of Isis, who stands on a lotus flower, and close by are two priests; on this wall part of the decoration is in outline, and part in low relief. There are several Arabic *graffiti*, a specially well written one being dated in

1310 A.H. On the lower part of the wall are several small figures carrying branches, offerings, &c. On the south wall of the chapel is a large relief wherein a queen is seen sitting upon a throne, the arms of which are ornamented with heads of lions.

Whilst digging before the door of the chapel, at a depth of about 2 feet from the surface, we found in the mud a set of iron fetters, which had been worn by some poor slave or captive. According to the opinion expressed by some natives the fetters were of the kind which the Dervishes put on captives of the better class. It is to be hoped that the captive who found temporary safety in the chapel here, and managed to bury his fetters afterwards, finally escaped.

On the north side of the north wall of the chapel are sculptured in relief several figures of bulls of a fine Sûdânî breed.

PYRAMID No. 3 (Cailliaud C, Hoskins U, Lepsius No. 18). This pyramid is built of well cut blocks of good stone, but its angles are without the usual borders. One-third of it is in ruins, and its north and west sides have suffered considerably; the west side has been burst by internal pressure. The layers of stone in the casing are fourteen in number, the height of the highest point (at the S.E. corner) is 17 feet, and the length of the east side at the base is between 31 and 32 feet. The chapel is well built, and massive, and some of its roof stones are still *in situ;* the jambs and other parts of the doorway have disappeared. There is neither relief nor inscription in the chapel.

PYRAMID No. 4 (Cailliaud D, Hoskins T, Lepsius No. 17). This pyramid stands on a layer of black basaltic stones, which are laid upon a deep bed of reddish material, and beneath them is the sandstone of the district. It is well and solidly built, and its angles are without borders; the layers of stone in its casing are twenty-two in number, and its "angle of rest" is greater than is usual. The length of the north side at the base is nearly 47 feet. A few of the rows of casing stones have been removed from the top. The chapel and pylon had almost disappeared in Cailliaud's time, and all that was left of the former was one slab, which Lepsius saw and had copied. The work of cleaning and excavation which we did at this pyramid has already been described (see above, p. 353), and to this it is only necessary to add that we made a good wide path on its north side. A bird's-eye view of this pyramid is given by Cailliaud (*Voyage*, tom. i., plate 47, fig. 2).

From the relief which Cailliaud and Lepsius found on the portion of the south wall that was standing when each of these travellers visited the site, we learn that the pyramid was built for a prince called Amen- . . . ākha . . . en-ȧb.[1] He is seen seated under a canopy on a throne, the body of which is in the form of a lion. His ornaments are simple, and he holds a long staff in his right hand, and a whip , in his left; on his head is a tightly fitting cap, with a uraeus in front, and his feet, in sandals, rest on a footstool. Beneath his throne stands his favourite dog, and behind it, on a pedestal, stands Isis. In the foreground we see Isis pouring out a libation, a god or ministrant loading a table with cakes of bread, ducks, &c., Anubis making ready boxes of unguents (?), a priest bringing a censer containing burning incense, &c.

Pyramid of Ȧrkenkherel No. 5 (Cailliaud E, Hoskins S, Lepsius No. 16). This pyramid is well built, and good stones have been used in its construction; its casing contains eighteen layers of stone, and rests on a base made of two layers of stones. The length of a side at the base is about 32 feet. The chapel is massively built, and is 11 feet long, 5 feet 4 inches wide, and 5 feet 8 inches high. A portion of its roof appears to have been removed deliberately, with the view of letting in light upon the interesting reliefs which are sculptured on the walls. Through the opening thus made stones and rubble poured in, and when I first saw the chapel in 1899, it was filled up to the roof, and entrance through the doorway was impossible. In 1903 we cleared out the chapel down to the floor, and again in February, 1905. It must also have been cleared out by Lepsius's party, for he published excellent drawings of the reliefs in his *Denkmäler* (Abth. V. Bll. 43-45). The north side of this pyramid is buried under the ruins of No. 6.

Inside the chapel, over the door, is the boat of the sun, in low relief. In the centre of the boat are the horizons of the morning and evening, with the hawk of Horus in each. In the bows

1 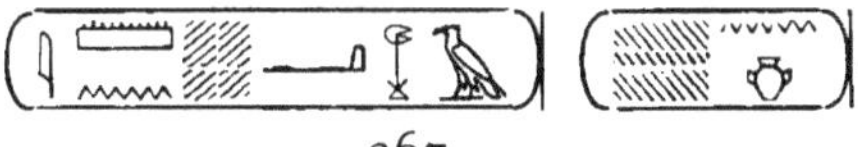.

kneels the deceased before a ram, sacred to Åmen, standing on a nome standard; the company of the gods who direct the boat is five in number. On the right of the door is a priest reading from an opened papyrus roll; he wears a cap surmounted by plumes, with a streamer which hangs down his back, and over his tunic he wears a panther-skin. Three lotus tassels are attached to his tunic. In the panel below are figures of oryges (?). On the left of the door is a figure of a *stem* priest, with a bandlet across his head; he wears a tunic with three lotus tassels, and a panther-skin. In his right hand he holds the sceptre, , and whip, 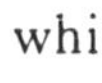, which when taken together, , are usually associated with Menu, or Amsu, the god of virility, fertility, and reproduction. The ceremony here represented was performed with the view of smiting those who had rebelled against the deceased in the two lands. In the panel above are six deities wearing feathers of Maāt, and in that below are figures of two horses being led by a groom (?). Over the door is cut the name GIORGIO TOMO, 1874, and on the body of the boat we read, in large letters, "P. C. LETORZEC, 1820"; the latter is the name of Cailliaud's travelling companion.

On the west wall of the shrine is the usual triad, within the ordinary decorated false door; on each side are five pairs of gods, and among them may still be identified several who in Egypt belonged to the companies of Rā and Osiris.

The reliefs of the north and south walls prove that this pyramid was built for ÅRKENKHEREL, whose prenomen was ĀNKH-KA-RĀ;[1] the deceased was the second priest of Osiris, a fact which, no doubt, accounts for the elaborate scenes from the *Book of the Dead* which are sculptured on his tomb.

On the north wall the deceased king, or prince, is seen seated on the usual lion-throne under a canopy; he wears a cap of imitation feather-work, in the front of which stand two uraei symbolic of his authority over the "two lands," an expression which in Meroë, as in Egypt, must have referred to the two banks of the Nile. These uraei appear to form the ends of a bandlet which is

1 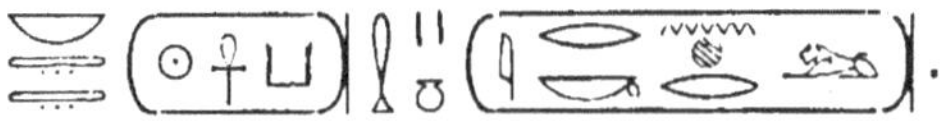.

fixed round his cap; this bandlet is ornamented with a winged disk. Behind the canopy stands the king in the embrace of the goddess of Ȧmenti, who has on her head the feather and hawk, . In front of the canopy stands a priest, whose name ends in RETL, , and he is throwing little pellets of incense into the fire-pan of the censer which he holds in his left hand. His panther-skin is fastened round him by means of three pairs of cords, and the ends of three of the cords terminate in tassels, or fastenings, in the form of lotus ends. By the side of the priest is a well-filled table of offerings. Above the priest, on a raised tablet, are seven lines of hieroglyphics, which refer to the "making of a royal offering, and the dedication of gifts to the great company of the gods of the Tuat," or Other World, and to the little company of the regions of the South and North, and to Osiris, the great god, the lord of the pure (i.e., holy) sarcophagus, and of Isis. In the mutilated lines at the end are enumerated the things which are to be offered by the thousand. Behind the priest, arranged in tabular form, are sculptured twenty of the "Pylons of Sekhet-Ȧaru in the House of Osiris." Each pylon is guarded by a god of the Other World, who holds a knife in his hand, and a figure of the king is seen outside each pylon with his hands raised in adoration or entreaty.

Here in fact we have all the vignettes save one of the CXLIVth Chapter of the *Book of the Dead*, in the form in which they are found in Saïtic and Ptolemaïc Recensions. The upper edge of this wall is ornamented with a row of figures of jackals, each of which has his whip, , and his sceptre, ; below these is a mutilated line of hieroglyphics, and then comes a border of stars. At the bottom of the wall is a row of attendants or servants bearing palm branches.

On the south wall is sculptured in somewhat elaborate detail the Judgment Scene from the *Book of the Dead* with which all are familiar. Osiris Khenti-Ȧmentet is seated at the end of the Hall of Maāti, along one side of which stand the Forty-two "Assessors." In front of the god, on a pedestal, is a lion, with two knives between his fore-feet and two feathers on his head; he represents the Amemit of the ancient versions of this scene. Behind him is the Balance, on the beam of which sits the dog-headed ape of Khonsu, the associate of Thoth, the scribe of the gods. Anubis and Horus stand by the support of the Balance, watching the heart balancing the figure of Maāt, and Thoth is seen recording the result on a long stick in his left hand. Two figures of the deceased stand by the Balance. In the first his hands are stretched out towards the figure of Maāt, as if he were in the act of addressing the goddess; and in the second he is standing in the embrace of a goddess, probably Maāt, and has both hands and arms raised exultingly. The legends which are cut in short lines of hieroglyphics above the figures are much mutilated, but sufficient remains to show that the first contained a petition similar to that found in Chapter XXXB of the *Book of the Dead*, and the second an address to the gods who were supervising the weighing of the heart, wherein they are besought to act justly, and the third the report by Thoth on the result of the trial of the heart in the Balance. Here, as elsewhere, the result is assumed to be satisfactory for the deceased Ȧrkenkherel, for we see him standing behind the god Osiris Khenti-Ȧmenti, with both hands raised in adoration. A glance at the Judgment Scene as presented in this tomb is sufficient to show that it was copied from a codex of the Saïte or Ptolemaïc Period, which had preserved several of the characteristic modifications due to the influence of the priests of Amen. Thus the monster which takes the place of Āmemit, or "Eater of the Dead," finds his counterpart as guardian of a pylon or Hall of the Other World in the Papyrus of Ȧnhai, as also does the figure of the deceased with his arms raised exultingly. The spelling of the words in the legends above the figures is that which was in use in Egypt in the Ptolemaic and Roman Periods, and it is a noteworthy point that Thoth is called the "Twice Great" . The contents of the texts were clearly modified to suit the views of the Meroïtic priests, but they retained all the essential points of the old Judgment Scene, and if the evidence of the Scenes on the walls of this pyramid is to be trusted, king Arkenkherel was a devout follower of Osiris, and was content to die professing the belief which the oldest dynastic inhabitants of Egypt had held

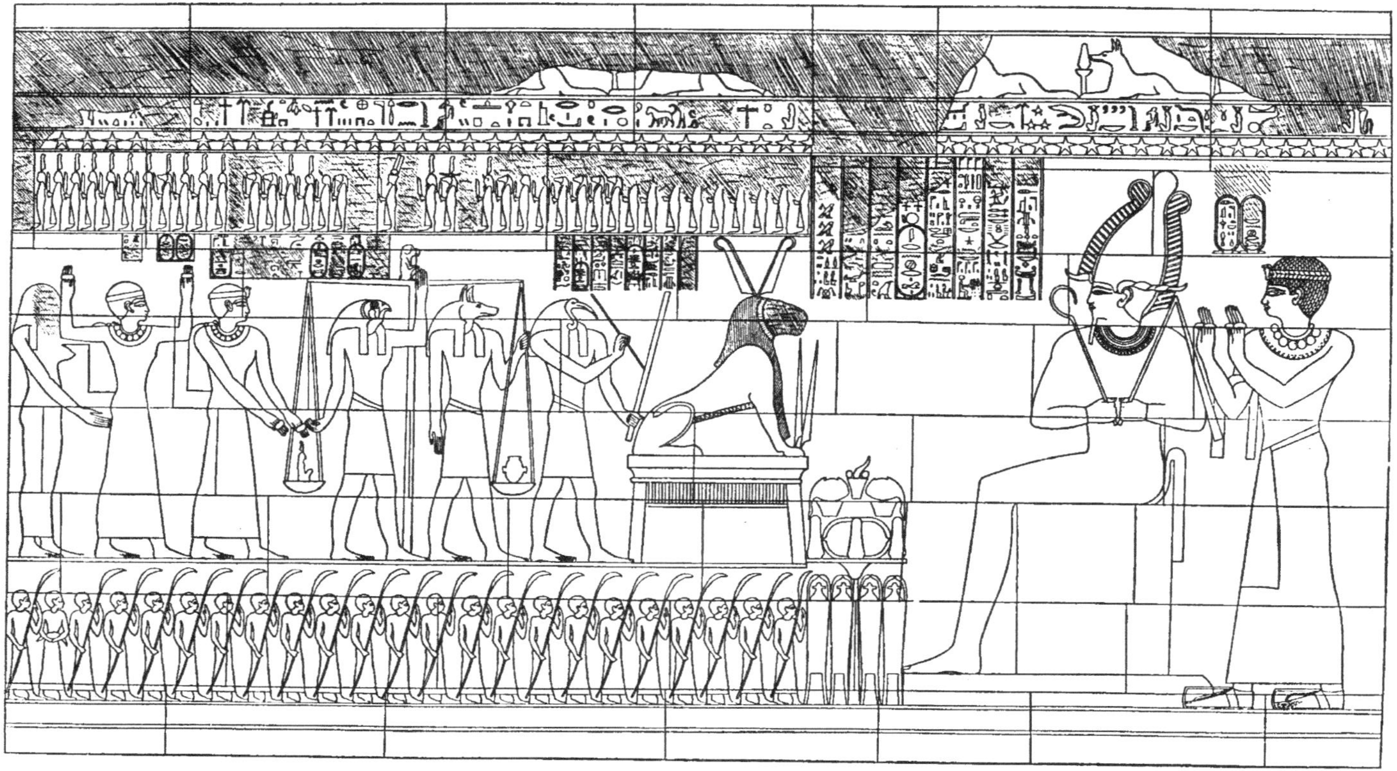

THE JUDGMENT SCENE FROM THE SOUTH WALL OF THE PYRAMID OF ARKENKHEREL (NO. 5).

[From Lepsius, *Denkmäler*, Abth V. Bl. 44.

Denkmäler, Abth. v., Bl. 43.

and promulgated at least five thousand years before his time. In connection with this it is interesting to observe that the name of Ȧmen is not compounded with his own, and that the king believed in the existence of the material heaven of Osiris, as well as in the kingdom of light of the Sun-god.

The ornamentation of the upper and lower portions of the relief on the south wall is the same as that on the north wall.

Pyramid of Queen . . . . Ȧmen-Shipalta,[1] No. 6 (Cailliaud F, Hoskins R, Lepsius No. 15). This is one of the largest of the northern group of pyramids, and according to the calculation of Cailliaud (*Voyage*, tom. ii., p. 157, and see plate 41), who saw it in an almost complete state, it was originally about 85 feet high. Its base is partially buried, and it is therefore impossible to make exact measurements of the lengths of the sides, but each must be, at least, 70 feet. The chapel covered a space about 18 feet square. In ancient days the pyramid showed signs of splitting on the south side, probably owing to some fault in the foundations, and a supporting wall was therefore built on this side to prevent further trouble. On the east side, near the top, was a rectangular niche, with a moulded cornice, like a window, and it was probably intended to be used by the soul of the great queen for whom the pyramid was built, when it came to revisit its body. The destruction of this pyramid was effected by Ferlini (see above, p. 290 ff.) who, because it appeared to be nearly complete, decided to pull it down, layer by layer, in his search for treasure. He asserts in the published account of his demolition of this pyramid that he found treasure in a chamber a little below the summit, and two metal vases in a hollow in it about half way down. When he reached the level of the top of the chapel he ceased his work of destruction.

When we began to make a road to the chapel of this pyramid we found its east and south sides completely blocked up by masses of very large stones and several tons of pieces of black basalt. When these had been removed, the inside of the chapel was found to

[1] The prenomen of the queen 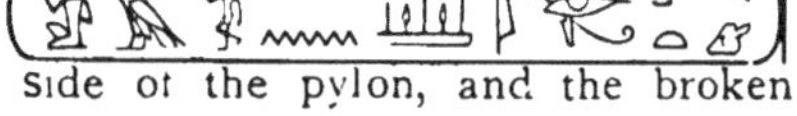 is found above the figure on the right side of the pylon, and the broken nomen 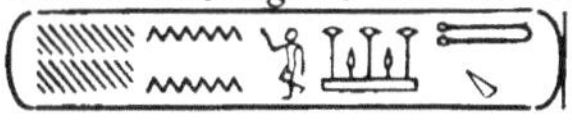 above the figure on the left side.

be filled, almost to the roof, with small stones, sand, dried mud, &c., which had been thrown there by some one who had been digging in the pyramid behind the chapel. This must have been done since Lepsius was there in 1844, for the chapel was in his time sufficiently

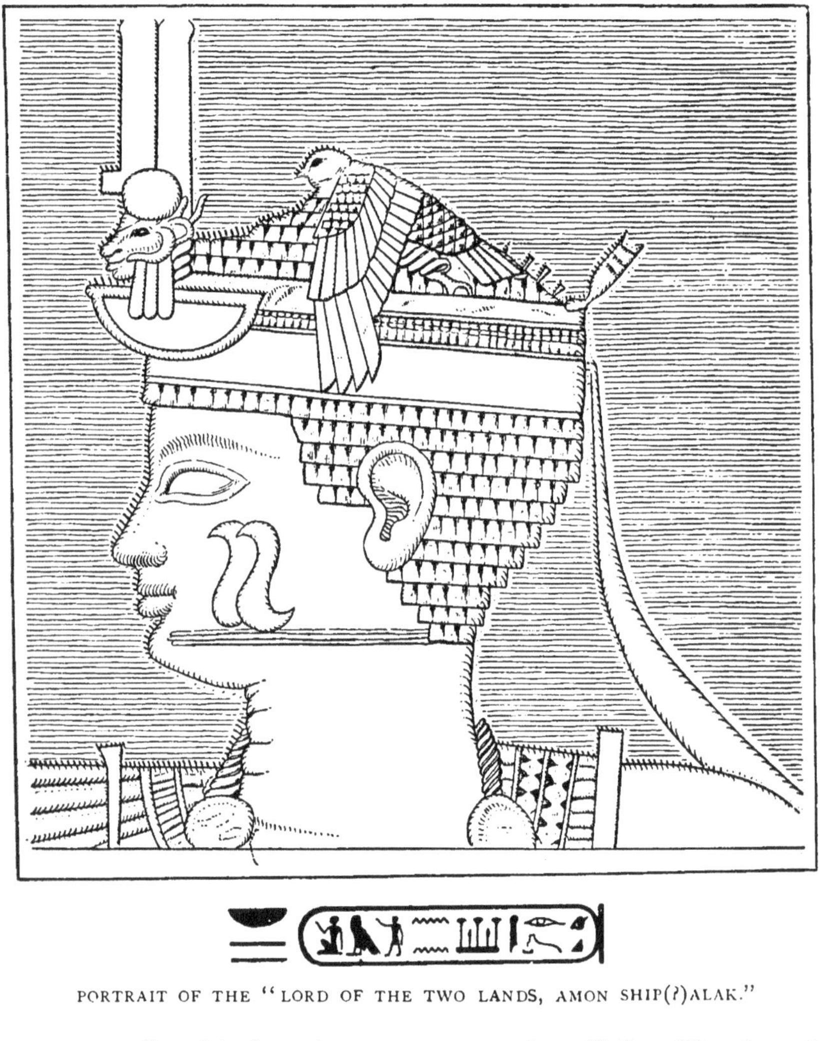

PORTRAIT OF THE "LORD OF THE TWO LANDS, AMON SHIP(?)ALAK."

empty to allow his draughtsman to copy the reliefs. We cleared out the chapel down to its floor, and removed everything which was piled up to the north and south of it, and a road was dug in front of the pylon, whilst search was being made for the foundations of the little portico which must have stood before it.

During the first visit to the site whilst the excavations were going on, Sir Reginald Wingate asked us to clear out the core of the

PORTRAIT OF AMEN-SHIPALTA, QUEEN OF MEROË, WHO BUILT PYRAMID NO. 6.
[From Lepsius, *Denkmäler*, Abth. V. Bl. 41.

portion of the pyramid which Ferlini had left untouched, as he wished to be quite certain that there was no chamber, or niche, behind the chapel. For if Ferlini really did find a chamber at the top of the pyramid, and another half way down, there was no reason why there should not be a third at the bottom. We therefore turned on a numerous party of soldiers, and in about a week they cleared out the core down to the bottom of the broad base on which the pyramid stood. No trace of the existence of any chamber was found, but the work was instructive, and helped us to understand how one of the largest of the pyramids of Meroë was built.

The chapel of this pyramid is one of the most interesting of its class on this site, and the reliefs on its walls are important for the study of the art of the period to which it belongs. The first thing which strikes the attention of the visitor is the fact that the roof is arched, and that each stone in it has been so cut that it forms a well-fitting segment of the arch. The arch is comparatively broad and low, and has still much strength in it. The walls of the chapel which take the thrust are solid, and, at the place where the arch springs on each side, are ornamented with a cornice of uraei. The inside of the arch was painted blue, and traces of this colour remain in many places.

To the right of the door, on the flat surface of the outer wall of the pylon of the chapel, is sculptured the figure of the deceased queen, who is represented in the act of driving a spear into the bodies of a group of captives, whose necks are tied together with a rope held in the queen's left hand. She wears a tight-fitting cap with a streamer, over which is a bandlet that terminates over the forehead in an aegis with a ram's head surmounted by a disk and plumes. Above the cap is a hawk with outstretched wings. Round her neck is an elaborate necklace, on her wrists are bracelets with fringes, and tassels hang from the front of the garment which ends near her feet. The queen is large in stature, her limbs are massive, and she is a fine representative of the steatopygous queens of the Island of Meroë, whose descendants of similar stature are said to exist in the neighbourhood to this day. On the left of the door is sculptured another figure of the queen, but she wears a somewhat different head-dress, and a lofty crown with horns, plumes, disks, pendent uraei, &c. Her collar is elaborate, and attached to her necklace is a pendent figure of an Egyptian goddess. Before her are the representatives of seven conquered

THE QUEEN OF MEROË WHO BUILT PYRAMID NO. 6 SPEARING CAPTIVES (RIGHT SIDE OF CHAPEL PYLON).

[From Lepsius, *Denkmäler*, Abth. V. Bl. 40.

THE QUEEN OF MEROË WHO BUILT PYRAMID NO. 6 SPEARING CAPTIVES (LEFT SIDE OF CHAPEL PYLON).

[From Lepsius, *Denkmäler*, Abth. V. Bl. 40.

nations, each with his characteristic head-dress; their arms are tied together behind their backs, above the elbows, and their necks are tied together by a rope held in the queen's left hand. Her bow and one arrow she grasps in the same hand, and with her right hand she drives her spear into the bodies of her captives.

Over the door between these reliefs is a deep and elaborate cornice, and in the centre of it stands a winged figure, wearing on her head a pair of horns with a disk between them. Heavy folds of feather-work fall by her feet, and behind her are two large pairs of wings outstretched. This ornamentation is unusual, for over doors of this kind we generally have the winged disks with pendent uraei.

The reliefs on the walls inside the chapel are much mutilated, but they are of interest. On the north wall the queen is seen sitting on a lion-throne under a canopy, wearing the triple crown, and holding a sceptre in one hand, and a palm branch in the other. Her jewellery is very elaborate, especially the armlets; from the smaller of her necklaces hangs a pendant in the form of a ram's head, and from the larger the figure of a goddess wearing plumes, probably Mut. Before her are her children and other members of her family bearing funeral offerings, and behind are remains of rows of ministrants bearing offerings. Here also we see the Balance wherein the heart was tried, with the dog-headed ape sitting on the middle of the beam. As this is the only element of the Judgment Scene represented, it seems to indicate that when the queen's pyramid was built, men had forgotten the other details. Its appearance on the wall, however, proves that the queen professed to believe in the Judgment of Osiris, and the trial of the heart before that god. Near the balance is inscribed the name AMIRO. On the south wall we see the queen seated in similar state, with a priest before her burning incense, and ministrants bearing palm branches. She wears a garment of a most unusual character over her right shoulder, and on one arm is an armlet, the centre-piece of which is formed by a massive scarab. In the upper eastern corner is an interesting representation of the funeral procession, and we see for the first time the funerary coffers mounted on wheels; the larger is propelled by six ministrants.

From what has been said above it is clear that the queen who built the pyramid possessed artistic tastes which found their expression in a love for fine apparel, ornamented with ropes and tassels, and elaborate jewellery, which in form and design was copied from the ornaments worn by women of high rank in Egypt in late Pharaonic times. It has already been said that the jewellery which Ferlini sold to the Royal Museum of Berlin and to the Antiquarium of Munich (see above, p. 299) was declared by him to have been found in a chamber at the top of this queen's pyramid, but it is interesting to note that the jewellery which the queen is represented as wearing in the reliefs is quite unlike that which he brought to Europe, and, in my opinion, it is purely Meroïtic. Reproductions of the objects in Ferlini's "find" which were acquired by Berlin were published in gold, and silver, and colours by Lepsius in the *Denkmäler* (Abth. V. Bl. 42), but as this huge and costly work is not always available for reference, tracings of some of the best examples have been made, and they are reproduced in black and white on pp. 298-306. It has been thought unnecessary to give drawings of all the armlets, &c., from the "find" which are now preserved in Munich, for, judging by the official description of it published in the "Guide to the Antiquarium,"[1] they are practically duplicates of the objects at Berlin. Specimens, however, are added for purposes of comparison. Those who wish to inquire further into the matter may consult Georg Hirth's "*Formenschatz*," 26 Jahrgang (1902), Nos. 27, 63, and 97.[2]

PYRAMID OF MURTER, OR ÅLU-ÅMEN, "LIVING FOR EVER, BELOVED OF ISIS" (ĀNKH-TCHETTA-MERI-ÅST), No. 7 (Cailliaud G, Hoskins Q, Lepsius No. 14. This pyramid is well built, its stones are squarely cut, and the twenty-six layers of stone of which it is formed are easy to climb. It is wholly ruined on the west side. The angle stone at each end of the tenth layer from the bottom, on the east side, has cut on it the *utchat* or Eye of Horus, or Rā, facing thus . I have not noticed

[1] *Führer durch das K. Antiquarium in München von* W. Christ, *Konservator, unter Mitwirkung von* H. Thiersch, K. Dyroff, *und* L. Curtius. München, 1901, p. 40.

[2] I owe this reference to the courtesy of Dr. Karl Dyroff, of the Royal "Antiquarium" of Munich.

utchats on any other pyramid. We cleared out the shrine, which was more than half full of stones and sand, and because we found fragments of inscribed stones fastened in the ground on the floor level, we removed the stones which formed the floor, and dug downwards for about 3 feet, but we found nothing. The chapel is large, and massively built, but in order to find a place for the pylon the builders were obliged to fill up the side of the hill with blocks of stone and earth. Strange to say, they did not bond their blocks into the hill-side, and did not even lay them with the outer end tilted up; therefore when a "settlement" took place, their foundations slipped away, carrying the pylon with it.

At the west end of the chapel is a false door, which is carved in such a way that the spectator might imagine he saw the jambs and cornices of three or four doors. In the centre we see the god Osiris seated and wearing the *atef* crown; on one side of him stands Isis, and on the other Nephthys. On the flat portions of the relief is the cartouche of "Osiris, the king, the lord of the two lands, Ȧlu-Ȧmen, living for ever, beloved of Isis."[1] Above the false door we see the Boat of the Sun sailing over the waters of heaven. In the centre is the sun on the horizon , and among the gods who are in the boat are Ḥāpi, the Nile-god, the Crocodile-god (Sebek), and the Hippopotamus-goddess (Ta-urt). At each end of the boat, but outside it, seated on a pylon, is the soul of king Ȧlu-Ȧmen, in the form of a man-headed hawk with a disk on his head, and with his hands raised in adoration of the rising and the setting sun. On each side of the false door are three small reliefs, and in each of the two top ones is a figure of the king, who is here called "MURTEK,[2] lord of the two lands"; he is in mummied form, and wears, therefore, the *atef* crown of Osiris. In the second relief on the left are two gods, and in the third are a form of the jackal-god, and a god with two serpents growing out of his neck instead of a head. In the second relief on the right are a hawk-headed god called Āa-Shāmu (?), and a god with two serpents growing out of his neck instead of a head; in the third are two ram-headed gods, the first being called KENUFI, and the

1 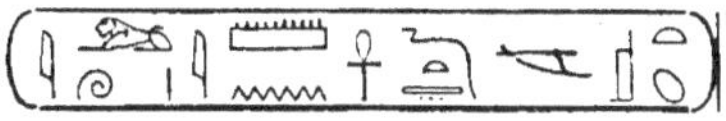.

2 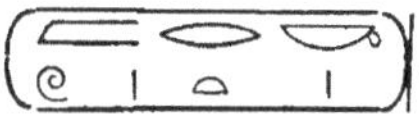.

second Lerā . . . . Each of these eight gods is armed with two knives. It is interesting to note that we have in the ram-god Kenufi the late equivalent of Khnemu, Khnoubis, Khnoumis, and in his name the original of the forms Khneph, Khnouphis, &c.

On the north wall are reliefs of considerable interest. Here we see the king seated on the usual lion-throne, by the side of which are laid nine bows, to indicate his sovereignty over the nine Sûdâni tribes that fought with bows and arrows; close by is his favourite hunting dog. Behind him stand two priestesses, each holding a sistrum, and one pouring out a libation; they are probably intended to represent his queen and his daughter.

VIGNETTES OF CHAPTERS OF "THE BOOK OF THE DEAD" IN THE CHAPEL OF THE PYRAMID OF MURTEK.

[From Lepsius, *Denkmäler*, Abth. V. Bl. 36.

Before him are sculptured the following:—*First Register.* The Judgment Scene in the Hall of Osiris, with figures of the forty-two "Assessors." Outside the hall are four bulls arranged as in reliefs of the Ptolemaïc Period. *Second Register.* 1. A priest standing by a pillar set up before a building which supports a shrine. On one side is the Bennu bird , and on the other Horus-Rā . This scene is the vignette of the XLVIIth Chapter of the *Book of the Dead* according to the Saïte Recension; it illustrates the text entitled, "The Chapter of not allowing the seat and abode of a man to be taken away from him in the Other World." 2. The king drinking water from the tree of Ḥathor in the Other World; this is the vignette of the LVIIth, or LIXth Chapter of the *Book of the Dead*, according to the Saïte Recension. 3. Anubis, the god of the dead, addressing the king. This is the vignette of the XLVth Chapter of the *Book of the Dead* according to the Saïte Recension, and illustrates the text entitled, "The Chapter of not decaying in the Other World." *Third Register.* 1. The king addressing three gods, each of whom holds the sceptre 𓌀. This is the vignette of Chapter XLIII. of the *Book of the Dead* according to the Saïte Recension, and illustrates the text, "Chapter of not letting the head of a man be cut off in the Other World." 2. The king standing at a table of offerings set before a hill, whereon are seated Rā, Temu, Isis, and a serpent. This is the vignette of the CVIIth Chapter

VIGNETTES OF CHAPTERS OF "THE BOOK OF THE DEAD" IN THE CHAPEL OF THE PYRAMID OF MURTEK.

[From Lepsius, *Denkmäler*, Abth. V. Bl. 36.

of the *Book of the Dead* according to the Saïte Recension, and illustrates the text entitled, "The Chapter of going in and of "coming forth from the Ṭuat (i.e., Other World) of the Åmentiu "gods, and of being among the followers of Rā, and of knowing "the souls of Amentet." At the end of the wall stands a priest, who wears a panther-skin and ministers at a table of offerings. The hieroglyphic texts are much mutilated, but parts of them give a connected sense, e.g., "The gates in the eastern horizon of heaven "are opened for thee, and thou findest Rā standing [there], and "he embraceth thee, O lord of the two lands, Ålu-Amen, &c." On the south wall we see the king seated on a lion-throne as before, but the place of the dog in the former relief is now filled by a lion. The king holds in one hand a staff, and in the other a whip, and his enemies are seen crushed beneath his sandals. Behind him stand two priestesses as before. The other scenes are:—*First Register.* 1. The priests bearing standards of the gods. 2. Anubis. 3. Nefer-Tem. 4. A sacred boat being carried by four priests. Beneath it are two plants, with buds on them, &c. *Second Register.* 1. Thoth, wearing plumes and a panther's skin. 2. Horus. 3. Menu, or Amsu, ithyphallic, and wearing disk and plumes. 4. Lotus flower and buds. 5. Isis and Nephthys standing one on each side of the funeral coffer which holds the body of the deceased, and which is surmounted by the hawk of Horus, wearing the double crown. *Third Register.* Priest at a table of offerings, loaded with fruit, flowers, joints of meat, &c., with jars and other vessels of wine, water, oil, &c., near him the text: a "royal oblation" from "Osiris, lord of Tattu, the "great god, the lord of Abydos, the lord of Ta-tchesert, and all "the gods who dwell in Statet (Restau)," and it entreats them "to "give bread, beer, oxen, ducks, incense, wax, linen swathings, "wine, milk, water, and every good thing which heaven giveth, "and the earth produceth, and the Nile bringeth forth out of his "cavern, to the double of" the king Ȧlu-Ȧmen. Along the lower border of each wall is a row of serpents, each having two arms and hands wherein it holds a knife. The gods in the first and second registers suggest that this portion of the relief is copied from the vignette of the First Chapter of the *Book of the Dead*, according to the Saïte Recension. The scenes described above make the chapel one of the most interesting of all on the site, and they show that the cult of Osiris was in a flourishing condition on the Island of Meröe when they were sculptured on its walls.

PYRAMID No. 8 (Cailliaud H, Hoskins O, Lepsius No. 13). This pyramid is fairly well built of good stones of moderate size; its base is formed of two or three layers of large stones, and on this there still exist thirty layers of stones of the pyramid itself. The length of the west side at the base is 63 feet. The south and east sides are ruined, and the chapel is entirely buried under the stones which have fallen from the top of the pyramid. The west side of the pyramid is in a tolerably good state of preservation.

PYRAMIDS NOS. 9 AND 10

PYRAMID NO. 9 (Cailliaud I, Hoskins K, Lepsius No. 12). The sides of this pyramid at the base are between 40 and 41 feet long, and the number of layers of stone in the building is thirty-one, or thirty-two. The stones are large and well cut. The east face, owing to some internal settling, has "crumpled," and is in an insecure state; if one or two stones were removed the whole side would collapse. The chapel is massively built, and it and the pylon are in an excellent state of preservation. There are no sculptured reliefs on any of the walls of the chapel, and it seems that the building was never finished. It is possible that, owing to the "crumpling" of the east side, the tomb beneath the pyramid was never occupied. The height of the chapel is 9 feet. We cleared out the chapel, which was choked with stones and sand, and also the spaces outside its walls, where we found great numbers of stones piled up; we also made a road on all four sides of the pyramid.

PYRAMID NO. 10 (Cailliaud K, Hoskins I, Lepsius No. 11). The base of the pyramid which once stood here is about 43 feet square. The pyramid has been almost entirely removed, and many of its casing stones may be seen in the two poorly built pyramids which stand near the base, on the east side. A portion of the core of the pyramid, which varies from 2 to 8 feet in height, still remains. The west side of the pyramid cannot be traced with exactness. No facts are available which throw any light on the disappearance of the pyramid, but it is probable that it collapsed in such a way that it was impossible to repair it, and that subsequent builders of pyramids employed the ruin as a quarry. The chapel, of which portions still remain, was 13½ feet long, and 6 feet wide, and its walls were fully 3 feet thick. On the west wall was a group of three figures of Osiris, Isis, and Nephthys, in relief. On the north wall are still to be seen portions of the Judgment Hall of Osiris, and of a representation of the ceremony of trying the heart in the Balance. On the south wall, in flat relief, is a figure of the king, and near him is Isis standing on a lotus; ministrants bearing offerings also appear. The outside of the chapel is without reliefs and inscriptions.

PYRAMID NO. 11 (Cailliaud L, Hoskins H, Lepsius No. 10).

This pyramid, with its chapel, fore-court, and pylon, forms the largest, and, in some respects, most important of all the sepulchral monuments on the site. The length of each side at the base is 65 feet, and its height, when complete, was nearly 80 feet, and, according to Cailliaud, its axis made with the magnetic north an angle of 60° towards the west. Its angle-stones are well shaped, and the layers of stone which form it are each about 15 inches high. The total length of the monument, including the pylon and its fore-court, was about 145 feet. The upper portion of the pyramid has been completely wrecked, and I cannot help thinking that it was brought about by the spreading of the report that Ferlini found the jewellery which he carried away in a chamber in the top of pyramid No. 6, which marked the burial-place of one of the great queens of Meroë. It is plain to all who visit the chapel of the pyramid which we are about to describe that the monument was set up in memory of a queen, and the wreckers of the pyramid would imagine that jewellery was to be found somewhere in the tomb of every queen. During our excavations on the site in 1903 we cleared out the whole of the first two chambers behind the pylon, and the greater part of the chapel, but we dared not go any further westward, or deeper, for we feared to disturb the heaps of stones which rested on the slant immediately above the chapel, lest the rubble being once set on the run, the whole of the ruined eastern face of the pyramid would slide into the chapel and bury the soldiers beneath it. In 1905, when, in connection with Mr. J. W. Crowfoot, I resumed work at the pyramids of Meroë, we decided that we would clear away from the eastern side of the pyramid all the stones, &c., which were likely to be dangerous, and to dig out the shrine down to floor level. This decision was carried out, and during the course of the work a stone hawk, fragments of a green glazed earthenware altar, and the greater part of the group of figures of Osiris, Isis, and Nephthys, which had originally been fixed against the west wall of the chapel, were found. The sculptured work under the feet of the deities was in high relief, the design was good, and the carving was excellent. An attempt appears to have been made to destroy the sculptured group by fire, for the figures were covered with a thick coating of

HORUS AND ANUBIS AS THEY APPEAR ON THE PYLON
OF PYRAMID NO. II.

[From Lepsius, *Denkmäler*, Abth. V. Bl. 28.

sooty matter, and they had all the appearance of having been smeared with grease or oil. The stone hawk was, I believe, originally fixed in the west wall of the chapel, either in a niche, or on a standard; it was probably thrown to the ground when the glazed altar was smashed, and the group of deities was dragged out of its place, and cast on the earth, face downwards.

The general plan of the building may now be briefly described. The pylon stands on a base formed of two layers of stones, and is about 20 feet high; the southern half of it still stands, and is in a good state of preservation, and on its face, in

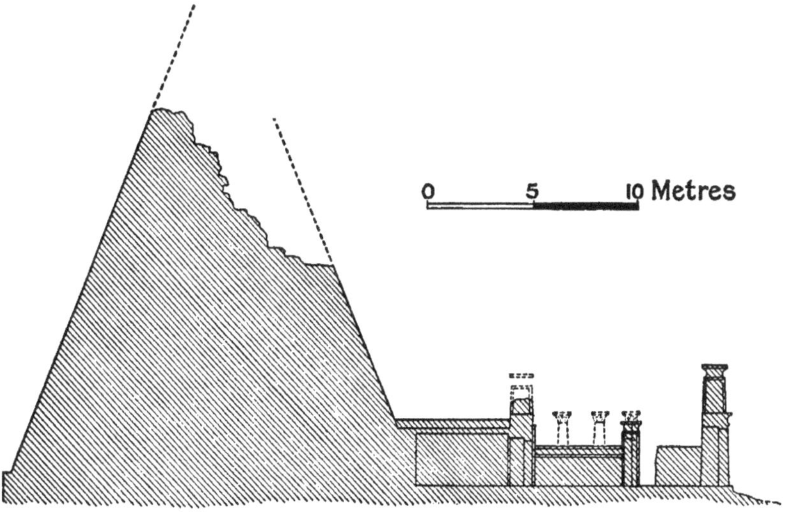

SECTION OF PYRAMID NO. II.

[From Cailliaud, *Voyage*, Plate XLV., No. 4.

sunk relief, is a large figure of one of the Horus gods. The god is hawk-headed, and wears the double crown of the south and north, 𓋖; in his right hand he carries the sign of "life," ☥, and in the left a libation jar, 𓏁; by his side stands a hunting dog, or Anubis. Behind the pylon is a small rectangular court, with a door in each of the south and north walls. There still remain a number of slabs let into the ground, with channels cut in their upper surfaces, and it is clear that these served as drains, and carried away rain water from the interior of the building. It is important to note this fact, for it shows that when the pyramid was built the summer rains at Meroë were sufficiently frequent and heavy to make it necessary to provide drains, and experience had, no doubt, shown the architect what a great amount of damage a little rain water would do. The walls of this small court were ornamented with a few roughly cut hieroglyphics, &c.

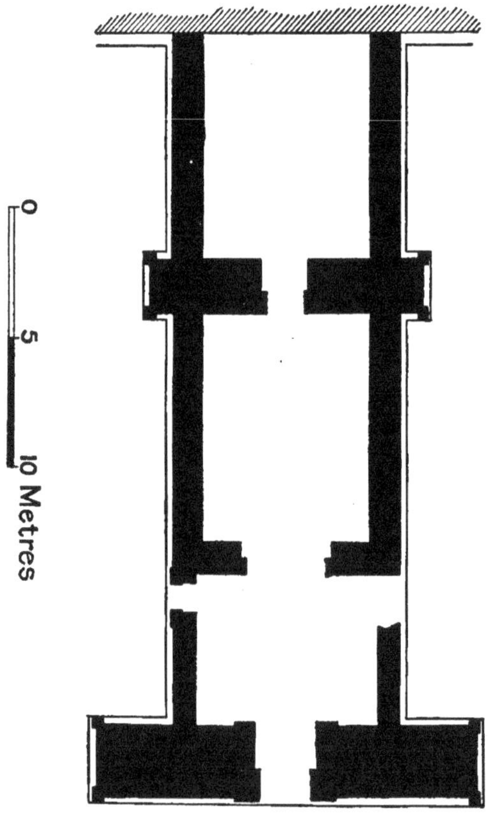

PLAN OF THE CHAPEL OF PYRAMID NO. 11.

[From Cailliaud, *Voyage*, Plate XLV.

The next court is somewhat longer, and the walls were provided with a decorated cornice, of which portions still remain. On the north wall are sculptured two rows of fine Sûdânî cattle, and above them a row of geese. On the south wall are more bulls, in groups of two, which are being led along to the sacrifice by the gods Horus, Thoth, and Anubis. Above this row are a number of figures of chickens, and a serpent having on its head a disk set between horns, and below it are ten figures of kneeling captives, each with his arms tied behind his back above the elbows. The roof of this court was supported by pillars, into which the beams ran; the capitals of these pillars were in the forms of lotus buds and open lotus flowers.

We now come to the chapel of the pyramid and its pylon. A

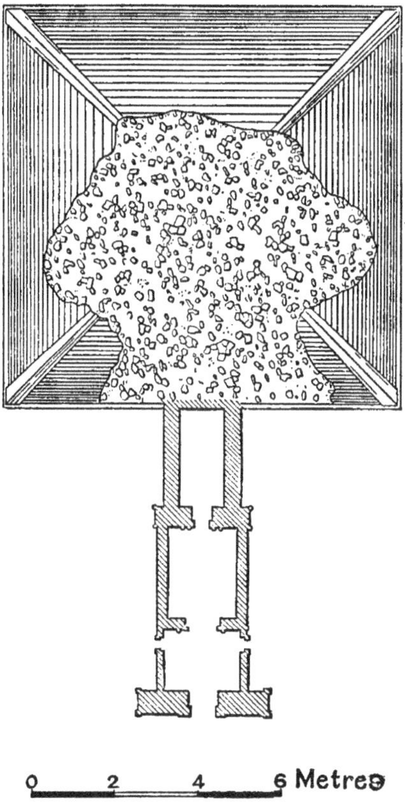

PLAN OF PYRAMID NO. 11 AND CHAPEL.

[From Lepsius, *Denkmäler*, Abth. I. Bl. 134.

very brief examination of the pylon will convince the visitor that the two courts and the pylon, which have already been described, belong to a much later period than the chapel; and if the ends of the walls of the second court which adjoin the chapel pylon be scrutinized, it will be seen that they do not "bond" into the pylon properly. In other words, after the chapel and the pylon had been built some time, the queen (or perhaps her descendants), determined to add another pylon and two courts to the tomb, and to make them join on to the chapel and pylon as best they could. They found it necessary to fill up the slope on the hill-side before the chapel, which was entered by means of a flight of steps, and on this made-up ground they erected the additions to the tomb. The work of the new portion is poor, and the reliefs, though well designed, are clumsy; the new courts do not "range" with the chapel, and they are out of proportion to the size of the pyramid.

SÛDÂNÎ BULLS AND POULTRY (PYRAMID NO. 11).

[From Lepsius, *Denkmäler*, Abth. V. Bl. 29.

On the north wall of the chapel the reliefs are most elaborate, and may be thus described:—The cornice is ornamented with: 1. A row of uraei, each represented full-faced, and each wearing a disk. 2. Disks, each having three pairs of wings and pendent uraei. 3. A row of five-rayed stars. On the west end of this wall we see the queen seated upon the lion-throne, the back of which terminates in the head of an animal. Above her brow is the uraeus of royalty, with the double crown, and on her head is the scorpion-goddess, Isis-Selqet. In her right hand she holds the uraeus sceptre and the end of a rope with which eight kneeling captives are tied together by the necks, and in her left she grasps a palm branch. She wears a garment with fringes and tassels, and her feet rest upon a footstool; behind her is a jackal-headed figure holding a fan with a very long handle, and close to her feet are the gods of the North and South Niles, who are supposed to be tying the "two lands" together. On a less elaborate throne immediately behind the queen is seated her consort; in his right hand is a palm branch, and his left is raised in adoration. On his head is a tight-fitting cap, and round his neck is a necklace, or collar, with a double row of disks, probably

SÛDÂNÎ BULL (PYRAMID NO. 11.)

[From Lepsius, *Denkmäler*, Abth. V. Bl. 29.

of gold. On his right arm and left shoulder are cartouches in pairs, but they are empty. We may note that the queen has *three* cartouches, but they also are empty, no doubt because no one knew how to write her names in hieroglyphics. By the side of the royal consort's throne we see his favourite hunting dog sitting, and two attendants standing. The canopy under which the queen sits is supported by light, Hathor-headed columns, round one of which is twined the long body of a winged serpent; the cornice is ornamented with five winged uraei. Behind the queen and her consort stands Isis, with her wings stretched out to protect both. Immediately in front of the throne are figures of Isis (?), Thoth, and Ḥāpi, and behind them in a rectangular space is a representation of a table of offerings, with attendant gods; below the queen is the Hall of Osiris, the arrangement of the Judgment Scene being that of the Ptolemaïc Period. The other reliefs may be thus described:—

THE QUEEN OF MEROË WHO BUILT PYRAMID NO. 11.

[From a photograph by Lieut. Percy C. Lord, R.E.

First register. 1. The queen adoring a sphinx, which is presenting to her a loaf of bread. 2. The queen standing at a lotus-shaped altar, adoring three gods. 3. Thoth, holding an inscribed papyrus, a Horus god, and Menu. 4. A fish-headed serpent, Maāt, Nephthys, and Horus, pouring out libations. 5. The queen adoring Thoth and Isis. 6. A serpent-headed god and Thoth. 7. Eighteen seated goddesses, Isis, Nephthys, Maāt, Mut, &c.

Second register. 1. Osiris seated at a table of offerings and holding a palm branch in his hand. 2. Four deities pouring out libations. 3. Isis making offerings. 4. Horus on a pedestal.

THE QUEEN MAKING OFFERINGS.

[From a photograph by Lieut Percy C. Lord, R.E.

5. The funeral procession. The body of the queen in her coffin is borne along in a boat-shaped bier on the shoulders of men, and is accompanied by seven gods and goddesses, among them being Thoth, Isis, Nephthys, and Maāt. Above the body are a winged disk and a disk without wings. 6. The queen leading four bulls for sacrifice. 7. Seven men carrying animals for sacrifice, and

gods, or men in the attire of gods, pouring out libations. 8. The tomb, the Persea tree, &c. (see above, p. 384.) 9. Eight hawk-headed and jackal-headed beings pouring out libations. 10. A priest, with two pairs of hands and arms, offering burning incense, and pouring out libations into a lotus-shaped vessel.

Third register. 1. A procession of men bearing branches of palms, &c. 2. A procession of women bearing branches of palms, &c.[1]

On the south wall, at the west end, is a relief wherein the queen is seen seated on the lion-throne, by the side of which kneel captives, with their necks tied together. Near her face are two empty cartouches; in her right hand she holds the sceptres  and , and in her left the whip, , and a palm branch, some of the leaves of which terminate in symbols of "life." Behind her is seated her consort, and Isis, who is pouring out libations, guards both with her wings. The queen's garment has fringes, and ropes and tassels, and she wears several deep, elaborately ornamented armlets; her consort wears a figure of the hawk of Horus on his breast. The reliefs sculptured on this wall are less elaborate, and less well preserved than those on the opposite wall. Here are represented a very elaborate table of offerings, the Hall of Osiris and the Judgment Scene, and numerous figures of gods making offerings and pouring out libations on behalf of the queen, who appears twice. In one register she stands in adoration before a sphinx, and in another she leads four bulls for sacrifice. We may note that her consort is also seen leading four bulls for sacrifice. Nearly one half of the space devoted to the representation of funeral ceremonies on this wall is occupied by rows of men and women, who bear palm branches in their hands.[2] The reliefs on the last wall of the chapel, i.e., above and on each side of the door, are not very interesting; they refer chiefly to the making of offerings and the pouring out of libations by priests, gods, &c. In the second panel from the top, on the right-hand side, are two

[1] We removed the north wall in February, 1905, to prevent its mutilation by natives and others: it is now preserved in the museum at Kharṭûm.

[2] This wall was presented to the British Museum by the Sûdân Government in 1905, and it has been built up in the last bay at the south end of the Southern Egyptian Gallery, on the west side.

male figures carrying bows, and wearing a kind of brimmed hat, of which I have seen the modern equivalent at Tanḳâsi Fair. For the Meroïtic inscriptions from the chapel, see *Denkmäler*, VI. Bl. 8, Nos. 29-32.

PYRAMIDS NOS. 12 AND 13 (Cailliaud M and N, Hoskins G and

THE OFFERINGS OF THE GREAT QUEEN AND THE JUDGMENT SCENE.

[From a photograph by Lieut. Percy C. Lord, R.E.

F, Lepsius Nos. 9 and 8). These two pyramids are oriented in exactly the same direction, they touch each other at their bases, and the length of each side of each at the base is about 63 feet. Rather more than one-third of each pyramid has been wrecked by treasure-seekers, and the chapels of each are buried under immense masses of stones, sand, &c., which have poured down upon them from the pyramids. In 1903, and again in 1905, we discussed the possibility of clearing out the chapels; in 1903 we had made some attempts, but it was found that the work required a greater number of men than we had with us, and to have removed the *débris* in a satisfactory manner would have necessitated the construction of a light railway from the top of the hill down to the level of the plain. These pyramids are in a very dangerous condition, for the eastern faces are cracked in all directions, and the greatest care will have to be taken in working at them lest they collapse suddenly. At some risk we removed some of the larger stones from the chapel of No. 12, and we found that its walls are ornamented with sculptures similar to those which are found in No. 11, only the relief is flatter. The stone is of a reddish tint, and is softer than the sandstone ordinarily employed in the pyramids.

The drawings which Lepsius's artist was able to make of the reliefs in the chapel of No. 12 are reproduced in the *Denkmäler* (V. 26 and 27), and may be thus described:—On the west wall, in the centre, standing beneath a canopy, is a prince of Meroë, making an offering to Osiris of a seated figure of this god, which has the feather of Maāt, 𓆄, on its knees, with his right hand; in his left is a palm branch. Round the prince's neck is a double necklace, with ram-headed pendants, and figures of the ram-headed god Àmen-Rā and Osiris. Isis stands behind him; her right hand rests on his right shoulder, and with her left she is pouring out a libation. Before him stands the goddess Maāt, who is also pouring out a libation. In the panels beside the centre relief we see:—1. Osiris, wearing the *atef* crown, and holding the sceptre 𓌀 and ☥. 2. Two gods holding knives: one has a lotus (?) in the place of a head, and the other a serpent, with a head at each end of his body. 3. The deceased adoring an ancestor (or I-em-ḥetep ?). 4. Figures of Seker-Àsȧr, Àmentet, and Taurt. 5. The deceased adoring the sacred bull, Ḥāpi, which has between its horns a disk and plumes. 6. Two gods with knives—Horus and Anubis. The ornamentation of the west wall of the chapel of this pyramid is unusual. On the south wall, at the west end of it, the prince or king is seen seated in royal state upon a throne, which lacks the usual decoration of lions' heads; the throne is, in fact, a stool with a very low back. The front of the canopy under which he sits terminates in a serpent, and the pillar on which it rests has a capital in the form of a ram's head surmounted by a disk. The prince wears the *atef* crown, from which

THE BUILDER OF PYRAMID NO. 12.

[From Lepsius, *Denkmäler*, Abth. V. Bl. 27.

a streamer falls behind his neck. In the one ear visible is an ornament made in the form of a ram's head surmounted by a disk; his garment is close-fitting, and is fringed across the chest. On the upper part of his left arm is a beetle, , wearing the triple crown, , a symbol of resurrection and regeneration which was very common in Egypt during the Ptolemaïc and

Roman Periods. The latchets of the prince's sandals are surmounted by uraei, and his feet rest upon a footstool with supports made in the form of lions with the object  between them; in his hands are the sceptre, , the whip, , the palm branch, and objects which appear to be intended to represent flowers. By the side of the chair of state, or throne, sits the prince's favourite hunting dog, with a deep collar round his neck. This dog was either very large, or is represented to be so as a mark of his importance, for his ears are on a level with the head of the man who stands behind him. Close to the throne stands Isis, pouring out a libation; as we should expect, the sculptor has endowed her with the chief physical characteristics of the full-bosomed, large-hipped queens of Meroë. The goddess has on her head the vulture headdress, with uraeus, and wears horns with a disk between them. Behind the prince stands his wife, barefooted, with her hands raised. In her right hand she holds what is intended to represent a sistrum; round her head is a bandlet, ornamented with stars and rosettes; and five rows of beads serve as bracelets. Her apparel is close-fitting, and falls to a point a little above her ankles. From the fact that she wears no uraeus over her forehead we may conclude that she did not belong to the house of the Meroë queens. The registers behind the queens are buried, and all that can at present be seen of the reliefs in them are:—1. A servant leading a horse. 2, 3. Attendants bringing some kind of weapons or objects used in the chase. 4. A female attendant, clad like the queen, and bearing a palm branch.

PYRAMID NO. 14 (Calliaud O, Hoskins E, Lepsius No. 7). The sides of this pyramid at the base measure 29 feet 9 inches. In 1903 the chapel was in an utterly ruined state, and only the lower layers of stone of one of its walls were *in situ*. On these, in flat relief, were the remains of a sculpture wherein was seen the figure of a prince, holding a bow and arrows in one hand, and the end of a cord, by which the necks of a number of kneeling captives were tied together, in the other. This pyramid is one of the latest of the Northern Group. We drove a passage through it from east to west, and pierced a hole in it from the top to the bottom; for the account of the work, see above, p. 349.

PYRAMID NO. 15

PYRAMID NO. 15 (Cailliaud P, Hoskins D, Lepsius No. 6). This was the most northerly of the pyramids of the Northern Group in 1903, for the pyramid which, according to the plan of

PORTRAIT OF THE MEROÏTIC KING RĀ-MAĀT-NEB (BUILDER OF PYRAMID NO. 17).

[Drawn from Lepsius, *Denkmaler*, Abth. III. Bl. 303.

Lepsius, stood to the north of it in his time, had disappeared. In shape it resembled the last pyramid on the south end of the ridge (No. 1). For the account of the demolition of this pyramid see above, p. 348. In his *Denkmäler* (V. 28, *a*) Lepsius reproduces a portion of the relief of a camel which was, no doubt, sculptured on one of the chapel walls.

PYRAMID No. 16 (Cailliaud Q, Hoskins P, Lepsius No. 37). This pyramid consists of eight or nine layers of stone, and its sides are about 16 feet long at the bases. It is unlike any other pyramid in the group, for its chapel is within the pyramid itself, its roof being formed by the stones of the sides of the pyramid, which project one over the other, and so make the enclosed space vault-shaped. On the west wall is a figure of the deceased making offerings to Osiris, and on the north and south walls are figures of ministrants in low relief. It is hard to give the reason, but in this chapel several Muḥammadan visitors have written *graffiti*.

PYRAMID OF NEB-MAĀT-RĀ, No. 17 (Cailliaud R, Hoskins N, Lepsius No. 39). This pyramid is in a very poor state of preservation, and of its chapel very little remains; the length of each side at the base is about 28 feet. It was built for a king of Meroë, who styled himself "The sun, lord of the two lands," and adopted the prenomen NEB-MAĀT-RĀ,[1] which belonged to Āmen-hetep III. king of Egypt, about B.C. 1450. His native Meroïtic name was rendered into hieroglyphics which appeared in the chapel of his pyramid under the form of .
The reading of these is doubtful. On the relief from the west wall, which was removed to Berlin by Lepsius,[2] the king is seen seated on the lion-throne; in his right hand he holds the whip, sceptre, &c., of Osiris, and in his left the peculiar Meroïtic sceptre. Before him are figures of Anubis and Nephthys, pouring out libations, and behind him stands Isis in her usual attitude. Above these figures are an Anubis frieze, and a row of stars, in relief. On the north wall is a figure of Osiris, seated, and holding the usual symbols of sovereignty and dominion, and before him are figures of a table of offerings and four bulls for sacrifice, the latter being depicted in the style common in the Ptolemaïc Period.

1 .

2 No. 2,260. See the official *Verzeichniss*, p. 406.

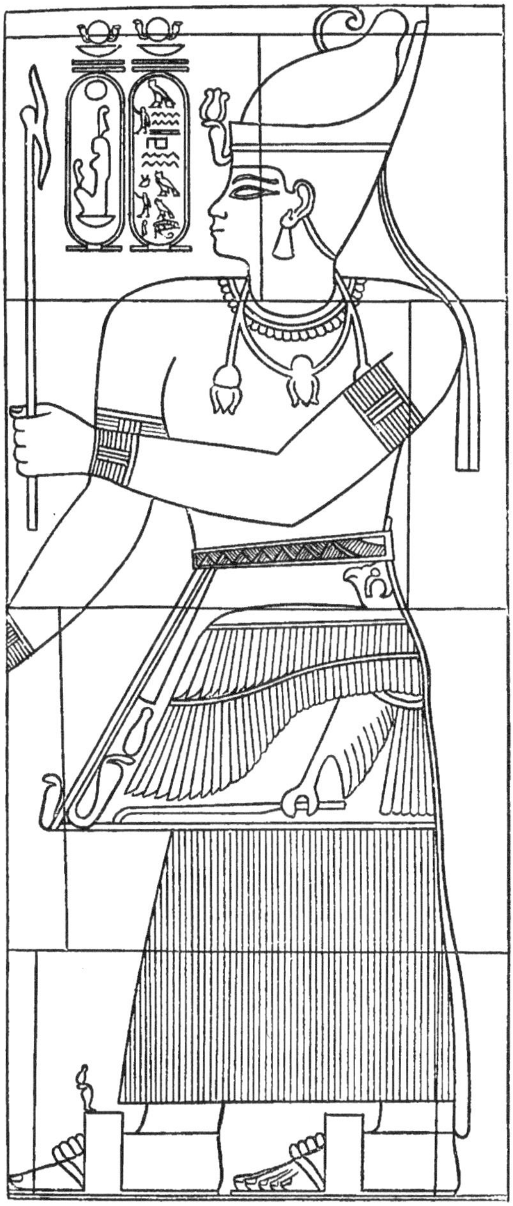

KING NEB-MAĀT-RĀ, THE BUILDER OF PYRAMID NO. 17.

[From Lepsius, *Denkmäler*, Abth. V. Bl. 51.

On the western end of the south wall, which was removed to Berlin by Lepsius,[1] the king is seen seated upon a lion-throne, arrayed in simple garb, but wearing many ornaments, including a tiara, earrings, collar, necklace, bracelets, armlets, finger-rings, with large bezels, &c. Behind him stands Isis, and before him stands a priest holding towards him a censer wherein incense is burning. It is important to note that the features of the king are of a distinctly Negro character, and that they resemble those of some of the figures on the walls of the temple at Maṣawwarât an-Nagaa. On the eastern portion of the wall the king is seen wearing the garb of a priest and the double crown, , and he is clearly officiating in some religious ceremony; behind him stand two rows of ministrants, and a number of cattle of different kinds, which have been brought for sacrifice.

PYRAMID OF AMEN-KHETASHEN (?), No. 18 (Cailliaud S, Hoskins L, Lepsius No. 38). This pyramid is one of the most striking objects in the Northern Group. It rests on a base, formed of three layers of stone, about 25 feet square, and its perpendicular height must be about 41 feet. Its sides are smooth, and they are inclined at an angle of 18 degrees. At a distance of six layers of stone from the top in the east face, there is an opening made in the form of a small door, with a deep cornice. This opening was probably intended for the use of the soul of the deceased when it returned from the Other World to visit the body in the tomb. The west side of this pyramid is wholly ruined, but its state is substantially the same as when Cailliaud drew a picture of it, and it is remarkable that the east side has not collapsed long ago. The north wall of the chapel is in ruins, but the pylon is in a good state of preservation. Before the chapel stood a little portico, the roof beams of which fitted into the pylon walls; it contained six columns, the bases of some of which were discovered by Cailliaud. This pyramid and its buildings stood in an enclosure which was surrounded by a brick wall. On the front of the pylon, on each side of the door, is a figure of the deceased king, who is represented in the act of smashing the heads of a number of enemies with his club; over his brow is a lion-headed

[1] No. 2,261. See the official *Verzeichniss*, p. 405; and *Denkmäler*, V. 51 *a*.

uraeus, and he wears an elaborate dress decorated with scale- or feather-work, and figures of gods. On the west wall of the chapel are figures of Osiris, Isis, and Nephthys, and on the south wall is a relief wherein the king is seen seated in state. In his right hand he grasps the characteristic sceptre, with a banner (?) at the top, and some object which resembles a mirror; and in his left hand he holds a club and whip. Isis, with the feather of Maāt in her right hand, stands behind him, and the legend above her head which reads, "Isis protecteth (or, giveth strength to) her son," proves that even when this chapel was built there were some priestly officials in Meroë who understood Egyptian hieroglyphics. In front of the king's face are his cartouches, but unfortunately the prenomen is obliterated. He styles himself, "Rā, lord of the two lands, lord of crowns, son of Rā;" his name was something like AMEN-KHETASHEN 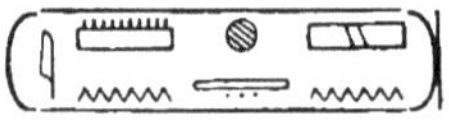. In front of the canopy under which the king is seated stands a priest presenting a censer with incense burning in its pan. The handle of the censer is in the form of a lotus, from which a hand projects to hold the pan; the end is in the form of a hawk's head. Attached to the handle is a small box, wherein the incense to be burned was placed; in front of it kneels a small figure of Anubis. The altar near which the priest stands is loaded with offerings.

Cailliaud mentions that he saw on the "face principal," to the south, a little inscription in what he imagined to be "Ethiopian characters;" this was removed by Lepsius, and is now in the Berlin Museum. See *Denkmäler*, VI. 8, No. 40.

PYRAMID NO. 19 (Cailliaud T, Hoskins M, Lepsius No. 31). This pyramid was built for Tirikanletau (?) whose name is found on the face of the pylon of his sepulchral chapel written in Meroïtic hieroglyphics thus . . Its faces are inclined at an angle of 16 degrees, its perpendicular height is nearly 30 feet, and the length of each side at the base is about 23½ feet. Before the chapel stood a portico containing four columns. On the face of the exterior wall of the pylon, on each side of the doorway, is sculptured in hollow relief the figure of a king who is represented in the act of smashing the heads of a

KING TIRIKANLETAU SLAUGHTERING CAPTIVES
(LEFT WING OF THE PYLON OF PYRAMID NO. 19).

[From Lepsius, *Denkmäler*, Abth. V. Bl. 49.

group of enemies with his club. He wears a sort of sleeved jacket which descends to his knees, and is ornamented with scale- or feather-work and figures of various gods; in each relief the captives are seven in number. The features of the king are of the Negro type with which we are already familiar, and he wears a close-fitting cap, or helmet, with streamers. Attached to the front of it is a ram-headed serpent, with an elaborate crown formed of horns, plumes, disk, uraei, &c., on its head. Near the head of each figure of the king is a single cartouche containing his name; so far as is known this king adopted no prenomen. For the Meroïtic inscription from this chapel see *Denkmäler*, VI. Bl. 8, No. 38.

PYRAMID NO. 20 (Cailliaud U, Hoskins C, Lepsius No. 3). This pyramid is well built with good stones of a large size, and it rests on a base which projects 3 feet on each of its four sides; the length of each side at the base is 53 feet. The chapel was built of large stones loosely piled one on top of the other, and is now in ruins; the slabs which formed its roof cracked in the middle, and when the pieces fell down they did much damage to the walls. High up on the east face is the pylon-shaped opening which we have already noticed in other pyramids. In 1903 we cleared large masses of broken stones, &c., from the base of this pyramid, and made paths all round it. We sank a shaft to the depth of about 20 feet on the east side, at the place whereon the chapel had stood, and found that the entrance to the burial-place beneath the pyramid was made in the usual manner.

PYRAMID NO. 21 (Cailliaud V, Hoskins B, Lepsius No. 2). This pyramid is built on the second little hill to the east of No. 20; the length of the north side at the base is about 44 feet. A pole has in recent years been driven through the platform at the top, but whether this was done by signallers, or by men who were searching for a treasure-chamber cannot be said. The chapel, of which the greater part still remains, is built of large blocks of stone, but they are not very carefully put together; the pylon is in ruins. At the west end of the chapel is a niche which was intended to hold figures of Osiris, Isis, and Nephthys, and the north and south walls are ornamented with the usual scenes, but they are in outline only, and the work is poor. Between 50 and

60 feet from the chapel is a shallow, flat-bottomed depression covered with sand. This is not the remains of a lake, as some have supposed, but it is the entrance to the passage in the side of the hill through which the body of the deceased was carried to its last resting-place under the pyramid.

PYRAMID OF ÅMEN-NETER, OR NETEK-ÅMEN, No. 22 (Cailliaud X, Hoskins A, Lepsius No. 1). This pyramid is built on the third little hill to the east of No. 2, and is the only one of the Northern Group which is oriented to the south. The length of one side at the base is 30 feet 8 inches. The pyramid itself is in a good state of preservation, but the chapel is partially ruined and its pylon is destroyed. On the west wall is a figure of the king who is seated on a lion-throne, with nine bows by the side of it. Isis stands behind him in the usual attitude, and, by the side of an altar or table of offerings in front of the king, is a priest making an offering of burning incense. Behind the priest we see a row of ministrants, and some men leading forward several donkeys. The appearance of asses in sepulchral reliefs in the chapels of the pyramids at Meroë is rare. In this instance it seems as if they were intended for sacrifices; we found the bones of a camel and a horse, among others, under one of the small pyramids which we excavated, and it would not be surprising if, when cattle were not available, asses were sacrificed in their stead. Of the period of the reign of ÅMEN-NETER, 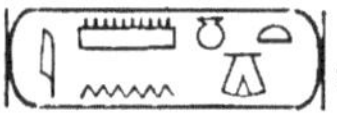, or 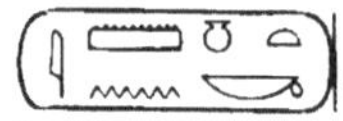, nothing is known; he adopted the prenomen of Usertsen I. , which we see not only on the walls of his chapel[1] but also on an altar which was found by Lepsius at Wad Bâ Nagaa, and removed by him to Berlin.[2] From this altar we learn that Åmen-netek's wife was called AMEN-TARIT, 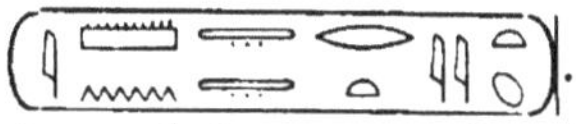.

Up to this point the order of the descriptions of the pyramids of the Northern Group is that of Cailliaud, the first traveller who published any account of them, only letters of the alphabet have been used instead of numerals; to the remaining pyramids of the group Lepsius's numbers are given.

[1] See Lepsius, *Denkmäler*, V. 25.

[2] See Lepsius, *Denkmäler*, V. 55; and the official *Verzeichniss*, p. 404.

PYRAMIDS NOS. 21 TO 32

PYRAMID NO. 21, a heap of ruins in Cailliaud's time.

PYRAMID NO. 22, a heap of ruins in Cailliaud's time, with only the false door standing.

PYRAMID NOS. 23-26, all these were excavated in 1903.

PYRAMID NO. 27, this pyramid was built for a king whose name is given, in a mutilated state, in Meroïtic hieroglyphics on the south wall of the chapel thus: ; like Amen-netek he adopted the prenomen of Usertsen I., . From the drawings published by Lepsius (*Denkmäler*, V. 48) we see that the north wall of the chapel was ornamented with reliefs in which the king is seen sitting under a canopy, with Isis behind him. A priest is making an offering of burning incense to him, and behind him come several women, each having her right hand raised in salutation and a palm branch in her left. On the south wall we again see the king seated under a canopy, and a priest making an offering of burning incense to him. The king's name and prenomen are contained in the two cartouches near his head. On the remainder of the wall are three rows of male figures, each having his left hand raised in salutation, and a palm branch in his right. Above the heads of the two figures of the priests and of the first two women are short inscriptions in the Meroïtic character; enlarged copies of these will be found in Lepsius, *Denkmäler*, VI. Bl. 8, Nos. 33-36.

PYRAMID NO. 28. A heap of ruins in Cailliaud's time, with the false door only standing; Lepsius found a Meroïtic inscription cut on one of the stones, and published it (*Denkmäler*, VI. Bl. 8, No. 37.)

PYRAMID NO. 29. A heap of ruins, with a false door only standing.

PYRAMID NO. 30. Wholly ruined.

PYRAMID NO. 31. Already described. See No. 19.

PYRAMID NO. 32. Pyramid of a queen, whose name is unknown, the cartouches being blank. A relief on the north wall (see *Denkmäler*, V. 50) of her chapel represents her seated on the usual lion-throne, and Nephthys pouring out a libation before her. In the upper register is a man leading a donkey wearing ornamental head-gear, and having on its back a skin and a saddle-cloth which reaches below its body. In the second register is a youth, presumably the queen's son, followed by three women bearing palm branches, with their right hands raised in salutation. Above the head of each woman is an inscription in the Meroïtic character.

PYRAMID NOS. 33-35. Wholly ruined. From a stone of the chapel wall of No. 35 Lepsius gives a drawing of an elephant (*Denkmäler*, V. 50 *c*).

THE BUILDER OF PYRAMID NO. 32.

[From Lepsius, *Denkmäler*, Abth. V. Bl. 50.

PYRAMID NO. 36. A mass of ruins, with the false door only standing. For the Meroïtic inscription see *Denkmäler*, VI. Bl. 8, No. 39.

PYRAMID NO. 37. Already described. See No. 16.

PYRAMID NO. 38. Already described. See No. 17.

PYRAMID NO. 39. Already described. See No. 18. For the Meroïtic inscription see *Denkmäler*, VI. Bl. 8, Nos. 40-42.

PYRAMID NOS. 40-43. All these we excavated in 1903. For the Meroïtic inscription from No. 41 see *Denkmäler*, VI. Bl. 8, No. 43.

From what has been said above it is clear that the pyramids of the Northern Group belong to all periods of the Meroïtic Kingdom. The oldest, I believe, are the first three or four which stand on the south end of the hill crescent. Next in point of age come those of the great queens of Meroë, some of whom bore the general name of "Candace," who appropriated to their tombs the best sites on the hill. And last of all come the pyramids which are built on the eastern slope of the hill, or on its skirts, close to the sandy bottom of the valley, and which form the tombs of the immediate descendants of the queens of Meroë, and of the kings with Negro features, who appear to have acquired dominion over the Kingdom of Meroë. In the present state of our knowledge it is futile to attempt to assign exact dates to these pyramids, for we have nothing to guide us except the sculptures on the chapels, which suggest that the oldest pyramids of the Northern Group belong to the end of the Ptolemaïc Period, say the first century before Christ, and the latest to the Roman Period, say the second or third century after Christ. It is certain that when some of the inscriptions were cut on the chapels there were people in Meroë who could read them, and who took care that the masons made the hieroglyphics correctly, and it is equally certain that when others were cut all knowledge of Egyptian hieroglyphics had died out, and that they were regarded merely as the traditional ornaments of the walls of funerary pyramids.

CHAPTER XI.

DESCRIPTION OF THE PYRAMIDS OF MEROË.

THE SOUTHERN GROUP, AND THE GROUPS ON THE PLAIN.

THE Southern Group of the Pyramids of Meroë lies across the sandy valley, a little to the south-east of the Northern Group. At the western mouth of the valley are the ruins of a pyramid of a very late date; it is unimportant, and except for its connection with the Southern Group would not have needed mention. The pyramids of this Group are about fifty in number, but of these, some forty are little more than shapeless heaps of ruins. A glance at the Group shows the visitor at once that its pyramids have no framework at their angles, and that they are less truncated than those of the Northern Group. The stones in the layers are often nearly square, and most of them were hewn from good quarry beds by skilful workmen. Several of the pyramids appear to have been built at a time when more care was given to the building of the monument proper than to the decoration of the chapel walls.

PYRAMID No. 1. The sides of this pyramid at the base were each about 20 feet long, and its chapel was a small one; a good deal of the south-east corner still remains, but the rest of the building is ruined. Its appearance suggests that many of its stones have been used in the construction of other pyramids.

PYRAMID No. 2. This pyramid contains eighteen layers of good well cut stones, but very little mortar was used in its construction; the length of each side at the base is about 22 feet. The chapel is in ruins; it was badly built, and was not ornamented with reliefs.

PYRAMID OF KENRETHREQNEN

PYRAMID No. 3. The area covered by this pyramid is about 25 feet square; with the exception of a few layers of stones the whole building has been taken down and carried away. Its chapel is in ruins.

PYRAMID OF QUEEN KENRETHREQNEN, No. 4. This pyramid covered an area about 20 feet square, but at the present time only the chapel remains. An attempt has been made to reach the sepulchral chamber by digging below the chapel, but when is

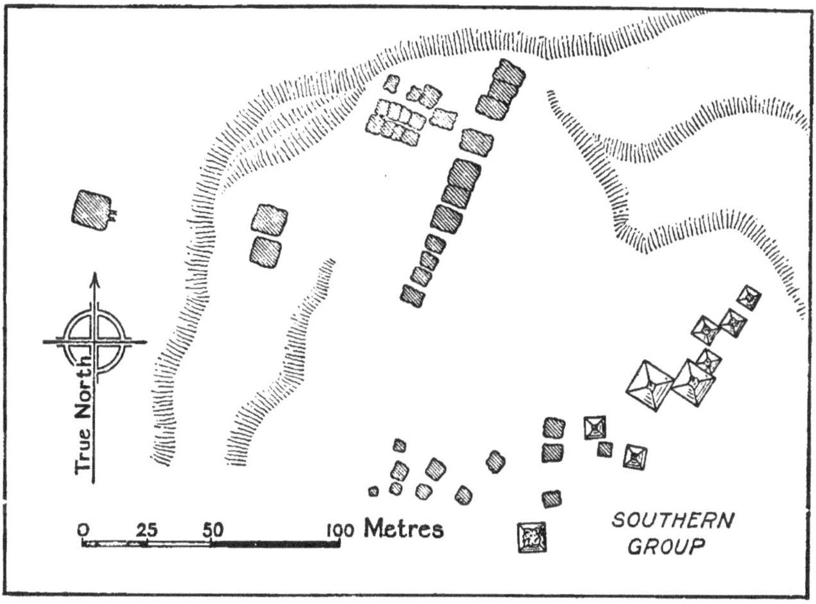

PLAN OF THE PYRAMIDS OF MEROË. GROUP B.

[From Cailliaud, *Voyage*, Plate XXXV.

not known. On the west wall, above the false door, are the remains of a relief of the Boat of Rā, with the deceased kneeling in adoration before Harpocrates, who is sitting in the bows. In the inscription below is a prayer on behalf of the deceased, who is made to ask the gods to grant suits of apparel of byssus, &c., incense, cakes, &c. On the north wall we see the queen seated under a canopy, the cornice of which is formed of uraei wearing disks; she has a whip in her right hand, and three lotus flowers in her left. Before her face are two cartouches which, together with those on the south wall, give her names as SERRENEN (?), and KENRETHREQNEN, or in its shortened form as KENRETH.[1] In the first register are women bearing offerings; in the second register the deities Ṭaṭ, Thoth, Horus, Anubis, Khnemu, and Qeb

QUEEN KENRETHREQNEN.

[From Lepsius, *Denkmäler*, Abth. V. Bl. 52.

; and in the third register Anubis pouring out a libation, two men bringing offerings, and two other men slaying an animal for sacrifice. Behind the canopy are traces of an inscription, which seems to have been of a historical character,

1 .

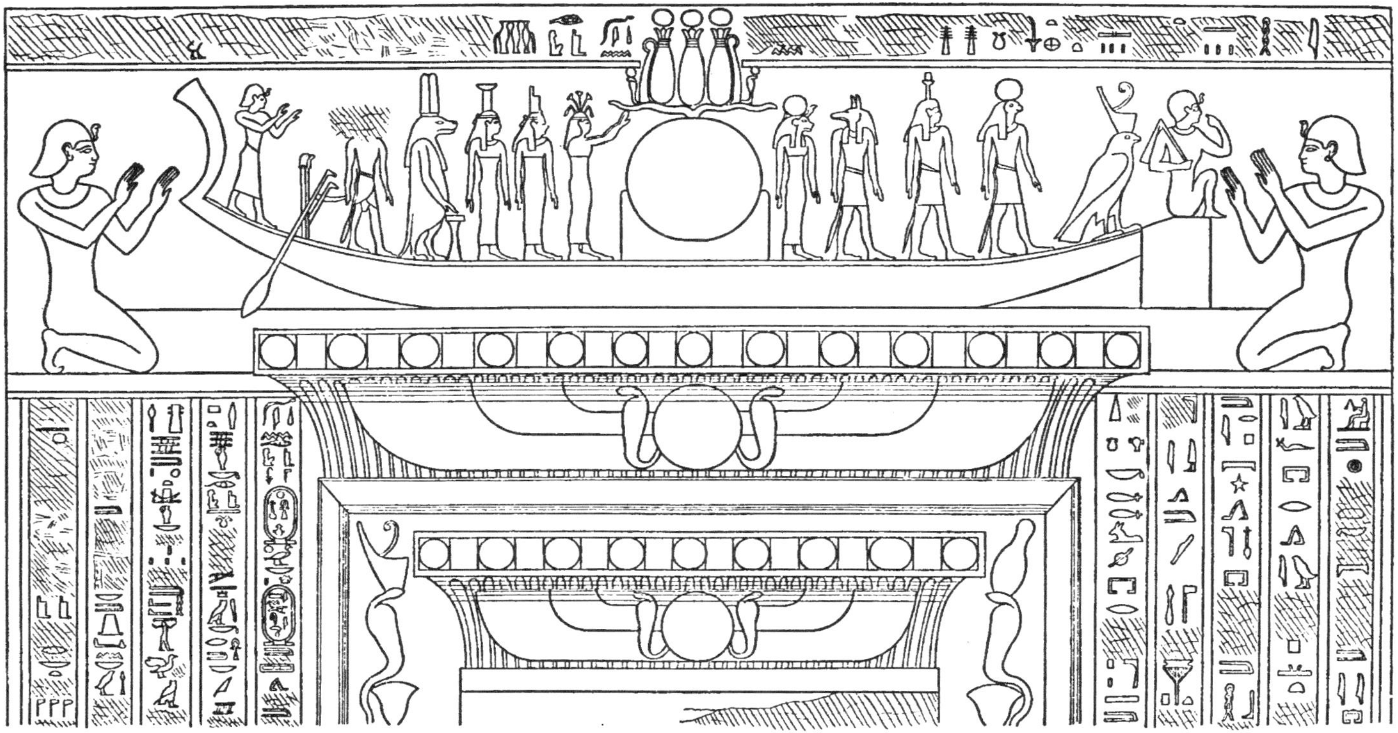

SCENE FROM THE CHAPEL OF THE PYRAMID OF ȦMEN-MERI-ȦSRU.

[From Lepsius, *Denkmäler*, Abth. V. Bl. 53.

for it begins with the word for "year," , followed by a number. On the south wall we see the queen under a similar canopy, by the side of which are four lines of hieroglyphics containing a prayer to Isis, Osiris, and Rā. In this inscription the queen is called KENRETH. In the reliefs close by the gods, headed by the queen herself, are pouring out libations, and men are bringing offerings. On the north wall is the cartouche 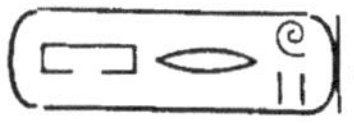 *Perui*, and on the south wall the cartouche 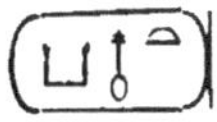 *Ka-nefert* (?).

PYRAMID OF KING ÅMEN-MERI-ÅSRU, NO. 5. When complete, this pyramid was one of the largest of the Southern Group, and was the best built; the length of each side at the base is about 50 feet, and twenty-six layers of stones still remain *in situ*. The whole of the south side, and part of the east, are ruined. On the west wall of the chapel are elaborate false doors, surmounted by winged disks with pendent uraei. Above these is the Boat of the Sun, with its divine crew. In the centre is the sun's disk on the horizon with a triple crown above. In the front half of the boat are Harpocrates, Horus, Rā-Harmachis, Nefer-Tem, Ånpu, and Sekhet; in the hinder half are a Nile goddess, Isis, Nephthys, Ta-urt, and the divine steersman. The deceased king's family clearly made up their minds that he would attain to a place in the bark of Rā, for we see a figure of him standing in the stern. Outside the boat, at each end of the relief, is a kneeling figure of the king with his hands raised in adoration. On the north wall of the chapel the king is seen seated, holding a whip in his right hand, and a long, uraeus-headed staff in the other. Behind him, on a pedestal, stands Isis, who has on her head , the phonetic value of which, Ås, is her name. Immediately in front of the canopy stands a priestess at an altar, pouring out a libation. In the first register are bunches of flowers, vessels of beer, &c., Anubis, and men bearing offerings; in the second register are Thoth, Horus, Khnemu, Ånpu, and Qeb; and in the third are Ånpu and men bringing offerings. At several places in the mutilated inscriptions the king's names and titles occur. He is styled, "King of the South and North, "the lord of the two lands, NEFER-ĀNKH-AB-RĀ, son of the Sun, "the lord of the diadem, Ȧmen-meri-Ȧsru," i.e., Ȧsru, the beloved of Ȧmen.[1] It is interesting to note that the words MAĀ KHERU 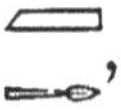, i.e., "whose spoken word must actually come to "pass," follow the name of the deceased as they do in an

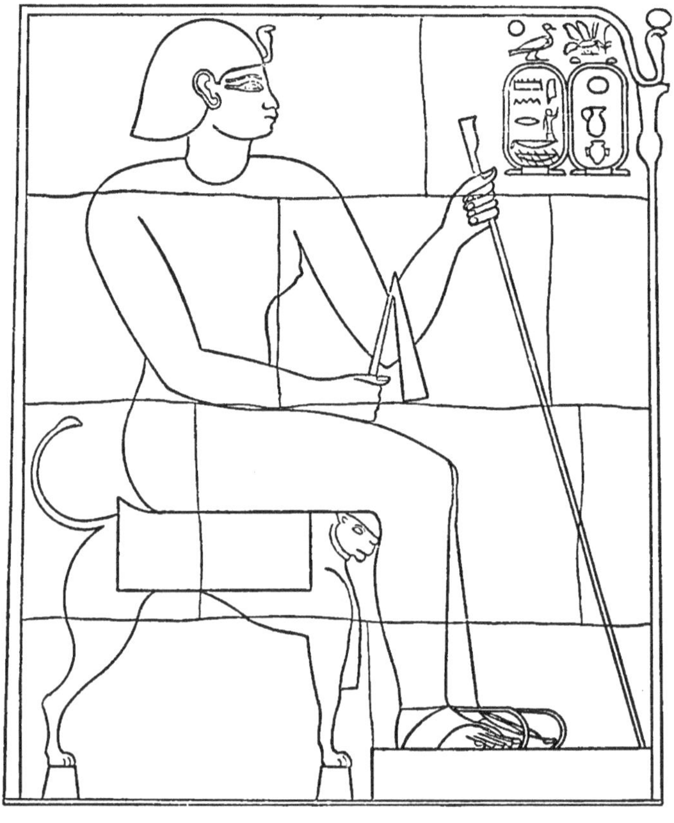

ȦMEN-ȦRK-NEB.

[From Lepsius, *Denkmäler*, Abth. V. Bl 54.

ordinary Egyptian inscription. The reliefs on the chapel walls of this pyramid are admirably executed, the hieroglyphics are well cut, and carefully formed, and they were certainly drafted by one who could read the language of ancient Egypt. There are

[1]  or .

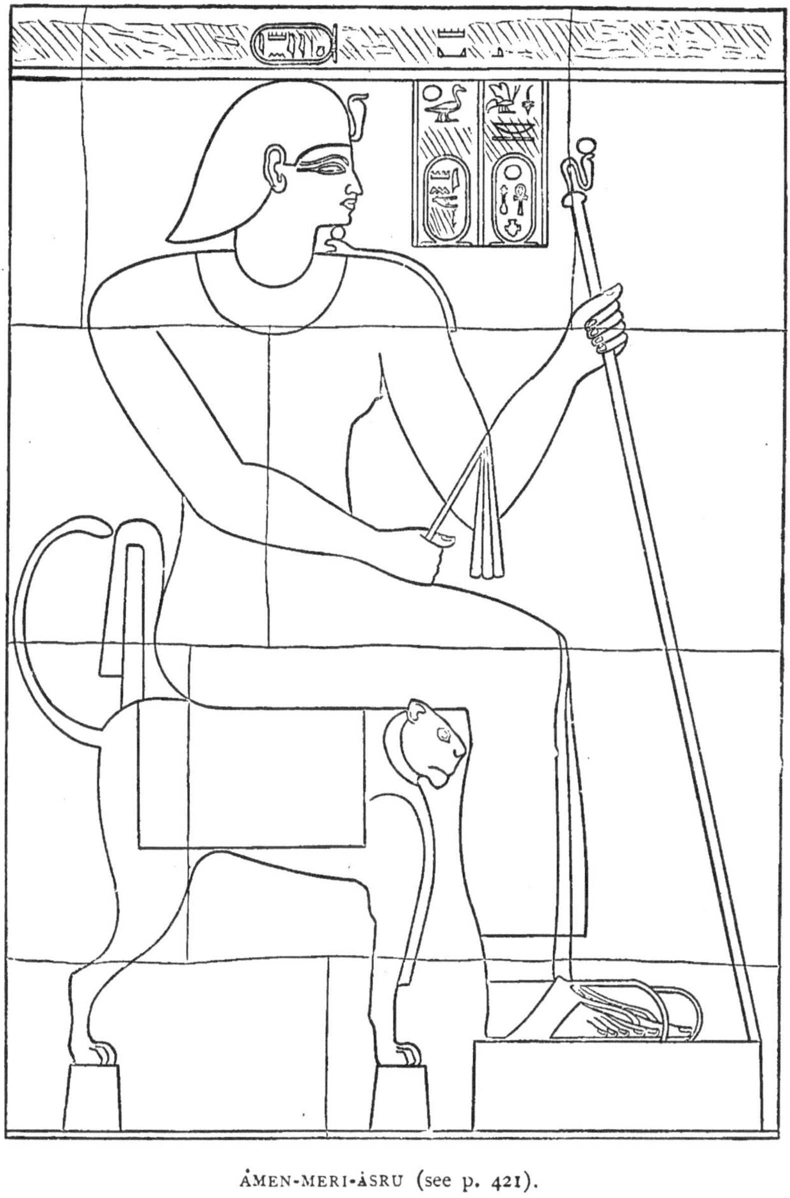

ȦMEN-MERI-ȦSRU (see p. 421).

[From Lepsius, *Denkmäler*, Abth. V. Bl. 54.

very few monuments on the Island of Meroë in which the ancient spirit and character of Egyptian art are so well preserved as in the chapel of the pyramid of ÅMEN-MERI-ÅSRU.

PYRAMID OF ÅMEN-ÅRK-NEB, NO. 6. This pyramid is practically complete. It consists of thirty-six layers of small-sized, but well-shaped, stones, and the length of each side at the base is 48 feet 6 inches. On the south side, near the top, is a projecting ledge, whereon a hawk has built her nest. In February, 1905, I saw lying on the ground below it the skins of several small animals, and the backbone and ribs of a lamb. The chapel of this pyramid is small. On the west wall is a relief of the Boat of the Sun, which much resembles that in Pyramid No. 6 of this Group. On the remains of the north wall of the chapel is a relief wherein the king is seated in the usual attitude, and the registers before him are filled with figures of gods and men, all occupied in providing sepulchral meals for the deceased. ÅMEN-ÅRK-NEB adopted the prenomen KHNEM-ÅB-RĀ, which originally belonged to Amasis II., a king of the XXVIth Dynasty, and his titles and cartouches are thus written: .

PYRAMID NO. 7. This pyramid is built of large, rough stones, and is nearly complete; a number of blocks have been thrown from the top, but fifteen layers of stones still remain *in situ*. The length of each side at the base is nearly 27 feet. Portions of the sides are in a tottering state, owing to a subsidence of the core. The chapel was massively built, and a portion of its south-east corner is still standing; over the door are figures of a winged disk and a winged beetle in high relief. The walls were ornamented with outline reliefs similar to those already described, but no traces of cartouches were visible.

PYRAMID NO. 8. This is a small and well-built pyramid, and at present consists of fourteen layers of good stones; the length of each side at the base is 18 feet 9 inches. The chapel was pulled down to make room for No. 9, which completely stops the light of the morning sun from shining on the place where it stood. The removal of the chapel caused the east face to fall, and then the east side of the core also collapsed. Several blocks of the chapel are lying on the ground, and it is easy to see that they were ornamented with the reliefs already described.

PYRAMID NO. 9. This pyramid is complete, and consists of twenty-two layers of well-cut stones; the length of the south side at the base is 25 feet 3 inches. The chapel was a small one, and is now in ruins. On the west wall of it is a carefully-cut false door, with winged disks and pendent uraei; in the middle of this is a cavity wherein figures of Osiris, Isis, and Nephthys once stood.

PYRAMID OF KING KALTELA, NO 10. The west side of this pyramid is in a ruined state, which permits the visitor to note that the foundation walls of the casings are in places 5 feet thick. At the present time twenty-four layers of stones are *in situ*, and the length of one side at the base is about 23½ feet, The roof and doorway are wanting to the chapel. On the north wall the king is seen seated, holding "life" in his right hand and lotus flowers in his left; in the second relief we see animals being brought for sacrifice, and in the third three human beings with their hands raised in adoration. On the south wall is another relief of the king, with his right hand stretched out, and his left grasping a whip. In the second register are seen men bringing offerings and pouring out libations, and the god Thoth presenting a plumed object, and a serpent-headed deity presenting a *menát*, , an object which symbolized joy, gladness, and happiness. The royal names and titles are found within the canopy and read:— , "King of "the South and North, KALKA, son of Rā, KALTELA." The other pyramids of the Southern Group are all in a state of ruin more or less complete, and are not worth description.

From what has been said above it is clear that the ten pyramids of which brief descriptions have been given probably belong to a period earlier than that of most of those of the Northern Group, and from the fact that the builder of one pyramid, No. 6, was called ARK-AMEN and adopted the prenomen of Amasis II., a king of Egypt of the XXVIth Dynasty, we may assume that his pyramid at least was built some time during the Ptolemaïc Period, or perhaps even a little earlier. The same idea is suggested by the fact that Asru, the builder of No. 5, adopted the prenomen of Psammetichus II., Nefer-àb-Rā, 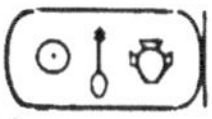, to which, however, he added *ānkh,* thus 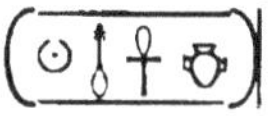. That he should call himself "beloved of Àmen" was only natural, seeing that the inhabitants of Meroë honoured above all other gods the gods whom their kinsmen at Napata, or Gebel Barkal, had learned to worship through the instructions of the priests of Àmen-Rā of Thebes, who had fled thither on the downfall of their rule in Egypt. In any case, it seems that the ten pyramids of the Southern Group all belong to the same period, for the system followed in decorating the walls of the chapels is practically the same in each, and the same groups of gods occur in each set of reliefs, and the similarity of the work, especially as concerns the manner in which the hieroglyphics are cut, indicates, in my opinion, that the masons belonged to one family or school, just as the kings and queens for whom they built the pyramids belonged to one dynasty. The first three or four pyramids of the Northern Group were probably built by the same dynasty, for both they and their chapels have much in common with those of the Southern Group. The measurements of the lengths of the sides of the pyramids at their bases given above are only approximately correct; much clearing will have to be done before exact details can be given. The site chosen by the builders of the Southern Group is admirable for the purposes of a necropolis, for it is surrounded by low, barren hills, which hide the pyramids almost entirely from travellers going north or south on the plain. When their tops are seen from a little distance it is quite easy to mistake them for the little pointed hills which abound in the Sûdân. The stone used in their construction appears to have been taken from the nearer of the two quarries in the hills to the east, where the layers of sandstone are thick and of nearly the same colour; the grain, too, is closer than that of the stone used in the Northern Group, and it is not so quickly affected by the weather. The stones which form the pyramids of the older group are more massive than those of the later pyramids, and squarer, and the blocks used in the walls of the chapels are larger, and the walls themselves are thicker and better built; the severity and grimness of the Southern Group have no equivalents in the Northern Group. When both Groups have been seen from the highest and most northerly point of the crescent-shaped hill on which the larger group stands, many travellers in recalling the view will agree with Hoskins (*Travels*, p. 68), who says, "Never "were my feelings more ardently excited than in approaching, "after so tedious a journey, to this magnificent Necropolis. "The appearance of the Pyramids, in the distance, announced "their importance; but I was gratified beyond my most "sanguine expectations, when I found myself in the midst of "them. The pyramids of Geezah are magnificent, wonder- "ful for their stupendous magnitude; but for picturesque "effect and elegance of architectural design, I infinitely prefer "those of Meroe. I expected to find few such remains "here, and certainly nothing so imposing, so interesting, as these "sepulchres, doubtless of the kings and queens of Ethiopia. I "stood for some time lost in admiration. From every point "of view I saw magnificent groups, pyramid rising behind "pyramid, while the dilapidated state of many did not render "them less interesting, though less beautiful as works of art. "I easily restored them in my imagination; and these effects "of the ravages of time carried back my thoughts to more "distant ages."

To the west of these groups, at a distance computed by Hoskins to be 5,600 feet, lies another group of small ruined pyramids, between twenty-five and forty in number. They are more than half buried in sand, and are unimportant. The greater number of them consist of little more than heaps of stones piled carelessly one upon the other, and few, if any, of them ever had any chapels on their east fronts. They stand immediately over the graves of the dead in whose honour they were raised. Some of them are built, obviously, of stones which were taken there from the thirty-five pyramids of the Southern Group, of which little more than the foundation-stones now remain. We thought it useless to make excavations here, for the bodies of the dead under the pyramids have probably been destroyed long ago by

SEPULCHRAL STELE, WITH MEROÏTIC INSCRIPTION. (Fourth Group, No. 15.)

[From Lepsius, *Denkmäler*, Abth. VI. Bl. 10.

the infiltration of water which must take place whenever the plain is flooded by summer rains.

Still further to the west, and a little to the south, partly on the edge of the strip of cultivated land and partly on the skirt of the desert, stands a very large group of pyramids, which Cailliaud called the "Pyramids of Aṣ-ṣûr, and Lepsius "Group C." This

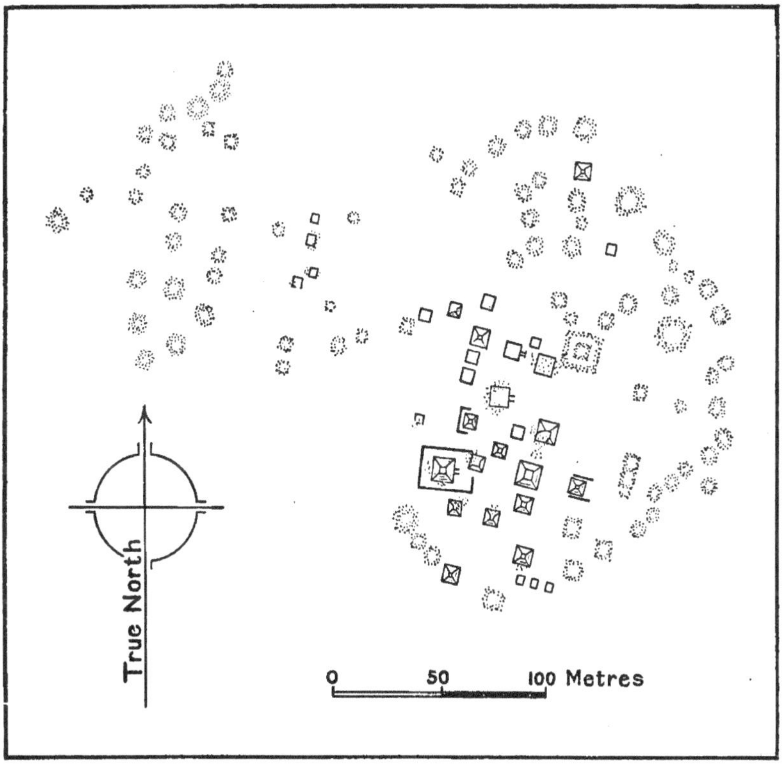

PLAN OF THE PYRAMIDS OF MEROË.—FOURTH GROUP.

[From Lepsius, *Denkmäler*, Abth. I. Bl. 133.

group, according to Lepsius's plan, contained at least 112 pyramids, varying in size from about 40 to 16 feet at the base; the height of the largest must have been about 60 feet, and of the lowest about 12 feet. Even in the days of Cailliaud all of them were in a ruined state, and Lepsius found that only five or six possessed remains of chapels. The largest stood in a walled enclosure and bears the No. 18 on his plan. In No. 15 there was a false door on the west wall of the chapel, ornamented with the winged disk and a cornice of uraei wearing disks, and in the lower part of it was inserted a sepulchral stele, with a rounded top. On the upper portion are cut in outline figures of the deceased and Osiris and Isis; the god is seated on his throne, with Isis behind him, and in front of him stands the deceased, who holds in his right hand a palm-branch and flowers. On the throne of the god is the symbolic representation of the union of the South and North, , which is found at a very early period in Egypt, and above is the solar disk with large outspread wings. Below this scene is an inscription of six lines, in cursive Meroïtic characters, the divisions between the words being marked by double dots, : , as in Ge'ez or Ethiopic, and in Amharic, the modern language of Abyssinia. This stele was taken to Berlin by Lepsius, and is now preserved in the Royal Museum (No. 2253); the accompanying illustration is taken from the facsimile of it which he published in the *Denkmäler* (V. 54 *e*, VI. 10. 45). From No. 27 of this group also came the inscribed altar whereon are cut figures of Anubis and Nephthys pouring out libations on behalf of the deceased. This object also was taken to Berlin by Lepsius, and is now preserved in the Royal Museum (No. 2254); the illustration here given is from the facsimile published in the *Denkmäler* (VI. 9).

The pyramids of this group appear to belong to a later period than that of either the Northern or the Southern Group, and we shall probably be not far wrong if we assign some of them to the second or third century of the Christian Era, and some to even a later date. The careless building of these structures betokens not only haste in construction, but want of knowledge, for it is evident from many particulars that the masons who put them together were not so well skilled in their art as those who built the pyramids of the kings and queens on the hills to the east. It is, of course, open to argue that they are not all necessarily royal, and that we should not expect them to be so well or so solidly built as royal sepulchres, but, on the other hand, some of them are certainly royal, and these exhibit the same defects of construction as the smallest and meanest of the pyramids, which may mark the resting-places of royal children or mere state officials. An idea of the class and style of the reliefs which ornamented the walls of the best of the chapels may be obtained from the

ALTAR WITH MEROÏTIC INSCRIPTION (BERLIN, NO. 2,254).

[From Lepsius, *Denkmäler*, Abth. VI. Bl. 9.

drawing published by Lepsius in *Denkmäler*, V. 54. The drawing here given is taken from the chapel of pyramid No. 25, and the relief from which it was made appears to have been almost the only one which was worth reproducing. The ruined state of the pyramids of this group is not due to any work of destruction carried on in the nineteenth century, for when Cailliaud visited them their condition was such that he regarded them more as

THE WEST WALL OF PYRAMID NO. 15 (FOURTH GROUP).

[From Lepsius, *Denkmäler*, Abth. VI. Bl. 10.

heaps of rough stones piled up over every tomb, like modern Arabs' burial mounds, than as pyramids, although he says they must have been pyramids. He measured the bases of twenty, and measured their angles of inclination, and found the traces of seventy-five others.[1] What their condition was when Hoskins was on the Island of Meroë cannot be said, for he states that he did not see Aṣ-Ṣûr (*Travels*, p. 84). It may be noted, in passing, as Lepsius pointed out, that this group of pyramids ought not to have been called by Cailliaud the "Pyramids of Assur, or Hachour," but the "Pyramids of Meroë," for "Aṣ-Ṣûr" is the name given by the natives to the whole of that part of the plain whereon are the ruins of the ancient city of Meroë and the pyramids, and it also includes a portion of Bagrâwîya, which Hoskins (*Travels*, p. 84) wrongly spells "Bagromeh."

[1] À un quart de lieue dans l'est 32° sud des ruines de la ville, sur la plaine déserte, se voit le premier et le plus petit groupe de pyramides. Toutes celles dont leur état de conservation m'a permis de mesurer les bases et l'inclinaison, sont au nombre de vingt ; mais il a dû en exister un plus grand nombre. Autour de ces monumens, je retrouvai les traces de soixante-quinze autres constructions, qui, sans doute, étaient autant de petites pyramides destinées à recouvrir des puits de momies. Au désordre qui régnait parmi les décombres de celles-ci, je conjecturai qu'elles consistaient pour la plupart en pierres brutes amoncelées sur chaque tombe, comme le font encore aujourd'hui les Arabes du désert. . . . Les pierres d'assise n'ont que 35 à 40 centimètres de hauteur ; seulement quelques assises de pierre de taille forment les quatre murailles de la pyramide ; le massif inférieur n'est qu'un remplissage de pierres brutes, entassées et mastiquées sans ordre avec de l'argile. On remarque que tous les sanctuaires, ou entrées supposées des tombeaux, sont tournés au levant, et que toutes ces pyramides sont orientées à peu de chose près dans la même direction ; en général, l'axe de chacune avec le nord magnétique présente un angle de 70° vers l'ouest ; et, par conséquent, elles n'ont pas leurs angles placés dans un rapport aussi exact avec les quatre points cardinaux de la sphère, que celles de Nouri. (*Voyage*, tom. ii., p. 152.)

CHAPTER XII

FOURTH MISSION TO THE SÛDÂN (1905).

THE work connected with my mission to the Sûdân in 1903 having been concluded, Sir Reginald Wingate approved of the results, and determined to continue archaeological investigations in that country so soon as funds were available, and the opportunity for making use of them presented itself. During the winter of 1903-4 no actual excavations were carried out by the Government, but the importance of preserving the antiquities which still exist in the Sûdân was generally recognized, and the Governor-General and his staff were actively employed in formulating plans on a comprehensive scale, with the view of establishing a central authority having power to excavate ancient sites systematically, and, when possible, to remove all important monuments to a place of safety in Kharṭûm. In fact, besides contemplating the making of excavations, Sir Reginald Wingate determined to found a Museum at Kharṭûm, wherein monuments belonging to all periods of Sûdân history might be made available for examination and study by travellers of all kinds.

The idea was an extremely good one, for it is manifestly useless to dig up antiquities until a place exists wherein they can be stored. When Sir Reginald came to England in the summer of 1904 he told me about his plan, and I at once urged him to begin to collect from various sites between Ḥalfa, at the foot of the Second Cataract, and Kerma, at the head of the Third Cataract, the monuments which I had seen lying about when I visited them some years previously, i.e., in 1897 and 1898. It was then quite impossible to remove these monuments to Europe, or even to put them in a place of safety, and as it seemed most unlikely that they had been carried off between 1898 and 1904, it was certainly worth while trying to find out if they still existed, and if so, what had become of them. Sir Reginald approved of the suggestion, and, after consultation with Sir Edward Maunde Thompson, K.C.B., Director of the British Museum, applied to the Trustees for the loan of my services, and the Trustees and the Treasury consenting, I was despatched to the Sûdân in December to assist Sir Reginald in forming the nucleus of a collection for his proposed museum at Kharṭûm.

At Wâdî Ḥalfa I was met by Mr. J. W. Crowfoot, Inspector of Education in the Sûdân, whom Sir Reginald had appointed to carry out the work with me. This appointment was a very fortunate one, for, apart from his knowledge of the natives and the country, Mr. Crowfoot possessed the official authority necessary to crown our endeavours with success. He provided me with a very comfortable house to live in whilst we were making arrangements for carrying out our work, and the cordial welcome which Major Midwinter and other friends in the Ḥalfa Mess extended to me made the days which I spent there pass very pleasantly. Mr. Crowfoot was able to collect men and tools and materials for our work without much difficulty, and the officials, both military and civil, Major Midwinter, Mr. C. G. Hodgson, the Hon. H. G. G. Pelham, Mr. W. H. Horton, and others, assisted us in a prompt and effective manner. In two days all was ready, and we left Ḥalfa one afternoon with our workmen in a special train. Our destination was Dulgo, or Deligo [1] as the natives sometimes call it, which is about 170 miles south of Ḥalfa. Our plan was to go there without delay, and to examine all the sites on both banks of the river between that place and Sarras. Major Midwinter had given us a very good coach wherein we could lay out our beds, and as there was a kitchen at one end of it and a *zîr*, or water jar, on a firm stand and full of fresh Nile water, we travelled in comfort. Mr. Crowfoot's cook was an experienced and resourceful man, and the youth I engaged at Ḥalfa to look after me was very sharp and attentive. He was small for his age, but he had travelled as servant in many parts of the Sûdân with Englishmen and knew their ways, and, as

[1] Burckhardt has "Delligo." (*Travels*, p. 65.)

he approved both of Mr. Crowfoot and myself, he served me well.

The journey to Dulgo was uneventful. We arrived at Sarras about 8 p.m., at Ambigôl Wells two or three hours later, and at Kôsha about ten the following morning. Here we were met by a very courteous Egyptian Mâ'mûr, or governor, who explained that our train could not proceed for a couple of hours, because the engine had to go to the water-shed near the river, and the driver and fireman wanted rest, and he invited us either to go to his house or to his office in the Government building close by. Mr. Crowfoot had various items of business to attend to, so we went to the latter. After coffee, he discussed with the Mâ'mûr the purchase of many hundreds of palm shoots (*shatl*), which Mr. James Currie, the Director, had decided to plant in the grounds of the Gordon College at Kharṭûm. The Mâ'mûr, being a soldier, knew little about such things, but he called in some civilian dealers in dates and palms, and then followed a most interesting conversation on the habits and customs of the palms which grew in the province of Dâr Sukkôt, and on the qualities of the dates which they produced. One realized at once what an important part the palm played in the life of the people of the district, and the knowledge about its varieties which the natives displayed was to me astonishing. Mr. Crowfoot's work as Inspector of Education was not limited to taking care that the natives learned how to read and write, but he set himself to acquire all kinds of information, down to the smallest details of the daily life of the people. At length a decision was arrived at as to when the shoots were to be cut, and all arrangements made for their packing, and their being watered during their journey by rail to Kharṭûm, and after a walk through the village we returned to the train.

Two or three hours later we arrived at Dulgo, and the Inspector ordered the Mâ'mûr to prepare a boat to take us up across the river to examine the ruins of the temple of Dulgo. Whilst the boat was being sought for, our baggage was removed to the Government rest-house which has been built at Dulgo within the last few years, and we found it very convenient. The house stands in a compound, in which attempts have already been made to create a garden, and its walls are fairly thick and substantial. The roof is flat, and forms a convenient place to sleep on in hot weather; the verandah is tiled and is spacious, and the walls are white-washed within and without. This rest-house is one of several which Sir Reginald Wingate has had built in the Sûdân, and every one must appreciate the soundness of the Government policy which provides for the housing of its Inspectors. In former days when an official arrived at a village in the evening after a long, hot day's ride, he had either to pitch his tent somewhere or pass the night in a native house, which is never a very clean place. If he decided to sleep in the native house, it was generally necessary to dispossess the master and mistress, with the family goats and chickens, who had to go and sleep elsewhere, and few Englishmen care to put the natives to such inconvenience. The rest-house is undoubtedly a useful institution, but it can only be properly appreciated and enjoyed by those who have travelled for weeks and months in countries wherein it does not exist.

Meanwhile the boat had been made ready, and a crew found, and ten minutes' walk through luxuriant crops of dhurra brought us to the river. The boat was large, and round-bottomed, like most of the craft that have to sail among the rocks in the cataracts, for experience has shown the native that boats built in this shape do not suffer so much when they strike on rocks hidden under water, and that the current carries them better through rocky shoals than those of deep draught. There are very few boats on that portion of the Nile, and the natives for generations appear to have neglected boat-building, for several travellers have recorded in their narratives that they were unable to visit such and such a site across the river, because no boat was available. A classical instance is the case of Burckhardt,[1] who wished to cross over to the Island of Sâî, but there was no ferry of any kind, and none seemed to be required by the natives, for when they had business on the oppposite shore they used to swim over, with their spear, or lance, fastened on top of the head. And again,[2] on his return from Tinâra along the east bank of the Nile, he wished to cross over and examine the ruins of the famous temple of Ṣûlb,

[1] *Travels*, p. 56.

[2] *Ibid.*, p 74.

or Soleb. But though he offered some peasants, who were watering the fields upon an island opposite the temple, all the dhurra remaining in his provision sack to carry him over and back again, an offer which was equivalent to that of a guinea to a London waterman, he was refused. Not only was there no ferry-boat, but the natives had no goat-skins, which when inflated help to support them when they cross the river. The crossing of the Nile in the Cataract country is even now a difficult business, and I am convinced that nothing but the "order of the Government," backed up by the Inspector's quiet but determined demand, would have caused the boat to be forthcoming so quickly. The ordinary traveller would have had to spend a day or two in bargaining for the use of the boat, and another day in finding a crew, and even then some unforeseen hitch would probably have caused the owner of the boat to cry off his bargain. Mr. Somers Clarke experienced the same difficulty some five or six years ago when he was examining the antiquities between Sarras and Semnah, and travellers who wish to spend some time in the Cataract country should do as he did,—take a boat with them.

So soon as all were aboard, the boat was pushed off, and three or four men towed her a little way up the river, so that we might take advantage of the northerly wind, and when the sail was unfurled we started at a fair rate of speed. We sailed by the side of an island which looked very fresh and green in the sunlight, and at a little distance it seemed to be a veritable paradise. On it were a few goats, and their owners, who wore nothing but waist-cloths, sat on the dry mud and watched them placidly as they grazed. We skirted some dangerous rocks, and the man at the helm showed great skill in avoiding some fierce whirlpools, which would have smashed to pieces any boat as small as ours which had the misfortune to get into them. After some forty minutes' sail we stopped by the side of a high mudbank, and ten minutes' walk through dhurra brought us to the ruins of the temple of Sese, or Sisi, which Cailliaud calls the "Temple of Sesceh,"[1] and Lepsius the "Temple of Sesebi."[2] This temple was built by Seti I, king of Egypt, about B.C. 1370, and ruins of the walls which

[1] *Voyage*, tom. i., p. 388.

[2] *Letters*, p. 236. Hoskins spells the name "Sescé,' but he did not visit the ruins.

THE RUINS OF THE TEMPLE OF SETI I. ON THE WEST BANK OF THE NILE NEAR DULGO.

[From Lepsius, *Denkmäler*, Abth. I. Bl. 118.

enclosed its grounds are still visible. When Cailliaud visited it, four of its pillars were still standing, and the bases of the remainder existed; everything else had been carried away, probably by the orders of some governor of the province of Dâr Mahass, to build some fortified castle. Nothing was to be seen of the temple's stones except some fragments of sandstone which were strewn about the surface of the ground. This temple, like all the rest of its kind, was oriented to the east, and it stood in one corner of a large enclosure which, judging by the ruins of the walls to the north of it, was strongly fortified. The pillars are ornamented with palm-leaf capitals, but on their bases the decoration consists of figures in relief of the bodies of captives, with the names of the tribes to which they belonged cut on them. The faces of the captives are nearly all the same, but their headdresses are different, and these, no doubt, indicated to the visitor to the temple in Seti's days the various Sûdânî tribes which had been conquered by the Egyptian soldiers. As Cailliaud said, some of the figures resemble those of women, but it is possible that an effeminate appearance was given to them by the architect's orders, with the view of insulting the tribes they represented.

A little distance from the ruins is the site of a large, ancient town, which, as Lepsius noted, stood on an artificially raised piece of ground, of which the regular encircling walls may still be recognized. I was very much surprised to find the temple site so bare, for when I first visited it, there were several fine drums of pillars there, and inscribed portions of the doorway, though half buried, were still in existence. A great deal of building has been going on in the neighbourhood during the last few years, and there is no doubt that the ruins on ancient sites have, whenever possible, been made to serve as quarries, which have supplied large quantities of good stone. And when we consider how well the ancient Egyptians built their temples in the Sûdân, no matter how far from Egypt were the sites chosen for them, and what excellent stone was used in their construction, we need not be surprised that the modern inhabitants of the country treat them as quarries. Whenever it could be found, the Egyptians selected their stone for building from the hardest layers of stone in the mountains, taking care in cutting their blocks to make allowance for waste in transport and weathering. When only inferior stone was to be had, they quarried larger slabs, and attempted to make up by quantity what the stone lacked in quality; this fact may be noted in Egyptian buildings all over the northern Sûdân. A mile or two distant from the ruins of the temple of Sese is the hill of Sese, or Gebel Sese, on the brow of which are the ruins of a fortress; to build this, the temple of Sese was probably stripped of its stones. Lepsius relates a tradition which he learned from his servant Aḥmad, a native of Derr, to the effect that at the death of every king of the district, his successor was led up to the summit of Gebel Sese, and there was made to put on a royal cap of peculiar shape and make,[1] no doubt as a part of a coronation ceremony.

An examination of the ruins of Seti's temple convinced both the Inspector and myself that it would be waste of money to dig there, and we were therefore obliged to modify our plans. It had been our intention to start at Dulgo, and to sail and float down the river to Kôsha, examining all the sites where ancient remains were to be found, on both banks of the river, as we went, and as we were provided with all the materials for digging, we decided to make excavations wherever it seemed desirable to do so. On making inquiries of the watermen we learned that it would take about a fortnight to float down stream to Ṣûlb, the site of the largest Egyptian temple in the Sûdân, for there was little water in the river, and we should have the north wind against us the whole way. For about twenty miles, i.e., from Sueki to Aggeh, we should have the wind broadside on, and it would be necessary to use the tow-line all that way. It is a simple matter to use the tow-line on a river with a good, firm bank, but in the Cataract country it is a very difficult matter. Trees, rocks, and shoals, occur with aggravating frequency, and when the wind is strong it blows the boat into the bank and keeps her there. Further inquiries showed us that we could sail up to Ṣûlb from Kôsha quicker than we could float down to it from Dulgo, and as we returned from the temple of Sese we determined to do so. When we landed and were about to return to the rest-house we found that the Egyptian military governor and his brother had prepared tea,

[1] *Letters*, p. 236.

and were expecting us to visit their house. Thither therefore we went, and found a tray, with china cups and saucers, a teapot, a sugar basin, and a box of English biscuits. Our hosts were most hospitable, and their large brown and white hunting dog made friends with us in a very engaging manner. The Inspector had heard of a native school somewhere to the south of Dulgo, and even whilst drinking his tea, plied our hosts with questions as to its whereabouts, and the number of people in the village, and the best way to get there. I fear that he with difficulty resisted the temptation of setting off to inspect the school then and there.

We returned to the rest-house, intending to stay the night there, for we had been assured that the train would not return from Kerma till the following day. After dinner, when the beds were ready and we were about to turn in, the telephone porter rushed in saying that the train was coming, and would only be able to stop half an hour, and that if we were going by it we must get ready without delay. With difficulty we found our servants and woke them up, and when they had realized that we had to pack up and be off, they were in despair. Just then we heard the hoot of the locomotive, and a few minutes later we saw the lights of the train as it pulled up. At that time the railway between Kerma and Kôsha was being taken up, for the rails, being quite good and nearly new, were required for the Atbara and Sawâkin Railway. When near Kerma the driver of the train which brought us to Dulgo found that a load of rails was ready, and he decided to couple up and to return without delay. Hence his unexpected appearance. To save him trouble our coach had been taken to the main line, and our baggage, beds, tools, water-pots, &c., had to be carried nearly a mile over rough ground, on a moonless night. The Sûdânî folk hate being disturbed in their sleep, especially to work in the dark, which they dread, but the soldiers worked well, and by midnight we and our belongings were once more in the train.

The following morning at dawn we found ourselves at Kôsha, and we took up our abode in the excellent Government rest-house which is there. The Mâ'mûr knew of a boat which was suitable for our work, but it was working up the river, and would not be available until the next day. Meanwhile the Inspector devoted himself to hiring men to come with us to dig, and he found several who were willing to work for the Government; so soon as they were engaged they set out to walk up the river to Sauardà, where we expected to make some excavations. On the following morning the boat arrived from the south, and we got her loaded in a few hours, and started about noon. Up to that time the day had been beautiful, but the wind began to freshen, and by one o'clock was blowing hard. We went along at a good speed, but gave up all idea of stopping anywhere for work on the way up with such a wind behind us. Our captain, one Muḥammad, was an expert boatman, and he handled his craft with great skill; he seemed to know every rock, whether sunken or visible, in that part of the river, and time after time steered us away from rocks which I felt certain would wreck us. We passed Ginnis, Kurar, and Attab on the east bank by two o'clock. Another hour brought us abreast of 'Amâra, and having passed Arnitti Island and Sâkiat al-'Abd, we were soon abreast of Abri, which is close to the north end of the Island of Sâî. We sailed on and passed the long Island of Sâî, taking of course the eastern channel, but as the wind became less strong our progress was slower. The next island we saw was Nilwitti, and after that came Wussi Island, and about five o'clock we arrived at Ḳubba Idris.

It was useless to attempt to continue our journey that evening, for the wind had dropped, and towing was an impossibility; we therefore stayed the night in the comfortable house of Shêkh Idris, of whom more will be said later on. The Inspector and I were glad to accept his hospitality, and to be able to eat our evening meal in a place so well sheltered from the wind and cold. The evening turned out to be beautiful, for so soon as the wind dropped, the sun came out, and painted the great clouds crimson and gold, and lit up the turquoise and emerald stretches between them with living splendour. The village has many palms and other trees along the river bank, and these and the large patches of vegetation which assumed a soft, restful green colour in the light of the setting sun, gave to the spot an indescribable beauty. It was a great shock when one turned from the luxuriant vegetation on the river bank and saw that the dreary Sûdân desert was less than half a mile away, and that the greedy sand was everywhere trying to encroach on and cover up the "strip of herbage" which was grown with such difficulty.

We left Ḳubba Idrîs early next morning, and by the help of the north wind we arrived at Ṣûlb about two o'clock in the afternoon. We were received by a few shêkhs, who seemed glad to see the Inspector, and spoke many pretty words of welcome to us both. A walk of about half a mile brought us to the ruins of what Cailliaud rightly calls "an Egyptian monument of the first order" (*Voyage*, tom. i., p. 376). The size and importance of this

VIEW OF THE RUINS OF THE TEMPLE OF ṢÛLB.
[From a photograph by J. W. Crowfoot, Esq.

"monument" or temple may be imagined from the following facts and figures.[1] It was built by Ȧmen-hetep III. in the fifteenth century before Christ, to commemorate his conquests in the Sûdân, and to consolidate his hold upon the country, and to help him to control the trade between Egypt and the country on both sides of the Blue Nile, which even in those days must have been very considerable. The temple consisted of:—1. A propylon now quite ruined. 2. A court, 155 feet long, with side walls, which joined the first propylon to the second. In this court was a flight of

[1] A plan with further details is given elsewhere in the account of the Sûdân conquests of Ȧmen-hetep III., king of Egypt, B.C. 1450.

steps, leading up to a smaller court about 70 feet long and 45 feet wide, and containing six columns, each with a diameter of 10 feet. 3. A second propylon 167 feet wide and 24 feet deep. 4. A court 90 feet long and 113 feet wide; it contained twenty-eight columns, and had a double row of them on the west side. 5. A court 78 feet long and 113 feet wide; this contained thirty-two columns, which were arranged in double rows on the north and south sides, and in single rows on the east and west sides. 6. A small court which led into the sanctuary. 7. The sanctuary, which was divided into sections by walls, and contained the symbol of the god to whom the temple was dedicated. The total length of the whole temple was about 540 feet, i.e., it was between 30 and 40 feet longer than St. Paul's Cathedral. The temple is built on the edge of the desert, and its first propylon stood about 600 feet from the river bank. Even in its decay it possesses considerable grandeur, and the picturesqueness of its surroundings gives these ruins an appearance which is most striking. Every traveller has been much impressed by the effect which the sight of it has produced upon him, and every one must regret the state of ruin into which it has fallen. The first question which the visitor asks himself is, "What has wrought the ruin of this massive building?" The answer is not difficult to find. Its ruin has been caused by the want of foresight on the part of the architect, who allowed the foundations of the pillars to be built of crude brick, as Cailliaud observed (*Voyage*, tom. i., p. 379). At some time or other the water of summer rains has found its way into the courts, and pillar after pillar has fallen because its foundations were melted under it. The general equilibrium of the rows of pillars having been disturbed, the massive stones, which formed the upper framework of the temple, fell, and in their fall broke the pillars which they struck. The sanctuary and the pro-naos have suffered most of all.

When I first saw these ruins seven or eight years ago there were in the second large court a number of inscribed and sculptured slabs which I hoped would one day come to the British Museum. They appeared to have formed a sort of screen wall between the pillars, and being of hard sandstone, they had suffered less than the other stones in the building. The Inspector and I went at once to look for these, but when we came to the place they were nowhere to be seen. Looking round we saw that several large blocks and slabs of stone showed signs of having been recently broken, and the fractures were so clean and fresh-looking that they might have been made only the day before. The Inspector began to ask questions of the natives who were with us, and little by little he learned that during the last two years parties of men had come in boats, and had carried away many loads of stone to be used in erecting Government build-

VIEW OF THE RUINS OF THE TEMPLE OF ṢÛLB.

[From a photograph by J. W. Crowfoot, Esq.

ings. These men had naturally rejected the blocks which were weathered badly or soft, and they selected the hardest and firmest for removal; when the blocks were too large to haul away they broke them into pieces of a size convenient for transport and stowage in the boats. The sculptured slabs which I had seen there were about 4 feet long and 3 feet wide, and as they were made of good, hard sandstone, they were undoubtedly chosen by the men who came with the boats, and were broken and carried away first of all. The natives of Ṣûlb were powerless to prevent this work of destruction, even if they had wished to do so, because there were officials of the Government with the boats, and they had the "order of the Government" to get stone. In spite of this, however, it is impossible to blame the Sûdân Government for such an act of vandalism, for it was committed without the knowledge of any responsible official. The overseer of works told his men to get stone, meaning of course that they were to go to the quarries in the hills, but it was far easier for them to go to the ruins of the temple and break up the blocks there, especially as the stones lay near the river, and this they did with the result already described. One could not help feeling sorry that such a thing should be done under British rule in the Sûdân, and done too at the very time when Sir Reginald Wingate and his officials were making every effort possible to preserve ancient monuments and buildings all over the country!

As the result of the examination which we made of the ruins we decided to make a few trial excavations on the site, and we therefore took steps to provide ourselves and our servants with a place to live in. The natives of the village a mile or so distant went and fetched trunks, and branches of small trees, and a number of mats, and in about an hour they had constructed a rectangular *tukl*, with a sort of inner room, and had roofed it over with palm-leaf matting which was tied to the tops of the tree trunks which formed the framework. This *tukl* gave us shade by day, but it did not keep out the cold by night, nor the sand which was driven against it by a strong north wind that blew almost continuously for three days. There were a number of good mud-huts near the river which were uninhabited, but they were in such a filthy state that it was better to live in our palm-matting *tukl*. When our beds and baggage had been taken into our abode the Inspector and I went over the ruins a second time, and we examined the second court carefully. Some of the sculptured work was extremely good, and the ornamentation of the bases of the pillars, which is still well-preserved, was interesting. Here we saw a series of turreted ovals (above which are human heads and torsos), each containing the name of some city, or district, or country, which had been conquered by Ȧmen-hetep III., the builder of the temple. The arms of each captive are tightly tied behind his back, above the elbows, and as the face and features of each are different it seems tolerably certain that the sculptor intended each man to be a typical representative of a tribe, and that he tried to reproduce likenesses easily recognizable. Many were portraits of men who belonged to tribes of the Northern Sûdân, that is to say, men of the districts now called Dâr Sukkôt and Dâr Mahass; on the other hand, many reproduced the wide nostrils, high cheek-bones, and thick lips of Negroes. The turreted ovals give the names of places in Palestine, Northern Syria, and Western Mesopotamia, as well as of districts in the Sûdân, but as the natives of the last-named country can never have heard of most of the Asiatic names, Ȧmen-hetep must have had them placed on the bases of the capitals solely with the view of magnifying his exploits generally. Be this as it may, the figures are well cut, and one can only regret that more of them are not preserved.

On the following morning we began to excavate the bases of the pillars that formed the portico before the second propylon, for it was likely that altars, and votive and commemorative statues of priests and officials would be found there. Several of the bases were laid bare, and much clearing was done, but nothing was found. We next dug through the ground at the foot of the flight of steps which led to the above-mentioned portico, and here three granite altars and a hawk were brought to light. How these monuments came to be here it is difficult to say, but they were no doubt votive offerings, which having been overthrown became buried and forgotten. The enclosure of the temple of Ṣûlb was large, and traces of its boundary walls are still to be seen. The ancient city must have covered a considerable tract of land, for its ruins extend both to the north and south of the temple. About a furlong to the north of the temple there is on the river-bank the lower portion of a well-built pier; its age is uncertain, but the stones of which it is formed are large, and they may date from Egyptian times. A little further to the north of this pier are the remains of a stone wall, which is built out from the bank, and which was intended either "to train" the river, or to form a shelter for boats behind it. There is nothing on the stones which would help us to assign a date to it. These constructions suggest that Ṣûlb must have been, at one period of her history, the centre of the trade of the district, and a town or city of considerable importance, and her position on the river would give her the command of all the river-borne commerce going south and north.

Having finished the work which had to be done at Ṣûlb, we determined to drop down stream to Suwârda. We left early one morning, and crossed over to the eastern bank, where we landed the Inspector, who wished to visit one or two places between Eru and Suwârda. He proposed to ride part of the way, and to walk the rest, and I was to come on in the boat ; we agreed to meet that evening at Suwârda. So soon as he had started the captain of the boat discovered that he had some friends in the village, and he went off to smoke a pipe and have a chat with them. In a general way this would not have mattered, for Suwârda is only seven hours distant from Ṣûlb by boat. Whilst he was gone, however, the north wind arose with considerable force, and was blowing a gale by the time he came back. It was hopeless to start in the teeth of such a wind, and we therefore remained tied up to the bank until one o'clock. The wind having dropped a little by this time, we started, but our progress was slow, and at three o'clock we were still a mile to the south of the famous rock called Gebel Dôsha, i.e., we had not passed the village of Ṣûlb. Quite suddenly the wind arose with renewed violence, and as we neared the great rock, and met its full force, we were caught by a squall and well-nigh capsized. The captain was, however, very alert, and, letting go the sail, he steered straight for some huge boulders on the west bank, a little to the south of the rock, and ran us in under the shelter of the high bank just behind them. The sail had suffered a good deal, and needed some patching, and there was nothing to be done except mend it, and wait for the wind to drop. The captain landed and said his prayers, and the crew went off to the great slope of bright yellow sand close by, where there was no wind, and lay down on it, and went fast asleep.

Meanwhile I took the opportunity of visiting Gebel Dôsha, which marks the boundary between Dâr Sukkôt and Dâr Mahass. This rock is of sandstone and contains here and there veins of iron ore. Some portions of it have become very dark in colour, and these give it a striking appearance, especially in the afternoon when the sun shines full on the bright yellow sand which lies about it. The ascent is made by means of a path cut in ancient days, and this leads to a sort of platform, whence a magnificent view of the surrounding country is obtained. From the platform the visitor steps into a cave hewn out of the rock after the manner of an ancient Egyptian tomb, and at the far end of this are the remains of three seated statues of gods. At the present time these are so much mutilated that they cannot be identified. On the walls are the remains of the cartouches of Usertsen III. and Thothmes III., kings of Egypt of the XIIth and XVIIIth Dynasties respectively, but the general look of the cave gave me the impression that it was not older than the XVIIIth Dynasty. The appearance of the cartouche of Usertsen III. proves nothing to the contrary, for we know that Thothmes III. was in the habit of placing his name side by side with that of the first great Egyptian conqueror of the Sûdân. On the rock, above the cave, or tomb, are sculptured a relief in which a king is represented making offerings to a god, and a tablet inscribed in hieroglyphics which are too much mutilated to read. On the south side of the cave is another relief, wherein a king is seen making offerings to Ȧmen-Rā; the name of the king has been hammered out. When I came down from the rock I found that several men had come from the village of Ṣûlb with two stones, which they believed to be antiquities of the greatest value; these objects were of a flinty nature and were certainly marked in a fantastic manner. With difficulty I explained to the owners of the stones that the markings were not writing, and they were greatly disappointed when I refused to buy the objects. It seems that they were regarded in the light of fetishes in the village, and whilst some of the natives were ready to sell them, others were strongly opposed to such a course.

Meanwhile the sail had been repaired, and as the day was turning to sunset, we started once more for Suwârda; the wind was still blowing with some force, and we made very little headway. About two hours after sunset, when the wind had dropped, the river became covered with mist, and as we were continually hitting rocks and running aground, we decided to tie up for the night. There was no village wherein to take shelter, and we therefore cooked our evening meal in the boat, and made the best arrangements we could for sleeping there. About midnight the mist disappeared, the moon rose, and it became bitterly cold. Blankets and rugs were powerless to keep in the warmth, and at length we lit a fire in the bottom of the boat and huddled over it. The captain, finding it too cold to sleep, pushed out into the stream, and we floated quietly down the river, over which silence brooded. The scene was one of real beauty, for hills, and desert, and palms stood out with intense sharpness under the wonderful Sûdân moonlight, and it was they that seemed to be in motion, and not ourselves. The only sounds audible were those made by some animal in coming down from the desert to drink at the river.

We were all too cold, however, to enjoy the scene thoroughly, and it was with thankfulness that we saw the blue-black of the sky before dawn change to that wonderful tint which heralds the day. A slight mist again appeared on the river, and the palms loomed out of it like shadowy phantoms as we slid by their roots. After what appeared to be hours of waiting, the sun appeared, and in a very short time we began to feel the benefit of his heat. About eight o'clock we tied up near the village of Suwârda, and I at once made enquiries for the Inspector, and found that he had not arrived there on the previous evening. A little later, however, he appeared, and I heard his adventures. As already stated, he started from Ṣûlb for Suwârda on foot, meaning to ride part of the way, and to arrive at the latter place in the evening in time for dinner with me. He found the distance longer than he imagined, and when night came he was several miles from Suwârda, and was hungry and thirsty, and very tired. The only provisions he had with him were a few dates and three cigarettes! He stayed in a wretched village for the night, and the natives made some bread from dhurra for him, but it was so dark and heavy that he could not eat it, although there was absolutely nothing else to be had. When he tried to sleep in the hut which the natives gave him, he was so cold and hungry that he could not do so, and so passed a miserable night. It is almost impossible for a European who has not travelled through this part of the Sûdân to realize the bareness of the villages and the poverty of their inhabitants. Each man grows just enough dhurra for his own needs, and every kantar of dates he can possibly spare he sells; meat is, of course, exceedingly scarce, for pasturage for sheep and goats is scanty in the extreme. Few people suffer from actual hunger, but I am sure that every creature, both man and beast, would be the better for a little more food.

Soon after our arrival in Suwârda the shêkh waited upon the Inspector and offered us the use of a house so long as we were there; the offer was gratefully accepted, and our baggage was moved there without delay. When this had been done we went off with our diggers to look at some antiquities which were near the village, and found among them a headless basalt statue of a high

THE TEMPLE BUILT IN HONOUR OF QUEEN THI AT SADDÊNGA.

[From Lepsius, *Denkmäler*, Abth. I. Bl. 114.

Egyptian official of the XVIIIth Dynasty. We arranged for this and other things to be dug out of the holes wherein they were half buried, and then decided to cross the river and examine the site whereon lie the ruins of the ancient Egyptian temple, generally known as the Temple of Saddên, or Saddênga. Cailliaud mentions it (*Voyage*, tom. 1, p. 368) in connection with the village of Nulwa, and Hoskins describes it as the Temple of Sukkôt (*Travels*, p. 254). The Temple of Saddênga is a mass of ruins, and only one pillar is now standing. It was quite a small building, and it is puzzling to find out what purpose it could have served. It dates from the reign of Amen-ḥetep III., who appears to have dedicated it to his favourite wife Thi. It was built on an unusual plan, and was, I believe, intended to be rather a fortified place on the great caravan road from Egypt to the south than a house of worship. The blocks of stone used in its construction are large, and well shaped, but the work on the Hathor capitals of the two pillars is flat and poor. From the ruins we passed southwards over mounds of rubbish which must mark the site of the ancient city, and came to the remains of another small temple, which Hoskins says the natives call "Bibân," i.e., "Gates." Among these we discovered a slab of black basalt, on the sides of which was sculptured the standard of a god ; it had evidently been used as the pedestal for a figure of a god or sacred animal, and was the first specimen of the kind I had seen. The workmanship was good and certainly ancient Egyptian, and we made arrangements to bring this interesting object away with us. The remains of the temple, which may have been a restoration of the late Ptolemaïc or Roman period, were neither important, nor interesting.

We returned to Suwârda in the early afternoon, and spent the remainder of the day in trying to obtain information as to the whereabouts of the antiquities which were there in 1898, but which had since disappeared. We could hear nothing of the granite sphinxes and the large stelæ which were then near the village, and the only conclusion possible is that they have been used for building purposes or smashed. Several shêkhs came and consulted the Inspector on all sorts of matters, and some of them were anxious to send their sons to Kharṭûm to be educated. Everybody wanted something for nothing, and the Inspector's patience and forbearance were astonishing. The natives, who are a mixture of simplicity and cunning in about equal parts, delighted in having an official of the Government to talk to in this unceremonious manner, and visits paid to them in this unassuming fashion, by suitable officials, will, I am sure, increase the confidence of this suspicious people in the Government. The mind of the Sûdânî man is set on a different plane from that of most folk, and his mental attitude to things in general can only be learned by informal intercourse with him.

Early the next morning we crossed the river again, and the shêkhs from the villages round Ḳubba Salim came to pay their respects to the Inspector. We went to the first shêkh's house, and were taken up into a good-sized room with a mud bench running round three of its sides; all the openings except the door were plastered up to keep out the cold, for the wind was very keen. The birds came in and made themselves at home, and were wonderfully tame. After a few minutes a servant came in and placed upon a small *kursi*, or table, two or three baskets of very fine Sukkôt dates, and he was followed by another with a tray containing a tea-pot of tea and cups and saucers. It will be remembered that most of the men in the district have at one time or other been domestic servants in Egypt, and it is there that they learned of the Englishman's fondness for tea. They buy and take back to their native country trays, spoons, plates, cups and saucers, &c., hence when an Englishman appears in their midst they are prepared to set before him his favourite beverage. The Inspector felt it to be his duty to call on the other shêkhs in the neighbourhood, and each of them gave us tea, which we were bound to drink. As we walked from one village to another it was interesting to observe the traces which the British officials of the Government had left behind them in the execution of their duty. Each village is now connected by a good broad road which, though generally ankle-deep in sand and dust, is a great improvement on the sheep and goat tracks which are usually found in and about villages in the Sûdân. The borders of the roads are marked out by stones in such a way that no native could plough any part of it up and sow a crop on it, and then plead ignorance that he had encroached on public property. On each man's property is a white-washed stone whereon is inscribed the number of acres of land he possesses, and in future the collector will have no doubt as to the amount of tax which each man has to pay him, and the native will find it difficult to evade any part of his liability. In the last village of the group which we visited is the well-known shrine of Ḳubba Salim, or Ḳubbat Salim. It is a large, dome-shaped building some 30 feet high, it is made of crude mud bricks, and it has a low door on the south side. Salim was a Sûdânî Muhammadan who is said to have flourished about the middle of the nineteenth century, though some place his date much earlier. He was a doer of wonders and is much venerated in the neighbourhood, but his fame and works are eclipsed by those of the great Shêkh Idris, whose tomb will be described later on. Ḳubba Salim is kept up by the gifts of those who make pilgrimages thither, and the care of it is hereditary in the saint's family. Though Salim is so much venerated it is astonishing how little the people seem to know about him. Many of the mud houses in the villages here have low benches of mud, with slightly concave tops, built on their north side; they form very pleasant shady places to sit on in the afternoon, and the natives sleep on them during the hot weather.

On our return we had our boats loaded up, and so soon as possible we bade farewell to the hospitable Omdah, or chief shêkh of the district, and set out for the Island of Nilwitti, where we intended to sleep. Our journey was a pleasant one, for the day was lovely and there was no wind. As we dropped down the river we passed many beautiful little islands, the trees of which harboured whole colonies of small birds, but so soon as the sun had set it became cold, and we were glad to land on Nilwitti, and take up our quarters in two *tukls* which had been recently built, I think, for one of the Government Inspectors. Early the following morning Mr. Crowfoot and I set out to visit a building on the island which was said to be extremely ancient; it was situated about half a mile inland, and was surrounded by mounds of rubbish, the remains probably of an ancient town. When we came close to it, we saw that it was solidly built of crude mud bricks, and that it had a dome. In walking through it we noticed two or three cell-like rooms and doorways, which had been walled up, and the building more resembled the martyrium of a Coptic saint, or high ecclesiastical official, than anything else. The central portion probably contained the tomb, and the rooms at the side served for the chapel and the sleeping-place of the caretaker, who was probably a priest. The natives told us that many years ago a holy man "from the East" came and lived there for several years. One night, however, the pinnacle or ornament from the top of the dome fell to the ground with a crash, and the next day the holy man departed, no one knows where. When we saw the building it was quite uninhabitable.

After our visit to the "martyrium" we went to see the school in the village which Mr. Crowfoot had to inspect. We went to the mosque, in the buildings of which it was situated, and were received by a number of grave men who took us into the room where the schoolmaster was giving the boys a lesson. The children were seated on the ground and were engaged in learning by heart some verses from the Ḳur'ân, but they were told to stand up, and to go into the courtyard and arrange themselves in a line. We went out and looked at them, and the Inspector asked the master questions about the subject of their lesson, and spoke to some of the boys. They were all dark-skinned; most of them were children from the neighbourhood, but a few came from a distance and boarded with the master. We looked at the queer little rooms in which they slept at night and marvelled. They were quite small, and had neither door nor window in them; they were entered through little low openings which were close to the ground, and reminded one of the door of a rabbit hutch The Inspector seemed satisfied with what the boys were doing, and we each made a small present to the master to be spent as he thought best on their behalf. We were then taken into the other rooms of the mosque, and our guides led us into a court which had at one time been partially roofed over, but was now in a ruined condition. We asked what had caused this state of things, and they answered briefly, "The Dervishes." It seems that one of the Khalifa's hordes had invaded the island, and, wanting firewood, had deliberately wrecked the whole roof, and most of the building, in order to get the beams! The natives of Dâr Sukkôt and Dâr Mahass were hated by the Dervishes, and suffered greatly at their hands.

About nine o'clock we left the Island of Nilwitti, and two hours later we were abreast of the island of Sâî, where we stopped and landed to go and look at some ruins which the natives were anxious for us to see. The island is about seven miles long, and in its widest part is about three miles wide The principal channel of the Nile is on the east side, for the channel on the west side dries up in the late spring. The natives of the island who acted as guides were full of stories of inscribed stones which they had seen, but when we arrived at the places where these were, we generally discovered them to be stones with rough chisel marks on them. We passed a great many ruins of workmen's houses near the old quarry and mining works, but found no inscription of any sort or kind among them. It was quite clear that in ancient times Sâî owed its importance to its quartz strata, from which gold was dug out by the natives. We walked over immense layers of agglomerate containing flints, agates, carnelians, &c. As we were re-embarking a native woman brought one of the largest water melons I had ever seen in the Sûdân and wanted to sell it; money she declined, saying that it was useless, but the purchase was effected by means of an exchange of some tobacco, and the crew were delighted to receive the melon as a gift.

After leaving the southern half of Sâî we passed through some lovely river scenery, and about two o'clock reached Kuwêkka, where we were welcomed by that most kind and hospitable man, Shêkh Idris. He insisted on our staying the night in his house, and had our beds and baggage taken out and carried to two large rooms, which he reserved for guests whom he delighted to honour. The shêkh was an old friend of the Inspector, to whom he appeared to be greatly attached, and he valued his opinion highly. He is a somewhat spare man, about 5 feet 8 inches in height, and dark-skinned; his face is open and pleasing, and his eyes are bright and intelligent, and see everything. His wit is quick, and he has a most pleasing smile. Had he lived in the days of the Pharaohs he would assuredly have been an "inspector of the countries of the south," and his astuteness would certainly have "filled the heart" of the king, his lord, with satisfaction. Years ago he and his people laughed at the pretensions of the Mahdi and the Khalifa, and remained loyal to the Government during the Dervish Rebellion, but their devotion cost many their property, and some their lives. Idrîs himself was too quick for the Dervishes, and managed to escape from them, although they succeeded in wounding him; the narrative of his escape is most interesting, and the story of his encounters with the rebels deserves to be done into writing. Idris is descended from a

KUBBA IDRIS.

[From a photograph by J. W. Crowfoot, Esq.

very old family, the heads of which have been shêkhs in Sukkôt and possessed property there for hundreds of years. I heard him tell the Inspector that a native, I think in Akâsha, possessed documents which showed that Idris's family was settled in the neighbourhood in the XVth or XVIth century. If this be so, it is much to be hoped that steps will be taken to preserve such writings, for they will probably throw some light on the condition of the country during a period of its history of which nothing much is known.

Soon after our arrival Idris took us into one of his cowbyres and showed us a number of stones which had been used in the building, and we found them to be parts of the inscribed front of an Egyptian tomb. Without any ado he had the portions of the wall in which they were imbedded knocked down, and the stones taken out and placed ready for loading in one of our boats. We then went to look at the famous Ḳubba Idris, or tomb of the ancestor of our host, who flourished in the early part of the XIXth century. This Idris was a follower of the great Shêkh Morghânî, who was learned in the doctrines and tenets of an important class of Muḥammadan religious thinkers, and he was venerated for his great spiritual powers. Idris the Great, as we may call him, was renowned in his generation for his piety and learning, and for at least three-quarters of a century Muḥammadans in the Sûdân have been in the habit of visiting the place of his burial, and it was believed throughout the country that a blessing rested on those who performed this meritorious act. Women came to the tomb with their husbands and prayed for offspring, and all who were about to set out on a journey, or to embark on any undertaking, endeavoured to visit the tomb in order to ask the blessing of Idris on their exertions.

The present Ḳubba is a solidly built structure of stone and mud brick from seventy to eighty feet high, and it stands among palm trees, at no great distance from the river, in a most picturesque position. The most striking feature of Ḳubba Idrîs is the dome which, though simple, is a really imposing object, and its stages, whilst adding a suggestion of considerable strength to the edifice, do not give it a heavy appearance. An excellent idea of the general look of the building will be obtained by examining the illustration given on the plate opposite, which is made from a photograph by my friend the Inspector. I was unable to find out the name of the architect, and could therefore obtain no clue as to what building served him for the model. This, after all, is not important. It seems pretty certain that the builder, whoever he may have been, was acquainted with western methods, and with the general appearance of late Byzantine ecclesiastical edifices. It is certainly the finest building of the kind in the Sûdân.

On the invitation of the shêkh we entered the Ḳubba and walked round the large rectangular hall, which appeared delightfully cool and shady after the outside glare. In the middle were two raised tombs, one of Idris the Great, and the other of his brother. These were formerly covered over by a costly canopy, which the Dervishes seized and carried away, and the present shêkh has not been able to afford another of the same kind. Round the hall were several graves, marked out by the palm branches and small earthenware cups which were laid upon them. Everything in the hall was simple and primitive, and one could not fail to remember in connection with it Burton's description of the tomb of Muḥammad the Prophet.

In the evening Mr. Crowfoot went to inspect the little school of Ḳubba Idris. The shêkh led us out to a small shed near the Ḳubba, on the floor of which a smoky fire was burning. Squatted on the ground round the fire were seven or eight little boys, each with his head bent over a whitened board, which served the purpose of a slate, whereon were inscribed in black ink some extracts from the Kur'ân, which the young student was trying to commit to memory. The children were rocking their bodies backwards and forwards, and straining their poor little eyes to read their texts by the uncertain firelight, and were striving hard to repeat correctly what they saw. The schoolmaster helped them out from time to time, but the strain on the minds and bodies of the little fellows must have been considerable. Next the boys stood up, and we could see their faces with tolerable clearness. The oldest was about ten years of age, but many were much younger, and it was hard not to question the wisdom of making such pinched little bodies work in this way by firelight. The large skull, pointed chin, and vacant face of one little boy seemed to me to betoken an idiot, but the parents were very anxious that the children should be taught, and they all contributed towards the expenses of the school. The Inspector spoke kindly words as usual to the teacher and the taught, and then, having made a small present to them, we left. The Inspector told the shêkh that working by firelight must be stopped, and then discussed with him the steps which would have to be taken for amending existing arrangements. In the Sûdân, as in England, education is a question of money, and the boys, having to work during the day, had only the evening in which to study. It really was pathetic to see how anxious the men were to have their children educated, and how ready each was to contribute his few *millîms*[1] towards the expense. Happily the Inspector knows the circumstances of the people from personal intercourse with them, and we may be sure that he and Mr. Currie will find the means for establishing schools in Sukkôt, wherein children may learn their lessons in the day-time, and not in the evening with only smoky fires to give them light.

After this, to me at least, novel experience, we returned to the house, and persuaded the shêkh to dine with us. He chatted during dinner and told us many interesting things about the invasion of his district by the Dervishes, and when the meal was over, he produced some books in which his ancestors were mentioned, and pored over them with the Inspector for some time. We questioned him about the ruins of some ancient building which were said to exist in the northern part of the Island of Sâî, and found that he knew them well, and having promised to take us to them, he departed for the night.

On the following morning we had our boats loaded early, and dropped down the Nile with the current; as there was no wind we made good progress. In about two hours we sighted a mass of ruined walls which were built on the extreme edge of the Island of Sâî, close to the river. We found a convenient place on the bank and landed, and then climbed up a steep, rough path to the remains of what is called the "Castle of Sâî." About half way up, lying on one side of the path through the walls, was a large portion of a stone figure inscribed with hieroglyphics in a style which suggested that it belonged to the XIXth Dynasty; this we

[1] One *millîm* = one farthing.

had put aside for removal to our boat. When we reached the top of the ruin, the scene which met our eyes was a remarkable one. We found ourselves in a kind of fort which contained several rooms and passages, with immensely thick walls; the outer walls were still thicker, and they were in places about forty feet high and crenellated. The inside space was filled with heaps of broken stones and crude and baked mud bricks, all scattered about in hopeless confusion, and it was clear that the upper portions of many of the walls had been overthrown by main force. In one portion of the enclosure we came upon the remains of bases of columns which were manifestly of Egyptian work, and we turned on our workmen to dig round in the hope of finding inscribed stelae. In a very short time they found a large granite stele, with a rounded top, lying face downwards; we raised it with some difficulty, and then saw that it was inscribed with several lines of hieroglyphics of a large size which were almost illegible. Brushing and rubbing revealed the fact that the stele was set up by Ȧmen-ḥetep III., to commemorate his conquest of the country, and the building of the temple among the ruins of which we were then standing. The stele was too large for us to remove, but the Inspector made a note to send men to bring it away at the end of the summer, when its transport by river to Ḥalfa would be easy. We selected for removal also several inscribed stones and portions of the ornamental stone-work from the pillars of a Coptic church.

The site on which the Castle of Sâî is built is one of great strategic importance, and, though there is no proof of it at present, I believe it was first fortified by Usertsen III., a king of the XIIth Dynasty. Under the XVIIIth Dynasty it was occupied by troops under the command of Egyptian officers, and a very strong fort was built there. Within the fort was a temple, built as we have seen by Ȧmen-ḥetep III. As Seti I. built a temple at Sesebi, and his son Rameses II. built another at Gebel Barkal, we are justified in assuming that they were masters of the Island of Sâî. Of the history of the Island in late dynastic times nothing is known. During the Christian Period the Copts turned the temple of Ȧmen-ḥetep III. into a church, of which we found some of the decorations. From what we saw about us, however, it was clear that the fort had been rebuilt in comparatively modern times, and that the remains of Egyptian and Coptic edifices had been used in its reconstruction. According to Burckhardt,[1] Sâî was garrisoned by a troop of Bosnian soldiers who were sent there by the Sultân Selim in the first quarter of the sixteenth century, and like Ibrîm and Aswân, it had its own Aghâ, or chief, who was independent of the governors of Nubia. The guns which were formerly in the Castle, were, according to Burckhardt, carried off by the Mamlûks, but Cailliaud says that several small Turkish cannon were still to be seen there.[2] A little to the north of the Castle are the remains of a temple which appears to have been founded by Thothmes III. and restored by Àmen-ḥetep II., and towards the middle of the island are four gray granite pillars, which mark the site of a Coptic church. Each pillar is a monolith, and has the Coptic cross cut on its capital. A few heaps of rubbish indicate where stood other portions of the church to which these pillars belonged, but every stone of any value for building purposes has been removed. From what has been said above it is clear that Burckhardt was mistaken in believing that there were "no remains of antiquity whatever" on Sâî, except the Castle, which he believed to be of the same date as that at Ibrim. Hoskins states boldly that Sâî "contains no remains of Egyptian antiquities" (*Travels*, p. 257), which is remarkable, seeing that he actually visited the island; Burckhardt did not, and was obliged to rely on the best information he could obtain. Sâî is a difficult place to reach, unless the traveller has his own boat with him. On January 2nd, 1821, Cailliaud crossed the river on a raft made of reeds and pieces of palm trunk; Hoskins in June, 1832, needed no raft, for the water in the Western channel only came up to the camel's knees, and he passed over to the island from the mainland without difficulty; Burckhardt, who must have been there in the winter, could obtain the use of neither ferry nor raft, and was therefore obliged to abandon his projected visit.

The Inspector and I spent some hours among the ruins of the Castle, and we should have liked to turn on a couple of hundred

[1] *Travels*, p. 56.

[2] *Voyage*, tom. i. p. 367. On y voit encore plusieurs petites pièces de canon turques.

men to excavate the whole site. This, however, was impossible, but it is to be hoped that the work will be taken in hand some day, for the clearing out of the Castle would, no doubt, bring to light many important historical facts. Having collected the stones which we had marked, we had them taken to our boat, and then the Inspector paid a visit to the local shêkh, who received us very kindly, and regaled us with tea and dates. We resumed our journey about one o'clock, and floated down the river through wild and interesting scenery. We passed the village of Sâî, on the right bank, and soon afterwards we saw a man running along the west bank and shouting to us. We saw that he was carrying something on his shoulder, and we stopped to see what he wanted. When he came up we learned that he had been running after the boat for some time, and that he had brought with him a little rectangular slab of sandstone with an inscription upon it. He told us that it had been in his village for many years, but that on hearing that we were collecting antiquities for the Government, he had brought it to us.

The Inspector rewarded the man for his trouble, and we took the little monument, of which a picture is given in the annexed illustration, with us for transport to Khartûm. When complete the stone contained twenty-three lines of Coptic text, but the last line has been rubbed away. The slab is fifteen inches long, and ten and a half inches wide at the top and twelve inches at the bottom. The text, after making reference to God, the Demiourgos of the Universe, Who hath power to kill and to make alive, Who said unto our first father Adam, "Thou art earth, and to earth thou shalt return," goes on to say that by His command the most worthy bishop and monk Abba Iêsou went to his rest (i.e., died) at the sixth hour on the twentieth day of the month Pakhôni (i.e., May 16th) [which fell] on a Sunday. The writer of the text then prays the Master of the Universe to give the deceased rest in the bosom of Abraham, Isaac, and Jacob, and says that he lived on this earth fifty years before he was consecrated bishop, and that he sat on the episcopal throne for thirty-two years. Bishop Iêsou was, therefore, eighty-two years old when he died. The last line but one gave, I think, the year of the Era of the Martyrs[1] in

[1] This Era began A.D. 284.

which he died, and the last line of all the number of the Indiction, but these lines are so much mutilated that little can be said about them. The year 92 seems to be mentioned, but the ninety-second year of the Era of the Martyrs would be A.D. 374, and this sepulchral stele belongs, in my opinion, to a

SEPULCHRAL TABLET OF IÊSÔU, BISHOP OF THE ISLAND OF SÂÎ, WHO DIED AGED EIGHTY-TWO YEARS.

much later date, probably to some period which lies between the seventh and tenth centuries. But whatever be its date, the importance of the little monument is considerable, for it proves that at some time during the Christian Period of the history of Dâr Sukkôt the Christians who were in this portion of the Sûdân were sufficiently numerous to need the care of a bishop. Remains of Christian churches have been found at many places between Sâî and Merawi, and these suggest that the Coptic Church in the Northern Sûdân was in a flourishing state for some centuries, and that the care of it was in the hands of properly appointed bishops and spiritual directors.

Three more hours of sailing brought us abreast of the southern end of the Island of Arnitti, and we landed to examine the antiquities which were said to exist there. We found, however, that some mistake had been made, for the ruins were on the west bank of the Nile, some distance to the north of this island. We therefore resumed our journey, and sailed on to that part of the bank which was nearest the ruins, where we landed and set out to find them. The river bank was very steep, and the space between its top and the water's edge was a mass of sand, into which we sank up to the knees at every step. The ruins were about half a mile from the river, and the ground was covered with a thick layer of bright yellow sand, beautiful to look at, but very unpleasant to walk through. The "antiquities" turned out to be the remains of a little stone temple, oriented to the east, which was built by Rameses II. We uncovered several inscribed slabs, and began to dig out a little chamber in the sanctuary, where we found a large limestone stele, covered with a copy of the bombastic "standard inscription" of Rameses II., similar to those which this king set up at Abû Simbel and elsewhere. Meanwhile the sun was setting, and we had made no arrangement about our sleeping-place; we therefore went back to the boat, and sailed across to Amâra. We found it extremely difficult to land, for the water was shallow near the east bank, and was strewn with boulders. At length we discovered a suitable place for landing to the south of the village, and were kindly received by the Omdah, or chief shêkh, who placed his house at our disposal for the night.

The next morning we were able in the strong light to obtain a good view of the plain of Amâra,[1] and to note that the cultivated land extended southwards for some miles, and that in some places the "strip of herbage" was two miles wide. The Omdah was

[1] See Cailliaud, *Voyage*, tom. i. p. 363; Burckhardt, *Travels*, p. 55; Hoskins, *Travels*, p. 263; and Lepsius, *Letters*, p. 237.

greatly interested in agriculture, and he was then engaged in making experiments to find out whether cotton could be grown in sufficiently large quantities to make the undertaking commercially profitable. He had made several wells in his fields, and the crops we saw were in as thriving a condition as any one could desire, it seemed to me. The village is large, and straggles along the river bank for a considerable distance, and everywhere are the palm trees which yield in large quantities the fine dates for which the district is so famous. About a mile and a half from the village are the ruins of the temple of Amâra, which have been so often mentioned by travellers. The temple was a rectangular building about 55 feet long and 31 feet wide, and contained eight pillars; six of these are still standing, but their capitals are wanting. The temple is entered by a gateway about 20 feet wide, and on each side of it are the remains of a pillar, about 3 feet 9 inches in diameter. The foundations of the temple are made of crude brick; the building is oriented due east. On the pillars inside are sculptured reliefs in which a queen and her consort are seen making offerings to the gods of the South and North Niles, to Khnemu and to other deities, and a column of hieroglyphics on each pillar sets forth the name and titles of the builder. Two names are enclosed within cartouches, one being that of a woman, and the other that of a man; they appear to be native Meroïtic names. Lepsius "recognized directly on the columns the fat Queen of Naga and Meroë, with her husband," and there is no doubt that the temple of Amâra belongs to the period of the dynasty of the great queens of Meroë. The name of the queen which is found on the pillars of Amâra certainly appears at Nagaa, but there the name of the prince or king is different from that at Amâra. The style and workmanship of the reliefs on the pillars suggest that the building is pre-Christian, and the fact that the little space over each group of figures has been left unfilled with hieroglyphics confirms the view that the temple was built at a time when masons no longer knew how to cut Egyptian inscriptions, or, if they did, that there was no man attached to the works who was sufficiently acquainted with hieroglyphics to write out the drafts of the inscriptions for them to copy. The fact that a temple was built on the plain of Amâra proves that a city of considerable size stood here at one time, and the fragments of pottery which are strewn about in all directions for a considerable distance probably mark its site and its extent. The town was no doubt an important centre of trade, and a halting place for caravans.

Having collected our workmen and tools, we dropped down the river about nine o'clock, and landed on the west bank, and were soon at work clearing portions of the ruins of the temple which we had visited the evening before. After about an hour's digging we found that the stele of Rameses II. had at some time or other been broken to pieces, which had been roughly stuck together with mud and plaster, and that the monument had been re-erected and was held in position by a thick mud wall built up behind it. The inscription, so far as I could see it, gave no new facts, and as the stele was made of very soft stone, we decided to cover it up again and leave it there until men could go with a wooden frame and cement, and remove it carefully. We made several trial diggings in other parts of the site, but we found nothing worth carrying away. We noticed the serious disintegrating effect which the wind-driven sand had upon the stone slabs of the temple, and it seemed to me that this was the principal cause of its destruction. The approaches to the temple are covered with sand to the depth of several feet, and those who excavate them will find it necessary to build a high mud wall as a screen, for the wind fills up the trenches almost as fast as they are cleared.

Having covered the bases of the pillars, &c., which we had laid bare, we returned to our boat and set out for Kôsha without delay. In about two hours we reached the southern end of the Island of Atab, where we landed in order to examine the remains of a fortified building which our captain had pointed out to us. At a little distance from the island the "Castle" could hardly be recognized, so well had its walls been made to join on to the foundations of the living rock on which it stood. We climbed the rocks and found that this "Castle" covered much ground, and that the mud walls were enormously strong, being in some places as much as 20 feet thick. Huge slopes formed of well-made bricks served as buttresses to the upper walls, and made approach on the sides where they existed practically impossible. Several of the inner walls were built in alternate layers of pieces of black basalt and mud bricks, and when in a complete state must have been very strong. On the east side were some small chambers, with little side rooms, which may have been used for prisoners or for bedrooms. We searched everywhere, hoping to find something which would give us a clue to the age of the building, but found nothing. The scenery of this portion of the Cataract was wild and picturesque in the extreme, and the view of the river to the south, in which bright green eyots, massive black rocks, yellow sand, patches of emerald green vegetation, stretches of rugged desert, and hills sloping down to the water's edge on both sides were mingled together in harmonious confusion, is one which, of its kind, cannot be surpassed. From the southernmost point of the "Castle," which must have been about 50 feet above inundation level, a splendid view of the country for many miles was obtained. The numerous rapids round the island make the work of landing, even at low Nile, very difficult, and during the inundation it must be almost inaccessible.

Between the Island of Atab and Kôsha, our destination, the river contains many rocky barriers which are visible, and large numbers of sunken rocks, of which the whereabouts are only known to the most expert watermen. Our captain knelt down on the sand and prayed with great fervour before he started to take us to Kôsha, and when we were floating between the treacherous rocks which his skill enabled us to avoid, we noticed that he had tied a small cotton bag to his rudder post. In answer to our question he told us that the bag contained a small quantity of dust which he had taken from the tomb of Shêkh Idris, and that he had brought it with him to secure the protection of the shêkh, who, he believed, would vouchsafe us a safe journey. Every traveller in the East is familiar with the native belief that dust taken from the grave of a holy man forms an effective amulet, but it was interesting to note the survival of this belief and the practical expression of it in the Sûdân in the twentieth century. When we had been floating down the river for an hour or so, we began to realize that there were reasons for the precautions which the captain had taken, for we found ourselves hemmed in with rocks. We steered to the bank and the crew got out and began to tow the boat, but in spite of all their efforts we ran on sand-banks frequently, and the reefs gave the men a good deal of trouble. The captain took the opportunity of getting out on a rock and of praying again, and then we began to make our way slowly through a reach of broken water, the boat grazing rocks with uncomfortable frequency. At length we passed into open water again, and we reached Kôsha about one hour after sunset.

The next two or three days we spent in bringing the antiquities we had collected to the railway station and putting them into a truck, and at intervals we had time to look about the village. In the market there was the inevitable Greek, with a stock of tinned provisions and bottled fruits, and in a room which opened out of his shop the natives found both time and money to play games of chance. The postal official was an expert telegraphist whom I remembered seeing in the submarine cable office at Suez years before; he did not like Kôsha as a permanent place of residence, and was hoping to be transferred to Abû Ḥamed at an early date. We found the natives of Kôsha greatly disturbed by the recent decision of the Government to take up the Ḥalfa-Kerma line south of Kôsha, and to discontinue the carriage of goods to Ḥalfá. The district of Sukkôt has always been famous for its dates, and since the opening of the railway to Kerma in 1896, the trade in this commodity has increased greatly. The natives collected the dates from the villages, and then packed them in large bags which they were able to send by rail to Ḥalfa for a few piastres per hundredweight. But as Lord Cromer has told us, the Ḥalfa-Kerma line was worked for years at a loss, and in 1903 the authorities decided to take up the rails from Kôsha to Kerma, which were in good condition, and use them in the construction of the new line between Atbara and the Red Sea. The section of the line between Ḥalfa and Kôsha was declared to be unsafe, and as the existing traffic did not justify its reconstruction it was further decided to discontinue mercantile traffic. The result was that many hundreds of bags of dates, each weighing three hundredweight, were lying by the line at Kôsha when we were there, and the merchants were in despair of ever disposing of them with benefit to themselves. Camel transport to Ḥalfa was very expensive, i.e., about three shillings per hundredweight, and the merchants declared this rate to be prohibitive. The captain of the boat who had taken us to Ṣulb entreated the Inspector on behalf of his friends to take a few bags of dates with him to Ḥalfa, as personal luggage, but this was, of course, impossible. It seemed a pity to see the dates lying on the sand spoiling, but no one who knew the circumstances of the case could pity their owners, for they had been warned for months beforehand that after such and such a day goods trains would cease to run. In spite of this warning, however, they continued to pile their dates at the station, even after the day mentioned had expired, believing that they would by this means force the railway authorities to run special trains to carry their wares to Ḥalfa.

It is almost impossible for an outsider to arrive at a right conclusion about any business or trade with which he is not familiar, but it has always seemed to me that if the date trade of Sukkôt were in experienced and capable hands, it might be made a very profitable undertaking. The dates of this district are large, sweet, fleshy, and of a good flavour, especially those which are known by the names of Gundîla, Barakâwî, Bintemôda, Kilma, and Shurwa,[1] and they are highly appreciated wherever they are known. Unfortunately they are almost unknown in many parts of Egypt, i.e., they are not obtainable, and they are rarely seen in Europe; no dates in Egypt are to be compared, in my opinion, with those of Sukkôt, and the fruit-merchants in the market at Cairo told me that they could sell large quantities of them if they could get them, packed neatly in small cardboard boxes, like the dates of Ḳena. What is wanted in Sukkôt is a central establishment, which should be conducted on the lines followed by the date-merchants at Al-Baṣra (Bussorah) on the Persian Gulf, where the dates would be sorted, selected, and packed under European supervision. The choicest fruit, packed in attractive, paper-lined boxes, would command a ready sale, and a competent authority assures me that they could be retailed in Egypt at a highly remunerative price. The less fine varieties packed in wooden boxes, or sacking, might be exported, and they would find at least as good a market as the inferior kinds of

[1] Shêkh Idrîs gave me specimens of all five varieties, saying that they were among the best dates he had ever seen.

Turkish dates, which sell freely in London. It is hopeless to expect the shêkhs of the district to work such an undertaking successfully, for they have neither the business qualifications of the kind necessary, nor capital ; if it is ever done, the initiating and controlling power must be European.

Our stay at Kôsha was prolonged somewhat because we were obliged to wait for a train from Kerma, and we did not succeed in leaving until Saturday evening (we had arrived on the Monday) ; the railway authorities allowed us to keep the saloon coach at Kôsha whilst we were collecting antiquities, and we therefore returned to Sarras in comfort. The train to which we were coupled was heavily loaded with railway lines, and the engine succeeded in climbing the gradients only with the greatest difficulty ; on one section of the journey the engine was placed in the middle of the train, and men had to walk on each side of her and throw sand on the rails. We descended the hill leading down to Ambiḳôl Wells at a dashing pace, for the load was a heavy one, and the only breaks used were those on the engine. We arrived at Sarras a little before dawn, and as soon as the Omdah was out of bed the Inspector sent for him, and told him to get a boat ready for us to sail up to Semna, where we had some work to do. When the boat arrived the men loaded the planks, ropes, picks, &c., into it with our luggage, but this work occupied a considerable time, for the river bank is very steep at Sarras, and we had to make détours so as to avoid destroying the crops sown on it.

We started with a strong north wind behind us, and in about an hour reached a village, where we landed so that the boat might be used in ferrying our camels across to the western bank. We decided to send our servants on with the camels to Semna, so that they might prepare a place to sleep in, and have a meal ready by the time we arrived in the evening. Whilst the camels were being ferried across we went and sat in a hut in the village, which is the most miserable I have ever seen in the Sûdân. The huts are made of stones and mud loosely piled together against the hillsides, and many of them are only partially roofed over. There are no palm trees to give shade, and the natives told us that the Dervishes had cut down every tree they could find in the district because the people would not join their rebellion. This says a good deal for the sense of the natives of this portion of the Second Cataract, but the practical result is that the villages are most uncomfortable. The people are exceedingly poor, and possess hardly anything except their scanty clothes; many sleep on the ground because they have no *ankaribs*, and the children we saw were nearly all mother-naked. We found them sitting and lying in the sun, usually under the shelter of some mud wall which the sun had made hot, like so many dogs; we gave piastres to each of them, but what they were most in need of was food.

The passage of the camels seeming to occupy a long time we went down to the river to see what had become of the boat, and we learned there that in being dragged out one of the camels had smashed a pole connected with the rigging, and had put his foot through the sail. When the beast was extricated from the wreckage he had made, the captain set to work to repair the damage; hence the delay. At length the boat came over, and we loaded her up, but as we were pushing off a large number of the workmen jumped on, and all but capsized her. She was a crazy craft at the best, and so shallow that, with a load on board, it was difficult to trim her; this boat was the only one on the river, and we were therefore obliged to hire her. Having made most of the workmen get out, we started to sail up to Semna, and so long as we were under the shelter of the high, rocky sides of the gorge, which is so striking a characteristic of this portion of the Nile Valley, we made steady progress. Soon, however, we came to a place where, on the west bank, there is a valley with its mouth opening on to the river, and along this the wind swept with great force, blowing us into the east bank. To avoid this we had to keep the head of the boat to the wind, but before we could get under the lee of the rocks again, a rope broke and the sail split from top to bottom, and we were blown on to the river bank again. To attempt to mend the wretched sail was hopeless, for it was made up of bits of stuff of all shapes, sizes, and thicknesses, and the numerous holes in it were patched with native calico! Several of the crew got out on the rocks and began to tow, but we made little headway because it was found impossible to haul on the rope continuously. Then a Berberi waterman jumped into the water and swam to a rock with a rope, and when he had mounted it he pulled the boat up to it; we then held on to the rock whilst he swam on to another and pulled us up to it as before.

Between these rocks the current was rushing at the rate of five or six knots an hour, and in some places we had to leave the main stream and creep along the side channels. We beguiled the tediousness of the journey by examining the huge blackened sandstone natural barriers in the river as we passed quite close to them, or touched them, and we saw at work the forces which had enabled the Nile to break its way through them. It seems that small pieces of hard stone and pebbles are brought down by the river, and deposited in the inequalities of the surface of the top of the sandstone. As the water flows over them it imparts motion to them, and by degrees they bore in the sandstone holes which become deeper and deeper, and we saw some holes several feet long, the sides of which had been rubbed through by the stones inside them. At low Nile the sandstone is exposed to the heat of the sun by day and to the cold by night, and the sides of the holes split open and they run into one another, and pieces split off their sides until at length gaps are made in the barriers. During the inundation the torrent pours between the rocks in a nine knot current, the boring of new holes begins, and the sandstone is scoured away. These facts were pointed out to me by Mr. John Ball, of the Egyptian Geological Survey Department, who was, I believe, the first to ascertain them.

In the course of the afternoon we approached a "gate" in the Cataract through which the river was rushing with mighty force, and the captain insisted that, with two or three exceptions, every one should leave the boat whilst he tried to work her through. We therefore got out on the rocks and watched the result of his labours with some anxiety, for though he was confident of success, we had our doubts about the matter; our beds, baggage, and tools we left with him, for the boat was some distance from a suitable landing-place. We had a coil of 60 yards of thick rope with us, and having tied one end of this to the main cross-beam of the boat, the captain told every man available to haul on it, whilst he pushed out a little into the current, and gradually poled the boat along the sides of the rocks towards the "gate." When the water became too deep for poling we had to depend entirely upon the rope, on which every one of us hauled with all his might. Gradually the boat came through the "gate," but only a few inches at a time, and for nearly an hour it was doubtful if the river would not conquer us in the end. We dragged the boat into a little bay just before sunset, and then discovered that we were little more than half way to Semna. We had spent the whole day in coming about ten miles! To attempt to reach Semna that night was hopeless, so we pushed on a little further to the Island of Gazîrat al-Malik, where we heard there were some natives living. We reached the island soon after sunset, and determined to stay there for the night. We climbed up the west bank, passing through crops of dhurra, and came to a small collection of mud huts which were situated at the foot of the hills that line the east bank of the island. A few men came out to receive us, and they seemed much astonished at our coming, but they found a couple of disused huts, which were without roofs, and so soon as these were cleared out we took possession of them.

The Inspector sent a messenger on to Semna to bring back our servants with the food, for we assumed that they had arrived there by that time, but we knew that some hours must elapse before they could appear, and we therefore set going the spirit lamp which we had in our "emergency box," and boiled some Bovril. We also lit a fire before the huts, for the night was bitterly cold. The women of the hamlet ground some dhurra, and made "wafer" bread, which was most acceptable, and the men brought branches of trees and a little palm leaf matting, and put roofs on our huts. About ten o'clock the Inspector's servant appeared with his cooking-pots containing the dinner he had had waiting for us at Semna, and after the exertions of the day we enjoyed our meal. The next morning we sailed up the river until the channel became blocked with rocks, and then we landed and rode on camels to Semna, which we reached a little before noon. When we arrived at the temple there were several natives awaiting us, and we were glad to find that they had brought *ankaribs* and firewood; as the village of Semna is about a mile and a half to the south of the Cataract, which is just below the temple, we decided to move our beds into the temple and live there.

Thoûgh as a historical monument the temple of Semna is of the greatest importance, yet it is impossible not to admit that, at first sight, its appearance is distinctly disappointing. It is a small building about 30 feet long, 10 feet wide, and 13 feet high, and is formed of massive blocks of stone, which are wholly out of proportion to the size of the edifice. It is perched up on the top of the steep, high rocks which are on the western side of the Cataract of Semna, and seems absurdly small when we remember that it was, under the XVIIIth Dynasty, the chief Egyptian sanctuary of the first frontier town of the Sûdân, which Usertsen III. founded there some forty-four centuries ago. The vastness and magnificence of the deserts and hills to the north and south of the great rock-barrier which Nature threw across the Nile valley here emphasize the comparative insignificance of the Egyptian buildings, both at Semna on the west bank, and at Kumma on the east bank, and we can only assume that, when the architects of Usertsen III., and of the Thothmes and Ȧmen-ḥetep kings threw away opportunities of setting up temples on a scale commensurate with the natural surroundings of the site, they did so at the behests of the most practical utilitarianism.

The temple of Semna[1] is oriented towards the south. It is built of limestone, and its form resembles the small temples which were built by the Egyptians in almost every large fortress in the Sûdân. On the east and west sides are the remains of the covered colonnades, each of which contained four pillars. On the east side there are at the present time three square pillars *in situ*, and on the west side there are two pillars, one square and one polygonal; portions of the architraves still remain. The main door is on the soûth side, but there is a smaller door on the west side, near the south end, which was made after the temple was built. The slabs which formed the ceiling were painted blue, and traces of the colour are still visible; Burckhardt says[2] that he saw

[1] For other descriptions see Burckhardt, *Travels*, p. 81, Cailliaud, *Voyage*, tom. i. p. 341; Hoskins, *Travels*, p. 269; Lepsius, *Letters*, p. 239.

[2] So also Cailliaud: "Dans l'intérieur, on reconnaît que les sculptures étaient "peintes, ainsi que le plafond, en couleur bleu-de-ciel, avec des étoiles."

traces of colour upon "several of the figures" in the reliefs, but I did not notice any. Their disappearance is probably due to the rubbings and wet paper "squeezes" which appear to have been made by archaeologists since Burckhardt visited the temple. The walls, both inside and outside, are covered with inscriptions and reliefs, chiefly in the style which was in vogue under the XVIIIth Dynasty, but portions of the original ornamentation of the front of the temple were erased by the officials of later kings, who cut in their stead inscriptions commemorating the dedication of offerings, and the greatness of their masters. Mention of these is made in the chapters which deal with the history of the ancient Egyptian occupation of the Sûdân.

The temple as it stands is substantially the work of Thothmes III., who seems to have rebuilt it on the site whereon Usertsen III. established his temple, and to have dedicated it to this king, who seems to have been worshipped in it conjointly with the ancient Sûdân god called *Ṭeṭun.* Certainly on the west wall we see Thothmes III. and his *sem* priest making offerings to Usertsen, who in the form of Osiris is seated under a canopy in a sacred boat. The temple built by Thothmes III. was not finished, and the northern end of it is formed of stones of different sizes, roughly cut and laid. We found nothing inside the temple except a headless statue of Osiris, about 3 feet high, which was lying half-buried in the sand at the west end. We cleared away the sand, and carried this statue to Kharṭûm, where it may now be seen in the Government Museum. Although, in my opinion, the statue does not belong to the period either of the founding or rebuilding of the temple, yet it was high time to remove this venerable object to a place of safety, and it is far better that it should be preserved in the capital of the Sûdân than in some continental Mûseum. In taking the statue of Osiris away from the temple we were not tearing the god from his own shrine, but from that of Ṭeṭûn, an old, indigenous god of the country, which the votaries of Osiris, during a late period of his cult, made the Egyptian god usurp. The walls of the temple rest upon the living rock, and are formed of slabs of sandstone, some of which are nearly 10 feet long, and 3 feet thick. Near the temple, a little to the north, were lying some capitals of pillars, which suggest that a temple of a later period once stood here.

On the walls inside the temple of Semna are cut the following names:—

B. Hanbury.
G. Waddington.
F. Hetley.
J. Paget.
J. G[ardner] Wilkinson.
J. S. Wiggett. April 21st. 52.
A. Burlingham. 1832(?).
Holroyd. 1835(?).
Melly B.

On the west wall, outside are cut the following names:—

Fatme.
Lafargue. 1853.
P. Candy. 1861.
P. C. Letorzec. 1820.
G. S. Eval. 1820.
E. F. A. 1848.
Paoletti. 1884.
I. W. Leigh. 1861.

From the top of the hill it is easy to see that the walls which surrounded the temple enclosure also protected the buildings of a large camp or garrison. These ruins are, as Burckhardt says,[1] certainly of high antiquity. They cover the top of the hill which overhangs the river bank, and are enclosed by a double wall, or rather by a wall within a parapet; the former is of brick, from 8 feet to 12 feet thick, and, wherever it is entire, is upwards of 30 feet in height. The parapet is constructed of stone, 20 feet in breadth, with sides sloping towards the declivity of the hill; the stones of the parapet are thrown irregularly upon each other, without cement, but those which form the sloping side are either cut, or dexterously arranged, so as to present a perfectly smooth surface, which, at the period when the work was taken care of, must have rendered it impossible for any one to climb over it.

[1] *Travels*, p. 82.

VIEW OF THE CATARACT AT SEMNA AND KUMMA.

[From a photograph by J. W. Crawfoot Esq.

CATARACT OF SEMNA

The famous Cataract of Semna is situated a little to the south of the temple, and is a most picturesque feature of the landscape. The barrier itself is formed of black basalt, in which at intervals are layers of quartz, varying in thickness from 1 to 5 inches. The main channel of the Nile through this is about 150 yards wide. Through this, even at low Nile, the river rushes with great rapidity and force, and the roar of its waters can be heard on a windless day at a considerable distance. The Inspector and I found it necessary to visit the ruins of Kumma, which stand on the high rock on the east side of the Cataract, and we inquired of the natives what means they employed in crossing the river. We learned that they had neither boat nor raft, and that when they were compelled to cross the Nile they usually went some distance either to the north or south of the Cataract, and then swam across it in the narrowest part they could find. They went on to say that one of their young men knew how to make a *tôf*, or raft, and that he should take us across. One afternoon we were told that the *tôf* was ready, and we went down to the river where it lay. It was made of four large bundles of reeds, about 12 feet long, tied together with ropes made of palm fibre, and was about 4 feet wide; on these we placed an *anḳarîb*, and then took our places upon it. The raftsman sat on one end of it, with a flat piece of wood, which he used both as an oar and a steering pole, in his hand, but the real motive power was supplied by four men, who, having tied their garments in bundles and placed them on their heads, stepped into the water, and began to swim, pressing the raft forward with their breasts. The wind, fortunately, was in our favour, and we passed over to Kumma in about half-an-hour. The shêkh and several men of the village met us, and escorted us through the defiles which led to the top of the rock. There were scores of hieroglyphic *graffiti* on the rocks [1] and boulders, and we noticed in several places layers of beautifully white quartz from 3 inches to 6 inches thick. The *graffiti* were only short sepulchral inscriptions, roughly hammered on the rock, to commemorate ancient Egyptian officials who must have died at the Cataract, or in its neighbourhood.

The village of Kumma is built inside the temple and its

[1] A selection of these will be found in Lepsius, *Denkmäler*, Abth. ii., Bl. 139.

precincts. Its inhabitants are not numerous, and they appear to lead miserable lives; on the patches of mud near the river they grow small crops of dhurra, but how they manage to find money to buy clothes and other necessaries is a mystery, unless it be that they obtain remittances from their relatives in Egypt. A native led us through a few huts and we found ourselves standing before a solidly built stone wall, on which appeared the cartouches of Thothmes II., Thothmes III., and Ȧmen-ḥetep III. Crawling through some low doors we entered chamber after chamber of an XVIIIth Dynasty temple of considerable size, but it was quite impossible to realize exactly what its plan was, because the floor of every chamber was covered to the depth of several feet with sand and stones, and with the rubbish which several generations of modern natives have left behind them. All the plans hitherto published are incomplete, and nothing final can be arrived at until the Sûdân Government has expropriated the natives and cleared out the whole site. It is to be hoped that Sir Reginald Wingate will cause this important work to be taken in hand at an early date, and have the best reliefs removed to Kharṭûm, for if the walls be uncovered, and be exposed to the full force of the wind and the heat of the sun, both the colours and the reliefs themselves will soon disappear. The situation of the temple is a fine one, and whether as a look-out station or a fort could not be improved upon; it stands, like all the temples of its class, in one corner of an enclosure which is about two hundred feet square, and was well protected by very strong walls on all sides. The garrisons of Kumma and Semna, which are exactly opposite each other, were intended to protect the Cataract, and to prevent the passage down the river of tribes from the south.

The view from Kumma is very fine, and the eye is able to wander over an enormous tract of country to the south, but the terrible deserts which seem to thrust themselves into the Nile itself must always strike awe into the hearts of the most casual spectator. The contrast between the bright green of the patches of cultivation and the few palms in the villages on the south, and the brilliant yellow of the sand, which stretches for miles in all directions, is very striking. The natives told us that in a hill about two miles distant there were quarries, probably those from which the sandstone used in building the temples of Semna and Kumma was taken, but we had not time to visit them. At no great distance from Kumma, to the south, there are some mud-brick buildings which are thought to be those of a Coptic church and monastery; these also we could not visit.

We returned to the river, and, having said farewell to the shêkh, took our places on the raft, which we noticed was somewhat water-logged. When we pushed off we found that the wind which had helped us to cross to Kumma was now against us, and in spite of all the efforts of the men who were swimming behind the raft and pushing it on, our progress across the river was slow. The raftman persisted in working his paddle on the wrong side of the raft, and this helped the current to carry us down stream some distance. One of the swimmers became numbed with cold, and his clinging to the raft kept one end under water, and allowed the little waves to pass freely all over it. Our *anḳarîb* was soon awash, but we reached the west bank again in about an hour, and were glad to step on to the rocks and walk back to the temple of Semna. On our way we noticed some Egyptian tombs hewn in the rock, and near the top of a bold bluff we saw an inscription in large hieroglyphics, which commemorated an official called Ȧmeni: this name suggests that it was cut under the XIIth Dynasty, when probably more than one Ȧmeni was associated with the Egyptian occupation of the Sûdân.

The examination which we made of the temple enclosure at Semna convinced the Inspector and myself that only excavations carried out on a very large scale could reveal the general history of the fortress, and we therefore determined to confine our investigations to the buildings in the immediate neighbourhood of the temple of Thothmes III. Directly opposite to the main door of that temple is a large mud-brick building, which up to the time of our visit had always been declared to be the ruin of a Coptic Church. Its walls are about 20 feet high, and inside it was filled with mud, sand, &c., to a depth of about 12 feet. Beyond the southern end of this building we saw several capitals of sandstone pillars lying about, and some very large stones, and we made some small experimental diggings with a view to finding out if they belonged to some temple which had been demolished. Digging northwards we found the bases of several columns, and when we arrived at what appeared to be the foundations of the end wall of the temple, we concluded that there was nothing more to be discovered. Still there remained the large, mud-brick building already mentioned to be investigated, and we turned on all the men to dig.

After a few hours' work the men came upon the end of a stone slab, which when cleared turned out to be the lintel of a doorway. It is 7 feet 1 inch in length, 2 feet 3½ inches in width, and about 10 inches thick. On the upper part of it is sculptured a disk with wings and pendent uraei, which is described by the accompanying hieroglyphics as "the great god of Beḥuṭet," i.e. Horus of Beḥuṭet. So soon as the mud was washed off the face of the slab, we saw from the line of hieroglyphics below the winged disk that the stone belonged to a building, presumably a temple, which had been dedicated to Ȧmen-Rā by Taharq, or Tirhâḳâh, who flourished in the second quarter of the seventh century before Christ, and was the second Sûdâni conqueror of Egypt. This king's cartouche appeared twice on the slab, prefixed by the ancient Pharaonic title , meaning "King of the South and North."

The digging continued, and next the men struck the jambs ot the doorway on which the slab had rested. These were formed of well cut stones, which were carefully laid and were ornamented with figures in hollow relief. It became evident from the course of the thick mud walls in which this stone doorway was set that the chamber we were clearing out was a small one, and that there must have been a space all round it, between it and the main walls of the building wherein it stood. The chamber had clearly been filled with mud up to the roof, which had served as the floor of a chamber of a later period. The mud came away easily from the walls and the roof, and revealed the fact that the interior had once been whitewashed, and that the roof was vaulted.

The digging was continued northwards, and at a depth of about 6 feet the picks began to strike against a stone, which was flat and square. Having cleared away the mud surrounding the

VIEW OF THE TEMPLE OF TIRHAKAH AT SEMNA, SHOWING THE PILLAR AND A PORTION OF THE VAULTED ROOF.

[From a photograph by J. W. Crowfoot, Esq.

stone we saw that it rested on a sort of square pillar, and when the mud was removed down to its base we saw that the object was an altar, similar in shape to those represented in the reliefs on the walls of the pyramid chapels at Meroë. This altar is about 4 feet high, 2 feet 7½ inches square at the top, and its sides are slightly concave; the upper slab is 3¼ inches thick. The altar has, during the centuries which have passed since it was set up, tilted a little forwards. An examination of the sides brought to light traces of hieroglyphics, and when we had scrubbed the front with water the following inscription appeared :—

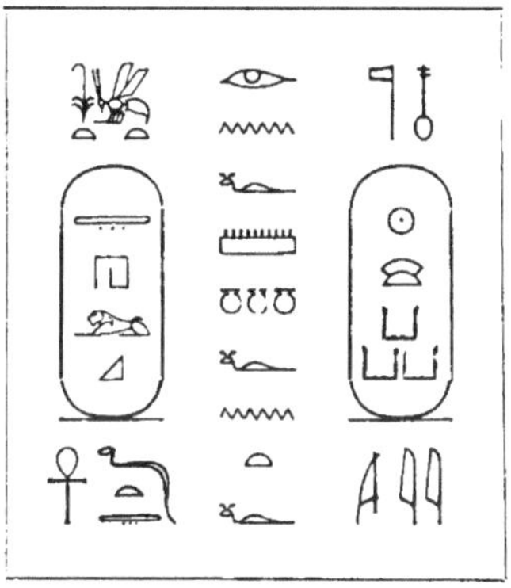

This inscription reads :—"Taharq (Tirhâḳâh), King of the South and North, the ever-living, hath made his monument to his father, the good-doing god Khā-kau-Rā, [by whom he is] beloved." In other words, Tirhâḳâh records the fact that he made the temple, the sanctuary of which we were then excavating, and that he dedicated it to Usertsen III., whom he places among the gods, and regards as his father by whom he is beloved. This "find" is an important one, for it tells us not only that Tirhâḳâh built a temple at Semna, but that he regarded Usertsen III., the first Egyptian king who occupied the Sûdân effectively, as a divine ancestor. He passes over Thothmes III. and the other great kings of the XVIIIth Dynasty, who built temples at many places in the Sûdân, and chooses to honour the first great Egyptian conqueror of his native land. The form of the inscription of Tirhâḳâh given above is evidently copied from the inscriptions of Thothmes III., wherein this king brackets himself with Usertsen

III. Thus on the walls inside the temple of Thothmes III. we find the following :—

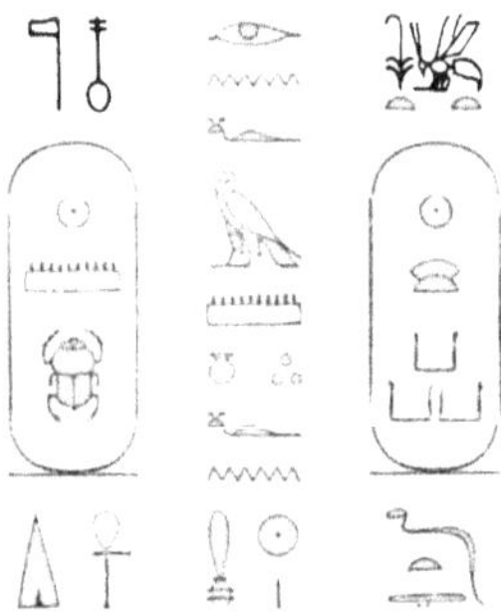

"The good-doing god, Men-kheper-Rā (Thothmes III.), hath made his building to [his father] the King of the South and the North, Khā-kau-Rā (Usertsen III.)." The other words "giver of

STATUE (SIDE VIEW) OF KING KHU-TAUI-RĀ AND ALTARS FOUND IN THE TEMPLE OF TIRHÂḲÂH AT SEMNA.

life, like Rā, for ever," are so placed that they may be made to refer to either one king or the other, or both. Apart from the historical importance of the inscription, the altar has a special value of its own archæologically, for it is the only altar *in situ* known to me in the Sûdân. It should be removed to Kharṭûm.

We continued our diggings in the sanctuary, and to the left of the altar was found a rectangular stone, 3 feet 3 inches high, $15\frac{3}{4}$ inches wide, and from $12\frac{1}{4}$ inches to $13\frac{1}{4}$ inches thick. It stands to the left of the altar as one looks in through the doorway, but is not set square with it. It was placed in position by what masons call a "plug and feathers," and remains of the pieces of wood ("feathers") were in the hole for the plug when it was cleared. Whilst we were removing the mud between the altar and the wall on the right hand side a group of objects of considerable importance was brought to light. The first object was a headless, limestone seated statue of a king, 8 inches high, who is represented as wearing a collar of three rows of beads and pendants, and holding a whip, , in his right hand, and a sceptre in his left. On the side of the throne are inscribed three rows of hieroglyphics, which read:—

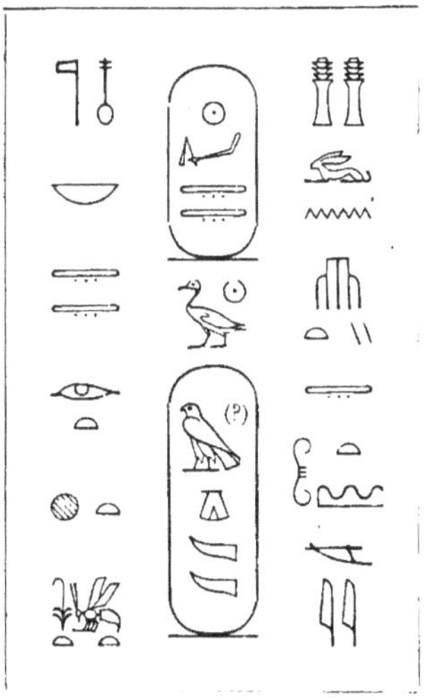

I.e., "The good-doing god, the lord of the two lands, the maker of "things, the King of the South and North, Khu-taui-Rā, the son of "Rā, Ḥeru-nest(?)-aṭebui (?), of ṬEṬUN, the governor (literally, at "the head) of Ta-Kenset, beloved." The reading of the name of this king is doubtful, but about that of his prenomen there is no doubt whatever. Its form suggests that king Khu-taui-Rā reigned soon after the end of the XIIth Dynasty, and in the Tablet of Karnak there is mentioned a king with this prenomen who must have been one the kings of the XIIIth Dynasty. Whether the Khu-taui-Rā, of whom we have a statue, is the same as the king with this prenomen of the Tablet of Karnak cannot be said definitively, but the probability that he was almost amounts to certainty. Both Brugsch and Wiedemann make Khu-taui-Rā the first king of the XIIIth Dynasty; the former said that his name was Sebek-ḥetep, but this is unlikely, as the latter has shown.[1] Apart from these considerations the work of the statue is in the style of that which we meet with under the XIIth Dynasty, about B.C. 2300-2000. The inscription given above is remarkable for the fact that it mentions the great Sûdân god Ṭeṭun, the governor of Ta-Kenset, or Nubia; this is one of the earliest references we have to this god in the Middle Empire, and it suggests that Khu-taui-Rā was a man of Sûdâni or Nubian origin, of whom a title rather than the name may be given in the second cartouche. In front of the king's statue was found also a curious little altar, of which an illustration is given on page 484; it is 12½ inches high, and 5½ inches square, and belongs to a class which is rare in Egypt. Near this was a brown sandstone model of a table of offerings, about 8 inches long, and 7 inches wide in the broadest part; on it were traces of figures of offerings cut in outline. We also found two pieces of a brown sandstone figure of a priest, with traces of hieroglyphics down the front; the work was in the style of that of the XIIth Dynasty.

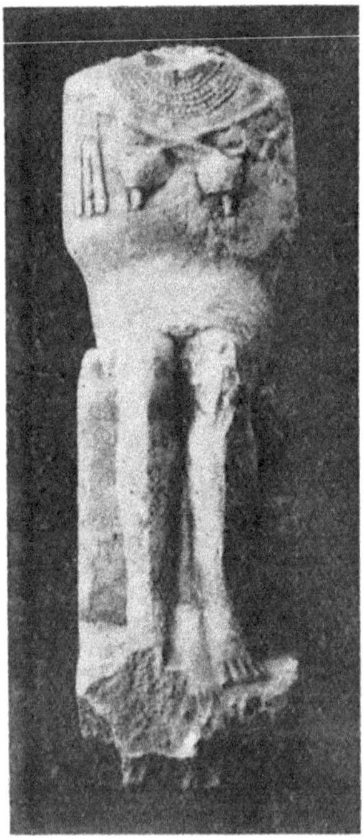

STATUE OF KHU-TAUI-RĀ (FRONT VIEW) FOUND AT SEMNA.

During the clearance of the remainder of the sanctuary the men came upon pieces of alabastra and fragments of blue faïence

[1] See my *History of Egypt*, vol. iii., pp. 84 and 85.

of the XVIIIth Dynasty, several pieces of pottery, and a terra-cotta lamp which appeared to belong to the Coptic Period. All these objects we took away, and they are now in the Museum at Kharṭûm. The discovery of small objects belonging to the XIIth or XIIIth Dynasty in the sanctuary of the temple of Tirhâḳâh, a king of the XXVth Dynasty, who did not reign until some fifteen hundred years after Khu-taui-Rā, and in such positions, is to me inexplicable. Yet such is the case. The presence of the Coptic lamp is easy to explain. The room above the filled-in sanctuary of Tirhâḳâh was used as a Coptic church, as we have already said. The lamp dropped, or was put on the mud floor, and was then forgotten, and little by little, with the help of some rain, it worked its way downwards until it reached the place where we found it. A somewhat similar case happened at the mound of Kuyunjik, wherein the palaces of Sennacherib and Ashur-bani-pal were buried. In February, 1889, we found at a depth of 30 feet from the surface a silver Sassanian bracelet, and a piece of a terra-cotta tablet inscribed in cuneiform side by side. The bracelet cannot be older than the fourth century after Christ, whilst the fragment of the tablet belongs to the reign of Ashur-bani-pal, B.C. 681-668!

Having cleared out the sanctuary of Tirhâḳâh's temple, and various other portions of the ruins, it became possible to make out the general plan of the building. The temple was rectangular, and was entered by one door only, which is on the south side. It consisted of a court with six sandstone columns, and a hall, in the centre of which was the sanctuary containing the altar. The whole building was about 75 feet long, and 41 feet wide. Mr. J. W. Crowfoot, Inspector of Education, carefully measured every part of it, and the excellent plan which is here reproduced I owe to his kindness. Like the temple of Thothmes III., which stands to the north of it, Tirhâḳâh's temple is oriented to the south. The stone pillars in its court were probably brought from the temple which stood a little to the north of that of Thothmes III., of the pillars of which we saw some capitals lying about. The general use of mud brick in Tirhâḳâh's temple indicates that the quarries in the hill on the opposite bank at Kumma were not being worked extensively under his reign. The funds at our disposal did not permit a general excavation of the site, but it is hoped that such a work may be undertaken, for there is always a possibility that a stele inscribed with a historical text of the builder may lie hidden among the ruins. With the clearing of Tirhâkâh's sanctuary we brought our work at Semna to an end. We removed the lintel of the door of the sanctuary and other inscribed blocks to the space before the temple of Thothmes III., and the Inspector made arrangements to have them taken to Ḥalfa later on in the year. From Ḥalfa they were to be transported to Kharṭûm by railway, and by this time they are probably housed in the Museum there.

From Semna we rode to the nearest point where the river was navigable, and then crossed over to the Island of Gazîrat al-Malik. On the following morning we went up the hill with our workmen to examine the ruins of buildings which we had been told about, and we found much to interest us. Having reached the highest point we saw that it had once formed the site of a large fortress, the walls of which were enormously thick and strong, although only made of mud bricks. Portions of the walls were still standing, and they had much in common with the massive mud-brick walls which we had seen at Semna. In the north-east corner of the enclosure were the remains of a small, solidly-built stone temple of the XVIIIth Dynasty, about 24½ feet long and 11½ feet wide. It is oriented to the east; the main doorway is in the east side, but there is also a smaller doorway at the eastern end of the north wall. The west end of the little temple is built into the living rock, as is also a portion of the north side. The blocks of stone are well cut, and well put together. The walls inside were ornamented with large figures of the king making offerings to the local gods, &c., but of these only the feet remained; the figures were painted in bright colours on a white, lime-washed ground. The inside of the temple was filled with bright yellow sand, and as this was being cleared out a good, black granite statue of the "Royal son Tcha-àb"[1] was found. On the back of the figure are three lines of inscription which contain a prayer to "Àmen-Rā, the lord of the thrones of the two lands," and a dedication of it

[1] 

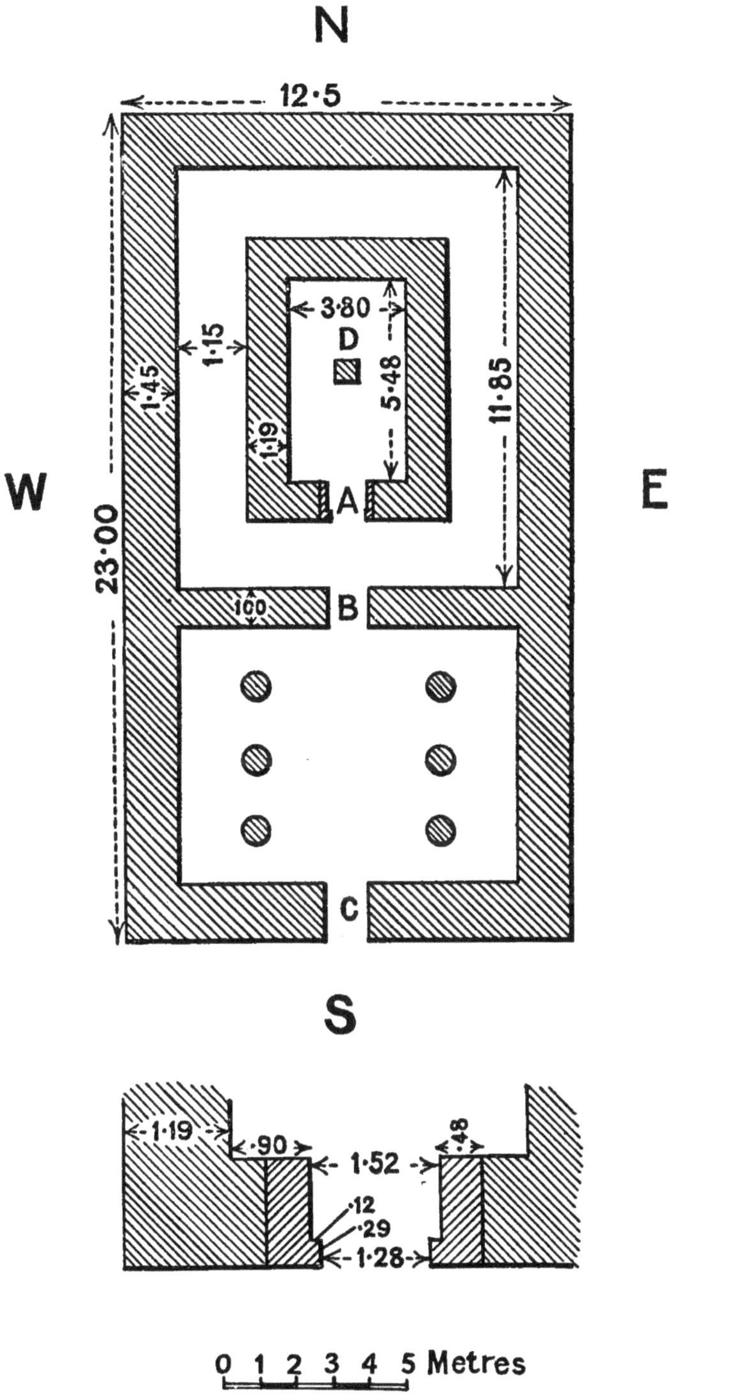

PLAN OF THE TEMPLE OF TIRHÂḲÂH AT SEMNA, DRAWN BY J. W. CROWFOOT, ESQ.

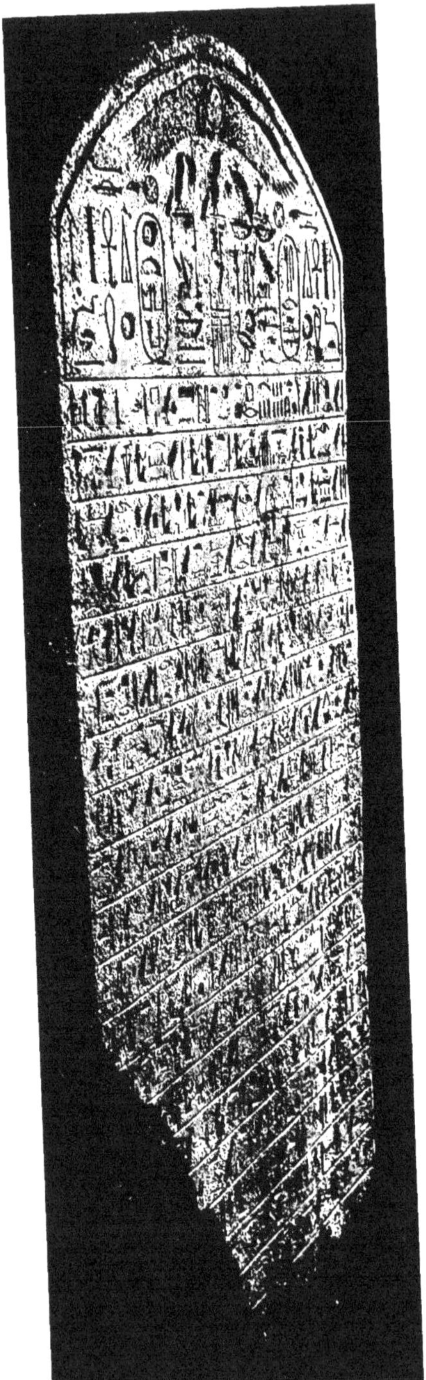

STELE OF KING USERTSEN III., DATED IN THE SIXTEENTH YEAR OF HIS REIGN.

[Found on the Island of Gazirat al Malik.

to this god, whose name is coupled with that of Usertsen III.,
, the first Egyptian conqueror of the Sûdân. The figure, I believe, dates from the period of the XVIIIth Dynasty.

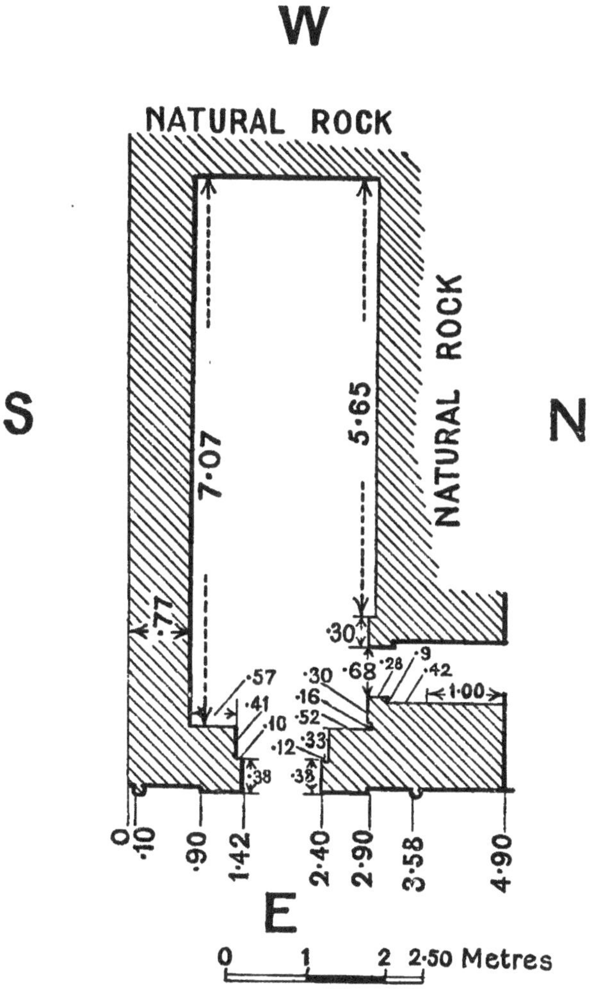

PLAN OF THE TEMPLE OF GAZÎRAT AL-MALIK, DRAWN BY J. W. CROWFOOT, ESQ.

On a mound in front of the temple we saw lying a large stone stele, with a rounded top, inscribed with twenty-two lines of hieroglyphics, and a glance showed that it bore on the surface of the rounded portion the names and titles of Usertsen III., with symbols of sovereignty and dominion. This stele, a photographic illustration of which is annexed, is dated in the sixteenth year of the king's reign, and the text sets forth the fact that he conquered the country and extended the boundary of Egypt on the south more than any of his fathers, in language which must have cut to the quick any native who understood its contents. As a rendering of the inscription will be given in the section of this book dealing with the invasion and conquest of the Sûdân by Usertsen III., nothing further need be said about it here. The stele had, it seems, once stood in or near the temple, and the position in which we found it suggests that it had been dragged from its place by the people who wrecked the temple, and who wished to cast it down the precipitous east face of the hill into the river which runs at its foot. They seem to have found the task too difficult, and to have abandoned it. Great force must have been employed in removing the stele, for the left hand bottom corner was broken away; we searched carefully for the missing piece, but could not find it. Whilst I was copying the inscription the Inspector examined the east face of the hill to see if there were any other monuments lying on it, and when he came to the mass of rocks and boulders near the river he found a black granite headless statue of Usertsen III., about 3½ feet high, and a statue of Osiris, of about the same height. It seems clear that these had been dragged from their places in the temple, and thrown into the river by those who overthrew the stele and wished to treat it in the same manner.

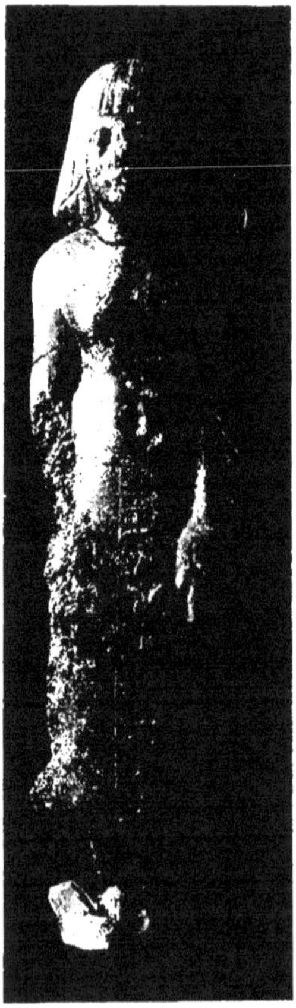

GRANITE STATUE OF PRINCE TCHA-ÂB FOUND ON THE ISLAND OF GAZÎRAT AL-MALIK.

Having carefully gone over the site of the old fortress, and finding no other remains similar to those described above, we decided to remove the stele and take it by boat to Sarras, whence we should be able to transport it by rail to Kharṭûm. To have left the monument where it was would have been a mistake, for though it was heavy, weighing about one ton, a dozen determined men could have turned it over and over until its own weight took it down the hill, in which case it would certainly have been broken to pieces, and fanatical people are to be found in the Sûdân, even under British rule. We therefore brought up our planks and rope, and, having lashed timbers under it, we turned on all the men to pull it over the crest of the hill, and down the west side, and along the plain to the high river bank. In this way we spent the whole of a long afternoon, but by sunset the stele was down on the river bank, through which, having cut a gap, we lowered it by ropes on to the soft gray sand near the water's edge. The men worked splendidly, and the Inspector increased their wages for the day. Our next difficulty was to find a boat in which to carry it to Ṣarras, for the owner of the solitary boat in the place strongly objected to allow it to be used for this purpose. Under the influence of a promise of liberal pay and a few emphatic remarks by both of us, he withdrew his opposition, and we built a staging of railway sleepers across his boat and dragged the stele on to it. We next took steps to move the statues of Osiris and Usertsen III. out of the reach of the waters of the inundation, and then our work on the Island of Gazîrat al-Malik was ended. We questioned the natives carefully with the view of finding out if there were any other antiquities on the Island, but we had exhausted its resources in this respect. A native said there was "writing" on a rock at its southern end, but when we went to the place we only found a *graffito* hammered on the stone by an official, who was either stationed on the Island or landed there under the XVIIIth Dynasty.

Before we left the Island of Gazîrat al-Malik the Inspector paid the inhabitants for the damage which we had done to the crops on the river bank by dragging the stele over them, and for the use of the boat, and for every service the men had rendered, and we made presents to the shêkh and the men and women who had served us personally whilst we were there. Some of them asked for medicines, which we were able to give, and we found that nearly all of them suffered from fever. That is no matter of surprise, for they lack sufficient covering at night and food. The cold both on the Island and at Semna was intense, and the natives must have felt the inconvenience of it at least as much as we did. When we saw their huts and the places where they slept we understood why they were up and about long before dawn, and why they sat outside and waited for the sunrise. Their life is indeed a hard one. They cultivate a little dhurra and *dokn* (millet), and they rear a few cows, sheep, and goats, but as they only kill a beast every now and then, fresh meat is a great rarity. The women rub down the grain and extract the flour, which they make into large "wafer" cakes and cook on hot stones, and the milk which the goats give forms an important contribution to their food. If they can obtain dates they consider themselves fortunate. The droppings from the animals are carefully collected and used as fuel. The animals live on dry dhurra stalks, the twigs and shoots of the trees on the banks, and anything they can pick up. There are on the Island a few dogs which act as scavengers. Matches, salt, and a little sugar are obtained at intervals from Ḥalfa, but we saw neither tea nor coffee on the Island. But as the wants of the people are few, and as they love their independence, they are content to endure hardship, and hunger when necessary.

On our way down the river from Gazîrat al-Malik we passed an island which is formed wholly of rocks, or more correctly, of one rock from which rise several rugged peaks; on one end is a ruin which was formerly occupied by a Muḥammadan saint, and on the other is a fortress built of mud bricks.[1] The rock which supports the latter has a great crack running down it from the top to the bottom. Lower down, on the west bank, perched high up on the rocks, we saw the ruins of another fortress, and we landed and visited them. The main entrance was on the south side, and to reach this we had to climb up a steep slope covered with yellow sand. The gate, even in its ruined state, is a massive piece of work, and when the walls which guard the approach to it were manned, the entrance to it by a hostile force must have been

[1] This is, probably, the "brick castle called Esest," mentioned by Burckhardt (*Travels*, p. 86).

impossible. We passed through the gateway and up a second slope, and then found ourselves on a large, flat, open, space, whereon rows of barracks must have stood. This is surrounded by mighty walls made of crude brick, portions of which, in an excellent state of preservation, still remain. We searched carefully everywhere, but could find no trace of the existence of Egyptian antiquities, and from this fact and the general plan of the gate and its approaches, which seemed to me to resemble the fortifications of mediaeval castles in Eastern Europe and Asia Minor, I came to the conclusion that this fortress was built about three hundred years ago. From the river side, before the days of modern artillery, it was impregnable, but there was one part of it, on the land side, which, it seemed to me, might be captured without great difficulty by a large force. So far as we could see there was no well in this castle. The general appearance of the stronghold suggested the possibility that it had been built and held by foreign troops, say the Turkish soldiers of Sultân Selim in the first quarter of the sixteenth century, who swept down from its heights and seized whatever they could find on the river banks, or plundered passing caravans in the Western Desert. The agricultural produce of the country round about is little now, and it never can have been great, and it is therefore clear that the large garrison stationed here must have drawn upon other resources for its means of subsistence. This fortress is very interesting, and every one who travels in that portion of the Nile Valley should certainly visit it.

The time passed so quickly in exploring the fortress that when we came back to our boat the day was turning to sunset; we therefore hurried away from the bank, and the crew rowed with a will. We were all anxious to reach Sarras before nightfall, for there are many rocks in the channels, and navigation in the dark is difficult. We made good progress, and the crew began to sing and to invoke the aid of the Prophet to second their efforts. Every now and then they also called upon one Îsa to help them. Now Îsa is the Arabic form of the name "Jesus," and some travellers who have heard the Nubian boatmen calling upon Îsa have thought that they were invoking Jesus of Nazareth, and have declared that the knowledge of His Name must have come down to the modern inhabitants of the country from the Copts, who were settled on the islands in the Cataracts. Subsequent inquiry, however, showed me that it is not Îsa "the Prophet" upon whom the watermen call, but Îsa the Robber, who was the terror of the Northern Sûdân in the early part of the nineteenth century. This Îsa, as we know from Hoskins (*Travels*, p. 275), was a shêkh of the Kararîsh tribe, who was driven into open revolt by the exorbitant demands made upon him by the Turkish governor of the district. He gathered together a few followers, and then proceeded to attack the caravans in the desert between Korosko and Abû Ḥamed, and to plunder them without mercy. He raided the cattle which were sent from Dâr Fûr to Cairo, and supplied himself with ammunition and arms from the Government convoys to the south. Every Government caravan was regarded by Îsa as fair game, and scores of hands were ready all over the country to help him to seize the property of the hated Turk; many robberies with violence of which he was wholly innocent were laid at his door. For five years he led the life of a robber-chief with great success, but the Government succeeded in bribing the 'Abâbdah shêkhs to drive him out of the Korosko desert, and at length he took refuge in a valley near Kumma, of which we have already spoken. Whilst hiding here one day he was betrayed by a friend into the hands of a party of soldiers, who were led to the rock where he was, and then simply fired a volley into him whilst he was asleep. His daughter An-nûr, who generally accompanied her father on his marauding expeditions, and who was a brave woman, married the only member of the band who did not run away when her father was shot. The life and deeds of Îsa have appealed for some generations to the romantic side of the Nubian character, especially as he resisted for five years with brilliant success the tyranny of the corrupt Turkish Pâshâ, under whose rule it was his misfortune to come.

We reached Sarras about sunset, and shortly after the boat bearing the stele of Usertsen III. and the other antiquities arrived safely. The Inspector made arrangements with our overseer Shêkh Shellabi to unload the boats, and to drag the antiquities up the steep bank to the railway, and to load them on a truck, and we were fortunate enough to be able to proceed by train to Ḥalfa the same night. Three days later Shêkh Shellabi arrived with his men and the antiquities, and we made ready to go to the Pyramids of Meroë, where we intended to clear up certain work which I had been obliged to leave unfinished in 1903. We sent one of our men who had been taken very ill with fever at Gazîrat al-Malik to the Military Hospital, where under the care of the British Director he received every attention; the same kind-hearted surgeon treated another man—who, in helping to move a big stone, had torn a hole in the side of his leg—with success and healed him. As we had grave doubts about the possibility of finding labour near the Pyramids of Meroë, the Inspector made arrangements to take on by train the best of the men who had been with us from Ṣulb to Sarras, and when we had done with them to draft them on to the railway between Atbara and the Red Sea, which was then in course of construction. The Inspector paid their railway fare, and their wages up to date, so that they might have means wherewith to obtain provisions sufficient for their needs during their stay with us. Major Midwinter, the Commandant, Mr. C. G. Hodgson, Locomotive Superintendent, and the civilian railway officials, the Hon. H. G. G. Pelham and Mr. W. H. Horton, gave us most friendly assistance, and on the third day after our return to Ḥalfa we left by the *train de luxe* for Shendî, which we reached the next evening. Here I enjoyed the hospitality for which the Railway Mess is famous throughout the Sûdân.

Having accomplished the object for which we had visited Shendi on the following morning, we left by the North Express the same evening, and about 10 p.m. arrived at Kabûshîa, the station nearest the Pyramids. About 2 p.m. the next day Shêkh Shellabi and the workmen arrived in the truck with the antiquities, and an hour later we were on our way to the Pyramids, which are about five miles distant to the north-east. By sunset our tents were pitched, and the camels had brought loads of water, and the workmen had lighted fires and were cooking their evening meals. There was a marked difference between the temperature of Semna and that of Meroë, for the air was now soft, and it was sufficiently warm to make sitting outside the tent in the evening pleasant.

The following morning the Inspector and I went over the ground and marked the work which the men were to do. We found that the pits which had been made in 1903 had been covered over with railway sleepers, and that the trenches had been provided with barriers to prevent the unwary traveller from falling into them. The roads and paths which we had made in 1903 had been widened and improved, and visitors could walk up to most of the chapels and examine the reliefs in comfort. These works had been carried out by the orders of Sir Reginald Wingate, who has done everything possible to make the Pyramids easily accessible to the tourist. As the result of our examination we decided to clear out the chapels which we had not time to attend to in 1903, and also to dig down to floor level in the fore-court and chapel of the Pyramid of the great queen (No. 11), whose funeral procession is illustrated in such wonderful detail in the reliefs sculptured on the north and south walls of her chapel. We were unable to carry on any more work in the passages under the Pyramids, for the men were afraid, and flatly refused to dig anywhere underground. It has already been said that the work of clearing out the queen's chapel was of a hazardous nature, because there was always the danger that the lower part of the east face of the Pyramid might collapse as soon as the mass of stones below it was disturbed, and bring down with it many tons of broken stones and sand which formed the core of the Pyramid, and which were heaped above and behind it. We therefore began to remove from the upper part of this ruined Pyramid every stone which was likely to slide down, and when a sufficient angle of rest had been given to the mass, we devoted our energies to digging out the chapel and fore-court. Meanwhile another party of men was engaged in clearing out chapels at the southern end of the crescent-shaped hill whereon the Pyramids stand.

Whilst these works were in progress their Royal Highnesses, the Duke and Duchess of Connaught, and the Princesses Margaret and Patricia, attended by Miss Pelly, Lord Edward Cecil, and Brigadier-General Sir John Grenfell Maxwell, visited the Pyramids and inspected the diggings. Their Royal Highnesses took keen interest in all they saw, and were graciously pleased to express their approval of the work. Their enthusiasm concerning everything relating to the ancient history of the Sûdân urged them to make this visit at much personal inconvenience and discomfort, for they arrived at the Pyramids so early as 8 a.m.; the day was exceptionally hot for the time of the year, and the spot at which their special train was stopped on the railway was nearly three miles from the Pyramids. When on the hill they spared themselves no fatigue, for they went from the southern to the northern end of it, and examined with great

THE QUEEN OF MEROË, WHO BUILT PYRAMID NO. 11, MAKING OFFERINGS.
[From a photograph by Lieut P Lord, R E

thoroughness the reliefs in all the principal chapels and several of the trenches, on their way.

After digging a few days, the men drew near the floor level of the chapel, and there they came upon a large stone slab, which appeared to have fallen face downwards. This was carefully cleared and raised, and we saw that the front of it was sculptured in high relief with figures of the triad Osiris, Isis, and Nephthys, figures making offerings, altar vessels, flowers, &c. This very important object had been wrenched from its position against the west wall of the chapel, and thrown down, and in its fall, several pieces had broken off the edges. An attempt appears to have been made to destroy it by fire, for the front was embedded in a layer of black, greasy soot, which remained like a mould of the figures in the sand below. In the sand near the slab a stone figure of a hawk was discovered. There is no niche in the west wall of the chapel in which it could have stood, and it must therefore have rested upon a small stone shelf above the figures of the Osirian triad. The finding of these objects was quite unexpected, for Lepsius could not have made the excellent drawings of the reliefs on the north and south walls without clearing out the sand and stones from the chapel. How his men came to overlook these objects is inexplicable, but it was fortunate for us that they did.

The next question to be considered was the preservation of the reliefs on the north and south walls. In 1903 I urged Sir Reginald Wingate to remove the whole chapel to Kharṭûm and to rebuild it in some sheltered spot in the gardens of the Palace. I did this, first, because the reliefs are the finest monuments of the kind which exist on the Island of Meroë, and illustrate in a remarkable manner the high pitch of perfection to which the Meroïtic sculptors attained in the early centuries of the Christian era. The fundamental design in the reliefs is, of course, Egyptian, but the details of its treatment are so essentially Meroïtic, that these sculptures form a class of monuments which stands by itself, and represents a most instructive phase of funerary art. Secondly, it needed a very brief examination to see that the reliefs had suffered a good deal from weathering and from abrasions, caused by the sand and stones which had fallen into the chapel from the core of the Pyramid since 1844, when Lepsius had drawings of them made. The preservation of these valuable reliefs could be effected in three ways:—1. By filling up the chapel to the top of the walls with sand, but if this were done they would be seen and enjoyed by no one. 2. By erecting a building over the chapel with glass sides and a roof sufficiently strong to keep out the wind, drift-sand, and falling stones. The objection to this proposition was a serious one, namely, the cost of the work, and the necessity of keeping a guardian always on the spot. 3. By removing the reliefs to some well-sheltered spot or museum. Sir

Reginald was of opinion that it would be best to remove the chapel to Kharṭûm, and subsequently sent an official to report on the cost of the project, but his report was unfavourable, and I under-

THE WEST WALL OF THE CHAPEL OF PYRAMID NO. 11, SHOWING WHERE THE TRIAD OF FIGURES HAD STOOD.

[From a photograph by J W. Crowfoot, Esq.

stand that he declared the removal of the chapel to be an impossibility.

A few days after our arrival at the Pyramids the Inspector

received an intimation that Sir Reginald Wingate was about to visit Kasala on a tour of inspection, and that he would have his train stopped at the point on the line nearest the Pyramids, and that he wished us to come and report to him concerning the work we had done. He was to arrive about six o'clock in the morning, and at dawn on the day he was expected we walked across the desert to the railway, and the special train made its appearance soon after we reached the line. Sir Reginald approved of the work which had been done at Ṣûlb and Semna, and of the antiquities which we had collected for the Kharṭûm Museum, and then discussed at length the plans for the preservation of the reliefs in the queen's chapel. In the course of our talk he asked, "What "examples of funerary sculptures from the Island of Meroë have "you in the British Museum?" and I told him that we had none, for all the stone altars and other objects which had formerly existed at Wad Bâ Nagaa and Gebel Barkal, as well as several reliefs from the chapels which we had cleared out, had been taken to Berlin by Lepsius in 1844. To this he replied that he would present to the Trustees of the British Museum all the reliefs from the south wall of the queen's chapel, whilst those from the north wall should go to Kharṭûm, where he would have them built up in the new Museum when it was ready to receive antiquities. Thus the Trustees of the British Museum would be able to fill up a gap in their unrivalled collection with an important example of Meroïtic sculpture, the Kharṭûm Museum would receive its counterpart, and make accessible to every visitor to Kharṭûm the finest set of Meroïtic funerary reliefs known, and both walls of the chapel would be lodged in places of safety once and for all. Sir Reginald then gave the Inspector and myself permission to take down the walls stone by stone, and ordered the boxes, in which we were to pack the stones of the wall which he had given to the Trustees of the British Museum, to be sent carriage free so far as the First Cataract (Shellâl). A little later his train moved off on its way to Ad-Dâmar, and we returned to the Pyramids to carry out his instructions.

Taking down the north and south walls of the chapel was not a difficult task, and when all the stones had been carefully

VIEW OF THE DOORWAY LEADING TO THE CHAPEL OF PYRAMID No. 11.

[From a photograph by J. W. Crowfoot, Esq.

received an intimation that Sir Reginald Wingate was about to visit Kasala on a tour of inspection, and that he would have his train stopped at the point on the line nearest the Pyramids, and that he wished us to come and report to him concerning the work we had done. He was to arrive about six o'clock in the morning, and at dawn on the day he was expected we walked across the desert to the railway, and the special train made its appearance soon after we reached the line. Sir Reginald approved of the work which had been done at Ṣûlb and Semna, and of the antiquities which we had collected for the Kharṭûm Museum, and then discussed at length the plans for the preservation of the reliefs in the queen's chapel. In the course of our talk he asked, "What "examples of funerary sculptures from the Island of Meroë have "you in the British Museum?" and I told him that we had none, for all the stone altars and other objects which had formerly existed at Wad Bâ Nagaa and Gebel Barkal, as well as several reliefs from the chapels which we had cleared out, had been taken to Berlin by Lepsius in 1844. To this he replied that he would present to the Trustees of the British Museum all the reliefs from the south wall of the queen's chapel, whilst those from the north wall should go to Kharṭûm, where he would have them built up in the new Museum when it was ready to receive antiquities. Thus the Trustees of the British Museum would be able to fill up a gap in their unrivalled collection with an important example of Meroïtic sculpture, the Kharṭûm Museum would receive its counterpart, and make accessible to every visitor to Kharṭûm the finest set of Meroïtic funerary reliefs known, and both walls of the chapel would be lodged in places of safety once and for all. Sir Reginald then gave the Inspector and myself permission to take down the walls stone by stone, and ordered the boxes, in which we were to pack the stones of the wall which he had given to the Trustees of the British Museum, to be sent carriage free so far as the First Cataract (Shellâl). A little later his train moved off on its way to Ad-Dâmar, and we returned to the Pyramids to carry out his instructions.

Taking down the north and south walls of the chapel was not a difficult task, and when all the stones had been carefully

VIEW OF THE DOORWAY LEADING TO THE CHAPEL OF PYRAMID No. 11.

[From a photograph by J. W. Crowfoot, Esq.

laid in rows to await transport to the railway, we struck our camp and went to Kharṭûm to find a cart or waggon. We arrived unfortunately just at the beginning of the celebration of the festival of Bairâm, during the early days of which all work is suspended, and the people devote themselves assiduously to feasting and the cult of pleasure. The Inspector worked very hard to find a cart, or carts, to take back with us to Kabûshîa, and for the first day or two his efforts were ably seconded by those of our overseer of works. On the morning of the third day, however, this worthy appeared to receive instructions as usual, but he was in a bemused condition, and he had been evidently keeping the feast. After the Inspector had been talking for a few minutes, he said, " O Pâshâ, I ask your Excellency to excuse my not understanding you to-day, for I have been keeping the feast and am drunk, but I will come to-morrow, and then I shall understand you ! " We could therefore do no work that day, but the man's honesty delighted us. On the following day arrangements for a supply of carts were made, and we left Kharṭûm for Kabûshîa with the understanding that they were to follow by the first goods train. When the train did arrive there were no carts in it, for the railway official, who was probably under the influence of the delights of the Bairâm festival, had refused to send them. Final careful instructions having been given to the overseer as to the removal of the stones from the Pyramids, the Inspector returned to his duties in Kharṭûm, and I proceeded north to Ḥalfa on the way to England. I learned subsequently that the carts arrived in the course of time, and that the overseer brought the stones safely from the Pyramids to the nearest point on the railway line, where he laid out the stones of each wall by themselves. Railway trucks were then sent on to the spot, and under the personal direction of the Inspector the stones for Kharṭûm were loaded into one of them, and those for London into another, and in due course each set was sent on to its destination. At Ḥalfa Major Midwinter, R.E., most kindly arranged to have Sir Reginald Wingate's gift to the British Museum packed in stout boxes, and this work was carried out by Mr. C. G. Hodgson, Locomotive Superintendent, assisted by Mr. C. C. F. Mackenzie. The stones which formed the south wall of the queen's chapel arrived, together with some specimens of the sculptured reliefs from other chapels, in London at the end of June, and the wall was built up in the last bay of the west side of the Southern Egyptian Gallery in the British Museum during the summer of 1905.

PART II.

A HISTORY

OF THE

EGYPTIAN SUDAN, ANCIENT AND MODERN

PART II.

A HISTORY

OF THE

EGYPTIAN SUDAN, ANCIENT AND MODERN.

CHAPTER I.

AWAY to the south of Egypt, beyond the mighty granite rocks which form the first Cataract, and beyond the region which is commonly called "Nubia," lies a vast country, peopled chiefly by tribes of men whose skins are dark-coloured or black, and by Negroes. The earliest designation known to us of this country is that which is given to it in the inscriptions of the ancient Egyptians, who called it vaguely "TA-NEḤESU, i.e. the "Land of the Neḥesu," or "Blacks." Ta-Neḥesu was originally one of the four quarters into which the Egyptians divided the world as known to them, the other three being the "Land of the Theḥennu," or Libyans, the "Land of the Āamu," or Asiatics, and the "Land of Men," or Egyptians. In other words, the Blacks occupied the southern quarter of the world; the Asiatics, i.e., the inhabitants of the deserts of the Peninsula of Sinai, Palestine, Syria, and the shores of the Red Sea, the eastern quarter; the Libyans, the western quarter; and the Egyptians, who regarded themselves as "Men," *par excellence*, the lower portion of the Nile Valley, or northern quarter. The Egyptians divided a portion of the Other World also into four quarters, and we learn from a text inscribed on the sarcophagus of Seti I[1] that the Egyptians, the Asiatics, the Blacks, and the Libyans will live again in separate groups in the Fifth Division of the Ṭuat, or Other World. This text, which declared that the "Men," or Egyptians, came into being from the tears which fell from the eye

[1] See my *Egyptian Heaven and Hell*, vol. ii., p. 151.

of the Sun-god, incidentally proves that they regarded the Neḥesu, or Blacks, with contempt, for they imputed to them a scandalous origin, and therefore considered them to be an inferior people.

At a comparatively early period after the rise of the Muḥammadan power in Egypt, Arab historians and others gave to the country to the south of the First Cataract, which is the natural boundary of Egypt on the south, the name of "Balad Sûdân," i.e., "Country of the Blacks." Mediaeval writers call it simply "Sûdân," i.e., "Blacks," or "Negroes," and this is the name which it bears on all modern maps. Thus "Balad Sûdân" is merely the Arabic translation of the words "Ta Neḥesu," and in giving this appellation to the country they have perpetuated the characteristic description of it made by the ancient Egyptians some six or seven thousand years ago.

It seems that, strictly speaking, the "Land of the Blacks" is the country which lies to the south of the modern city of Kharṭûm, and includes both the valley of the Congo, or Western Sûdân, and the valley of the Nile, or Eastern Sûdân, but the ancient Egyptians made it to include the territory of the dark-skinned peoples which extends from that city northwards so far as the First Cataract. In modern times the looseness with which the name Sûdân is used is perplexing, but the same complaint was made by the intrepid traveller, Mr. W. G. Browne, who says, "Nothing can well be more vague than the use of the word Soudan "or *Sûdan*. Among the Egyptians and Arabs *Ber-es-Soudan* is "the place where the caravans arrive, when they reach the first "habitable part of Dar Fûr; but that country seems its eastern "extremity, for it is never applied to Kordofân or Sennaar. It "is used equally in Dar Fûr to express the country to the west; "but on the whole seems ordinarily applied to signify that part "of the land of the blacks nearest Egypt."[1]

In no Egyptian inscription have we any description of the limits of the Land of the Blacks, and even Greek and Arab geographers and historians fail to give any clear idea of what they considered the extent of the Sûdân to be. This, however, is not to be wondered at, seeing that neither the Egyptians nor the Arabs explored the Sûdân thoroughly, and that they only obtained

[1] *Travels in Africa, Egypt, and Syria*, London, 1806, p. xxi.

descriptions of it from merchants or the leaders of raiding expeditions, or from stray travellers who had visited certain portions of it. That the Arabs believed the Sûdân to be an immense region is evident from a tradition quoted by Masûdi (cap. xvi.) to the effect that it required at least seven years to travel all over the Sûdân and Abyssinia, that the Sûdân was sixty times as large as Egypt, and that it represented one-sixtieth part of the earth's surface. From a practical point of view this tradition is of no value, for it is, clearly, one of the artificial calculations which the Arab writers rejoiced in, but it proves that the Arabs believed the Sûdân to be an immense country, and they probably included in it a number of the provinces which lie to the west of Dâr Fûr, and a large portion of sub-tropical Africa. For the purpose of this book the Sûdân means the country which is ruled by Great Britain and Egypt, and which extends from Abû Simbel, or let us say, Wâdî Ḥalfa, on the north to Gondokoro on the south, i.e., a distance of about 1,200 miles as the crow flies, and from the frontier of Dâr Fûr on the west to the Abyssinian frontier on the east, i.e., a distance of about 1,000 miles; thus the Sûdân may be said to cover an area of about 1,250,000 square miles, and to include the greater part of the Nile valley. Scattered over this vast extent of country numberless tribes have lived from time immemorial, and among these there have always been representatives of all the most important Negro peoples of East Africa.

The most important natural feature of the Sûdân is the Nile, and, in the brief account of the history of the country which is given in the following pages, it will be seen that the river has always been the highway by which civilization has made its way from north to south, and that all the kingdoms which have sprung up and flourished in the Sûdân during the past 4,000 years have owed their success to the fact that they were situated on the Nile, or on one of its main tributaries or branches. A glance at the map of north-east Africa will show the reader that the greater part of the Sûdân consists of deserts, wherein men may travel from north to south for a month at a time without seeing a town, or even village of any size. These deserts are ribbed with apparently interminable ranges of low hills of sandstone, of bare and forbidding aspect, and many thousands of square miles of territory are covered with nothing but sand, out of which nothing grows. Even by the Nile itself, the strip of mud which is cultivable on each side of the river is always narrow, and is far from being continuous, and can in no way compare with the mud of Egypt for depth and productiveness. The islands in the river are also very important as dwelling-places for the natives, who can sow and reap their crops there without disturbance, and can readily obtain an abundant supply of water for themselves and their families, their crops, and their cattle. On the lands away from the river, which lie within the rainy zone, large crops of various kinds of grain are grown, and herds of fine cattle find pasture; but when the deserts, and ranges of hills, and swamps, have been deducted from the area of the Sûdân the cultivable land is reduced to a relatively small amount.

In spite, however, of its savage and waterless deserts the Sûdân has been traversed by trading caravans from time immemorial, and the profit to be gained by barter from the Sûdâni folk, both from those who live on the river banks and those who breed cattle on the plains to the south of Kharṭûm, has tempted men in all ages to journey from the north-east coast of Africa to regions which lie only a very few degrees north of the Equator. In all ages the merchants of Lower Egypt, who carried on business with the Sûdân, sailed up the Nile to some convenient stopping place, where, having landed, they made up their caravans, and set out for their destination, travelling thither by way of the desert, and stopping at the Oases to water their animals, and to replenish their stores of dates and grain. In the earliest times of all, and probably down to a period so late as the XVIIIth Dynasty, the beasts of burden were asses. If some place near the modern town of Asyût were chosen for a starting point, which was most likely, the caravan of asses or camels marched to the Oasis of Khârga, and then, in a direction which is almost due south, on to the valley which is now known as "Baḥr bila-ma," i.e., the "Waterless River." This crossed, the journey was continued in a south-westerly direction to the Oasis of Selima, where a halt was made. From Selima the track ran, still in a south-westerly direction, nearly to the famous swamp wherein, according to an ancient tradition, tortoises lived and bred, and then, bending almost due south, it went on to settlements which probably lay near the modern towns of Kôbi, Dâr Mâra, and Dâr Fûngâra.

Thus was reached the kingdom of Dâr Fûr, and the route between that country and Egypt has practically remained unchanged for century after century.

The journey from Lower Egypt to the Sûdân by the desert was, in some respects, more difficult than by river, but the desert route was, on the whole, safer, quicker, and cheaper. The four great chains of cataracts on the Nile between Syene and Berber must always have formed insuperable obstacles in the way of cheap river transport, and the long bends and windings of the river lengthened the journey to the Sûdân by several hundreds of miles. Egyptian merchants who traded with the Eastern Sûdân could despatch their goods by two routes. By the first they followed the road described above until the Oasis of Selima was reached, and then, bearing to the south-east, marched to Dongola and Korti. Thence they crossed the Bayûda Desert to some spot on the Nile, nearly opposite to the modern town of Shendi, and having crossed the Nile, they proceeded in a south-easterly direction to the cities on the Blue Nile, where they disposed of their wares. By the second route, which lay to the east of the Nile, merchants sailed up the river into Upper Egypt, and, making some village near the modern town of Darâw their starting point, then proceeded in a direction almost due south until the Nile was again reached near the modern village of Abû Ḥamed. From this place they marched along the east bank, crossed the Atbara river, and continued their route to the settlement which must have stood near the modern town of Shendi. From Shendi they bore away in a south-easterly direction, crossed the eastern end of the Wâdî of Nagaa, and then directed their steps to the cities on the Blue Nile. The first of these routes has always been the more popular, for the traveller by it escaped the journey through the terrible and practically waterless desert which extends from Darâw to Abû Ḥamed.

The questions which will force themselves naturally into the reader's mind are:—If the Sûdân consists chiefly of waterless deserts, why should merchants or travellers journey thither? And what is it that the Sûdân produces which has, in all periods of history, drawn men irresistibly into its remotest parts? There are no manufactories in the country, the natives have never made with their hands any goods which would find such a ready sale in the civilized world that merchants should deem it worth while to send caravans to the Sûdân to bring them away, why, then, have the ancient Egyptians, the Ptolemies, the Romans, the Arabs, the Turks, and the modern Egyptians, fought so long and so fiercely for its possession? The answer to such questions is not far to seek; men in all ages have gone to the Sûdân in search of GOLD, and they have found it there with comparative ease. Under the earliest dynasties the ancient Egyptians were content with such quantities of that valuable metal as could be obtained by the ordinary methods of barter. At a later period, i.e., under the XIIth Dynasty, the Egyptians realized that they could get gold more easily and more cheaply if they were the acknowledged masters of the Sûdân, therefore did Usertsen III. set out and conquer the country, and occupy it. The kings of the later dynasties consolidated the Egyptian power in the Sûdân as much as possible, but they only did so because it paid them to do so. They did not encourage the advance of Egyptian civilization in that country because they wished to improve the mental and physical condition of the Sûdâni folk, and they did not build temples in the Sûdân for the purpose of propagating ancient Egyptian theology and converting the natives to their own beliefs. They built temples in garrison towns, and in mining and trade centres, whenever it paid them to do so, and they maintained them just so long as they were able to squeeze out of the Sûdânî folk gold enough to justify their policy, and to return them a handsome revenue. As further reference will be made to this matter later in the book, we may at once pass on to notice briefly the usual condition of its inhabitants.

The greater number of the inhabitants of the Sûdân must, in all ages, have been pagan savages, who were ruled by the grossest superstitions and beliefs. There is every reason for believing that the whole of the vast extent of this country was broken up into petty kingdoms and principalities, each of which was ruled in an arbitrary manner by some head of a tribe, who had forced himself into the supreme office of chief. The road to sovereignty lay through many a bloody battle-field, and the methods followed by a successful rebel in the Sûdân, in dealing with the opposition of foes, and with conquered enemies, have been the same in all ages. A man only became king and all-powerful when he had killed every one who had the will and the power to resist him in the smallest particular. Wars, small inter-tribal fights, and raids undertaken for the purpose of obtaining women or cattle were carried on perpetually, and such influence as was possessed by the local medicine-man, or magician, certainly leaned to the side of the man who had the largest body of warriors. It is not unreasonable to assume that every now and then a king would arise who succeeded in making his power felt over a large tract of country, and when such an event happened a comparative state of peace would exist for perhaps a generation. But the strong man would be conquered ultimately by one stronger than himself, or be driven from his seat of power by a son or nephew who rebelled with success, and then in the fights which followed men would be killed, women and children carried off as slaves, crops destroyed, huts burned, and a whole province laid waste. In spite of all this, however, a certain number of men must have earned a living by trade and barter, and the produce of one district, or at least certain articles, such as skins of animals, feathers, gold, and various kinds of wood, must have found ready buyers in another. Fighting and trading have always been the chief occupations of tribes in the Sûdân, and when war failed to give them employment, they devoted themselves diligently to the haggling and bargaining which never failed to give zest to the business of buying and selling. Unfortunately the ancient Sudânî kings who were not influenced by foreigners have left few monuments behind them, and when we consider the conditions under which they must always have lived, this fact should not surprise us. The largest city in the Sûdân can never have been more than a large collection of palm-leaf houses, either round with pointed roofs, or square with flat roofs, and in most places the government buildings, under which we may group palaces, forts, and temples, have usually been made of crude brick. We are now able to trace historical facts connected with the relations which have existed between Egypt and the Sûdân back for a period of some six thousand years, and these show that of all the remains of ancient buildings which now exist in the Sûdân, not one-tenth are the result of pure Sûdânî suggestion or enterprise. Many archaeologists have imagined that we shall find in the Sûdân the ruins of purely native buildings and monuments which will enable them to construct a connected history of the country, but none of the surveys and explorations which have been made by ancient and modern travellers has resulted in the finding of any ruins which are not the remains of temples, forts, palaces, monasteries, &c., in fact, the work of foreigners. We may now consider briefly the principal foreign influences which have made themselves felt in the Sûdân.

Of the influences which, in ancient times, were exercised upon the inhabitants of the Sûdân, the strongest and most lasting was undoubtedly the Egyptian. It is impossible to assign a date to the period when the people who lived in the Valley of the Nile to the north of Syenė began to trade systematically with the Sûdâni tribes, but we are justified in assuming that frequent intercourse went on between Egypt and the Sûdân from time immemorial. After the union of the Egyptian kingdoms of the south and north under one authority by Menȧ, or Menes, we may also assume that this intercourse developed, and that the vigorous kings of the first three dynasties took care to make their power felt by the peoples to the south of Egypt. Semerkha, a king of the Ist Dynasty, and Tcheser, a king of the IIIrd Dynasty, carried on wars against the tribes in the Peninsula of Sinai with great success, and it is quite certain that such monarchs could have subdued the peoples of the Northern Sûdân, had there been the least necessity for doing so. It is very probable that they did make them pay tribute at fixed intervals, and although there is no proof of this, still, probabilities must be considered. It is interesting to note that the Egyptians themselves always appear to have had some idea that they were connected with the people of the land of Punt,[1] which they considered to be peopled by "Neḥesu," or "Blacks," and some modern authorities have no hesitation in saying that the ancient Egyptians and the inhabitants of Punt belonged to the same race.[2] Now Punt is clearly the

1 .

2 See Naville, *Deir el Bahari*, pt. iii., p. 11, Müller says (*Asien und Europa*, p. 113), "Unsere hypothetische Meinung ist die, dass die Bewohner von Punt zu derselben Rasse gehörten, wie die alten Ägypter selbst, dass sie als Verdränger der dunklen Rasse gemeinsam mit diesen einwanderten und die Fühlung mit dem agyptischen Volksstamm frühzeitig verloren, auch mehr Negerblut in sich aufnahmen als dieser. Ja es scheint, dass sie den Ägyptern näher standen als die ebenfalls Ägypter, wie es vor ihrer höheren Entwicklung beschaffen sein musste."

name of a portion of Africa which lay far to the south of Egypt, and at no great distance from the western coast of the Red Sea, and, as many of the Egyptians appear to have looked upon this country as their original home, it follows that, in the early period of dynastic history at least, the relation between the black tribes of the south and the Egyptians in the north were of a friendly character. Certain it is that the tradition that the Egyptian civilization sprang from the Ethiopians, or Blacks, was believed by some classical writers, who had opportunities of finding out what the best informed people of the day thought about the subject, and there is little doubt that this tradition was based upon statements made by the ancient Egyptians themselves. We may note in passing that the plaited, turned-up beard, which is a characteristic of the Egyptian gods, is found to have been worn by the inhabitants of Punt in the time of Queen Hatshepset; and also by the Egyptians of the Ist Dynasty, though never at a later date.

Reminiscences of the wars which the Egyptians probably carried on against the black tribes of the south may be found on the green slate objects of the early period, about which so much has been written in recent years. To what use these objects were put need not trouble us here, and the reader who wishes to investigate this point will find it discussed in a sensible way by Mr. F. Legge in his valuable paper [1] on these interesting antiquities; but it is important to note that they are sculptured not only with hunting scenes, but also with representations of fights and of the defeat and slaughter of enemies. The men who are vanquished have curly wool for hair, and are bearded and naked, and it is evident that they were circumcised. On one of the objects of this class preserved in the British Museum[2] we see a naked captive in the hands of an official who wears a garment which reaches down nearly to his ankles; the wretched creature had a weight, a portion of which is visible, suspended before him from his neck, a method of punishment which is, I am told, in use in the Sûdân to

[1] *Proceedings Soc. Bibl. Arch.*, May, 1900. See also a very interesting paper by Prof. Naville in *Comptes Rendus* of the *Académie des Inscriptions* for 1906, entitled, *Le Dieu de l'Oasis*.

[2] No. 20,791, Third Egyptian Room.

this day. On the reverse of the object are the lower portions of the bodies of two giraffes, which evidently were feeding upon the leaves of a palm tree. Now, the giraffes on the reverse suggest that the scene sculptured on the obverse took place in some country which was situated to the south of Egypt, and the wool on the heads, and the noses and thick lips of the men, proclaim that they belonged to some negroid race. That the men are circumcised need cause no surprise, for circumcision has undoubtedly been practised by the peoples of North-east Africa from time immemorial. The observance of this rite can be traced back to the earliest dynasties in Egypt, and, as Prof. Maspero has pointed out, the inscription on the walls of the pyramid of king TETÁ, about B.C. 3300, actually mentions a being called Tu-ā, or Tchu-ā, whose title was the "Circumciser."[1] These facts taken together indicate that the Egyptians in Predynastic and in early Dynastic times went to hunt in the deserts of the Sûdân, and that subsequently disputes of a serious character arose, which in the end developed into fierce fights. The early kings of Egypt and their followers were stronger and better armed than the natives, and were therefore able to work their will on them. The appearance of the giraffe among the sculptures on the slate objects makes it certain, in my opinion, that the country wherein these fights took place was the Sûdân, and the physical characteristics of the men render it impossible for them to have been anything but negroes. In connection with the fact that they were circumcised it may be mentioned that ancient Christian tradition in Ethiopia asserts that circumcision was known and practised in that country long before Christianity entered it, and the history of Ethiopia shows that the preachers of the Gospel, when they introduced the Christian rite of baptism, permitted their converts to retain their ancient custom of circumcision.

The earliest mention at present known of the Sûdân in Egyptian inscriptions is found on the now famous stele of Palermo, which was first published by Signor A. Pellegrini.[2]

[1] The word rendered "circumciser" is *thesebu* ; it is akin to the Coptic ⲥⲉⲃⲓ, and the determinative is conclusive.

[2] *Nota sopra un iscrizione egizia del Museo di Palermo*, Palermo, 1895.

SENEFERU IN THE SUDAN

This important monument contains a list of festivals and of the gifts which certain early Egyptian kings offered to the gods, and among these kings is mentioned Seneferu,[1] the first king of the IVth Dynasty, about B.C. 3766. Of him it is stated that he sent an army into the Land of the Blacks, and that he carried away captive seven thousand men, and two hundred thousand children and cattle. It is difficult to understand what Seneferu did with his captives, unless he set them to work in the turquoise mines of Sinai,[2] and to build his tomb near Dahshûr, and the Pyramid of Mêdûm. Seneferu was the first king of Egypt who carried war into foreign countries on a large scale, and his conquest of the Sûdân was, no doubt, only one of the many feats of arms with which he must be credited. We possess no details of the conquest, but it was probably made necessary by the Black Tribes refusing to pay tribute or send gifts. Under the immediate successors of Seneferu the authority of Egypt in the Sûdân seems to have been well established, for under the reign of Ȧssȧ, the last king but one of the Vth Dynasty, the governor of the region of the First Cataract, whose stronghold was at Ābu, or Elephantine, and whose name was Ba-ur-ṭeṭ, went so far south as the land of Punt and brought back, among other things, a pygmy, whom he sent to the royal court at Memphis to amuse the king with his dancing. To assume that this official made such a long journey merely for the purpose of bringing back a pygmy[3] is unwarrantable, and the statement which we have on the authority of Ḥer-khuf,[4] a governor of the First Cataract under the Ist Dynasty, indicates that Ba-ur-ṭeṭ had, during the course of a trading expedition, penetrated far to the south, and into the region where

[1] See Wiedemann, *Aegyptische Zeitschrift*, 1885, p. 77; Müller, *Aethiopien*, p. 7.

[2] The latest publication of the representations of Seneferu slaughtering his foes in Sinai is that of R. Weill, *Recueil des Inscriptions Egyptiennes du Sinai*, pp. 103, 104, Paris, 1904.

[3] See Schiaparelli, *Atti del R. Accademia dei Lincei*, Rome, 1893, pp. 22-25; Erman in *Zeitschrift D. Morgen. Gesell.*, Bd. 46, p. 574 ff., and Erman, *Aegyptische Zeitschrift*, Bd. xxxi., p. 66.

[4] The word for "pygmy" is *ṭenk* , and it finds its equivalent in the Amharic word *denk* ድንክ፡

the pygmies lived, and that he brought one of these interesting people back with him, and sent it to the king much in the same way that a soldier or high official in modern times sends a giraffe or some other rare beast to a European sovereign. Ba-ur-ṭeṭ was probably not the first Egyptian official to present a pygmy to his sovereign, for dwarfs of the kind were well known in Egypt in the Ist Dynasty; in the small chambers close to the tomb of Semempses the skeletons of two dwarfs were found, and dwarfs are sometimes depicted on stelae of the Archaic Period. All such facts go to prove that the relations which existed between Egypt and the Sûdân under the first five dynasties were close, and that a considerable amount of trading was done between the two countries.

Under the VIth Dynasty we find Egypt drawing levies of soldiers from the Sûdân to fight in her wars, and on this point we obtain some valuable information from the biographical inscription of Unȧ. This officer was born in the reign of Tetȧ, the first king of the VIth Dynasty, and when quite young he was attached to the service of the court. We hear nothing of him under Tetȧ's successor, but when Meri-Rā Pepi I. came to the throne, he gave Unȧ the rank of *smer*, and made him an inspector of the priests of the pyramids of his family. Pepi I. next made him a judge, and Unȧ acted with such discretion and skill in certain legal matters which were then being tried, that he gave the king great satisfaction, and he was allowed to fetch from the quarries at Tura the stone necessary for a sarcophagus, &c. Unȧ was next promoted to the rank of *smer uāt*, and was made governor of the Red Sea littoral, and given great power over the southern parts of the kingdom. He was so much trusted by his master that he was commissioned by him to investigate some dispute which the king had with his queen Amtes, and he performed his work in a highly satisfactory manner. If we may believe his own statement, no servant had ever before been so greatly trusted by his lord as he, "but," he says naïvely, "I was good, and I was well pleasing "unto His Majesty, and I filled (or satisfied) the heart of His "Majesty." As the result of some disturbance among the tribes of the Eastern desert, i.e., the inhabitants of the country between the Nile and the Red Sea, Pepi I. determined to wage war against

Āamu-ḥeru-shā,[1] i.e., "the Āamu, who are on the sand." He next sent into all the countries away to the south of Elephantine,[2] and enlisted the inhabitants in his army, and he brought "many times ten thousand" bowmen and spearmen to help him. He drew his allies from Setcher, and Khen-setcher, and Årthet, and from the negro-lands of Tcham, or Metcha, Amam, Uauat, Kaau, and Tathem; at the head of all these the king set Unȧ, who says that all the arrangements for the great campaign were in his hands. The contingent from each district was placed under the command of local governors and chiefs, but it was Unȧ who gave the word which set the whole of the vast host in motion. In due course Unȧ and his army forced their way through the land of the desert peoples (Ḥeru shā), and conquered it, and then the work of destruction began. The Egyptians and their negro allies razed to the ground all the fortified buildings of the natives, which are represented as oval buildings with crenellations;[3] they cut down all the fruit trees[4] and the vines, they set fire to everything which could be burned, they slew "many tens of thousands" of the natives, and over and above all this they captured alive a vast multitude of the people. Unȧ's treatment of the rebels was so satisfactory to the king, and no doubt so profitable also, that his sovereign sent him through the land of the dwellers on the sand five times, and Unȧ tells us explicitly that he acted in such a manner that His Majesty loved him "more than anything else." In fact, whenever there was any rising among the desert tribes, Unȧ took boats loaded with troops and set out to harry the wretched folk with fire and sword. Whilst he was carrying on his work of repression of the "Ḥeru shā," king Pepi I. died, but his successor approved of Unȧ's deeds, and, having appointed him to be the bearer of his throne and sandals, raised him to the rank of a *ḥā* prince, and made him governor of Upper Egypt. In this important office he performed his duties with the greatest

1 . Other officials who made expeditions into the Sûdân in the VIth Dynasty were Pepi-Nekht and Sabnȧ.

2 .

3 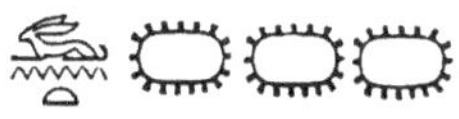.

4 .

thoroughness and zeal, and his king gave him a new proof of the confidence which he placed in him by sending him to the country of Abhat, to obtain for him a stone sarcophagus, with its cover, and a little pyramid. He was next sent to Elephantine Island for the granite which was required in the building of his sovereign's pyramid at Ṣaḳḳâra called Khā-nefer. To transport the granite he took with him six large broad-beamed boats, three barges of the kind called *sath*, and three other barges of another kind, the whole being protected by one "war-boat." Unȧ tells us that work on such a large scale had never been done at Abhat and Elephantine Island with only one war-boat to protect the workmen, and the stones, and the boats, and we may therefore conclude that the fame of the five expeditions which he had made to the south had produced a good effect throughout the country. His next duty was to go to the quarries at Ḥet-nub (Alabastronpolis), and hew out a table for the offerings which would be made in the king's tomb; the work of quarrying the slab and floating it down to Memphis occupied seventeen days. Unȧ next superintended the building of a large *usekht* boat, 60 cubits long, and 30 cubits wide, and he managed to bring it down the Nile in seventeen days during the third month of summer (June-July), although the river was very low.

Unȧ's next labour was a very important one, for his king sent him to the south to dig out five lakes, or canals (?), which were to be used in connection with the floating of stone down the river. Where these lakes or canals were made is unknown, but it is most probable that they were in the First Cataract, and that they were intended to facilitate the passage of broad-beamed barges and rafts through the Cataract at low Nile. This work being completed, Unȧ went on to the country of Uauat, in order to build three *usekht* barges, and three *sath* barges of the acacia trees which grew there. When he told the local chiefs the object of his mission they made the people of Ȧrthet, Uauat, Amam, and Metcha bring wood, and the barges were built in one year. Taking advantage, no doubt, of the high Nile, Unȧ floated his empty barges and rafts through the Cataracts, and, having loaded them with granite at Elephantine, let the river carry them down to Memphis. Now these facts are important, for they prove that

Unȧ must have made his way very far to the south, probably a considerable distance beyond the modern city of Kharṭûm, or his mission may have taken him into the neighbourhood of Sennaar. There seems to be no possible room for doubt that Unȧ found the wood for his barges in the "big tree country," which is situated on the west bank of the White Nile, or on the Gazîra, i.e., the land on the east bank between the White and Blue Niles. Another important fact is indicated by Unȧ's narrative, namely, that the power of Egypt in the Sûdân was sufficiently firmly established to induce the governor of the countries of the south to make the men of Uauat and other districts bring the wood necessary for building the barges and lighters.

Unȧ and his men lived in Uauat for nearly a year, a fact which suggests that he waited until the inundation filled the river bed with water sufficiently deep to enable him to float his barges through the Cataracts without difficulty. He says nothing about trouble raised by the natives, so we may assume that about B.C. 3230 the relations between Egypt and the Sûdân were of such a peaceful character that an Egyptian official could, at a distance of about sixteen hundred miles from Memphis, the capital of Egypt, carry out his king's orders without let or hindrance. The wood used in building the barges is described as "shentch of Uauat, and the trees from which it was cut were, no doubt, finer and larger than the trees of the same species which are found in Egypt at the present day, and are called by the same name, i.e., *ṣunṭ*. The inscription of Unȧ is a very valuable document, but it only supplies us with a certain amount of information about the works which he carried out for kings Pepi I. and Mer-en-Rā, and their Governments, and tells us nothing about the Sûdân except from the point of view of an administrative officer. Fortunately, however, we are enabled to gain some idea of the possibilities of the country from a trader's point of view from the inscription of Ḥer-khuf, the governor of Ābu, the ancient frontier city of Egypt on the south, which was represented by Syene of the Greeks, and Aswân of the Arabs. This officer was a relative of the great chief Mekhu, whose tomb is at the top of the staircase which is cut in

1 

the solid rock in the hill of Contra Syene, on the left bank of the Nile, opposite to the modern town of Aswân. He was a man of high rank, and was chancellor of the civil and ecclesiastical revenues of his town ; he was also a priest highly placed, and his dignity was that of a *smer uāt*. It seems that his father Ȧrȧ was a merchant, for king Mer-en-Rā sent him on a trading expedition to the country of Amam, and Ȧrȧ took his son Ḥer-khuf with him. The journey to and from Amam occupied seven months in all, and father and son returned laden with Sûdâni products. The king approved highly of the result of Ȧrȧ's expedition, and forthwith sent Ḥer-khuf a second time to the south ; he went without his father, and visited the countries of Meskher, Teres, Arthet, and Sethu, the last two of which, he says, had never been visited by any official before.

Ḥer-khuf's second journey occupied eight months, and it seems that he went further south than his father had been ; he returned laden with Sûdânî products as before. The king was again satisfied with the results of the mission, and he sent him to Amam a third time. On his way thither he found that the king of Amam was engaged in war against the king of the land of Themeḥ,[1] and, having made gifts to him, Ḥer-khuf joined his forces, and marched with him to Themeḥ. The king of Themeḥ was, apparently, beaten, and it seems as if this result was brought about either by the advice or help of Ḥer-khuf, for we next read that the king of Amam sent a company of his soldiers to Egypt with Ḥer-khuf's caravan,[2] which consisted of three hundred asses, laden with incense, ebony, skins of animals, boomerangs, &c. On his way back to Memphis Ḥer-khuf passed through the lands of Arerthet, Sethu, and Uauat, and, when the king of these regions saw that he was accompanied by an armed force, he made haste to send him a gift of oxen and goats. In due course Ḥer-khuf reached the Nile, and as he was sailing down the river, he met his brother official Unȧ on his way up to meet him with a number of boats, laden with wine and other luxuries, which king Mer-en-Rā had sent to him as a reward for all the toil and trouble of his travels.

It has already been said that the positions of the lands of

[1] .

[2] More correctly *Ḳayrawân* قيروان

Arerthet, Amam, and Uauat cannot be given accurately in the present state of our knowledge, but it is pretty certain that none of them was situated to the north of Kharṭûm.[1] According to some, Amam was the name given to the desert which lay east and south of Aswân, and extended so far as the shore of the Red Sea; according to others, Amam was the country on the right or east bank of the Nile, the most southerly borders of which included the northern parts of the region round about the Blue Nile. The first mission of Ḥer-khuf occupied seven months, and the second eight months, and from these facts it is certain that he must have gone so far as the modern province of Dâr Fûr on the White Nile, or the region of Sennaar on the Blue Nile, for the deserts on the left bank of the Nile between Aswân and Kharṭûm cannot have produced many of the Sûdân products which he and his father brought to Egypt. These deserts could not have supported the herds of elephants from which he obtained his ivory, and there is no proof that either incense or ebony trees grew there. Under the word "incense" we are probably to include the kind of gum which the Arabs call *libân*, and which is even now gathered in the same way as gum arabic by the natives who live in the deserts between Kordôfân and the Shilluk country. It was, and still is, in great demand over all north-east Africa, and in Burckhardt's day it was "considered as the frankincense, and called Incenso" (*Travels*, p. 294). In his narrative of his third mission Ḥer-khuf tells us that he went to Amam by way of Uḥat,[2] from which statement it may be inferred that he passed through some Oasis. Now on leaving Aswân he would probably travel by the road which leads directly to the Oasis of Kurkur, and thence to the Oasis of Selîma; the latter Oasis has been the halting-place of caravans journeying from Egypt to Kordôfân and Dâr Fûr, or from Egypt to the regions on the Blue Nile, from time immemorial, and it is this to which Ḥer-khuf probably refers.

There is also another point in his narrative to be noticed. He tells us that the king of Amam sent a company of soldiers with

[1] F. W. von Bissing, *Geschichte Aegyptens im Umriss*, Berlin, 1904; and see my *History of Egypt*, vol. ii., p. 101.

[2] .

him to Egypt, and it is difficult not to think that these men were, to all intents and purposes, slaves. If this were so, we can only regard Ḥer-khuf's caravan as the prototype of the modern slave dealer's, which always contained a large number of negroes who were forced to leave their country to perform service in Egypt. In the account of the first and second expeditions we hear nothing of the bringing of natives to Egypt, although Ḥer-khuf tells us that his father and himself returned laden with the products of the countries which they had visited. Ḥer-khuf's two visits to the south had taught him that "the Soudan supplies slaves,"[1] and it seems to me that his third expedition was neither more nor less than a slave *razzia*, carried out, let us hope, without bloodshed or any of the awful scenes of violence which disgraced the middle of the nineteenth century of the Christian Era in Africa, and will ever testify to the laxity of the policy of the nations of Europe which professed to regard the slave trade as an abominable thing, and a blot on Christian civilization. There is unfortunately no doubt that the Sûdân has supplied Egypt and other oriental countries with slave labour for thousands of years, and it seems almost as if the natives of that country have been found fit for nothing else. The earliest *razzia* of which we have any mention is that of king Seneferu, which has already been referred to, but it is most unlikely that it was the first which took place under royal Egyptian auspices. The example set by Seneferu was followed by his successors, and the expedition of Ḥer-khuf to Amam was, no doubt, only one of many which were carried out under the VIth Dynasty.

Finally, we may note that on his arrival at Aswân, after his third expedition, Ḥer-khuf reported to his king, Pepi II., what he had done, and that he received from his master a letter which filled him with pride and pleasure. The king says that he has read with approval the statements in the letter which Ḥer-khuf had written about his mission, and then refers to the paragraph wherein his energetic servant reported that he had brought back a "ṭenḳ," or pygmy,[2] who was one of "the dancers of the god,"

[1] Baker, *Albert Nyanza*, p. 11.

[2] Gr. πυγμαῖος, i.e., a being whose length is a πυγμή, i.e., the distance between the elbow and the knuckles. For classical accounts of the pygmies see Homer, *Iliad*, iii. 6; Aristotle, *Hist. Animals*, viii. 12; Aelian, *Hist. Animals*, xv. 29; Philostratus, *Icon.*, ii. 21; &c.

from the land of the spirits, and was like the pygmy that had been brought to Egypt from the same neighbourhood in the reign of king Assȧ. Pepi II. applauds his official's devotion to his interest, and promises to bestow on his grandson very high honours. Following these words comes the royal command for Ḥer-khuf to proceed without delay to Memphis by boat, and to bring the pygmy with him, for Pepi II. would rather see the pygmy than all the tribute of Bata and Punt. Ḥer-khuf was ordered to provide capable people to look after the pygmy whilst he was on the boat, so that he might be watched all night long, and not be allowed to fall into the river, and the king promised that if Ḥer-khuf brought him safe and sound to Memphis he would confer upon him honours far greater than those which king Assȧ bestowed upon his officer Ba-ur-ṭeṭ, who had brought a pygmy to his court [about one hundred years before]. The despatch of Pepi II. closes with some words which appear to form an order to the temple officials between Aswân and Memphis to furnish Ḥer-khuf and his party with whatsoever they have need of on their journey. From the fact that the pygmy is described as one of the dancers of the god,[1] we must conclude that he belonged to the company of the dancers who performed before one of the gods, or perhaps the chief god, of his native country, and that the knowledge of the particular dance which they danced was rare in Egypt.

Professor Maspero has pointed out[2] that the type of the pygmy whose dancing amused and delighted the heart of the king is well illustrated by the god Bes, who is represented as a thick-set, strongly-built dwarf, with a large head, and a broad face, which is sometimes jovial and at other times warlike. As Bes was the dwarf who pleased the gods by his dancing, so the pygmy from the south, by his dancing, amused and delighted the king. Apart from the pleasure which the pygmy caused by his dancing, he possessed a special interest from the fact that he came from the "Land of the Spirits," i.e., from the region which was supposed to lie between the border of this world, and that of the Other World, and near

[1] *Ȧbau neter* . Compare also, Wiedemann, *Die Anfänge dramatischer Poesie im alten Aegypten* (Mélanges Nicole).

[2] *Sur un Formule du Livre des Pyramides* (*Études de Mythologie*, ii., p. 431).

the Islands of the Blessed. The pygmy who could dance the divine dance, which the divine dwarf Bes danced before the god, was a being with whom to identify themselves the early kings of Egypt thought it no disgrace, for they hoped to learn from him the dance which would please Osiris when they should be obliged to pass from this world into his presence in the Other World. It is true that the *rôle* to which they were ready to lend themselves was that of a buffoon,[1] but in this case the *rôle* of the buffoon was also that of a god, i.e., Bes. Hence we find from the Pyramid Texts[2] that two of the kings of the VIth Dynasty, Pepi I. and Mer-en-Rā,[3] or Meḥti-em-sa-f, identified themselves boldly with the "ṭenḳ" or pygmy, for they hoped that by assuming this *rôle*, the gods, whose duty it was to lead them from this world into the kingdom of Osiris, would perform their task with all speed, being convinced that they were taking into the divine presence a being who would give pleasure to Osiris, and that the great god, being pleased, would pass judgment in their favour and would permit them to pass quickly into the region where the beatified dwelt. The Texts of Pepi I. and Mer-en-Rā were writen before the pygmy which Ḥer-khuf brought from the south arrived in Memphis, but the religious importance of the pygmy was well known to their writers, and we may be certain that the pygmy brought to Memphis for Åssà, a king of the Vth Dynasty, was not theonly one who was seen in Northern Egypt under the preceding dynasties.

About the meaning of the word which the Egyptians used for "pygmy" there is no doubt, for the determinative which follows the letters *ṭnḳ*, i.e., , is decisive. If the position of the country of Amam could be located with tolerable accuracy it would help materially in fixing the limits of the pygmy country to the north. According to Stanley,[4] the pygmy folk are scattered among the Balessé, and inhabit the land situated between the Ngaiyu and Ituri Rivers, and between Ipoto and

[1] Maspero, *op. cit.* p. 435.

[2] The identification of the ṭenḳ in these texts was first pointed out by Erman, *Zeitschrift der Deutsch. Morgenl. Gesell.*, 1892, p. 579.

[3] See the texts of Pepi I., ed. Maspero, lines 400-404; and text of Mer-en-Rā, lines 570, 571.

[4] *Darkest Africa*, vol. ii., p. 92.

Mount Pisgah; they are called Wambutti, but are also known by the names of Batwa, Akka, and Bazungu. They live in the Equatorial forest and support themselves on game, which they are very expert in catching. They vary in height from 3 feet to 4 feet 6 inches. A full-grown male may weigh ninety pounds. They shoot arrows, the tips of which are thickly coated with poison, from their little bows, and they are adepts in the use of the spear. They are such expert huntsmen that no game would be left in the forest round about them in a short time, and they are therefore compelled to move to other settlements so soon as game becomes scarce. They kill elephants for their ivory, birds for their feathers, and they collect honey from the woods, and traffic largely in poison. Every road from any direction runs through their camps, and their villages command every cross-way. They are more crafty and cunning than the tribes of men of larger stature among whom they live, and their wonderful methods of collecting intelligence enable them to know of the coming of strangers long before their neighbours. They arrange their dwellings in a circle, with an open space for the chief's hut in the centre; these dwellings are in the form of an oval cut lengthways, and have doors, 2 or 3 feet high at the ends. On each track leading from their villages, about 100 yards in advance, is a sentry house which is just large enough to hold two pygmies, and its doorway faces the track.

Stanley distinguishes two species of pygmies, the Batwa and the Wambutti: the former have longish heads, long narrow faces, and round reddish eyes set close together, and the latter have round faces, gazelle-like eyes, set far apart, and open foreheads which give one an impression of undisguised frankness, and are of a rich yellow, ivory complexion. The Wambutti live in the southern part of the great Equatorial forest, and the Batwa in the northern, and extend to the Awamba forests, which lie on both banks of the Semliki River, and east of the Ituri. The Semliki River leaves Lake Albert Edward, near its north-western corner, in lat. 0° 8′ 30″ south, and it discharges its waters into the south end of Lake Albert Nyanza in lat. 1° 9′ north.[1] Assuming now,

[1] Sir W. Garstin, *Report upon the Basin of the Upper Nile*, p. 65. Cairo, 1904.

as we are entitled to do, that Ḥer-khuf journeyed some hundreds of miles to the south of the junction of the White and Blue Niles, there is no reason why he should not have come in contact with pygmies who were engaged in the ivory and skin trade, and so have been able to persuade one of them to journey with him to Egypt. Although Pepi II. was so anxious to see the pygmy whom Ḥer-khuf had brought, it must not be imagined that pygmies were unknown in Egypt before that time, for, as objects in ivory and ebony have been found in tombs of the earliest dynasties at Abydos, it is evident that the Egyptian traders in the Sûdân must have come in contact with them during their trading transactions in the far south, and they must have had knowledge of their physical and mental characteristics.

From the facts enumerated above we see that communication for administration and trade between Egypt and the Sûdân was frequent under the IVth, Vth, and VIth Dynasties, and that the authority of the king of Egypt over the Sûdân was sufficiently established to make it possible for an Egyptian official to build barges and lighters, using native labour for the purpose, so far to the south of Egypt as Amam. In fact, it seems that the Sûdân was, even at an early period, regarded as a continuation of Egypt, and an interesting passage in one of the texts inscribed on the walls of the pyramid of Pepi I. makes it perfectly clear that the greatest of the Sûdân gods was recognized by the Egyptians as being of sufficient importance to rank with their own. The passage is found in Professor Maspero's edition of the text, lines 199 ff.; in which, after referring to the appearance of Pepi I. as a divine being in the sky, with "his soul on him, and his words of power on both sides of him, and his book [of magical texts] at his feet," it goes on to say that Temu hath brought to Pepi the towns, and hath made him embrace the nomes and unite the lands, that is to say, the domains of Horus, and the domains of Set, and Sekhet-Åaru (i.e., the Elysian Fields), according to the decree which was uttered by Seb, the hereditary chieftain of the gods. The text then continues, "Khensu, that is Åuḥa, the governor of the Land of the South, and Ṭeṭun the great, the governor of Ta-Kenset, and Sept, who is under his trees, adore[1] this Pepi, and they carry the ladder for this Pepi, and they set up the ladder for this Pepi."

The god , whose name is read Khensu by Professor Maspero, and is glossed by Âuḥȧ, was the god of the whole Sûdân, and Ṭeṭun was the god of that portion of it which lies between the First and Second Cataracts, and Sept was the god of the Eastern Desert, and Eastern Delta, and the Egyptian colonies in the Peninsula of Sinai. The mention of the "ladder" recalls the old legend according to which the god Osiris was obliged to make use of a ladder whereon to mount from this earth to the iron platform of the sky. The ladder was set up by Horus and Set, who stood one on each side of it, and, as Osiris lacked the strength necessary for mounting it, each of these gods placed two of his fingers under one of his shoulders, and gave him the impetus which took him up the ladder into heaven. Whether the writer of the passage intended to pay a compliment to the Sûdânî folk, or whether he merely wished to indicate that his sovereign's power extended not only over the people of the Sûdân, but also over their great gods, cannot be said. In either case the passage is of singular interest, for it contains, I believe, the earliest mention of the god Ṭeṭun, and proves that the gods of the Sûdân were held by the Egyptians to be of sufficient importance to justify their introduction among their own divine companies. In respect of the god Khensu, it is interesting to note that the symbol of his name , which is given in the Pyramid Texts, is also found in a scene on the wall of a chapel of one of the Pyramids of Meroë (Northern Group, No. I, see

1 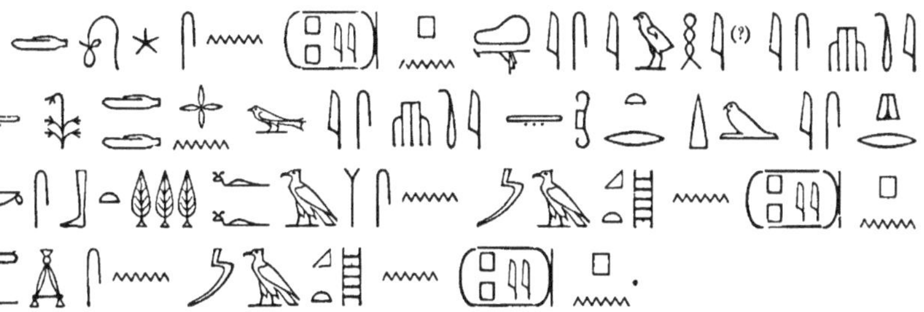

page 362). This symbol is one of four which are represented as being borne on standards by priests in a procession, and its appearance here proves that, at a period so late as that wherein the pyramid was built, this god was still regarded as one of the four great gods of the country.

CHAPTER II.

THE SÛDÂN UNDER THE XITH, XIITH, AND XIIITH DYNASTIES.

AFTER the reign of Pepi II. the monuments of the VIth Dynasty are silent concerning the Sûdân, and we hear nothing of that country for several hundreds of years. The immediate successors of Pepi II. were weak monarchs, and the prosperity of their capital, Memphis, declined rapidly; as their names are not mentioned in the quarries of Egypt and Sinai, we may conclude that no architectural works of any great scale or importance were undertaken during their reigns. The worship of the gods languished, and their sanctuaries became impoverished, trades and the arts declined, and, as the strong hand of a vigorous king was not forthcoming to keep order, the local chiefs began to arrogate to themselves new powers, and to attack each other, and in a few generations Memphis sank into a city of no importance. Now whilst Memphis was decaying and the rule of its last feeble kings becoming more and more ineffective, the princes of Herakleopolis succeeded in gaining their independence, and their descendants became the kings of the IXth and Xth Dynasties. Of these Herakleopolitan kings the most important, so far as we know, were Khati I., Tefaba, and Khati II. Whether any one of these kings asserted by force of arms his authority over the Sûdân there is no evidence to show, but we may note that Khati II. declares that he "spread awe of himself "throughout all the land of Egypt, and inflicted punishment "upon the Lands of the South." Whether these words refer to some victory which he gained over the princes of Thebes, who were the steadfast opponents of his Dynasty, or over the country to the south of the First Cataract, is, at present, uncertain.

It is, however, unlikely that, whilst warfare was going on between the Princes of Herakleopolis and the Princes of Thebes,

Egyptian power and influence would extend in the Sûdân ; on the contrary, it is more than probable that the dwellers on the Nile immediately to the south of the First Cataract would not leave unimproved the opportunity which the dissensions of the rival claimants to the throne gave them of fortifying and consolidating their position to the south of Egypt. We may also be very sure that whenever it was possible they would fail to bring gifts and tribute to the kings of Egypt. The feudal chiefs of the First Cataract were powerful folk, their city of Sunnu (Syene, Aswân) was the great market for the produce of the Sûdân ; it was to the interest of the owners of caravans as well as to that of the merchants, that Egypt should have no effective hold on the city, for such hold would result in the levying of dues and taxes. Whilst Egypt was in the throes of civil war, the Sûdân trader carried on a lucrative trade with the natives of Upper Egypt, and little by little the governors of Ābu, or Elephantine, and Sunnu extended the bounds of their territory northwards so far as the modern town of Darâw, and perhaps even to Edfû or Esna. They did not do this with the view of acquiring territory only, but because the neighbourhood of Darâw was the starting-place for caravans to the far south, and to mining places in the Eastern Desert, and it formed a more convenient halting-place for caravans from the south than Aswân, which is surrounded by hills. Edfû and Esna, on the western bank, formed convenient termini for the trading caravans of the Western Desert, and the people who thronged into Upper Egypt from the south settled in any place north of Sunnu which they were able to keep possession of.

At length, however, the day came which witnessed the defeat of the Princes of Herakleopolis by the Princes of Thebes, who forthwith proclaimed themselves masters of all Egypt. The founder of the dynasty of Theban kings was a feudal chief and hereditary duke called Āntefȧ, who, however, did not make use of a cartouche in writing his Rā-name. After his death, one of his immediate descendants, when he became king, adopted the titles which the great kings of the earlier dynasties had assumed, and had his prenomen and nomen written within a cartouche. This king, whose name was Menthu-ḥetep, at once took steps to assert his authority over the dark-skinned folk who had settled in his country, and in a short time he was master of that portion of the Nile Valley which lies between Thebes and the modern village of Korosko. The evidence of the hieroglyphic inscriptions of the period suggests that certain tribes, which are to-day known by the name of Barâbara, had been so bold as to plunder the Government caravans, and to invade Egyptian territory, and loot unprotected villages. Menthu-hetep proceeded to the First Cataract, where he reopened the granite quarries, and on the Island of Konosso are to be found rough reliefs on the rocks, in which we see the deities Khnemu, Menu, Menthu, Net (Neith), and Satet standing by his cartouche, and in the accompanying inscriptions they declare that they have placed the whole country under his sandals. In one place the god Menu stands upon fifteen bows, each of which represents a Sûdâni tribe, and they indicate the fifteen barbarian countries which Menu has given into the king's hands.

During the reign of Menthu-ḥetep II. we hear nothing of the Sûdân, and this king appears to have devoted his energies to quarry work in the Wâdî Hammamât.[1] By his orders a well was dug ten cubits square, and the magnitude of his operations may be gauged by the fact that his chief official, Åmen-em-ḥat, had under him several thousands of men, including three thousand boatmen.

By the time his successor Menthu-ḥetep III. came to the throne,[2] the tribes of the south appear to have begun again to cause trouble, and this king found it necessary to deal with them in the ordinary way. Among the ruins of a temple at Gebelên in Upper Egypt, near Shêkh Mûsa, M. G. Daressy[3] found the remains of a bas-relief whereon this king is represented in the act of slaying Nubians, Asiatics, and Libyans. At this period such a scene is no mere conventional ornament of a temple wall, but is a representation which must have some direct relation to the events which it commemorates. Owing to her geographical situation

[1] For the inscriptions concerning him, see Lepsius, *Denkmäler*, ii. 149.

[2] The correct reading of his prenomen, Neb-ḥep-Rā, was first pointed out by Mr. F. Ll. Griffith.

[3] *Recueil de Travaux*, tom. xiv., p. 26, No. 32.

Egypt could not exist as an independent kingdom unless the nomad tribes on three of her borders were in subjection to her. When once the Princes of Thebes had overcome their opponents among their own countrymen, they proceeded without delay against the southern tribes who menaced their peace, and thus under the XIth Dynasty we find Egypt endeavouring to regain in Nubia and the Sûdân the authority which her sovereigns possessed under the VIth Dynasty.

The last king of the XIth Dynasty was Seănkhka-Rā, and it is important to mention him because he sent an expedition to Punt under the command of an officer called Ḥennu. The immediate object of the expedition was to bring back in ships loads of the precious myrrh or balsam called *ănti*, which was highly prized throughout Egypt. Menthu-ḥetep III. appears to have attempted to bring to Egypt by sea ship-loads of the same substance, and Seănkhka-Ra followed his example. We have already seen that Ba-ur-ṭeṭ, the feudal lord of the First Cataract, brought back a pygmy from Punt, in the reign of king Åssȧ, but so far as we know he journeyed thither by land. Whether the expeditions to Punt under the XIth Dynasty indicate that the desert route thither was unsafe for Government caravans is a little doubtful, but, as will be seen a little further on, it is by no means impossible. It must be remembered that when Thebes became the capital of the Kingdom of the South and the North in the place of Memphis, the balance of power throughout Egypt was disturbed. It was more easy to reduce the southern tribes to order from Thebes than from Memphis, but it was also more difficult to keep a firm hand on the desert dwellers on the east and west of the Delta. It is quite certain that even at this early period the tribute of the Sûdân was of considerable importance to Egypt, for otherwise her kings would never have made such strenuous efforts to maintain their authority in that country.

With the accession of Åmenemḥāt I., the first king of the XIIth Dynasty (about B.C. 2466), a new era of conquest dawned for Egypt. This king first set to work to put Upper Egypt in order, and to fix the boundaries of the great feudal chiefs of Beni-Hasan, Gebelên, Al-Kâb, and presumably also of Elephantine, and to bring the Delta under his effective control. He seems to have made no attempt to restore Memphis, the ancient capital of the country, to its former position of greatness, but he built a fortress called Thet-taui, a little to the south of that city, which he used as a residence and for administrative purposes. Probably with the view of strengthening his hold on the Delta, he built, or rather rebuilt, the temples of Bubastis and Tanis. These works done, Ȧmenemḥāt I. was able to consider seriously the state of affairs in the country to the south of the First Cataract, for he was master, as he himself says, of all Egypt, "from Abu (Elephantine) to the reed-swamps of the Delta." For his buildings he needed the labour of slaves, and for their decoration and for temple ceremonials he needed gold. Both slaves and gold had been brought from the Sûdân from time immemorial, and it seems certain that his determination to conquer that country was rather the result of his need for these objects than his love of conquest, or than the mere desire to "enlarge the borders of his country." His love of the chase and of the slaughter of lions and crocodiles took him into the Sûdân, and he probably learned there, at first hand, concerning the sources whence the natives obtained their supply of gold. At all events, he decided to conquer the country, and to take possession of the mines.

In the papyrus which contains his account of the conspiracy against him and the attack upon his life,[1] he tells us that he conquered the Mātchaiu,[2] the Uauaiu,[3] the Satiu,[4] and the Ḥeriu-shā. With all these peoples Ḥer-khuf, the feudal lord of Elephantine, under the VIth Dynasty, had come in contact. The Mātchaiu were probably the most warlike of them all, and we hear of their being employed as guards and policemen under later dynasties. The

[1] See Birch, *Select Papyri*, Sallier ii., plate 10 ff.; the Ostrakon in the British Museum, No. 5,623; Birch, *Egyptian Texts*, p. 16; Dümichen, *Aeg. Zeit.*, 1874, p. 30; Maspero, *Recueil*, tom. ii., p. 70; Maspero, *Records of the Past*, vol. ii., p. 9 ff.

[2] 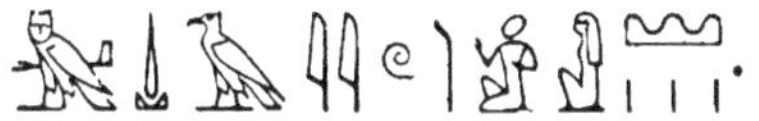

[3] 

[4] 

conquest of the country south of Egypt, so far as Korosko at least, was effected by the twenty-ninth year of the king's reign, for an inscription on a rock at the entrance to the Valley of Girgaui, on the road from Korosko, accidentally discovered by Dr. Lüttge in 1875, states that Ȧmenemḥāt I. came there in that year to smite the inhabitants of Uauat.[1] Whether the neighbourhood of Korosko formed a part of Uauat is uncertain, but the possession of this portion of Nubia would make him master of the gold mines in the Wâdî al-'Alâḳi. This Wâdi was entered from the Nile near Kubbân, and in the Wâdi al-Khawânib the remains of the tools and implements used in working the gold may be seen to this day.

Usertsen I., the son and successor of Ȧmenemḥāt I., who had reigned jointly with his father several years before he became sole monarch of Egypt, carried on the work of the conquest of the Sûdân which his father had begun. In the forty-third year of his reign he led an expedition into Nubia, some details of which are supplied by Ȧmeni or Ȧmeni-emḥāt, the feudal lord of Menāt-Khufu, in an inscription which is cut on the walls of his tomb at Beni-Hasan.[2] The campaign was directed against "four peoples,"[3] the text does not give us their names, but we are probably to understand the natives of Amam, Uauat, Arthet, and Metcha. Usertsen I. sailed up the river into Nubia, defeated the tribes, and compelled them to bring him tribute; the collecting of the offerings fell to the lot of Ȧmeni, who says that he brought them back safely to Egypt, and that not a single man of his contingent was missing when he returned. Ȧmeni was despatched a second time to the Sûdân by his lord, and went thither at the head of four hundred men; the avowed object of his mission was to bring back gold,[4] and he tells us that he did so. This mission was so successful that the king sent him once again to the south, and he and his four hundred men brought back with them the objects of

1 See Brugsch, *Aeg. Zeit.*, 1882, p. 30.

2 See Champollion, *Monuments*, tom. iv., pl. 395; Lepsius, *Denkmäler*, ii., 121, 122.

3 

4 The word for gold is *nubu* 

tribute for which he had been sent, and landed them at the city of Coptos. We must here note that Ȧmeni tells us in his inscription that the king "overthrew his enemies in the abominable country of KASH;"[1] this is an important statement, for it shows that one part of the Sûdân was called by the Egyptians "Kash."

STELE OF USERTSEN I. IN THE BRITISH MUSEUM (NO. 963) FOUND AT PHILAE.

Now this is the first appearance of the name Kash in the Egyptian inscriptions, and it is the original of "Cush," the name given to Nubia by the writers of the Old Testament, and by most of the peoples with whom the Hebrews came in contact. The Hebrews, however, unlike many classical authors and post Christian writers, never included "Ethiopia" in the term.

1 

The extent and limits of Kash in the time of Usertsen I. are unknown, but it seems that its northern frontier was a little to the south of the modern town of Korosko, whilst its southern border was probably near the junction of the White and Blue Niles. Speaking generally, the Egyptians divided the northern Sûdân into two parts; the northern part was called Uauat, and the southern Kash. Uauat was conquered by Ȧmenemḥāt I., who set up his boundary inscription near Korosko, and his son certainly overran all the northern part of Kash, and set up his boundary stone not far from the modern town of Wâdi Ḥalfa. Near this town Champollion[1] discovered a stele which refers to the conquests of Usertsen I. in the Sûdân, and on it this king claims to have conquered the countries of Huu, Kas,[2] Shemik, Khasaȧ, Shaāt, Akherkiu, Uau, Khemer (?), and Amau, and it is probable that this stele formerly marked the limit of Egyptian territory on the south. The stele is now exhibited in the Museum at Florence.[3] Whatever may have been the size of the army which Usertsen I. led into the Sûdân, it is quite clear that the expeditions of Ȧmeni bear a striking resemblance to the modern slave-hunting expeditions so graphically described by the late Sir Samuel Baker in his *Albert Nyanza* (p. 12). In his account of them Ameni says never a word to indicate that the Egyptians attempted to administer the country which they raided; but he boasts that he went to the Sûdân for gold and "stuff," and brought both back.

In the summer of 1892, Captain H. G. Lyons, R.E., carried out a number of important excavations on the west bank of the river opposite Wâdî Ḥalfa, and made an examination of the remains of all the temples of the XIIth and XVIIIth Dynasties which are to be found on the site. He found the little mud-brick temple and fort of Usertsen I. and completely cleared it, and in the course of his work he discovered another temple which was built by Thothmes IV., a king of the XVIIIth Dynasty. The

[1] See his *Letters*, p. 101; *Notices*, p. 692; *Monuments*, tom. i. pl. 1., No. 1; Rosellini, *Monumenti Storici*, pl. 25, No. 4; Birch, *Aeg. Zeit.*, 1874, p. 111 ff.

[2] 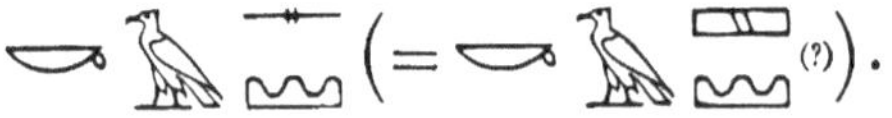

[3] No. 2540.

temple lies about 200 yards to the north of the temple of Thothmes II. and Thothmes III., and it was first cleared out by Captain Lyons. In the sanctuary he found the remaining or lower portion of the famous stele, which was set up by the officer Menthu-ḥetep to record the victory of Usertsen I. over the tribes whose names were duly recorded on it, and portions of a duplicate. We have already referred to the upper half of the stele, which was found by Rosellini and taken to Florence, and as Captain Lyons sent to the Museum there the

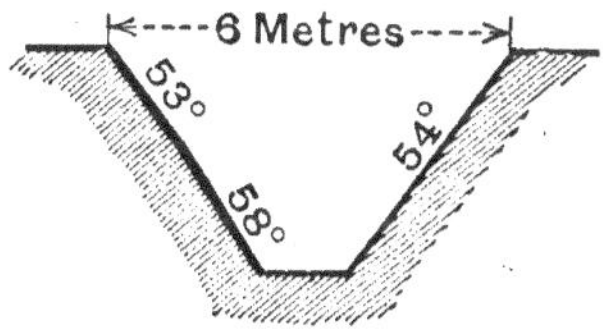

SECTION OF V-SHAPED DITCH.

lower half which he discovered, this important monument may now be seen in a complete state. Besides these objects he recovered from the second temple the interesting stele of Erṭā-Ȧntef-Ṭeṭi, a "governor of the South," i.e., Nubia, in the reign of Usertsen I., and four or five smaller stelae. The stele of Erṭā-Ȧntef-Ṭeṭi he presented to the Trustees of the British Museum, where it is now exhibited in the Southern Egyptian Gallery (No. 1177), and the smaller stelae to the Ashmolean Museum, Oxford. The

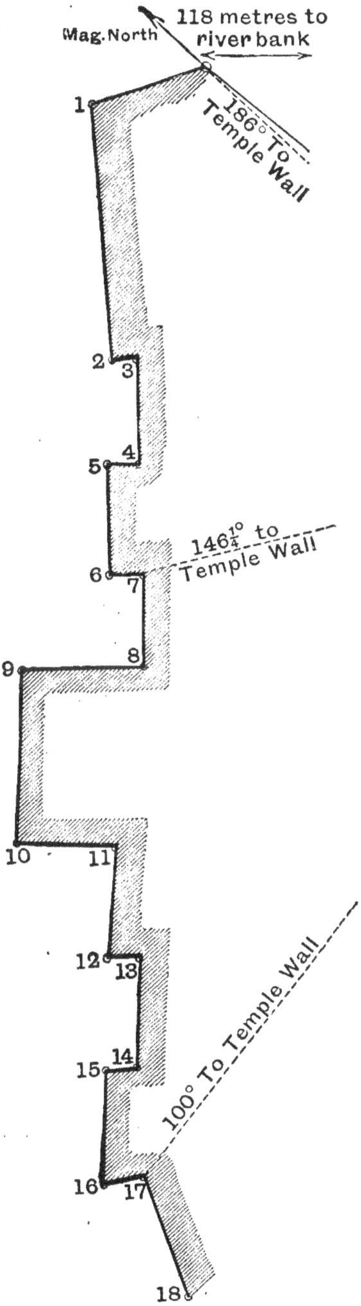

TRACE OF FORTRESS WALL AT WADI HALFA (SULU-N-DIFFE) WEST BANK.
Surveyed by Capt. H. G. Lyons, R.E.

temples of Usertsen I. and Thothmes IV. stood in a large enclosure which was surrounded by a line of fortifications, of which a few bricks of the base of the wall alone remain ; in front of this line was a ditch, which is now sanded up. Captain Lyons learned from the people round about that the name given to the site by the Barâbara is "Sulu-n-diffe," i.e., "Fort of Sulu."

Ȧmenemḥāt II., the successor of Usertsen I., continued the policy inaugurated by Ȧmenemḥāt, and succeeded in forcing the Nubians to pay tribute in gold and precious stones. In his reign the Egyptians gained firm foothold in the country of Ḥa, by which we are, perhaps, to understand the district which lies between Wâdi Ḥalfa and Semna; in fact, they advanced some fifty or sixty miles further to the south than they had done in the time of his predecessor. A high official, called Sa-Hathor, tells us in his sepulchral inscription, which was found on a stele at Abydos,[1] that he journeyed into the country of Ḥeḥ, and made the people to labour in the mines there. The young men dug out the ore, and crushed it, and the old men washed out the gold. This mention of young and old men forcibly reminds us of the description of the method of working the gold mines given by Diodorus Siculus[2] (Bk. iii., chap. 13 ff). Sa-Hathor says that the natives were terror-stricken, and greatly afraid of his lord, and that they came to him, and when we think of the methods which the Egyptians used in dealing with the Nubians, it is clear that this official is telling the truth. In the twenty-eighth year of the reign of Ȧmenemḥāt II. Prince Kheut-khat-ur returned safely from an expedition to Punt, and thus we see that the Egyptians were bringing the products of the Sûdân to their country both by sea and by land. From the Peninsula of Sinai also they were obtaining turquoises during this reign, and these, with the gold and carnelians which came from the Sûdân, were made into

[1] It is now in the British Museum, No. 569. The text is published and described by Birch in *Aeg. Zeit.*, 1874, p. 112, and *Egyptian Texts*, p. 21.

[2] 
, "I worked a mine with young men, I forced "the old ones to wash out gold, I brought turquoises."

jewellery, of which such splendid specimens were discovered by M. J. de Morgan at Dahshûr.

Here we may note that the inscriptions which belong to the reign of Amenemḥāt II. supply us with another name for the country to the south of the First Cataract, namely Ta-Kenset,[1] or more fully "Ta- Kenset of the Neḥesu," i.e., "Ta-Kenset of the Blacks." This is the name given to Nubia by Sa-Hathor, who also speaks of a journey which he made to the land of Ḥa.[2] Also the feudal lord of Elephantine, who must have been a contemporary of Sa-Hathor, described himself as "great chief of Ta-Kenset, and superintendent of the desert lands [of the south]."[3]

Under Usertsen II., the next king of this dynasty, the Government quarries at Elephantine were kept working, and an official called Menthu-ḥetep, who was overseer of them, tells us that he successfully repulsed the attacks which the local Nubians made upon his men. A statement of this kind goes to show that the authority of Egypt was not accepted by the natives, and it seems that, after all, Egypt's hold on the country was slight, and that so soon as her soldiers left the First Cataract after an expedition, the "conquered vile Nubians" rose up in rebellion behind them. Usertsen II., who was identified with Sesostris by Manetho, appears to have made no expeditions into the Sûdân, but, if his governors of the frontier succeeded in extorting tribute from the natives regularly, they would be unnecessary.

Soon after the next king of Egypt, Usertsen III., ascended the throne, about B.C. 2333, he decided to complete the conquest of the Sûdân, and to occupy it, if not with Egyptian troops, at least with native levies under Egyptian officers. He set to work to carry out his plans in a systematic manner. Knowing well how difficult it would be to take large boats through the First Cataract, especially if his men were to be attacked by the natives whilst they were hauling them through the "gates," he determined to make a canal,[4] or rather to clear out and enlarge an old one, which appears tohave existed under the VIth Dynasty. When

1 . 2 .

3 See my account of the Aswân tombs in Proc. Soc. Bibl. Arch., 1887, p. 32.

4 See Wilbour, in Maspero's *Recueil*, tom. xiii., pp. 202, 203.

his men had finished their labours on it, the canal was 250 feet 4 inches long, 34 feet 7 inches wide, and 25 feet 10 inches deep; from inscriptions on a rock on the Island of Sâḥal we learn that this canal was used for the transport of war-boats in the reign of Thothmes I., and that Thothmes III., in the fiftieth year of his reign, had it cleared out, and passed a law to the effect that the boatmen of the Cataract were, in future, to clear it out every year. Usertsen III., having made a way for his boats and passed them through the Cataract, proceeded to sail up the Nile to the Second Cataract. This took place in the eighth year of his reign. He traversed the difficult country between Ḥalfa and Sarras, and then occupied the Island of Gazîrat al-Malik, a few miles to the north of Ṣemna. On the highest point of the hill on this Island, probably near the site of the remains of the temple of the XVIIIth Dynasty which now stands there, he built a huge fort, and erected presumably a small temple at its north-east corner. In the sanctuary was a seated statue of the god Osiris, and near it another of himself. When this temple was wrecked during the period which followed that of the XIIth Dynasty, the heads were knocked off both statues, and the statues were thrown down the steep face of the hill, at the foot of which they were found by Mr. J. W. Crowfoot when we were working on the Island in January, 1905. Close by, we may be sure in some prominent place, Usertsen set up a stele on which were set forth in large well-cut hieroglyphics an account of his conquest of the country, and a very unfavourable opinion of the mental and physical characteristics of the natives. We found this stele lying near the top of the precipitous side of the hill, whither it had been dragged with the view of throwing it down into the river. It is dated in the sixteenth year of his reign, and the text on it is a duplicate of that found on the stele which he set up in the same year at Kumma, the companion fort to Semna.

Passing up to Semna, a few miles further to the south, Usertsen III. came to the most important of all the "gates" of the Second Cataract. On each side of this "gate" are masses of rock which stand at a considerable height above the river, and on the highest points of these he built forts. Strategically the whole site is of the first importance, for it commands a good view of the river both to the north and to the south, and it is situated in the very heart of the country in which are found the strata of quartz, whence gold was obtained. For miles and miles along the river banks the traveller finds the remains of the broken basalt strata which Nature alternated with quartz strata, and it is clear that the whole neighbourhood was worked by men seeking for gold for many generations. Of the strength of the garrisons which were maintained here by Usertsen III. we know nothing, but the size of the fortified enclosures at Semna and Kumma suggests that they were sufficient to keep in order the wretched workmen who dug out the gold ore, and to quell any ordinary rebellion which might break out among the natives. The worship of the gods was not neglected, for in each fort was a small temple, strongly built of stone, or of stone and brick, wherein the Egyptian officials might adore the gods whom they knew and worshipped in their own land, and also store the gold until it could be sent northwards on the backs of asses. Thus trade and religion went hand in hand, and the weary workmen had the opportunity of admiring the skill of their conquerors in business, and the devotion of their rulers to their gods. As a matter of policy the local gods were duly recognized, and, when sufficiently important, were included among the gods of Egypt.

When Usertsen III. became master of Nubia so far to the south as Semna, he set up a stele to mark the boundary of his kingdom, and that of the land of Ḥeḥ. This stele is dated in the eighth year of his reign, and was probably inscribed when he was actually at Semna. The text is an interesting one, for it shows that although he had conquered the country to the north of Semna, the natives to the south were able to give him a good deal of trouble. Judging from its contents it appears that the people of Ḥeḥ were in the habit of passing through the Cataract in their boats, and stirring up discontent and revolt among the vanquished Nubians, and the mischief which they caused seems to have been so great that the king was obliged to prohibit any "Black" from passing Semna, except for purposes of trade or embassy. His decree reads:—[1]

[1] For the hieroglyphic text see Lepsius, *Denkmäler*, Bd. ii., Bl. 136. For renderings see Brugsch, *Egypt under the Pharaohs*, vol. i., p. 182; Chabas, *Études sur l'Antiquité Hist.*, p. 135; Müller, *Aethiopien*, p. 10.

THE DECREE AGAINST THE BLACKS PROMULGATED BY USERTSEN III. IN THE EIGHTH YEAR OF HIS REIGN.

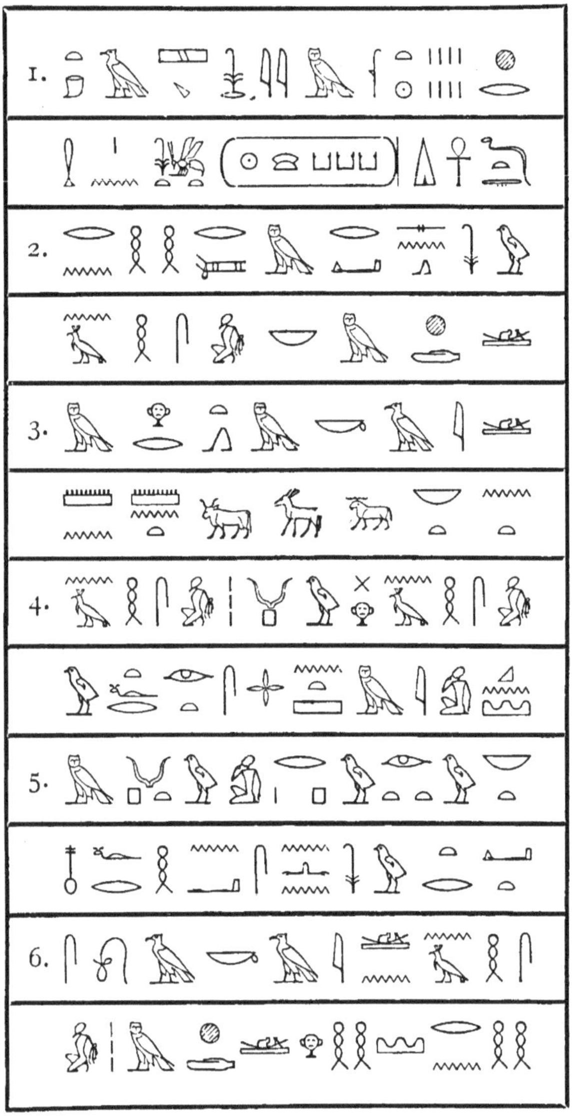

DECREE OF USERTSEN III.

1. "The southern frontier in the eighth year under the "Majesty of the King of the South and North, "(Rā-khā-kau) (i.e., Usertsen III.), giver of life for ever.
2. "No Black whatsoever shall be permitted to pass [this "place] going down stream,
3. "Whether travelling by the desert, or journeying in a "boat, with cattle, asses, and goats of various kinds "belonging to
4. "Blacks, with the exception of such as cometh to do "business in the country of Åqen,[1]
5. "Or on an embassy. Such, however, shall be well "entreated in every way whatsoever.
6. "No boats belonging to the Blacks shall in future be "permitted to pass down the river by the country of "Ḥeh."[2]

Eight years later Usertsen III. set up two inscribed stelae, one at Semna and one on the Island of Gazîrat al-Malik, and from these we learn the views which he held about his conquest of Nubia, and the people whom he had brought into subjection. The text on each stele, with the exception of the first line, is the same, and the king's names and titles are the same, though arranged somewhat differently, but on one the inscription occupies nineteen lines, and on the other twenty-two. On the rounded portion we see the vault of heaven, in the centre of which is the solar disk, winged, and with pendent uraei, having symbols of eternity on their necks. On the right and left is written the name of the city Beḥuṭet, which indicates that the Winged Disk is the symbol of the great warrior-god Horus of Edfû. Below this are the titles of the king: 1. The living Hawk (Horus). 2. The divine of origin. 3. Lord of the Vulture and Uraeus diadems.

[1] Brugsch believed Åqen to be the Acina of Pliny, Bk. vi., chap. 35.

[2] Brugsch's version is as follows:—"Here is the southern frontier, which was "fixed in the eighth year under the reign of king Usurtasen III., the dispenser "of life for ever, in order that it may not be permitted to any negro to cross it, "with the exception of the ships which are laden with cattle, goats, and asses "belonging to the negroes, and except the negroes who come to trade by barter "in the land of Aken. To these, on the contrary, every favour shall be allowed. "But otherwise it shall not be permitted to any vessel of the negroes to touch "at the land of Heh on its voyage nevermore."

4. He whose birth is divine. 5. King of the South and North. 6. The living Creator. 7. The Golden Hawk (Horus). 8. The Son of the Sun. 9. Lord of the two lands. 10. Rā-khā-kau, giver of life. 11. Usertsen, giver of life, stability, and power, for ever! The text below reads:—

1. "In the third month of the season Pert, His Majesty "fixed the southern boundary at Ḥeh.
2. "I made my boundary, and I advanced up the river "[beyond that] of my father's. I added
3. "greatly thereunto, and I give commands (or, I pass "decrees). I am the king (*suten*), and what is said [by "me] is done. What
4. "my heart conceiveth is that which my hand bringeth "to pass. [I am] a crocodile to seize and carry off, and "one who beateth down [his foes]
5. "mercilessly. Words do not remain still in my heart. "The coward among the flatterers standeth [in ex- "pectation of]
6. "mercy, but the compassion of [his] enemies reacheth "not to him. He (i.e., the king) attacketh him that "attacketh him; he is silent to him that is silent,
7. "and he returneth the answer to a matter according to "what hath happened. Now inaction (or, silence) after "an attack giveth strength
8. "to the heart of the enemy; mighty must be the attack, "[like that of a] crocodile. For the man who retreateth "is vile and a poltroon, and no man is he who on his own
9. "territory is defeated and brought into servitude. "Therefore thus is the Black, for he falleth down pros- "trate at the word which is
10. "spoken to him, and he turneth back when any attacketh "him, and he giveth his back in flight to his pursuer, "and he runneth away.
11. "The Blacks are not men of boldness, but they are "timid and weak, and they have nothing but buttocks "for hearts.
12. "My Majesty hath seen them, and I have not erred con- "cerning them. I seized their women, I carried off

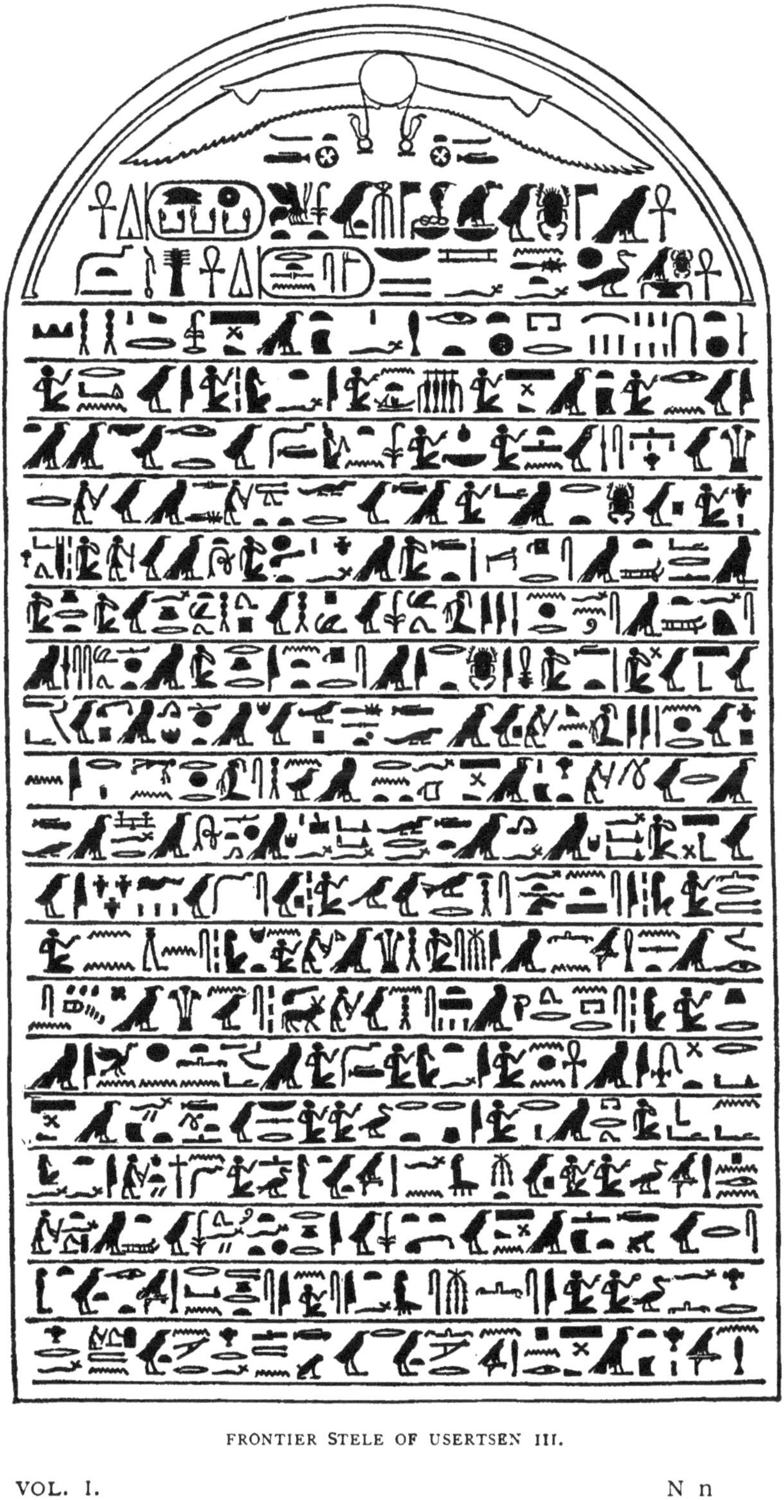

FRONTIER STELE OF USERTSEN III.

13. "those who had possessions [when I] appeared at their "wells, I slew their bulls, I destroyed their grain,

14. "setting fire to their houses. This I swear by my own "life and by my father; I speak truth, there is no doubt "about the matter, and

15. "that which cometh forth from my mouth cannot be "gainsaid. Furthermore, every son of mine who keepeth "intact this boundary,

16. "which my Majesty hath made, is indeed my son, and "one begotten by my Majesty, and he is the son who "protecteth his father,

17. "and keepeth intact (literally, makes to flourish) the "boundary of him that begot him.[1] Besides, he who "alloweth it to be set back, and doth not do battle

18. "for it, is not my son, and behold, he hath not been "produced by me. And moreover, my Majesty hath "caused to be made [and set up] a statue

19. "of my Majesty on this boundary, not only with the "desire that ye should prosper thereby, but also that ye "should do battle for it."

The stele from which the above rendering has been made is preserved in the Royal Museum in Berlin (No. 1157), where it was taken by Lepsius. In the official *Verzeichnis* (p. 111) it is said that the upper portion of it was inadvertently left at Semna, and that this is now in Cairo. In the last edition (1904) of his *Histoire Ancienne* (p. 126), Prof. Maspero says in a note to his remarks on Usertsen's decree of the eighth year of his reign, and on the stele set up in the sixteenth year, that "these inscriptions, which had been mutilated by the travellers who wished to carry them away, have passed from the Museum of Giza to that of Berlin." The stele with the duplicate text in twenty-two lines, the left-hand bottom corner of which is broken off, was, as we have already said, removed with great difficulty by Mr. J. W. Crowfoot and myself, from the top of the hill on the Island of Gazîrat al-Malik to Khartûm, where it now is.

[1] I.e., this son is the counterpart of Horus, who protected his father Osiris.

[2] The stele with nineteen lines of text was first published by Lepsius, *Denkmäler*, Bd. ii., 136.

The inscription of Usertsen III. quoted above is interesting from several points of view. Portions of the text are difficult to translate, and no rendering of the inscription yet published is satisfactory. The general drift of it is, however, quite clear. It opens with a statement that he has enlarged the boundary of his kingdom to an unprecedented extent, and goes on to say that he is a king whose thoughts are turned into action promptly and vigorously. His abuse of the Blacks whom he has conquered is violent, and is truly oriental in character, for he calls them cowards, who run away when they find themselves attacked, poltroons, and impotent folk, and says that they fall prostrate at the mere sound of a warlike word. Timid, feeble, and foolish he reckons them to be. The next few lines throw a lurid light on Egyptian methods in the Sûdân, and they help us to realize that the slaughter of men and cattle, the ravishing of women, the destruction of crops, and the burning of villages, were the results which always followed an invasion of Nubia by Pharaoh's hosts. We have already seen (see p. 517) how Unȧ treated the natives, and how he cut down their vines and fig-trees, and laid waste the fields, and slew the people by tens of thousands, and we know that whether it was the king in person who conducted an expedition, or merely a high official, the result, so far as the native was concerned, was the same.

Now although Usertsen's arms were victorious in the Sûdân, he appears to have realized that the only way to ensure their success uniformly was to build a line of forts in places of strategic importance. Thus he built a fortress called Ḥeru-Rā-khā-kau, near the Island of Elephantine, and also a temple, which he dedicated to the Cataract deities Sati and Anuquet, on the Island itself; we derive this information from the stele of his official, Ȧmeni, which was discovered by Mr. Gadsby in 1874, and[1] from rock inscriptions on the Island of Sâḥal. At Amâda, a few miles to the south of Korosko, he built another fort, and the site was so well chosen that Thothmes III. restored it, and established the worship of his great predecessor, to whom, even in those early times, divine honours were paid. The fort and temple built by Usertsen I. were, no doubt, still standing at Behen, or Buhen,

[1] See Birch, *Aeg. Zeit.*, 1875, p. 50 ff.

which was on the west bank of the river, a little to the south of the modern town of Wâdî Ḥalfa, therefore Usertsen III. had no need to establish a fortress here. Three miles to the south of the famous rock of Abûṣîr (Abû-Ṣîr), at the foot of the Second Cataract, he built another fort and a temple, and their remains are to be seen to this day close to the Ḳa'lat Ma'atûḳa. The fort stood at the mouth of the Wâdî Ma'atûḳa, which was at one time much frequented by caravans. About thirty-five miles further to the south he built the fortresses of Semna and Kumma,[1] but of the temples which he, no doubt, founded there, no remains exist. The next place to the south where the name of Usertsen III. is found is Gebel Dôsha, the bold sandstone rock which serves as the boundary between Dâr Sukkôt and Dâr Mahass. The other royal name which occurs here in the chamber high up in the rock is that of Thothmes III., and it seems as if this king carried out works here with the view of perpetuating the memory of his great ancestor. According to Prof. Maspero,[2] Usertsen III. made a *razzia* among the natives on the Tacazze river, or southern part of the Atbara. We know that this king began his conquest of the Sûdân in the eighth year of his reign, and that he was still fighting in person in that country in the nineteenth year of his reign;[3] it is therefore possible that he built forts at many places between Semna and the Fourth Cataract, of which all traces have been obliterated. The above facts show that his conquest of the Sûdân was complete, and we may be certain that he made himself master of all the great trade centres, and levied taxes in slaves, gold, &c., on every caravan.

Àmenemḥāt III., the son and successor of Usertsen III., had no need to wage war in Nubia during his long reign of nearly fifty years, and his chief work in that country was the fortress which he built at Dakka. It stood near the terminus of the road which leads to the gold mines in the Wâdî 'Ulâkî, or Akita, as it is called in the hieroglyphic inscriptions, and this fact suggests

[1] See a valuable paper by M. de Voguë entitled "Fortifications de Semneh en Nubie," in the *Bulletin Archéologique de l'Athenaeum Français*, 1855, p. 81 ff.

[2] *Hist. Ancienne*, p. 127; Naville, *Bubastis*, pl. xxxiv. A., and pp. 9, 10.

[3] See Maspero, *Mélanges*, tom. i., p. 217.

that in the reign of this king the mines passed entirely into the hands of the Egyptians. The important building operations which he carried out in Egypt absorbed the greater portion of his energy, but he appears to have made his officers at Semna and Kumma undertake the duty of registering on the rocks the maximum height of the waters of the Nile during the Inundation, for several years. These observations were, no doubt, intended to assist the irrigation officials in Egypt in calculating the times when the great canals and basins should be opened, and their waters discharged on the surrounding fields. They were made many times during the king's reign, i.e., in the 3rd, 5th, 7th, 9th, 14th, 15th, 22nd, 23rd, 24th, 30th, 32nd, 37th, 40th, 41st, and 43rd years, and the greater number of them are cut on the rocks on the east bank, at Kumma.[1] The inscription referring to the

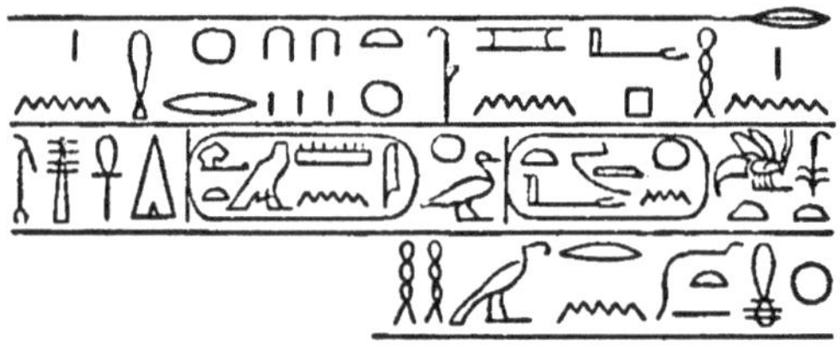

INSCRIPTION ON A ROCK AT SEMNA RECORDING THE LEVEL OF THE NILE IN THE 23RD YEAR OF THE REIGN OF ÀMEN-EM-ḤÀT III.

30th year was cut out by Lepsius and taken to Berlin, where it is now preserved in the Royal Museum (No 1161).[2] If these register marks really represent the height reached by the waters during the Inundation, it appears that the summer Nile flood rose about twenty-six feet higher than it does at the present time.[3]

The belief that the Nile levels marked on the rocks at Semna and Kumma had some special connection with Lake Moeris in the Fayyûm has long held the field, but in recent years the view has been gaining ground that Lake Moeris never existed, and if this be so, we must cease to think that the registers of Nile levels at Semna and Kumma were anything more than records made for general irrigation purposes in ancient Egypt. Many authorities

[1] See Lepsius, *Denkmäler*, Bd. ii., 139.
[2] See the official *Verzeichnis*, p. 111.
[3] See Lepsius, *Letters*, p. 239.

have been content to accept the identification of the site of the Lake Moeris, described by Herodotus, made by M. Linant de Bellefonds,[1] who thought that the road-ways which exist between the towns of Al-Lâhûn and Madinat al-Fayyûm were the remains of the dams within which Ȧmenemḥāt III. confined the waters of his lake. M. Linant maintained that Lake Moeris occupied the gap in the hills by which the Bahr Yûsuf enters the Fayyûm, and covered the so-called " plateau " on the south-east of Madina, the encircling bank commencing at its north-east end at Edwah, and being continued through Al-A'alâm, Bîhamû, *Zâwîyat* al-Karâdsa to Madina. The area given to the supposed lake by Linant is 405,479,000 square metres, but the true area is 257,800,000 square metres; the Lake described by Herodotus had a circuit of 450 miles, but the perimeter of Linant's Lake is 110 kilometres. The depth given to the Lake by Herodotus is 92 metres, whilst that of Linant is 9·60 metres.

The first to point out these facts, and to show that Linant's identification, which has been accepted by almost every writer, is incorrect was Major R. H. Brown, R.E.,[2] who sums up the matter thus:—" The Linant theory, examined in the light of the " more accurate knowledge gained by the physical features of " the Fayûm, and tested by the application of figures to determine " its possible performances, can no longer stand, but falls to pieces; " and the wonder is that, based as it was upon erroneous data and " propped up by no solid support of fact, it stood so long. It may " be said of it, to the credit of its author, that it was ingenious, but " not that it was true." Major Brown's facts are accepted by Prof. Maspero, who, in speaking of the accounts of the Labyrinth and Lake Moeris given by classical writers, says, " These are only " legends, in which the truth only holds a very small place. The " famous reservoir, which regulated the inundation, and assured " the fertility of Egypt, never existed. What Herodotus saw " was the inundation, and that which he took for the dams " which formed the enclosure of the reservoir, are the road-ways " which separated the basins one from the other. When he visited

[1] See *Mémoires sur les Principaux Travaux d'utilité publique exécutés en Égypte depuis la plus haute antiquité jusqu'à nos jours*, 1872-1873, chapter ii.
[2] See the *Fayûm and Lake Moeris*, London, 1892.

"Egypt, the natural lake which spread itself out at the east of the "valley, occupied a far larger surface than that which it has in "our days, and its level was sufficiently high that at the moment of "the rise of the Nile the whole country seemed to form only a single "sheet of water [extending] from the mountain to the desert. The "Labyrinth itself was not the wonderful palace which Herodotus "described, but the town which Àmenemḥāt founded as a depend- "ance of his pyramid, the ruins of which are visible near the modern "village of Ḥawâra.[1]

The identification proposed by Linant is a matter which, after all, can only be discussed satisfactorily by irrigation experts, and if Major Brown declares the existence of Lake Moeris as described by Herodotus to be impossible, and gives good reasons for his opinion, the Egyptologist must, because he lacks the necessary expert knowledge, be content to defer coming to a decision until the engineers have threshed out the subject. The two greatest Egyptologists of modern times, Lepsius and Brugsch Pâshâ, accepted Linant's identification of Lake Moeris, and the former "n'a pas hésité à déclarer dans un Mémoire spécial que le "savant français avait fait la découverte la plus brillante et la "plus indubitable quant à la véritable position topographique "du fameux lac Moeris." Lepsius, the Egyptologist, examined the site personally, and was convinced that Linant was correct in his views; Major Brown, the eminent irrigation engineer, also examined the site, and is certain that Linant was wrong. Here we have another instance of the Egyptologist passing judgment on a question which lies outside his province, and of the very patent fact, which is even at the present time only partially recognized by Egyptologists and Egyptian archaeologists, namely, that a knowledge of hieroglyphics does not necessarily make its possessor a competent authority on irrigation questions, or on architecture and the mechanical arts of ancient Egypt.

Of Àmenemḥāt IV., the successor of Àmenemḥāt III., but little is known. During his short reign records were kept of Nile levels in Nubia, as the inscription on the rocks at Kumma, dated in the fifth year of his reign, testifies. We have no evidence to show that he made any expeditions into the Sûdân, and, when we remember

[1] *Hist. Ancienne*, p. 132.

the completeness of the conquest of the country by Usertsen III., it is impossible not to conclude that warlike demonstrations by the Egyptians were unnecessary in the reign of Ȧmenemḥāt IV.

We may now briefly summarize the various steps in the conquest of Nubia under the XIIth Dynasty. Ȧmenemḥāt I. conquered the Māṭchaiu, the Uauaiu, the Sitiu, and Ḥeriu-shā, and fixed his boundary near Korosko. Usertsen I. conquered the four great tribes of the country, and fixed his boundary at Behen, or Wâdî Ḥalfa, one hundred miles further to the south than his predecessor. He drew large quantities of tribute from the natives, and sent, among others, Ȧmeni to bring gold to Egypt. He was perhaps the first king of Egypt to build a fort and found a town a few miles to the south of Korosko. The remains of both the fort and town were discovered in 1892 by Captain Lyons, R.E., who noticed on the rocks near several *graffiti* belonging to the XIth, XIIth, and XIIIth Dynasties. These clearly indicate that the site was occupied by Egyptian officials under the Menthuḥetep kings of the XIth Dynasty, and this being so we may assume that it was a centre of Sûdân trade of considerable importance. In the reign of Ȧmenemḥāt II. the officer Sa-Hathor went into Nubia and began to work the gold mines of Ḥeḥ by means of native labour, on behalf of the Egyptian Government. The young men dug out the ore, and the old men carried out the operations connected with the final stages of washing out the metal. Under Usertsen III. the Egyptian frontier on the south was moved to Semna, and an edict was passed forbidding any negro to pass north of that place except for purposes of business or embassy. For eleven years at least, i.e., from his eighth to his nineteenth year, this king carried on a series of wars, which resulted in the complete subjugation of the country. He built a line of forts, which were occupied by native garrisons under Egyptian officers, between Elephantine and Semna, and in many of them he placed temples; he appears to have established a fortified outpost about eighty miles south of Semna, in the neighbourhood of Gebel Dôsha. From a portion of a monument discovered by Prof. Naville[1] we learn that Usertsen made a raid in a country called Ḥuā.[2]

[1] *Bubastis*, plate 34.

[2] 

Now a country called Ḥuā is mentioned in an inscription of a later period in connection with Punt, and if it be the same region it follows that he invaded the country on the western shore near the southern end of the Red Sea. If this be so, this king must have been absolute master of all the great trade routes of the Egyptian Sûdân, as well as of all the gold mines throughout the country. Before Usertsen's death arrangements were made for a systematic supply of gold for Egypt, and the caravans travelled on from fort to fort, bearing their precious loads to the old Egyptian frontier city of Elephantine in safety. It is probable that each caravan was provided with an escort of soldiers of sufficient strength to repulse any attack which was likely to be made upon it by the marauding tribes of the desert. It is clear from the inscriptions that each Egyptian settlement in the Sûdân was ruled by an officer who possessed powers of summary jurisdiction, and that at places like Behen, or Wâdî Ḥalfa, he was sometimes a man of high rank, i.e., an *erpā* or a *ḥā*, and that one of the tribes of such an officer was "superintendent of the South," or, "governor of the South," is certain from the evidence of the monuments like that of Erṭā-Ȧntef-Ṭeṭi.

Under the XIIth Dynasty, however, there seems to have been no one official who was in charge of the whole Egyptian administration of the Sûdân, and at that time there was no equivalent of the term "royal son of Kash," or viceroy, who was regularly appointed by Egypt under the XVIIIth Dynasty. The governor of each town was allowed to do as he pleased, provided that he succeeded in making the natives of his district contribute a satisfactory amount of gold, precious stones, skins, &c., to the revenue of the country, which had to be despatched to Egypt, and at this period the state of affairs in the Sûdân must have been much like that in which they were under the rule of such "strong men" as Muḥammad 'Alî. To get everything possible out of the Sûdân, slaves, gold, ivory, skins, &c., was the order of the day. The contempt which the governing classes felt for the natives is, as we have seen, clearly expressed in the words of the king himself, who called them timid, cowardly, vile, impotent, and stupid beasts.

In the reign of Ȧmenemḥāt III., the successor of Usertsen III., a fort was built at Dakka with the view of strengthening the hold which the Egyptians had on the mines of Wâdî 'Ulâḳî, but further raids were necessary, for the Sûdân had not recovered from the ruin and devastation which had been spread through it broadcast by Usertsen III. The reign of Ȧmenemḥāt IV. was short and unimportant, and the Sûdân was not troubled by any *razzia* on a specially large scale.

The only work of public utility undertaken in Nubia by the kings of the XIIth Dynasty was in connection with the Nile. Usertsen I. appears to have constructed a series of dykes on the west bank of the river, and to have made some attempt to "train" its waters. Usertsen III. cleared out and enlarged the old canal which ran through a portion of the First Cataract, and Ȧmenemḥāt III. caused records of Nile levels to be cut on the rocks at Semna and Kumma, no doubt in connection with a scheme for the regulation of the water supply of Egypt. In all these efforts, however, the advantage which would accrue to the Egyptians was first calculated, and the effect which they might have on the prosperity of Nubia was not specially considered. The main objects were to keep a clear water-way for the passage of boats employed in the business of the Government, and to use the data collected at Semna in connection with the working of the irrigation basins in Egypt.

The kings of the XIIIth Dynasty, who were of Theban origin, succeeded in maintaining their hold upon the Sûdân, but few details of the period during which they ruled have come down to us. The first king of the dynasty, according to the King-Lists, was he whose prenomen is Khu-taui-Rā. Nothing is known about him, and no monument of him was known until the discovery at Semna of the small statue of him by Mr. J. W. Crowfoot and myself in January, 1905 (see Vol. I., pp. 485, 486). The fifteenth king of this dynasty, Sebek-ḥetep I., caused records of the Nile levels during the first four years of his reign to be cut on the rocks at Semna and Kumma; the record of the fourth year was cut out by Lepsius and taken to Berlin, where it is now exhibited in the Royal Museum (No. 1,160).[1] During this king's reign the

[1] See the official *Verzeichnis*, p. 111.

governor of Nubia was a prince called Ren-seneb.[1] The twenty-first king of this dynasty, Nefer-ḥetep, apparently caused work to be carried on in the quarries at Elephantine, for on a rock on the Island of Konosso he is represented standing before the God Khnemu, and close by his cartouche is seen by the side of Menthu-Rā, Menu, and Satet. On the Island of Sâḥal he is seen adoring Anuqet, and figures of himself and the members of his family are roughly sculptured on the rocks near Aswân. The twenty-third king of this dynasty, Sebek-ḥetep III., was the greatest of the dynasty. The extent of his sway is proved by the fact that he set up colossal statues of himself at Tanis and Bubastis, the

COLOSSAL STATUE OF A KING ON THE ISLAND OF ARḲÔ.

[From Lepsius, *Denkmäler*, Abth. I. Bl. 120.

seats of his power in the Delta, and on the Island of Argo, or Arḳô.

This Island is about twenty miles long, and its southern end is about two hundred and five miles from Wâdî Ḥalfa; it lies a little to the south of the head of the Third Cataract, and between it and the Fourth Cataract boats can sail up and down the river every day in the year. Arḳô was visited by M. Cailliaud in 1821, and he describes the vegetation upon it in glowing terms.[2]

[1] See Lepsius, *Denkmäler*, Bd. ii., Bl. 151.

[2] "Les végétaux respirent sur cette île la fraicheur et la vie : les arbres qui "ont péri desséchés par la main du temps ou étouffés par les violentes "étreintes des lianes, présentent eux-mêmes les apparences de la vigueur et de "la jeunesse, sous le tissu de verdure dont les enlacent ces plantes gigan-"tesques, qui forment de toute part de magnifiques berceaux que l'art aurait "peine à imiter" (*Voyage*, tom. ii., p. 2).

SEBEK-HETEP III.

Towards the middle of the Island are two gray granite colossal statues, lying on the ground; one statue broke into two pieces when it fell down, or was overthrown, and the other has lost parts of its arms. The height of each statue, including the pedestal, which is nearly 3 feet, is between 23 and 24 feet. Lepsius attributed them to the Hyksos period, but they seem to me to belong to a far later date.

The king is represented as bearded, and wearing the crown of the south; round his neck is a collar formed of circular ornaments. His tunic is fastened round his waist by a knotted cord, and is held in position by a strap passing over each shoulder. In the unbroken statue the king wears anklets, and in the broken one armlets; in front of the right leg of the latter is a small statue of Harpocrates, with the fore-finger of his right hand raised to his lips, and wearing a pair of horns with a disk between them. Cailliaud calls them "colossal statues of Memnon,"[1] and Hoskins thought they be-

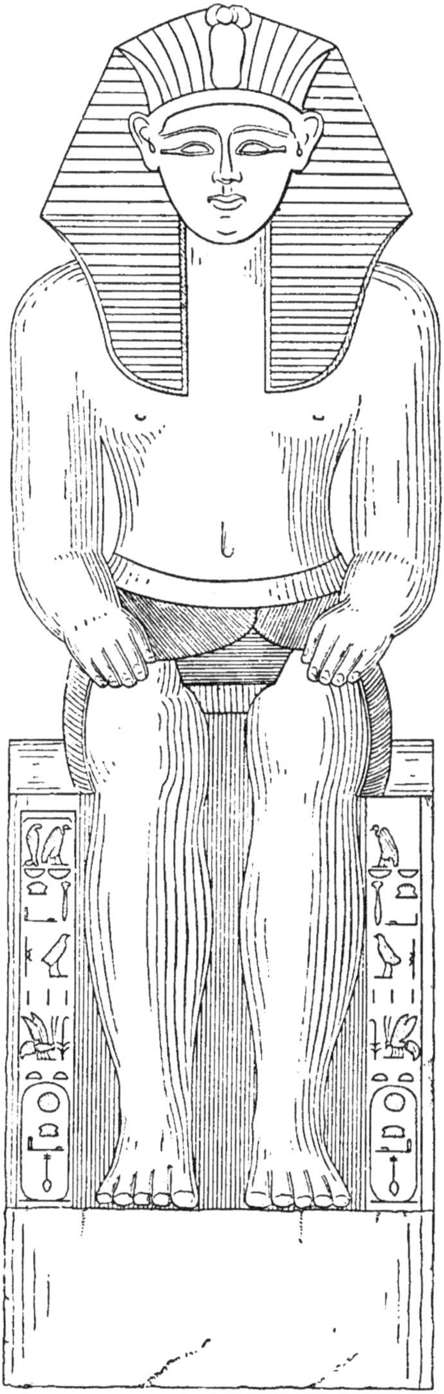

STATUE OF KING SEBEK-HETEP III. ON THE ISLAND OF ARḲÔ.

[From Lepsius, *Denkmäler*, Abth. II. Bl. 120.

[1] *Voyage*, tom. ii., p. 2.

longed to the Ethiopian period.[1] These statues stood, undoubtedly, one on each side of the door of a temple, the site of which was about 260 feet long, and about 163 feet wide. The stones which formed the temple have been removed, and there is absolutely nothing left to suggest that it would be worth while making excavations there. A little distance behind the statues are the remains of a headless black granite seated statue.

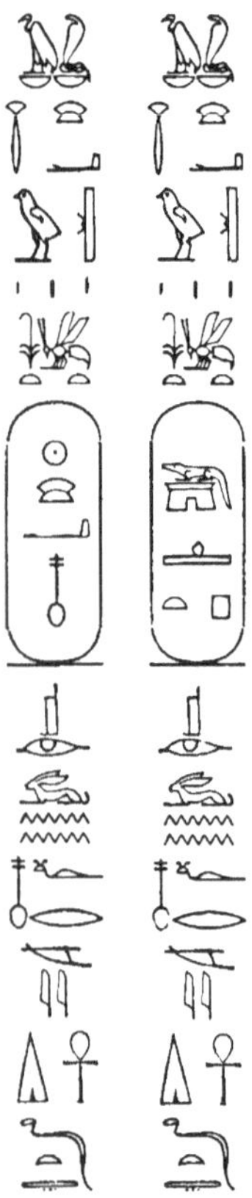

Hoskins says[1] that this statue was half-buried in the ruins, and that the name of Sabaco [i.e., Shabaka] is engraved on it in hieroglyphics. Viewed in the light of his observations on p. 296 of his *Travels*, to the effect that the name Shabaka is not found on any of the monuments of Ethiopia, this statement is difficult to understand. Lepsius in his great work[2] publishes an outline drawing of a seated statue on the Island of Arḳô, and on each side of the legs is a column of hieroglyphs containing the names and titles of the king whom it represents. From the inscriptions, which are here given, we see that in the one column we have the king's prenomen and his titles, and in the other the king's nomen and a repetition of the titles. These read, "Lord of the vulture shrine, lord of the "uraeus shrine, abundant of risings [like Rā], "King of the South and North, Rā-khā-nefer, "beloved of Osiris Un-nefer, giver of life for "ever." In the second column, besides these titles, we have the king's name, Sebek-ḥetep. It seems that Hoskins knew the value of the first sign in the second cartouche, and that he assumed Sebek to be the equivalent of Sabaco. This black granite statue in many ways resembles the statues of Usertsen III. set up by himself in various shrines in the Sûdân, and it belongs, in my opinion, to a period much earlier than that of the two colossal statues which have already been described.

[1] *Travels*, p.2.

[2] *Denkmäler*, Abth. ii., Bl. 120.

SEBEK-HETEP III.

Behind the statue of Sebek-ḥetep III., at about the same distance, sculptured in gray granite, is a group of monkeys standing on their hind legs , and having their fore-legs raised in adoration before them. The town which stood near the temple must have been of considerable importance, and Lepsius saw[1] the traces of one extending far across the plain, with an immense necropolis attached to it, in which two huge monumental tombs were distinguished above all the others, one of which was called Kermân and the other Dafûfa. They are oblong in form; the larger is 150 feet long and 66 feet wide, and the smaller 132 feet long and 66 feet wide. Each is about 40 feet high, and is solidly built of crude mud bricks; in front of each is a building, which may have served as a chapel wherein prayers were said for the dead, and offerings made.[2] Lepsius thought that the oldest Egyptian settlement of any importance on Ethiopian territory must have been on this spot; it was probably occasioned by the Egyptian power having been driven back towards Ethiopia during the rule of the Hyksos in Egypt. In connection with the statues on the Island of Arḳô, reference must be made to the granite quarries wherein these were hewn. These quarries are situated on the Island of Tombos,[3] which is about two hours down stream, at the head of the Cataract of Hannek, and a little north of Ḳubba Abû Fâṭma; here among the blocks of granite which are scattered about is still to be seen another colossal statue, about 12 feet long, which is in a much ruined state.[4] The quarries are on the right bank of the river, and are sufficiently far away from the Island of Arḳô to make the work of transporting the statues there one of no small difficulty.

Towards the close of the XIIIth Dynasty there reigned in the Delta a king who styled himself "King of the South and North, Rā-Neḥsi," or Neḥsi-Rā.[5] Now the word "Neḥsi" means

[1] *Letters*, p. 234.

[2] For views of these see Hoskins, *Travels*, p. 216; Lepsius, *Denkmäler*, Abth. i., Bl. 120.

[3] More correctly ṬUNBUS طنبس.

[4] For a view of it see Hoskins, *Travels*, p. 218.

[5] .

"Black," or "Negro"; therefore this king's name means "the Negro of Rā." It is quite certain that he was a king of foreign extraction, for the sign  stands after his name, and as he is styled in an inscription at Tanis, "the Royal son Neḥsi," it is probable that he was in reality a black man, and a son of one of the kings of Egypt who led expeditions into the Sûdân, and that he had by some means established himself, by virtue of his descent, on the throne of Egypt.[1]

Of the history of the Sûdân under the XIVth Dynasty we know nothing.

[1] See Naville, *Recueil*, tom. xv., p. 99; and my *History of Egypt*, vol. iii., p. 103.

CHAPTER III.

THE SÛDÂN UNDER THE XVIIITH, XIXTH, AND XXTH DYNASTIES.

OF the history of the Sûdân under the XVth, XVIth, and XVIIth Dynasties, i.e., during the period of the rule of the Hyksos kings, nothing is known. The seat of the Hyksos power was in the Delta, their capital being at Avaris;[1] for some centuries they were masters of Lower Egypt, and probably of a large portion of Upper Egypt also. Whether they attempted to exercise any authority over the Sûdân cannot be said, but it is probable that they did not; if they did, they left no traces of their rule behind them. Under the second dynasty of Hyksos kings a dispute broke out between these rulers and the Princes of Thebes, and after a series of fights, which were probably spread over a long period of years, the latter succeeded in expelling the Hyksos and making themselves lords of all Egypt. A legend found in the First Sallier Papyrus says that the Hyksos king was called Rā-Āpepi and the Theban Prince Seqenen-Rā, and that the dispute between these kings arose because Seqenen-Rā would neither worship the Hyksos god Sutekh, nor acknowlege his supremacy. This may or may not be true, but there is probably a substratum of fact in the statement, and when we remember the devotion which the Princes and Kings of Thebes always displayed towards their god Āmen, it is easy to understand the contempt which they would feel for the chief god of their conquerors. In any case, the Thebans vanquished the Hyksos, and Āāḥmes the younger son of Tauāaqen, whose prenomen was Seqenen-Rā, and who appears to have died in a fight with the Hyksos, ascended the throne as lord of all Egypt, and as the first king of the XVIIIth Dynasty, about B.C. 1700.

1 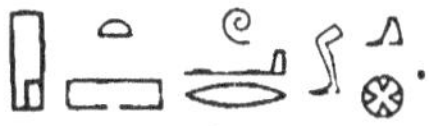.

Áāḥmes, or Amasis I., continued the war of independence which Tauāaqen had begun, and having besieged and captured the city of Avaris, the Hyksos stronghold, he pursued the Hyksos themselves to the city of Shârûhen, whither they had fled for refuge. This took place in the fifth year of his reign. When Amasis had subdued the tribes and peoples in the desert to the north-east of Egypt, he realized that it was time to reduce the Nubians to submission. For two or three centuries the grasp of the iron hand of the Egyptians on their country had been relaxed, and the people had well-nigh forgotten how to pay tribute. The account of the campaigns of Amasis in Nubia written by one of his generals, who also bore the name of Amasis,[1] gives us a few interesting facts, for he says, "When His Majesty had chastised sorely the Mentiu of Asia, he sailed up the Nile to Khent-ḥen-nefer."[2] The exact position of this region is unknown, but it seems tolerably certain that it included all the Nile Valley so far south as the Fourth Cataract, and probably all the cultivated lands between Kharṭûm and Dâr Fûr. "Khent" is a very old Egyptian name for the Sûdân, and it is probable that the portion of it which is indicated by the words "Ḥen-nefer" may describe the "park-like country" on both sides of the White Nile, which is fertile, and contains trees and vegetation of all kinds in abundance, and is full of wild and domesticated animals. To this country Amasis went, "in order to punish the "Anti[3] among the people of Kenset (i.e., the Nubian Troglodytes), "and His Majesty made a great slaughter among them. I rose "up, and I brought in two prisoners alive, and three hands, and "the king again gave me a gift of gold, and also two female slaves. "Then His Majesty sailed down the river with joy, his heart being "elated with conquest and strength, because he had conquered and "obtained possession of the lands of the South and those of the "North." The narrative is simple, and its meaning clear: Amasis made a military demonstration in Nubia, killed a great many people who resisted his progress, or declined to pay tribute, and

1 For the text see Lepsius, *Denkmäler*, Bd. iii., Bl. 12.

2 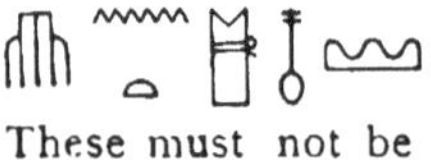.

3 These must not be confused with the Anti of Syria and the Peninsula of Sinai.

then, having collected a large amount of Sûdân produce, he returned "in peace" to Egypt. We may note in passing that the only people of Nubia mentioned by Amasis are the Anti[1] and the Kensetiu, the former probably referring to the wild and lawless desert tribes whose homes were in the hills and mountainous districts at some distance from the river banks, and the latter to the inhabitants who dwelt on and near the Nile itself. It was, obviously, necessary to bring the desert tribes into subjection, for otherwise the Government caravans could not travel from Nubia into Egypt in safety.

Soon after Amasis I. returned to Egypt, a serious revolt broke out in the south, and the people rose, and headed by a leader, to whom the Egyptians gave the name of "Aata," i.e., "Filthy one," or "Plague," or "Fever,"[2] marched towards Egypt, and "laid waste the shrines of the gods of the South." What these words mean exactly it is hard to say, but they seem to indicate that the Nubians, driven to desperation by the recent invasion of their country by the Egyptians, and stirred up by a brave and fanatical leader, who mixed religion with his politics and tried to persuade his followers that he was preaching a religious war, advanced to places like Semna, Kumma, Gazîrat al-Malik, Ma'atûḳa, and Behen, and overthrew the temples which had been built by the kings of the XIIth Dynasty, and broke the statues of the gods. Against this rebel Amasis I. marched, accompanied by his generals, Amasis the son of Baba, and Amasis the son of Pen-nekheb, and they succeeded in catching him alive on the Nile at a place called Thent-taā. Amasis the captain, and each member of his crew who took part in his capture, received five heads as the reward of his bravery, and a grant of land in his native city. What was done with Aata is not said. Soon after this, our narrator tells us, "there rose up a vile one, whose name "was Tetáān, and he gathered unto him a number of runagates "and rebels, but His Majesty smote him and his companions so "sorely that they could never again rise up." The slaughter of the rebel and his companions no doubt put an end to the

[1] 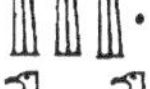. On this name see the remarks of Müller, *Asien*, pp. 21, 22.

[2] .

rebellion; at all events we hear nothing more of expeditions to the Sûdân in the reign of Amasis I.

After the death of Amasis I. Egypt was ruled by his widow, Queen Åāḥmes-nefert-ȧri and her son Åmen-ḥeṭep I. Soon after his mother died, Åmen-ḥetep I. decided to go to Nubia "to enlarge the borders of Egypt," a euphemism probably for "making a *razzia*." He put himself in the hands of his father's old officers, Amasis the son of Baba, and Amasis the son of Pen-Nekheb, and the former says in his inscription, "I conveyed by "boat up the river the king of the South and North, Åmen-ḥetep "(I.), when he sailed up the Nile to Kesh (Cush), to enlarge the "borders of Egypt. His Majesty took captive the chief of the "Ånti of Kenset when he was among his soldiers, for they were "caught in an ambush and could not escape, and they were "scattered, and could make no further resistance. And, behold, "I was the captain of our soldiers, and I fought with all my "might, and the king observed my valour. I brought in two "hands and carried them to His Majesty, whilst he was searching "for his (i.e., the rebel's) men (i.e., slaves) and his cattle, and I "rose up and captured a man alive and brought him into His "Majesty's presence." The mention of men and cattle suggests that Åmen-ḥetep I. had reached some part of the Sûdân where slaves and good cattle abounded, and we naturally think of the region south of Kharṭûm. Within the last few years large numbers of fine cattle have been brought down to Kharṭûm, and despatched by train to Ḥalfa, and thence by boat into Egypt; the district occupied by the Baḳḳâra (i.e., "cattle-keepers") was then, as now, famous for its cattle, which have been much appreciated in Egypt in all periods. How far Åmen-ḥetep I. penetrated into the Sûdân is uncertain, but his name occurs on a wooden tablet, which is said to have been discovered at Meroë,[1] and if this be so, it shows that this king emulated the example of Usertsen III., who marched all over the Egyptian Sûdân.[2]

[1] See C. Gazzera, *Descrizione dei Monumenti Egizii del Regio Museo a Torino, contenenti leggende reali*, Turin, 1824. Plate i., No. 8.

[2] In Signor Gazzera's drawing we see the king's cartouches mounted on the symbol of the union of the Two Countries. On each side of these is a palm branch standing in the symbol for "eternity." (British Museum, press mark 7703 *aa* 23).

Whilst Åmen-ḥetep I. was collecting the slaves and cattle which he had raided, a rebellion broke out in the north, and he was obliged to hurry back to quell it; the king travelled in great haste, and Amasis the captain says, "I brought His Majesty in "two days to Egypt, from the Upper Well,[1] and His Majesty "rewarded me with a gift of gold." In addition to the women whom he brought to His Majesty, he captured two for himself, and the king promoted him to the rank of Āḥatiu-en-ḥeq, i.e., a "warrior of the Royal Guard." Amasis the son of Pen-nekheb also distinguished himself in this expedition, and he captured one Nubian alive. When the king returned to the north he engaged in a fierce conflict with some people called Åmu-kehek, or Åmu-neb-hek, the exact position of whose country is unknown. In this expedition the general Amasis, the son of Pen-nekheb, was again with him, and this officer distinguished himself by capturing "three hands," which he no doubt cut off himself from the king's enemies.[2] The Åmu-kebek were vanquished, and, as we know that Åmen-ḥetep I. conquered a number of Asiatic foes, we may assume that they were among them. The king certainly fought personally in the regions to the north-east of Egypt, and he went into battle in a chariot drawn by horses.[3] Thus we see that the Egyptians soon recognized the value of this animal, which appears to have been introduced into Egypt by the Hyksos.

As we hear nothing more of expeditions into Nubia, we may conclude that the king found his hands very full of Asiatic affairs, as the result of his conquest of the southern portion of Syria. About this time he appears to have realized that it was impossible for him to make expeditions both into Nubia and Syria, so, as the tribute of Western Asia was likely to be far more valuable than that of Nubia, he determined to fight in person in Syria, and to place the government of the Sûdân in the hands of a viceroy. Having decided to appoint a viceroy, Åmen-ḥetep I. selected his own son, Thothmes I., to fill the position, and bestowed upon him

1 .

2 See Maspero, *Aeg. Zeit.*, 1883, p. 78.

3 See the wooden tablet in the British Museum, No. 2429.

the title of "Prince of Kash"[1] (or, Cush). It is possible that Ȧmen-ḥetep I. had himself held the same position and borne the same title, and some colour is lent to this view by the statements made in the inscription of Amasis the son of Baba, to which reference has already been made. We have seen that this officer followed Amasis I. into Nubia, and that he also took Ȧmen-ḥetep I. there, and in the last lines of the text in his tomb he adds the information that he also conveyed Thothmes I. up the Nile when he went to Kheut-ḥen-nefer to punish the natives who had broken out into open rebellion. Ȧmen-ḥetep I. was very fortunate to be able to avail himself of the services of his father's old, trusted, and experienced captain of the boats, and he was more fortunate still when he knew that his son would be accompanied by this capable veteran.

When we consider the importance of the Sûdân to Egypt it is difficult to understand why the kings of the XIIth Dynasty had not appointed their sons to be "Princes of Kash." The traffic up and down the river, in which the king was the most interested party, must have been enormous. The boats from the south were filled with negroes, cattle, gold, precious stones, grain, ivory, ebony, frankincense, gum, skins, etc., whilst those from the north were loaded with food with which to feed the Egyptian officials and the thousands of wretched men who toiled in the gold mines, and at crushing the ore and washing out the gold. Such traffic was far too valuable to leave entirely to the management of the local governors, and that this fact was recognized by Ȧmen-ḥetep I. is clear from his appointment of a "Prince of Kash." At first the holders of the viceroyalty were all princes of the blood, but long before the close of the XVIIIth Dynasty, the Government found it to be expedient to allow high officials who were not of royal birth to bear the title. Sometimes, it seems, an Egyptian prince accepted the title, but lived at court in Egypt; in such cases a deputy was appointed who administered the country in the name of the Prince of Kash. Thus we see that Ȧmen-ḥetep I. made the Sûdân a province of Egypt, and there are many indications in the inscriptions that it was divided into districts, each of which

[1] .

was under the rule of a governor who was responsible to the Prince of Kash.

On the death of Ȧmen-ḥetep I. the desert tribes of the Sûdân rebelled according to their custom, and the first result of the revolt was the suspension of the payment of tribute by them, and interference with the caravans. The news of the death of the king spread rapidly through the desert, and everywhere the nomad tribes closed in on the Egyptian forts along the Nile, and began to harass the officers of the Egyptian Government. Their attempts were seconded by the thousands of wretched natives who worked in the mines, and who, naturally, were always hoping that something would happen which would enable them to escape from their life of hard labour. When Thothmes I., the son of Ȧmen-ḥetep I., ascended the throne, he sent out an announcement of the fact to the governors of the provinces of Egypt, and set out in it the names and titles which he had adopted. At the end of the royal message he commands that the offerings, i.e., tribute, which are due to the "gods of the south" at Elephantine shall be offered, together with wishes for his happiness, and that all whom it concerns shall take the oath of allegiance to him.

These things, however, the tribes of the Sûdân refused to do, and Thothmes I. was therefore obliged to go to Nubia with an army to punish the natives and to make them pay their tribute. Amasis, the son of Baba, conveyed the king to Khent-ḥen-nefer, i.e., to the regions south of Kharṭûm whence came the slaves, and ebony and ivory, and fought with his usual bravery and success. The Egyptian fleet of boats met the enemy in their boats on the river, and a fierce fight took place. During the conflict some of the enemy's boats were capsized in mid-stream, and floated on to the mud banks; Amasis the captain must have played a prominent and decisive part in the fight, for he was promoted to be "Chief of the sailors," or Admiral of the Fleet.

The king attacked his enemies in person, and Amasis tells us that "he raged at them like a lion (or panther). He hurled "his javelin, which pierced the body of his foe, who fell down "headlong before the king. The enemy suffered a great defeat, "and large numbers of them were captured alive. Then his "Majesty sailed down the river, and all the people made submission "unto him. And the dead body of the vile king of the Nubians "was tied to the bows of the boat of His Majesty, who returned "to Thebes."[1] This formed an object lesson, the significance of which was not likely to be misunderstood by the natives as they watched the royal barge float down the river. This expedition was directed specially against the people of Khent-ḥen-nefer, a name which, according to Brugsch,[2] comprehended all "the "countries of the African continent, and therefore included the "countries and peoples situated to the west of the Nile as far "as the Libyan north coast;" it is, however, far more likely that the region to which Thothmes I. went was situated in the country which is to-day known as the Western Sûdân. There was nothing to be gained by traversing the desert to the west of the Nile, and as the Egyptians were a practical folk and undertook expeditions into remote countries, not for settlement but for what they could gain, they naturally attacked the regions which abounded in slaves and wild animals and cattle.

To commemorate his expedition into Nubia Thothmes I., in his second year, caused an inscription of eighteen lines to be cut on a rock on the Island of Tombos, near the head of the Third Cataract, about five hundred and forty miles south of Thebes,[3] but it, unfortunately, supplies us with very few facts of a historical character. After an enumeration of the royal names and titles, the text goes on to say that the king has become sovereign of the two lands, that his rule extends as far as the sun's course, the South and the North being the domains of Horus and Set, that he has united the Two Lands and taken his seat on the thrones of Seb, &c. He seated himself on the throne of Horus to enlarge the boundaries of Thebes, and to acquire the cultivable lands, to make to work the Ḥeriu-shā (i.e., the nomad tribes of the desert), and the Hill folk, who are abominable before the gods, and the Aqabet. "The people of the south shall float down the river, and "the people of the north shall sail up it, and all the mountain and "desert lands shall unite in bearing their gifts to the well-doing "god [of] primeval time"—says the king. Thothmes I. boasts

[1] See Erman, *Aeg. Zeit.*, 1891, p. 16.

[2] *Egypt under the Pharaohs*, vol. i., p. 329.

[3] For the text, see Lepsius, *Denkmäler*, Abth. iii., Bl. 5.

that he enslaved the Ḥeru tribes,[1] and that their villages "smelled the earth" before him. The Khennutiu[2] folk sent messengers to bring their submission to His Majesty, and the chief of the Semti folk[3] was overthrown by him, and the "miserable and "contemptible negro fled as the king advanced up the river. He "gathered together the boundaries on both sides of the Nile, and "not a head of hair was absent" (i.e., no native was absent), and the Qeṭu[4] people rallied to him. He attacked the Ȧnti of Kenset, i.e., the Troglodytes, he slaughtered them in the places where they lived, and they collapsed under his blows, and their bodies turned into carrion (?). Then His Majesty swept through the valleys and khôrs like a mighty flood which destroys and lays waste everything which stands in its way, and drove out the people like flocks of frightened birds. Then the "lords of the great house" built a fort for his soldiers which could not be captured by all the Nine Tribes of the Bow together, for His Majesty was to the Nubians as the young panther is to a cow which is frightened and blind. The souls of His Majesty extended the boundaries of his kingdom in all directions, he marched even to the uttermost limits of the country carrying his victorious sword with him, he sought battle everywhere, but found no one strong enough to resist him. He penetrated to mountains and deserts, wherein his predecessors had "not only never been, but which they had never even seen." The southern boundary of his kingdom was the uttermost limit of Nubia, and the northern was that river whereon if a man travel a southerly direction he journeys down stream.[5] The river here referred to is the Euphrates, and all the writer of the text wished to convey by his circumlocution was that, unlike the Nile, the Euphrates enters the sea at its southern end. Never, continues the text, was the like done by other kings. His name went forth to the bounds of the sky, it penetrated the Two Lands, and reached the Other World, and by it men were in the habit of swearing throughout all countries.

1 

2 

3 

4 

5 

From the above extracts from the inscription of Tombos it will be seen that the text has little historical value, and that it tells us few things which we did not know from other sources. We may notice in it the claim which is made for Thothmes I. of sovereignty over Syria and Western Asia so far as the Euphrates, but as the inscription is dated in the second year of his reign, it is clear that the expeditions to Nubia and Syria were neither difficult nor protracted, and that they were undertaken rather for the purpose of collecting tribute than conquest. In the reign of Thothmes I. the Sûdân was divided into districts like Egypt, and every portion of it except the deserts, which were occupied by the nomad tribes which successfully evaded every attempt to force upon them a settled government and civilization, was administered by a properly appointed official.

Thothmes I. was succeeded by Thothmes II., his son by a wife called Mut-nefert; his reign was short and unimportant, but his officials made the usual expeditions into Nubia and Southern Syria, and compelled the natives to acknowledge the supremacy of their lord. On the death of Thothmes I. the desert tribes of the Sûdân revolted, and they invaded the lands of those who lived under the protection of Egypt, and raided their cattle. Thothmes II. despatched his forces to Nubia without delay, and his commander-in-chief declared that he would not leave a single man alive in the country. The Egyptian troops marched through the country, killing men, burning crops and villages, and raiding the cattle, and finally they captured alive a son of the "chief of Kash," whom they bound and carried into the king's presence and set under his feet. The Nubians, seeing that their revolt had failed, brought in gifts as usual until the Egyptian officials were satisfied, or knew that the natives had nothing else left to bring, and having bowed their backs in homage, and "smelled the earth" at the feet of the king's representative, they proclaimed the glory and power of Thothmes II., and retired to their deserts to await the next opportunity for a revolt. These details are supplied by Amasis Pen-Nekheb, who played a prominent part in the Nubian expedition, and was rewarded by the king with rich gifts for his prowess. In the reign of Thothmes II. the block of buildings belonging to the XVIIIth

STELE SET UP IN THE TEMPLE OF THOTHMES II AT WADI HALFA BY SETI I., ABOUT B.C. 1370, IN THE FIRST YEAR OF HIS REIGN. THE KING IS REPRESENTED IN THE ACT OF BURNING INCENSE BEFORE AMEN-RA, MENU, AND ISIS.

[British Museum, No. 1189.

Presented to the British Museum by Sir Charles Holled Smith, K.C.M.G., 1887.

Dynasty at Kumma was begun, and the cartouches of this king are to be seen to this day over the door of the temple which he built there in honour of the god Khnemu.[1] His prenomen is also found, together with those of his father, grandfather, and great-grandfather, on the outside of the south wall of the temple of Semna,[2] and it is clear that he carried out some work in connection with the famous fortress founded by Usertsen III.

Thothmes II. married his sister Ḥātshepset, by whom he had two daughters, and the lady Åst, by whom he became the father of Thothmes III. At his death Ḥātshepset, who had been associated with her father in the rule of the kingdom, became virtually Queen of Egypt, for, although she was nominally the regent, and acted on behalf of her nephew Thothmes III., it is easy to see that she managed the affairs of Egypt according to her own will and pleasure. The most important event in the reign of the Queen was an expedition to Punt, which was planned and carried out under her directions. The expedition consisted of five ships, which sailed down the Red Sea to some point on the African coast, probably near Cape Guardafui, and the captain of the fleet, having landed and found the governor of the district, Pa-rehu, presented the Queen's gifts to him, and proceeded to do business with him. Finally the Egyptians took back gold rings, boomerangs, *ānti*, i.e., gum for incense, or myrrh, ebony, ivory, green gold, eye-paint, apes, monkeys, and panther-skins. As Ḥātshepset had nothing to do with conquests in the Sûdân we may at once pass on to the reign of her nephew, Thothmes III.

When Thothmes III. ascended the throne of Egypt he found that the rule of his aunt Ḥātshepset, however peaceful and "progressive," had only paved the way for a general revolt in all the countries which were subject to Egypt. Whilst the queen was amusing herself in sending off the expedition to Punt, and in beautifying her capital, the Syrians, and the tribes in the Eastern Desert, and the natives of the Sûdân, were making a firm stand against the payment of the tribute which had been laid upon them by the early kings of the XVIIIth Dynasty. Envoys bearing tribute had ceased to arrive at Thebes, the local governors in all

[1] See Lepsius, *Denkmaler*, Abth. iii. 58.

[2] *Ibid.*, 47*c*.

parts of the kingdom failed to collect the revenues, for the simple reason that the tribes laughed at their demands, and even at their threats, and the treasury of the temple of the great god Amen, which had hitherto supplied the queen with funds, was being depleted. When Thothmes III. became sole king, in the twenty-second year of his age, he saw that he had a gigantic task before him, which was nothing less than the reconquest of every province of the kingdom which he had inherited. With promptitude he set out for Syria, and when he arrived there he learned that all the tribes of Western Asia were in a ferment, and that they had cast off the yoke of Egypt. He attacked Megiddo and captured it, and thus broke up the conspiracy ; the spoil which he carried back to Egypt was enormous, over two thousand mares, nearly one thousand chariots, two thousand goats, twenty thousand sheep, thousands of slaves, gold, silver, metal vases and vessels of all kinds, and over two hundred thousand measures of corn.

It is unnecessary here to describe the Syrian expeditions of Thothmes III. in detail, and it will be sufficient to state that the towns, cities, and districts which he conquered in Western Asia were at least three hundred and fifty-eight in number, and that he conquered the country eastward as far as the Euphrates, near which, at Nī, he set up his memorial stele and the mark of the boundary of his kingdom in Asia. In the thirty-second year of his reign the Kenbetu,[1] or people of Punt, and the people of Uauat sent tribute to the king. That of the former country consisted of two hundred and thirty bulls, one hundred and thirteen oxen and calves, ten negroes, and boat-loads of ivory, ebony, panther-skins, &c.; that of the latter, sixty bulls, thirty-one oxen and calves, and boat-loads of Sûdân products. We may note in passing that the Sûdâni folk did not wait for the king to come and fetch their tribute, but that they brought it to Thebes. Two years later the people of Punt sent 1685 measures of incense, a large quantity of gold, negroes, male and female, oxen, calves, bulls, goats, &c. Uauat also sent similar offerings, but in smaller quantities and numbers. In one place in the tribute-lists the offerings of the "vile country of Kash" are enumerated separately from those of Uauat and

[1] 

Punt, and this fact seems to suggest that in the reign of Thothmes III. the three great provinces of the Sûdân were Kash, Uauat, and Punt. These countries appear to have sent tribute to Egypt every one or two years, and the kinds of gifts they sent were always the same. At this period Uauat appears to have been Nubia so far as Wâdi Ḥalfa, Kash extended from Wâdî Ḥalfa to Kharṭûm, and Punt represented all the region to the south, east, and west of that city for a considerable distance.

The detailed account of the expeditions of Thothmes III. given upon the walls of the temple of Karnak contains no information which would lead us to suppose that the king marched into Nubia in person. We see from it that his time was fully occupied in collecting the tribute from Western Asia, which was far more valuable than any which Nubia could set before him, and we learn from the inscription of his general, Amen-em-ḥeb,[1] that he found relaxation in hunting elephants, of which he killed one hundred and twenty. In spite of this, however, more buildings were set up in Nubia in the reign of Thothmes III. than under any other king, and, if we may believe the list of places conquered in the Sûdân which appears on the wall of a pylon at Thebes, we are justified in saying that Egyptian rule in Nubia was never so effective as at this period. The list is divided into three parts, which contain the names of places conquered by the king, and "wherein he made a great slaughter," in "Kash the vile," Uauat and Punt, respectively;[2] the first includes twenty-three names, the second twenty-four, and the third one hundred and ninety-five. There is no reason to doubt the reality of the king's power in the Sûdân, but we have no evidence which would justify us in assuming that he took any personal part in the formation of it, or that it was the result of the efforts of any except Neḥi,[3] the fearless and vigorous "Prince of Kash." Reference may now be made to the temples, &c., in Nubia which bear the names of Thothmes III.

[1] His tomb is at 'Abd al-Ḳûrna at Thebes. For the text, see Ebers, *Aeg. Zeit.*, 1873, pp. 1-9; and for English translations, see Birch, *Records*, vol. ii., p. 53; Brugsch, *Egypt under the Pharaohs*, vol. i., p. 395.

[2] Brugsch, *Egypt under the Pharaohs*, vol. i., p. 406.

[3] See Lepsius, *Denkmäler*, Abth. iii., Bl. 45, 46.

On the Island of Elephantine he built a temple in honour of Khnemu, the great god of the First Cataract. This was in a good state of preservation when the members of the French Expedition visited the island in the early years of the nineteenth century, but it was pulled down by the local ma'amûr, or governor, of Aswân about the year 1821, who used the blocks of stone to build a palace for Muhammad Alî. In the year 1886 the natives of Aswân were found breaking up granite slabs bearing the cartouches of Thothmes III., but some of them were saved from destruction, and two or three lay for years near the station buildings of the Aswân-Shellâl Railway. In the First Cataract itself Thothmes III. ordered the old canal, which appears to have existed in the VIth Dynasty, to be cleared out, and his boat passed through it on the twenty-second day of the ninth month of the fiftieth year of his reign. The inscription which records this fact says that His Majesty "sailed on it, his heart being glad, he slaughtered his enemies,"[1] but there is no statement that he went into the Sûdân, and it seems tolerably certain that the king only opened the canal by sailing down it when it was ready for use. It may be noted that the word used for "sailed" is *khet*, which means "to sail *down*" the river, as opposed to *khent*, which means to sail up the river. On the Island of Bigga slabs inscribed with the cartouches of Thothmes III. were found by Wilkinson, and at Kalâbsha the Emperor Augustus drew some of the stones for his temple from an old temple-fortress built by Thothmes III. At Dakka and Ḳubbân Thothmes III. founded forts and temples in connection with the gold mines in the Wâdî 'Ulâḳî, and he appears to have chosen for these the sites which the kings of the XIIth Dynasty had selected for their temples. Another small temple stood a few miles to the south of Dakka, near Ḳûrta, and its foundation dates clearly from his reign.

At 'Amâda, to the south of Korosko, he built a temple to Rā-Ḥerukhuti, probably on the site of a temple of the XIIth Dynasty. On a relief is sculptured a figure of the god, who is

1 
Recueil, tom. xiii., p. 203.

seated with a table of offerings before him, and who tells the king that he has given him life and sovereignty, &c. In the reliefs found at Ellesîya, a little to the south of Derr, on the east bank of the river, the king is seen burning incense to the hawk-headed god Sepṭ,[1] and being embraced by Ṭeṭun,[2] the lord of Ta-Kenṣet, and standing before his great ancestor Usertsen III., whom he worships as a god.[3] On a stele at the place, which

TEMPLE OF THOTHMES III. ON THE ISLAND OF ELEPHANTINE.

[From *Description de L'Égypte*, tom. I., pl. 34.

is dated in the forty-second year of the reign of Thothmes III., the king is represented making an offering of milk to the goddess Sati, and another of bread to the god Horus of Mȧām, i.e., the classical Primis. At Ellesîya also is a cave wherein are sculptures representing the king seated between the goddesses Nekhebet and Uatchet, and making offerings to

1 

2 

3 See Lepsius, *Denkmäler*, Abth. iii., Bl. 45.

Hathor, Horus of Mâām, Horus of Behen, and Thoth.[1] These were made by the "royal son, the superintendent of the lands of the South, Neḥi."[2]

At Behen, or Wâdî Ḥalfa, Thothmes III. enlarged the temple which was began there by Thothmes II., and decorated it in a striking manner. This building was dedicated to Horus of Behen, and it stands a little to the south of the mud-brick temple of Usertsen I. on the west bank of the river, about two miles from the Sirdarîya. This temple was approached from the river by a flight of steps, of which Champollion gives a drawing,[3] and when in a complete state must have presented a fine appearance, placed as it is on the top of the river bank. The temple enclosure was surrounded by a good mud-brick wall, of which in many places remains still exist. The pillars, some of which are Doric in shape, and the main walls are built of thick blocks of stone, which appear to have been brought from Egypt, and the painted decorations are in a good state of preservation. Under the floor of the main building are cellars, wherein the temple property, and perhaps also consignments of gold from the south, were stored. On some of the pillars there are sepulchral

PORTION OF A PAINTED STELE SET UP BY THOTHMES III. IN THE TEMPLE AT WÂDÎ ḤALFA, IN THE 35TH YEAR OF HIS REIGN.
(British Museum, No. 1021.)
Presented to the British Museum by Sir Charles Holled Smith, K.C.M.G., 1887.

[1] See Lepsius, *Denkmäler*, Abth. iii., Bl. 46.

[2] 

[3] *Notices*, p. 37.

GENERAL VIEW OF THE TEMPLE OF THOTHMES II. AND THOTHMES III. AT WADI HALFA FROM THE WEST END.

SEPULCHRAL STELE SET UP UNDER THE XIXTH DYNASTY IN THE TEMPLE AT WADI HALFA.

[British Museum, No. 1188.

Presented to the British Museum by Sir Charles Holled Smith, K.C.M.G., 1887.

GENERAL VIEW OF THE TEMPLE OF THOTHMES II. AND THOTHMES III. AT WÂDÎ ḤALFA, FROM THE EAST BANK.
[From a photograph by Lieutenant P Lord, R E.

inscriptions set up to commemorate the officials of the district, and to the left as the visitor enters is an inscription dated in the twenty-third year of Seti I., wherein this king's victories over the Libyans and Syrians are recorded.

VIEW OF THE TEMPLE OF THOTHMES II. AND THOTHMES III. AT WÂDÎ HALFA, FROM THE SOUTH-EAST CORNER.
[From a photograph by Lieutenant P. Lord, R.E.

Thanks to the efforts of Sir Reginald Wingate, the remains of this important little temple have now been made available for study, and the preservation of the paintings in it is, for some years

VIEW OF THE TEMPLE OF THOTHMES II. AND THOTHMES III. AT WÂDI ḤALFA. FROM THE WEST END.

[From a photograph by Lieutenant P. Lord, R.E.

at least, assured. Through the kindness of Colonel (now Sir Charles) Holled Smith I was enabled to visit this temple in December, 1886, and it was then in much the same state as when Champollion saw it. In 1887 Colonel Holled Smith cleared

ENTRANCE TO THE TEMPLE OF THOTHMES II. AND THOTHMES III. AT WÂDÎ ḤALFA, FROM THE RIVER, OR EAST END.

[From a photograph by Lieutenant P. Lord, R.E

out the whole building, and in the course of the work he discovered some stelae, and the figure of an official, &c., which he presented to the Trustees of the British Museum in the same

STATUE OF KA MES, A SCRIBE OF THE TOWN OF BEHEN, OR WADI HALFA.

[British Museum, No. 1022.

Presented to the British Museum by Sir Charles Holled Smith, K.C.M.G., 1887.

VIEW OF THE TEMPLE OF THOTHMES II. AND THOTHMES III. AT WÂDÎ ḤALFA, FROM THE SOUTH.

[From a photograph by Lieutenant P. Lord, R.E.

year. Whilst this officer was at Ḥalfa he kept the temple clear, but soon after his departure it became choked by the drift-sand which the north wind carried into it. In 1892 Captain H. G. Lyons, R.E., cleared out the temple once again, but was not rewarded by the discovery of any object of importance. In recent years the British Commandants at Ḥalfa, e.g., Colonel Hayes Sadler, have done much good work there, and in 1904 Sir Reginald Wingate made a grant of money for the purpose of

PAINTINGS IN THE TEMPLE OF THOTHMES II. AND THOTHMES III. AT WÂDÎ ḤALFA.

[From a photograph by Lieutenant P. Lord, R.E.

THE TEMPLE OF THOTHMES III. AT SEMNA, EAST SIDE.

[From a photograph by Lieutenant P. Lord, R.E.

VIEW OF THE TEMPLE OF THOTHMES III. AT SEMNA, FROM THE SOUTH-WEST CORNER.

[From a photograph by Lieutenant P. Lord, R.E.

USERTSEN III. DEIFIED, SITTING IN HIS DIVINE BARK.

THE GOD ṬEṬUN EMBRACING THOTHMES III.

[From Lepsius, *Denkmäler*, Abth. III. Bl. 49.

clearing away the sand from the inside and outside of the temple, and the building of a wall and a roof to protect the paintings and reliefs. All the arrangements for these works were made by Mr. J. W. Crowfoot, Inspector of Education in the Sûdân, and they would have been carried out by him in the winter of 1904-05, but for his departure with me to make excavations on ancient sites in the country of the Cataracts further to the south. The work was, however, only postponed for a few months, for in November, 1905, the temple was cleared and the wall built, under the

VIEW OF THE TEMPLE OF THOTHMES III. AT SEMNA, FROM THE SOUTH-EAST CORNER.

[From a photograph by Lieutenant P Lord, R.E.

direction of Mr. J. W. Crowfoot, by a native contractor, Mr. P. D. Scott-Moncrieff, of the British Museum, being in charge of the work. By means of a grant made by Mr. Crowfoot and sanctioned by Sir Reginald Wingate, Mr. Scott-Moncrieff was enabled to clear out a small vaulted mud-brick building which lies a little to the north of the temple of Thothmes II. and Thothmes III., and in it he found some sepulchral stelae of the XIIth or XIIIth Dynasty, and a figure of Sebek-em-ḥeb, of very fine work and finish, and belonging to the same period as the stelae.

DOOR JAMB INSCRIBED WITH NAME AND THE TITLES OF THOTHMES III.
Found on the east bank of the Nile at Wâdî Ḥalfa (British Museum, No. 1,019). Presented to the British Museum by Sir Charles Holled Smith, K.C.M.G., 1887.

Thothmes III. also appears to have built a small temple on the east bank of the river, on a site not very far from the position occupied by the British Camp in 1886. When I visited the camp in that year I saw in a wall of one of the huts a long slab of sandstone with an inscription on it which was almost covered with mud; this being removed, the hieroglyphics showed that it had formed part of some edifice which was dedicated to Horus of Behen by Thothmes III. Colonel Holled Smith had the slab removed at once from the wall, and sent it home by me to the British Museum, where it now is (No. 1,019). Inquiry showed that the slab was found among a heap of ruins on the east bank, close to the river. In connection with this, it must be mentioned that Captain Lyons noted that "there was visible at low Nile in 1902, "at the north end of the Ḥalfa lines, a "flight of steps, which certainly be- "longed to some ancient building on "the east bank."

Passing on now to Semna, we find the stone temple which Thothmes III. dedicated to the gods Ȧmen, Khnemu, Menthu, and Ṭeṭun, in commemoration of his great predecessor Usertsen III., to whom divine honours were paid here and elsewhere in the Sûdân. The general situation of the building has already been described,[1] and we may therefore pass on to note briefly the reliefs which adorn it, and the inscrip-

[1] Vol. I., pp. 476-8.

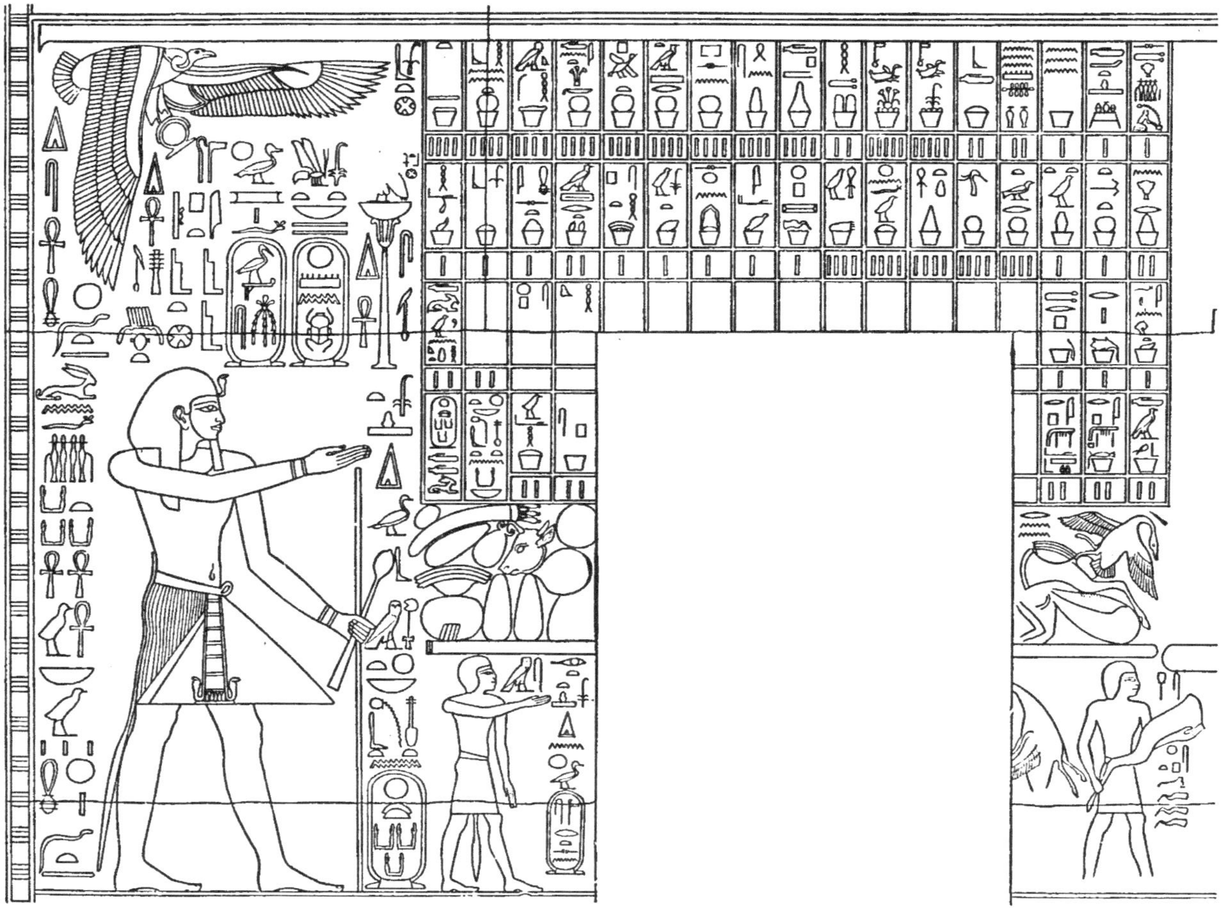

THOTHMES III. DEDICATING OFFERINGS TO USERTSEN III.

[From Lepsius, *Denkmäler*, Abth. III Bl. 48.

tions. On the outside of the south wall, above and by the sides of the main doorway, we see the king making offerings to Ṭeṭun, Khnemu, Usertsen, and other gods. On the inside of this wall, over the door, is the dedication to the four gods whose names are mentioned above, and, on the right, a text saying that Thothmes III. builds this monument to Father Ṭeṭun, and Usertsen III. On the inside of the west wall are seen:[1] 1. a tabular list of the

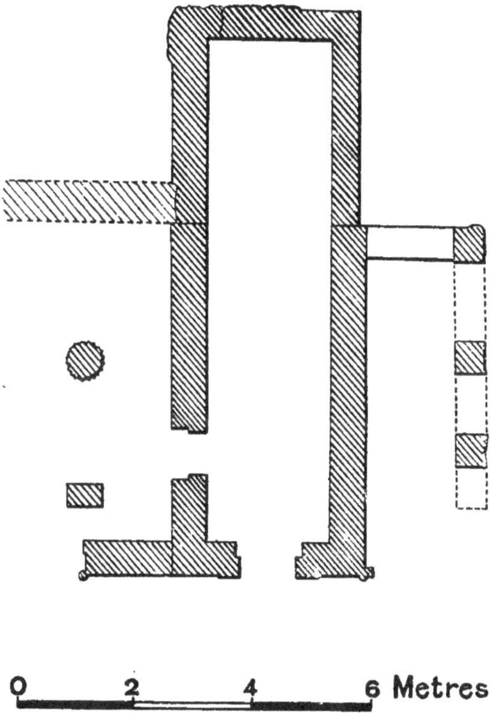

PLAN OF THE TEMPLE OF THOTHMES III. AT SEMNA.

[From Lepsius, *Denkmäler*, Abth. I. Bl. 113.

offerings which were to be made in the temple, and a figure of Thothmes III. dedicating these to the god Usertsen III., who is seated in his divine bark. 2. Ṭeṭun embracing Thothmes III. 3. Thothmes III. making offerings. 4. A sepulchral coffer in a boat. 5. Ṭeṭun giving "life" to Thothmes III. On the north wall, inside, Thothmes III. is seen adoring Ȧmen-Rā, who promises to give him everlasting life. On the inside of the east wall are:

[1] See Lepsius, *Denkmäler*, Abth. iii., Bl. 47 ff.

1. Thothmes III. making offerings to Åmen-Rā and Ṭeṭun. 2. Usertsen III. seated in his divine boat. 3. Åmen-Rā embracing Thothmes III. 4. Thothmes III. making offerings before a sepulchral coffer in a boat. 5. Ṭeṭun embracing Thothmes III. On the outside of the west wall are: 1. Thothmes III. offering a pectoral to Ṭeṭun. 2. Ṭeṭun seated on a throne, with his hands stretched out over the crown of the king, who kneels at his feet, and who is supposed to be inhaling stability, power, and life for millions of years. Before the king stands the priestly official Ån-Mut-f, who addresses the god

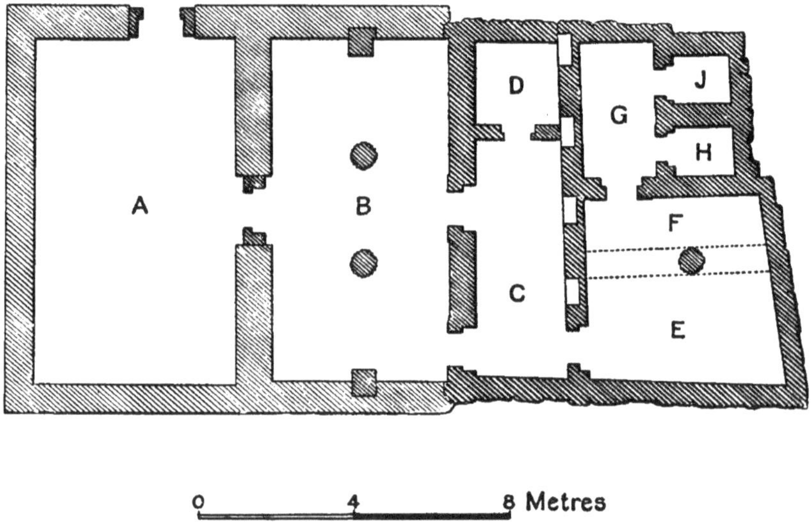

PLAN OF THE TEMPLE AT KUMMA.

[From Lepsius, *Denkmäler*, Abth. I. Bl. 113.

Ṭeṭun, and says, "Thy dear son Rā-men-kheper hath seated "himself upon thy seat, he hath inherited thy throne, he hath "made himself the supreme king in this land, and his rule shall "never change. Grant thou thy support to his souls, and let awe "of him be in the hearts of the Hill-men (Ånti) and the Cattle-"men (Mentu) as a gracious reward to him for building this "beautiful, solid, and well-constructed temple to thy honour." To the left of this scene stands Uatchet, and to the right, before the doorway was cut in this wall, was a figure of Nekhebet. 3. Thothmes III. standing before "Satet, lady of Elephantine."

4. Ṭeṭun and Thothmes III. in converse. 5. Usertsen III. presenting "life" to Thothmes III. On the architrave and pilasters are inscribed the ordinary formulae of dedication, and also on one of the fluted pillars.

On the outside of the east wall are: 1. A figure of Thothmes III. 2. The text of a decree, dated in the second year of the king's reign, in which are enumerated the offerings of bulls and grain which are to be offered at stated periods of the year to the gods of the temple. In line 12 a queen called Merseḳer[1] is mentioned. 3. Usertsen III. seated on a throne, receiving, presumably, the endowment which is to be provided out of the revenues of the land for ever. 4. Thothmes III. standing between Thoth and the goddess of time and years. 5. Amen-Rā giving "life" to the king. 6. The king pouring out a libation. 7. The king standing between Menthu and Isis. 8. A figure and an inscription of Neḥi,

UATCHET, LADY OF SEMNA.
[From Lepsius, *Denkmäler*, Abth. III. Bl. 52.

1 .

USERTSEN III. PRESENTING "LIFE" TO THOTHMES III.
From the Temple of Thothmes III. at Semna.
[From Lepsius, *Denkmäler*, Abth. III Bl. 54.

the Prince of Kash in the reign of Thothmes III., who superintended the building of the temple at Semna, and made arrangements for its endowment.

At Kumma, on the west bank, we find several reliefs of Thothmes III. in the portion of the temple which he added to his father's building. The dedication over a doorway tells us that the temple was dedicated to Hathor, lady of the city of Satu, and to Khnemu, the repulser of the tribes who fight with the bow. It is interesting to note that it is expressly stated that the temple was built of "beautiful white stone of the country of Shaăt,"[1] by which we are, no doubt, to understand stone taken from some quarry in the neighbourhood. The reliefs represent: 1. Thothmes III. sitting between Khnemu and Usertsen III. 2. Thothmes III. making an offering to Khnemu. 3. Thothmes III. dancing before Hathor, and presenting a bird to her. 4. Thothmes III. receiving

[1]  Lepsius, *Denkmäler*, Abth. iii., Bl. 57 *a*.

"life" from Ṭeṭun, "the chief of Ta-Kenset, the great god, his lord." 5. Khnemu who driveth back the people armed with bows from "the great gate of the lands [of the south]," and who saith unto him, "Come thou to us into the temple, and look thou

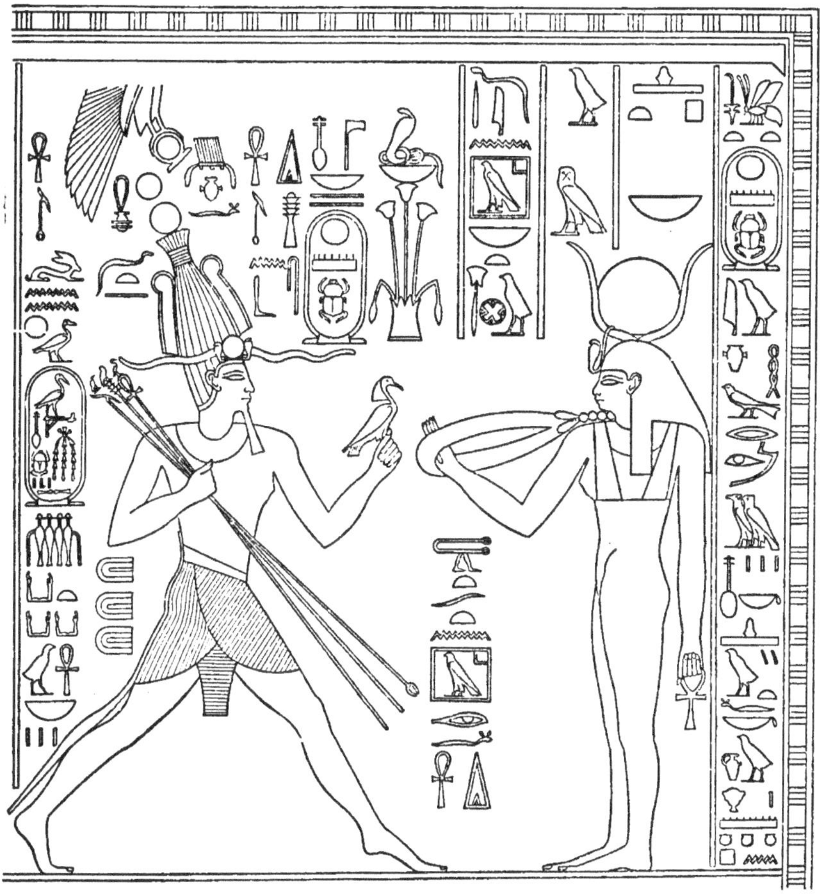

THOTHMES III. DANCING BEFORE HATHOR.

[From Lepsius, *Denkmäler*, Abth. III. Bl. 57.

"upon thy fathers who smote the southern tribes, and all the "gods of the Land of Kenset, and I will make thy stability to be "like unto that of the heavens." 6. Thothmes III. presenting a table of offerings to Khnemu. By the side of this scene is a line of inscription which mentions Thothmes II., who added to the temple, and below this is a figure of Sen, the Prince of Kash, who stands with his hands raised in adoration.[1] A little beyond this is an interesting scene in which we see Thoth marking on a palm branch held by Khnemu the number of the years of life of a king. Above the centre are two cartouches, which are filled with the signs which form the prenomen and nomen of Thothmes I.

RELIEF REPRESENTING THOTHMES III. MAKING AN OFFERING TO A GOD (GEBEL DÔSHA).

[From Lepsius, *Denkmäler*, Abth. III. Bl. 59.

The prenomen was originally written , but across the last sign  the sign 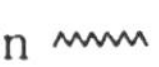 was cut at a later date, the sign  thus becoming ; this was done in order to make it appear that the temple was built by Thothmes II., whose prenomen was

[1] Lepsius, *Denkmäler*, Abth. iii., Bl. 58.

. This fact shows that the oldest portion of the temple buildings at Kumma dates from the reign of Thothmes I.

Passing southwards, the next place where the name of Thothmes III. is found is on the Island of Sâî, which is about eighty miles from Semna. Near the northern end of this island, and to the north of the "Castle of Sâî," down on the plain, are the remains of a small temple whereon are found the names of Thothmes II. and Thothmes[1] III. They stand on the east side of the island, and are not far from the river, the main channel of which runs by

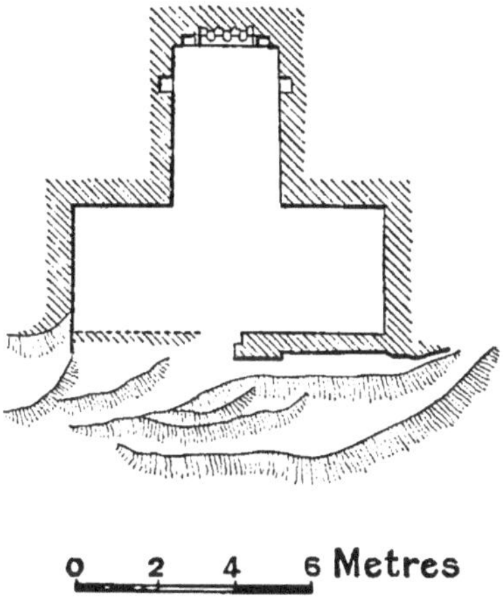

THE ROCK-HEWN TEMPLE OF DÔSHA.

[From Lepsius, *Denkmäler*, Abth. I. Bl. 115.

the east bank of the Nile. This temple was built under the direction of the famous Neḥi, Prince of Kash, whose name was found inscribed on a stone there; it was a small and quite ordinary building, the exact plan of which it is not now easy to trace, for most of the stones in it have been carried away, probably to serve as material for the "Castle of Sâî." Between Sâî and Gebel Dôsha no monument of Thothmes III. has yet been found, but in the latter place, inside the chamber hewn in the rock, we see on the walls a figure of this king making an offering to "Horus, the Bull, the lord of the Land of Kenset." Elsewhere in the chamber is a relief, the lower portion of which is broken

[1] See Lepsius, *Denkmäler*, Abth. iii., Bl. 59 *b* and *c*.

away, and near the taller of two royal figures are cut the cartouches of Usertsen III. and of Thothmes III., side by side, thus:—

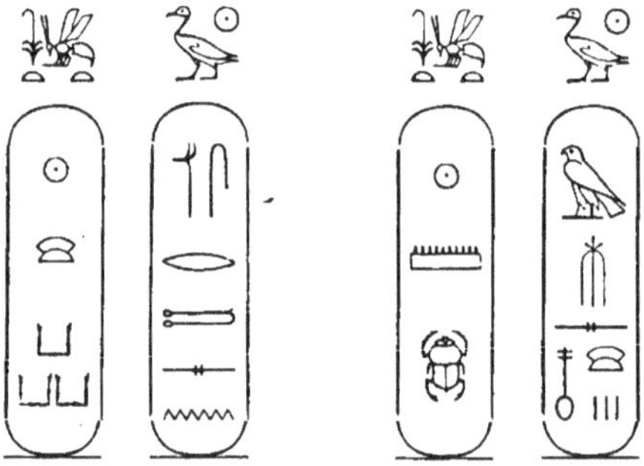

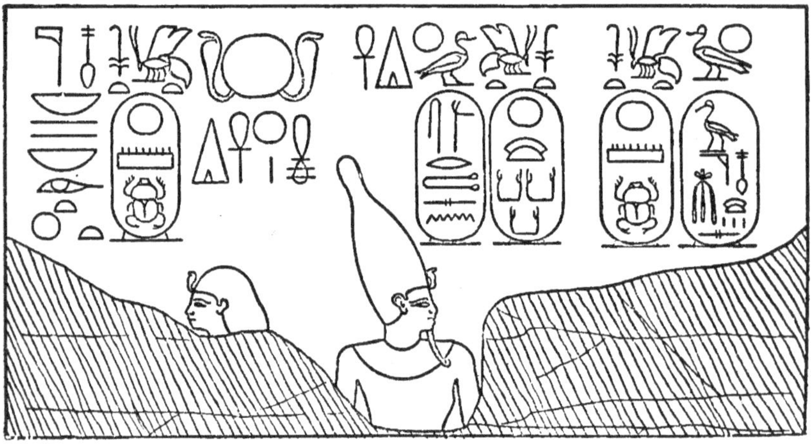

USERTSEN III. AND THOTHMES III. AT GEBEL DÔSHA.

[From Lepsius, *Denkmäler*, Abth. III. Bl. 59.

Although very few remains of buildings inscribed with the name of Thothmes III. have been found in the country to the south of Gebel Dôsha, it is tolerably certain that this king built a temple at Ṣulb, and that he erected forts all the way along to the head of the Third Cataract. We know that Thothmes I. made the natives build him a fort near the Cataract of Tangûr, and it is unlikely that the able and vigorous officers of Thothmes III. would relax their hold upon any site which was essential for the protection of those engaged in bringing the tribute of the Sûdân to Egypt. Thothmes III. appears not to have taken so much interest in the Sûdân as in Western Asia; had he done so, we may be sure that he would have made his line of forts and temples extend to the northern boundary of the region which produces cattle and great trees, i.e., to the south of Kharṭûm.

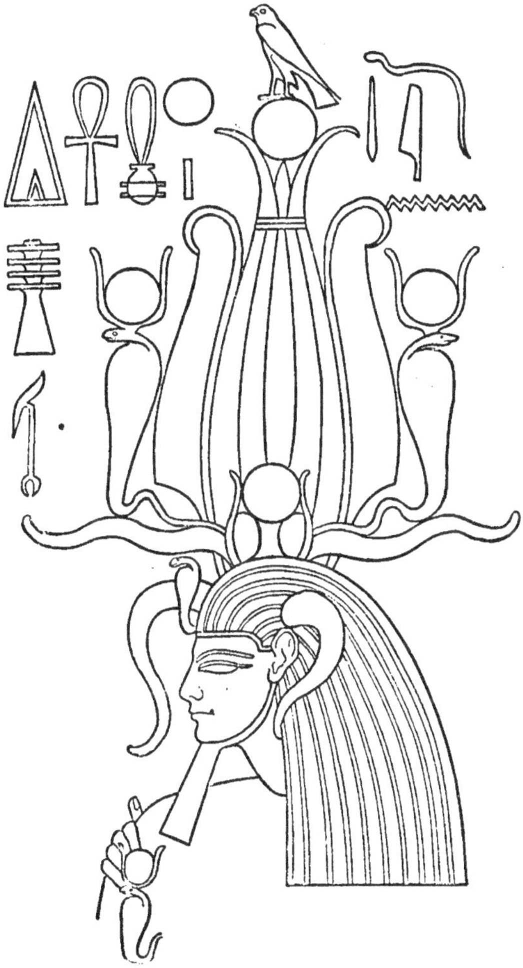

AMEN-HETEP II. WITH THE HORNS OF THE NUBIAN RAM SACRED TO AMEN.
[From Lepsius, *Denkmaler*, Abth. III. Bl. 63.

The facts given above concerning the dealings of his officers in Nubia justify the words which the priest put into the famous address of Åmen-Rā, who says to the king, "I have magnified "thy irresistible might in the bodies of all men, and I have made "the sounds of the roarings of thy Majesty to go round about "among the Nine Tribes who fight with the bow. The chiefs "of all the deserts and mountains in the south are gathered "together within thy grasp. I have stretched out my arms wide, "and I have bound in fetters and made prisoners for thee the " Hill-men (Ȧnti) of Kenset by ten thousand times ten thousand, "and have led captive the dwellers in the north by hundreds of "thousands." Thothmes III. reigned fifty-four years, but during the last few years of his life Ȧmen-ḥetep II., his son by Ḥātshepset, the daughter of the great queen of that name, was associated with him in the rule of the kingdom.

Soon after Ȧmen-ḥetep II. succeeded to the throne some of the tribes and peoples of Western Asia revolted, and, as usual, refused to pay tribute. The king promptly set out for Syria, and, marching through the country, reduced the natives to submission; he visited the city of Ni, which was either near or on the Euphrates, and its inhabitants appear to have welcomed him gladly. The disaffection seems to have originated in the country of Thȧkhisa,[1] which was probably situated to the north of Kadesh, for he slew seven of its kings and brought their bodies to Egypt. We read of Ȧmen-ḥetep II. attacking the natives with such fury that his own troops declared he was as terrible as Set, when the god was in a fierce rage, but when the spoil which he gained after the fight was told, it is found to consist of twelve bows, a quiver full of arrows, and its leather straps. Thus the fight proves to have been an attack on a passing caravan! A few cities undoubtedly rebelled against the authority of Ȧmen-ḥetep II., and the whole country would probably have done the same, only the people had not had time since the death of Thothmes III. to prepare an organized resistance.

The expedition to Syria probably took place in the first or second year of the king's reign, for the stele at 'Amâda, which gives a description of some of the events which happened in the country of Thȧkhisa, was set up in the third year. His dealings with Nubia are illustrated with tolerable completeness by the building operations which he carried out in that country. His name is found on the Island of Bigga, or Senmut, as it is called

1 .

in the text,[1] and he must have repaired or added to the temple at Termes, or Telmes (Kalâbsha), for he is represented on one of its walls making offerings to Menu (Amsu) and the Nubian god Merul, or Meril.[2] This god was of Sûdânî origin, that is to say, the worship of him was brought from Ta-neter, or Punt; he is the Mandulis of classical writers. At Mâām (Primis, or Ibrîm) he appears in the company of Horus of Behen and is seen making offerings to Khnemu, Satet, Ānqet, Horus, Hathor, and Nekhebet.[3]

The most important work which Åmen-ḥetep II. did between Elephantine and Wâdî Ḥalfa was in connection with the temple of 'Amâda, with the refounding of which he had been associated by his father Thothmes III.[4] This temple was built under the XIIth Dynasty, but during the period of the rule of the Hyksos in Egypt it had fallen into ruin. The chief work of restoration was done by Åmen-ḥetep II., who, in a stele which he set up in it on the fifteenth day of the third month of the season of the Inundation (Epiphi), records some interesting facts. The temple was built, he tells us,[5] of stone, with endless labour, the walls round about it were of brick, its doors were of a special kind of wood, and their settings were made of good stone, so that the name of his father Thothmes III. might be perpetuated. When the foundation-stone had been laid, Åmen-ḥetep II. built a great sandstone pylon, with its complementary buildings, and a colonnade, and he provided the sanctuary with vessels of all kinds in silver and copper. He did all this because the gods had brought him back in safety from the country of Upper Retennu (Northern Syria), where he had vanquished his foes, and extended the borders of Egypt. He returned with great joy of heart and gratitude to father Åmen, for "he had slain seven chiefs with "his own club, who were in the country of Thåkhisa, and he "hung them up head downwards at the bows of the boat of His

[1] Lepsius, *Denkmäler*, Abth. iii., Bl. 63 *c*.

[2] 

[3] Lepsius, *Denkmäler*, Abth. iii., Bl. 63 *d*.

[4] The two names are found on two doors; see Lepsius, *Denkmäler*, Abth. iii., Bl. 65 *b*.

[5] *Ibid.*, Bl. 65 *a*, line 12.

"Majesty. Six of these he had stretched out and displayed high "up on the walls which were opposite to the pylon of Thebes, "together with their hands, and the other he placed in a boat "and had conveyed to the rebel chief of Ta-Kenset, and hung "upon the walls of the city of Nept (Napata), so that all the folk "there might understand the mighty acts and adore him for ever "and for ever in all the countries of the world, and in all the "mountains and deserts of the Land of the Blacks,[1] and might "know that he had seized with his hands and conquered the "Āamu, and the northern folk who lived away in the swamps in "the remotest regions of the earth." As a confirmation of the bloodthirsty character which the king gives himself, Brugsch[2] calls attention to the scene painted on one of the walls of an officer's tomb at Ḳûrna (Thebes). Here the king is represented as a child sitting on his nurse's knees, whilst his feet rest upon the heads and backs of nine hereditary foes of Egypt, but it seems to be only an allegorical picture intended to show that the king, even when a babe, was able to set his feet on the necks of his enemies.

One point of special interest for us in the extract quoted above is the statement that Ȧmen-ḥetep sent the body of the seventh Syrian chief to be hung up on the walls of Nept, for all the Blacks to see. Now from the words which follow it is clear that Ȧmen-ḥetep II. had this done in order to terrify the Blacks, and this being so it is equally clear that the city of Nept must have been situated in the country of the Blacks, and that it was of considerable importance. It fact, since it was to the Sûdân what Thebes was to Egypt, it must have been the metropolis of the country. The city which it is most natural to identify with Nept is that which in the later inscriptions is called Nept, or Nepita, i.e., the capital of the Nubian kingdom established by Piānkhi-meri-Ȧmen. Nept, or Nepita,[3] called "Napata" by classical writers, lies on the west bank of the Nile, opposite to

[1] 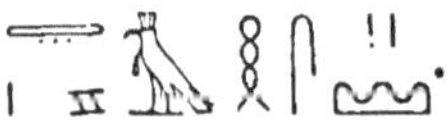.

[2] *Egypt under the Pharaohs*, vol. i., p. 459.

[3] , or .

Gebel Barkal, and is about fourteen hundred miles, by river, from the Mediterranean Sea. If this identification be correct, and it certainly seems to be so, it shows not only that an important city existed in the Dongola province in the reign of Amen-ḥetep II., but that Egyptian influence was paramount in it.

Returning now to the building operations of Ȧmen-ḥetep II. in the Sûdân, we may note that he enlarged the temple of Usertsen I. at Behen, or Wâdi Ḥalfa, and set up therein several pillars whereon he caused his names and titles to be cut. A plan of this temple was published by Champollion,[1] and among its remains was found the stele of an official who flourished in the reign of Usertsen I., which gives the names of a number of Nubian tribes; the work carried out there by Captain Lyons has already been described. At Kumma Ȧmen-ḥetep II. made

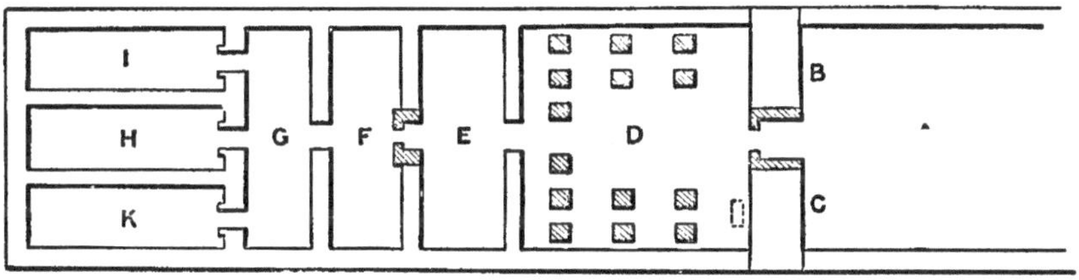

PLAN OF THE TEMPLE OF ȦMEN-ḤETEP II. AT WÂDÎ ḤALFA.

[From Champollion, *Monuments de l'Égypte*, p. 50.

additions to the temple, and on several reliefs there we see[2] him making offerings to Khnemu, the god of the Cataract, to whom he dedicated his buildings. In one place we see him standing face to face with Usertsen III., whose right hand rests upon his shoulder in an encouraging manner; an inscription states that the temple was built of *shāt* stone. The only place further south where his name has been found on the ruins of buildings is the Island of Sâî,[3] but when the site of Napata has been cleared out we may expect to find traces of his rûle, and probably of buildings which he set up there.

The inscriptions unfortunately tell us nothing about the extent

[1] *Notices*, p. 50.
[2] Lepsius, *Denkmäler*, Abth. iii., Bll. 66, 67.
[3] See Lepsius, *Letters*, p. 257.

of the travels of Åmen-ḥetep II. in the Sûdân, but it seems that he must have undertaken a journey so far to the south as Wad Bâ Nagaa, which is only about seventy miles from Kharṭûm, and

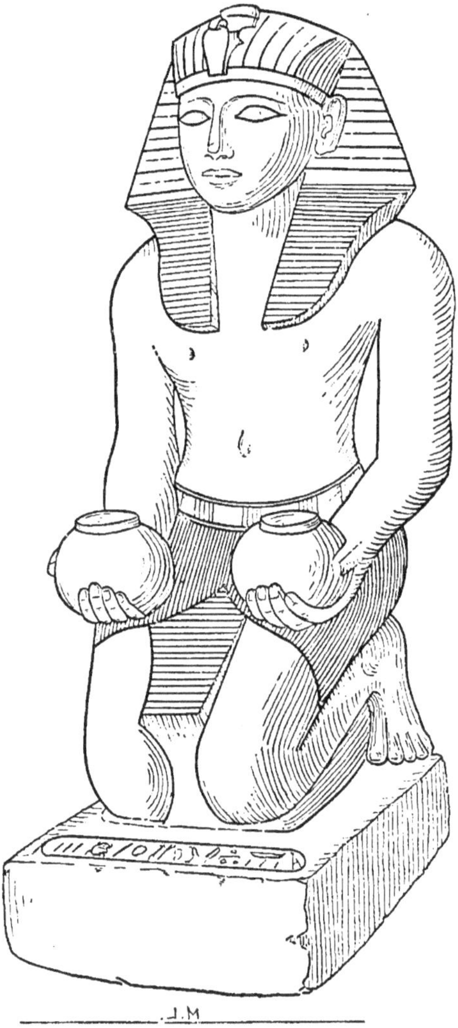

KNEELING FIGURE OF ÅMEN-ḤETEP II. OFFERING TWO VASES TO HIS GOD.
Found at Wad Bâ Nagaa.

have founded a temple there. This supposition is based upon the fact that two statues of the king were found by Lepsius's party at this place; in each of these the king is kneeling, and making an offering of two vases, which he holds one in each hand. The material used is red Nubian sandstone. Just in front of his knees is the cartouche:—

,

and on the back is the inscription—

,

THOTHMES IV. SLAYING HIS ENEMIES IN THE PRESENCE OF THE GODS.
[From Lepsius, *Denkmäler*, Abth. III. Bl. 69 *e*.

i.e., "Beautiful (or, well-doing) god (Āa-kheperu-Rā), beloved "of Khnemu, repulser of the tribes who fight with the "bow, son of Rā, (Āmen-ḥetep, god, prince of Thebes), "beloved of Khnemu, repulser of the tribes who fight "with the bow."

These statues are now in the Museum at Berlin (Nos. 2056, 2057), and form the most southerly remains of Egyptian civilization which have, up to the present, been found in the Sûdân.[1]

Ȧmen-ḥetep II. was succeeded by Thothmes IV., who during his short reign made one expedition into Syria, and another into Nubia. A rock-sculpture on the Island of Konosso shows us the king in the act of slaying a typical Nubian in the presence of the old Nubian god Ṭeṭun and the god Khas ; the former declares that he has given Thothmes IV. sovereignty over the Ȧnti, or Hill-men of Nubia, and the latter that he has made him master of all the countries thereof.[2] This scene is dated in the seventh year of the king's reign. An inscription on the same island,[3] dated the eighth year of his reign, refers to this expedition, but though it is full of high-sounding phrases about the king's valour, and his resemblance to various gods, there is nothing in it to show that he did anything in the Sûdân worthy of special note, or that he did anything more than perform a journey and collect tribute. Ȧmen-hetep, a high-priest of the god Ȧn-Ḥer, says on his stele that he accompanied the king when he went into Neherin, and Kari, or Kali . Neherin, as we know, was the country near the Euphrates and in the neighbourhood of Aleppo, and was the frontier of Egypt in Syria to the north; Kari, or Kali, must therefore have been the southern limit of Egypt's possessions in the Sûdân, but where it was situated exactly we cannot say. The place furthest south where the name of Thothmes IV. appears is 'Amâda; here we find inscriptions recording his names and titles, and among others one wherein his prenomen stands immediately above that of Usertsen III. Neither Thothmes IV. nor his predecessor, Amen-ḥetep II., had need to attack the natives of the Sûdân, for these had not had sufficient time or opportunity to organize resistance on a large scale. Thothmes IV. married, among other women, the daughter of Artatama, king of Mitani (the Māthen, 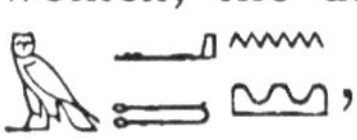, of the hieroglyphic inscriptions) in Western Asia, and made allies of some of the leading kings of the country

[1] See the official *Verzeichnis*, p. 130.

[2] Lepsius, *Denkmäler*, Abth. iii., Bl. 69 *e*.

[3] J. de Morgan, *Catalogue*, p. 66.

with the view of protecting his interests against the Kheta and other peoples of Northern Syria. He is also famous for having cleared away the sand from the Sphinx, and restored, or rebuilt, the temple of Ḥeru-khuti which stood between its paws.

Thothmes IV. was succeeded by his son Ȧmen-ḥetep III., the Ἀμένωφις of the Greeks, who was about twenty years of age when he came to the throne; he reigned for between thirty and forty years, and under his rule Egypt and her provinces enjoyed peace and prosperity. During the first four years of his reign nothing serious happened to disturb Egypt, but in the fifth year, according to a stele published by Lepsius [1] and M. J. de Morgan,[2] "one came" and told His Majesty that the abominable chief of Kesh,[3] for so the name is spelled, had rebelled, and that his insolent heart had stirred him up to declare himself independent. Amen-ḥetep III. set out promptly, and in a very short time reduced the rebel to submission. The centre of the rebellion was at Ȧbhat, to the south of Behen or Wâdî Ḥalfa. The forces of the Prince of Kash were reinforced by the king's personal troops, and the wretched Nubians were, as usual, defeated with great slaughter. From three hundred and twelve natives the hands were cut off, and seven hundred and forty were made prisoners,[4] and a large quantity of booty captured. On a stele [5] dated in the fifth year of his reign, we see the king standing between Khnemu and Ȧmen-Rā, behind whom are representatives of the four great divisions of the Sûdân which had been conquered by him, their names being: 1. Vile Kesh. 2. Arek or Alek. 3. . . . ar or al. 4. Ur . . . These Amen-Rā, whom the king declared to be his actual father, is supposed to have given to his son, who went into Nubia to "place the boundaries of his country wheresoever he "pleased,[6] even so far as the four pillars which supported the sky." As we have already seen (p. 533), Nubia was divided into four parts under the XIIth Dynasty.

[1] *Denkmäler*, Abth. iii., pl. 82 *a*. [2] *Catalogue*, p. 67. [3] .

[4] This number is made up thus: Men 150, boys 110, women 250, old me 55, children 175. See Birch, *Archaeologia*, vol. xxxiv., pl. 28, and p. 378.

[5] Lepsius, *Denkmäler*, Abth. iii., Bl. 82 *a*.

[6] 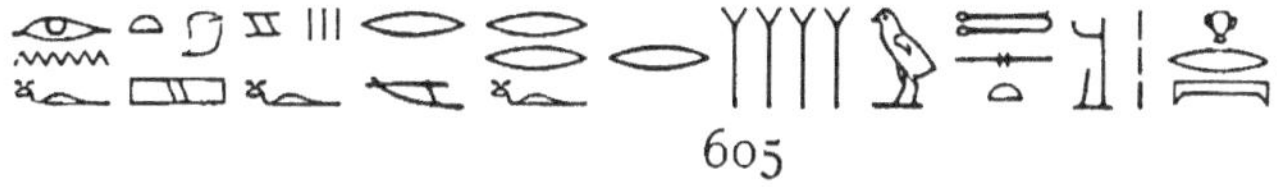.

If we examine the account of Åmen-ḥetep's expedition into Nubia in his fifth year, we shall see that it was no war, but a mere raid. The natives who were bringing their accustomed gifts, or tribute, were stopped on the road by some Nubian brigand (like Îsa, who flourished early in the nineteenth century of our era, and who kept the Government of Egypt in a state of terror for five years or more), whereupon the local governor, with his local irregular troops and those of the king, set out, and slew the brigand and his followers, and brought in the tribute from the desert and sent it down the river to Thebes. Cutting off the hands of the vanquished was a custom which flourished under the rule of the Mahdî and Khalifa, and in the remote parts of the Sûdân, to the south, it is not unknown even at the present day. The result of the raid was eminently satisfactory for Åmen-ḥetep III., and we do not read that another was necessary during his reign.

Apart from the rock-sculptures and inscriptions in the First Cataract there is little in Nubia at the present time to testify to the activity of this king in the country before we come to the district south of the Island of Sâî. We have already seen that a line of fortresses and temples extended from the Island of Elephantine[1] to the Island of Sâî, and that a fortified building of some kind existed near the Tangûr Cataract; but between this last and the Island of Sâî, i.e., for nearly eighty miles, there appears to have been neither temple nor fort of any importance before the reign of Åmen-ḥetep III.

Taking the buildings of this king in Nubia in the order in which they come as we proceed to the south, the first to be mentioned is the temple of Saddênga, which stands on the west bank of the Nile, at no great distance from the river, not far from the tomb of a famous Muhammadan saint called "Gubba (Ḳubba) Salim." The building is now a mass of ruins, amid which a single Hathor-headed pillar still stands. According to the plan[2] which Lepsius's party was able to make, we see that the temple was rectangular, and that a portico supported by eight pillars, four on each side of the door, stood before the entrance. The building is oriented to the east, and it is still possible to see that it was divided into two

[1] The temple which he completed at Elephantine, in its main portion, measured 40×30×13 feet; it was approached by a short flight of steps and a portico ran round the building.

[2] See *Denkmaler*, Bd. ii., Abth. i., Bl. 115.

chambers of unequal size, the smaller containing eight round pillars on square bases, and the larger twice this number. About the sanctuary nothing can be said, for no remains of it exist. The temple was built, as we learn from an inscription found on the spot, by Ȧmen-ḥetep III. in honour of his wife Thi,[1] the daughter of Iuaa and Thuȧa, whose tomb at Thebes was opened in 1905 by Mr. Theodore N. Davis.[2] Thi was not of royal birth, but it is perfectly certain that she was accorded the highest rank and honour which a woman could attain in Egypt, and the king gave her name prominence everywhere equal to that of his own.

In the winter of 1904-5 some natives dug up near the Fayyûm one or two beautifully executed statues of Thi, which were evidently intended to be portraits of this remarkable woman, and it was interesting to see that her face possessed all the physical characteristics with which we are familiar in exaggerated forms in the sculptures and pictures which represent her son Ȧmen-ḥetep IV. Her influence over Ȧmen-ḥetep III. must have been very great, for her name appears with his own on the large green glazed steatite scarabs which he made to commemorate historical events, and even on that whereon he declares that the northern boundary of his land is Neharina,[3] and the southern boundary Karei.[4] The temple built for Thi was a comparatively small edifice, but it is of interest as being, perhaps, the only building which was dedicated by a king of Egypt to his wife. Why the site now known by the name of Saddênga was chosen for the purpose it is impossible to say, but it was no more remarkable for Ȧmen-ḥetep III. to build a temple in the Sûdân to please Queen Thi, than for him to dig a lake in the city of Tcharukha three thousand six hundred cubits long, and six hundred cubits wide, whereon she might sail when she felt disposed. The decorations and inscriptions on the temple

1 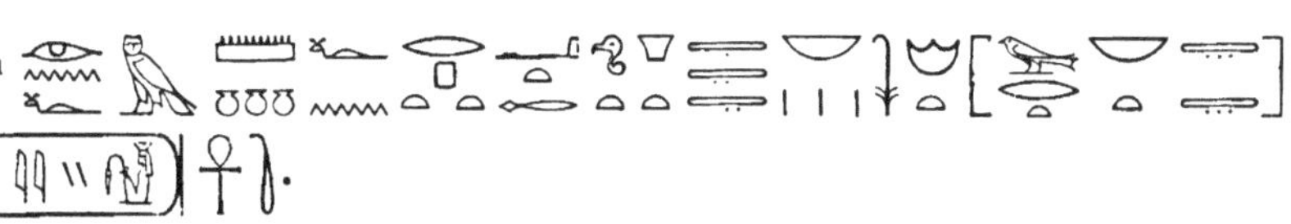

2 For the account of the discovery, see the narrative by Mr. Davis in his *The Tomb of Hâtshopsîtû*, London, 1906, 4to.

3 , i.e. Bêth Nahrîn of the Syrians, or Mesopotamia.

4 

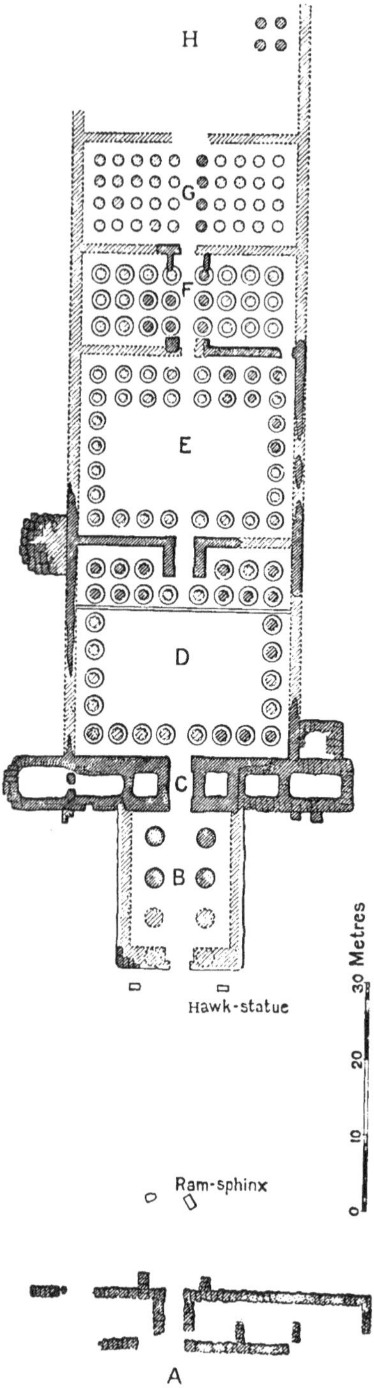

PLAN OF THE TEMPLE OF ÂMEN-HETEP III. AT ṢÛLB.
[From Lepsius, *Denkmäler*, Abth. I. Bl. 117.

of Thi were not very elaborate, but fortunately sufficient of the latter have come down to us to show when and by whom and for whom it was built. Away to the west of the temple is a large necropolis, and this suggests that a town of considerable size must have stood near.

Passing southwards, the next temple of Âmen-ḥetep III. is that which this king built at Ṣûlb, or Ṣolib, or Ṣoleb, on the west bank of the Nile, about six hundred yards from the river. When in a perfect state the temple must have presented a grand and noble appearance, but every one must lament the short-sightedness of the king's architect who allowed Nubian sandstone to be used in its construction, and who took no trouble to make good and solid foundations for this edifice, which is massive and imposing, even in its present sad state of decay. The visitor to the temple, which is oriented almost due east, passed through a large pylon, which must have been about one hundred and sixty feet wide, immediately behind which were two ram-headed sphinxes, one on each side of the path. He then passed on to a flight of steps which led to a portico with eight circular pillars, on very large bases, which stood before the second pylon. The portico is about seventy feet long and forty-five feet wide, and at its north-east end stood a high pedestal with the figure of a hawk upon it.

The second pylon is about one hundred and seventy feet wide, and is about onc hundred and fifty-five feet from the first; its depth is about twenty-five feet. This pylon contains five rooms, two in the north wing and three in the south, and it is probable that they were inhabited by religious or civil officials. On each

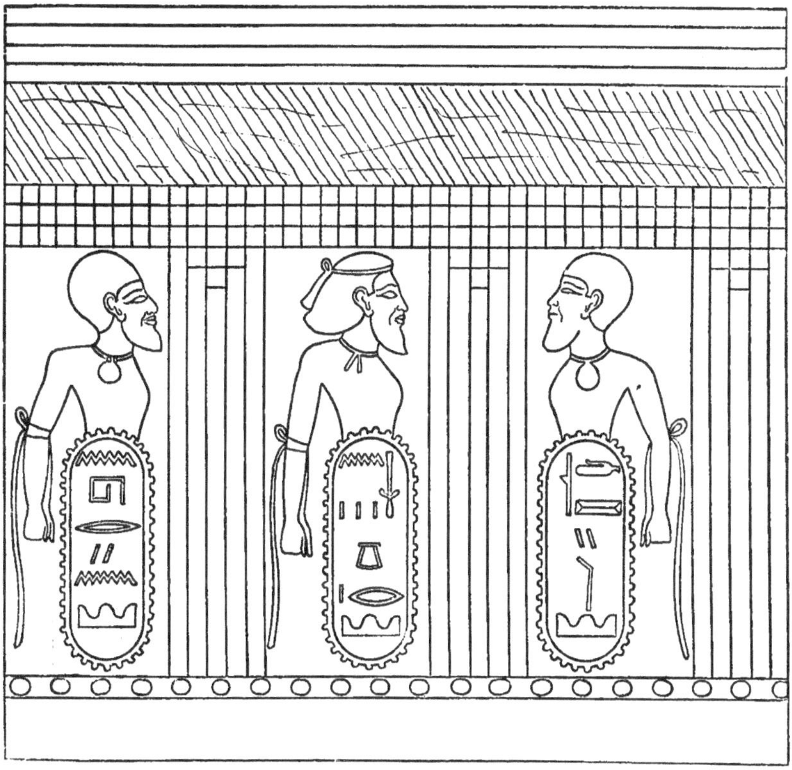

NEHERIN (MESOPOTAMIA). SENḲERU (SINGAR). QEṬSHI (KEDESH).
CARTOUCHES OF CAPTIVE NATIONS IN THE TEMPLE OF ṢULB.

side of the passage through the pylon is a recess, which lightens somewhat the severity of the pylon. The first court, A, contained twenty-six pillars, with lotus capitals, a single row on the north, south, and east sides, and a double row on the west side; its length is about ninety feet, and its width about one hundred and thirteen feet. The second court, B, contained thirty-two pillars, arranged like those of the first court; its length is about seventy-eight feet. Beyond this court are two chambers, each about fifty feet long; the first contained twenty-four pillars, twelve on each side of the path, and the second forty pillars, twenty on each side of the path.

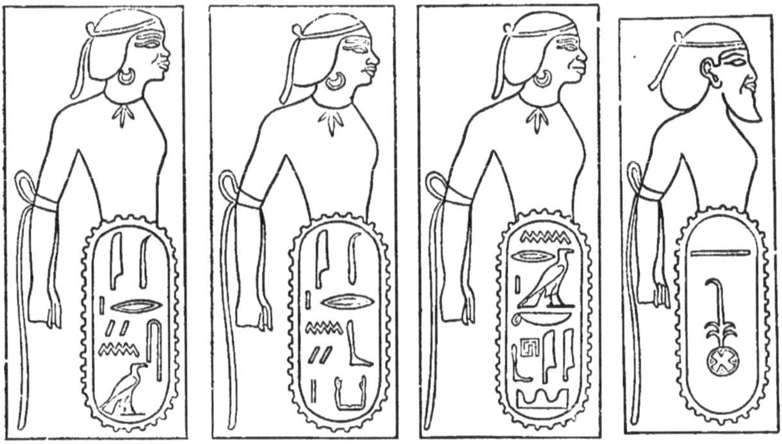

THÀRESINA. THÀKEBENIKA. NAREKIHEB. TA-RESU (THE SOUTH).

CARTOUCHES OF CAPTIVE NATIONS IN THE TEMPLE OF ṢULB.

The pillars of the first chamber had palm-leaf capitals, and on their bases were sculptured figures of a series of prisoners represented with their heads and breasts resting on "turreted

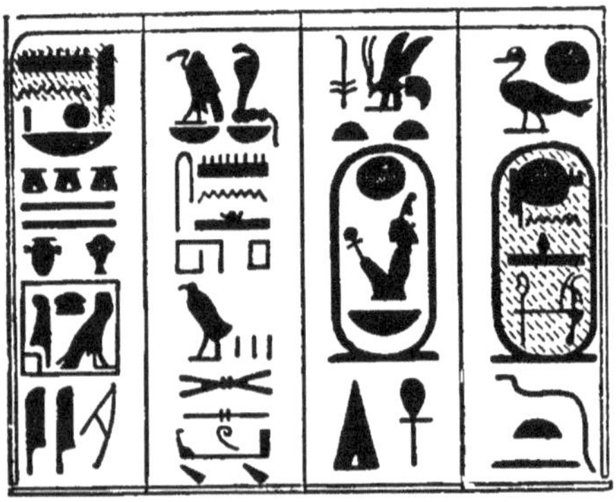

NAMES AND TITLES OF ÀMEN-ḤETEP III., BELOVED OF ÀMEN-RÀ.

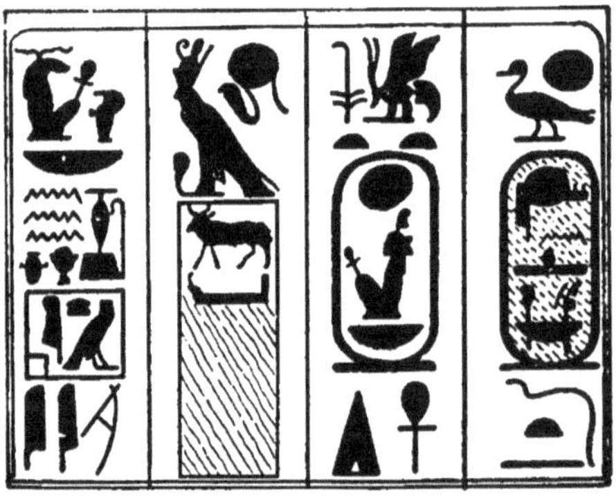

NAMES AND TITLES OF ÀMEN-ḤETEP III., BELOVED OF KHNEMU.

ovals," containing the names of the countries to which they belonged. Some of the pillars were decorated with reliefs wherein the king is seen making offerings to the gods of Egypt. Beyond the chambers, at the distance of about seventy feet, are masses of stone and portions of round pillars, which probably formed parts of the sanctuary, and as these extend to a distance of about forty feet, it is clear that the total length of the building cannot have been far short of six hundred feet, as we see from the following details:—

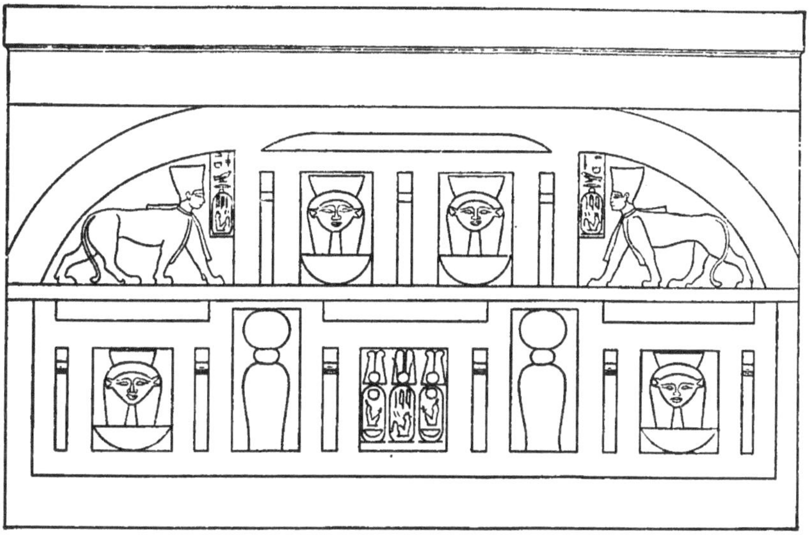

ENTABLATURE INSCRIBED WITH THE PRENOMEN OF ÅMEN-ḤETEP III. AND THE NAME OF QUEEN THI.

Depth of first pylon, say	... ...	20 feet.
Distance between first and second pylon		155 ,,
Depth of second pylon	... ...	25 ,,
Length of First Court	... ...	90 ,,
,, Second Court	... .	78 ,,
,, First Chamber	... ...	50 ,,
,, Second Chamber	... ...	50 ,,
,, Sanctuary, &c.	... ...	110 ,,
Total	...	578 feet.

The number of pillars in the whole building cannot have been less than one hundred and fifty.

There appears to have been an enclosure in front of the first pylon surrounded by a wall, but its length is quite uncertain;

any statement about its dimensions can only be based on guesswork.

The name given to the temple of Ṣulb in the hieroglyphic texts is Ḥet-khā-em-Maāt, 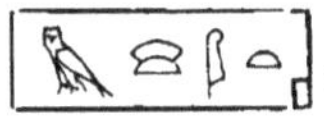,[1] i.e., "the house diademed with Truth," and was dedicated to Ȧmen-Rā, Khnemu, and Ȧmen-ḥetep III. Of the reliefs with which it was decorated we can get a good idea from the drawings published by Lepsius.[2] We see the king, assisted by the *sem* and *kher ḥeb* priests engaged in the performance of religious ceremonies, and in making offerings to Ȧmen-Rā and other gods; in some of the scenes he is accompanied by the "Great Queen. Thi." Some of the ceremonies appear to be connected with a passage through gates; both texts and figures are, however, very fragmentary, and it is difficult to make connected sense out of them.

The face of the second pylon was sculptured with large figures of the king, who was represented in the act of slaying his enemies. On one of the door-posts is an inscription which states that Ȧmen-ḥetep III. built the monument, both to father Ȧmen, the lord of the thrones of the Two Lands, and to his own Image living upon earth;[3] the name of this Image was the king's own prenomen, i.e., NEB-MAĀT-RĀ, . The Image is represented in the usual form of a god, and he wears on his head a sort of cap surmounted by a figure of the crescent moon with a disk within it; its title was "lord of Ta-Kenset, great god, lord of heaven." On the bases of the pillars are the names of several conquered cities, provinces, and countries, e.g., Turusu, Tharutharu, Akhenthek, Akaritha, Tanpu, Ḳeṭshi, Senḳeru, Neherin, Kefa, Mai, Kathȧ . . ., Māithȧriȧa, Qurui, Samānirku, Māturu, Ta-tchennian, Shāt, Ta-resu, Sekhet-am, Theḥennu, Mātbann, Menti-nu-Satet, Atharumȧqu, Maqu, Ḳuruses, Aruruk (?), Serunik, Akina, Ȧbhet, Māthaka . . . ., Ȧken, Ȧurusha, Narukiheb, Tharubnika, Tharusmȧ, Pasunka, Ȧihethȧb, Punt, Thita,

[1] Or, Ḥet-Menen-en-khā-em-Maāt 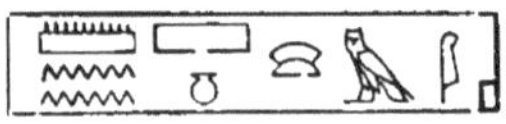.

[2] *Denkmäler*, Bd. v., Abth. iii., Bl. 83 ff.

[3] 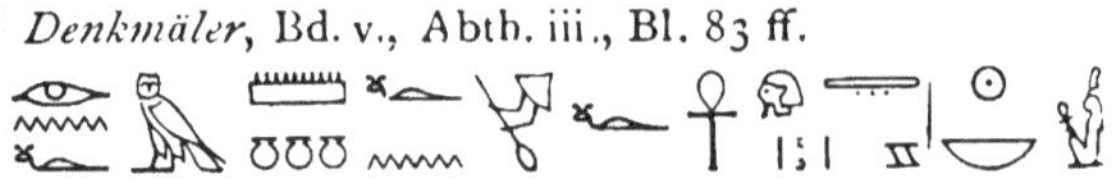.

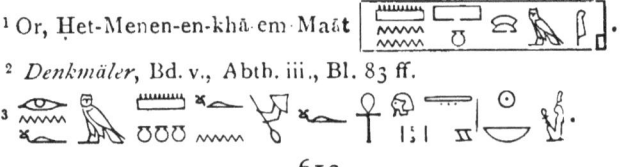

Ȧrrpakha, Qaruqamisha, Ȧsuru, Ȧpthethna. A large number of the above names are found in the lists which were drawn up for Thothmes III., and cut on the walls of his temple at Karnak, and it is possible that these formed the sources whence the architects of Ȧmen-hetep III. and later kings drew the names of conquered peoples and countries with which they filled their annals. It has been thought that the temple of Ṣulb was founded by

AMEN-ḤETEP III. WORSHIPPING HIMSELF UNDER THE FORM OF THE LORD OF KENSET.

[From Lepsius, *Denkmäler*, Abth. III. Bl. 85.

Thothmes III., and though no definite proof for this view can now be furnished, this may well be the case; if so, the names on the base of the pillars would be those of tribes and nations vanquished by him, and not by Ȧmen-ḥetep III.

The existence of the large temple which has been briefly described above makes it certain that there must have been a city of considerable size in the neighbourhood of Ṣulb, and that it must have been of great importance as a trading centre. Amen-ḥetep III. no doubt wished to pay great honour to Thi by dedi-

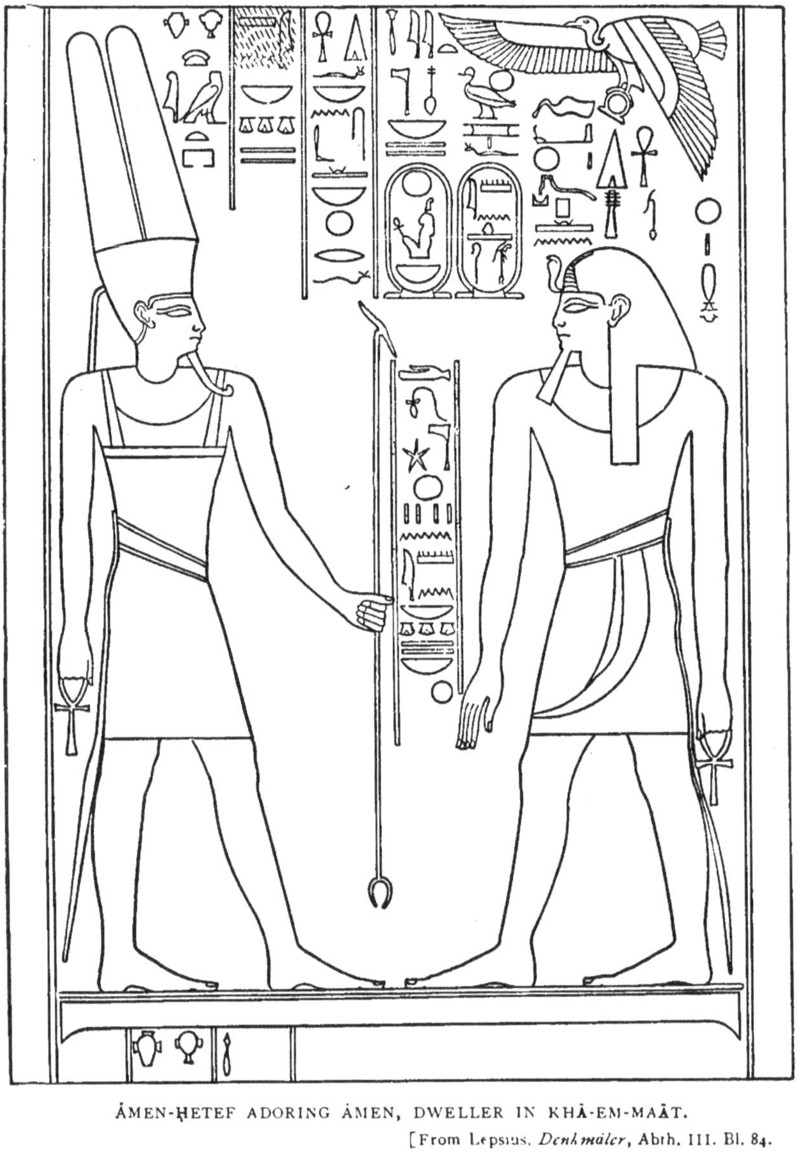

ÅMEN-ḤETEF ADORING ÅMEN, DWELLER IN KHÅ-EM-MAĀT.
[From Lepsius, *Denkmäler*, Abth. III. Bl. 84.

cating a temple to her at Saddênga, and also to do himself honour as the god of the Sûdân by dedicating a temple to his own "living Image upon earth," but we may be sure that he would have indulged neither of these sentiments unless the profits which accrued to him from legitimate trading, and from the raids which his officers made in the Sûdân, justified him in undertaking these works. The kings of Egypt did not build merely for the glory of their gods temples on the skirts of the desert, or in places where no markets were held, and no caravans passed; travellers rested in the shade of the colonnades, and exposed their wares to those who went in and out of the temple, and, of course, made offerings duly to the gods in return for successful bargaining or lucky business. The temple of Ṣulb was built by Sûdânî labour, and was maintained by the work of Sûdânî folk, and it played a very important part in the system of government, or mis-government, whereby the revenues of Egypt from the Sûdân were squeezed out of the wretched natives.

Of the other buildings of Ȧmen ḥetep III. in the Sûdân very little is known. It is impossible to think that the temple of Ṣulb is the most southerly of his monuments, for there must have been forts or temples, or both, at intervals all the way from Ṣulb to Napata. We have already mentioned[1] the temple of Sesi, the remains of which stand on the west bank of the Nile opposite to Dulgo, or Deligo, but it must be referred to here in connection with the reign of Ȧmen-ḥetep III., because it was probably founded by him. The same may be said of the temple which once stood near Kerma, about two hundred and three miles from Ḥalfa, and of that of Khandaḳ, about forty-five miles from Dongola Al-Ûrdî. Unfortunately a mosque has been built over the remains of the temple in the latter place, and until that is removed excavations are impossible.

The next place to the south most likely to have been chosen as the site for a fort under the XVIIIth Dynasty is that which is called to-day Donḳola Al-'Agûz, or Old Dongola; it stands on a hill on the east bank of the Nile, and is about ninety miles from New Dongola. It was the capital of the Nubian kingdom in Christian times, and was probably a place of importance even when Ȧmen-ḥetep III. was king. Its commanding position on the river gives it great value strategically. Last of all we come to Napata, which, if it be identical with the Nept

[1] Vol. I., p. 440.

mentioned in the inscription of Ȧmen-ḥetep II., was certainly a flourishing city under the XVIIIth Dynasty, and perhaps the capital of the district. That it was chosen by this king as a fit place wherein to display the dead body of the Syrian chief, whom he had slain with his six comrades, speaks volumes for

THE RAM OF ȦMEN MADE BY ȦMEN-ḤETEP III. AND PLACED BY HIM IN THE TEMPLE OF KHĀ EM-MAȦT (SÛLB).

its importance. Whether Ȧmen-ḥetep III. built a temple there or not cannot be said definitively, but the probabilities are that he did; no mention of his name has, however, been found on any portion of a building there, but this fact counts for little at present because the site has not been thoroughly excavated. On the opposite side of the river, that is to say, among the ruins of the temples which stood on the plain at the foot of Gebel Barkal, several fine monuments inscribed with his name and titles have been found, and among these may be specially mentioned a ram,[1] a pair of red granite lions,[2] a hawk,[3] &c.

THE RAM OF ÅMEN MADE BY ÅMEN-ḤETEP III. AND PLACED BY HIM IN THE TEMPLE OF KHĀ-EM-MAĀT (SÛLB).

The ram represents the variety of that animal which has horns

[1] Taken by Lepsius to Berlin; see the official *Verzeichnis*, No. 7262, p. 122. Published by Lepsius, *Denkmaler*, Abth. iii., Bl. 91.

[2] [illegible] from Gebel Barkal by Lord Prudhoe, and presented to the British Museum in 1835.

[3] Taken by Lepsius to Berlin; see the official *Verzeichnis*, No. 1622, p. 122.

that curve round, their tips being parallel with his face, and which is found in the Sûdân, and he is lying down with his fore-legs doubled back ; as the type and symbol of Ȧmen or Ȧmen-Rā he has a disk upon his head. Between his fore-legs stands a small figure of the king who dedicated the figure to the god Ȧmen, and to himself. On the four sides of the base are inscriptions which read:—

RED GRANITE LION MADE BY ȦMEN-ḤETEP III., AND USURPED BY THE NUBIAN KING ȦMEN-ȦSRU.

The Lions were brought from Gebel Barkal and presented to the British Museum by Lord Prudhoe in 1835.

[From Lepsius, *Auswahl*, Pl. XIII. (British Museum, No. 34)

I. " Beautiful god, (Neb-Maāt-Rā), son of Rā, (Amen-ḥetep, "prince of Thebes). He hath made his monument to his father "Amen, the lord of the thrones of the Two Lands. He hath "built a magnificent temple, making it very spacious, and very "great, and exceedingly beautiful. The pylons thereof pierce "the sky, and the poles (for the flags) touch the stars of heaven. "It can be seen for leagues both up and down the river, and is "visible from afar on both banks. Giver of life!"

II. " Beautiful god (Neb-Maāt-Rā), son of Rā, (Amen-ḥetep, "prince of Thebes). He hath made his monument to his Image,

GRANITE LIONS OF AMEN-HETEP III.

"(Neb-Maāt-Rā), the lord of Ta-Kenset, the great god, lord of "heaven. He hath made a magnificent building. It is surrounded by a great wall, and the battlements thereof project into the sky like great obelisks. This hath the king "(Amen-ḥetep, prince of Thebes), made for millions of millions "of years for ever and for ever."[1]

RED GRANITE LION MADE BY ÀMEN-ḤETEP III., AND USURPED BY THE NUBIAN KING ÀMEN-ÀSRU.

The Lions were brought from Gebel Barkal and presented to the British Museum by Lord Prudhoe in 1835.

[From Lepsius, *Auswahl*, Pl. XIII. (British Museum, No. 1.

¹ The texts read :—

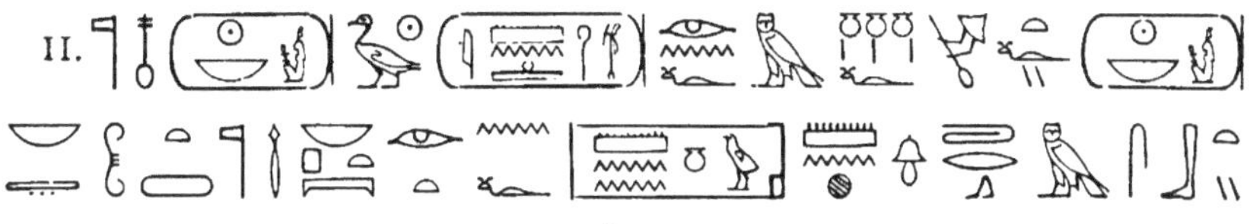

These interesting inscriptions prove clearly that the king who had the ram made was Amen-ḥetep III., and that it came from a *mennu* which he built in honour of Ȧmen and of his own Image. We have already seen that the ancient Egyptian name for the temple of Ṣulb was Mennu-Khā-em-Maāt, and because *mennu* is mentioned in the inscription translated above it has been boldly declared that the ram was made for the temple of Ṣulb, and that it was taken to Gebel Barkal by one of Ȧmen-ḥetep's successors. This evidence does not appear conclusive, for the king may quite well have built one *mennu*, to which he gave the name of "Khā-em-Maāt," at Ṣulb, and another at Gebel Barkal, or at Napata. He built the temple of Luxor at Thebes, the capital of Egypt, with the express purpose of informing the Egyptians that he was a god sprung from the actual seed of Ȧmen, and, as we have seen that he determined to establish himself as the equal and counterpart of Amen in the Sûdân, and that he built a temple at Ṣulb in honour of his living Image upon earth, the probabilities are that he also founded at Napata, which city was certainly regarded by Ȧmen-ḥetep II. as the capital of the Sûdân, another *mennu*, or temple, with the view of spreading the doctrines which he held about his divine origin and nature.

The two granite lions and the hawk already mentioned do not help us out of the difficulty. The inscription on one of the lions[1] repeats the words with which we are already familiar, viz., "He made his monument to his Image living upon earth, "(Neb-Maāt-Rā), the lord of Ta-Kenset, the dweller in the *mennu* "of Ḥet-khā-em-Maāt,"[2] and goes on to say that the king is a

These, with the variant texts from other rams, are given by Lepsius, *Denkmäler*, Abth. iii., Bl. 89.

[1] British Museum, No. 1.

[2] 

"mighty lion,"[1] and beloved of Åmen-Rā. There is nothing in these words to indicate that the lion was brought from Ṣulb to Gebel Barkal, for they only say that king (Neb-Maāt-Rā) built a temple to his Image, the god Neb-Maāt-Rā who dwelt in Ḥet-khā-em-Maāt. The inscription on the base of the other lion[2] gives the names and titles of Tut-ānkh-Åmen, one of the last kings of the XVIIIth Dynasty, and adds the important information that he "repaired the temple-building of his father, the king of the "South and North, (Neb-Maāt-Rā), son of Rā, (Åmen-ḥetep, "prince of Thebes), and built a temple to Father Åmen-Rā, the "lord of the thrones of the Two Lands, and to Tem, lord of "Heliopolis, and to the Moon-god Åāh." Now here there is no mention whatsoever of the temple of Ṣulb, and it is clear that if Tut-ānkh-Åmen says on a monument found at Gebel Barkal that he restored his father's buildings, there must have been something there to restore.

The portion of the stone hawk and its standard found at Gebel Barkal by Lepsius proves nothing, for the inscriptions upon it merely record the names and titles of Åmen-ḥetep III. A figure of this particular variety of hawk, which was dedicated to the god Sept, who was a tutelary deity of the Peninsula of Sinai, as well as of the Sûdân, existed in many temples in Nubia. There was one at least at Ṣulb, one at least at Gebel Barkal, and Mr. J. W. Crowfoot and myself sent a portion of the black basalt standard of one, which we found near Ḳubba Salim, to Kharṭûm.

From the facts given above it is clear that on the whole the rule of Åmen-ḥetep III. in the Sûdân was a beneficent one, and that, under the peace which his rule assured to the country, trade flourished and the material prosperity of the natives increased. The mines, of course, had to be worked, and the supply of slave labour required by Egypt to be provided, but in spite of all this there was a large class of people in Nubia who were benefited by the Egyptian rule, and who, seeing that there was no likelihood of overthrowing it, began to adopt quietly certain phases of Egyptian

[1] 

[2] British Museum, No. 34.

civilization, and the manners and customs which it brought in its train. Ȧmen-ḥetep III. must have spent a good deal of time in the country during the first ten years of his reign, and it is probable that of the one hundred and two lions which he boasts on his scarabs that he has shot with his own hand, the greater number were slain in the hills to the east of Wad Bâ Nagaa, in the Island of Meroë. More than all the other kings of Egypt he appears to have wished to make the Sûdân prosperous, for, after the great fight which took place early in his reign, we hear nothing of raids and wars, or of the burning of crops and villages, or of the slaughtering of the natives. Egypt had been in continuous possession of the Sûdân for about two hundred years, and Hill-men and Cattle-men alike had by this time learned that it was ill to attempt to obstruct the passage of slave and gold caravans, or to interfere with the administration of the country by the Princes of Kash, and that the arm of Pharaoh was long and his hand heavy.

At the death of Ȧmen-ḥetep III. the kingdom of Egypt passed into the hands of his son, Ȧmen-ḥetep IV., whose mother was the great Queen Thi. The inscriptions of his reign make no mention of any expedition into Nubia or Syria, and it is probable that neither the king nor his officers found it necessary to make raids or carry wars into these countries during the early years of his reign at least. It does not fall within the scope of this book to discuss the religious opinions of Ȧmen-ḥetep IV., and it is only necessary to say that he declared himself to be the foe of Ȧmen, the great god of Thebes; that he declined to call himself "Ȧmen-ḥetep," because this god's name formed a part of that name, and gave himself a new name, "Khu-en-Ȧten";[1] that he quarrelled with the priests of Ȧmen, and withdrew to a place on the Nile north of Thebes, called to-day Tell al-'Amarna, and founded a new capital; and that he built there a temple to Ȧten, an ancient form of the Sun-god of Heliopolis, whom he proclaimed to be the greatest of the gods and the creator of the universe.

The greater part of his reign of twenty years was occupied by him in religious controversy, and in carrying out his own peculiar views concerning Ȧten and his worship, but in passing

[1] I.e., "Spirit of Ȧten."

judgment upon him it should be remembered that he came of a family which had for generations held opinions about the origin and nature of its members of such overweening pride and arrogance that they appear ludicrous to modern students of mankind. Àmen-ḥetep I. was a blind adherent of the god Àmen, and founder of the great college of the priests of this god at Thebes. Ḥātshepset declared that she was the veritable daughter of Àmen by Queen Aāhmes, and was incarnate of this god. Thothmes IV. cleared away the sand from the Sphinx, and rebuilt the temple of Ḥeru-em-khut, or Harmachis, as the result of the appearance of this god to him one afternoon after a hunt near the Pyramids of Giza. Àmen-ḥetep III. believed that one portion of his nature was divine, and built a temple to his *Khent* , or Image, and worshipped it therein. His son denounced Amen and all his works, and proclaimed Aten to be the true god, though he tolerated the worship of certain solar deities, among them being Harmachis, for whose temple his grandfather had done so much. Nearly all the kings of the XVIIIth Dynasty were religious enthusiasts of one kind or another, but none of them allowed their opinions to affect their rule over Egypt, and none shirked their duty to the state of making Syria and Nubia pay tribute at the appointed times, except Amen-ḥetep IV.

Amen-ḥetep III., his father, certainly had a decided leaning to the cult of Àten, but he avoided a break with the priests of Àmen, and, in Nubia at least, allowed that god precedence over his divine counterpart. His son, unfortunately for him, did break with the priests of Amen, and whilst he was leading a life of artistic luxury in Khut-en-Àten, the new capital which he built, the great empire which his ancestors had made in Syria and Nubia began to fall to pieces. The royal treasurer of Àmen-ḥetep IV. says that he brought back tribute for his master from Syria, from the Islands of the Mediterranean, and from Nubia; but, when we remember the evidence of the Tell al-'Amarna tablets, it is clear that he was a courtier who told his lord only what was acceptable to him. The letters found at Tell al-'Amarna are full of appeals by Syrian governors for help which never came, and they prove that whilst the king of Egypt was declaiming to his followers on religious matters, and playing the high-priest, and offering up bloodless sacrifices, province after province, and city after city were being captured by the enemies of Egypt, who attacked her vassal princes with impunity.

In Egypt itself Ȧmen-ḥetep IV. caused building and repairing operations to be carried out in many places, but in Nubia we find his name only in one place, namely, Ṣulb. Here, by the entrance to one of the pylons,[1] are two reliefs in which the king is seen making offerings to the "Image" of his father "living upon earth," in whose honour the temple was built. As Ȧmen-ḥetep IV. never went into Nubia, we must assume that this was the work of some of the temple officials who were on his father's foundation. At the death of the king, the cult of Ȧten declined in Upper Egypt, and the throne passed to successors who were faithful adherents of "Ȧmen-Rā, the lord of the thrones of the Two Lands." Ȧmen and his priests had triumphed.

Ȧmen-ḥetep IV. was succeeded by Tut-ānkh-Ȧmen, a son of Ȧmen-ḥetep III., who married a daughter of Ȧmen-ḥetep IV. called Ānkh-s-en-pa-Ȧten; this lady, after her father's death, changed her name to Ānkh-s-en-Ȧmen. The only work carried out in Nubia by the new king was the restoration of a temple built by his father at Gebel Barkal, and the erection in the same place of a temple to Ȧmen, Tem of Heliopolis, and Aāh, the Moon-god.[2] We owe this information to an inscription on one of the two granite lions in the British Museum (No. 34), which were found at Gebel Barkal by Lord Prudhoe, and brought home and presented by him to the Trustees of that Institution in 1835. The fellow-lion (No. 1) bears an inscription of Ȧmen-ḥetep III., wherein the temple which he built at Ṣulb is mentioned. It is probable that the lion inscribed with the name of Tut-ānkh-Ȧmen was begun by the father and finished by the son,

[1] See Lepsius, *Denkmäler*, Abth. iii., Bl. 110 *k*.

[2] 

who added his name to it. On the name of the lion of Tut-ānkh-Ȧmen is an inscription which shows that it was usurped by a later Nubian king called Ȧmen-asru.

Under the next king, Ȧi, who succeeded to the throne through his marriage with the lady Thi, a kinswoman of Ȧmen-ḥetep IV., the Nubians continued to pay tribute to Egypt, and on account of the efficient rule of Pa-ur, the Prince of Kash and the governor of the South, the king found it unnecessary to make any expedition into the Sûdân. At Shataui, near Abû Simbel, Ai built a shrine, and on its reliefs we see[1] him in company with a high official making offerings to Ptaḥ, Rā, Horus, Sebek, Ānuqet, and Satet, and to the deified king Usertsen III. It is important to note that no mention is made of Thothmes III., or Ȧmen-ḥetep III., the first kings who attempted to administer the Sûdân systematically.

By the time that Ḥeru-em-ḥeb, the last king of the XVIIIth Dynasty, ascended the throne, the priests of Ȧmen and the people in general realized that the prosperity of the country of Egypt was not so great as when the tributes of Syria and Nubia were pouring into Thebes at frequent intervals and in large quantities. Ḥeru-em-ḥeb was a wise and prudent ruler, and when he became king one of his first acts was to destroy the Ḥet-Benben, or "Obelisk House," which the "heretic king," Ȧmen-ḥetep IV., had set up in the midst of the buildings of Ȧmen-Rā at Thebes. He carried out many administrative reforms of a far-reaching character, and restored the temples of the old gods throughout the country, and re-endowed them with lands and other possessions. This done, he began to make arrangements for increasing the revenues of Egypt, and therefore planned expeditions into Syria and Nubia. Whether he succeeded in making the Syrian tribes pay tribute in any large quantity is extremely doubtful, but his expedition into Nubia appears to have been attended with good results. In a rock-hewn temple at Silsila we see[2] him dancing before the god Menu (Ȧmsu), and in the text above it is said that he was "chosen [to be king] by Amen himself."[3] This statement is

[1] See Lepsius, *Denkmaler*, Abth. iii., 114 *e-h*. [2] *Ibid.*, 119-121.

[3] 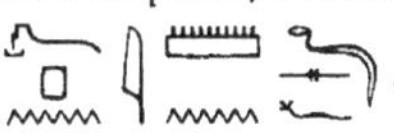.

interesting, for it indicates, as Prof. Maspero has shown, that the king was actually pointed to, or touched, by the hand of a figure of Àmen, in front of which he was presented by the priests of that god. Elsewhere we see him making offerings to Thoth and Hathor, and to Sheps (?) and his consort, and in the text on the lintel and jambs of the doorway he mentions Àmen-Rā, Khnemu, Ḥeru-khuti, Sebek, Mut, and Ānqet. On another relief he is being suckled by the goddess Taurt,[1] and on yet another he stands, with his battle-axe over his right shoulder, before Àmen-Rā. The other reliefs represent scenes connected with his journey into Nubia. The king is seated on a throne which is borne by poles on the shoulders of twelve Nubians, a priest burning incense walks before him, and by his side a number of Nubians are led by soldiers.

The texts describe these men as "princes of the abominable Kash," whom he has conquered, and they are roped together by their necks. He is addressed as "king of Egypt, Rā of the Nine "Nations who fight with the bow; thy name is great in the land "of Kash, thy roarings are in their habitations, and thy mighty "strength, O beautiful governor, hath turned the mountain lands "of the South into pillars of Pharaoh." Further on he is said to be "more learned than any scribe, and to be wiser than the lord "of Khemennu," i.e., Thoth, and his entrance into Kash is described as that of a lion. The historical facts supplied by these reliefs are few, and they unfortunately give no idea as to the part of Nubia from which the king brought his captive chiefs. From another inscription[2] we learn that Ḥeru-em-ḥeb received offerings from Punt, but whether these were brought as tribute, or as the result of trade, it is difficult to say. On the portion of the relief from Karnak, published by Mariette, the "chiefs of Punt" appear with their hands raised in entreaty, and some of them bear skins, precious stones (red), bags of spices, metal buckets, &c. They were strangers in Egypt, for they say, "We know not Egypt, "and our fathers have never trodden its soil."[3] The absence of

1 

2 Mariette, *Mon. Divers*, pl. 188.

3 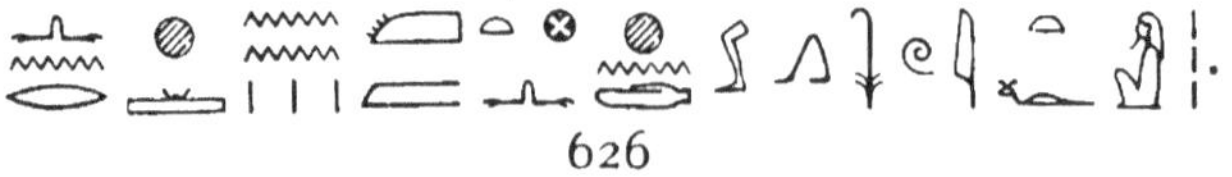

any details as to the countries in the south which were forced to pay tribute suggests that the power of Egypt in Nubia was on the wane, and when we remember the unsettled state of Egypt during the reign of Ȧmen-ḥetep IV., and the disturbed times which followed after his death, it is not surprising that the desert tribes seized every opportunity of throwing off their allegiance to the Pharaohs.

With Rameses I. we begin a new dynasty of Egyptian kings, the XIXth. During the reign of this king matters went from bad to worse, and Egypt was practically obliged to relinquish her hold upon the rich, tribute-producing countries of Western Asia, from which Thothmes III. had drawn such great treasure. The confederation of tribes in Northern Syria, which was headed by the Prince of the Kheta, was now so strong that Rameses was powerless to stay their encroachments, and he was glad to make a treaty with Sapalul, the Prince of the Kheta. It is not known in what year of his short reign this treaty was concluded, but it was probably soon after his accession to the throne. In either the first or second year of his reign he made an expedition into Nubia, but he waged no war there, and he conquered no tribes. He appears to have visited Behen (Wâdi Ḥalfa), for a limestone stele sculptured with figures of the king and his son, Seti I., making offerings to Menu, and dated in his second year, was found there by Champollion[1] in the temple founded by Usertsen I. and restored by Amen-ḥetep II. The object of this visit was probably to re-assert the authority of Egypt in Nubia, but otherwise it was without results.

When Seti I., the son of Rameses I., became the sole ruler of Egypt, he found that the tribes living in the deserts to the east and north-east of Egypt and in Palestine were in open revolt. The peoples who were in Northern Syria, headed by the Prince of the Kheta, refused to acknowledge his sovereignty, and as these were joined by the nomad tribes who lived by pasturing flocks, the payment of tribute to Egypt was out of the question. Seti I. took the field against this league of peoples, and marched into Syria, with the object of reducing the "abominable Shasu" to subjection. He passed through Palestine and advanced into

[1] See *Notices*, p. 32 ff.; E. de Rougé, *Notice Sommaire*, Paris, 1876, p. 48.

Northern Syria, where he vanquished the tribes without any great difficulty; the court historian says that the "Sun of Egypt and the Moon of all other lands" drove the people before him like Bāru,[1] and that he slew their chiefs and passed through their soldiers like a flame of fire, and that all who could fled before him. He collected large quantities of spoil, and every tribe hastened to appease his wrath with gifts, and as he retraced his steps to Egypt he left ruin and desolation behind him. He had conquered the country for the time, but the minds of the vanquished were filled with hate and lust for vengeance. It is difficult to understand why the great kings of the XVIIIth Dynasty did not appoint a permanent official in Syria, with the title of Prince of Syria, in the same manner that they appointed a viceroy in Nubia with the title of Prince of Kash. Had they done so the Egyptians would probably have had no need to invade that country time after time, and to crush frequent revolts at great cost and with much difficulty. When Seti I. returned laden with spoil he was warmly welcomed by his people, and especially by the priests of Àmen, to whom he gave large gifts.

From Lebanon he brought back much cedar wood, which was employed in making a boat for Àmen-Rā, and flagstaffs for the pylons of the temples. The Syrian campaign over, Seti I. was at liberty to turn his attention to Nubia, but, although his name is found on buildings and rocks so far to the south as Gebel Sesi, there is no mention anywhere of a great expedition into the country by him. Among the list of the countries which he claims to have conquered[2] we find the names Punt, Ànti of Kenset, Theḥennu, &c., but it is probable that this list is made up of selections from that of Thothmes III., and that it is not to be regarded as a strictly historical document. On one of the walls of the desert temple of Redesîya[3] the king is seen slaughtering "the chiefs of Kesh the abominable," and Àmen-Rā, in whose presence he stands, says, "I have given to thee the South, even as the whole of the North, to be under thy sandals."

[1] .

[2] See Lepsius, *Denkmäler*, Abth. iii., Bl. 129.

[3] *Ibid.*, Bl. 139.

Behind Åmen-Rā are ten "turreted ovals," with human heads and busts above them, inscribed with the names of conquered lands and people, e.g., Ḥa-nebu, the abominable Kash, Ta-resu, Shaāt, Sekhet-en-Åm, the Menti of Asia, and the Ånti of Ta-Kenset. These are roped together by the necks, and the rope is in the hand of the god.

INSCRIPTION DATED IN THE 23RD YEAR OF SETI I., CUT ON A PILLAR IN THE TEMPLE AT WÂDÎ ḤALFA.
[From a photograph by Lieutenant P. Lord, R.E.

The building operations carried out by Seti I. in Nubia were not very important. On a relief at Kalâbsha the king is seen standing between Horus and Set, who are pouring water over him; at Dakka and Ḳubbân he repaired portions of the temples which had been built there by kings of the XVIIIth Dynasty; and at 'Amâda he restored some portion of the temple of

Thothmes III. Thanks to the devotion of the "Governor of the South," Ȧmen-em-ȧpt, a relief was sculptured on Gebel Dôsha, wherein the king is seen making an offering to "Khnemu, the lord of Ȧb, the dweller in Ṭu-ăb, the great god, the lord of Ta-Kenset," to Satet, lady of Ṭu-āb, and to Ānuqet.[1] Further south, on one of the four remaining pillars of the Temple of Sesi, is sculptured a scene wherein the king appears standing in adoration before Ȧmen-Rā. On the bases of the pillars are "turreted ovals" inscribed with the names of conquered lands and peoples, very few of which are legible.[2] This temple appears to have been founded by Ȧmen-ḥetep III. Thus, judging by the evidence before us, it seems clear that Seti I. built no forts in the Sûdân, and that works which he carried out, about which there can be no doubt whatsoever, stopped at 'Amâda. The reason for this is not far to seek. He found that the sources of the gold supply in the Sûdân were becoming exhausted, or at least that they did not yield so much as formerly, and he gave his attention to the development of new mines. For at least a thousand years before his time it was well known that there were gold mines in the Eastern Desert between the Nile and the Red Sea, and Seti I. determined to take possession of them, and to work them systematically as he had worked the emerald mine of Gebel Zâbara.

According to a stele of Rameses II., his father, Seti I., sent men into the desert of Wâdî 'Ulâḳi, the entrance to which from the Nile is near Dakka, and they dug a well there one hundred and twenty cubits deep. This well, no doubt, yielded water for several years, but its supply gave out at length, and in the third year of Rameses II. men and asses died of thirst on the road to the mines, because there was no water in it. To Seti I. also belongs the credit of having either cleared out an old well or dug a new one on the old road to Gebel Zâbara, and of having dug some new wells near the Temple of Redesîya, which is about forty miles from the Nile. These facts indicate that he was developing the mines in the Bega country, now occupied by the Bishârîn Arabs, and that he was less interested in the Sûdân

[1] See Lepsius, *Denkmäler*, Abth. iii., Bl. 141. [2] *Ibid.*

from a mining point of view than many of his predecessors. The roads to his mines in the Eastern Desert were patrolled by Nubian soldiers called "Matchai," who were also employed as police in the cities and towns. The personal interest which Seti I. took in gold-mining is proved by the inscription from the Temple of Redesîya, published by Lepsius,[1] wherein it is said that the king wanted to see the place whence came the gold, and that having travelled thither, he was struck by the terror of the waterless road, and forthwith ordered a well to be dug in one part of it. The well was dug, and water gushed up in great abundance, and the temple was built, and a small town grew up about it. The fact that Seti I. could obtain gold from the Wâdi 'Ulâḳî, and from other places nearer to Egypt, rendered him almost independent of the supply of gold from the districts far to the south, and this being the case he had no need to maintain the ancient forts and temples beyond Dakka, with the exception of 'Amâda, which served as a kind of advanced outpost.

Rameses II. succeeded his father on the throne of Egypt when he was about twenty-five years of age; he had been trained in the profession of arms from his boyhood, and during the lifetime of Seti I. he had taken part in many successful raids on the Libyans and other nations on the borders of Egypt, and was well accustomed to desert fighting of all kinds. The great campaign against the Kheta, which was the chief event in his long reign of sixty-seven years, does not concern us here, and we therefore pass on to note the principal facts in connection with his dealings with Nubia, or the Sûdân, which had by this time been in the almost continuous possession of the Egyptians for nearly four hundred years. It is possible that he raided certain parts of Nubia during the early years of his reign, but there is no proof of it. In the stele from Ḳubbân[2] he says that he was a "mighty bull against Kash the abominable,"[3] and "a raging monster that trampled down the Blacks"[4] and the Ânti (Hill-men), that he gored them

[1] *Denkmaler*, Abth. iii., 140 *b*.

[2] Prisse d'Avennes, *Monuments*, pl. xxi.

[3] 

[4] 

mercilessly with his horns, that his "souls" gained the mastery [1] over Khent-ḥen nefer and that his terror penetrated to Kari,[2] but we cannot accept these statements literally. Rameses II. undoubtedly asserted his authority in Northern Nubia with vigour when he became king, and he probably passed the first two years of his reign in the country, but there is no evidence that any rebellion on a large scale broke out there, and none of the known facts warrant our thinking that he conquered Khent-ḥen-nefer, or even visited that region, or that Kari, wherever it was situated, acknowledged his supremacy. Åmen-ḥetep III. asserted, no doubt truthfully, that Kari was the limit of his kingdom to the south, and Rameses II. merely copied the statement, thus claiming glory to which he was not entitled.

There is, however, no reason for doubting that he was greatly interested in the gold mines of the Eastern Desert, and we gain some important information about his share in their development from the stele of Ḳubbân. According to the text, the king was in the temple of Ptaḥ at Memphis for the purpose of prayer and thanksgiving, when he began to think about the country in which the gold mines were situated, and to work out plans for sinking wells on the road to them, for he knew that water was exceedingly scarce there. He had been told that there was much gold in the land of Åkaita,[3] but no water was to be found on the road. Of the men who had been sent to the mines one half had died of thirst, and also the "asses which were in front of them," and neither in going nor coming from the Nile did they find anything to drink. The result of this was that the mines were not worked. The king then told his chancellor to call the chiefs of the country, and question them as to the plan to be followed in sinking a well, and when they came into the presence they told Rameses II. that the country had always been short of water, that many kings had wanted to dig a well, and that only Seti I. had been able to carry out his purpose. According to them, Seti's well was unsatisfactory, for although it was 120 cubits deep, no water came in

1 

2 

3 

it; finally they suggested that the king should ask his father the Nile to send water out of the mountains, for they were sure that if he did his command would be obeyed. Thereupon Rameses II. ordered a well to be dug, and we may be sure that water appeared, for otherwise the Stele of Ḳubbân would not have been set up. The well was dug in the third year of the king's reign.

The greatest of all the works of Rameses II. in Nubia are, unquestionably, the Temple of Bêt al-Wali, and the Temple of Abû Simbel; but he repaired some of the buildings of his ancestors, or at least did sufficient work on them to enable him to add his name to those of their founders. He added to the temple on the Island of Elephantine, or perhaps built a new one, for in 1887 several large blocks of granite and sandstone inscribed with his name might be seen lying there. The temple of Bêt al-Wali, on the west bank, consists of a vestibule and two small chambers, and is dedicated to Åmen-Rā, Horus, Isis, Khnemu, Satet, and Ānuqet. The vestibule is the most interesting section of it, for on the north wall are sculptures representing the conquest of the Theḥennu, or Libyans, and on the south wall we see the king engaged in conquering the people of Kesh. As illustrations of these are given elsewhere in this volume no further mention of them is needed here. The actual temple is hewn in the rock, and in front of it are two fluted Doric columns, similar to those at Beni Hasan; on the architrave is an inscription which states that Rameses II. renewed buildings and erected a temple in honour of his father's father, by which words he may refer to Åmen-Rā, or to Khnemu, or to his grandfather, Rameses I. At Garf Ḥusen, the Tutzis of the Itinerary of Antoninus, Rameses II. built a rock-hewn temple which has been generally known as the "Temple of Kirsh," because it faces the village of that name. This temple was called "Pa-Ptaḥ," i.e., the "House of Ptaḥ," and was dedicated to several gods; Rameses II. included himself among the gods who were to be worshipped here. When Champollion visited the site he saw the remains of a pylon, but these have since been washed away by the river. An avenue of sphinxes led to the large hall, and of these several are still *in situ*. The hall contained eight pillars with statues of Osiris on them; it is about 90 feet wide, and 65 feet long. The second chamber contains six Osiris pillars, and is about 45 feet square; its height is nearly 30 feet. Beyond this is a third chamber, about 40 feet wide and 18 feet long; it contained two square pillars. In the north and in the south wall is a recess; and in the west wall are three recesses, the centre one, which is the largest, contained the shrine wherein stood the statues of the gods. The total length of the temple buildings. chambers is about 300 feet. Why Rameses II. built this temple is not clear, but it was probably used in connection with the work at the gold mines, and it was certainly a convenient halting-place for caravans in the Western Desert.

At Ḳubbân, the Contra Pselcis of classical writers, Rameses II. repaired the old fort which was built by Thothmes III., probably on the site of the older building which was founded by the kings of the XIIth Dynasty. At the end of the Wâdî Sabû'a, i.e., "The Valley of the lions," Rameses II. built another temple in honour of Amen and Ptaḥ; it was approached by an avenue of sixteen lion-sphinxes, arranged eight on each side. Before the pylon, which is about 44 feet wide, stood statues of the king, and on its eastern face are the remains of sculptured reliefs wherein the king was represented in the act of slaughtering his foes. The great court, which is about 63 feet square, contains two rows of Osiris pillars; on its walls are lists of the names of the sons and daughters of Rameses II. His sons were one hundred and eleven in number, and his daughters sixty-seven. Behind this court are two smaller chambers, the first containing twelve pillars, and the second five recesses, one in the north and one in the south walls, and three in the west wall, the centre one containing figures of the gods worshipped in the temple. At Derr[1] Râmeses II. built another rock-hewn temple. The fore-

[1] The description of the temple of Derr by Burckhardt is well worth reprinting here. He says (*Travels*, p 27), "The temple is situated on the declivity "of a rocky hill, just behind the village. It is entirely hewn out of the "sand-stone rock, with its pronaos, sekos or cella, and adytum. The pronaos "consists of three rows of square pillars, four in each row. The row of "pillars nearest the cella, which were originally joined by the roof to the main "temple, are of larger dimensions than the rest; they are nearly 4 feet "square, and about 14 feet high, and are still entire, while fragments of the

court, about 45 feet wide and 43 feet long, contained three rows of pillars, the most westerly row having statues of Osiris. The sides of the court are formed of the living rock, and on this are sculptured war-scenes, wherein Rameses II. appears in his chariot. The first chamber contains six pillars, and beyond this is the sanctuary containing two recesses. The temple was called "Pa-Rā," i.e., "House of Rā," and was dedicated to Āmen-Rā and Rā-Ḥeru-Khuti, or Rā-Harmachis. At Ibrîm, in the second

"shafts only remain of the two outer rows. In front of each of the four pillars "are the legs of a colossal figure, similar to those of the temple of Gorne, at "Thebes. A portion of the excavated rock which had formed one of the walls "of the pronaos had fallen down; on the fragments of it a battle is "represented; the hero, in his chariot, is pursuing his vanquished foe, who "retires to a marshy and woody country, carrying the wounded along with "him. In a lower compartment of the same wall, the prisoners, with their arms "tied behind their backs, are brought before the executioner, who is represented "in the act of slaying one of them. All these figures are much defaced. On "the opposite wall is another battle, but in a still more mutilated state: in "this, prisoners are brought before the hawk-headed Osiris. On the front wall "of the cella, on each side of the principal entrance, Briareus is represented in "the act of being slain, and Osiris, with uplifted arm, arresting the intended "blow. This is the same group which is so often seen in the Egyptian "temples; but Briareus has here only two heads, and four arms, instead of the "numerous heads and arms represented in Egypt. On the four pillars "in front of the cella, variously dressed figures are sculptured, two "generally together, taking each other by the hand. The Egyptian Mendes, "or Priapus, is also repeatedly seen. The cella of the temple consists of "an apartment thirteen spaces square, which receives its light only through "the principal gate, and a smaller one, on the side of it. Two rows of "small pillars, three in each row, extend from the cella to the adytum: these "pillars show the infancy of architecture, being mere square blocks, hewn out "of the rock, without either base or capital; they are somewhat larger at the "bottom than at the top. The inside walls of the cella, and its six pillars, are "covered with mystic figures, in the usual style; they are of much ruder work-"manship than any I have seen in Egypt. Some remains of colour prove "that all these figures were originally painted. On one of the side walls of "the cella, are five figures, in long robes, with shaven heads, carrying a boat "upon their shoulders, the middle of which is also supported by a man with "a lion's skin upon his shoulder. In the posterior wall of the cella, is a "door, with a winged globe over it, which leads into the small adytum, "where the seats of four figures remain, cut out of the back wall. On both sides "of the adytum are small chambers, with private entrance into the cella; "in one of which a deep excavation makes it probable that it was used as a "sepulchre."

of the five caves there, are figures of Setan, the Prince of Kash, and other officials, adoring Rameses II.

The finest and most impressive of all the buildings of Rameses II. in Nubia is the rock-hewn temple of Abû Simbel, which he built to commemorate his victory over the league of Asiatic tribes who were led by the Prince of the Kheta; for simple grandeur and majesty it is second to none in all Egypt. The temple is oriented due east, and was dedicated to Rā-Harmachis. When Burckhardt visited the temple[1] it was so much buried by the sand that he found it difficult to determine whether the statues in front of it were in a sitting or standing posture! The façade of the temple was formed by cutting away the sloping side of the hill and smoothing the surface for a space measuring 120 feet by 105 feet. At the top was cut a row of dog-headed apes, twenty-one (?) in number, each being about 6 feet high. In front of the façade are four colossal statues of Rameses II., each about 66 feet high. On each side of the colossi are smaller figures, chiefly of women; thus we have Queen Nefert-ȧri, Ȧmen-ḥer-khepesh-f, the eldest son of Rameses II., Tua, mother of Rameses II., Nebt-tatet, and Bent-anṭa. The large hall, which measures nearly 58 feet by 55 feet, contains eight massive pillars, with statues of Osiris attached to them. The walls are decorated with battle scenes in relief, those on the north wall illustrating the king's Asiatic campaign, and those on the south his raids in Nubia. From the large hall a chamber, containing four square pillars, is entered; beyond this is a chamber about 35 feet long, entered by three doors, and beyond this again is the sanctuary, with an altar. At each end of the long, narrow chamber, in the west wall, is a recess. Behind the altar are painted four gods, Ȧmen, Ptaḥ, Rameses II., and Rā-Harmachis. On the north side of the large hall are two doorways which lead into corridors, and at each end of it, in the west wall, is another doorway which leads into three corridors. The total length of the chambers in a straight line is about 185 feet.

To the north of this temple is a smaller rock-hewn temple, which Rameses II. built in honour of the goddess Hathor and his

[1] See his *Travels*, p. 91.

wife Nefert-ȧri. The hall is about 35 feet long and 26 feet wide, and contains six Hathor-headed pillars, each of which bears the cartouches of Rameses II. and his wife Nefert-ȧri. In the sanctuary is a figure of the queen, with the attributes of Hathor, standing within a shrine, and in front of the shrine is a figure of the king making offerings of flowers to her. To the north of this temple is the stele of Ani, a Prince of Kash, and to the south is the stele, dated in the thirty-fourth year of the reign of Rameses II., recording his marriage with the daughter[1] of the Prince of the Kheta. Another stele close by describes the king's victories over the land of Kheta and of Kash. A little further on is a small building, consisting of two chambers, which was dedicated to Thoth and Harmachis by Rameses II.; quite unaccountably the cartouche of Usertsen II. is found inscribed on one of the walls. Rameses II. also built a temple in honour of Horus in this neighbourhood, but its site is unknown. At Shataui, or Mashakit as it is called by Champollion, the modern Adda, is the small rock-hewn chapel of Pa-ur, the Prince of Kash, who flourished in the reign of Rameses II.; on a relief here we see this officer worshipping the king and the goddess Ānuqet. Some thirty miles further to the south, near Faras and Aksha, is a small temple wherein Rameses II. worshipped Ȧmen, and was himself worshipped. Curiously enough, we find no mention of Rameses II. at Behen (Wâdi Ḥalfa) or at Semna, and his name does not appear again until we reach 'Amâra. Here, on the western bank, are the ruins of a small temple, and in the course of some "trial" clearings which Mr. J. W. Crowfoot and myself made there in January, 1905, we found a large sandstone stele inscribed with a text of Rameses II. The stele was much broken, and the text appeared to be a duplicate of that of Abû Simbel; we re-buried the fragments, and left them where we found them. We have it on the authority of Lepsius[2] that Rameses II. built a temple to Ȧmen-Rā at Napata, but nothing was to be seen there of the remains upon which he based his statement.

Thus we see that Rameses II. directed his attention to building temples on the Nile between Elephantine and Abû Simbel, that

[1] Her Egyptian name was Rā-ma-uā-neferu.

[2] *Letters*, p. 222

is to say, in that part of the Nile Valley from which he drew the greater portion of his revenues. The country south of Wâdî Ḥalfa yielded a comparatively small quantity of gold in his day, and it was therefore unnecessary for him to build forts and temples beyond the best gold-producing districts. The Stele of Ḳubbân tells us that the king meditated upon the fact that no gold came from the land of Akaita because there were no wells on the roads, and its existence proves that he tried to remedy this state of things. It would be wrong to assume that the well which he dug in the third year of his reign was the only one which he made in Nubia during the long period of his rule over Egypt; on the contrary, there is every reason to believe that he sank many wells, and thus made the whole of the Wâdî 'Ulâki, which extends from the Nile nearly to the Red Sea, accessible to his workmen. The fact that he built temples at Kalâbsha, Garf Ḥusên, Wâdî Sabû'a, Derr, Abû Simbel, and Aksha, and repaired the fort at Ḳubbân, proves that people congregated near these places, and that they did so for purposes of trade goes without saying. There must have been other temples on the road between Elephantine and Abû Simbel, where caravans could halt and find rest and security for the night, for clearly Rameses II. spared no pains to make the road on the western bank of the Nile safe for the transport of his gold, and we see that there was a temple or government building at intervals of from twelve to twenty miles the whole way from Kalâbsha to Aksha. If the gold was sent north by river the boats could tie up for the night at the nearest temple or fort, where, no doubt, a guard sufficient for all purposes of protection of the royal property was stationed.

Rameses II. was succeeded by his thirteenth son, Mer-en-Ptaḥ (I.) ḥetep-ḥer-Maāt, and in the fifth year of his reign the Libyans, to whom a large number of Mediterranean peoples joined themselves, revolted and began to invade the frontiers of Egypt. The king collected his forces, and defeated the rebels in a pitched battle, and their leader, king Mārеiui, fled; the king of Egypt captured large quantities of spoil, which he had packed on the backs of asses and sent to Egypt. The Libyan king left behind his wife and children, and six of his brothers and sons, and 6,359 officers and soldiers were slain and mutilated, according to the barbarous fashion of the day. Some 9,376 prisoners were taken alive, and the conquerors seized 9,111 swords, 120,314 weapons of various kinds, and 120 horses. Whilst Mer-en-Ptaḥ was engaged in crushing the Libyan revolt he had neither time nor attention to give to Sûdân affairs, and the government of the country was left to the Prince of Kash, whose name, Mes, appears

SETI II. MER-EN-PTAḤ MAKING OFFERINGS TO HORUS OF BEHEN IN THE TEMPLE AT WÂDÎ ḤALFA.

on a rock near Aswân.[1] Lepsius found at Dakka some blocks of stone inscribed with Mer-en-Ptaḥ's name, and it is therefore possible that he carried out some works of repair on the ancient temple, but it is unlikely that he built on a large scale anywhere

[1] See Lepsius, *Denkmäler*, Abth. iii, Bl. 200.

in Nubia, for his father's temples must have been in a tolerably good state of preservation.

Mer-en-Ptaḥ was, it seems, succeeded by Seti II. Mer-en-Ptaḥ II., whose reign was uneventful; he neither waged wars nor built temples in Nubia. His cartouches are found cut on the second colossal statue of Rameses II., on the north side of the entrance to the temple at Abû Simbel.[1]

Sa-Ptaḥ Mer-en-Ptaḥ was one of the immediate successors of Seti II. Mer-en-Ptaḥ. On a rock near Aswân a seated figure of the king is scûlptured;[2] before him stands the Prince of Kash and governor of the south, Seti,[3] and behind him the chancellor Bai,[4] his name is also commemorated on a rock on the Island of Sâḥal, where Seti, Prince of Kash, is adoring cartouches containing his name.[5] This sculpture was made in the third year of the king's reign, and in the inscription the official says, "Praised be thy *ka* (i.e., double), O mighty king! Grant thou grace to the *ka* of the fan-bearer on the right hand of the king, the Prince of Kash and governor of the south, Seti." Like his predecessors Mer-en-Ptaḥ I. and II., Sa-Ptaḥ neither waged wars nor built temples in Nubia. It was supposed that, owing to the shortness of his reign, Sa-Ptaḥ did not build a tomb in the Valley of the Tombs of the Kings at Thebes, but this was a mistake, for it was discovered there in the winter of 1905-6 by Mr. Theodore N. Davis, assisted by Mr. E. R. A. Ayrton.

With the death of Sa-Ptaḥ the XIXth Dynasty came to an end, and for several years no man was able to make himself master of the country, which fell into a state of lawlessness and anarchy. According to the great papyrus of Rameses III., "every man did that which it seemed to him right to do, and "for very many years the people had no chief governor who was "able to maintain dominion over the other rulers." In Syria a certain man called Ȧrsu[6] succeeded in seizing the supreme

[1] See Lepsius, *Denkmaler*, Abth. iii., 204.

[2] *Ibid.*, Bl. 202 *c*.

[3] 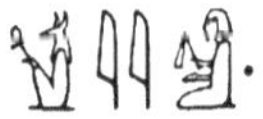

[4] 

[5] Lepsius, *Denkmäler*, Abth. iii., Bl. 202, *b*.

[6] 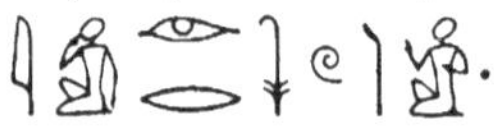

power over the country, and in making the local princes and chiefs pay tribute to him instead of to the gods, but after a few years a relative of Rameses II., called Set-Nekht, was placed by the priests on the throne of Egypt, and he succeeded in suppressing Ȧrsu and other claimants to the sovereignty of the country. During his reign Egypt possessed but little authority in Syria, and Nubia was ruled by the Prince of Kash and his subordinates.

Set-Nekht was succeeded by his son Rameses III., who during his father's lifetime had assisted in governing Egypt, and to him belongs the credit of having developed the commerce of the country considerably. For some time before he ascended the throne a number of Mediterranean peoples were preparing to invade Egypt, but it was not until the fifth year of his reign that the conspiracy came to a head, and the enemy dared to carry out their plans. The Egyptians were victorious, and they mutilated about twelve thousand of dead rebel warriors. In the eighth year of the reign of Rameses III., Egypt was threatened by several nations and tribes, who determined to attack her by sea and land simultaneously. The king was, however, equal to the occasion, for having placed his ships with their hired crews in certain positions, his army set out to attack the land forces of the enemy. The Egyptians routed their enemies, who fled to their ships and tried to escape, but these found themselves blocked by the king's fleet, and large numbers of the rebels were killed or taken prisoners. Rameses III. marched into Syria, and collected tribute and gifts, and where these were not forthcoming he cut down the fruit trees, burned the crops, and destroyed the villages. After his return to Egypt the king was compelled to undertake two more campaigns, one against the Libyans, who were led by Kapur, and another against several Shasu tribes; in both of these he was successful, and he captured much spoil.

On the road between Egypt and Syria, at a place called Aina, Rameses III. dug a well, which he surrounded by a strong building, twenty cubits square and thirty cubits high; this indicates that he attempted to provide a regular supply of water for the men and beasts of the caravans which passed to and from

Syria into Egypt. Rameses III. appears not to have visited Nubia, and there is no mention in the inscriptions of any expedition into that country in his reign. A portion of his fleet sailed at regular intervals to Punt, and in his summary of the principal events of his reign the king himself tells us that his ships returned laden with all the marvellous products of the country or region called Neter-taui, which is situated on the African coast to the south of the Red Sea. These ships set out on their journey from the "mountain of Qebti," or Coptos, by which we must understand some port near the modern Ḳuṣêr, and there they were unloaded when they returned. The goods were taken overland to some spot on the Nile, near the modern town of Ḳena, probably by way of the Wâdi Hammâmât. To the same Red Sea port the copper from the mines in the Sinaïtic Peninsula was brought, and the metal, in ingots, was carried across the Eastern Desert into Egypt on the backs of asses. There is no reason to doubt that the gold mines in the Wâdî 'Ulâki were worked successfully by the king's agents, and it is quite clear from his own testimony that the natives of the Sûdân gave him no trouble.

In summing up the results of his rule he says: "I made the "whole country to be covered with blossom-bearing trees, and "I made all the people to sit under the shade thereof I made it "possible for an Egyptian woman to walk with a bold and "free step whithersoever she pleased, and no man or woman "among the people would molest her. In my time I made the "horsemen and the bowmen of the Shairetana and the Qehaq "to dwell in their towns, and to lie down stretched out at full "length on their backs, and they were not afraid, because there "was no fighting with Kash (Nubia), or with the Syrian foes. "Their bows and their weapons of war were laid up inside their "guard-houses, and they were filled with meat and drink, of which "they partook with rejoicings, and their wives and their children "were with them, and they looked not behind them, because "their hearts were glad."[1] Thus it is clear that there was no war in Nubia in the reign of Rameses III., and that when we see the name of Punt among the names of the peoples and countries

[1] Brit. Mus. Papyrus, No. 9900, plate 78, lines 9-12

which he is said to have conquered, its appearance proves nothing more than that the scribe, who drafted the inscriptions for his temple, copied it out from the list of Thothmes III., together with several others, without any regard to the history of his master's reign. The latter part of the reign of Rameses III. was a period of peace, for the king's aim was not conquest, but the prosecution of commercial enterprise. The wealth of Egypt at this time must have been enormous, otherwise the king could not have presented to the gods of the temples of Thebes, Abydos, and Memphis the valuable series of gifts which are enumerated in his great papyrus preserved in the British Museum. The farthest place in the south where the name of Rameses III. is found is Semna, where it appears near a door built by Thothmes III.[1]

The reign of Rameses IV. was short, and in it nothing of importance happened in Nubia; the greatest work undertaken by him was the construction of a road in the Wâdî Hammâmât from the Nile to the Red Sea. In the reign of Rameses V. the Prince of Kash was called Pa-ur. He was a devoted servant of his lord, for in his grave near Ibrîm (Primis) are sculptured figures of the king and his queen Nefert-art. Rameses VI. appears to have carried out some works at Emmáāt,[2] the modern 'Amâda, in Nubia, for the Prince of Kash, one Pennut, who was the Åṭennu,[3] or Viceroy, of Uauat and Akita, dedicated the revenue from a piece of land for ever to the maintenance of the service which was connected with the worship of the statue of the king. The area of the "parcel" of land was 320,000 square cubits. This information is derived from the inscriptions on the walls of the tomb of this official at Aniba, near Ibrîm, wherein are also depicted several scenes connected with the burial and worship of the deceased. Pennut is seen worshipping the Cow-goddess Hathor, and in a shrine within the funeral mountain is the goddess Apet, holding a frog in her hand. Elsewhere are reliefs of the presentation of the deceased and his wife to Osiris, the Great Scales in the Judgment Hall, the

1 See Lepsius, *Denkmäler*, Abth. iii., 47 *a*.

2 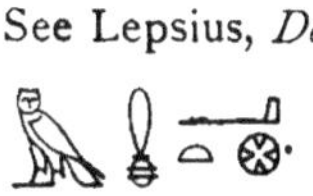

3 

Sekhet-Ȧaru, or Elysian Fields, &c.[1] A rock sculpture on the Island of Sâḥal shows us the official Maā-Ȧmen worshipping Rameses VI.[2]

The reigns of Rameses VII. and Rameses VIII. were unimportant, and their names do not appear in Nubia.

In the reign of Rameses IX., which lasted eighteen years, the Sûdân continued to send gifts to Thebes,[3] but the king carried out no building operations in that country. The actual ruler of Egypt at this time was Ȧmen-ḥetep, the high-priest of Ȧmen, whose power was practically unlimited, and who built for himself a great house, with wooden doors and copper bolts, and set up a statue to each of the high-priests of his god in a courtyard which he planted with trees. The position of the priests of Ȧmen had become precarious, and poverty was staring them in the face, for their treasury was nearly depleted. As their royal masters, since Rameses III., had carried on no wars, there was no spoil from which they could maintain their god and his temples and his services, and as the prosperity which had come over the country as a result of the commercial enterprises of Rameses III. had declined, their revenues had dwindled considerably. Out of this difficulty they found a way by persuading the king to give the high-priest of Ȧmen power to levy taxes on the people for the support of the temple and priesthood of Ȧmen-Rā. This authority was given to the high-priest Ȧmen-ḥetep in the tenth year of the reign of Rameses IX. at a solemn assembly, whereat the god Menthu, and the names of Ȧmen-Rā, Ḥeru-khuti, Ptaḥ, Thoth, and Rameses IX. were invoked as witnesses, in the following words[4]:—"Let the "taxing and the usufruct of the labours of the inhabitants for "the temple of Ȧmen-Rā, the king of the gods, be placed under "thy administration. Let the full revenues be given over to "thee according to their number. Thou shalt collect the duties. "Thou shalt undertake the interior administration of the

[1] See Lepsius, *Denkmäler*, Abth. iii., 229-232.

[2] Mariette, *Mon. Divers*, pl. 72, No. 48.

[3] See Lepsius, *Denkmäler*, Abth. iii., 235, 236 *a*.

[4] Brugsch's rendering; see *Egypt under the Pharaohs*, vol. ii., p. 187. The text is given by Lepsius, *Denkmäler*, Abth. iii., Bl. 237 *e*.

"treasuries, of the store-houses, and of the granaries of the "temple of Åmen-Rā, the king of the gods; so that the income of "the heads and hands for the maintenance of Åmen-Rā, the "king of the gods, may be applied to his service." The passing of this decree was the beginning of the downfall of the power of the Theban kings, and the first of the series of great events which resulted, a few years later, in the usurpation of the supreme power by the high-priest of Åmen.

In the reign of Rameses X. the prosecution of the thieves who systematically robbed the royal tombs and mummies of the great kings and benefactors of the temple and priesthood of Åmen, which had been begun by Rameses IX., was continued, and in his first year some sixty people were arrested. Of the reign of Rameses XI., which must have been short and unimportant, nothing is known. In the reign of Rameses XII. the high-priest of Amen was called Ḥer-Ḥeru. This official was the "commander-in-chief of the army," and "governor of the South and North," and as his predecessor had obtained authority from the king to levy taxes on the people, he was master of both the spiritual and material resources of the country. Rameses XII. possessed merely nominal power, and Upper Egypt and Nubia, at least, were ruled by Ḥer-Ḥeru; when the king died the high-priest of Åmen declared himself to be the king of Egypt. Meanwhile the popularity of the priests of Åmen was not so great in Lower Egypt, for it was evident to the local chiefs and nobles that the priests of Åmen were absorbed wholly in promoting the interests of their god and of themselves, even at the expense of the country's welfare, and that they had neither the means nor the wish to maintain the supremacy of Egypt in Syria. The people of the Delta, moreover, quickly realized that they could not rely upon them for defence against the attacks of the lawless tribes on the north-east frontier of Egypt, and that, if they wished to preserve their independence and their trade, they must find means to protect both.

The state in which the Delta folk found themselves was not new, for even in the reign of Rameses III. the actual power possessed by the priests of Amen was greater than that of the king. The successors of Rameses III. were inert and incompetent rulers, and during their reigns the influence of the priests increased so quickly that before the death of Rameses XII. it became evident that they would usurp the sovereignty of the country at the first opportunity. In spite of their power, they were, however, unable to keep order in Thebes, and more than one riot of a serious character broke out in the city, and their authority was so lightly esteemed that the professional thieves of the day broke into the royal tombs on the western bank of the river, and stole the jewellery which had been buried with the mummies of the great Theban kings and queens, wrecked their coffins, and even tore the mummies in pieces to get at the valuable amulets, rings, necklaces, &c., which were wrapped up in the swathings. Thus we see that the priests of Ȧmen were not able even to protect the mummies and tombs of the greatest benefactors of their brotherhood, and it is therefore not to be wondered at that they failed to keep the peace among the civil population in general. As a result of the rule of the priests all military expeditions ceased, no building operations were carried on, the works in the quarries were stopped, and the vassal tribes paid no tribute.

The first priest-king, Ḥer-Ḥeru, however, attempted to prove that Syria paid tribute to Ȧmen by declaring that the products of that country which had been obtained in the ordinary way by trading caravans were offerings made by the Syrians to his god! That he had no real influence there is proved by the fact that his envoy, Unu-Ȧmen, whom he sent to Bêrût to buy cedar wood to make a new boat for the god Ȧmen, was robbed of all the money he had with him at Dôr, and was obliged to send back to Egypt for a fresh supply. For an important official entrusted with a high mission, and carrying a considerable sum of money with him, to be robbed in Western Asia is an event which has frequently happened, even in modern times, and which need not surprise us, but when such a thing takes place it is a tolerably sure sign that the hold of the Government on the country is a slight one.

The result of Ḥer-Ḥern's incapacity as a ruler was that the Delta folk set up over themselves as king a descendant of Rameses II. called Nes-Ba-Ṭeṭ, which name was changed by the Greeks into Smendes. He chose for his capital the ancient city of Tanis, and little by little his power extended to Thebes.

At length Ḥer-Ḥeru, the high-priest of Ȧmen, appears to have come to some understanding with him about the limits of their respective dominions, for it is clear that Smendes ruled from Tanis to Saut, the modern Asyût, and the high-priest from Saut to the First Cataract, or perhaps even to the Second Cataract. In spite of this arrangement, however, we find that Smendes possessed the means of making his authority felt in Upper Egypt, and a proof of this, which we owe to M. G. Daressy,[1] is the fact that, when a portion of the temple of Ȧmen at Luxor was in danger of falling down because its foundations had been undermined by the waters of the Nile, it was this king, and not the high-priest Ḥer-Ḥeru, who repaired or rebuilt it.

Smendes heard of the danger which threatened the temple when he was at Memphis, and promptly gave orders that three thousand of his own men should go to Thebes and repair the damage, and he made large numbers of the natives of Upper Egypt to work under their instructions. It seems that every man who was physically able was made to work, and the great quarry opposite was reopened so that suitable stone in abundance might be forthcoming. We have already seen that the priests of Ȧmen were unable to prevent the robbery of the royal tombs, and that they could not keep order among the people, and from the above facts it is clear that, when the second greatest temple in Thebes was in danger of collapsing, they were content to allow the king of the North to undertake the labour and expense of the restoration of its stability. They were, in fact, unable to protect the property of the god whose devoted and faithful servants they declared themselves to be. Under the priests of Ȧmen, Egypt was once more divided into two distinct kingdoms, and two sets of kings ruled the country, the one from Tanis, and the other from Thebes. These kings formed the XXIst Dynasty.

Meanwhile there flourished in the Delta a certain Libyan called Buiuuaua,[2] or Buiuua-Buiuua, who was a man of great importance among the Libyan Māshuasha tribes, and was

[1] See Maspero's *Recueil*, tom. x., p. 133 ff., "Sur les Carrières de Gébéléin et le roi Smendès."

[2] .

probably their leader. His descendants appear to have held positions under the kings of Tanis of the XXIst Dynasty, and Shashanq, his great-great-great-grandson, married the high-priestess of Ȧmen, called Meḥtet-en-usekht. This marriage, of course, gave him a claim to the throne of Egypt. Shashanq's son, Nemareth, married Thent-sepeḥ, who also had the divine blood of Ȧmen in her veins, and thus the claim of the descendants of Buiuuaua to the throne was still further strengthened. Among the offspring of Nemareth and Thent-sepeḥ was a son called after his grandfather Shashanq, better known from the Bible narrative[1] as "Shishak," who, a few years before the death of the last Tanite king of the XXIst Dynasty, established himself at Bubastis in the Delta, and declared himself king of Egypt. He was the founder of the XXIInd Dynasty,[2] the kings of which ruled Egypt for considerably more than one hundred years. Shashanq's eldest son, Osorkon, married Tasheṭ-Khensu, and succeeded him on the throne at Bubastis, and his second son, Ȧuapeth, married a priestess of Ȧmen, and became a sort of viceroy in Upper Egypt, with Thebes for his capital.

We may now leave the Kingdom of the North out of consideration, and note the consequence of the appointment of Ȧuapeth in Upper Egypt. During his rule at Thebes the robberies of the royal tombs continued, and it seemed impossible either to prevent them or to arrest the malefactors. Early in the period of the rule of the priests of Ȧmen the mummies of Seqenen-Rā III., Ȧāhmes I., three of the kings called Thothmes, Seti I., Rameses I., Rameses II., Rameses III., Rameses X., and of several queens, had been removed from their respective tombs to the tomb of Ȧmen-ḥetep I., which was strictly guarded, but in spite of all the precautions taken, the thieves succeeded in effecting an entrance and in plundering the mummies. Although we cannot suppose that the Libyan Ȧuapeth looked upon the mummies of the great kings with the same reverence as the priests of Ȧmen, yet we may suppose that he was anxious to put

[1] See 1 Kings xiv. 25; 2 Chronicles xii. 2-9.

[2] The Libyan origin of this dynasty was first noted by Krall. Dr. Birch attributed to it a Babylonian origin, and was partially followed by Brugsch, and Oppert thought that some of its members might have been Elamites.

an end to lawlessness and sacrilege, and with a view of doing this he determined to remove the royal mummies, with their coffins and all their funeral furniture, to a more secure hiding-place.

The spot chosen by him was the tomb of Ȧst-em-khebit, a princess, at Dêr al-Baḥari. The pit by which the tomb is reached is about one hundred and thirty feet deep, and from the bottom of this there runs a corridor about two hundred feet long which ends in a mummy chamber. To this chamber were brought all the mummies from the tomb of Ȧmen-ḥetep I., and such coffins, &c., as had been left by the thieves were placed along the corridor. This done, the entrance to the corridor in the pit was carefully closed with mason's work, and then the deep pit was filled up with stones, sand, &c. For more than twenty-seven centuries the royal mummies remained undisturbed, so well was their hiding-place concealed by Ȧuapeth, but a means of getting into the princess's tomb was discovered in 1871 by some natives, and ten years later the Egyptian Government took possession of its contents and removed them to the old Museum at Bûlâḳ.[1]

This work of Ȧuapeth was productive of far-reaching results, and it is difficult not to think that in carrying it out he was actuated by more than one motive. We know that the priests of Amen performed memorial services in the chapels of the royal tombs at stated intervals throughout the year, and also that the first priest-king caused periodic examinations of the mummies to be made, in the course of which such mummies as required it were re-swathed,[2] and new coffins were provided for them. When Ȧuapeth removed the royal mummies to the hiding-place described above, he not only placed them beyond the reach of the robbers of tombs, but he made it impossible for the priests of Amen to continue their memorial services near the mummies, and so practically took away one of their chief occupations, and the principal reason of their existence at Thebes. These facts they realized at once, and seeing that it was hopeless to expect

[1] See Maspero, *Les Momies royales de Deir el-Bahari* (Mémoires de la Mission du Caire, tom. i., p. 511 sqq.)

[2] Thus in the sixth year of his rule he had the mummies of Seti I. and his son Rameses II. re-swathed.

any recrudescence of their former wealth, influence, and power, they began to consider the advisability of betaking themselves to

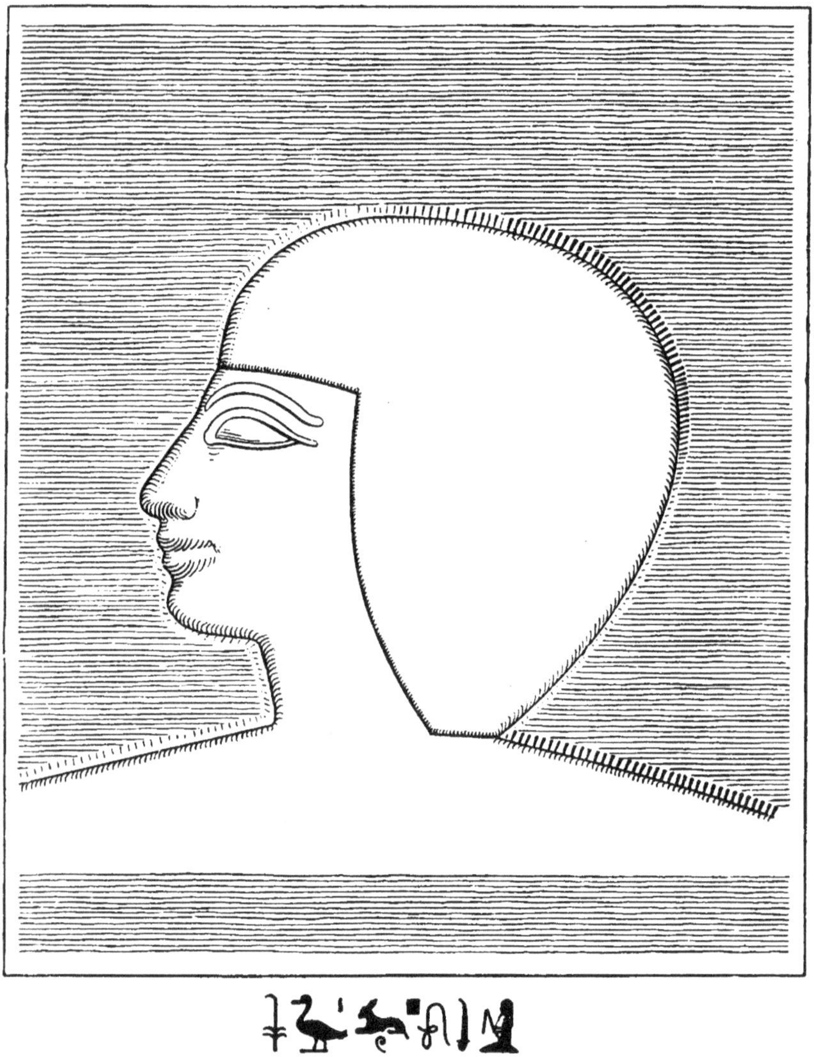

PRINCE ÂUPUATH, WHO CAUSED THE ROYAL MUMMIES TO BE REMOVED FROM THEIR TOMBS TO HIDING PLACES AT DÊR AL-BAḤARÎ.

[From Lepsius, *Denkmäler*, Abth. III. Bl. 300.

some place where they could enjoy fuller opportunities for the development of their peculiar religious views. The north was closed to them obviously, but the south was open, and there they determined to go. We have already seen that king after king of Egypt, from the XIIth Dynasty downwards, had dedicated temples in the Sûdân to Åmen-Rā, and for a period of fifteen hundred years that god held paramount power in every region of the country where the influence of Egypt had penetrated. Thus it was certain that the priests of Åmen would be well received in Nubia, and that the upper class of that country would welcome the leaders of the Åmen cult from Thebes, the principal seat of the worship of the god. Between the First and Fourth Cataracts there was in the tenth century before Christ a long series of forts and temples, the priests attached to the latter having themselves probably come from Egypt. There were Egyptian settlements at Ḳartassi, Kalâbsha, Garf Ḥusên, Dakka, Ḳubbân, Ḳûrta, Wâdî Sabû'a, 'Amâda, Derr, Abû Simbel, Wâdî Ḥalfa, Ma'atûḳa, Semna, on the Islands in the Second Cataract, 'Amâra, on the Island of Sâî, at Suwârda, Saddênga, Ṣulb, Dulgo, Tombos, Arḳô, Khandak, Old Dongola, Merawi, Gebel Barkal, and probably at many other places on the river up to the foot of the Fourth Cataract, but not beyond.

Many of these settlements were occupied by miners, who were fed by food imported either from Egypt or from the south, and were unsuitable as homes for bodies of priests who had lived in comfort at Thebes, and some were merely forts which were garrisoned by soldiers. The only place at all suitable for the purposes of the priests of Åmen was Napata, a town at the foot of the Fourth Cataract, which had long been regarded by the Egyptians as the capital of the Egyptian Sûdân. The town of Merawi is the modern representative of Napata, and the fertility of the Nile Valley in its neighbourhood makes the site an ideal one for a Sûdânî town. For a few score miles down-stream the banks on each side of the river are capable of cultivation, and palm trees and vegetables of all kinds have always grown there luxuriantly. Napata stood at the end of the great valley through which caravans passed to and from the countries near the Atbara and the Blue and White Niles, and the fact that there was much gain to be made from the pious traveller and the prosperous merchant was not forgotten by the priests of Åmen, when they selected that city as a place of refuge in the Sûdân.

When, and under exactly what circumstances, the departure of the priests of Ȧmen took place from Thebes cannot be said, but it is probably correct to say that their exodus began under the rule of Shashanq I., the founder of the XXIInd Dynasty, and that it continued until the greater number of the priests had left Thebes. We do not, unfortunately, know what became of the endowments belonging to the god Ȧmen, but it seems certain that the priests would carry away with them a certain amount of temple property, apparel, &c., connected with the worship of their god, and treasure sufficient for establishing themselves in their new abode. The remaining revenues were, no doubt, devoted to the maintenance of the sanctuary of the god, the temple-buildings, and the remnant of the priests who, for one reason or other, preferred to remain at Thebes. After the departure of the main body of the priests of Ȧmen from Thebes, the sanctuary of their god lost much of its splendour, and the fame of Ȧmen himself dwindled, in proportion as that of the gods of Abydos increased, and the worship of the deities of Tanis and Bubastis spread into Upper Egypt. The followers of Ȧmen in Thebes continued, however, to be tolerably numerous, and his shrine was well worth plundering by the Assyrians, who captured the city in the seventh century before Christ.

END OF VOL. I.

www.ingramcontent.com/pod-product-compliance
Lightning Source LLC
Chambersburg PA
CBHW040337300426
44111CB00029B/2938
9781639236190